Lecture Notes in Computer Science 2783

Edited by G. Goos, J. Hartmanis, and J. van Leeuwen

Springer
Berlin
Heidelberg
New York
Hong Kong
London
Milan
Paris
Tokyo

Wanlei Zhou   Paul Nicholson
Brian Corbitt   Joseph Fong (Eds.)

Advances in Web-Based Learning – ICWL 2003

Second International Conference
Melbourne, Australia, August 18-20, 2003
Proceedings

 Springer

Series Editors

Gerhard Goos, Karlsruhe University, Germany
Juris Hartmanis, Cornell University, NY, USA
Jan van Leeuwen, Utrecht University, The Netherlands

Volume Editors

Wanlei Zhou
Deakin University, School of Information Technology
221 Burwood Highway, Burwood, 3125, Australia
E-mail: wanlei@deakin.edu.au

Paul Nicholson
Deakin University, School of Scientific and Developmental Studies in Education
221 Burwood Highway, Burwood, 3125, Australia
E-mail: pauln@deakin.edu.au

Brian Corbitt
Deakin University, Pro Vice Chancellor (Online Services)
221 Burwood Highway, Burwood, 3125, Australia
E-mail: bcorbitt@deakin.edu.au

Joseph Fong
City University of Hong Kong
Department of Computer Science
Kowloon, Hong Kong
E-mail: csjfong@cityu.edu.hk

Cataloging-in-Publication Data applied for

A catalog record for this book is available from the Library of Congress.

Bibliographic information published by Die Deutsche Bibliothek
Die Deutsche Bibliothek lists this publication in the Deutsche Nationalbibliografie;
detailed bibliographic data is available in the Internet at <http://dnb.ddb.de>.

CR Subject Classification (1998): H.4, H.3, I.2.6, H.5, K.3, D.2, I.2

ISSN 0302-9743
ISBN 3-540-40772-3 Springer-Verlag Berlin Heidelberg New York

Springer-Verlag Berlin Heidelberg New York
a member of BertelsmannSpringer Science+Business Media GmbH

http://www.springer.de

© Springer-Verlag Berlin Heidelberg 2003
Printed in Germany

Typesetting: Camera-ready by author, data conversion by PTP-Berlin GmbH
Printed on acid-free paper   SPIN: 10931547   06/3142   5 4 3 2 1 0

Preface

The 2nd International Conference on Web-Based Learning (ICWL 2003) took place in Melbourne, Australia.

ICWL 2003 followed the tradition of the successful ICWL 2002 held in Hong Kong and aimed at providing an in-depth study of the technical and pedagogical issues, as well as incorporating management issues of Web-based learning. Additionally, there was a focus on issues of interest to the learner, offering the optimal Web based learning environment to achieve high academic results. Deakin University organized this conference in conjunction with the Hong Kong Web Society, to provide a forum which gathered educators, researchers, technologists and implementers of Web-based learning from around the world to discuss, collaborate and advance all relevant issues pertaining to this area of research.

The main focus of ICWL 2003 was on the most critical areas of Web-based learning, in particular, Web-based learning environments, virtual universities, pedagogical issues related to Web-based learning, multimedia-based e-learning, interactive e-learning systems, intelligence in on-line education, e-learning solutions, CSCL, and authoring tools for e-learning. In total, the conference received 118 papers from researchers and practitioners from 13 countries. Each paper was reviewed by at least three internationally renowned referees. Papers were rigorously examined and selected based on their originality, significance, correctness, relevance, and clarity of presentation. Among the high-quality submissions, 50 papers were accepted and included in the proceedings. Later, the proceedings editors will recommend that some high-quality papers from the conference be published in a special issue of an international journal.

We believe the conference provided a forum for discussion among educators, researchers and technologists for addressing the various aspects of Web-based learning; provided a suggestive guide for the implementation of the Web-based mode of learning, and addressed the technical, pedagogical, management and social issues associated with the implementation; explored concepts and examples of good practice in developing, integrating and delivering e-learning solutions; and provided an opportunity for conference participants and solution providers in e-learning to exchange views and provide feedback on Web-based learning

We would like to take this opportunity to thank all the authors for their submissions to the conference. Many of them traveled some distance to participate in the conference. We also thank the Program Committee members and additional reviewers for their efforts in reviewing the large number of papers. Thanks also go to the local conference organizers for their great support.

Last, but not least, we would like to express our gratitude to all the organizations who supported our efforts to bring the conference to fruition. In particular, we are grateful to Deakin University and the Hong Kong Web Society for their sponsorship and assistance.

August 2003

Wanlei Zhou, Paul Nicholson
Brian Corbitt, Joseph Fong

Organization

ICWL 2003 was organized by Deakin University in conjunction with the Hong Kong Web Society.

Executive Committee

General Co-chairs: Brian Corbitt, Deakin University

Joseph Fong, Hong Kong Web Society

Program Committee Co-chairs: Wanlei Zhou, Deakin University

Paul Nicholson, Deakin University

Local Organization Chair: Malcolm Campbell, Deakin University

Steering Committee

Shi-Kuo Chang	University of Pittsburgh, USA
Joseph Fong	Hong Kong Web Society (Chair)
Qing Li	City University of Hong Kong
Xiaoming Li	Beijing University, China
Maria Orlowska	University of Queensland, Australia
Timothy Shih	Tamkang University, Taiwan
Wanlei Zhou	Deakin University, Australia

Program Committee

Peter Albion	University of Southern Queensland, Australia
Leicha Bragg	Deakin University, Australia
Stéphane Bressan	National University of Singapore, Singapore
Wentong Cai	Nanyang Technological University, Singapore
Malcolm Campbell	Deakin University, Australia
Jiannong Cao	Hong Kong Polytechnic University
Ronnie Cheung	Hong Kong Polytechnic University
Jo Coldwell	Deakin University, Australia
Brian Corbitt	Deakin University, Australia
Brian d'Auriol	University of Texas at El Paso, USA
Caroline Dowling	Australian Catholic University, Australia
Joseph Fong	Hong Kong Web Society
Alex Fung	Hong Kong Baptist University
Wen Gao	Chinese Academy of Sciences, China
Andrzej Goscinski	Deakin University, Australia
Minyi Guo	University of Aizu, Japan
Sarah Guss	RMIT University, Australia
Bernard Holkner	Monash University, Australia
John Hughes	University of Ulster, UK

Program Committee (Contd.)

Ali Hurson	Pennsylvania State University, USA
Kai Hwang	University of Southern California, USA
Beverley Jane	Deakin University, Australia
Weijia Jia	City University of Hong Kong
Zongli Jiang	Beijing Polytechnic University, China
Han Jin	Huazhong University of Sci. and Tech., China
Stephen Keast	Deakin University, Australia
Leissa Kelly	Deakin University, Australia
Chung-Ta King	National Tsing Hua University, Taiwan
Irene Kwan	Lingnan University
Reggie Kwan	Open University of Hong Kong
Keqin Li	State University of NY at New Paltz, USA
Xiaoming Li	Beijing University, China
Qing Li	City University of Hong Kong
Craig Linn	University of Western Sydney, Australia
Zhiyong Liu	National Natural Science Foundation, China
Dennis McLeod	University of Southern California, USA
Christine Morin	IRISA/Université de Rennes, France
John Murnane	Melbourne University, Australia
Paul Nicholson	Deakin University, Australia
Maria Orlowska	University of Queensland, Australia
Yi Pan	Georgia State University, USA
John Pearson	University of Hong Kong
Raj Raje	Purdue University, USA
Jeff Richardson	Monash University, Australia
Geoff Romeo	Monash University, Australia
Jackie Silcock	Deakin University, Australia
Peter Smith	University of Sunderland, UK
Philip Steele	Monash University, Australia
Chengzheng Sun	Griffith University, Australia
Boleslaw Szymanski	Rensselaer University, USA
Arthur Tatnall	Victoria University of Technology, Australia
Y.-M. Teo	National University of Singapore, Singapore
Ulrich Thiel	GMD-IPSI, Germany
Choonhapong Thaiupathump	Chiang Mai University, Thailand
Juhani Tuovinen	Charles Sturt University, Australia
Julia Walsh	Deakin University, Australia
Craig Warren	Deakin University, Australia
Yue Wu	University of Electronic Sci. and Tech., China
Zhengda Wu	Bond University, Australia
Jianwei Zhang	Tsinghua University, China
Wei Zhao	Texas A&M University, USA
Si Qing Zheng	University of Texas at Dallas, USA
Weimin Zheng	Tsinghua University, China
Wanlei Zhou	Deakin University, Australia

Additional Reviewers

In additional to all members of the Program Committee, the following people were also involved in reviewing the papers:

Scot Aldred
Pui On Au
Penny Baillie-de Byl
Keith Chan
Alvin Chan
K.W. Chau
Kai Chow
Bouras Christos
Steve Drew
Geoge Fernandez
Junyan Geng
Hermann Gruenwald
Om Kumar Harsh
Suk-Ki Hong
Nikolai Joukov
Woochun Jun
Elicia Lanham

Elvis Wai Chung Leung
Paul Cheng Leung
MeiYi Li
Qinghu Li
Cheng-xin Liu
Hongen Lu
Yi Mao
Elspeth McKay
Joan Richardson
Kamaljeet Sandhu
Siranush Sargsyan
Raghavendran
   Sethumadhavan
Nalin Sharda
John Shepherd
Runting Shi
Sean Wolfgand

Marc Spaniol
Congyong Su
Herman Surjono
Marvin B.L. Tan
Alexandra Uitdenbogerd
Adriana Vivacqua
Weiyuan Wang
Feng-Hsu Wang
Matthew Warren
Huang Weitong
Jason Wells
Cao Yanhua
Li Yang
Fan Yang
Xinyu Zhang
Degan Zhang

Table of Contents

Web-Based Learning Environment

Virtual University

Pedagogical Issues

Multimedia Based E-learning

Interactivity

Intelligence in Online Education

Innovative Curriculum in E-learning

E-learning Solutions

CSCL

Challenges of Web-Based Learning Environments: Are We Student-Centred Enuf?

Judithe Sheard[1] and Julianne Lynch[2]

[1]School of Computer Science and Software Engineering
Monash University
Melbourne, Australia
judy.sheard@csse.monash.edu.au
[2]Faculty of Education
Deakin University
Melbourne, Australia
jlynch@deakin.edu.au

Abstract. The last decade has seen a phenomenal growth in the use of the Web in university education, with various factors influencing the adoption of Web-based technology. The reduction of government funding in the higher education sector has forced universities to seek technological solutions to provide courses for a growing and increasingly diverse and distributed student population [13,14]. Another impetus has been a shift in focus from teacher-centred to learner-centred education, encouraging educators to provide courses which enable students to manage their own learning [6]. In this paper we discuss challenges associated with the design and provision of Web-based learning environments that are truly student-centred. We draw on interview and questionnaire data from an evaluation study to raise issues surrounding the provision of online environments that meet learners' needs. We discuss the challenges of catering for the needs of different learners and the challenges associated with helping students to make the transition into new online learning environments.

1 Introduction

Within university teaching programs the use of the Web ranges from occasional, supplementary use (sometimes initiated by the learner) to the provision of fully integrated electronic environments where all learner interactions happen online [8,10]. Increasingly educators incorporate a range of Web-based resources in their teaching programs. The organisation of these into an integrated environment is typically referred to as a *Web-based learning environment* [16]. Piguet and Peraya [15] describe a Web-based learning environment as "a place where learners and teachers interact" and defines it as "a hypermedia based program or system that uses the attributes and resources of the WWW to facilitate learning" (n.p.). The use of Web-based learning environments is increasingly supported by university administrators. In fact, universities educators are now often required to demonstrate the *Web presence* of their units [10,11]. A factor in this trend is the reduction of government funding in the

W. Zhou et al. (Eds.): ICWL 2003, LNCS 2783, pp. 1–11, 2003.

higher education sector which has forced universities to seek technological solutions to problems associated with a growing and increasingly diverse and distributed student population [13,14]. However, research must be undertaken to ensure that these so-called *solutions* do not cause new problems.

What do we know about how students experience these environments? Although the Web can potentially be used to provide exciting and engaging learning spaces, it should not be assumed that learners will find these spaces a comfortable and easy environment in which to learn. Arif [2] questions the assumption that all students are ready to use these environments effectively. Using an electronic environment requires skills and learning processes that are different from those used in a paper-based or face-to-face environment. Carlson, Repman, Downs and Clark [3] maintain that "even experienced students face challenges in a new kind of learning environment and they may find that skills that served them well in a traditional classroom are inadequate for learning via the World Wide Web" (n.p.).

An important consideration in the provision of Web-based learning environments is determining students' reactions to these environments in terms of the way they interact with them and their affective and attitudinal responses. Davis [7] determined that users' attitudes towards a technology system have a significant impact on their acceptance and usage of these systems [7]. An investigation of the literature by Harrison and Rainer [9] determined that the main causes of resistance to using technology systems are negative attitudes towards computers, high levels of anxiety and low self-efficacy. In their study investigating these factors, Coffin and MacIntyre [5] found that they were related to inexperience with computers and low motivation to learn to use computers. Studies have shown that inhibitive affective responses can stem from characteristics of both the learning environment and the learner. Akerlind and Trevitt [1] claim that the change to a new learning environment can produce discomfort or anxiety which may inhibit the learning process. Their research suggests that the extent of feelings of anxiety experienced by learners is related to their previous experience and the degree to which the new environment is different from or similar to environments previously experienced, with environments that are less familiar more likely to engender feelings of discomfort. Furthermore, characteristics of individual learners have also been found to affect the extent of these reactions [4].

These studies are founded on an understanding that different learners will respond to a learning environment in different ways. They demonstrate the usefulness of examining students' reactions when evaluating a learning environment. The findings of studies that examine the range of learner reactions to particular types of environments and that identify the antecedents of particular reactions have important implications for the design and effective use of Web-based learning environments. Although many university educators view the primary impetus behind moves towards Web-based learning environments to be top-down directives based on non-educational rationales [12], a more palatable rationale is that these environments can facilitate a shift in focus from teacher-centred to learner-centred education, encouraging educators to provide courses which enable students to manage their own learning [6]. Enabling the learners more control of their learning has become the "central goal or a desirable side benefit" of computer technology [1, p.96]. Examining student reactions to Web-based learning environments can give insights into the possible effectiveness of these environments and to the possible problems they give rise to. If students are to use these environments effectively then factors which could inhibit their learning should be determined [11]. These factors should be considered when providing Web-based learning environments.

2   Context of the Research

This paper draws upon data collected as part of an evaluation of a website that was developed to supplement face-to-face components of an undergraduate education unit. The Web-based learning environment provided general information about the unit of study and various resources including a synopsis, definitions, extended reading, scenarios illustrating concepts ('snapshots') and interactive forums. Two drop down menus known as "Global Navigation" and "Local Navigation" provided access to most resources on the site. The site was largely static: it was designed and created prior to the commencement of the semester and most of the content (outlines of topics, examples illustrating concepts, definitions, links to external sites) remained the same for the duration of the semester. The only exceptions were discussion forums that asked students to post in responses to classroom scenarios. Students were able to choose if and when they would view particular topics, but they had no control over the format of the information provided.

3   Research Methods and Participants

A decision was made to work with a small number of students intensively to get deeper insights into their experiences. Twenty students enrolled in the education unit as part of a Bachelor of Education participated in this study. Volunteers were sought from three of a possible 14 tutorial groups. The students were aged from 18 to 47 years; however, only four students were over the age of 25. Eight students were male and 12 were female. Eight students were enrolled in a Primary Teaching course and 12 in a Secondary Teaching course.

Each participant attended an interview with the evaluator. During the interview, students were asked to complete a questionnaire that asked for demographic data and for information about students' usage of computers, the education unit website and their opinions of its usability and the usefulness of its contents. Each participant was then observed as they completed a series of tasks *inside* the unit website. Tasks ranged from locating a page on the site to completing an entry in a discussion forum. The evaluator then asked follow-up questions, following a semi-structured interview schedule. Each session was from 30-45 minutes in duration. The data was collected from the 6th to the 8th week of 2nd semester 2002.

4   Computer Usage

The students generally rated themselves as having an average skill level with computers. Using a seven point Likert scale, where 1 indicated *beginner* and 7 indicated *expert,* half the students rated their skill level at the midpoint ($M = 4.15$, SD

= 0.99). However, their reactions to computers tended to be positive. Using a scale where 1 indicated *negative* and 7 indicated *positive*, they rated their experiences with computers ($M = 4.75$, $SD = 1.16$, $t = 2.8$) and feelings about computers ($M = 4.95$, $SD = 1.36$, $t = 3.1$) significantly above the mid-point of the scale as measured using one sample t-tests.

All except three students had access to the Internet outside the university and indicated that they had moderate use of the Internet for coursework ($M = 4.10$, $SD = 1.45$) and for general use ($M = 3.80$, $SD = 1.74$). Their frequency of access varied, with nine students accessing it daily, six twice weekly, four weekly and one monthly.

The students were not frequent users of the education unit website. Twelve students claimed that they had only accessed the site three times or less and most mentioned that at least one of these accesses had been during class. They were generally positive about the usefulness of the site for their work in the unit and indicated a very purposeful use of the site. Most of the accesses to the site appeared to be for their assessment tasks, which required them to post a response or comment to a discussion group. Most showed a scant knowledge of the content of the site beyond what they had used for their assessment tasks.

5   Reactions to the Website

The students expressed a range of affective reactions to the unit website, from positive feelings of satisfaction and comfort to negative feelings of anxiety, frustration, confusion, annoyance, lack of confidence and being overwhelmed. The mini case studies provided below illustrate the range of responses reported by participants.

5.1   Graeme

The most common negative effective responses reported by the students were confusion and frustration. These were often reactions to problems locating information and navigating within the site and in some cases involved students becoming disoriented within the site. Many students indicated that there were initial problems learning to use the site. Graeme illustrates this type of response.

Graeme was a mature age student who had returned to study after a variety of careers. He claimed to be a "traditionalist" but was also interested in online education. He was comfortable using computers however rated his computer skills as low. He accessed the Internet daily, mainly for personal use; however, he had only accessed the unit website three times and was concerned that these were sketchy and not competent sessions.

Graeme was enthusiastic about the unit and expressed a keen desire to fulfil the online assessment requirements; however, throughout the interview he expressed annoyance and frustration with various difficulties he had experienced with the website:

> *It is frustrating because I know I have got work to do, same as we have assignments and readings to do for tutes and there is a barrier to being able to*

do it. You want to do it but it is very frustrating when you can't get the thing to work.

Most of Graeme's negative reactions seemed to relate to the organisation of the website and the accessibility of information. He spoke of barriers and hurdles to overcome to access the information. He described his reaction to the site as "problems – how am I going to get in there" and spoke of being intimidated by the site. Graeme did not seem comfortable with inherent nature of the hypertext environment in which material is organised with a multidirectional rather than sequential format. He maintained he would have felt more comfortable if the website was organised in the same way as the printed materials for the unit. He liked things to be straightforward and clear. He spoke of the information on the website as being hidden:

I'm sure there is an awful lot in there …it's very hidden …I like to see what I'm dealing with before I go in one at a time, and I like that, I want to see what I'm dealing with.

However, despite these difficulties he was eager to persist with the site and saw that his confidence would build with familiarity and practice.

But there are always pluses and minuses. I am really eager to do it now, not only because we have to but because I want to make a comment or two on the topics we are doing. But the mechanics …it's almost like the form is the problem not the content. The content of [the website] is no problem – but it's the form of it that is holding me back a little.

5.2   Rosie

Some students did not have confidence in the site as a safe and useful learning space. Rosie illustrates the responses of learners who do not trust the information on the Web.

Rosie indicated she was comfortable using computers and she rated her skill level as above average. She was a regular user of the Internet for general use however had only used the unit website twice and claimed that this was because she did not like using it. There appeared to be several reasons for this. First, she stated that she found that the information on the site was not clearly laid out, commenting that "It's all confusing and I hate it – its just a blobbery mess". During the interview she spoke several times about being confused by the site and mentioned feeling lost. She further explained:

It's just totally confusing. You get in there and it's just like – "where am I supposed to go, what am I supposed to do", there's no clear "you need to go here". It's just Global Navigation, Local Navigation. It reminds me of the big Internet and how you do searches – it's just not clear.

Second, the appearance of the website did not appeal to her and did not inspire her curiosity:

Dull and boring. Considering it's education I think they need to make it nice and bright and welcoming, easy to use, treat it as if we were kids and teenagers and we really don't know what we are doing. Flashing stuff – you know - news for this week.

She expressed annoyance at having to use the website and stated that she only used the site because it was mandatory.

...I've just gone to where I had to go.... If it was easier for me to get around and understand then I would probably use it more often than I do.

Furthermore, she had a general mistrust of the Internet claiming "there is so much dodgy stuff" and she commented on the difficulty of finding original sources of information.

5.3   Chris

The mature-aged students who participated in this study appeared to experience particular difficulties with anxiety. They were keen to use the technology effectively and recognised the significant role it has in education. However they had little experience with computers and appeared to lack confidence when using them and to have less access to peer support than did other students. The case of Chris illustrates some of the challenges faced by mature aged students.

Chris was a mature age student who had returned to study. She rated her skill level with computers as low and did not use computers much for general use. She indicated that she did not feel uncomfortable with computers, however while performing the tasks she seemed anxious and unsure of what she was doing. Chris came to the interview with her login details written down on a piece of paper and was the only student who did this.

Chris commented several times throughout the interview that she liked the website and indicated that she thought it was a good idea. She claimed the site was useful as it reinforced the material covered in class. Furthermore, it forced her to use computers and this had increased her confidence in using them.

... I quite like it, when I give it a go - generally I like it – as long as it's easy enough to get into – I like it. I've found I do all my readings as well and in class there is usually only about two of us who do this - so maybe they jump on the Net and do it that way, I don't know.

She expressed frustration in the many small difficulties that she had faced while attempting to use the site. As a mature age, female student who had not used a computer before the course she felt isolated in her class and the lack of readily available support at university and home had caused problems. She suggested that a special class for people in her situation would be beneficial.

... it took me a long time to figure out how to get into it. And I think, also, because I am so much older that anyone else, if I had been in a group I could have just said "well how do you get into it", but I didn't, I struggled and struggled for so long, nights, and didn't get in there and once I got in there it was easy, but oh gee, it was so long.

In spite of these difficulties, she was determined to use the website and quietly confident that eventually she would succeed:

I know it is very limited what I know. I would like to know more and have it all make sense – put it all together...It doesn't look like I do today but when I am in there at home I can work it out.

Chris acknowledged the benefits of online education but felt that in her situation, with difficulties in gaining access to computers, she needed to also work in a paper-based environment.

5.4 Elizabeth

Some students expressed irritation and annoyance with the site. Elizabeth was an interesting case because the source of her irritation was a fundamental dislike of working with computers. She expressed a preference for more conventional teaching and learning environments.

Elizabeth rated her computing skill level as average and was one of the lowest users of the Internet amongst the students interviewed. She did not indicate in the survey that she had had any negative experiences working with computers, however during the interview she commented several times that she did not like working with them. She claimed that she preferred face-to-face classes, "I learn better if I have someone explaining it to me. Even lectures - I would rather blackboard and chalk". In a previous unit she did an assignment in which all the work was done on the Internet, which she had hated. She further stated that she had "little motivation when it comes to using the Internet to learn".

Elizabeth had accessed the site six times and claimed that she had explored the site. There were aspects to the site that she liked:

*I like that it has general information – so for the topics you can get a fairly general rundown on the information and then it has links to go to more detailed sites. That is one of the things I **do** like about it – it makes it easy to search other areas of the Internet that is the only thing I really think, "oh, that is good".*

However, a dislike of working in an electronic environment seemed to influence her reactions to the site.

I think it's really good it's just I don't like using it. It's just a personal thing - I don't like sitting in front of a screen – I can't learn that way – I just get really tired and lose concentration quickly. But I think the site's really good.

She also mentioned that accessing and finding the information on the site was a problem and had led to some confusion, but that was mainly because of a lack of familiarity with the site caused by infrequency of access.

Every time I go into the site I always feel like, "where do I have to go again". It still doesn't register – it is not in my memory bank to go straight to that one or straight there, because, every time I have been looking for something different as well – so it's not always really clear to me.

5.5 Kim

Students who gave positive comments about the unit website usually referred to the usefulness or potential usefulness of the site for their work. The case of Kim illustrates his comfort and satisfaction with the site as a learning environment.

Kim rated his experience with and reactions to computers as average. However, he used the Internet every day and had accessed the unit website every week during the semester. He was the only student interviewed who appeared to be using the website in the manner intended by the unit teaching staff.

Our tasks are to go into each week, then each module and each topic – you sort of follow on each week.

Kim's use of the website appeared to be both purposeful and exploratory. He demonstrated a good knowledge of many of the features of the website and had contributed to the discussion topics more than was required for assessment. He appeared confident using the website and attributed this to regular use. While using the website and during the interview he commented that the website was well organised and the navigation was straightforward.

… the Local Navigation in there makes it so much easier – rather than searching for anything - it's all there. It helps if you know what you are going after, but to have it all in that one drop down menu makes the searching for links here and there easier.

Kim found that the website compared favourably to other websites he had used.

Probably one of the easiest websites to use …You go to some websites and there are icons here, there and everywhere, you have got to follow through - here it is all there in the one place.

6   Discussion

Students who participated in this research made many positive comments about the usefulness of the Web-based learning environment provided for them; however, they also reported affective responses that the literature suggests would be inhibitive to their learning. Such affective responses are of interest here because research suggests they impact negatively on students' acceptance and usage of new learning environments (Davis, 1993). Addressing the causes of students' reactions which could adversely affect learning presents challenges to the designers and implementers of Web-based learning environments.

6.1   Different Needs

The Web-based learning environment used in this study was designed and fully implemented prior to the commencement of the semester by instructional developers in consultation with the educators. This approach to provision of a Web-based learning environment differs from other possible approaches where content is developed incrementally, responding to the needs of the students as they progress through their course. The approach used in this study affords the advantage of the educator being able to think through the aims of the unit and provide high quality information that is presented in a consistent format. Another advantage is that it reduces the time needed during the semester to update and maintain the website. However, although the design of such an environment is informed by the anticipated experiences of student-users, it is teacher-centred. The educator's control over the form and content of the website is maximised. The design of the website is based on the educator's view of how the students will use the website but this is not an easy thing to anticipate given the diversity among student cohorts. The content of the unit website in this study was organised into topics which were provided to summarise and complement content covered in class each week; however, Kim was the only student who had visited the website each week as the unit educators intended. The other students appeared reluctant to incorporate the website into their chosen learning space.

6.2   Competing Needs

The website used in this study made use of hyper-linking and navigation tools to organise information so that the need to scroll down the screen would be minimised. This design principle has become part of our popular understanding of how to build good websites. Yet Graeme found this characteristic of the environment inhibiting: "I'm sure there is an awful lot in there … it's very hidden … I like to see what I'm dealing with before I go in one at a time." The technologies that currently predominate in the online provision of university course materials do not afford students any control over format. Both Graeme and Rosie were uncomfortable with the hyperlinked environment and both expressed dissatisfaction with Web environments more generally. No one format is going to meet the needs of all students. Just as not all students learn effectively in a one-to-many lecture, not all students can be expected to learn effectively in the same online environment. Digital technologies have the potential to provide environments that can be tailored to individual students' needs and to offer students some choice and flexibility in the way they engage with the content of their courses. This principle is beginning to be seen in the provision of adaptive websites which cater for to the learning styles and needs of individual students [17]. This type of website may be able to provide the flexibility required to accommodate the needs of Graeme and Rosie.

6.3   Dilemmas of Motivation and Authentic Use

Common reactions to the website used in this study included the confusion, frustration and annoyance that often accompany early encounters with new learning environments. For most students, these inhibiting affective responses lessen as they become more familiar with the environment. However, familiarity is difficult to gain if use is infrequent. Unless a website is accessed regularly users tend to forget the website structure and the location of information. Elizabeth indicated that each time she used the website it was an effort to remember where she had been before. A difficulty here is that most of the students appeared to access the website only when necessary. Students' assessment in the unit included hurdle tasks, one of which was a requirement to contribute to two of the discussion forums. These tasks acted as an extrinsic motivator for students to access and explore the website. However, in the case of Rosie and Elizabeth, this limited use was not enough to overcome difficulties they faced in using it

The use of mandated hurdle requirements is a common feature of university teaching where a Web-based environment is used to complement a predominantly face-to-face unit. However, the setting of such tasks is not unproblematic for educators. Most educators would prefer to believe that learners' motivation for accessing and exploring their online materials is intrinsic and bolstered by the value that they gain from their online activities.   However, this would appear to be unrealistic. Most students in this study gave no indications of any intrinsic motivation to use the website and the use of extrinsic motivators appeared necessary to encourage use of the website. Graeme indicated that his motivation for using the website had developed from the initial extrinsic requirement to a desire to contribute to online discussions: "I am really eager to do it now, not only because we have to but because I want to make a comment or two on the topics we are doing." In the case of Graeme, the provision of extrinsic motivation for developing basic skills in using the website lead to the development of intrinsic motivation.

6.4   Overcoming Anxiety

Another reaction to the website used in this study was anxiety. This particularly affected the students who were unsure about computers and the Web environment. Graeme and Chris as mature age students had had very little experience with computers and felt particularly vulnerable in a class of predominantly younger students who they assumed had used computers extensively at school. Chris had the added difficulty of gaining access to a computer outside class time. Confidence can develop with familiarity and practice however this becomes difficult to achieve when access to computers and the Web is limited or problematic. Educators need an awareness of the possibility of these difficulties to help students overcome the initial hurdles they may face using an environment they are unused to. Responding to student needs is challenging and the introduction of an electronic learning environment, which is unfamiliar to both students and educators, provides a new range of challenges.

7   Challenges

This paper highlights a number of challenges that face those involved in the design and implementation of Web-based learning environments, including the challenge of catering for students with different needs (particularly in terms of learning style and preferred modality), the challenge of motivating students to use environments that complement face-to-face teaching, and the challenge of assisting students to overcome initial affective responses that might inhibit their learning or cause them to discontinue their use of the environment. When incorporating Web-based learning environments into teaching programs it is important to recognise factors that may inhibit their effective use.   Students bring a great diversity of experiences and expertise to an electronic learning environment and educators should be sensitive to these and adapt their teaching programs to cater for the needs of all students. Addressing these issues will ultimately enhance the students learning experience.

Online environments offer the possibility of providing access to education that is more flexible and more responsive to students' needs. However, it is possible that such environments, while responding to the anywhere-anytime needs of students, fail to address the diversity in students in terms of learning style, modality preference, computer skills and experience. Future developments in online course provision technology, if such technology is to facilitate truly student-centred teaching and learning, need to be smart enuf to respond to these challenges.

References

1. Akerlind, G.S., Trevitt, A.C.: Enhancing self-directed learning through educational technology: When students resist the change, *Innovations in Education and Training International*, 36 (1999) 96–105.
2. Arif, A.A.: Learning from the Web: are students ready or not?, *Educational Technology & Society*, 4 (2001) 32–38.
3. Carlson, R., Repman, J., Downs, E., Clark, K.F.: So you want to develop Web-based instruction - points to ponder. *SITE '98*, AACE, Washington, DC, 1998.
4. Chua, S.L., Chen, D.-T., Wong, A.F.L.: Computer anxiety and its correlates: a meta-analysis, *Computers in Human Behavior*, 15 (1999) 609–623.
5. Coffin, R.J., MacIntyre, P.D.: Motivational influences on computer-related affective states, *Computers in Human Behavior*, 15 (1999) 549–569.
6. Collis, B.: New didactics for university instruction: Why and how?, *Computers & Education*, 31 (1998) 373–393.
7. Davis, F.D.: User acceptance of information technology: system characteristics, user perceptions and behavioral impacts, *Journal of Man-Machine Studies*, 38 (1993) 475–487.
8. Harmon, S.W., Jones, M.G.: The five levels of Web use in education: factors to consider in planning online courses, *Educational Technology*, 39 (1999) 28–32.
9. Harrison, A.W., Rainer, R.K., Jr.: An examination of the factor structures and concurrent validities for the Computer Attitude Scale, the Computer Anxiety Rating Scale, and the Computer Self-Efficacy Scale, *Educational and Psychological Measurement*, 52 (1992) 735–745.
10. Ingram, A.L.: Using Web server logs in evaluating instructional Web sites, *Journal of Educational Technology Systems*, 28 (1999) 137–157.
11. Lund, C., Volet, S.: Barriers to studying online for the first time: Students' perceptions. *EdTech'98*, Perth, West Australia, 1998.
12. Lynch, J., Collins, F.: Academics concerns about the "push for flexible delivery". *18th Annual Conference of the Australasian Society for Computers in Learning in Tertiary Education (ASCILITE)*, Melbourne, Victoria, 2001, pp. 377–386.
13. McDonald, J., Postle, G.: Teaching online: Challenge to a reinterpretation of traditional instructional models. *AusWeb99*, Lismore, NSW, 1999.
14. Oliver, R.: Partnerships in teaching and learning: An emerging role for technology. *EdTech'98*, Perth, West Australia, 1998.
15. Piguet, A., Peraya, D.: Creating web-integrated learning environments: an analysis of WebCT authoring tools in respect to usability, *Australian Journal of Educational Technology*, 16 (2000) 302–314.
16. Wang, L.-C.C., Beasley, W.: Effects of learner control and hypermedia preference on cyber-students performance in a web-based learning environment, *Journal of Educational Multimedia and Hypermedia*, 11 (2002) 71–91.
17. Wolf, C.: iWeaver: Towards 'learning style'-based e-learning in computer science education. *5th Australasian Computing Education conference*, Adelaide, Australia, 2003, pp. 273–279.

Cognitive Scaffolding for a Web-Based Adaptive Learning Environment

George Fernandez

School of Computer Science and Information Technology
RMIT University, Melbourne, Australia
gfernandez@rmit.edu.au

Abstract. On-line Web-based learning environments with automated feedback, such as WebLearn [5], present subject questions to the student and evaluate their answers to provide formative and summative assessment. With these tools, formative learning activities such as quizzes and tests are mostly pre-planned, since testing instruments are generated by selecting questions in a pre-specified manner out of question banks created for the purpose. Although this approach has been used with a significant degree of success, the real challenge to support students' learning is to mimic what a human instructor would do when teaching: provide guided learning.

The main difficulty associated with creating such an 'electronic tutor' is to implement the required intelligent dynamic behaviour during learning. That is, at any stage of a student's learning session the system should take into account his/her demonstrated cognitive level to generate the next appropriate formative testing instrument. For students to be able to make the higher-level cognitive contributions as they progress through a session, the system must keep a history of students' answers and must react accordingly. We call here that behaviour *adaptive learning* by *adaptive formative assessment*.

We propose on this paper a strategy to implement an adaptive automated learning system, based on establishing an incremental cognitive path from the lowest to the highest level questions related to a concept. In the research literature this has been often called 'cognitive scaffolding'. For our on-line automated environment, the first hurdle has been how to define the scaffolding and how to implement it from question banks that have not been created for this process. Our approach is embodied in WebTutor, a 'black box' component being developed at RMIT University to work in combination with the generation, presentation and feedback capabilities of the WebLearn system.

1 Introduction

Cognitive scaffolding represents what an instructor does when working with a student "to solve a problem, carry out a task, or achieve a goal which would be beyond his unassisted efforts" [10, pp 90]. It is generally a dynamic process, with the student interacting with the instructor, who attempts to understand from the student responses what the cognitive gaps are, and accordingly provide guided support to progress along the intended learning path. Instructors do this by presenting appropriate examples to reflect on and problems to solve, and demonstrating skills that student can imitate.

W. Zhou et al. (Eds.): ICWL 2003, LNCS 2783, pp. 12–20, 2003.

This typically follows a "from shallower to deeper" approach, as a sequence of steps intended to guide the student to the desired depth of understanding. The best instructors are the ones who, during a session, follow a student's demonstrated progress and adapt the learning activities to promote as much as possible reflection by the student. To do so, they present content to stimulate inquiry in the students, present alternative points of view on a concept, raise points for consideration, and decide on subsequent steps in the instruction. During that process, often students are asked to perform learning activities for which they are unprepared. If that happens, a skilful instructor follows the student's answers and evaluates the shortcomings, and backtracks looking for a place to start again on a firmer footing. The teacher's model of instruction includes a continuous evaluation of what are the difficulties with the problem at hand, and what would be the necessary steps for helping students advance towards their goals.

In on-line teaching and learning there is much less teacher-student face-to-face contact than traditionally, thus changing the emphasis from a teacher-centred to a student-centred approach [3, 8]. The main purpose of teaching is now to properly manage the learning process rather than to transmit information in a clear and organised manner, (a la Level 1 and Level 2 in [9]). Learning environments with automated feedback have been used rather successfully in online learning, albeit mostly for rote learning by focusing on drilling exercises. As discussed above, however, creating an 'electronic tutor' would require engaging students in appropriate self-directed learning activities that foster question, reflection and analysis along an incremental cognitive path. With the support of an appropriate environment, well-structured learning tasks should induce consideration, inquiry and discovery in the students, progressing students through their learning process to the higher levels required for deeper learning (See for example [6, 7]).

However, on-line learning environments today are not capable of adequately supporting learning processes in such a way. Not only they are typically restricted to questions with a given simple format, such as Multiple Choice, Multiple Answer, or Short (Key) Text, but they lack the human instructor's ability to retrace steps and dynamically change the angle of instruction based on what the student seems to have learnt/not learnt up to that stage. We argue that an automated learning system providing formative assessment might, to a certain extent, be able to do that if the system keeps the history of the previous student answers during a session and decides on what testing instrument to generate next based on what the student has already learnt and is still required to achieve.

This issue is naturally related to Computer Adaptive Testing (CAT), where there has been considerable research attention focused on Item Response Theory (IRT) [1]. IRT is attractive because it is based on solid statistical foundations, and because, with the right item bank and variance of examinees, it may be very effective for computer based automated testing. Our interest here is not, however, adaptive testing but adaptive learning by adaptive formative assessment. By this we mean that we intend to endow the learning environment with the capability of guiding students through a learning session where questions are presented as a response to their previous answers in the session, following a strategy resembling a human instructor.

The rest of this paper is organised as follows. Section 2 presents previous research on WebLearn, a Web-based learning environment with which WebTutor is tightly associated. Section 3 presents the basics of Item Response Theory (IRT), a line of research closely related to this paper. Section 4 discusses the conceptual differences between IRT and our line of research. Section 5 presents the proposed strategy to establish the cognitive scaffolding for a given item bank related to a concept or concepts. Section 6 concludes, and presents suggestions for further research.

2 WebLearn, a Web-Based Online Learning Environment

WebLearn is a WWW-based tool that supports self-learning by presenting questions of different types and providing student with automated feedback. The system is easy to use by non-computer experts, it is highly configurable to reflect diverse subject objectives and personal teaching preferences and it can accommodate subjects in many different disciplines. The system supports the teaching of 'WebLearn subjects', divided into modules, each divided into set of learning objectives (e.g. Bloom's Taxonomy of Educational Objectives, [2, 4]). Each module requires questions addressing the learning objectives, compiled into quiz and tests question banks. For formative assessment, WebLearn automatically generates random quizzes from the stated learning objectives, according to the instructor's directions, checks the answers given by the students, and provides immediate feedback. Quiz questions can be Multiple Choice and Multiple Answer (more than one correct answer), Short Text, and a variety of numeric and other types with and without random generation of parameters.

Over the last two years, WebLearn has been working in combination with Maple, a Mathematics symbolic manipulation package. Systems such as Maple provide an environment with which students can interact in mathematical terms, since they include specialised 'engines' that interpret abstract mathematical language. On the other hand, environments such as WebLearn have been designed to present questions to students and analyse their answers against predefined correct answers supplied by the instructors. Our approach combines the generation, presentation and feedback capabilities of WebLearn with the analysis capabilities of the Maple engine. When required, WebLearn automatically generates a formative or summative — a quiz or a test — testing instrument. Students' answers are captured by WebLearn and fed through Maple. The response from Maple is then caught back by WebLearn to be analysed, massaged into an appropriate form, and fed back to the students. This makes possible the correct evaluation of questions with no unique answer, for example, providing proper assessment of any right answer provided by the students. WebLearn treats Maple essentially as a 'black box', making possible to quarantine software changes to either system. The interoperation between Maple and WebLearn offers a wide variety of unique features, including handling of symbolic mathematics in areas such as general calculus, differential equations, Fourier and Laplace transforms, algebra, finite mathematics and geometry.

The development of WebTutor follows the same 'black box' approach.When WebLearn requests the generation of a new testing instrument to present to the students, WebTutor generates the new quiz by inspecting the student's history and deciding on the best way forward. Currently the system uses a very simplistic approach to make this decision, so this research intends to provide a sound strategy to move the student along an incremental cognitive path. Thus, we are developing a formal framework on which to base these decisions, effectively implementing the above mentioned scaffolding. The two main problems we currently face are the development of appropriately graded question banks, and the provision of a set of criteria and structures to progress students up the cognitive ladder. This paper discusses our progress on the first one of these issues.

3 Item Response Theory

Item response Theory (IRT) was first introduced to provide a formal approach to adaptive testing. The theory establishes how to estimate the unknown 'ability' θ of a student being tested with a test consisting of a number of items (questions). Each of these items measures an aspect of the ability being estimated. Answers to an item are assessed as correct or incorrect; the student receives a score of one for a correct answer, zero otherwise. The main goal of IRT is to determine the true ability of an examinee by studying the probability of a correct response to each individual item in a test. Therefore, the primary interest of IRT is whether an examinee answered each individual item correctly or not, rather than a total test score. The theory considers each examinee to have a numerical ability value θ somewhere on the ability scale. The value of θ is measured on a scale having a midpoint of zero, a unit of measurement of one, and a range from negative to positive infinity.

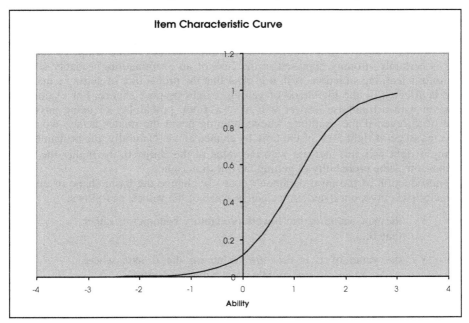

Fig. 1.

Although IRT has been used for free-response items, more often automated tests consist of multiple-choice items. One of the main applications of IRT has been to implement adaptive testing within an automated system by providing a carefully chosen sequence of questions. IRT determines at each step of the testing process which is the best next item to be presented to a given student, provides a stopping condition for the test, and a statistical estimation of the value of θ at the end of the exercise. The fundamental construct of the theory is the Item Characteristic Curve, which for each item represents the probability P(θ) that an examinee with ability θ will give a correct answer to the item. In the case of a typical test item, this probability will be smaller for examinees of low ability and larger for examinees of high ability (See Figure 1).

The shape of the curve is typically a smooth S, with differences depending on the value of some parameters. The first of these is the difficulty of the item b, determined – somewhat arbitrarily – by the point on the θ axis where the probability P(θ)=0.5. The second parameter is the item discrimination a, which describes to what extent an item discriminates between examinees having abilities below and above, and close to, b. The discrimination parameter is often interpreted as the slope of the curve at abscissa b, although the value is actually a/4. There are actually several models in use – with one, two and three parameters – so this model is identified as the two-parameter model.

The 1-parameter model fixes the value of a=1, so there is only necessary to determine the difficulty parameter to establish the characteristic curve for the 2-parameter model. The three-parameter model includes the guessing parameter c. Although this last model lacks the mathematical elegance of the one and two parameter model – mainly because it doesn't follow a logistic model – this third parameter c is very important for CAT. In automated testing, it is reasonable to assume that if students don't know the answer to a Multiple Choice question they will attempt to guess it. This is certainly strongly expected in the case of an examination, probably slightly less so in a learning situation. Still, it is clear that the probability of getting a question right is affected by the likelihood of getting it right by pure chance. For example, a question with a true/false answer will have a 'floor' probability of being answered right of .5; even if the examinee knows nothing about the matter he/she would be expected to get it right 50% of the time by chance alone. Naturally, the probability of getting it right will still increase with the value of the ability θ, the higher the value the closer to 1 the probability of getting the question right.

The introduction of the third parameter does not change the basic shape of an item characteristic curve, but it certainly changes some of the values, as follows:

- the new value of the lowest probability becomes c rather than 0;

- the value of b is now the value on the θ axis where P(θ)=(1+c)/2 (the middle point between c and 1);

- the actual value of the slope at b is a(1-c)/4.

4 IRT and Adaptive Formative Assessment

Our first step to implement adaptive learning is the definition of the scaffolding. Although there are many similarities between IRT and the requirements for adaptive learning, there are also important differences:

- The value of θ under IRT is loosely defined as the 'ability' of an examinee at the moment of taking the test. This is assumed to embody the knowledge and cognitive capabilities of the examinee at the time of the test. The examinee is not supposed to learn during the examination process. However, adaptive learning as defined here perceives the value of θ to change as learning progresses. Actually, our intention is not to try to determine θ• as adaptive testing tries to do, but to move students along an incremental cognitive path so their value of θ increases on a particular topic.

- The discrimination parameter a is very important for adaptive testing, since it indicates the sensitivity of the estimation of θ. Given that the purpose of the examination is to determine the level of θ, a high value of a indicates that the item is capable of discriminating between two very close levels of ability within a certain range. For our purposes, though, an exact value of a is less relevant, since the intention is not to determine the value of θ but to increase it as a result of the learning process. In practice, however, questions are to be divided into categories, and the discrimination parameter may be used as a decision mechanism to trigger item selections from a higher cognitive category: a correct response to an item close to the category edge with a high value of a may indicate that is time to move the student to next category up.

- The difficulty parameter b is crucial to our research, specifically to create the cognitive scaffolding based on increasing values of b. If the learning system consists of questions with an established level of difficulty, it is possible to progress up the learning path until a certain stopping condition occurs.

- During an examination under IRT, the sequence of items presented to an examinee is determined by selecting, at each step in the procedure, the 'best next item'. Intuitively, this should be:

  o   an item with difficulty close to the examinee's θ value, since selecting an item that is too easy or too hard will provide no new information about the value of θ;

  o   an item with a high value of a, since it is desirable to have an item that is most useful in discriminating between examinees with abilities close to the unknown value θ.

For adaptive learning, however, these considerations are not that important. Students are supposed to learn during a session, and therefore there is no fixed value of θ to estimate in this case. The intention is to present a sequence of items that challenge, but don't discourage, students. We are only interested in a reasonable estimate of the value of θ at any stage of the learning session, to be able to make a decision about when to move the student up the incremental cognitive path.

5   The Cognitive Ladder

In systems such as WebLearn, the question banks have not been developed with cognitive scaffolding in mind, so regardless of how questions have been grouped they need to be re-classified so the system can progress the students up the cognitive ladder. To this end, the items in a question bank must be classified from lower to higher in a chosen cognitive taxonomy. A question may be classified higher than another question in a given taxonomy for different reasons, such as when the higher-level question is perceived as harder, more abstract, or requiring a deeper understanding than the lower-level question. We argue that it is unreasonable to put this classification burden on the instructor, for several reasons:

- Given that a bank used for this purpose may contain thousands of different items, the large number of questions may be too much for an instructor to categorise. If more than one instructor is used, problems of consistency would arise.

- The resulting classification by an instructor would be a very subjective one, and highly dependent of the opinion and experience of the instructor.

- Such a long and demanding task will inevitably result in an inconsistent categorisation, even by one instructor.

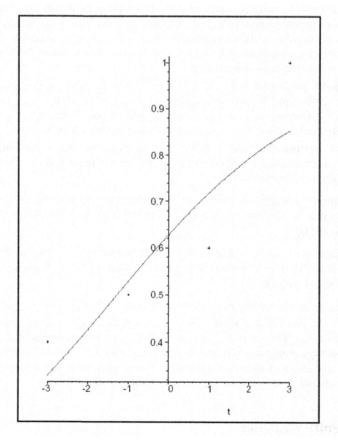

Fig. 2. An item classified, a = 0.411, b = -1.273

Regardless of the taxonomy, the only known invariant is that, given a question in a bank, students of higher ability are more likely to answer the question correctly than students of lower ability. It is possible to use this invariant to automatically classify a whole bank if the abilities of a group of students are known, or estimated by other means. The chosen strategy for this project was to use historic students' results as an estimate of their ability, and to use this information to provide a classification for the whole item bank. It was then possible to establish a correspondence between the estimated difficulty of the students' answers to the question banks for a first year programming subject. Two different, parallel approaches were considered for this project, as follows:

- The results of student tests were considered from the historical records. The unknown ability θ of the student cohort was estimated by their subject and examination results, and divided into categories θ_j. The proportion of correct answers to total number of answers pj/mj was then established for students in each category θ_j and used as an estimator of the probability value for the item response curve. This is an estimation of the true probability $P(\theta j)$, and it is then possible to obtain corresponding pairs $(\theta j, P(\theta j))$ to fit the characteristic curve and obtain the parameters a and b. This approach directly classifies automatically all the questions in the bank. Figure 2 depicts one of the characteristic curves obtained.

- A group of five experienced instructors was given a set of 30 questions to categorise into five categories: from 1 (Very Easy) to 5 (Very Hard). This gives a reasonable estimation of the difficulty of the items in the small question sample, with the intention to try to infer from this grading a classification for the whole collection. For this second approach, a Neural Network was then trained with the values obtained from the experts, and made to classify the whole item bank based upon the students' results and the classification by the experts. Once the Neural Network learns the ranking process, any number of questions can be ranked using just their historical information. It was then possible to automatically estimate the value of b for each question of the whole bank.

With both approaches, different strategies are being tried on this phase:

- It is possible to consider the final subject results, or only its examination component, as a measure of students' ability. Preliminary results seem to indicate that examination marks are a better indicator than overall subject marks.

- It also remains to be determined whether the experts' opinion is a good estimation of the difficulty of the questions in the sample, so it may be used when there are no historical data available.

- There are several ways of aggregating the experts' opinion, likely to produce different results. Data collection and analysis is progressing in this area.

- There are also several ways of categorising students' abilities θ_j, such as using equally spaced intervals or equal population segments (quartiles, deciles and so on). These are also likely to produce different results.

A complete analysis of the results obtained is currently progressing.

6   Conclusions and Further Research

Preliminary results are very encouraging. The scheme makes possible the automated classification of the items in a question bank to implement the cognitive ladder, even when the bank has not been developed for the purpose. The analysis of the results is currently in progress, in an attempt to establish the best strategies to follow in the near future. Some questions remain unresolved, in terms of the best indicator of the students' ability, whether the experts' opinion and Neural Network strategy provides a good estimator for when there is no historical results available, what is the best way of categorising the experts' opinion, etc. Research is progressing on these issues. After this phase is concluded, the research will attempt to establish an appropriate strategy to progress students up the cognitive ladder.

References

1. Baker, F.: The Basics of Item Response Theory. Second Edition, ERIC Clearinghouse on Assessment and Evaluation, Boston C., & Rudner L. (Eds), USA, ISBN 1-886047-03-0
2. Bloom B.S.: Taxonomy of Educational Objectives, David McKay Company Inc, New York, (1964).
3. Chalmers D. & Fuller A.: Teaching for Learning at University: Theory and Practice. Edith Cowan University, Perth., (1995).
4. Doran M. and Langan D.: A Cognitive-Based Approach to Introductory Computer Science Courses: Lessons Learned. SIGCSE Bulletin. Proceedings of the 26th ACM SIGCSE Technical Symposium. March, Nashville, TN, (1995), pp 218–222.
5. Fernandez G.: WebLearn: A CGI-Based Environment for Interactive Learning. Journal of Interactive Learning Research. Vol 12, No 2, (2001), pp 265–280.
6. John S., Netherwood G., Sudarmo & Fernandez G.: Learning Taxonomy Analyses Of Student-Based Activities Using The Lego Mindstorms System. Proceedings of the 13th AAEE Conference. Canberra, ACT, Australia, September, (2002).
7. Fernandez G., John S. & Netherwood G.: Objective-Based Teaching of Science and Engineering With an On-line Student-Centred Environment. Proceedings of the 12th AAEE Conference. QUT, Brisbane, Australia, pp 332–337, (2001).
8. Laurillard D.: Rethinking University Teaching: A Framework for the Effective Use of Educational Technology. Routledge. London, (1993).
9. Prosser M. & Trigwell K.: Teaching for Learning in Higher Education, Open University Press. Buckingham, (1998)
10. Wood, D., Bruner, J. S., & Ross, G.: The role of tutoring in problem solving. Journal of Child Psychology and Psychiatry, 17, 98–100, (1976).

Information Security – An E-learning Problem

M. Warren[1] and W. Hutchinson[2]

[1] School of Information Technology, Deakin University,
Geelong, Victoria, Australia, 3217.
mwarren@deakin.edu.au
[2] School of Computing & Information Science, Edith Cowan University,
Western Australia, Australia, 6018.
w.hutchinson@ecu.edu.au

Abstract. The paper describes the issues relating to the security of e-learning systems. The security perspective in e-learning systems is often ignored. This paper introduces the major information security issues as a primer for the research being carried out by the authors into the developing of generic, baseline information security standards for the e-learning environment.

1 Introduction

E-learning involves more than the availability of texts or lecture notes online or merely the use of the Internet within a course. Different electronic media may be used including computers, the Internet, intranet, CD-ROMS, DVDs, audio and video tapes, and virtual environments.

E-learning provides a convenient and flexible learning experience that can complement or replace traditional face-to-face teaching for on campus students. For off campus students, e-learning is a more engaging and interactive method of learning than conventional approaches such as the post and telephone. Students can work in an environment that seems much less isolated from their lecturers and fellow students. Accessibility is also improved to students with geographical or time issues. Students can work at their own pace, have up to date course information that can revisited at any stage and have synchronous or asynchronous contact with the unit's staff or other students.

Some of the key features that have been identified by (Smissen, 2002) for online teaching and learning include:

- Easy to use;
- Platform and browser compatibility;

W. Zhou et al. (Eds.): ICWL 2003, LNCS 2783, pp. 21–26, 2003.

- Synchronous communication;
- Asynchronous communication;
- Collaborative work;
- Online assessment;
- Result management;
- Assignment submission.

It should be noted that the security requirements of E-learning seldom appears in the literature in relation to E-learning. But security is an important aspect of all IT systems.

2   The Australian Security Problem

A recent AusCERT Survey (Auscert, 2002) has focused upon the state of E-security within Australia, the following is a summary of the main results:

- 67% of all organizations surveyed have been attacked in 2002 - twice the 1999 level and 35 per cent of these organizations experienced six or more incidents;
- 98% of companies had experience either computer Security incidents / crime or other forms of computer abuse (such as network scanning, theft of laptops, employee abuse);
- of Australian organisation who were victims of computer incidents, 65% of these attacks were from internally parties within the organisation and 89% came from external sources;
- 43% of Australian organizations were willing to hire ex-hackers to deal with security issues, three times more than in the US.

The survey showed that E-security and computer misuse are a major problem within Australia. The survey showed that external attacks were the source of the majority of attacks. An Australian Federal Government department NOIE (National Office of the Information Economy) sponsored project tried to determine the risks associated with the Information Economy. They determined that 43% of survey respondents were concerned with privacy issue and 42% of survey respondents were concerned about fraud (Allen Consultancy Group & NOIE, 2002).

These previous security studies indicate that Australia has a major problem with security in the corporate world, there has however been no studies into the security problems that face Australian Universities. One can only guess at what level the problem of IT security relates to Australian Universities.

3 E-learning Technologies

Deakin University is an Australian university that is at the leading edge of using the latest E-learning technologies. They use a number of e-learning technologies and these include the following:

WebCT
WebCT is a web-based tool that incorporates the school's intellectual and technical resources to serve as a store of information and facilitate a more flexible learning experience for students. Course notes, class news, results and other relevant materials are kept online for individual units and updated when required. Additional features include: facilities for asynchronous or synchronous discussions, a whiteboard, student tracking, internal course email and quizzes. The WebCT folder for a particular unit is accessible only by the teaching staff and students associated with that unit (Trondsen, 1998).

FirstClass
FirstClass is an Internet based communication system which provides real-time chat, group conferences with threaded messaging, email, a community directory, file sharing and many other useful features. Staff and students involved in a unit have access to meet online and communicate with each other in small, private, study groups or in more public discussions (Deakin University, 2003).

4 Security Considerations

Security problems have arisen through the use of e-learning technologies. A number of different situations have developed which show the weaknesses associated with the security mechanisms underpinning the e-learning systems. The following scenarios indicate major security flaws and suggest a poor level of Information Security being implemented within these systems.

The security problems that the authors have found include:

Passwords – a single default method is used to generate students' passwords. The problem is that the same simple method is used to generate thousands of students' logins. If the method of password creation were made public it would compromise thousands of passwords at the start of the semester. The other problem is that students are then expected to change their default password. The problem is that there is not a mechanism to force the students to change their password and some students use the default password for the entire semester.

Guessing URLS – students can bypass the security authentication mechanisms by directly guessing a URL address. For instance if a lecturer calls an assignment solution – solution.htm and stores it in the SCC209 (unit) directory, the student can directly go to SCC209/solution.htm page avoiding the security authentication mechanism. The only solution to this problem is to use abstract names for the naming of pages e.g., instead of solution.htm use ssdddccc.htm. An example is shown by figure 1, where a person has directly entered the URL to an obtain an assignment solution, this action has by passed all the security mechanisms associated with Web-ct.

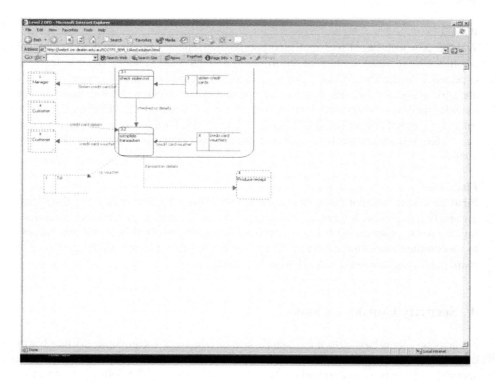

Fig. 1. Direct Link to Assignment Solution

Problems with Software – the E-learning systems do not log students out of the system when they finish. This means that another student can use the computer after the authorized student has finished their session and gain access to their E-learning ac-count. This allows some one to masquerade as an authenticate user and then for exam-ple post offensive messages to other students or staff.

Non-Repudiation – the e-learning systems allow students to submit their assignments. The problem is that the systems do not allow non-repudiation to be carried out. Staff cannot prove that the correct student did the assignments submitted. Also, the system also does not show that a student has tried to submit an assignment and failed e.g. a session crashing during the upload process.

Complexity of e-learning systems – due to the complex nature of the e-learning sys-tems novice users may mis-configure the system they are using. This means that staff may not set-up the security features correctly which allow students to gain access to information that they should not have for example, assignment solutions.

Many of the security problems and weaknesses described are often not discussed by e-learning researchers. The authors' experiences have shown that e-learning systems are not secure and can easily be open to abuse. Of course, the security dimension often seems at odds with the 'open' and flexible requirements of a university environment. Many universities (for example, Edith Cowan University) allow a certain access to non-students as a marketing tool.

5 The Security Issues

The Security implication of e-learning needs to be fully considered. The authors are conducting the development of security guidelines that focus upon e-learning. These guidelines will be focused towards the protection of systems from the user viewpoint and administrator viewpoints.

The authors are using the baseline approach to dealing with the problems of Information Security within e-learning. Baseline security offers an alternative to conventional risk methods as they represent the minimally acceptable security countermeasures that an organization should have implemented. These countermeasures are applied in a generic manner for example; every organization should have the same baseline security countermeasures implemented.

The advantages of using baseline methods include (Warren and Hutchinson, 2000):

- cheap to use;
- simple to use;
- no training is required to use the method;
- it is quicker than undertaking a full security review.

The authors are using this security rationalize to develop a series of baseline security guides that will assist users of e-learning technologies as well as the staff who develop such systems. The authors are focusing upon developing security awareness programs for users of such systems. The research will be validated at the universities of both authors and will be the source of future research papers.

6   Conclusion

E-learning is a powerful tool that all Australian Universities are now using. E-learning is here to stay but the security issues and problems need still to be addressed. The major advantage of e-learning out weighs any disadvantages relating to security problems.

The security implication of e-learning needs to be fully considered. The authors are developing guidelines that could have implications of all users and developers of E-learning systems within Australia.

References

1. Allen Consultancy Group & NOIE (2002) Report: Australia Information Economy – the Big Picture, Sydney, Australia.
2. AusCert (2002) 2002 Australian Computer Crime and Security Survey, University of Queensland, Australia.
3. Deakin University (2003) Online teaching and learning – Firstclass.
    URL: http://www.deakin.edu.au/students/teach_learn/firstclass.html
    [Accessed: Jan 3rd, 2003].
4. Smissen, I. (2002) Requirements for Online Teaching and Learning at Deakin University: A Case Study, Deakin University, Australia.
    URL: http://www.deakin.edu.au/~ismissen/ausweb02/paper.html.
    [Accessed: Jan 3rd, 2003].
5. Trondsen, E. (1998) The New World of Technology-Based Learning, SRI Consulting Business Intelligence.
6. Warren, M., Hutchinson, W (2000) The Australian & New Zealand Security Standard AS/NZS 4444, New Zealand Journal of Computing, 8,1/2: 37–43, November, New Zealand.

Building an Effective Learning Management System

Joan Richardson

RMIT University, School of Business Information Technology, 239 Bourke Street,
Melbourne, Victoria 3000, Australia

Abstract. The designer of a subject was involved in creating a learning management system for use by 1400 students, in several countries with varying delivery modes, educational requirements and different technology infrastructures. The learning management system described currently consists of a CD-Rom, a Web site and a textbook. The product is utilised not only by the learner, but also as a support to the facilitators of the learning. Database concepts need to be adopted to ensure that the subject stored resources acquire the attributes of a relational database. A number of advantages are provided by way of storing educational components in a Web site as reusable objects. The system is a work in progress. There will be a resultant reduction in the redundancy of knowledge components of the subject and an improvement in the production time for online courses. This paper will discuss the process involved in the development of this learning management system.

1 Introduction

At the core of the work undertaken to create a Learning Management System is the constant evaluation of student's perceptions of effective teaching and learning processes and staff review. The aim is to use available human and technological resources to provide a quality, flexible, learning, environment for staff and students. In particular "It is intended that the resources provided assist undergraduate students in the early stages of their programs. Students at this level typically have limited work experience and practice applying taught skills in a problem-solving context."(Richardson et al, 2003)

The learning management system described is currently comprised of a CD-Rom, a Web site and a textbook. The system is however a work in progress. It has been designed to not only be used by a learner, but also as a support to the facilitators of the learning. This was not intentional, but emerged from the fact that the designer/manager of the subject was involved in creating a learning resource for use by 1400 students in several countries with varying delivery modes, educational requirements and different technology infrastructures.

Several essential factors describing the student population underpinned decisions relating to the design of the subject. The large and diverse group of students requires the use of various teaching processes to cater to individual learning needs. Students are culturally and geographically diverse. Commonalities included an interest in business and a need for end-user high order computing skills. The fact that the unit aims to provide students with current business computing skills and concepts is

W. Zhou et al. (Eds.): ICWL 2003, LNCS 2783, pp. 27–36, 2003.

secondary when assessing available technologies to add to the repertoire of teaching tools and processes.

Flexibility was an imperative to ensure a robust product as the learning spaces and student groups varied between the locations where the subject was delivered. The choice of applications software used for development and storage of resources affects the delivery due to differing infrastructures and platforms. For instance, there was no point in using Windows XP if the materials could only be used in one location. The environmental differences also impacted on technology based design decisions. The approach was to use an authoring tool that created a product that could be accessed by a range of browsers and be easily portable across platforms and technologies. The authoring software and the versions of productivity tools initially used enabled the same product to be presented via a CDROM and/or a Web site.

The engagement of learners and facilitators to address the tasks at hand is traditional. Problem-solving tasks in a business context bind the learning activities and the delivery of these activities is augmented by new technology. Continual improvements to existing resources have been built for the unit. The early adoption of technological tools as they become available provides a rich teaching and learning environment for the students and staff.

To mobilize the desired functionality for the subject materials a strict adherence to a design process was required. The initial design of the unit included a description of content, educational processes and relevant student outcomes. Once the content was outlined technological tools aimed at augmenting the quality of the student experience were chosen. Each traditional use of teaching spaces and contact hours was examined with a view to improving the quality of the student experience and augmenting or replacing the traditional content with technologically supported media.

2 Lectures and Demonstrations

The conceptual base necessary to provide a basis for student's understanding of end-user computing in a business context was to be delivered in a traditional lecture format. The content was delivered using PowerPoint and enriched via business context case studies. As the delivery options were broadened to include CDROM and the WEB, the focus in the lecture theatre shifted. Time was spent interacting with the students as they were expected to complete exercises aimed at ensuring an understanding of conceptual material covered.

The lectures explained concepts and terminology. The case studies were used to provide real life problems and opportunities to which end-user applications software could provide optional solutions. Demonstrations used the case studies to illustrate the solutions to problems posed during lectures. The solutions described also covered all skills required to obtain a higher grading in the assessment tasks for the unit. The tying of the examples provided in demonstrations to real-life problems and assessment tasks provided an abstract linking of the different components of the unit.

Several staff was responsible for creating audio files of the lectures and demonstrations that were stored on the CDRom. These learning activities could be accessed by students and completed in a similar fashion to the actual lecture theatre experience as the audio was synchronized with the PowerPoint slides. The design of the site enabled students to listen and type their own notes in PowerPoint.

3 Workshops and Case Studies

Detailed instructions that could be used to create the case study FrontPage, MS Excel, MS Word, PowerPoint and MS Access real-life solutions to problems were included in the CDROM and WEB site as workshop exercises and samples that provided assistance for completion of assessment tasks. This was extended in recent versions of the Web site and CDROM for the unit to include videos of real life business problems.

For the last three semesters all continual assessment tasks have related to a problem posed for one of the four case studies included in the design of the unit and Web-based descriptions of the case studies. The assessment solutions require the integrated use of Word, Excel, Access and PowerPoint. Exceptional solutions created by the students are included in the WEB site and CDROM. This enriches the existing case studies, provides experience of complex problem solutions and enables students to learn from each other.

The continual improvements to existing resources built for the unit, the focus on problem solution and the early adoption of technological tools as they become available provide a rich teaching and learning environment for both the students and staff. The paradigm for both stakeholders has shifted. Staff access resources from the CDRom or online and in doing so can multitask and modify resources depending on the current interactions occurring with a student group and save then modification for later use. Students can also multitask, save modifications to existing resources and completed work and print if required. The system has the potential for growth as the number of choices for staff delivery increases as well as student learning activity choice.

4 The Learning Management System

As additional resources have been created for the subject supported by the differing types of technology usage the site has become large and complex. Lectures can be attended, listened to or read. Problems can be read, discussed or a case based video watched. The book contains the concepts and theory required by end-users to enable them to solve problems in business using standard technologies. A thorough description of the knowledge base is accompanied by examples of the processes utilized to solve the business problems in each chapter of the text. New problems based on the case studies described on the CDRom are also provided. Problems posed require the application of systems thinking tools and/or the application of software productivity tools. These are supported by extra resources on the CDRom.

The CDRom contains the case studies, the application based workshop activities, problem description videos and audio and PowerPoint's of the lectures and demonstrations. Until now the Web site has been the continuous improvement point replica of the CDRom. Now the intention is to utilise the Web site to enable the staff to schedule learning activities, choose resources and create assessment tools and contextualising material. The site will also be accessible for students to interact with staff and each other, to choose resources and check on their learning.

The effective usage of each of the resource delivery modes is slowly becoming delineated according to effective use by staff and students. This represents a point in time for the identification of the capacity of the technology and therefore may change. However it also reflects staff and student needs. Over time students have become accustomed to using a split screen and multitasking. A paradigm shift has occurred when they accept using online workshop activity instructions which requires that they build a web site or develop an Excel model.

5   Implementation Issues to Enable Development – A Case Study

The need for the creation of a subject development process underpinned by database design concepts has been driven by the placement of tertiary education in the marketplace. This has necessitated the creation of subject resources suitable for flexible delivery modes and media. The web and CDROM technologies have been particularly useful. As a by-product of the subject content end-user applications and new technologies are integrated into the teaching and learning resources to inform students of potential usage.

Time constraints imposed by the requests for variations of the course, changing technologies and the inclusion of new technologies demand an alteration in the subject creation process. It is not advisable to create a subject for traditional and online delivery that is built in a top-down manner without recognition of a future need for modification and the re-use of educational components. In order to ensure that subject content is stored in a modular reusable fashion the design needs to be approached in a bottom up fashion. The knowledge capability content stored in the educational components needs to be dynamically addressable to compress the subject design process time line.

Database concepts need to be adopted to ensure that the subject acquires the attributes of a relational database. A number of advantages are provided by way of storing educational components in a Web site as reusable objects. There will be a resultant reduction in the redundancy of knowledge components of the subject and an improvement in the production time for online courses.

6   Outcomes and Objectives

The first step in the subject design process (Figure 1) is the definition of objectives and outcomes. The learning objectives are set out in two categories, those specific to the knowledge capabilities of business computing and those more general ones, the generic capabilities. The knowledge capabilities for this subject represent the business computing specific knowledge that would be expected of a business graduate. The generic capabilities refer to the means by which students utilize and apply the knowledge components required in a broader context.

The outcomes required at the conclusion of the subject include both knowledge and broadly based generic capabilities and these are described. Specified outcomes necessitate the application of knowledge capability components utilizing mapped generic capability characteristics. An outcome specified for the course described in this case study is "Effectively use a variety of software packages widely employed in business practice".

The entire subject mapping process retains a focus on the learning experiences provided for students via the description of subject outcomes, the inclusion of education components containing generic capabilities, technological augmentation and assessment tools that combine both. The effectiveness of the subject is determined by the successful completion of assessment tasks.

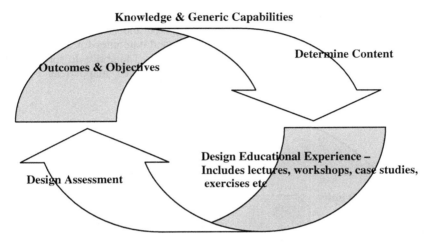

Fig. 1. The Subject Design process

7 Mapping

7.1 Knowledge and Generic Capabilities

The education components containing the knowledge and generic capability content required for the subject are mapped. The process of mapping the knowledge content for end-user applications requires the collection of resources relating to the skills, concepts and terminology needed in order to achieve specified outcomes for students. The knowledge capabilities need to be collected in educational components and stored in a manner that enables reuse

In a traditional delivery mode these resources may include material from textbooks, workshop manuals and PowerPoint presentations. As part of this new mapping process each resource chosen to be included in an educational component needs to be matched with technologies that mimic or augment the traditional learning experience. In reality each resource probably needs to be stored for flexible delivery and perhaps requires storage in a series of ways.

During a traditional subject design process the academic responsible for the subject design and development may or may not feel ownership of the individual knowledge component resources included. The ownership relates to the actual creation of resources. So usually the academic owns the design, scheduling and delivery modes of the course.

In the new mapping process the academic is responsible for the choice of resources to be included, the technologies to be used to provide specified modes of delivery and the navigational pathways through a web site that mimic the traditional schedule. The academic designs the learning experiences required to enable the acquisition of knowledge. These learning experiences integrate the knowledge based educational components of a course.

The part of a subject that entails the application of knowledge in a real world context is an important part of all learning completed and is included in the subject map as the generic educational components. Designed outcomes for a subject become deliverables by virtue of the use of generic capabilities. The ability to solve problems, to build models and to communicate solutions has been mapped as educational components of this course.

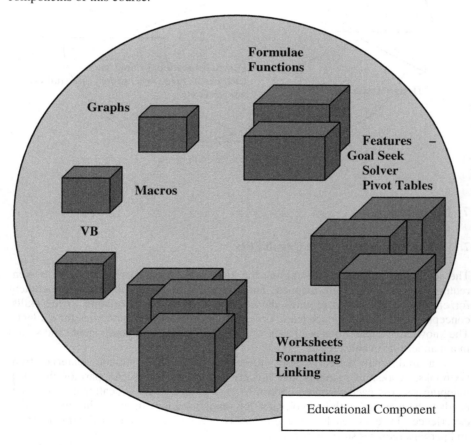

Fig. 2. Learning Object Comprised of Knowledge Based Educational Components

7.2 Determine Content

Discipline expertise is utilized to choose topics to be included in the course. The number and nature of topics incorporated into a subject to be undertaken over a specified period of time is determined. This part of the design process matches the content to the level or depth required.

A number of related skills and concepts make up an educational component, as per Figure 2. A number of educational components make up a learning object. All are topics abstractly linked by generic capabilities and assessment tasks.

7.3 Design Educational Experience

Learning experiences were chosen to suit the knowledge content, level of expected achievement and generic capabilities. The academic controlling this process incorporates knowledge expertise, educational experience and personal preference for delivery modes into the product. Consequently the academic owns the mapping procedure and resultant course. The modes of delivery required for the subject impact on the selection of technologies needed to transmit or enable learning.

Traditionally decisions relating to whether a type of learning was best delivered by a lecture or a demonstration, or a workshop exercise were all that was necessary. Now options are possible and another layer has been added to the decision process due to available technologies. Each topic within an educational component has to be assigned a preferred delivery mode as per Figure 3.

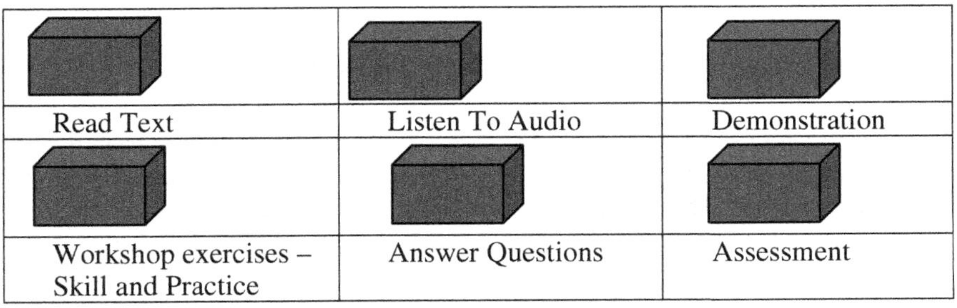

Read Text	Listen To Audio	Demonstration
Workshop exercises – Skill and Practice	Answer Questions	Assessment

Fig. 3. Delivery modes

7.4 Design Assessment

The assessment is then designed and mapped across both the knowledge and generic capability components of the course. Attention also needs to be paid to the level or depth of learning required by the group of students in question. Case studies were used to perform this task and also integrated throughout the subject materials to enhance the abstract integration and contextualisation of subject resources.

7.5 Navigational Pathways

Once the content and learning experiences for all of the educational components for a particular subject have been created the on-line version needs to be built. Each learning experience is assessed and matched with a range of suitable delivery technologies. To suit the database methodology imposed upon this process each educational component needs to be an addressable entity in its own right. This design enables an increased flexibility in usage as demanded by the market.

The educational components are then sequenced and combined by the navigational pathways created for the online delivery. Order of delivery is scheduled via the pathways of the site and content of the subject by the addressable packages. The navigational pathways created provide alternative scheduling or flexible delivery of knowledge content. The choice of knowledge expertise, assesment mechanisms, scheduling and mode of delivery are designed by the academic. The envisaged developer interface assists in the creation of Web sites underpinned by modules of knowledge content. By replacing the traditional resource choice, collection and development processes subject development productivity is increased. Knowledge becomes reusable. An example of a repository map for the Business Computing Applications Area is included as Figure 5.

The focus of the developer is maintained for complex resource development, scheduling or ordering and the creation of integrative components for the system. The scheduling of learning experiences to suit delivery models, the integration of fragmented content by way of assessment mechanisms and even the creation of knowledge components not currently available are all important tasks performed by the developer or academic in this instance.

8 The Learning Management System – The Future

Authoring software used to develop educational Web-sites is now user friendly. The software however operates from an end-user perspective and all building is completed in a top down manner. This approach was initially effective due to two factors:

- The developer only had to manage the conceptual understanding of the outcome desired
- The simplicity of the functionality required.

Now the complexity of the technical and functional requirements of the outcomes or Web-sites require a database design approach be taken in the building of the underpinning storage site for Web-sites. The amount of resources stored has become unwieldy in a number of instances. A bottom up approach to the design of the site needs to be enabled. Storage would be more ordered and easier to modify. To enable this it is suggested that a second interface specifically built for the developer or academic be created. The graphical design of the end-user interface to ensure attention to metaphors etc could then be completed in a top-down manner and connected to the underpinning content and functionality.

At the current time the site described in this case study has a business learning environment metaphor that is clearly articulated using Flash animated pictures for the

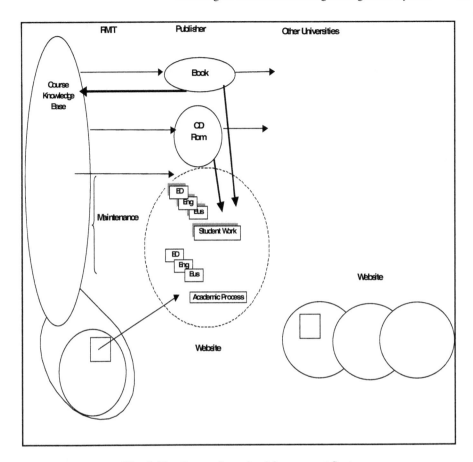

Fig. 4. The Current Learning Management System

first two levels. The continuation of the metaphor to the detailed description of the learning environments the student would traditionally be utilizing is vaguely embedded via the backgrounds used for each of the workshops, lectures, demonstrations, case studies and scheduling pages. The extension of the metaphor to include the navigation via the buttons was restricted by time and technology. It is however intended to use identified objects drawn from the context pictures in the text to assist navigation throughout the site. These objects will also support an abstract graphical connection between the concepts delivered in the text and the context technology driven applications or solutions to problems on the CDRom and Web site.

Historically the building of sites in education has been predominantly completed by educational designers (experienced end-users of applications software) who are not working at the operational level. The focus of development has therefore been at the level of the interface rather than functional usability. These workers have not been integrated by the organizational structure, project management or the description of roles and responsibilities. As the technologies have matured the gap between those developing sites and those using them has become greater and hidden by the creation of complex compliance processes and the use of technology to re-brand and market.

Attention needs to be paid to the integration of content by the application of content in context by students to solve problems. The technology is the tool used. The processes relate to the application rather than the structure and design of the sites. This contextual layer of activities require academic decisions relating to delivery mode, and learning activities

The design and usage has not been addressed from both the subject developer (academic) and student perspective. The technology is mature enough for common work practice processes to be recorded and utilized to inform the design of the end-user interface. It is necessary to fragment the content and then decide on technology usage to digitize. This then needs to be re-built by the interaction between teachers and students and the assessment tasks. Figure 6 depicts the intention for the system under construction.

9 Conclusion

At the time of writing this paper the components of the learning management system for the introductory end-user computing subject are built. The design for the underpinning of a web-site comprised of learning objects is also complete. The next step is to tag the learning objects to enable a search engine to operate at the web-site level. The database layer description and the course developer interface also need to be created. As the system has developed the type of resource to be stored in any part of the system has been attached to effective usage. The distinctions between the types of resources to be stored traditionally, or as learning objects in digitized means or merely as transient communication is becoming clearer. Figure 4 illustrates the knowledge base that can be developed as re-usable objects. The illustration also identifies the components of the system to be stored traditionally and the components of the system that need to be altered for delivery of the resource into different contexts.

References

Laurillard, D.M. (1994). Multimedia and the Changing Experience of the Learner, *Proceedings of the Asia Pacific Information Conference*, June 28–July 2, Brisbane. apitite

Lines, R. (1999). Teaching with technology: the space between strategy and outcomes. *Proceedings of the Technology in Training and Education Conference and Exhibition* (pp.19–25). Retrieved from http://ultibase.rmit.edu.au/Articles/online/lines1.htm

Richardson, J, Beiers, H, Bruno, V, Deng, H, Henschke, K,. *Computing For Business Success*, Pearson Education Australia, 2003

Wireless AnyServer – A Mobile ad hoc Web-Based Learning System*

L. Cheng, Pui On Au, and Weijia Jia

Department of Computer Engineering and Information Technology
City University of Hong Kong, 83 Tat Chee Avenue, Kowloon, Hong Kong
{plcheng, itjia}@it.cityu.edu.hk, poau@cs.cityu.edu.hk}

Abstract. Wireless technology can enhance the Web-based learning applications with efficiency and effectiveness. This paper presents the design and implementation of a novel Wireless Web-based Learning system (called Wireless AnyServer) that enables web-based learning system to be accessed in the wireless communication environment.

Keywords: Wireless communication, Web-based learning, Wireless LAN, Mobile navigation, IEEE802.11b, Ad Hoc communications.

1 Introduction

Web-based learning systems become the main trend for e-learning environment and help the learning process of students with efficiency and convenience. Web-based learning, on the one hand, possesses vast information base that may play a major role in enriching educational resources. On the other hand, greatly improve the quality of traditional teaching by providing efficient and fast way of resource detection, accessing and sharing. There are many well-known systems existing in the market, such as WebCT platform [6, 7] that provides students with web-learning environment for accessing various course materials.

However, web-based learning still requires lecturers or students to approach to those online systems in order to receive the helps or access the information resource. When applying in real environment, such as in the large conference theaters, large recreation centers etc, the learning or training process may not have the fixed network connection for web accessing. In this situation, wireless accessing to the learning information resources becomes necessary. Based on our intelligent platform AnyServer, this paper presents a novel system (called Wireless AnyServer) using wireless connection and accessing to enable the web-based system to be accessed through wireless devices such as PDA or laptop. Therefore, both instructors and students can interactively access/share the course information and resource in the motion without physically relying on fixed the internet or machines. This is particularly convenient for instructors

---

•* The work is partially supported by CityU Applied R & D Funding no. 9640006 and Hong Kong RGC, China grant nos: CityU 1055/01E and CityU 1039/02E, and CityU Strategic grant 7001355.

W. Zhou et al. (Eds.): ICWL 2003, LNCS 2783, pp. 37–45, 2003.

and students to interact with the on-line teaching / learning resource in the mobility. For instance, when students are in the campus area, they can retrieve the course materials through the Palm or PDA.

The rest of this paper is organized as follows: Section 2 gives the background information and supporting technology of the system. Section 3 discusses the detailed system design and implementation using ad-hoc wireless connections. Section 4 introduces a pilot system we are currently using and testing for the teaching at City University of Hong Kong and we conclude the paper in the final section.

2   Background Information and Supporting Technology

2.1   Wireless Technology

Wireless LAN standard is provided in the IEEE802.11 specification [2], it first relies on the Physical Layer to define the modulation and signaling characteristic for the sake of data transfer. IEEE802.11b defines two distinct modes of MAC layer [2, 3]: the Infrastructure network and the ad-hoc network. Infrastructure network may require the device to access wireless network through calling access point and then the traffic from the mobile radio signal is transferred to the wired network. In ad hoc network, peer mobile nodes communicate through mutual connection of wireless LAN card. A simple network is formed and the communication channels are established between the multiple hop devices in a given coverage range without the use of wireless access point [3]. IEEE802.11 wireless technology offers the following advantages [4]: (1) appliance interoperability; (2) faster product development; (3) stable future migration; (4) price reductions and (5) avoiding incompatibility.

2.2   AnyServer [9]

AnyServer is an intelligent platform that provides smart information and system integrations. It allows users with an easy way for the organization and management of information base such as teaching materials in a semantically way and enables multimedia documents and different software to be organized/synthesized under the same platform. Various documents in the form of MS Word, MS PowerPoint, PDF, video clips, audio, executable files etc. can be easily integrated and presented in AnyServer. AnyServer not only synthesizes the information but also sets links for the entities and concepts within the information objects. To make the system easy to use, the interface design of the AnyServer applies the similar interface such as Windows Explorer and allows the information nodes in the branch to communicate with each other; this is different from Windows Explorer in which the different files are just physically integrated together whereas files cannot communicate with each other.

In particular, AnyServer organizes the teaching materials into a tree structure. The tree in the server not only provides the text-based descriptions for each node, but also indicates the relationships (associations) among all nodes on the tree. The associations are established by adopting the conceptual network [1], which is used to model and express the internal relationships among objects (concepts). In order to facilitate the students to effectively and efficiently access and study the materials, the concept association mechanism has been designed and implemented by specifying the overall picture of the study paths through various concepts. Thus, AnyServer enables educators to organize and associate their course materials semantically and logically through tree structures by simply adding/deleting/editing the tree nodes, a set of common primitive operations have been implemented such as CREATE(), DELETE(), MERGE() and SPLIT() for the tree nodes. With these operations, we can integrate different information objects together to form a single semantic and relational structure.

With the intelligent information/system, AnyServer has been implemented with efficient web-mapping mechanism. With WebMapping subsystem, once the teaching information is installed or integrated into AnyServer, with the help of WebMapping, the integrated material can be easily shift to web server for custom presentations.

3   Overall System Architecture

Wireless AnyServer is a 3-tier system: 1st tier: the mobile clients; 2nd tier: the ad-hoc front ends that provide connection to the mobile clients; and 3rd tier: the web-intelligent server: AnyServer. In the following, first we briefly illustrate Wireless AnyServer in terms of client and front-end design and we finally show a pilot system that we have implemented at the moment.

3.1   Wireless AnyServer

Wireless AnyServer can be installed into a laptop that becomes an ad-hoc front end. The overall architecture of Wireless AnyServer is shown in Fig. 1 in which both instructors and students can work in two ways of connections, i.e., through connection to servers in the wired network or ad-hoc multi-hop connections to Wireless Any-Server Front-end that is installed with customized information. Wireless AnyServer supports two different kinds of modes of wireless accessing to the information: (1) through mobile connection while the mobile nodes connect to the servers which is fixed in the locations (such as in a large conference room, thereat etc); (2) Ad-hoc mode where the nodes may use multi-hop connections to access the learning material through front end system.

At the client side, students can use thin client devices such as PDA or laptop to access the Wireless AnyServer front-end through multi-hop connections. The front-end can be a laptop equipped with wireless LAN card and it can be further customized with specific information resource with local installation or connected to the Internet.

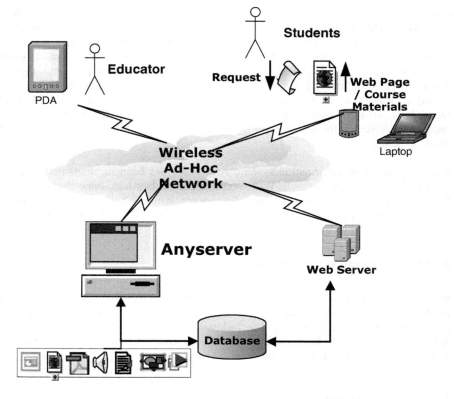

Fig. 1. System Overview of Wireless AnyServer

3.2   Client and Front End Connection

Based on IEEE802.11 standard, the wireless connection can be supported through two different kinds of modes: (1) Infrastructure mode that has the involvement of wireless access point to front end or (2) Ad hoc mode that relies on the ad-hoc connection from one hop to another directly. We focus on the second approach as it offers easy implementation and instant connection flexibility without the need to establish a wireless infrastructure like access point.

For the ad hoc network, one has to set up the establishment of ad hoc network ID inside the each device wireless LAN card (see Figs. 2 and 3). When considering the use of PDA and Pocket PC (applied in our applications), the effective range of controller application actually depends on the wireless LAN coverage area. The overall IEEE802.11b wireless range is around 100m in an open area [2], it guarantees that the mobile client can function at any position in a large lecture or conference room.

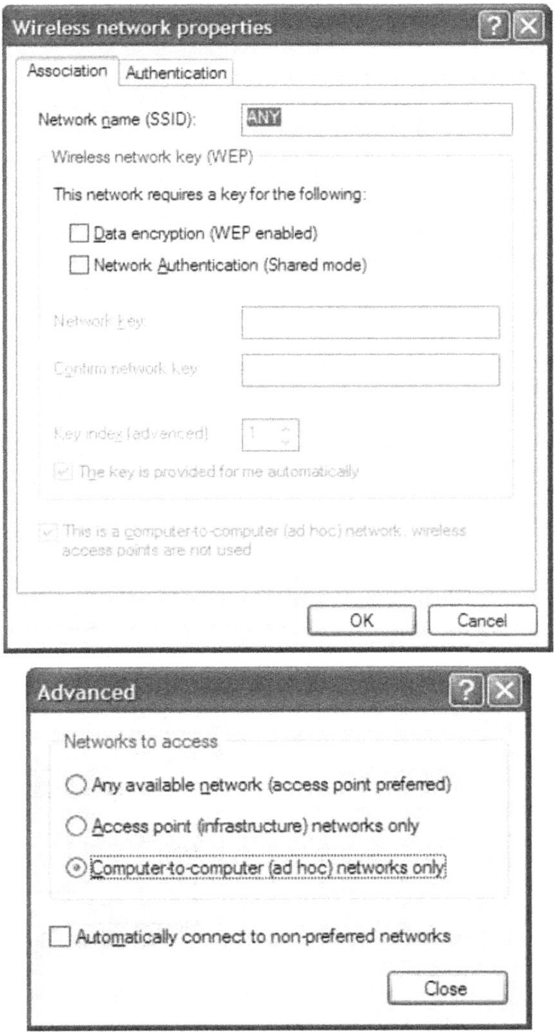

Fig. 2. Configuration in Ad Hoc mode with Network ID to "ANY" in desktop PC

We use Win CE and Pocket PC as the implementation OS with applying WinSock [8] Window component and eMbedded Visual Basic [5] for system developments. Fig. 4 shows the communication architecture between PDA and front-end using a TCP port.

When an application in PDA needs to send message to the laptop, it transmits the data through the TCP port. Through the MAC layer of the PDA driver, the data will be processed to fit the signal specification of IEEE802.11b in the Ad Hoc Mode. When the front-end device wireless LAN card receives the signal and assembles it back to computer digital data, the upper application finally collects that data through TCP port. The corresponding source codes concerning the connection between 2 devices are shown in Fig. 5.

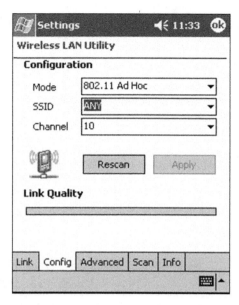

Fig. 3. Configuration Ad Hoc mode with Network ID to "ANY" in Pocket PC

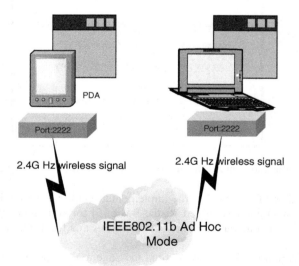

Fig. 4. Ad-hoc Connection Architecture

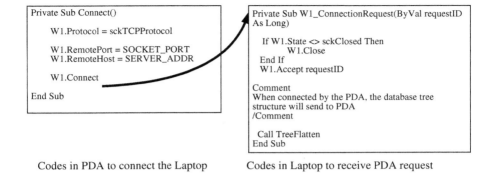

| Codes in PDA to connect the Laptop | Codes in Laptop to receive PDA request |

Fig. 5. Source Codes of Making Connection between 2 devices

On the PDA side, when the subroutine *Connect()* is initialized, the WinSock [8] component in eMbedded Visual Basic is used. It is first set to use TCP connection and the remote network address and the corresponding port number is assigned to the WinSock component. Finally, the codes call the *Connect* Method in WinSock to start the connecting process. On the Laptop side, after the data is transferred through the wireless ad hoc mode network and received at Laptop, the corresponding WinSock event method *W1_ConnetionRequest()* is initialized. In the method, it first checks current WinSock component is in used or not, then it accepts the connection request made by the PDA. Finally, the data processing method *TreeFlatten()* is called to analyze the incoming data as shown in Fig. 5.

Fig. 6 shows the thin client interface in which the tree structure of AnyServer has been downloaded into the PDA screen. The thin client interface can be used for both instructors and students. An instructor can use the thin client to control the display and an action of the front-end. On the other hand, the students may use the thin client device to browse the text outline of study material and perform some interactive tasks with the front-end (e.g. asking questions). In general, users can choose the PDA working mode through downloading the contents from Wireless AnySever or work in the interactive way with the front-end system to interact with each other. In the later mode, using PDA interface may control the ad-hoc node to show the message in the front-end or send a command to the front-end for some actions.

Since the thin client (PDA, Palm or mobile phone) has very limited resource (less memory and small screen), it is difficult to transfer the entire tree structure information from internet or front-end to the thin client device screen for presentation. Therefore, the notations and management of the course information in a concise way are essential. To solve the problem, we have designed a XML form tree markup representation. As a result, the entire tree representation will be marshalling into the text list that is easy to transmit in the narrow band wireless network. Fig. 7. gives an example how a course lectures are represented with tree markup tags.

Fig. 6. Thin client tree format presentation

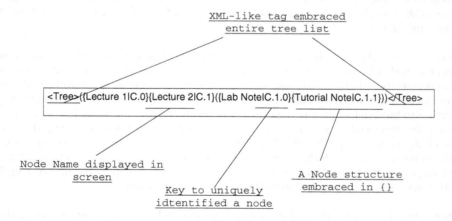

Fig. 7. Example of text list of tree content

When the tree information is retrieved, the corresponding data will be marshaled by a series of layout. According to the layout showing in Fig. 7, the entire tree list is embedded in the tag format of <Tree>... </Tree> and each tree node is embraced in the parenthesis. The node name and node key will be separated by a pile and the nodes of sub tree list are further included in an additional rounded parenthesis. Through this marshalling scheme, the entire tree formation can be marshaled and sent to the thin client. After unmarshalling at the PDA side for instance, the tree list will be then reformatted on the PDA screen.

3.3   A Pilot System: Remote Slideshows Controller

Currently we have implemented a pilot system using PDA to access the remote teaching slides of courses (powerpoint). With the system, during the lecture in a large theatre, a lecturer is able to easily control the slide transformation. Thus, the lecturer may approach students who may need help, or provide the direct guidance without going back to the machine to control the overhead projector for showing the slides. Besides, this application is also interested to the lecturer who may need to teach the students in different lecture rooms. Through this technology, we actually arouse the student learning interests at the City University of Hong Kong by increasing the class interactivity between students and instructors. On the other hand, if the students bring back their laptops, they may even download the on-line learning material on spot from the front-end through ad-hoc wireless connection.

4   Conclusions and Future Works

We have designed and implemented a pilot wireless web-based e-learning system using the ad-hoc mode of IEEE802.11b standard communication in our intelligent platform AnyServer. The wireless systems can facilitate web-based learning with more flexibility and easy accessing the teaching materials for users. Thus, adopting the state-of-the-art wireless technology can greatly improve the accessing efficiency and convenience. Currently, we are working on the process to develop the Wireless Any-Server into an interactive system which is a kind of wireless chartroom that enables the students to interact with instructors directly without interrupting the teaching process of instructors. Furthermore, the features of handling multimedia teaching material to present into the thin client mobile device are also under the development.

References

[1]   S. Luo, S. Sha, D. Shen and W. Jia, "Conceptual Network Based Coureware Navigation and Web Presentation Mechanisms", Proc. of First International Conference on Web-Based Learning (ICWL) 2002, Hong Kong, China, Aug. 2002.

[2]   L. M. S. C. of the IEEE Computer Society. Wireless LAN medium access control MAC and physical layer (PHY) specifications. IEEE standard 802.11, 1999 Edition, 1999

[3]   Raytheon Company, The IEEE 802.11 Wireless LAN standard, 1998
      http://www.raytheon.com/re/adc/raylink/80211.htm

[4]   Jim Geier, Benefits of the IEEE802.11 Standard,
      http://www.wireless-nets.com/whitepaper_benefits_80211.htm

[5]   http://www.microsoft.com/mobile/developer/downloads/default.asp

[6]   WebCT Homepages at University of Georgia, http://webct.uga.com

[7]   WebCT Homepages at http://www.webct.com

[8]   http://msdn.microsoft.com/library/default.asp?url=/library/en-us/vbceide/htm/project_108.asp.

[9]   http://anyserver.cityu.edu.hk.

A Web-Based Platform for E-learning Based on Information Management System [*]

Pui On Au, Leung Cheng, Weijia Jia, and K.O. Chow

Department of Computer Engineering and Information Technology
Department of Computer Science
City University of Hong Kong, 83 Tat Chee Avenue, Kowloon, Hong Kong
poau@cs.cityu.edu.hk

Abstract. This paper presents an intelligent *Information (course materials) Management System*, (called AnyServer) which can serve as an Web based Learning platform (WLP) and enable course educators to easily manage and organize their teaching materials into conceptual and semantic associations among "pieces-wise of knowledge" and publish their materials in web in a "well-organized" format. Our platform is different from the traditional web-based learning tools in the sense that educators can dynamically organize the teaching knowledge with tools in AnyServer and then convert the teaching materials into web-publishing materials with easy way. The interfaces and the features of the systems are very sophisticated, flexible and enable users to effectively navigate the materials and search for the learning material to their needs.

Keywords: Web based Learning platform; Information system; e-Learning; Internet Intelligent System.

1 Introduction

In the traditional learning pattern, educators have to act as an active role to publish the course materials so as the students can access through downloading or some simple searching mechanism. Through the downloaded notes, the students normally read the notes page by page for learning. However, this kind of learning pattern is passive and only suitable for the students who have sufficient time to study page by page. If the students intend to learn particular concepts only, they have to hurry to search all related concepts without going through all course notes. For example, if a user intends to learn a concept *A* only, but the concept *A* will refer to another concept *B*. Then one has to search the concept *B* from his notes or other ways while learning the concept *A* if there is no association mechanism is built. It is usual that one concept often associates many other concepts and the concept associations are not explicitly

---

[*] The work is partially supported by CityU Applied R & D Funding no. 9640006 and Hong Kong RGC, China grant nos: CityU 1055/01E and CityU 1039/02E, and CityU Strategic grant 7001355.

W. Zhou et al. (Eds.): ICWL 2003, LNCS 2783, pp. 46–54, 2003.
© Springer-Verlag Berlin Heidelberg 2003

indicated. Consequently, there is no clear picture for the study paths and the concepts for given materials. The searching and setting up the associations may overwhelm or even confuse students' study life. In the worst case, the students may give up using these tools.

In order to facilitate the students to effectively and efficiently study the materials with the clear picture of the study paths, we designed and implemented an *Information Management System* (called AnyServer) and a *Web-based Learning Platform* (WLP) with concept associations. AnyServer enables educators to organize and associate their course materials semantically and logically through tree structures by simply adding/deleting/editing the tree nodes. The formatted material through AnyServer thus may be published to the web with easy tools provided by WLP backend system. The WLP front-end thus is an environment for students to access the teaching materials with convenience and efficiency. Students may study those course materials from Web with additional personalized or customized services. Figure 1 illustrates the overview of our prototype e-learning system.

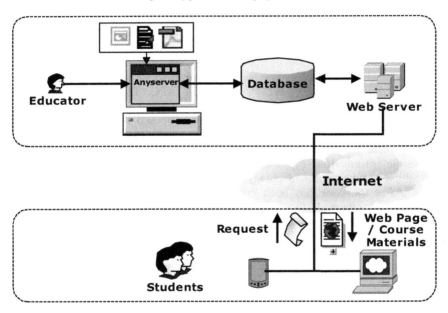

Fig. 1. Overview of our e-learning system

2 Overview the System

AnyServer is such a system that provide users with easy organization and management for course materials in a semantically way. It enables multimedia documents and different software to be organized under the same root – i.e., in the same platform such as the documents in the form of MS Word, MS PowerPoint, PDF, video clips, audio, executable files etc. To make the system easy to use, the interface design of the AnyServer applies the similar interface of Windows Explorer. However, AnyServer allows the information nodes in the branch to communicate with each other, this is different from Windows Explorer in which the different files are just put together whereas files cannot communicate with each other basically.

AnyServer is able to organize and synthesize the teaching materials and various systems into an integrated tree structure. The tree in the AnyServer does not only provide the text-based descriptions of the associated tree node like file path, last modified date and access modes, but also includes the relationships (associations) among all nodes on the tree. The associations are established by adopting *Conceptual network*, which was proposed by [1]. Moreover, the integrities of the associations among nodes are maintained through a set of pre-defined and user-defined rules. The idea of the integrity maintenance is more or less same as the idea in the database management system. *Conceptual network* is used to model and express the internal relationships among objective objects (concepts). In this paper, the terms of *information entity* and *concept* are used interchangeably.

The tree nodes either associate with local resources or remote resources. The remote resources are located on remote machines that may not under the educator's control. For those remote resources, some communication/transport protocols and authentication mechanisms are required to make the resources accessible. Using which communication protocols for accessing the resources from the AnyServer depends on what communication protocols are used at the remote machine. The common protocols are FTP, HTTP, SOAP and RPC. Therefore, the protocol for accessing one node's resources may be different from each other's. In order to achieve the access transparency, AnyServer is proposed to enable users to access every node using the same set of operations regardless of the locations of the resources once the node is created. In the phase of node creation, the user must provide the information (e.g. location, authentication information, resource name, protocol used at the remote machine) for accessing the new resource with the help of wizard. After the node has been created, all operations of this node are mostly identical to the others. In this paper, the detailed design and implementation of the resource access will not be discussed.

Apart from organizing information semantically, AnyServer can act as an information browser which can recognize the type of the selected information and display them appropriately. At the current development stage, AnyServer can present and playback the most common file and multimedia documents like MS Word, MS PowerPoint, FLASH, PDF and video stream etc. For those files that are composed of text, they can be converted to artificial speech using Text-To-Speech (TTS) technology. Currently, AnyServer supports both English and Mandarin. This feature enables the users to have an alternative way to browse (i.e. listen to) the selected information by voice. Since the different kinds of information are organized as a set of trees structure thus AnyServer provides a set of common primitive operations such as CREATE(), DELETE(), MERGE() and SPLIT() for the tree nodes. With these operations, we can integrate difference information objects together to form a single semantic and relational structure.

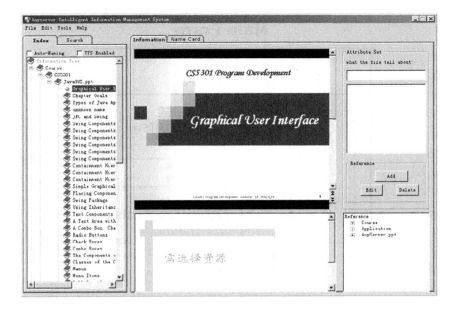

Fig. 2. The main panel of the AnyServer

2.1 Framework of AnyServer

The AnyServer can be divided into three layers: Presentation, Functional and Database. MS Visual Basic 6 is mainly used for implementing the prototype of the AnyServer.

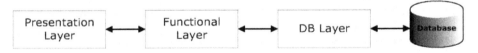

Fig. 3. The framework of the AnyServer in three-tires

2.1.1 Presentation Layer and Functional Layer

In AnyServer, the user interface is divided into several user controllers. Each user controller has its own interface and is also responsible for handling the events triggered within the controller. Therefore, each controller has its separated functional modules to perform the corresponding functionalities related to the controller. If the functional module changes the shared resources such as the content and the associations, the changes will be reflected on the *InformationTree* which is shared among all controllers. Figure 4 shows the interactions and the relationships among all components in AnyServer.

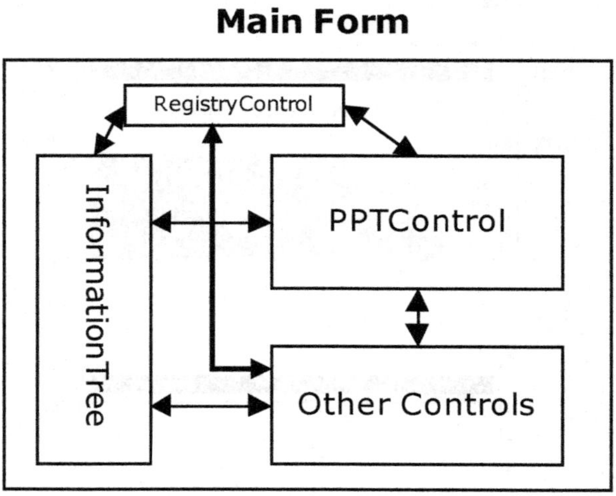

Main Form

Fig. 4. User controls in the AnyServer

At the current development stage, three user controls are defined: *InformationTree*, *PPTControl* and *RegistryControl*. Each user control can communicate with each other through the published APIs. The *RegistryControl* acts as the directory that records the name and reference of every control in the main form. If one control intends to call a method in another control, it contacts the *RegistryControl* to get the references of the callee control first.

- *InformationTree:* This control customizes the *TreeView* control. The user interface of this control and most events associated with this control are similar to the tree in the Windows Explorer. When we right-click on the node, the context menu pops up and let the user to quickly select options such as *Cut, Copy, Delete, Rename* and *Properties* etc. The options in the context menu may be different for node to node because different nodes may associate with different objects that have their own properties and actions.

- *Multiple ObjectHandler:* Since different objects have different properties and behaviors, different program modules are required to handle different objects. For example, when we want to initiate/create a PPT object, *PPTHandler* is called to process the corresponding tasks. If we want to create a PDF object, *PDFHandler* is called instead. Those handlers are extended from the *ObjectHandler* that provides common methods and properties for all other specific handlers that extend from it.

- *PPTHandler:* *PPTHandler* is one of the specific handlers extended from the *ObjectHandler*. It processes all operations related to Power Point file. Here is the example of showing how a PPT file is added on the *InformationTree*: When a user created a PPT file as a node, AnyServer will create a folder named as the prefix of the file name and automatically split the PPT slides into leaf nodes under that folder. For example, with the file fold CS5301, if one wants to create a PPT objects under the course name CS5301 folder, one can click the creation menu to add a node named "CS5301" and then right-click the CS5301 folder and choose "new". After specifying the path of the PPT file called Lecture_1.ppt, AnyServer automatically generates the Lecture_1 folder and the leaf nodes (Slide_1 to

Slide_*n*). AnyServer can also analyze and extract the text in the PPT slide. To formulate the text file enables text mining and also serve as the source for TTS (text-to-speech) subsystem (to be introduced later) to read the contents of the slides.

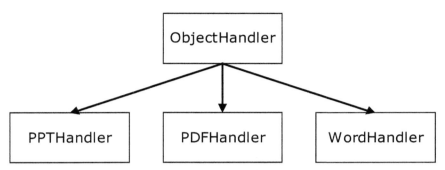

Fig. 5. ObjectHandler and its subclasses

- *PPTControl:* This control is specifically for displaying the user interface and manipulating the PPT slides. The operations include: 1) slide preview; 2) configuring of the relationships among slides and 3) changing the logical order of the slides.

2.2 Database Layer (*DBHandler*)

This layer (class) is responsible for directly manipulating the database. All controls in the presentation layer do not manipulate the database directly; they must submit the request to the *DBHandler* for executing the corresponding operations on behalf of the controls. The advantages with the *DBHandler* can be illustrated as following:
- The user controls do not need to deal with the communication with the database. Thus the database is transparent to the users so that the database can be protected.
- To minimize the number of changes on the controls if the database design is changed. The database thus is de-coupled from the user interface to maintain the integrity of the database system.
- The database implementation can be concealed. For example, if a node is deleted from the *InformationTree*, the *DBHandler* may decide to either delete that node permanently from the database or set the status of that node is "deleted".

3   Web-Based Learning Platform

The Web-based Learning Platform (WLP) provides the environment for users (students) to browse information (course materials) using Web browsers. The WLP serves as front-end system and allows e-learning system to be installed in the web. It also relies on technology of ASP.NET and the database system that is shared by both the AnyServer and the WLP.

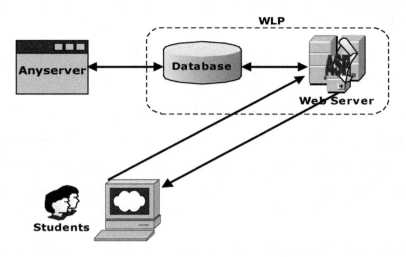

Fig. 6. The Web-based Learning Platform

The figure above illustrates the design of the WLP. After the instructors have prepared and processed their course materials using AnyServer, all course information and the associations are stored in the central database. When a student uses a Web browser to access a main page (index.htm) of the WPL and successfully logon, the ASP.NET pages are invoked to process the requests for that user. Since the WPL provides personalized service for each user (student), different authorized users will have different access right for reviewing the contents of the web pages. This is usual that different students have their own habits and progress-speed of learning, so that it is inappropriate to make a system that treats all users as the same. Therefore, personalized services are required for the effective and efficient e-learning system. The personalized service subsystem includes:

1. The customized layout and style of content pages;
2. The personal information of the user;
3. The information of people who are related to the user;
4. The progress of the e-learning study of the user;
5. The personalized course materials which are delivered based on the past progress and the knowledge level of the user;
6. The personal notes written by the user;
7. The personal bookmarks of the course materials;
8. The recommended course materials suggested by the WLP. The recommendation is based on the past progress and the past results of the user. The recommendation is also represented in a graph, which can give the visual overview of the past and the future study paths to the user.

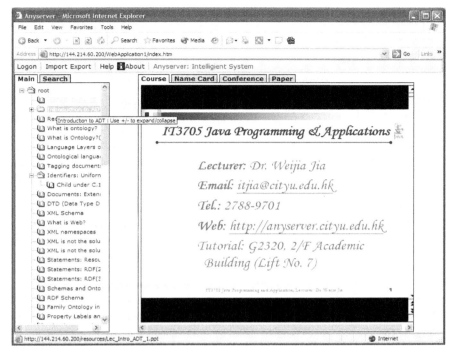

Fig. 7. Web-based interface for e-learning

Figure 7 shows the preliminary layout of the personalized content page. The page shows the content of the course materials in a tree structure at the left-hand side. The contents can be any types that can be displayed or interpreted by the Web browser and they are organized semantically. The *Search* function is also provided to search the keywords and their associations. The figure also shows that the page contains some other kinds of personal information like name cards, upcoming conferences and papers published. Another two special features are *Import* and *Export* which are explained in the followings:

Import: This feature allows the user to upload data files which must be supported by the WLP. Then the WLP recognizes the types of the files and validates the file contents. If the files are supported and validated without errors, the WLP integrates the import files with the existing contents. For example, a user may get a course material in PPT format from a third party and he wishes to access it anytime and anywhere. In this case, one may import that MS PowerPoint file to the WLP which integrates it with the existing contents and makes the PPT be a part of the tree.

Export: This feature enables the user to export the information such as course materials, personal information and the tree structure into certain supported formats and lets the user download it. For example, the user may export the tree structure into a XML file and export the personal information into a Web page, so that one may save those exported files and customize for one's own purposes.

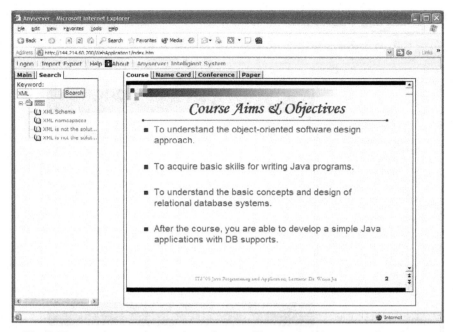

Fig. 8. The search page: the search results are still maintained in a semantic structure

4   Conclusions

We have presented an integrated e-learning systems that supported by dynamic information management and web-based development systems, targeting at the help for both educators and students to easily prepare the course materials and effectively search contents respectively. In fact, the two systems can be used independently. AnyServer system provides the environment for instructors to easily manage and semantically organize their course materials. WLP provides the personalized web-based services for students to learn effectively and efficiently. The prototype of the system is under the development and we are currently using the system in City University for several thousands of students to access.

References

1. S. Luo, S. Sha, D. Shen and W. Jia, "Conceptual Network Based Coureware Navigation and Web Presentation Mechanisms", Proc. of First International Conference on Web-Based Learning (ICWL) 2002, Hong Kong, China, Aug. 2002.
2. S. Walther, "ASP.NET Unleashed", Sams Publishing, 2002.
3. M. Spenik, A. Indovina, D. Jung and P. Boutquin, "Sams Teaching Yourself Visual Basic 6 Online in Web Time", Sams Publishing, 2000.
4. WebCT, http://www.webct.com/.
5. Microsoft Speech Technologies, http://www.microsoft.com/speech/ .

Experiences in Developing and Running WebCMS

Siew Siew Ong and John Shepherd

School of Computer Science and Engineering,
University of New South Wales,
Sydney NSW 2052 Australia
{ssong, jas}@cse.unsw.edu.au

Abstract. This paper describes our experiences in developing and running the WebCMS course management system in the School of Computer Science and Engineering (CSE) at the University of New South Wales. We analyse the usage of the system via a range of techniques, draw some conclusions on its current usage, and suggest some future directions for the project.

1 Introduction

WebCMS [3] is a course management system that allows lecturers to create courses and manage student- and course-related matters through a web-based interface backed by a centralised database. It was developed in the School of Computer Science and Engineering (CSE) at the University of New South Wales as a replacement for and extension of a suite of X-windows-based class management tools also developed in CSE. One aim was to provide the convenience of web-access to class records. Another was to see precisely how difficult it would be to build a system similar to WebCT, but tailored for local needs. The system is built on top of an Apache/PHP/MiniSQL platform.

WebCMS was installed in July 2001 and has been used by 35 courses since then. The system has not been promoted as an official teaching tool within the School nor have we conducted any training in how to use the system. All usage has been by staff interested in what the system might provide, and most have kept using it.

The system provides a wide variety of functionality (including a Group Management Tool, a MessageBoard, and templating mechanism for writing course introductions). This paper aims to analyse how this functionality is actually being used, to gauge the success of the system thus far, and to use this as a basis for suggesting future changes.

The remainder of the paper is structured as follows: section 2 provides an overview of the functionality of WebCMS; section 3 describes our experiences in developing and users' experiences in using the system; section 4 discusses current usage of the system; and section 5 concludes what we have learned and suggests directions for future development.

W. Zhou et al. (Eds.): ICWL 2003, LNCS 2783, pp. 55–68, 2003.

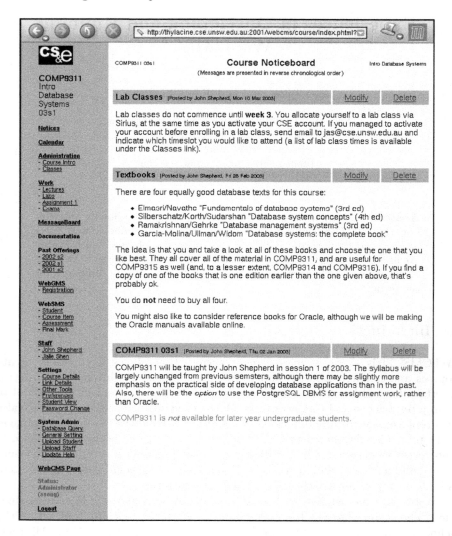

Fig. 1. Course Main Homepage

2   Overview of WebCMS

In this section, we summarise the functionality of WebCMS; further details may be found in [4].

WebCMS users are broadly categorised as staff and students, with sub-classes of staff such as lecturer-in-charge and tutor. WebCMS aims to allow lecturers to produce a course website in a style similar to existing CSE course websites, but with minimal effort. Since WebCMS promotes a common look-and-feel across all course websites, students find the website of a new course instantly famil-iar and can access relevant information with little effort. In addition to effort minimisation, WebCMS provides interaction features (such as a NoticeBoard and MessageBoard) that were previously only available on course web sites in an ad hoc fashion and with considerable effort by the course staff. An example WebCMS course page is shown in Figure 1. All course websites are displayed via a sidebar menu, with a main frame for displaying content and carrying out interactions. The following are the main features of WebCMS:

Course Creation. The course website is created by the lecturer-in-charge of the course. This involves simply supplying a name and course code and selecting a colour. After this, a basic website is immediately available, with tools such as NoticeBoard and Calendar.

Course Look and Feel. WebCMS provides an interface for limited customisation of course Web pages. Lecturers can select a colour scheme to be carried throughout the web site, and can select which tools and other links appear in the sidebar menu.

Course Content Management. WebCMS allows course material such as lecture notes, tutorial questions/solutions and laboratory exercises to be integrated into a website either by uploading them into a central file store or by setting up links to material stored elsewhere. Some kinds of material (e.g. course introductions) can be generated via a template and stored in the WebCMS database.

Notice Board. This allows lecturers to post messages of interest to the class. The NoticeBoard appears in the main frame when students initially access the course website (see Figure 1).

Calendar. This allows staff to post information about class events (such as assignment due dates). WebCMS displays a list of these events along with the number of days remaining before each event.

Student Management (WebSMS). WebSMS provides four major components for lecturers to manage and track student assessment. The Student component allows staff to add, delete and search for students in the class list. The Assessment Item component allows staff to store details of graded classwork (e.g. assignments), including various styles of grading or marking, and validation constraints on the values that can be entered. The Assessment component enables staff to update student results on the assessment items. The Final Mark component allows lecturers to generate final course marks by defining an overall mark formula and by scaling marks with an interactive graph-based scaling system.

Group Management (WebGMS). WebGMS provides facilities for creating and managing project groups for courses that run group-based assignment work. Students create and register groups online. Once a group is created all members of the group have access to shared group website under the class website where they have a range of private facilities for managing group work (e.g. noticeboard, calendar, todo list, and a web-based interface to CVS for managing software development). Staff initially set group size limits and a registration timetable. As groups begin to use their sites, staff can monitor their progress via simple activity indicators such as number of intra-group messages.

Message Board. An asynchronous threaded discussion board provides means for students and staff to engage in collaborative exchange about topics in the course. This allows staff to answer common questions in a well-defined forum to reduce the number of repeated questions that arise in a forum such as one-to-one email. All posters on the MessageBoard need to be authenticated.

Tool Incorporation. A tool is a feature supplied by WebCMS that provides a specific service such as Message Board or Group Management. It can be incorporated into any course. A particular tool may not be appropriate in all courses, and so WebCMS provides a facility enabling lecturers to add/delete these tools when necessary.

The above features/modules form the basis for the original WebCMS system that is analysed later in this paper. New modules for on-line marking, running multiple-choice quizzes, and allowing class registration will be discussed in Sections 3.4-3.6.

3   Experiences

WebCMS was developed by the first author during March-June 2001. It was first deployed in the UNSW semester from July-November 2001, and used by one course (taught by the second author). After this initial trial, it has been steadily adopted by more courses, and, in the current semester (March-June 2003), is being used by 10 courses, some for the third time. The courses range from first-year classes with enrolments of over 700 to specialist postgraduate courses with enrolments of less than 20. The students in CSE come from a range of backgrounds, including widely different skill levels with computer technology and many different ethnic backgrounds.

   This section analyses the current usage of the WebCMS, as well as giving details of ongoing developments. Feedback on usage was obtained in three ways: questionnaire, web server access log analysis, and informal suggestions/comments given by users. The questionnaires were administered in March 2003 with the aim of discovering the system's accessibility, tool effectiveness and usability, and collecting other general comments. WebCMS runs on its own web server and the access log was available for the period April 2002 to March 2003 (comprising over 700MB of data). We used both ordinary statistical analysis as well as data mining on the log to ascertain usage patterns. This is discussed in detail in section 3.7. The informal comments from users were drawn from a number of different sources, including email, face-to-face discussions, and comments on MessageBoards where topics had been set up specifically to discuss WebCMS.

3.1   Message Board (Bulletin Board)

The MessageBoard has been used extensively and is incorporated in most WebCMS-based courses. It is largely used by students to post/answer questions on assessment-related matters such as assignments, projects and lab exercises, and other course-related matters such as looking for group members, reporting bugs, etc. For lecturers, it provides a common area for them to answer student questions (similarly to an FAQ), saving them from having to repeatedly answer similar questions. 71% of respondents agreed that Message Board provides mean for students to collaborate with lecturers apart from using email. 87% of respondents agreed that Message Board provides a way for students to share knowledge with each other. Students also reported that they always find the answer they want in the Message Board. However, there are some students who do not read the existing messages before posting a question, resulting in repeated messages in the Message Board as noted by one respondent the respondents:

"There seems to be a lot of repeat messages, because people don't read other ones first..."

One possible solution is to include a filtering feature to check whether a message is similar to any current messages and display these messages to the poster. If they think that none of these messages is similar to the one they want to post, then they can proceed in posting the message.

A new feature added to the Message Board in response to user requests was a notification service where users can opt to have new messages emailed to them. The email contains the message itself, along with a hyperlink referring to a WebCMS page where the user can view and reply to the message. A future improvement (suggested by users) is to allow users to add filters to restrict notification only to messages of a certain kind e.g. messages on a certain topic, or responses from the course staff.

"Email notification is great, but it would be nice to be able to ignore certain thread."

"Email notification for responses to selected thread."

A variation on this would be to modify the way messages are presented on WebCMS course websites, e.g.

"Highlight messages posted by the lecturer and tutors as they are the most newsworthy."

There are several limitations in the Message Board: it uses only a two-level hierarchy (a list of broad topics, and a list of messages within each topic); and, the searching system does not provide sufficient recall. The rationale for using a two-level hierarchy was that users would be likely to "lose themselves" in a deeply nested hierarchy. However, feedback from users suggests that the two-level hierarchy causes problems with topics becoming too large (too many messages). Converting the system to use a multi-level hierarchy is relatively straightforward because of the data structures used in the original implementation.

"Once you get above 30 or so messages on a topic, it is too hard to find relevant questions, so you start to get people asking questions that have already been answered."

"The current topic/category structure breaks down a bit when you've got a large number of posts under a topic. e.g. a topic like Assignment 2 accumulates a large number of posts around the assignment deadline, and it gets quite annoying for ppl looking at the messageboard for answers to click through post looking for what they want."

Analysis on the web server log revealed that of those people who accessed the Message Board, only 1% of them have used the search mechanism provided. One possible reason for this might be that the current search mechanism allows searching based only on the poster and the message title. A better search mechanism would clearly include content-based search. However this will need to wait until the system is ported to a more powerful database system (the current database MiniSQL, does not support search within long text strings). An alternative to full content-based search would be to require users to supply a set of keywords with their message. Whether users would supply sensible keywords is matter of conjecture.

Some users have indicated that having to identify themselves in their posts is threatening enough to discourage them from posting at all. At least one user has suggested the use of aliases to overcome this:

"I don't really like the feature in Message Board that it will list/post your real ID. I don't feel comfortable with that feature at allbecause sometimes I just want to be unknown and consider the case when you post a straightforward question or wrong comments. I suggest replacing this feature with a user-chosen nickname."

We do not support this. If students can hide their identity in posts, then there may be an increased likelihood of posting silly questions or giving incorrect answers to other students' queries.

While there is clearly some work required to overcome the problems described above, the Message Board was rated highly by users (3.7/5) in terms of overall usefulness.

3.2   Group Management (WebGMS)

WebGMS is one of the most popular modules, and has been used in many WebCMS-based course websites (primarily because group project work is quite common in CSE course). It was also rated highly (3.3/5) in terms of overall usefulness. Positive feedback was received for most WebGMS features, particularly the online group registration. Class administrators were especially pleased with online registration, because they previously performed this task manually via many rounds of email. Some indicative feedback from the questionnaire:

"This is a very good tool that assists in better project management."

"Generally it's a good tool that lets the groups find themselves."

Upon registration, a group web page is generated to allow collaboration among group members. A group-tracking feature is also available for lecturers to monitor the progress and activities in the group web pages. While 604 groups had been formed under WebGMS, only 60 of them have actually made use of the group website for any serious collaboration (based on activities such as posting messages, notices, meeting minutes, adding calendar entries, etc.) There were 242 groups who had at least "done something" in their group website, but the number of activities never exceeded five messages/notices. A possible reason is that these groups were initially testing out the features on the group website but decided not to use it for collaboration. When asked about this in questionnaire, the following comments were given:

"It is much more easier and faster to use email/phone/direct. Usually people just too lazy to specially log on to WebGMS."

"Not all the groups members have access to Internet regularly or would like to use this tool. Besides, there is lots of efficient substitute, i.e. SMS/mobile phone/home phone/ICQ."

"Initially used it, but then people got lazy to login all the time to check if there's anything new. We ended up communicating through email instead."

From the comments given, it shows that students prefer to use communication channels other than the group website for collaboration. This means that the tool is being used primarily for group registration. One possible solution to encourage participation is to force students to use more features of the tool by making it part of their assessment (e.g. using group web logs as records of the development process).

One problematic feature of the current registration process is that students form groups by selecting a list of group-mates from all students enrolled in the class not currently in a group. Students can be added to groups regardless of whether they actually want to work with the other people in the group, and need to explicitly remove themselves from a group once added. Allowing students to specify a list of people they would (or would not) be willing to work with might streamline this process somewhat.

3.3   Assessment (WebSMS)

WebSMS is the least used module. It provides functionality to manage class lists, course assessment items and student assessment records as well as marks finalisation. However, of these four features, only one of them is being used: class list management. Most staff continue to use the older X-windows-based class management tool (SMS [1]) for handling marks, even if they use WebCMS for the rest of their course website. Some users reported that they do not use WebSMS because they were not well-informed of the functionalities provided by this module, while other users commented that they would consider using WebSMS if it provided all of the functionalities available in SMS, such as producing reports of final marks in the precise format required for submission to the University.

Others did not use WebSMS because they were worried about the security of storing confidential information such as marks in a Web-based system.

3.4   Quiz (WebMCQ)

WebMCQ is a recent module implemented in March 2002. It allows lecturers set up multiple-choice quizzes. There are four major components: Category, Question, Quiz and Registration. The Category component allows staff to set up different question categories. The Question component allows them to add questions for each category. The Quiz component provides facilities for staff to generate an entire quiz. Quiz questions are selected from a question bank in one of three ways: manually, randomly selected from the entire question bank, or randomly selected from each topic (in which case the number of questions from each topic needs to be specified). Restrictions on the quiz can be specified such as opening/closing date (date which students can/cannot take the quiz), date on which the results can be released to students, specific times at which students can take the quiz, duration etc. The Quiz component is linked to the Course Assessment Item component of WebSMS. Upon generating a quiz, a course item for this quiz is also generated, allowing the student assessment result for the quiz to be stored. The Registration component allows staff to associate students to classes, to ensure that students can only take the quiz within the time specified for the class. For lecturers, it displays a list of students along with their results and answers for the quiz.

This module has been used in a number of courses and was rated 3.3/5 by the respondents. 68% of the respondents agreed that WebMCQ provides students with valuable and instant feedback on their performance. 87% of them said that having a summary of overall class performance in the quiz would be useful. One staff member was more specific on what information would be useful to them on class performance:

"I needed statistics that told me: a. how many students answered each answer (not just each question.) b. clustering of students to tell if there's a group of really bad/really good students that skews the results in a. c. how many students answered how many questions correctly."

One improvement to WebMCQ would be to link quiz Categories to course materials. At present, the course material (e.g. Lecture notes) is organised based on topics, which are quite similar to WebMCQ categories. Hence, instead of having staff to set up Categories in WebMCQ, they could make use of existing topics as the basis for question categories. Under such as system, we could develop a recommendation system that suggested useful course material for student, based on their quiz assessment results. When asked on this point in the questionnaire, 77% of respondents agreed that a mechanism to provide a recommended reading list of topics based on quiz performance would be useful.

3.5   Assignment Management

This is another new module, developed as part of an Honours Thesis project [2] in 2002. It provides facilities to allow electronic submission, marking and collection of CSE coursework assignments. There are three major components for this module: Assignment Setup, WebGive and WebMark. Assignment Setup allows staff to set up assignment submission and marking systems. WebGive presents a simple, straightforward method for staff to set up either an individual or group-based assignment submission system. Restrictions related to an assignment submission such as due date, late penalties, file size and file types can be specified accordingly to the needs of an assignment. It also includes the ability to activate assignment submission and/or collection functions for students. WebMark features the ability to run automated and subjective marking on assignment submissions. Markers are able to insert annotations and marks into submission source code files. This allows staff to provide detailed feedback to students.

3.6   Class Registration (WebCRS)

WebCRS is a new module currently being developed. This module allows students to register for laboratory or tutorial classes online. Restrictions on class can be specified such as the capacity (class size), whether it is a regular (e.g. lab, tutorial) or one-off (e.g. presentation) class, opening/closing date for registration, etc. Students will be notified if there is any class clash within the course or other courses in WebCMS. Waiting lists are provided to allow students to register for a class that is already full, and be notified by email if a place becomes available. Reporting facilities are available for staff to show confirmed registrations and waiting list lengths for each class.

3.7   Web Log Analysis

Prior to the web log analysis, we preprocessed the log via the following steps:

Data Cleaning. This step aims to remove unwanted or unnecessary data from the raw data such as image files, or URLs related to other applications running on the web server. Table 1 shows portion of the raw web server log.

Session partitioning. After the data cleaning step, we have to partition the log file into sessions to identify a collection of pages accessed by a single user (identified by their IP address). In WebCMS, sessions time out after 20 minutes, so we use this as a threshold for the partitioning. If an IP address does not access the server until more than 20 minutes after the previous access, we consider it to be a new session.

Course partitioning. Because a user can access several course Web sites in a session, it would be interesting to know what kind of pages were being accessed by users for each course. Hence, we further partition the session into courses. The course accessed can be obtained from the `cid` parameter in the URL.

Table 1. Raw web server access log

IP Address	Date & Time	Type	Request object	Protocol	Stat	Bytes
211.28.45.60	14/May/2002:23:07:17	GET	/webcms/image/cselogo.gif	HTTP/1.1	304	-
202.7.181.42	14/May/2002:23:07:18	GET	/webcms/course/menu.phtml? tid=&cid=12&mode=	HTTP/1.1	200	4203
129.94.241.59	14/May/2002:23:07:19	GET	/webcms/course/index.phtml? cid=16	HTTP/1.0	200	783
211.28.45.60	14/May/2002:23:07:21	GET	/webcms/lecture/view_lecture.phtml? tid=&cid=16&mode=	HTTP/1.1	200	9635
129.94.241.59	14/May/2002:23:07:22	GET	/webcms/notice/view_notice.phtml? tid=&cid=16&state=view&mode=	HTTP/1.0	200	10250
129.94.241.59	14/May/2002:23:07:22	GET	/webcms/course/menu.phtml? tid=&cid=16&mode=	HTTP/1.0	200	3997
129.94.241.59	14/May/2002:23:07:23	GET	/webcms/image/cselogo.gif	HTTP/1.0	304	-
211.28.45.60	14/May/2002:23:07:27	GET	/webcms/intro/view_intro.phtml? tid=&cid=16&mode=	HTTP/1.1	200	155
211.28.45.60	14/May/2002:23:07:27	GET	/webcms/intro/template.phtml? tid=&cid=16&	HTTP/1.1	200	14053
211.28.45.60	14/May/2002:23:07:28	GET	/webcms/class/view_class.phtml? tid=&cid=16&mode=	HTTP/1.1	200	11729

The WebCMS interface is designed using a two-frame system: the system has a sidebar menu containing a list of operations/modules available to the user, and a main frame containing the current content. Users typically access the system by going to the "home page" for a particular course (`course/index`). This script sets up two frames which are loaded with the sidebar menu (`course/menu`) and the course noticeboard (`noticeboard/view_notice`). The menu also loads a copy of the CSE logo. Subsequent accesses include clicking the options in the menu sidebar, which will invoke scripts in the main frame. When a user has only read privilege, the main frame will contain the current content of the module. When user has read/write privilege, the main frame is subdivided into a Control frame and a Display frame. The Control frame displays a set of functions related to a module (e.g. Add, Edit, Delete and View), whereas the Display frame is where user views information or provides input to the system.

The objective of this analysis is to gain some insight into how users actually make use of the system, as well as look for interesting access patterns using data mining tools. The analysis considered the following questions:

Question 1: What is the number of pages accessed in a typical session/course? How much time is spent in a typical session? What are the pages accessed in a typical session?

In determining session length, we include all pages accessed, including the three accesses that comprise the load up of the main course web page.

The maximum number of pages accessed (i.e. session length) in a single session is 2465 (1 occurence) whereas minimum pages accessed is 1 (21835 occurences). Subsequent analysis of the very long session revealed that it accessed many pages from a number of different courses in a very short time. Checking the IP address revealed that it was a robot for a search engine. Analysis of other sessions longer than 500 revealed a similar pattern. It seems that very few "real" sessions exceed 500 pages.

As noted above, there were 21835 sessions consisting of a single page access. This result is interesting, as we would have expected that all sessions would have accessed at least the course main homepage, giving a session of at least length 3. The most common kind of session of length one (4485/21835) involves a single access to the page `lecture/view_lecture`. It appears that people may have bookmarked individual pages within WebCMS for quick access to important parts of the site.

As expected, sessions of length 3 are the most frequently occurring. The vast majority of these consist of the three page accesses for a main course website. The interesting aspect of this is that very many people simply go to the main course web page and then go no further. Presumably they are simply checking the Noticeboard for new notices.

If we consider the initial access (which loads the frames and the menu and noticeboard in those frames) as a single access, the average number of pages accessed per session is around 6.

Question 2: What is the first page when session starts?

As expected, the first page that most users access when session starts is `course/index` (46076 occurences). This is followed by `view_lecture` (43933), `view_lab` (24416), `view_notice` (20102), `view_messagetopic` (19329), `view_tutorial` (15265) and `view_intro` (7625). It appears that these pages are bookmarked by very many users.

Question 3: What is the most frequent access to pages/modules

Table 2 and Table 3 show the ten most frequently accessed pages and modules. It is interesting to note that many people are making use of the collaboration tools, Message Board and WebGMS.

Question 4: What do users do after logging in?

It should be noted that users are not required to login in order to access the course home page. They can view the general information about the course (e.g. Notices, Lecture Notes) by simply accessing the main course web page. They need to authenticate themselves only when they want to have the "write" access to some module (e.g. to post a message). Therefore, it would be interesting to draw out the possible reason they login to the system (i.e. whether there is any relationship between login and the kind of activities performed after login). The number of sessions which involve login is only 10197 out of 328966 total sessions (i.e. only 3% of sessions result in a login).

The three pages most frequently accessed after login were the three pages loaded on initial access to the course site; this is expected since these three pages are reloaded after login. Note that the menu needs to be reloaded because login in can cause additional links to be displayed in the menu to reflect additional privileges from logging in. Other pages frequently accessed after login are the Message Board (as one has to authenticate him/herself in order to post any message), Course Creation (this functionality is only available to staff), and WebGMS.

Question 5: What are the interesting patterns such as pages accessed following some other pages accessed previously?

Table 2. Frequently accessed pages

Page	Frequency
notice/view_notice	540151
course/index	475583
course/menu	473333
messageboard/view_content	166476
lecture/view_lecture	164407
messageboard/view_message	115513
tutorial/view_tutorial	93907
lab/view_lab	92143
messageboard/view_msgtopic	69491
intro/view_intro	30749

Table 3. Frequently accessed modules

Module	Frequency
Notice	542321
Message Board	366990
WebGMS	264435
Lecture	170120
Tutorial	95871
Lab	93321
Course Creation	47067
Course Introduction	37699
Class	24240
Calendar	18038

To determine the answer to this question, we used association rule mining to reveal relationships between pages accessed in a typical session. Following are partial results from the initial mining (confidence level $\tilde{9}9\%$):

```
notice/view_notice, course/index,
                    tutorial/view_tutorial => course/menu
lecture/view_lecture, course/view_notice,
                    course/index => course/menu
notice/view_notice, course/index, lab/view_lab => course/menu
...
```

The first example is interpreted as: for those people who access pages notice/
view_notice, course/index and tutorial/view_tutorial, 99% of them will also access course/menu in a session. This is because of the two-frame system in WebCMS, which will load the menu frame (course/menu) and main frame (e.g. notice/view_notice) when accessing the course web site. It should be noted that this mining does not take into account the sequence of these pages (i.e. it is not sequential mining). Since these results are expected, in the subsequent mining, we remove the course/index, course/menu and course/notice since these are very frequently loaded at the beginning of a session. Some of the interesting results are (minimum support=0.1 minimum confidence=0.1):

```
tutorial/view_tutorial => lecture/view_lecture 57%
tutorial/view_tutorial => lab/view_lab 44%
lab/view_lab => lecture/view_lecture 40%
lab/view_lab => tutorial/view_tutorial 39%
lecture/view_lecture => tutorial/view_tutorial 30%
lecture/view_lecture => lab/view_lab 24%
```

This suggests either that students often make use of several kinds of course content together (e.g. look at the lecture notes while doing a lab exercise), or that they try to do all of their content access in a single session (e.g. printing lecture notes and also printing tutorial questions for the next week).

4 Discussion

When questioned about the most useful/interesting features in WebCMS, some of the comments received included consistent layout, ability to choose to login or remain public, ease of use and navigation, provision of a standard/centralised way to access resources, message board, group management system, and multiple-choice question. Comments received for the most useless/uninteresting features include lack of functionality to individualise course web site (this contrasts with our original aim of having a consistent look-and-feel to all course web sites), multiple-choice questions (one user complained about its complexity), group management system (the possible reason is the use of other communication means) etc. Features that users would like to see added: online class registration system (currently being implemented), greater customisation options, meeting agendas, moderated instant messaging system, chat room and linking of calendar events to the actual deliverable. Overall, users are satisfied with WebCMS. Some of the comments received:

> "Overall WebCMS is an excellent system that enables students to get any course information required as well as to provide a more interactive learning environment."

> "WebCMS is a great idea, it would be great if it was standard throughout all subjects and the entire university. Making it mandatory would be great as well. I believe it makes things easier for lecturers, students and administrators."

> "I think that people behind WebCMS have done a great job in providing this tool as it is easy to use."

> "Overall, I think it's a very nice system for course management."

Users who have experienced with other course management system include WebCT (94%) and customised systems developed in other UNSW Schools. When asked about how these systems compared to WebCMS, most of the comments related to efficiency and usability, including:

> "WebCMS is useful and easier to use, you do not need to follow a zillion links to get where you want to go, the helps provided are less ambiguous and it does not crash as often as WebCT."

> "WebCMS is better, no need to login unless need to post a message."

> "I find WebCMS much nicer. I found WebCT was quite cumbersome to use, and many of the features if offered were not used by the lecturer, although I guess that could apply to WebCMS too."

> "WebCMS provides more clear user interface."

> "The frequency of failure of WebCT is higher than WebCMS, WebCMS seems a bit more stable, but the user interface looks boring? it should allow greater flexibility on changing how it looks, with the functionalities stay unchanged."

5   Conclusions and Future Work

WebCMS, a web-based course management and online learning environment, has been in operation at the School of Computer Science and Engineering since July 2001. During this period, users have provided much useful feedback and many suggestions which have led to improvement of existing modules as well as development of new tools. Future work includes development of a more general framework that provides greater flexibility in determining user access to course items, development of new modules such as WebPoll (a survey system), a facility for copying courses from one semester to the next, and other module-specific modifications mentioned before. We are also planning to port the system from PHP3/mSQL to PHP4/PostgreSQL. The platform will also be used to explore ideas in the area of personalised learning environment.

Acknowledgement. We would like to thank all the staff and students in CSE for providing us with useful suggestions and comments throughout the development of WebCMS as well as those who participated in our survey.

References

1. Stephen Fischer, Geoff Whale, Mei Whale, and Charles Willock. *Manual: student database management, assignment submission and marking systems version 2.2.* School of Computer Science and Engineering, UNSW, February 2000.
2. Felicia Kurniawati. *An Assignment Management System for WebCMS.* Honours Thesis, School of Computer Science and Engineering, University of New South Wales, 2002.
3. Siew Siew Ong. *A Web-based Course Management System.* Honours Thesis, School of Computer Science and Engineering, University of New South Wales, 2001.
4. Siew Siew Ong and John Shepherd. Webcms: A web-based course management system. In *13th International Workshop on Database and Expert Systems Applications (DEXA 2002)*, pages 345–350, Aix-en-Provence, France, September 2002. IEEE Computer Society 2002.

A Dynamic Conceptual Network Mechanism for Personalized Study Plan Generation

Elvis Wai Chung Leung and Qing Li

City University of Hong Kong, {iteleung,itqli}@cityu.edu.hk

Abstract. In a web-based learning environment, *student-centered* study plan become critical since the target users who have the *self-learning expectation* and *individual academic background* are very different from those of a traditional classroom. In fact, designing individual study plan is very *complicated* and *time consuming* as the target users normally are very diversified. To the best knowledge of our understanding, most of existing course enrollment facilities are quite primitive. In this paper, we introduce a conceptual framework for setting up individual *student-centered study plan* through 1) a dynamic conceptual network mechanism for capturing the relationships among courses to facilitate the dynamic generation of a study plan, and 2) intelligent knowledge base facilities, such as personal profiles, to help understand students' behavior so as to provide student-centered results to different learning groups.

1 Introduction

To face up to the increasing trend of continued learning demand, most universities are taking advantages of technology for their Web-based education [8, 9]. One characteristic in Web-based education is that the learning initiative is driven by the students. Thus, there is an increasing need to explore a mechanism for helping learner design a personalized study plan.

In fact, the design of individual study plan is very *complicated* and *time consuming*. The target users are generally in a very wide range and of different background. In the traditional classroom learning, the design of a program is usually targeted to a student group rather than individual students. It may seem to be possible that personal mappings of the student's background to the study program can be done manually, the procedures and resources involved however are tremendous. The program designer has to consider individual user's academic study background as well as the vocational study background before admitting a student into a program. Apart from the study background, other issues like the prerequisites of each course (if applicable) the proper duration of the program to the student, and the student's progression will also need to be considered. It inevitably creates the problem of duplicating the efforts and wasting time and resources.

Meanwhile we have to realize the fact that users carry different knowledge and different goals. So *"One program with pre-defined courses for all"* approach is insufficient for today's Web-based education. The focus of online education is to understand individual student's background knowledge and learning needs in order to provide proper courses in the program for their study anytime anywhere. Currently the course

W. Zhou et al. (Eds.): ICWL 2003, LNCS 2783, pp. 69–80, 2003.
© Springer-Verlag Berlin Heidelberg 2003

choices provided in a program are quite limited and the duration and progression of the program are also pre-defined. There is little room to allow students to switch from one to the other or to proceed faster in their study route based on their own progress. One of the advantages of e-Learning is the ability to provide a bulk of courses in a particular period because it needs not take into account the issues of teaching man-power, classroom, student schedule, and so on. However, most of existing web-based education systems are quite unsatisfactory in providing sufficient flexibilities for the selection of courses, progression of study, and duration of study. Thus, there is a need for such systems to re-organize the courses contained in the program based on individual needs by using proper Web-based education system in an effective and efficient manner.

1.1 Paper Objective and Organization

To facilitate the Web-based individual study plan generation, we introduce in this paper an innovative mechanism that utilizes *user profile* and *dynamic conceptual network* to provide the *personalized study plan*. The proposed mechanism makes use of the user profile to determine the characteristics of the study group, including background knowledge and learning goals. The dynamic conceptual network is a *hierarchy tree* in association with *courses*. Each course is stored in a *node* of dynamic conceptual network. Apart from the course contents, each node also contains some *attributes* for construction of relationship among each node and self-description of each node. This paper aims at advocating the idea of *treating different students differently* in the generation of personalized study plan based on the hybrid use of user-profiles, XML, and Java technologies. Our proposed web-based mechanism is thus able to establish, in particular, the relations among the program and courses, and also adapt to users having very different backgrounds and learning goals.

Through designing the conceptual framework and algorithms for dynamic concept network, we aim to address the following main topic in this paper: *How to effectively serve individual student in preparing the personalized study plan?* The rest of this paper is organized as follows: Section 2 reviews the current e-Learning systems and discuss their pros and cons. The specific features of the proposed conceptual framework and algorithms are detailed in sections 3. The final section concludes this paper and makes suggestions for further research.

2 Related Work

For the past few years, some researchers have focused on the areas of agent-based, multimedia, and adaptive approaches for e-Learning system. Before we introduce our dynamic study plan generation approach, some related research projects are discussed as below.

For the agent-based research work, *Andes* [6] a collaborative project started since 1995 between the University of Pittsburgh and the US Naval Academy, has took a modular architecture, and is implemented in Allegro Common Lisp and MS Visual C++. The main agents of *Andes* contain a problem author, a problem solver, an action interpreter and a help desk. These agents function in the sequence of creating problem definition, generating the problem solution graph model, and referring to the student model to make decisions upon receiving appropriate feedback and assistance. *LANCA* [7] adopts an intelligent agent's approach to distance learning in a distributed environment by using a constructive approach instead of user profiles to assist students in difficulty by building a common and useful databank. Unlike *Andes* and *LANCA*, *DT Tutor* [12] uses decision-theoretic methods for coached problem solving to select tutorial actions that are optimal given the tutor's beliefs and objectives. It employs a model of learning to predict the possible outcomes of each action, weighs the utility of each outcome by the tutor's belief that will occur, and select the action with the highest expected utility.

Among the multimedia-based projects, *Classroom 2000* [14] is designed to automate the authoring of multimedia documents from live events. The researchers have outfitted classrooms at Georgia Institute of Technology with electronic whiteboards, cameras, and other data collection devices that collect data during the lecture and combined it to create a multimedia document to document the class activities. *Cornell Lecture Browser* from Cornell University [10] captures a structured environment (a university lecture). It automatically produces document that contains synchronized and edited audio, video, images and text, so as to synchronize the video footage in the live classroom with the pre-recorded slides used in the class. Last but not the least, *MANIC,* from University of Massachusetts [9], discusses the ways of effectively utilized WWW-based, stored materials and presentation paradigms. In particular, *MANIC* proposes that students be given the opportunity to browse the materials at their own pace, stopping and starting the audio at their will.

For the adaptive approaches for online course materials, *WebCT* [11] has been widely used in education sectors to produce online courses or to act as a tool for publishing supplementary materials for existing courses. A *WebCT* course is mainly created by using a series of linked HTML pages which are defined as paths or "road map", and all these interactions take place through a web browser. *InterBook* [15] is based on a specific concept-based approach to develop an adaptive Web-based LISP textbook while *NetCoach* [16], an authoring system, allows the users to create adaptive and individual course modules without programming knowledge. The concepts used in *InterBook* are basically elementary pieces of knowledge for the given domain, with a more advanced form of the domain model being a network. Each page has a set of outcome concepts and a set of prerequisite concepts associated with it to support adaptive navigation and hyperlink annotation. Unlike *WebCT* and *InterBook, NetCoach* implements two adaptive navigation techniques: curriculum sequencing and adaptive annotation of links. In *NetCoach*, the knowledge base of a course consists of concepts that are internal representations of the pages to be presented to the learner at the front-end.

However, individual or tailored instruction based on learners' needs and background has not been achieved yet. Therefore, the integration of multiple agents [4,5], user profile [13], and multimedia technologies into a collaborative learning environment remains a very challenging problem.

3   Conceptual Framework and Algorithms

In this section, we describe a conceptual framework of the dynamic conceptual network and study plan generation algorithms. In order to provide an overall picture of the implied structure, the conceptual framework for the dynamic conceptual network will be explained first.

3.1   Relationship for Program, Course, and Credit Units

With the existing online education systems, one of the most important limitations for study plan generation is that the relationships among the courses of a specific program are not well defined. Thus, preparing an individual study plan is very complicated and timing consuming. In order to provide a better solution, we need to identify the structure for courses of a particular program.

As an example, figure 1 shows the main structure of a particular program (Master of Business Administration) as an illustration. Due to the wide variety of target users in online education, a *credit unit system* for online learning is introduced in our model in order to serve the individual student needs. Normally, a *program* includes *core courses, elective courses*, and *minimum required credit units*. A student is required to complete the core courses as the fundamental training. Subsequently, he/ she also needs to determine the major study by choosing the elective courses. Both the core and elective course are assigned with a number of credit units. Upon completion of the courses, the credit units will be recorded in the individual user profile. Finally, an academic designation will be awarded if the minimum credit units of the program are reached.

In order to define the dynamic conceptual network, we need to identify the relationships among program and courses. As shown in figure 1, some *natural relationships* are implied and to be discussed as follows.

Fig. 1. Structure of an example program (Master of Business Administration)

- *Relationship among program and program.* A program is designed for under- and post-graduate level. Normally, a student is required to complete the under-graduate program first, and then the post-graduate program is provided for the advanced study consideration. To ensure the student with sufficient knowledge to learn the post-graduate program, usually the prerequisite (admission requirements) checking is used. The student is only allowed to enroll the program if the prerequisites are fulfilled.

- *Relationship among program and course.* A program includes a set of courses whose syllabus is designed based on the program nature such as science, business, philosophy, and so on. To meet the individual learning goals and study background, a student is allowed to choose from the set of courses those that can meet the individual program requirements for receiving an academic award.
- *Relationship among course and course.* A Course is a unit to contain concepts and knowledge for student's studying. Normally, a student is required to complete the foundation courses first, and then the advanced courses will be provided for further study. To ensure the student with sufficient knowledge to learn a particular course, usually the prerequisite checking is also used. The student is only allowed to take a course if its prerequisites are fulfilled.

3.2   Conceptual Framework for Dynamic Conceptual Network

In order to build up the relationship among the program and courses, we introduce a *dynamic conceptual network* for personalized study plan generation.

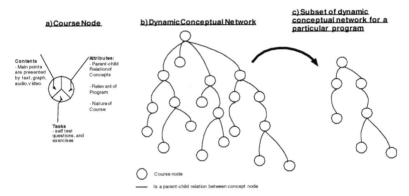

Fig. 2. Dynamic conceptual network

Definition: A dynamic conceptual network (figure 2b) is a *hierarchical tree* for developing the *inter-relationships* among *courses*. Each course is stored in a *course node* (figure 2a) of the dynamic conceptual network.

The dynamic conceptual network is composed of course nodes. Each course node has a unique identity for easy reference. As shown, the course node in figure 3a includes contents, tasks, and attributes. The contents are presented by text, graph, audio, and video. Tasks include self-test questions and exercises. In order to provide facilities for building up relations among the course nodes, three attributes are defined in each course node, i.e., Parent-child relation of concepts, relevance of learning objectives, and level of difficulty. The semantics of each attribute is explained below.

- Parent-child Relations. These inter-concept links are for building up the dynamic conceptual network. Each relation contains a *parent link* and *child link,* which refer to the identities of some other course nodes.

- <u>Relevance of Program</u>. This is the information for identifying the relevant course for a particular program and the program admission requirements.
- <u>Nature of Course</u>. As a means to serve the concept of personalization, this is a parameter to determine whether the course is core or elective for the targeted group.

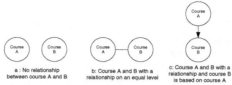

Fig. 3. Course nodes relationships

Based on the above attributes, figure 3 shows three possible scenarios among the course nodes, i.e., no relationship between course, courses A and B with a relationship on an equal level (level of difficulty), and courses A and B with a relationship and concept B is based on course A. A rule-based mechanism [4] is employed for the concept node's mapping using the following rules.

- **Rule A:** // Figure 3a shows no relation between courses A and B.
  *IF <no equal of parent-child attributes for the course nodes A and B>
     THEN <No relation between A and B>*
- **Rule B:** // Figure 3b shows that courses A and B are of a relationship on an equal level.
  *IF <the parent links of course A and B in their parent-child attributes are of the same object reference>
  THEN <A and B are of the relation on an equal level>*
- **Rule C:** // Figure 3c shows that courses A and B are of relationship and course B is based on course A.
  *IF <the parent link of course node B is of the same object reference as that of course node A's child link >
  THEN <A and B are of the parent-child relation; course node A is the parent and
  course node B is the child>*

3.3   Personalization of Course Materials for Target Study Group[1]

According to the above rules and mechanisms, we now show for a particular program how a subset of dynamic conceptual network is used to generate a set of personalized study plan for a target study group. The overall processes are divided into two stages: ***extraction*** of relevant courses from the program and ***filtering*** the most suitable course(s) for the target group based on the result set. For illustration, we assume that student A graduated with Bachelor of Computer Science and student B graduated

---

[1] We assume that the program requirements for those students who have similar user profiles are much the same. Thus, we can serve a target group of students based on their alike user profiles.

with Bachelor of Engineering. Now both two students want to take a Master of Business Administration program in order to strengthen his management skills.

Extraction of relevant courses for the program. Although the relations are only built on the course nodes, we can still extract the relevant course(s) for the particular program due to the attributes of each course node. Based on the attributes, a *multi-layer retrieval mechanism* is devised to retrieve the relevant information based on attributes' value and reconstruct the hierarchy based on the parent-child relations, as captured by the algorithm in figure 4. As an example, for the given program *"Master of business administration"* of figure 1, relevant course nodes within the program will be compared based on the pre-defined rules (cf section 3.2) so as to identify the relations among the course nodes for reconstruction of the hierarchy tree. Following the algorithm in figure 4, we obtain a preliminary subset of dynamic conceptual network (as shown in figure 5) in which the courses include *financial accounting, market analysis, operations management, modeling and analysis for management, management accounting, marketing management, organizational behavior strategic advantage, e-business, financial management services management* and *international business.*

```
DCN = Dynamic conceptual network
SRP = Student Required Program
RelevantSubset(DCN, SRP)
Empty(SubsetofDynamicConceptualNetwork)
While not Empty (DCN.CoursetNodes) do
 If DCN.CoursetNode.RelevantofProgram = SRP then
  /* Checking the relationship among course nodes based on the above rules */
  /* The comparison is below the DCN.CourseNode to nodes of the result set
     (subset of dynamic conceptual network) */
  /* If the rules B,C are true, the relationship link will be added to the result set */
     While do
        If Rule C  is true then
          Mapping the relation to the result set
          Exit do
        Else Rule B  is true then
           If  DCN.CoursetNode.NatureofCourse= core then
             Add a new dimension to the result set in core course root
           Else
             Add a new dimension to the result set in elective course root
           Endif
           Exit do
        Endif
     Until  Empty(SubsetofDynamicConceptualNetwork)
  Else
     Disregard
 Endif
 Enddo
 Return (SubsetofDynamicConceptualNetwork)
```

Fig. 4. Extraction of relevant courses for the given program

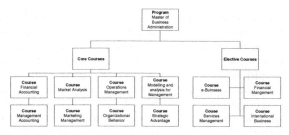

Fig. 5. A preliminary subset of dynamic conceptual network

Filtering the courses for the target group. In order to provide a personalized study plan for Web-based education, student profiles can be utilized [2,3]. In particular, a student is only required to identify the interested program, and then based on the student profiles available, the proposed mechanism will generate the relevant program structured for his/ her consideration. The information contained in a user profile includes student study history, preference and so on. To show the function of personalization, assume we have two individual user profiles: 1) Student **S1** who has studied the operations management; and 2) Student **S2** who has studied the financial accounting. The algorithm in figure 6 assumes that if the parent node is irrelevant to the target group, then the child node is also irrelevant. First, the user profile will be compared with the result set in order to identify the irrelevant course nodes based on the study history of the study group. The irrelevant course nodes will be marked "irrelevant" in the child link so as to ignore them in the dynamic concept network. The result of this filtering process is shown in figure 7 where **S1** is provided with such courses as financial accounting, market analysis, modeling and analysis for management, management accounting, marketing management, organizational behavior strategic advantage, e-business, financial management services management and international business. In contrast, **S2** is provided with the courses of market analysis, operations management, modeling and analysis for management, management accounting, marketing management, organizational behavior strategic advantage, e-business, financial management services management and international business.

3.4   Multi-layer Model for Study Plan Generation on the Internet

We now introduce a *Multi-layer Model* for Web-based study plan generation. Among others, it leverages various mechanisms of the framework's programming model, so as to produce efficient applications that are also maintainable.

Figure 9 shows the Multi-layer Model that facilitates the development of the study plan generation; it consists of *User View Layer* (UV), *Processing Layer* (PL), and *Knowledge Repository Layer* (KR). All layers have their own functions that can handle different tasks on behalf of the model. The UV layer, as the information collector, is located at the first to receive queries from the requesters. When a student submits a request, UV starts to function and passes the information to the second layer, PL that cooperates with KR for designing personalized study plan. The KR layer includes *XML-based study program and course information* and *User Profiles*. At the final stage, UV is requested by PL for the result sets' presentation.

```
h = study history of the target group
r = RelevantSubset(DCN, SRP)
t = true
ProcessFiltering(r, h)
While not is Empty (r) do
    t = true
    While not is Empty (h) do
        If h.course = r.CoursetNode then
            Assign "Irrelevant" to the r.CourseNode.Child.Link
            t = false
        Endif
    Enddo
    If t = true then
        If  the child link of parent node for the r.CourseNode marked with "Irrelevant"
then
            Assign "Irrelevant" to the r.CourseNode.Child.Link
        Endif
    Endif
Enddo
```

Fig. 6. Identifying the relevant learning courses for the target study group

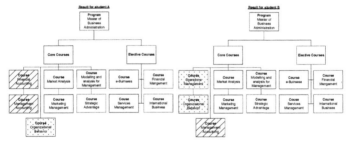

Fig. 7. Result of personalized course materials for students **S1** and **S2**

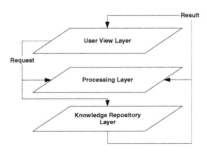

Fig. 8. Multi-layer Model

As a comparison on delivering study plan to students, UV depends on the student's user profile to determine the presentation layout as a frame for study plan delivery. In contrary, PL and KR are based on each individual request to generate the required results. Under this proposed model, each layer works independently in terms of its own tasks. Thus, no matter how any combination of courses for a program or how the user view is changed, the possible negative chain effects and cost of modification can be minimal. Eventually, the efficiency and effectiveness of development, implement and maintenance can be enhanced.

3.4.1 Implementation Aspects

To implement the proposed framework, the following techniques and tools are adopted for the elements in each layer:

User View Layer

- **Java server pages (JSPs)** – JSPs expect the servlet to provide data in the request context that is after formatting ready to be inserted into an HTML page. In general, the role of the JSP page is to make the final decision about the format and content of the response to an end user request

Processing Layer

- **Servlets** – Servlets provide the coordination between the programming and content elements of an application.

- **Java Architecture for XML Binding (JAXB)** – JAXB provides an API and tools that automate the mapping between XML documents and Java objects.

- **Command beans** – Command beans are beans that implement a basic business logic step. Their roles are to abstract and regularize the computations supported by the business logic of the application.

Knowledge Repository Layer

- **XML** – All course materials are stored in XML format. As an XML document is typically structured in a tree/hierarchical way, the relationships inside are mainly parent-to-child, which facilitate easier addition or removal of the nodes or documents. Relational databases do not deal well with highly flexible data relationships. XML-native data is treated more like a document, which is good for two key purposes: document-resident data is subject to changes, and documents need to be passed around intact to a number of people.

Based on the above, the servlets in PL can process HTTP requests and coordinate the rest of the application elements (such as Java Bean and JAXB) for study plan generation. As mentioned, the KR layer is to serve the PL in providing relevant source of the course and user profiles for the study plan generation. The responsibility for generating the user interface is assigned to JSPs in UV. For the study plan delivery, the JSPs take data provided by the servlet, format it and insert it into a HTML data stream to be sent to the client. Such a multi-layer decomposition provides a basis for rapid customization of dynamic pages and thus supporting the customization model of development.

4   Conclusions and Future Work

In this paper, we have presented a dynamic conceptual network mechanism for personalized study plan generation through the hybrid use of dynamic conceptual network, user-profiles, XML and Java technologies. Among the many desirable features offered by the proposed mechanism, the following ones are worth particular mentioning:

- **Dynamic conceptual network**. It provides a hierarchical tree for developing the inter-relations among individual courses. Each course is stored in a course node of a dynamic conceptual network, through which a student is supplied with the relevant study background information for a particular program.
- **Personalization of study plan for target study group.** The suggested study plan is generated based on individual learning group's expectation and learning goals, which supports the ideas of personalization and interactive learning [1] effectively. A win-win solution can be delivered in that the teacher has the relevant study plans for further advisory, and the student also has a personalized study plan for reference.

Currently, the presented study plan mechanism is being incorporated, together with a cooperative tutoring mechanism [3], into our agent-based e-Learning system [2]. In our subsequent research, we plan to design a *personalized scheduler* to help student arrange the online learning timetable for any given period.

References

[1]   Jonassen, D.H., Supporting Communities of Learners with Technology: A Vision for Integrating Technology with Learning in Schools. *Educational Technology*, 35(2). 60–63, 1995

[2]   Leung E., and Li Q., Agent-Based Approach to e-Learning: An Architectural Framework, in Kim, W., Ling, T.W., Lee, Y.J. and Park, S.S., *The Human Society and the Internet*, LNCS 2105, pp.341–353, 2001.

[3]   Leung, E. and Li, Q., Architecture and Algorithms of CPS – an Agent-based Tutoring System for Coached Problem Solving on the Web. *Proceedings of the First International Conference on Web-based Learning (ICWL2002)*, World Scientific Pub., pp.59–79, Hong Kong, 2002

[4]   Riley, G., *CLIPS, A Tool for Building Expert Systems*. http://www.ghg.net/clips/CLIPS.html.

[5]   Lesser, V. R., *Cooperative Multiagent Systems: A Personal View of the State of the Art*, IEEE Transactions on Knowledge and Data Engineering, vol. 11, no.11, Jan –Feb 1999

[6]   Gertner, A. S. and VanLehn, K., Andes: A Coached Problem Solving Environment for Physics in Gauthier G., Frasson C. and VanLehn K., *Intelligent Tutoring Systems*, pp. 133–142, 2000

[7]   Frasson, C., Martin, L., Gouarderes, G. and Aimeur, E., LANCA: A Distance Learning Architecture Based on Networked Cognitive Agents, in Goettl B., Halff H., Redfield C.

[8]   Pimentel M. G.C. and Abowd G.D., Ishiguro Y., Linking by Interacting: a Paradigm for Authoring Hypertext, *Proceedings of ACM Hypertext*, May 2000

[9]   Stern M., Steinberg J., Lee H. I., Padhye J. and Kurose J.F., MANIC: Multimedia Asynchronous Networked Individualized Courseware, *Proceedings of Educational Multimedia and Hypermedia*, 1997

[10]   Mukhopadhyay S., Smith B., Passive Capture and Structuring of Lectures, *Proceedings of ACM Multimedia*, October 1999.

[11]   WebCT: http://www.webct.com/Murray, R. C. and VanLehn, J., DT Tutor: A Decision-Theoretic, Dynamic Approach for Optimal Selection of Tutorial Acitons, in Gauthier G., Frasson C. and VanLehn K., *Intelligent Tutoring Systems*, pp. 153–162, 2000

[12] Bradley K., Rafter R. and Smyth B., Case-Based User Profiling for Content Personalisation, in Brusilovsky P., Stock O. and Strapparava C., *Adaptive Hypermedia and Adaptive Web-Based Systems*, pp.63–72, 2000

[13] Pimentel M. G.C., Abowd G.D., Ishiguro Y., Linking by Interacting: a Paradigm for Authoring Hypertext, *Proceedings of ACM Hypertext*, May 2000

[14] Brusilovsky, P., Eklund, J., and Schwarz, E. web-based education for all: A tool for developing adaptive courseware. Computer Networks and ISDN Systems, Proceedings of Seventh International World Wide Web Conference (1998) 291–300

[15] Weber, G., Kuhl, H-C, Weibelizahl, S. Developing adaptive internet based courses with the authoring system NetCoach. Proceedings of the third workshop on adaptive hypertext and hypermedia, UM2001, TU/e Computing Science Report 01/11. (2001)

GridFS: A Web-Based Data Grid for the Distributed Sharing of Educational Resource Files

Li Qinghu[1], Wang Jianmin[2], Kwok Yan Lam[2], and Sun Jiaguang[2]

[1] School of Software, Tsinghua University, Beijing, China
`liqinghu99@mails.tsinghua.edu.cn`
[2] School of Software, Tsinghua University, Beijing,China
`{jimwang,lamky,sunjg}@tsinghua.edu.cn`

Abstract. Platform for Distance Education of China will manage large amounts of educational resource files and large numbers of users, both of which are geographically distributed all over China. In such a grid environment, a high scalable, distributed file sharing approach with dynamic replication is needed. In this paper, we review existing related activities in file sharing and propose a web-based distributed file management architecture called Grid File System (GridFS). We describe its two fundamental services (namely, file access service and metadata service) followed with query processing and dynamic replication algorithm. Our query processing algorithm eliminates the duplication of query messages, and the simulation results show that our approach eliminate exponentially increase of the number of average per-site messages as the TTL (Time To Live) of a query increases to get higher query success rate. We believe GridFS would benefit most grid applications, web information systems and hierarchical web cache systems.

1 Introduction

Within a context of rapid technological change and shifting market conditions, the education system is challenged with providing increased educational opportunities without increased budgets [14]. Many educational institutions are answering this challenge by developing distance education programs. Chinese Ministry of Education is developing a platform for distance education of China (PDEC), which will provide services (rural and remote education) for nearly hundred millions of people all over the P.R.C.

Students, faculty and educational resources are key players in education. Since, in distance education face-to-face interaction between a teacher and students is restricted, educational resources play an important role in bridging the instructional gap.

Most of educational resources such as text, images, flash, courseware, audio and video exist in the form of files. These files in PDEC have the following characters:

W. Zhou et al. (Eds.): ICWL 2003, LNCS 2783, pp. 81–92, 2003.

- Large amount and continuously increased
- Various sizes from kilobytes-scale to gigabytes-scale
- Multifarious types and complex relationships between one and another
- Heavy load (hundred-million-scale users)
- Shared among different institutions and individuals
- Geographical distribution of themselves and their consumers

It is also necessary for these files to be writable, since it is required that PDEC should allow users not only to explore the shared files but also to edit/update them and create/publish new files as easy as operate files on their local traditional file systems.

In order to manage such educational resource files we have launched an effort to build a writable, serverless data grid with large scale, high performance, and high reliability. We call it Grid File System (GridFS) to emphasize that it is the extension to data grid [1] built over the web with self-governed internet-like topology and dynamic replication. We believe GridFS would be valuable to most grid applications, web information systems and hierarchical web cache systems.

The organization of this paper is as follows. We first discuss related activities in file sharing (section 2). Then, we introduce our GridFS architecture and describe two basic services of GridFS (section 3). Next, we propose a query processing algorithm (section 4) and a dynamic replication strategy (section 5) applied in GridFS. Section 6 is about the simulation of our methods. The paper ends with the conclusion and an introduction of the implementation status (section 7).

2   Related Work

The idea of large scale, high reliable file sharing with high performance is so fundamental that we might assume GridFS-like technologies must surely already be widely deployed. In practice, however, while the need for these technologies is indeed widespread, we find only primitive and inadequate solutions to PDEC problems.

Traditional distributed file systems like Network File System (NFS) [2] and Andrew File System (AFS) [4] provide a convenient interface for remote I/O with a uniform file name space. However, this approach does not support multi-site replication issues and also cannot achieve good performance due to a lack of collective I/O functionalities. In contrast, parallel/stripped file systems like DFS [3], HPSS [6] provide collective I/O but their parallel/stripped data transferring can only be applied in one cell, which is the basic administrative unit consists of some servers (master, replica, backup and metadata catalogue) and clients. Each cell is self-governed and one cell cannot cooperate with another one. This restricts their scalability and performance. SRB [5] provides a means to organize information stored on multiple heterogeneous systems into logical collections for ease of use. As the key part of a federated deployment of multiple SRB servers, MCAT (Metadata Catalogue) [5] is not distributed but centralized. This makes MCAT a bottleneck and restricts the scalability and reliability of SRB.

In peer-to-peer (P2P) file sharing systems such as Gnutella [16] and Freenet [15], files are stored at the end user machines (peers). Such systems identify resources (files) through their names. That is, P2P systems use names as their search criteria. However, in the context of PDEC, requests specify sets of desired attributes and values: for example, the type of educational resource, the keyword of resource content, and what course, which chapter is the desired resource file relevant to.

Our work is more closely related to data grid [1], which is a specialization and extension of the "Grid" [7]. Some data grid related projects (e.g. EDG [8], GriPhyN [9]) have been established to solve real and specific problems. Those projects are motivated by the requirement of an increasing number of scientific applications ranging from high-energy physics to computational genomics to access to large amounts of data. In each of these projects, the topology of all the sites is a tree designated in advance and only the root site contains the original files. This makes the root site a bottleneck and restricts the flexibility and makes it difficult for geographically distributed users to share their own files directly on the end user machines. Moreover, the original files can be replicated on the intermediate sites or leaf sites for clients to get high performance, but a file can only be replicated along certain branch from higher level to the next level [11]. This leads to the impairment of flexibility and performance.

3   GridFS Architecture

From section 2, we can see that current distributed file/storage systems do not address all of the concerns and requirements in PDEC. It is here that Grid File System (GridFS), the extension to data grid, enters the picture.

Our objective is to construct a decentralized distributed file system to share file objects across a mass of different institutions and individuals. GridFS should be decentralized in order to achieve high scalability so that it can accommodate large numbers of (e.g. 10^8) machines. Platform-independence should be another important feature of GridFS so that it can be deployed on diverse platforms from desktops, top end servers to clusters, even distributed systems with different OS and other software. Security problems across multiple administrative domains, which are not our focus in this paper, are also very important. All these requirements lead to our architecture design which makes GridFS achieve high performance and high trustworthy in file discovery, read operation and write operation.

3.1   Topology and Basic Components

As depicted in Fig. 1, the topology of our GridFS architecture is multi-level. A certain intermediate node (e.g. Site A) at certain level may have several children, which belong to the next level. The relationship of them is netlike and they can contact with one another. When a node is added, its parent node is specified. Through its parent node, the new node can find out all of its siblings. To avoid a single point of failures, a node can have several parent candidates with automatic failover.

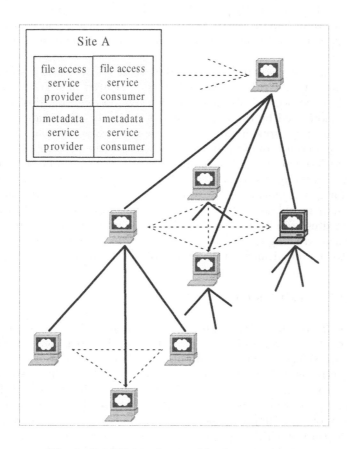

Fig. 1. GridFS topology and basic components

It is apparent that the topology is similar with that of the Internet. An intermediate site is similar to a gateway in the Internet and a leaf site is similar to a terminal computer.

Each site in GridFS is constructed into an atom grid and each intermediate site, along with all of its descendants, constitute a composite grid. Each grid, whether atom grid or composite grid, not only can work on its own but also can be combined with its sibling grids to provide more powerful service (This is also our vision about the "Grid"). The parent site in one grid is the bridge between this grid and other grids. It also can cache/replicate files that are frequently accessed to get high performance.

Each site can act as a service provider as well as a service consumer. A service provider provides two basic services: file access service and metadata service, which serves the service consumers. A service consumer can only access directly the metadata service on its parent or siblings, but it can access the file access service on any site in the system directly. Here, we merged concepts from P2P into our GridFS.

A service provider manages not only the files to be shared on its owner site, but also the replicas copied from other sites. Replicas are created automatically by a dynamic replication strategy which will be discussed in section 5. The main aims of replication are to reduce access latency and bandwidth consumption. Replication can also help in load balancing, striped file transferring for large files and can improve reliability by creating multiple copies of the same file.

3.2   File Access Service

In a grid environment, files may be stored in different locations and on different storage systems with different characters. The file access service hides the infrastructure differences among the underlying storage systems to present client applications with a uniform view of files and with uniform mechanisms for accessing these files. In this way, it is needless for client applications to be aware of the specific low-level mechanisms required when accessing to files at a particular location. On request to appointed file, the file access service at a particular site authenticate (beyond this paper) the client user first, if the authentication succeed, the file access service will go into operation by accessing the specific underlying file system through its own interface.

File access service provides partial access to a file. This made it possible for several sites, which hold the replica or original of the same large file, to cooperate in a stripped transfer. Our parallel/stripped transfer model assumes three entities: the control side (the logical entity initiating and finalizing a transfer), the source side (the source of file(s)), the sink side (the sink of file(s)). The control side could be a third party or a module collocated at either the source or sink side. Both the source side and the sink side can be composed of one, two, or more sites. That is, the source file object may be striped or replicated on different sites and so does that on the sink side. The control side specifies the distributed source file(s) and the distributed sink file(s) by using the metadata service (will be discussed in next sector), which manages the information about files and their hosts, and then initiate a transfer. When a transfer finishes, the control side will finalize it by adding or updating the metadata of the source or sink file(s) through the metadata service.

The model definition assumes reliable connection-mode transfer protocol. HTTP is a good choice since it is sophisticated, popular, secure (HTTPS), efficient, robust and easily extensible. HTTP combines control and data over single channel. This makes it simple, easy to bind with Web Service, and easy to get through a firewall. So we construct GridFS over the web and a site is a web server in practice. We believe web information systems and web caching would benefit from GridFS.

3.3   Metadata Service

Besides the file access service, GridFS includes another set of basic machinery, which manages the information about GridFS itself, including information about the contact among different sites, the underlying file system on each site, file instances, the contents of file instances, etc. This is called metadata service, which provides a means for publishing, accessing and filtering the metadata.

There are various types of metadata, application metadata, replica metadata, system configure metadata, runtime metadata. Application metadata describes two types of information about a file. One is the basic information such as file type, file size, file owner, and file access right, etc. The other is the information content represented by the file and other information useful to applications that access the file. Actually, application metadata defines the logical structure or semantics that should apply to the uninterrupted bytes that make up a file instance, a set of file instances or a sect of a file instance. The system configure metadata describes the fabric of GridFS itself. This information includes network connectivity and such details, about the underlying file system on each site, as their type, interface for access, capacity etc. The replica metadata, which is made up of the mapping information from file instances to particular locations, is used to manage replication of a sect of a file instance, a file instance, or a set of file instances. The runtime metadata describes the information about the status of the file: for example, being read or being written.

As discussed above, GridFS is a hierarchical and distributed system, so, in order to achieve scalability, avoid any single point of failure, the metadata service should be also treated as a distributed service. In most of current data grid projects, it is assumed that the replicated files are read only and the updates to metadata are infrequent. So, in such cases, distributed directory services, such as that provided by LDAP [10], are used to represent data grid metadata. In PDEC, where GridFS will be applied first, updates to both file objects and metadata are to be increasingly frequent both because there are more file objects and complicated relationship and because more and more file objects are published and replications are created or removed dynamically when needed. Unfortunately, the existing directory services (provided by LDAP, etc.) are well known to perform poorly in the presence of frequent updates. To meet the needs of PDEC, we start with implementing metadata service based on a relational database management system (MySQL), which not only can avoid the limitations of LDAP-like directory services in the presence of frequent updates, but also can provide powerful query language, SQL, which can execute more sophisticated queries that extract data from over the entire metadata domain.

4   Query Algorithm

In this paper, a "client" is referred to a site that initiates a request for a file handle. When a client (e.g. SA) wants to access a file, it first produces a query (Q) that describes the information about the file. Next, metadata service consumer (MSC_A) on SA sends the query to local metadata service provider (MSP_A) if MSP_A exists. If MSP_A does not exist or MSP_A cannot find corresponding file handle, MSC_A will pass Q to all metadata service provider on the siblings of SA along with a parameter TTL (time to live). At the same time, MSC_A passes Q to the metadata service provider on the parent node (SA_P) of SA. The parameter TTL is also sent to SA_P. The detailed query algorithm is described as follows.

Metadata Query Algorithm

```
Site.QueryProcess(Q, TTL, Sender){
/*
  Q: the information about the requested file handle
  TTL: the maximum times that Q can be transmitted.
  sender: the site that Q comes from.
*/
ExeQry(Q); //Execute query Q locally
if (there is a returned result!=null) return result;
if (TTL==0) return null;
if (Sender is myself or my child){
  //transmit Q to my siblings;
  for (each sibling Si){
    Si.QueryProcess(Q, TTL-1, this);
  }
  //transmit Q to my parent
  parent.QueryProcess(Q, TTL-1,this);
}
if (Sender is myself or my sibling or my parent){
  //transmit Q to my children;
  for (each child Ci){
    Ci.QueryProcess(Q,TTL-1,this);
  }
}
if (there is a result!=null returned) return result;
return null;
}
```

5   Dynamic Replication

5.1   Replica Selection

After receiving a list of replicas of the requested file, SA will make a selection among these replicas to get a replica that is predicted to provide the best performance. This process, namely replica selection, is based on response time prediction. With up-to-date status information about remote sites in its local metadata repository and that returned by query, SA can predict the response time of each replica accurately.

Response time (T_r) consists of two components: service time (T_s) and waiting time (T_w) and can be formulated as $T_r=T_s+T_w$. SA will select a replica that achieves a predicted minimum T_r. Waiting time denotes the time necessary for SA to establish the connection with the remote site which accommodates the particular replica. Service time is the time that the transfer will last and is computed by dividing the file size S, by the transfer speed V. So the formulation changes into the following:

$$T_r = S/V + T_w \qquad (1)$$

For a particular remote site (e.g. SB) that ever be accessed by SA, SA maintains lists of T_ws and Vs of N recent accesses. Variables V and T_w in Formulation (1) is respectively the average of those T_ws and the average of those Vs. If no information about SB exists in the metadata repository of SA, T_w will be assumed to be the average of the known average waiting-times, and the recent average output speed of SB will be assigned to V. The average output speed of SB is monitored and is periodically pushed to all the correlative sites by SB.

For a large file, SA can select two or more replicas and even cooperate with its parent, sibling, or children sites to start up a stripped transfer discussed above.

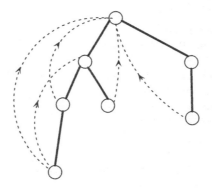

Fig. 2. Distribution of Replicas

5.2   Replica Acquisition, Release, and Reallocation

After the file transfer from the selected site (SB) to SA finishes and the lists of T_ws and Vs about SB are updated on SA, the average waiting time (avg(T_ws)) and the average of transfer speed (avg(Vs)) to the selected replica(s) are respectively calculated. If avg(T_ws) is larger than the waiting time threshold (TH_w) or avg(Vs) is slower than the transferring speed threshold (TH_v), a "replica acquisition" request will be sent to SB. Each site is free to select TH_w and TH_v differently. SB will accept the request by returning the metadata about the replica to SA and recording the information about SA. In GridFS, the distribution of replicas of the same file is tree-like, as depicted in Fig. 2. Besides the bidirectional link between itself and its parent replica, each replica has also a spare link to its grandparent replica so that it can turn the grandparent into a new parent if its old parent is to be released or becomes unavailable. In addition, each replica keeps a link to the original so as to acquire writer lock from the original (replica consistency is beyond this paper). Certainly, more ancestors are linked to in succession, more reliability will be achieved.

If the pool (on SB) of available replicas of the same file is full filled, the replica whose last access time is the earliest will be released. After the specified replica is released, all its children are notified and they will send "replica acquisition" requests to SB by themselves. The above process will be repeated.

If no storage space is available to accommodate a new file copy, SA will first examines the local cache, which holds replicas of different files, to see which replica is the most infrequently accessed one and then move it to SA's parent site (the motivation for this moving is that the parent site maybe be able to accommodate the replica and thus propagate the object up to make it cover more sites and have more chances to be searched). This replica reallocation processing will be repeated until SA shas enough free storage spaces.

6   Simulation

6.1   Metrics

Performance issues in GridFS are extremely complicated. In addition to issues such as load on the network, load on network participants, and delays in getting positive answers, there are a host of other criteria such as success rate of the query, the bandwidth of the selected provider nodes, and fairness to both the consumer and the provider. It is impossible for us to use all of these criteria in evaluating query and replication algorithms.

Instead, we focus on efficiency aspects of the algorithms solely, and use the following simple metrics. These metrics, though simple, reflect the fundamental properties of the algorithms.

- P(success): the probability of finding the queried object before the query terminates. Different values of TTL have different criteria for terminating the query, and lead to different probabilities of success.
- avg. #msgs per site : overhead of the algorithm as measured in average number of query messages each site in GridFS has to process. The motivation for this metric is that in GridFS, the most notable overhead tends to be the processing load that the network imposes on each participant. The load, usually message processing, is directly proportional to the number of messages that the node has to process.

6.2 Methodology

In the evaluation of our query method and replication strategy, we run a set of simulations constructed using PARSEC[12] and report aggregate results.

In our simulations, the internet-like topology consists of numlevel levels. For simplicity, we assume that each site, except leaf sites, has n children on the next level. The total number of all the sites in GridFS is denoted by N. We first place N files on these N sites randomly (This results in that none of these files is placed on some sites and some sites contains more than one files.) And q_i represents the relative popularity, in terms of the numbers of queries issued for it, of the i'th object. The values are normalized.

$$\sum_{i=1}^{N} q_i = 1; \; q_i \propto 1/i^{\alpha} (Zipf - like : \alpha \; is \; a \; constant) \qquad (2)$$

Since studies have shown that web queries tend to follow Zipf-like distributions [13] and GridFS queries are similar to web queries in practice, we generate 1000N different queries that follow Zipf-like distributions, each query starting at a random site (i.e., we randomly choose different site from which to initiate the query). Then, for each query, we simulate our query processing and dynamic replicating.

Statistics are collected from the 1000N queries for the N files randomly distributed on N sites. In our simulation, numlevel=6 and n=10. This results in that N=111111. For replication in our simulation, we assume that the more hops between two sites, the better is the network performance between them (i.e. the waiting time is shorter and the transfer speed is higher). We also suppose that one object (original or replica) on certain site can only be replicated 5 times at most. We calculate the aggregate results for the following metrics: P(success) is the number of successful queries divided by the total number of queries generated; avgMsgs is the average number of messages generated for each query divided by the total number of sites in that network.

As a final note about our methodology and metrics, we stress that they omit a lot of issues, including the message delays in the network, the service time for file transfer, the actual load on a site for processing and propagating messages, etc. However, these models help us understand the fundamental properties of our query processing and replication algorithms.

6.3 Results

GridFS uses TTL to control the number of hops that a query can be propagated. However, choosing the appropriate TTL is not easy. For files that are widely present in GridFS, small TTLs suffice; for files that are rare in GridFS, large TTLs are necessary.

Fig. 3 shows the probability of success and average per-site message overhead as TTL increases. We are likely to think that it is difficult to eliminate exponentially increase of the number of average per-site messages as the TTL increases

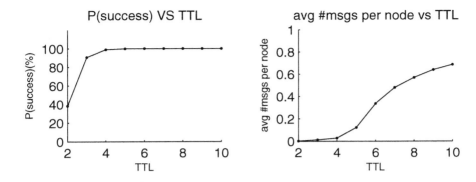

Fig. 3. How the probability of success and average per-site message overhead vary as
TTL vary.

to get higher probability of success, but our simulation results depicted in the
figures show that the probability of success approaches 100% quickly as the TTL
increases, and the number of average per-site messages increases smoothly as the
TTL increases. The reason is that the internet-like topology and our query processing algorithm eliminate the duplication of query messages and our replication
algorithm makes the hot files widely present quickly. The simulation results also
show that the appropriate value of TTL is 3 or 4.

7   Conclusion and Status of Implementation

In this paper, we present a web-based data grid, namely GridFS, for the distributed sharing of educational resource files. After introducing the architecture
of GridFS, we propose a query processing algorithm and a dynamic replication
strategy. Our internet-like topology and the query processing algorithm eliminate the duplication of query messages, and the simulation results show that
our methods eliminate exponentially increase of the number of average per-site
messages as the TTL increases to get higher probability of success.

We have made progress on several fronts in our effort to identify the basic
services for GridFS. We have a preliminary design of the file access API, which
provides a standard interface including create, delete, open, read, write and close
operations on file instances. This interface also support transfers started and
controlled by a third party. For this prototype API design, we have developed
a library in Java and SOAP to implement interfaces to web servers. In this
library embedded in Apache Tomcat, we have also implemented metadata service
including query processing and dynamic replica management. Metadata service
uses MySQL to store metadata of files, file contents, replica distribution, and
the fabric of GridFS itself. We can use SQL language to query these attributes
to find replicas associated with particular specification.

Acknowledgments. This work is supported by the Ministry of Education P.R.C under contract 2001BA101A12-02 and the National Key Basic Research and Development Program of China (973 Program) under Grant No.2002CB312006.

References

1. A. Chervenak, I. Foster, C. Kesselman, C. Salisbury, and S. Tuecke. The Data Grid: Towards an architecture for the distributed management and analysis of large scientific datasets. Journal of Network and Computer Applications, 23:187–200, 2001.
2. R. Sandberg. The Sun Network File System: Design, Implementation and Experience, Tech. Report, Mountain View CA: Sun Microsystems, 1987.
3. M. L. Kazar, B. W. Leverett, O. T. Anderson, V. Apostolides, B. A. Bottos, S. Chutani, C. F. Everhart, W. A. Mason, S. Tu, and R. Zayas. DEcorum file system architectural overview. In Proceedings of the Summer USENIX Conference, June 1990.
4. J. Morris, et al. Andrew: A Distributed Personal Computing Evironment. Comms. ACM, vol 29, no. 3, pp. 184–201, 1996.
5. A.K. Rajasekar and R.W. Moore. "Data and Metadata Collections for Scientific Applications", High Performance Computing and Networking (HPCN 2001), Amsterdam, NL, June 2001.
6. R.W. Watson, R.A. Coyne. The parallel I/O architecture of the High-Performance Storage System (HPSS). In IEEE MSS Symposium, 1995.
7. I. Foster, C. Kesselman and S. Tuecke. The anatomy of the grid: Enabling scalable virtual organizations. International Journal on Supercomputing Applications (2001).
8. European Data Grid (EDG). http://www.eu-datagrid.org/
9. Grid Physics Network (GriPhyN). http://www.griphyn.org/
10. M. Wahl, T. Howes and S. Kille. Lightweight directory access protocol (v3). RFC 2251, Internet Engineering Task Force, 1997.
11. K. Ranganathan and I. Foster. Identifying Dynamic Replication Strategies for a High Performance Data Grid. In Proceedings of the International Workshop on Grid Computing, Denver, Colorado, November 2001.
12. Parsec home page. http://pcl.cs.ucla.edu/projects/parsec
13. V. Almeida, A. Bestavros, M. Crovella, and A. de Oliveira. Characterizing reference locality in the www. In Proceedings of 1996 International Conference on parallel and Distributed Information Systems (PDIS '96), 1996.
14. Marchioro II, T.L., and Landau R.H., "Web-based Education in Computational Science and Engineering", in computational science engineering, IEEE Computer Society, April-June 1997, pp. 19–26.
15. I. Clarke, O. Sandberg, B. Wiley, and T. Hong. Freenet: A Distributed Anonymous Information Storage and Retrieval System. ICSIWorkshop on Design Issues in Anonymity and Unobservability, July 2000.
16. Gnutella. http://gnutella.wego.com.

A Virtual Laboratory for an Online Web-Based Course – 'Rapid e-Business Systems Development'

F. Leung, T. Chau, T. Tang, and S. Liao

Department of Information Systems, City University of Hong Kong, Hong Kong, China
{isfelix, istenson, istang, issliao}@cityu.edu.hk

Abstract. This paper is to report a previous project on showing how physically classroom training, web-based course materials and web-based communication can help in teaching an e-business development course. The various planning and implementation issues in this project will also be discussed.

The case addressed in this paper was about a virtual laboratory for an undergraduate course in City University of Hong Kong (CityU). One of the major objectives in this course is to design and develop an e-business application using existing programming tools and software packages. Students can learn the concepts of an Electronic Commerce (EC) website and follow the steps to build up a complete EC website. With the support of this virtual laboratory, the development and learning process can be carried out at any place of the world where Internet access is available.

1 Introduction

Hong Kong has an excellent telecommunications infrastructure boasting full broadband network coverage. By February 2002, broadband network covering 98% of households and all major commercial buildings through fiber-to-the-building and Digital Subscriber Loop (DSL) technologies. Broadband users in household totaled 624 thousands in February 2002 and reached 916 thousands in December 2002. Besides, the Internet traffic through broadband networks totaled 27 terabits in December 2002 [1]. The tremendous growth of Internet broadband network coverage, broadband penetration rate and broadband usage produces a new form of electronic community daily. For example, teaching and learning are no longer to be confirmed within the four walls of a classroom but can be on the Internet.

Due to the breakthrough of Internet bandwidth restriction, the materials transferred on the network are not limited to static texts or some graphical images but can also be audio and video. As the most important benefits of web-based learning are the use of hypertext and hypermedia to link plain documents or multimedia information [2, 3], it is why a fastest-moving change occurs is in the education sector. Also, a sufficient network bandwidth makes possible to implement a 'virtual classroom', which has many of the same features of a physical classroom such as access to lecture materials, to ask and answer questions, to turn-in homework, etc. As a result, web-based teaching and learning have been attracting more and more attention in Hong Kong.

W. Zhou et al. (Eds.): ICWL 2003, LNCS 2783, pp. 93–103, 2003.

The subsequent sections of this paper are organized as follows: Section 2 describes the background of our work and the reason why to build up a web-based virtual laboratory. The discussion about the design and implementation is given in section 3. In section 4, the selection and the use of EC package will be discussed. Section 5 describes the security issue in our virtual laboratory. Section 6 concludes the paper.

2 Background

The case addressed in this paper was about a virtual laboratory for an undergraduate course. The course was developed by Department of Information Systems, which is a department in the faculty of business from CityU, in 2001 autumn. We have used 4 months to design, implement and test our virtual laboratory. Meanwhile, we also have designed a 13-week courseware material. The first student intake started in January 2002 and there were 48 students who have registered this course in that semester.

2.1 About the Course

The course, was known as IS4338 Rapid e-business Application Development, was offered to third year students using a combination of physical classroom teaching and web-based training. These students have taken a year or more of high-level programming language (eg. Visual Basic) courses during their undergraduate education. The teaching pattern of this course was a mixture of on-campus lectures and off-campus virtual laboratory sessions. They were distributed alternately along a semester with 13 weeks. We considered our virtual laboratory was a part of web-based training in this course.

This course lasted for one semester and it covered the fundamentals of EC website with emphasis on developing and programming. One of the major objectives in this course was to design and develop an e-business application using existing programming tools and software packages. Upon successful completion of the course, students were expected to comprehend the concepts of an EC website. With the support of our virtual laboratory, students could follow the steps to build up a complete EC website.

2.2 Reason to Develop a Virtual Laboratory in Our Course

There are four major reasons to propose this project. Firstly, Electronic Commerce has already become the major focus of teaching and research in our faculty of business. EC related teaching is really in demand at the levels of both undergraduate and graduate and practice of implementing an EC website is a very useful way to enhance students' knowledge and skills which are a must for their careers in the field. This remote laboratory can provide an excellent means for our students to actually implement the EC concepts learnt from their classrooms.

Secondly, although virtual teaching is not a new concept, bringing an EC building laboratory to students' homes is a new practice, at least in the faculty of business. The price of an EC solution package, such as Microsoft® Commerce server from Microsoft Corporation [4] and INTERSHOP® from Intershop Communications [5], is far from being affordable for our students. Moreover, the installation of such a package involves a number of associated software packages and therefore is a complex task. For example, Microsoft® Commerce server requires Microsoft® SQL Server™ 2000 to host the database. Without a remote EC lab, our students have to physically come to a specific computing laboratory in order to learn the practical issues of EC systems development. Each workstation in this lab should have expensive software packages installed. Also, both hardware and software must be maintained by computing experts. The number of students who can benefit is then very small and the allocated time for an individual is limited. A remote EC lab can enable our students to implement EC applications by themselves, i.e., without any help from computing experts is required, without the constraints of time and location.

Thirdly, due to well-provided coverage of broadband network in Hong Kong, it has made possible greatly increased access to networked multimedia information. It is easier for us to distribute high quality audio and video materials on the Internet. Students can better make use of these multimedia materials to review the lecture or to look at our demo video clips.

Lastly, although several web-based course management system such as WebCT and Blackboard [6, 7] supporting on-line lecturing and tutoring have been adopted in CityU, these tools are not able to provide students convenient online access to programming facilities available in computer labs. One of the powerful features of our virtual laboratory is the integration of the existing EC software packages together with a remote development environment.

2.3 Courseware Development

We have developed 13 lectures and 12 tutorial training exercises. All these learning materials were available on the web, including lecturing PowerPoint slides, reference documents and demonstration video clips, etc. These materials were available 'on-demand', at times and locations that most convenient to students. For each week during the semester, the students were required to come to the campus to have the lecture. Each web-based training exercise on a specific topic was followed by a lecture accordingly. The topics, which were covered in this course, were followed in this order: DHTML, JavaScript, Active Server Pages (ASP), Active Data Objects (ADO), Component Object Model (COM) technologies in Microsoft® Commerce Server and XML.

One of the optimal modes for a web-based distance lecture is to use streaming video clips for the audio/video lecturing, and dynamically loaded HTML pages to present the lecture notes [8]. We have adopted Microsoft® Windows Media™ Technologies [9, 10] to help us to develop and deploy streaming multimedia content across the Internet. The ability of this Windows Media™ platform could stream our multimedia courseware. Students could render content while that content is being received over the Internet without downloading it first. Streaming was selected instead of downloading multimedia files because it could greatly reduce the waiting time and storage requirements of the students' computers. Otherwise, our students had to wait for the video files to fully download before they could start to view them. This was extremely helpful for those students did not have fast enough access to download large multimedia files quickly such as using 56K dial-up connection. Also, for our student there was no charge for any videotape.

The instructor recorded 13 one hour of lectures of IS4338 while having the physical classroom training. We have encoded the digital media content into Windows Media-based content by using the Microsoft® Media™ Encoder. The Advanced Streaming Format (ASF) codec was our selected file format, which is a highly flexible and compressed format, could contain streaming audio, video, slide shows, and synchronized events. With the help from Windows® Media™ ASF Indexer, we have integrated and synchronized the instructor's PowerPoint slides with the corresponding video clip. The finalized streaming materials were act like video-based presentations on the Internet. Students have taken advantages of the recorded lecture and were using them at home or elsewhere for review after lectures.

Those ASF media files and published PowerPoint slides were put on our Microsoft® Windows Media™ Service Server as on-demand contents. The streaming delivery technique was multicast that can preserve our network bandwidth. When we were going to provide streaming media, we have considered the line capacity that our student might have. As streaming video is quite sensitive to users' Internet-connection speeds, thus we have encoded the digital content at different data-delivery rates. We did not only just produce the high-bandwidth video clips but also the low-bandwidth one. We have both 100kbps (kilobit per second) and 300kbps encoding rate for streaming video. The faster the speed, the better the clip will look and sound. As we do not have to maintain a clear focus and smoothness of the lecture's movement, we use a frame rate of 12fps (frames per second) to produce the streaming video. Besides the multimedia courseware, other text-based materials will be saved in 'portable document format' (PDF) using Acrobat software and can be viewed directly on the web.

3   Design and Implementation of the Virtual Laboratory

The server operation system used in our virtual laboratory was Microsoft® Windows® 2000 Server edition. The software used to provide web services was Microsoft® Internet Information Server. The software adopted to be an EC application was Microsoft® Commerce Server 2000 and the software used to provide relational database management services was Microsoft® SQL Server™ 2000. The software used to provide streaming audio and video over the Internet was Microsoft® Windows Media™ Service Server. Besides the phpBB discussion board, most of the components of this web-based classroom environment were built in Active Server Pages (ASP). The system architecture of the remote lab is shown in the Figure 1.

3.1 Web-Based Environment

In order to provide a fast, reliable and high available server system to accommodate numerous simultaneous accesses, a 3-tier web-enabled architecture will be adopted in our EC virtual laboratory. Our platform has two servers and each was equipped with one Pentium III Xeon 1GHz CPU, 1 GB of SDRAM and a three-disk 18 GB RAID5 (Random Array of Inexpensive Disks) storage. With RAID support, our systems could tolerate the loss or failure on any one hard disk. The primary purpose of these two servers was to provide web, application and database services.

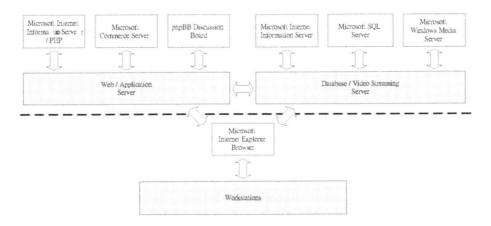

Fig. 1. System Architecture of the Virtual Laboratory

3.1.1 Web/Application Server
The Web/Application Server was the front gate of the whole system. We will not discuss the firewall and other Internet networking devices in our paper. The Web Server accepted requests from the users and sent the results back to the users. The Application Server provided all necessary facilities for the users to build an EC Web site. The users could use their own browsers to access the Web/Application Server building an EC website together with a SQL database located within our campus. Since only a browser was needed for the client side, all clients of our system were very "thin" and the users did not need to install or configure any thing before allowed to use the remote EC lab to build an EC website. The basic architecture of the remote lab is shown in Figure 2.

3.1.2 Database/Video Streaming Server
The Video Streaming Server was responsible for delivering compressed video to our students' request for a particular video stream. This was handled by Microsoft® Windows Media™ Technologies which were a commercial streaming media software packages. The Database Sever enabled the connections between the Application

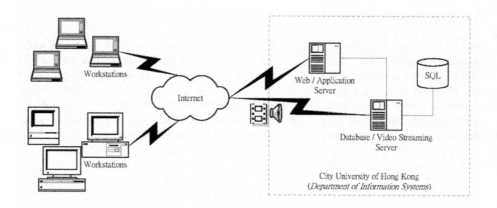

Fig. 2. Basic Architecture of the System Environment

Server and the SQL database. Data in Microsoft® Commerce Server and phpBB discussion board would be hosted in the Database Sever. As video streaming required a fairly high-performance system, that was why we separated the Application and the Video Streaming into two separate systems.

3.1.3 Workstation
In order to access our virtual laboratory, a Microsoft® Internet Explorer 5.5 web browser was a basic requirement which acted as an ActiveX container. We adopted ActiveX technology in our environment. For Internet Explorer, Windows Media™ Player was embedded as an ActiveX Control object in the web page. Windows Media™ Player needed a proprietary codec, which was called TechSmith Screen Capture Codec (TSCC), to play our streaming video.

3.2 Features and Functions

Our virtual laboratory was implemented in Windows 2000 environment. There were totally 10 functions in our virtual laboratory platform and they were done mainly in ASP. All students connected to our system through a graphic user interface as shown in Figure 3. Students needed to login to our system before they could get full access rights browsing through our website. The following features and functions were included in our EC virtual laboratory.

3.2.1 Course Materials
All the archived teaching materials were located in this section. Students could download the PowerPoint slides and exercises by simply logon to our web server. If students wanted to review the previous lectures, they could simply choose the encoding rate and click on the URL. Both the video and the presentation PowerPoint slides were played within the pop-up window with 780×550 pixels. This dimension

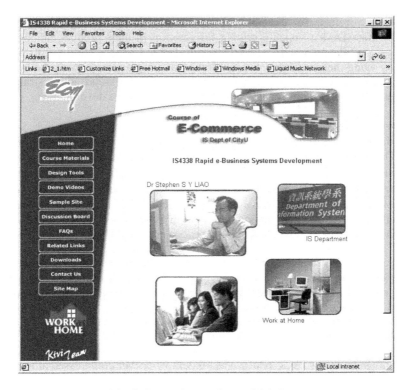

Fig. 3. Screen Layout for the Main Page

could suitable for those users who were still using 800×600 screen resolution. It was not recommended for our student to use 640×480 screen resolution because it was too small to display both.

A Windows Media™ Player was embedded in the top of the left frame while presentation slides were displayed on the right one. As the lecture proceeded, the slide refreshed automatically, synchronized with lecture audio. During streaming the video, student could pause the lecture at any point to take notes, or to repeat a section.

3.2.2 Design Tools

Since the development of an EC website under any EC solution packages was by default working locally, the adopted EC solution package in our virtual laboratory had to be reconfigured so as to allow remote website constructions over the Internet. A submission and deployment mechanism, which allowed the students to upload their web pages to our server and view their developed websites, were facilitated in this section.

Also, we have integrated a management tool, which was called Business Desk, from the Microsoft® Commerce Server for students remotely to manage their Commerce

Server 2000 websites. For example, students could access those pre-built modules within Business Desk to update pricing information in their product catalog or run reports base on sales transactions. Students can start to learn the components of an EC website by using these modules without doing any programming. As these beneficial features from the software package provided all basic back-end administrated tool, students would only need to focus on the front-end web pages development.

3.2.3 Demo Videos

Besides the video-based presentation, we also provided other video demo clips on our server. These videos were in streamed format showing all the necessary steps to install the commercial software packages such as Microsoft® Commerce Server and Microsoft® SQL Server™. In order to make the user guide in a more effective visual way for our virtual laboratory, we also captured the Windows desktop activities using those facilities provided. Students could simply play these pieces of streaming video from their browsers so as to understand the processes to build up an EC website.

All these multimedia screen capturing were done by Camtasia Studio [11] which was a video screen-recording studio. We have used TechSmith Screen Capture Codec (TSCC) to optimize for recording computer screens and to compress these videos. We first used Camtasia Recorder to record the Windows desktop activities into several AVI files and then used Camtasia Producer to convert them to streaming files in Microsoft Advanced Streaming Format (ASF).

The advantage on using TSCC codec was lossless whenever compressed at reasonable compression rates. We could produce the video exactly like the screen that was recorded. Although the TSCC codec was not part of the standard Microsoft distributed codecs, it was compatible with Windows. Students only needed to download and installed this freely available codec which was used by the Windows Media™ Player to play the video.

3.2.4 Sample Site

We have put together some sample sites that were built by using Microsoft® Commerce Server for our students. Students not only saw just how powerful this software package could be, but they also could get a few ideas that they might not have thought about such as the designs, the interfaces, the functions of different kinds of EC websites.

3.2.5 Discussion Board

Although there were many ways for people to communicate electronically with one another outside of class at their own convenience, our virtual laboratory was heavily relied on electronic discussion board to facilitate a communication channel. It was useful to find that we could now only need to answer a question once following by posting the answer on-line then all students could benefit from the answer. This could help us to increase our efficiency and productivity. At the end of the semester, we found that our students were more readily to interact with each other and thereby the discussion board could provide our student a new opportunity for peer-to-peer learning.

We have not built up our own discussion board. We simply implemented the phpBB [12], which was an open source bulletin board system, on our Windows platform to promote asynchronous interactions between students, lecturer and teaching assistants whenever after class. Students could access the phpBB from anywhere on the Internet. This tool allowed our student to post messages containing text (in various fonts, sizes and colours), graphics, and any type of file attachment.

3.2.6 Frequently Asked Question (FAQs)
Besides our interactive bulletin board system, we have also created a Q&A mechanism which provided effective assistance to help the users to overcome possible difficulties they might encounter in building an EC Web site. Those most commonly asked questions would be posted in this section. The users read some pre-set questions and answers before sending e-mail to ask us.

3.2.7 Related Links
This section contained extensive listings of related information that can be found on the Internet.

3.2.8 Downloads
If students wanted to download the evaluation copy of those commercial software packages and installed in their own machine, they could benefit from these hyperlinks.

3.2.9 Contact Us
The e-mail address and contact number of lecturer and those teaching assistants would be listed in this section.

3.2.10 Site Map
We have added a sit map which acted like a website index for student to access the web pages at their convenience.

4 Software Justification

Microsoft® Commerce Server is the latest EC solution package of Microsoft. It reduces the complexity and the time for building tailored, effective EC solutions. By providing the application framework together with sophisticated feedback mechanisms and analytical capabilities, Commerce Server allows our students to quickly develop an EC website. This software package provides the critical EC infrastructure needed to build an effective online EC business. User profiling and management, product and service management, transaction processing, and targeted marketing and merchandising are all integrated to create a comprehensive system customizable for our students' specific needs.

The Commerce Server Solution Sites provide a significant head start for developing a website based on Commerce Server 2000. They provide a highly structured approach to building a website that will be easy to extend and maintain. Students can use the

Solution Sites to build working websites that they can customize as needed. Most of the basic features needed for creating a commercial website are present in the Solution Sites, such as a shopping basket, a checkout procedure, a product catalog, user profiles, and so on.

5 Security Issue in Our Virtual Laboratory

Besides physical restrictions were in place for the two servers, additional security controls were needed and have been implemented in our virtual laboratory. We have divided these controls into two parts: restricting access to specific files or directories and verifying the identity of users who try to view those files.

5.1 File Security

As most of the files were located in the web server including the teaching materials and students' files, the first place where security was needed was to restrict access to specific files or directories on that server. File security relied on controls built into the operating system. Windows authentication was used to verify the identity of students who tried to write files to the server. "Course Materials", "Design Tools" and "Demo Videos" were restricted categories on which viewers were not allowed to access these facilities through an anonymous account.

5.2 Identity Verification

Each student has had a login user account on the web server and they were granted with write permission on his/her own working directories. Besides the file access level control, we also have implemented application level security. In the database server, each student was separately assigned a username and password for SQL Server authentication which were different from Windows authentication.

5.3 Security Lack

Streaming media servers have relied on the security features of web server to protect their media streams. This was done by only allowing authorized students to view the "Demo Videos" category. However, whenever the users could get access to that web page, they could view the source code and discover the actual "hidden" URL for those media files. If they really did so, we had nothing to prevent them from freely accessing the file and from sharing that address with others.

Streaming video which is unlike a progressive download and suppose to be not allowed to save on the viewer's computer. However, streaming digital media files are no longer necessary to ensure stream without downloading. Several programs are currently available that allow viewers to capture an audio or video stream and save it to a file on the their computer. As those streaming materials are not that confidential, we still convert the media files into streaming media files which already good enough to provides a certain level of security on our media content.

6 Conclusions

In this paper, Microsoft® Commerce Server has been successfully integrated in our virtual laboratory which help students to understand an EC website development. Being a computer-based learning and development platform, our virtual laboratory allowed students to gain access to course materials and to use those facilitates from Microsoft® Commerce Server. According to the usage of our virtual laboratory, it can only be considered as a supplement rather than a replacement of all physically classroom training. Because of the only requirement on the client side is a Microsoft® Internet Explorer 5.5 web browser, a Windows Media™ Player and a TSCC codec plug-in, it is very convenience for students to start developing their own EC websites.

References

[1]   Office of the Telecommunications Authority (OFTA), Statistics of Customers of Licensed Internet Service Providers in Hong Kong. Retrieved April 16, 2003, from *www.ofta.gov.hk/datastat/eng_cus_isp.pdf*.
[2]   Lynnette R. Porter, "Virtual Classroom", John Wiley & Songs, Inc., 1997.
[3]   James F. Kurose, Keith W. Ross, "Computer Networking: A Top-Down Approach Featuring the Internet", Addison Wesley, 2000.
[4]   Microsoft® Commerce Server, Microsoft Corporation. Retrieved April 16, 2003, from *http://www.microsoft.com/commerceserver/*.
[5]   INTERSHOP®, Intershop Communications Inc. Retrieved April 16, 2003, from *http://www.intershop.com/*.
[6]   WebCT, WebCT Inc. Retrieved April 16, 2003, from *http://www.webct.com*.
[7]   Blackboard , Blackboard Inc. Retrieved April 16, 2003, from *http://www.blackboard.com/*.
[8]   P. Thomas, Carswell L., Price B., and Petre M., "A Holistic Approach to Supporting Distance Learning Using the Internet: Transformation, Not Translation", British Journal of Education Technology, April 1998, Vol.29(2), pp.149-161.
[9]   Microsoft Corporation, "Inside Windows Media", Microsoft Press, Nov. 1999.
[10]   Microsoft Corporation, "Windows Media Control SDK", Microsoft Corporation, 1999.
[11]   Camtasia Studio, TechSmith® Corporation. Retrieved April 16, 2003, from *http://www.camtasia.com*.
[12]   phpBB, phpBB Group. Retrieved April 16, 2003, from *http://www.phpbb.com*.

A New Architecture for Web-Based Virtual Laboratory with CORBA Technology*

Jianxin Wang[1], Weini Lu[1], and Weijia Jia[2]

[1] College of Information Science and Engineering, Central South University,
ChangSha, 410083, China
jxwang@mail.csu.edu.cn
[2] Department of Computer Engineering and Information Technology,
City University of Hong Kong, Kowloon, HongKong
itjia@cityu.edu.hk

Abstract. This paper proposes a new architecture for web-based virtual laboratory with CORBA technology. In the architecture, Java Applet acts as the client tool, CORBA acts as the communication bridge between different objects. The integration of JavaBean, Matlab and COM/DCOM is implemented as the computing tools on the server side. By using the architecture, the efficiency of developing virtual laboratories can be improved markedly. This paper also introduces the implementation of virtual laboratory for communication principle based on the architecture. In the virtual laboratory, the instruments are developed as components, which improves the developing efficiency and the reuse of components. Matlab is also used for computing in the server, which enhances the simulation capability.

Keywords: Web-based virtual Laboratory, CORBA, Matlab, Architecture

1 Introduction

With the rapid development of Internet, modern long-distance education as a new education mode has became an important problem for discussion. Virtual Laboratory (VL) based on the Internet is a key on improving the quality of distance education since experiments are significant for most engineering and application courses. For most current virtual laboratories, there are some disadvantages. For examples, they are only fit for certain kind of course and may not be flexible; if they are modified to meet the needs of the other courses, substantial workload is to reform the system. Considering the dynamic changes, we design a new architecture for web-based virtual laboratory with CORBA technology, which can integrate the third party software developed with Java, C++ or others. The architecture has the following features: it has expansion capability, independence of platform, and software reuse. With these characteristics, we can construct various kinds of Virtual Labs.

* This work was partially sponsored by HK UGC grants CityU 1055/01E, CityU 1039/02E, and CityU Grant 7001355.

W. Zhou et al. (Eds.): ICWL 2003, LNCS 2783, pp. 104–113, 2003.

The rest of the paper is organized as follows. In section 2, we introduce related researches. Section 3 describes the design of system architecture. Section 4 deals with the implementation of system including client side and server side. Section 5 gives an example. Conclusion is given in section 6.

2 Related Work

VL can be classified into two categories according to its realization technologies. The former is developed with pure software while the latter is developed with the combination of software and hardware. The former mostly adopt these popular WWW technologies including HTML, CGI, Java, Applet, Java Servlet and so forth. Ref.[1] discussed the design and development of a virtual biology lab, most of which components, including all the virtual experiments are implemented as Java Beans. Extensible Markup Language (XML) is used for application and data description. Ref.[5] introduced a VL platform based on Internet, which is developed with pure Java language. It uses Java Applet in client side, and the experiment components are implemented as Java Beans. In the VL, users can design and run their experimental flow according to their requirements. Ref.[6] proposed a design of virtual programming lab for online distance learning. It uses HTML and Java Applet on the client side, and CGI and Java Servlet in server side. Before running an experiment, users need to write their program codes in the client, then the client sends the codes to the server. After receiving the request, the server invokes the corresponding language compiler, then returns the result to the client. Ref.[7] described an internet-based computer laboratory for DSP courses, in which all the programs are written as stand-lone Java Applets. Most of the experiments in the VL use the Java Digital Signal Processing (J-DSP) Editor, which allows users to design and simulate a large variety of systems.

Ref.[2] presents a virtual network laboratory for learning IP network, in which one Ethernet Switch and many personal computers running on Linux operation system act as simulation equipments in the server. Users input Linux network commands by using Web then receive output from the server. A VL for the disabled persons is introduced in Ref.[4]. The laboratory adopts Macromedia Company's Authorware to design the user interface thus makes the interface more lively. Their design uses LabView platform to carry out simulation. A realization scheme of VL given in Ref.[3] applies WWW technologies including HTML, CGI, Java and LabView platform to provide usage for real equipments with standard interface. A web-based distributed virtual educational laboratory discussed in Ref.[8] allows components of server side to be distributed in different host computers. Service components of the VL are developed with LabView platform.

Among these VL systems mentioned above, they all only can transfer information among the same type of objects. They failed to realize the communication mechanism among the various types of objects. In addition, integration of the existing virtual simulation systems is not possible. For overcoming the drawbacks, we thus propose a new architecture for web-based VL in order to improve the developing efficiency.

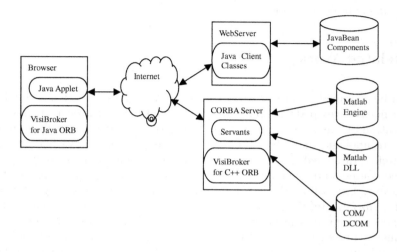

Fig. 1. The architecture of system

3 The Architecture of System

The Common Object Request Broker Architecture (CORBA) allows distributed applications to interoperate with each other, regardless of what language/tools they are used for the implementation or where these applications reside. The Object Request Broker (ORB) in Fig. 1 connects a client application with the objects whenever necessary. The communication is transparent. The client program does not need to know the detail implementation of the internal object regardless of the object locations (either local or remote). In our system, the client program only needs to know the object's name and knowhow to invoke the object's interface. The ORB takes care of the details of locating the object, routing the request, and returning the result. The interface is defined with the Interface Definition Language (IDL). IDL is a descriptive language used to describe the interfaces implemented by the remote objects. Within IDL, we can define the name of the interface, the name of each of the attributes and methods etc. Thus CORBA technology is used to implement our VL system.

Development efficiency and components reuse are key issues during our development of VL. Matlab is high-powered software for science and engineering computation, which provides us with powerful numerical computing capability and many simulation tool packets. By using Matlab, we can implement system modeling and simulation in multi-domain. So with the integration of Matlab, VL system's developing efficiency and simulating capability can be greatly improved.

The system requires interoperation among Java, Matlab and C++ objects. Therefore we choose CORBA as the right developing tool. The architecture of a VL falls into two parts: clients and server. Clients are Java Applets embedded in browsers, which makes clients have the independence of platform and security, and so on. The server mainly contains: CORBA server components written by using Matlab computing engine, Matlab DLL, COM/DCOM components supplied by the third party, Java Bean components. The architecture of web-based VL is proposed in Fig. 1.

Users can connect Web Server through browsers. After entering a VL, browsers automatically download applets from server to clients. Then applets will run on Java Virtual Machine (JVM). Through client side's ORB and server side's ORB, clients can connect and access server.

4   Implementing the System

4.1   IDL Interface Definition

Clients and server use the same IDL interface: CommPrinciple.idl. The IDL file describes the interfaces implemented by the remote objects. Once you've created the IDL file, you can use an IDL compiler to generate the client stub code and the server skeleton code. In clients, idl2java compiler generates client's stub code by compiling CommPrinciple.idl. The stub code which implements methods definition according to CommPrinciple.idl will be used to resolve long-distance CORBA objects by clients. In server, idl2cpp compiler generates skeleton code by compiling CommPrinciple.idl. The skeleton code will be used to transfer clients' service requests.

When a client makes a request, the client's ORB locates the object implementation, activates the object if necessary, delivers the request to the object, and returns the response to the client. The client is unaware that whether the object may be is on the same machine or across a network. A client program uses a remote object by obtaining a reference to the object. Object references are usually obtained using Naming Service. Then the object's reference will be passed to stub code. With the help of stub code and ORB, the client can transfer his request to skeleton code, then to the target service object. The compiling process of CommPrinciple.idl is proposed in Fig. 2.

4.2   The Design of Server

The server side mainly includes the entry of main program, the implementation of objects' methods, and the activation of the Matlab engine.

The main program is with responsibility for initializing ORB, setting up Portable Object Adapter (POA) to manage service objects, then, creating service objects based on the CommPrinciple.idl file, waiting for receiving requests. The implementation of objects' methods is written in C++ language.

Two methods can be used to invoke Matlab. The first is to invoke Matlab engine. By this way, Matlab, which acts as a service process, provides clients

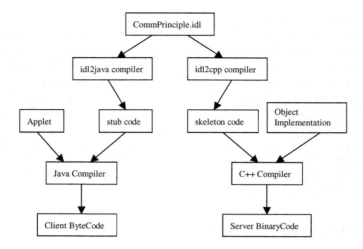

Fig. 2. The compiling sketch map of client and server interface definition CommPrinciple.idl

with a group of engine functions. With the help of these functions, clients can communicate with Matlab engine conveniently. The method provides programmers programming simplicity. However, the system can't run without Matlab runtime environment, and server can't provide clients with frequent visit. The second method is to invoke DLLs. With the compile tools provided by Matlab, the "M" files can be transformed into DLLs. In this way, the advantage of Matlab and C++ can be developed well including powerful computing capability and rapid executing speed. But the program developed in this way is hard to be modified and debugged, and the codes converted from "M" files are hard to be understood for programmers. So we choice one of these two methods or both to develop our server program according to the actual applications.

4.3   The Design of Client

The client side mainly includes the implementation of Java Applet and experiment components. The applet mainly answers for the implementation of the main interface. A component is written as Java Bean, which take charge of the obtaining and invoking of a service object.

The main interface mainly includes: menu bar, tool bar, attribute editor for components, experiment operating window and equipment bar, and so on. The equipment bar provides all the system components. By using it, user can select the required component. Then drag and drop the component to experiment operating window. The user needs to link the selected components in order to assemble an experiment flow. Finally, user can run his experiment by dropping the running button.The process of simulation is proposed in Fig. 3.

A Java Bean obtains service objects by using Naming Service. Server invokes the "bind" method of a Naming Context object in order to not only publicize

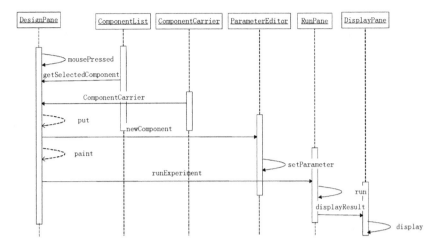

Fig. 3. The process of simulation in client of system

the object but also provide the object self and it's name framework. By invoking the "resolve" method of the very Naming Context object, client can discover the object.

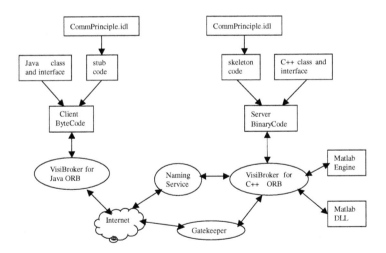

Fig. 4. The implementation of system

4.4 Implementation of the System

Just as the illustration of Fig. 4, the VL system falls into two parts: clients and server. They both compile the same IDL file: CommPrinciple.idl. Then clients will generate stub code while server will generate skeleton code. Based on the skeleton code, Server will implement the methods defined in the CommPrinciple.idl file then publicize service objects by using Naming Service. Based on the stub code, clients can activate the methods of service objects with the help of Naming Service, client ORB, and server ORB.

As a result of the restriction of "Sand-Box" in almost browsers, the Java Applet can't access the other servers besides the Web server. So without the help of the IIOP agent the Java Applet can't communicate with CORBA server, except that CORBA server and Web server reside in the same machine. In our system, we use VisiBroker as CORBA server, which provides Gatekeeper as IIOP agent. Clients' requests are sent to Gatekeeper at first. Then Gatekeeper transmits the requests to server. The answers are also sent back with the other way round.

5   A Virtual Lab for Digital Communication

The filtering experiment of digital communication can illustrate the development process of the system. The filtering experiment needs signal generator, signal adder, filter, and oscilloscope. The signal generator, signal adder, and oscilloscope are implemented as Java Beans, while the filter need to invoke the Matlab function "lowFilter()", which has been compiled in Matlab engine.

In the CommPrinciple.idl file, filter's interface has been defined, which has two methods: lowFilter and heightFilter. The input parameter is the sampled data of signals.

```
//CommPrinciple.idl
typedef sequence< double > mytype;
interface Filter{
    mytype lowFilter(in mytype inData);
    mytype heightFilter(in mytype inData);
};
```

In the server side, the main program is responsible for initializing ORB and creating filter service object "FilterImpl". The main code is showed as follows:

```
orb = CORBA::ORB_init(argc, argv);
rootContext = CosNaming::NamingContext::_narrow
            (orb− >resolve_initial_ references("NameService"));
rootContext− >rebind(name, reference);
```

The code of FilterImpl is followed:

```
mytype * lowFilter(const mytype & inData) {
    if (!(ep=engOpen(NULL))) { exit(-1); }
    b=mxCreateDoubleMatrix(1,inData.length(),mxREAL);
    mxSetName(b,"x");
    memcpy((void*)mxGetPr(b), (void*)num2,
            inData.length()*sizeof(double));
    engPutArray(ep,b);
    engEvalString(ep,"y=lowfilter(x)");
    t = engGetArray(ep,"y");
```

```
engEvalString(ep, "close;");
for(i = 0;i < length;i++)
   {data[i] =*(mxGetPr(t)+i); }
result = new mytype(0,length, data, 1);
return result;
}
```

The implementation of height filter is passed over because it is parallel to the low filter.

The code of the client's Applet is showed as follows:

```
<APPLET codebase="." CODE = "Entry.class" archive="vbjorb.jar"
   NAME = "vLab" WIDTH = 200 HEIGHT = 100 ALIGN = middle>
<param name="org.omg.CORBA.ORBClass"
   value="com.inprise.vbroker.orb.ORB">
<param name="vbroker.orb.alwaysTunnel" value="true">
<param name="vbroker.orb.gatekeeper.ior" value="gatekeeper.ior" >
</APPLET >
```

As a Java Bean, "LowFilter.java" use the followed code to look up objects and invoke methods.

```
orb = org.omg.CORBA.ORB.init(args,null);
......
Object = ((NamingContext)root).resolve(root.to_name(" Filter"));
Filter manager = FilterHelper.narrow(Object);
result = manager.lowFilter(sampleData);
```

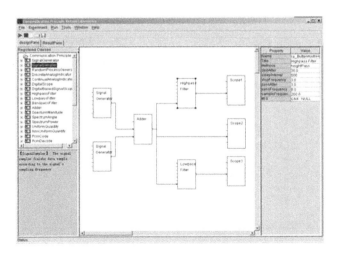

Fig. 5. Operating interface of Virtual lab

Fig. 5 gives the main interface of the VL, which can be accessed through Web by users. The main interface mainly includes: menu bar, tool bar, attribute editor for components, experiment operating window and equipment bar, and so on. The equipment bar provides all the components for the VL of digital communication. User choose the corresponding components from the equipment bar to do experiments, such as lowpass filter, highpass filter et.al.Then user wants to link the selected components in order to assemble an experiment flow. Finally, he can run his experiment by dropping the running button and the experiment results is shown as Fig. 6.

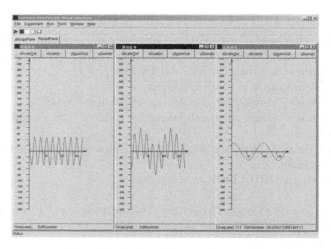

Fig. 6. Interface of processing result

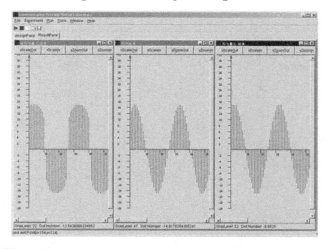

Fig. 7. Processing result interface of quantifying experiment

Fig. 6 shows the interface of the output, which is the result of filtering experiment. The left frame gives the result of height filtering while the right shows the result of low filtering. The middle presents the original signal, which is the overlap-add of $\sin(4\pi t)$ and $\sin(20\pi t)$.

Fig. 7 shows the result interface of quantifying experiment. The left frame gives the result of nonuniform quantification while the right gives the result of uniform quantification. The middle shows the quantified signal.

6   Conclusion

The development of remote education has played an important role in the world. Moreover, virtual laboratory based on Internet is the key on improving the remote education. This paper particularly discusses the architecture and implementation of the VL platform. In the architecture, the integration of Java Bean, Matlab and COM/DCOM improves the efficiency of developing the virtual laboratory. This paper also illustrates the key design and implementation technologies of communication principle virtual laboratory based on this architecture. In the virtual lab, Java Applet is used as client tools, which provides clients with the independence of platform and safety. Matlab is also used for computing in the server, which enhances the simulation capability. The system provides designers with an effective approach to develop virtual lab, at the same time providing users with an experiment environment without the restriction of time, place and equipments. By using the system, the reform of the colleges' experiment teaching will be expedited, and the quality of long-distance education will also be improved markedly.

References

1. R. Subramanian and I. Marsic, ViBE: Virtual Biology Experiments, In Proceedings of the Tenth International World Wide Web Conference (WWW10), Hong Kong, p. 316–325,May 2001.
2. L. Fabrega, J. Massaguer, T. Jove, and D. Merida, A Virtual network laboratory for learning IP network, The 7th Annual Conference on Innovation and Technology in Computer Science Education, June 2002, Aarhus, Denmark
3. A. Ferrero and V. Piuri, A Simulation Tool For Virtual Laboratory Experiments in a WWW Environment, IEEE Transaction On Instrumentation and Measuerment, 1999, 48(3):741–746.
4. M. Duarte and B. P. Butz, The Virtual Laboratory for the Disabled, the 31th ASEE/IEEE Frontiers in Education Conference S1C-23, 2001.
5. Wang Jianxin, Chen Songqiao, Jia Weijia, and Pei Huiming, The Design and Implementation of Virtual Laboratory Platform in Internet, Proceedings of The First International Conference on Web-based Learning, p. 169–177
6. Jiannong Cao, Alvin Chan, Weidong Cao, and Cassidy Yeung, Virtual Programming Lab for Online Distance Learning, LNCS 2436, First International Conference, ICWL 2002 Hong Kong, China, 2002, p. 216–227.
7. A. Clausen and A. Spanias, An Internet-based Computer Laboratory for DSP Courses, Proceedings of the ASEE/IEEE Frontiers in Education Conference 1998, Tempe
8. L. Benetazzo, M. Bertocco, F. Ferraris, A. Ferrero, C. Offelli, M. Parvis, and V. Piuri, A Web-Based Distributed Virtual Educational Laboratory, IEEE Transaction On Instrumentation and Measurement, 2000, 49(2): 349–356.

The Creation and Maintenance of an Online Subject: Some Practical Factors

John Murnane

Department of Science and Mathematics Education
The University of Melbourne
Victoria 3010, Australia
jmurnane@unimelb.edu.au

Abstract. This paper discusses some of the practical factors associated with the creation and maintenance of a Website supporting an online, postgraduate, tertiary-level subject, created and maintained largely by a single lecturer. The size of two subject Websites are described, some factors effecting maintenance, possible problems in adapting teaching styles to a simple Web page format and problems that may arise when the lecture of a subject changes or a visiting lecturer participates.

1 Introduction

This paper discusses some of the practical factors in the creation and maintenance of a Website supporting an online, postgraduate, tertiary-level, subject. Two subjects taught online by the author at the University of Melbourne are used as the main examples. Students in these subjects are all practicing teachers, from preschool to tertiary level. Most, but not all, have formal teaching qualifications, the notable exceptions being those from the training industry and the tertiary sector.

The subjects discussed were created largely by a single lecturer and maintained in the same way. Thus they represent only a small number of online subjects but their essential simplicity makes them relatively easy to study. Their basic structure and substance is sufficiently representative of the essence of online teaching to be usefully analysed. They utilise quite low-level technology which, while it does not give any comparison against courses utilising powerful, interactive multimedia, does make a first-approximation analysis on the basis of the size of the site practical. Their educational effectiveness is not analysed, although over the four years of their existence they have proven to be very effective.

2 The Creation of an Online Subject

The creation of an online subject is no small task. Even assuming the prior existence of a suitable subject description, the actual work that goes into the creation of the Website is but a part of the process. The educational approach, the means by which subject matter can be conveyed within the limitations of Web technology and

W. Zhou et al. (Eds.): ICWL 2003, LNCS 2783, pp. 114–121, 2003.

appropriate communication and means of assessment should all be thought out and decided upon before work commences on the site itself. The need for progressive evaluation and maintenance of the site will exist for the life of the subject and this may be compounded if the original creator leaves.

The structure of an online Website could conceivably stretch from being a list of linked resources with minimal original material and an assessment requirement, to a full self-contained original work. Most subjects will fall somewhere between these extremes. First year chemistry at Melbourne for instance, is almost totally online. A "tutorial package" [1] provides the lectures, exercises and much of the tutorial material online with the practical laboratory sessions 'live.' This structure is the work of a big, diverse and expensive team over many years, an investment that can be justified by the large number of students involved and the stability of the material. An analysis can be found in Fritze [2].

The two subjects forming the basis of this paper are Software Environments for Learning, and Teaching With Information Technology. These are offered online and face-to-face as part of the Masters level program in the Faculty of Education at the University of Melbourne. The major impetus for putting these subjects online was to allow remote students to take them, but it also solves some timetable and employment clashes. All subjects in the program run for one Semester (12 weeks), and form one quarter of a full time year. The assessment associated with these subjects is "the equivalent of 8,000 words."

These subjects have a long history reaching back to 1980. It was this accumulated background of experience, knowledge, evaluation and lecture notes which made it economically possible to offer then online within the budget available at the time, which, considering the task, was minimal: in the region of $2,000 per subject. That the subjects exist at all is due largely to overtime put in by their two creators. Both subjects were first offered online in 1999.

The Website for Software Environments was originally developed by John Warner[1] and the author built the Teaching With Information Technology site. Neither used, or uses, any particularly advanced Web or programming techniques. The nature of the existing subjects was such that text and simple graphics, largely screen grabs and simple line diagrams, sufficed. The inherent structuring characteristics of a Website provided the educational structure for the subjects. (Projected developments utilising more sophisticated and rich media are not discussed here.)

Software Environments concerns all the usual application software teachers expect to find on a personal computer: word processing, spreadsheets, graphic manipulation, multimedia creation, Web page editing and, lately, digital video and sound editing. The emphasis is on the educational significance and use of these products—the ability of students and teachers to take over the technology for their own purposes—but since many teachers begin the course with only a basic knowledge of word processing, it is necessary to provide descriptions of their operation, and examples to work through so they can become quite familiar and comfortable with the tools. (Face-to-face students get demonstrations and workshops—a superior solution.) Although assignments require a moderate level of competence in using the various

---

[1] John Warner is now a Senior Fellow in the Department of Science and Mathematics Education at the University of Melbourne.

tools as, essentially, a 'hurdle requirement,' grades above pass standard rely on the educational elements.

Teaching with Information Technology is a very different subject. It has a lecture-seminar format and is concerned with three main things:

1. An exploration and evaluation of the different ways that computer and communication technology could be used in educational contexts. The aim is to have each student consider uses to which they might put the technology in their classes in relation to their own educational psychology and philosophy. In the nature of things, the degree of detail and the scope of this section is severely limited by the time available.

2. An exploration of the many practical issues concerned with the use of computers in education: where to locate computers; Internet access; the IT budget; professional development; Web access and Acceptable Use Policies; data security; equable access to computers etc. This part of the program is carried out via a Seminar program and for online students an online Forum.

3. To start the students on their careers as researchers. Basic research skills, techniques and orientation are fostered and developed.

From 1996 the Education Faculty provided a basic vehicle, (SOCS), of their own design, into which material could be loaded to support online teaching of this type. Since 1999 the main University Information Technology Service has offered a slightly more versatile version of its own called WebRAFT. Material from the two complete subject Websites is loaded from lecturer's computers to one of these servers.

The size of the Websites required to support subjects of this nature and at this level may be surprising to anyone yet to involve themselves in an enterprise of this type. A raw word count on both subject sites produced, in round figures, the following numbers:

Software Environments for Learning, 2003: 63,400 words

Teaching with Information Technology, 2002: 95,500 words.

The word counts do not consider graphics and other embedded files, the work required to set up and maintain the structure of the sites or another considerable volume of work on the respective Forums, but they are interesting nevertheless. Pages specifically provided for face-to-face students (largely concerned with assignments) have been omitted from these word-counts.

Breaking down the site by general area produces the word-counts in Tables 1 and 2.

Table 1. Word Count: Software Environments for Learning

Area	Words
Administrative pages, main indexes etc.,	9,700
Assignments	1,280
Lectures	48,380
Workshops	4,040

The raw word count overestimates the actual scale of the intellectual property to some extent. Some material, for instance instructions for using the Net and finding the Websites, is common to both subjects and some is copied straight from Department and Faculty material and available elsewhere but repeated to make sure students take notice. This takes up roughly half the 'administrative material.'

Nevertheless, with the exception of standard page-footers giving creation date and creator etc., there is something approaching 48,000 words of original work in the lecture pages. This is supplemented with copious linked pages, scanned and electronic material and access to full text, online journals, not included in the word–count. Assessment in both subjects has to offer a considerable amount of latitude and guidance to make it suitable for all levels of education, hence the large number of words. Online assignments also include a wealth of detail provided to face-to-face students during the normal course of lectures.

Table 2. Word count: Teaching With Information Technology

Area	Words
Administrative pages, main indexes etc.,	8,360
Assignments	6,212
Lectures	80,930

In Teaching With Information Technology, probably 18,400 words should be subtracted from the lectures to account for one which is largely three scanned papers contributed by a Departmental staff member on software evaluation and not written specifically for the subject. This still leaves an 'original' lecture content of some 62,500 words (and the evaluation material will have to be replaced for the 2003 version).

Any body of electronic work of this size will require a considerable amount of maintenance. As new technology relevant to education becomes available it must be incorporated into the subject and the educational material revised to take account of it. This may require a very minor alteration, or it may require the complete replacement of a lecture. The sites have to be completely overhauled each year and the lectures, to a greater or lesser degree, rewritten. (This excludes any other educational revision to the syllabus, educational approach or a different selection from applicable material.)

3 Adapting Teaching to the Web

Not all material, and certainly not all teaching, is easily amenable to online education. One of the consistent lessons our students have delivered, in several ways and at different times to the lecturing staff, is that while teachers are generally happy to learn in whatever medium the material is presented through, provided they perceive it as relevant, they are, as group, far more reluctant to adapt their own teaching to suit a medium they perceive as restrictive. Thus while, for instance, they may be quite happy to take their own lectures from the Web and communicate with the lecturer via the Forum and email, when confronted with using the same medium for their own teaching, many exclaim that 'This isn't the way *I* teach!' Fortunately current technologies and computerised tools allow sufficient flexibility to satisfy many teaching requirements, but this still occurs and may also obtain at the lecturer level.

Two of the Teaching With Information Technology lectures were written by a colleague on the subject of Constructionism. He was not entirely happy with the idea of delivering a formal lecture on the subject since he considered a lecture to be inconsistent with the subject matter, but the lectures were given. When it came to putting this material on the Website for distance learners, after considerable thought and trial, he was forced to the conclusion that the Web was not an appropriate system in which to shape the content and his approach to it: his educational philosophy. This lecturer has considerable technical and practical skills with areas of computing, yet he eventually had to confess defeat and post two, quite inadequate, to him, MS Word files covering the lectures. He was not happy.

4 Maintenance

The subject Websites did not start out at their current sizes. Over the years both have grown. They are probably both now at about the maximum appropriate for their subject size. If they grew much more students would be faced with an inappropriate amount of material to get through. In the last two revisions, material added had to be roughly balanced by material deleted or relegated to 'further reading.' Teaching with Information Technology began in 1999 with 70,800 words. 63,600 of these were taken up by 11 lectures. Overall, although the lectures have grown somewhat, most of the subsequent inflation has been in the 'Administrative' area. The average lecture runs to around 5,600 words.

As an example, Lecture 10 is about "Life in CyberSpace." This would occupy a nominal one and a quarter hours, face-to-face. The 2002 version ran to 9,600 words. The 1999 version was 6,820 words. (In 1998 it didn't exist.) Differences between the 2001 and 2002 versions are marked and when rewritten for Semester 2, 2003, new material will have to be added at the expense of existing ideas. Obviously it is not just the process of typing that is important here, these lecturers are to a large extent totally original and the thinking and the research have to be done.

There have been many invited (face-to-face) guest lecturers, some paid by the University, some not. It is a rare invitee who is in a position to contribute a page to the online site and in the case of these subjects, it hasn't happened. (One did promise, but nothing eventuated—the 'missing' 12th lecture from 1999.) It is simply too much to expect an invited lecturer to produce the material and if they did there is an immediate issue of copyright. Certainly there is nothing in the Departmental budget to finance such a thing. In this case either the online students get a summary, placed on the site by me, or miss out on that facet entirely. Given time constraints and my reluctance to represent someone else's material as gathered by me in a lecture, usually they just miss out.

5 Changing the Guard

An emerging issue is the status of a Website when a subject is taken over by another lecturer. It is one thing to develop an online version of a subject while it is taught face-to-face and have it ready for the next year. It is something else to take over a subject with, say, a month or two to prepare an online version in that time. If a subject is running and the lecturer changes, the only possibility is to take over the existing Website. This raises immediate and very difficult issues in Intellectual Property and will probably raise educational issues as well. (Contracted online lessons or the work of a full team of developers where copyright issues are settled at the beginning and the institution retains full control are in a different category.)

Personally I have seen both sides—I took over an existing subject from a colleague and have bequeathed a subject to another lecturer. While there were no major Intellectual Property issues arising in either case the nature of the ensuing problems were different. The University of Melbourne's policy is that it owns the Intellectual Property to a subject developed by one of its employees and this can be used once an academic leaves a subject, but this is subject to a caveat that "the University recognises the moral rights of the author including rights of attribution and integrity of authorship." [3] Alteration, without permission of the original author of their original material can easily constitute a violation of that author's rights.

The subject I 'inherited' was Software Environments for Learning. I had worked closely with the original author for many years and had shared the face-to-face version. He trusted me with his material, something that definitely cannot be guaranteed in the general case—especially where philosophical material is involved an academic may well object to having their thoughts altered in any form whatever. As it happened Software Environments contained a comparatively small amount of material that involved controversial opinion, at least between John Warner and myself, and in parts where I did want to put an alternative view I simply included the initials of its author. It is important that alternative views can be stated and stated strongly, no matter what the subject.

I certainly had no qualms turning my Teaching With Information Technology material over for extension and/or modification but this subject provided different problems. This was the worst case in that it was only for one year so there was no question of the new lecturer spending much time introducing her own material, experienced though she was in this area. The syllabus is a very wide one and a considerable amount of selection of the actual ground to be covered is required. There is also considerable latitude in the educational standpoints adopted in different places and the way the material is presented. Teaching With Information Technology runs in Semester 2 and the lecturer concerned had Semester 1 to think about how she would approach things (both face-to-face and online), albeit while dealing with a full Semester 1 load! The nub was, when she got around to it, she found she simply could not follow my rather idiosyncratic lectures. In the end her Website consisted of the PowerPoint she used face-to-face linked to my version of the lecture from the previous year. As a stop-gap this worked, but it is obviously far from ideal and if she had continued with the subject would have to have developed a totally new version. Whether the University would have been prepared to allot another $2,000 dollars to rewrite the subject is untested.

It is significant that in late 1980's, when I relinquished a predecessor of Teaching With Information Technology, within a week the replacement lecturer told me that she simply could not treat the subject in the way I had. Nor could I follow some of what she had done when I took its successor back in 1995. The problem was not in what was being taught, but how. "That's not the way *I* teach."

6 No Easy Answer

Since the first Web pages appeared on Melbourne University sites in the mid-1990's there has been discussion on the 'vehicle' to be developed or purchased to carry the teaching content. One of the few common threads to come from these is the almost total insistence of academics that they want nothing to do with a system that dictates how their material is to be presented or how they have to teach. There is considerable existing literature about the individual differences between learners: perhaps it is time for educational institutions to give more emphasis to individual differences between teachers since there appears to be a general expectation at all levels that all teachers are quite interchangeable.

It is easy to find common factors in the successful creation and/or handover of a online subject. The one which stands out is the existence of a team. A team can have the flexibility to absorb and redistribute loads created while a site is created and working together in a face-to-face subject builds the content, approach and confidence needed to do the same online. This is not a useful insight since it is already established wisdom in both educational and Information Systems practice. There is a need for new insights in managing change where harmonious team-work is not operative.

Clearly the nature of the subject has a large part to play. John Warner characterises subjects as 'Folkloric' or 'Idiosyncratic.' These are, respectively 'a body of material that is part of the common consciousness and experience of most ... educators' and a subject 'depending for its success on the experiences of the lecturer using the anecdotes, experiences and insights of that lecturer, with many of these insights not being part of the common experience.' This matches experience with Software Environments, clearly Folkloric and easy to pass to another lecturer, and Teaching with Information Technology as Idiosyncratic and causing transition problems. A recognition of the nature of the subject at the outset will at least allow some anticipation of these but brings the danger that institutions will simply discriminate against Idiosyncratic subjects. This inevitably happens in the compulsory education sector where subjects must of necessity be standardised to the degree that any qualified person can teach them. It would be regrettable if this spread simply because of Web economics.

Consider too that just as some lecturers are better than others in face-to-face mode, some will be better or worse online. There is no a-priori reason to suppose that the two strengths should coincide and many reasons to suspect that they will not. It would be nice to think that lecturers could be allotted to subjects taught in the manner that coincides with their strengths!

7 Conclusion

The work involved in teaching an online subject at Postgraduate level may involve work, if not the original research, comparable to writing a doctorial thesis. Taken over several years, teaching online utilising simple Web technology can involve quite as much work and difficulties to maintain as it did to establish the subject in the first place. Difficulties inherent in teaching online should be addressed as part of the continuing business of education rather than factors influencing what is taught or how.

References

1. McNaught, C., McTigue, P. and Tregloan, P.: Students' Understanding of Moving Visual Images in Interactive Multimedia. *AUC Academic Conference 'From Virtual to Reality.'* The University of Queensland (1996). Available at: http://auc.uow.edu.au/conf/Conf96/Papers/McNaught.html. Accessed 13/3/03
2. Fritze, P.: *Innovation in University Computer-Facilitated Learning Systems: Product, Workplace Experience and the Organisation.* PhD thesis, Faculty of Education, Language and Community Services, RMIT (2002). Available at: http://eprints.unimelb.edu.au/archive/00000233/. Accessed, 13/3/03
3. The University of Melbourne: *Statute 14.1–Intellectual Property.* Melbourne, Australia: The University of Melbourne (1999).

SameView: A Large-Scale Real-Time Interactive E-learning System Based on TORM and AMTP

Yi Che, Runting Shi, Yuanchun Shi, and Guangyou Xu

Dept. of CS, Tsinghua University, Beijing 100084, China
{cheyi97,shirunting99}@mails.,
{shiyc,xgy-dcs}@tsinghua.edu.cn

Abstract. In this paper, we present the design and development of SameView, a real-time interactive E-learning system. It is designed for large-scale deployment over the Internet and provides a friendly user interface for various pedagogical activities. For efficient scalable multicast over the Internet, SameView is built on top of TORM (Totally Ordered Reliable Multicast), a transport layer multicast infrastructure exploiting a tree-based structure. Between the transport layer and upper level applications is an enhancement layer called AMTP (Adaptive Multimedia Transport Policy), an adaptive multimedia transport strategy to cope with heterogeneous network configurations. To enrich a user's learning experience, SameView offers a multimodal human-computer interface by incorporating audio/video presentation, as well as a synchronized whiteboard for collaborative web browsing and annotation. Several enhanced features are introduced, including a live record tool which could be used to record a classroom session for later viewing.

1 Introduction

With rapid advances in distributed multimedia technology, the notion of real-time interactive distance learning has received more attention than ever before. Whereas traditional classroom activities are characterized by their inherent geographical limitation, the advent of distant E-learning applications has enabled students to attend classes anywhere with an online computer. Among existent commercial products of media applications, two main categories are readily applicable for remote E-learning. The class of streaming media applications, including RealNetworks[1] and Microsoft Windows Media[2], allow a one-way streaming broadcast of on-demand media or stored contents. On the other hand, video conferencing software such as Microsoft NetMeeting[3], support real-time interactive two-way or multiway communications. Yet they both offer generic services and are not well suited for distance E-learning purposes. Then we witnessed the birth of several RTIVCs(Real-time Interactive Virtual Classroom), as marked by the virtual classroom at University of Washington[5]. Apart from combining these two types of services, RTIVCs have a well-designed user interface for pedagogical activities such as courseware browsing and class recording.

W. Zhou et al. (Eds.): ICWL 2003, LNCS 2783, pp. 122–133, 2003.
© Springer-Verlag Berlin Heidelberg 2003

Inspired by the very same notion, we designed and implemented our own version of an RTIVC. Compared with existent RTIVCs, our contribution is highlighted mainly in three aspects:

1) TORM(Totally Ordered Reliable Multicast), a transport layer infrastructure for multicast over the Internet;
2) AMTP(Adaptive Multimedia Transport Policy), an intermediate layer placed between the transport and application layers, to enable adaptive multimedia transport;
3) SameView's multimodal user interface specially designed for pedagogical activities, so that interactive communication could be achieved through audio/video presentation and an HTML-capable whiteboard for courseware browsing and remote discussion.

The rest of the paper is organized as follows. In Section 2, we present the overall architecture of SameView and explain the roles of different components. Section 3 and 4 will focus on TORM and AMTP respectively. In Section 5, we introduce SameView's multimodal user interface, and in Section 6, we report the various tests we have performed with our system. Finally, conclusion and future work will be given.

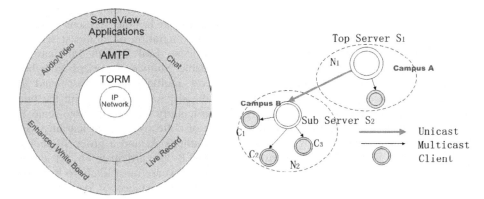

Fig. 1. Overall Architecture of SameView   **Fig. 2.** Collective Remote Learning

2   Architecture

There are several issues of concern in the design of a remote E-learning system.

● In order for the instruction to be carried out on a wide basis, the underlying transport layer must provide support for scalable and efficient dissemination of real-time interactive data. To address the problem, we build the application on the basis of a reliable multicast infrastructure named TORM, which is a hybrid approach employing both multicast and unicast to deliver data over a hierarchical tree structure.
● In order to cater to the heterogeneous networks over the WAN, it is necessary to provide differentiated services with regard to local bandwidth conditions. This is

achieved through AMTP, a presentation layer incorporated between transport services and high-level applications.

- In the case of E-learning, a friendly human-computer interface is crucial to ensure the quality of a user's learning experience. The goal of the interface design is to provide a remote student with as many luxuries of an in-class participant as possible. SameView provides a multimodal interface, with an audio/video channel broadcasting the live classroom session, an HTML-enabled whiteboard for courseware browsing and remote discussion, and a live record tool as an enhanced feature for class recording.

The overall architecture of our real-time E-learning system is illustrated in Figure1.

3   TORM

3.1   Hybrid Multicast

After more than a decade's research on multicast protocols and applications, it is now well-understood that multicast could efficiently utilize network resources and offer low-latency delivery to multiple receivers. Yet a number of crucial problems have hindered the global deployment of IP multicast over the present Internet infrastructure. While many researchers advocate the migration of multicast services into the application layer(Application-level Multicast, End System Multicast or Overlay Multicast), TORM(Totally Ordered Reliable Multicast) presents a hybrid scheme instead. By combining application-level multicast(IP unicast) and IP multicast, TORM exploits the virtues of both methods. As compared with the pure application multicast strategy, its privilege is particularly evident in large-scale E-learning applications. Consider the common case of collective distant learning (See Figure 2.), where the lecture is carried out on Campus A, and a group of remote students gather in a computer room on Campus B to participate in the online instruction. Because the Campus B students(C1, C2, C3) are most likely to be in the same LAN, communication overhead will certainly be reduced, if data could be multicast to every node on the IP level, instead of having a separate IP unicast stream per node, an inevitability with the pure application multicast scheme.

TORM adopts a hierarchical tree structure so that network load could be distributed among different nodes. This prevents potential dangers as exposed by centralized methods, e.g. the central MCU(Multipoint Control Unit) in UWashington's virtual classroom. Each node in the tree is assigned one of the three roles accordingly: the root acts as the top-server, non-leaf nodes as sub-servers, whereas leaf nodes act as clients. The top-server and the sub-servers are a collection of strategically placed network agents that collaboratively provide multicast service over the WAN. In Figure 3, N_1, N_2, N_3 are three *domains*(i.e. LANs in which IP multicast is possible), with no router support for IP multicast in between. In order for S1 to deliver data to clients in N2 and N3, a unicast link is created between the top-server S1 and each sub-server, namely S2 and S3. These unicast links are called *tunnels* in the TORM model. Upon receiving data through the tunnels, the two sub-servers will be in charge of multicasting it to other clients in the same domain.

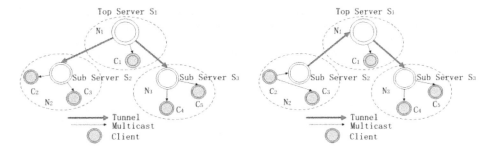

Fig. 3. Tree-structured TORM   **Fig. 4.** Data route with C2 as the data source

It is also possible for data to originate at a leaf node. Figure 4 explains the routing mechanism when client C_2 acts as the data source with every other member as a subscriber. First of all, C_2 multicasts the data within domain; upon receival, S_2 unicasts the data to S1 who then relays them to C1 and the N3 domain.

3.2   Reliable Multicast

In the process of a distant instruction, it is a requisite to guarantee the reliable distribution of certain categories of data such as electronic handouts, annotation, browse action, etc. While IP multicast provides only a best-effort service model, it is left for our own duty to introduce enhanced functionalities such as an error recovery mechanism.

Error control is usually done in two ways. In an ACK based error control scheme, it falls on the sender to assure reliability, whereas in a NAK based scheme, the receiver assumes the duty. TORM adopts the NAK scheme to declare packet losses, which is generally preferable to the ACK scheme in terms of less incurred network overhead. In order to prevent NAK implosion when data is lost or damaged for multiple receivers, all NAK frames are transmitted through unicast after a period of random delay. The NAK frame is always transmitted to the upriver node of the actual data flow rather than the parent node in the static tree structure(See Figure 5). Once a node receives a NAK frame from a downstream node, it will retransmit the specified packets if they are found in the local buffer. If not, it will have to wait for the retransmission from its own upriver node before it relays the lost packets downstream. The NAK frame need not be relayed by intermediate nodes, for a separate error detection process is run on each node, and should data loss occur, the intermediate node would have initiated its error repair procedure by its own discovery.

If a NAK comes from a different domain, the retransmission will occur through the linking tunnel. Because NAK frames from different domains are independent of each other, a retransmission is limited but to the requesting domain. In the case of an intra-domain NAK, however, it is likely that the same problem will afflict other local hosts as well. Thus it would be a good idea to multicast the retransmission so that if a node finds repair to the problem in time, it will cancel the scheduled NAK correspondingly, thereby suppressing repetitive NAKs. On the other hand, if, in a very short time interval, two or more intra-domain NAKs report identical problems, the sender will respond to the first one alone, discarding all others as repetitive NAKs.

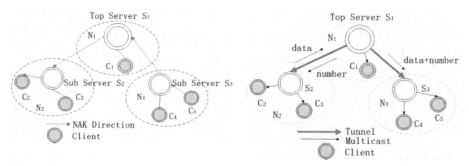

Fig. 5. The direction of the NAK when C5 loses the package from C2

Fig. 6. Data and the serial number can be combined

A theoretical analysis has been performed by comparing the error recovery mechanism of TORM with that of another reliable multicast protocol named SRM[6]. Based upon a mathematical model adopting the MM1 queuing theory, we have proved that TORM is advantageous over SRM in terms of recovery efficiency especially when the depth of the TORM tree is not large.

3.3   Totally Ordered Multicast

With multi-party interactive applications such as RTIVCs, it is important to guarantee the data consistency on each node. TORM incorporates an improved centralized serialization scheme to ensure unified global sequencing of messages on all hosts.

In a traditional centralized serialization algorithm, the data source first transfers the message to the root; after binding a global sequence number with the message, the root transmits it down the distribution tree to every receiver. If, however, all data need to be relayed by the root, the point of centralization is apt to become overburdened, thus presenting a potential bottleneck and greatly undermining scalability. TORM adopts an improved method instead. While the data source multicasts the data in compliance with the routing algorithm, it falls upon the root node to assign an incremental ordinal number for each instance of data upon receival. The root dispatches the generated sequence number as a separate message to all others nodes. Hence they will be able to sort the data packets, before they are submitted to the application layer, in a globally unified fashion as specified by the sequence numbers.

In some cases (See Fig.6), it is possible to reduce network overhead by combining the data and the serial number into one message, instead of having them relayed separately. In Figure 6, for instance, upon receiving data originated from domain N2, the top-server S1 binds an arbitrated sequence number to each data instance and transfers the two as a whole to domain N3 and Client C1.

4   AMTP

With an increasing diversity of network bandwidth, terminal capabilities and user preferences, it is imperative that content be delivered more intelligently[7]. On one hand data is transformed so that Qos could be attuned to accommodate available local resources with flexibility; on the other hand content is customized for individual preferences. While multimedia data propagated over the net is rich in variety, a unified adaptive delivery method is desirable. This is what AMTP aims to accomplish. The Adaptive Multimedia Transport Policy is so designed as to be readily applicable for the TORM model. Figure 7 depicts a simple scenario where the sub-servers in the TORM tree, by means of AMTP transformation, tailor the received information to local bandwidth conditions. A sub-server performing AMTP duties is called a *proxy* in our system. More complex frameworks can be achieved in practical application.

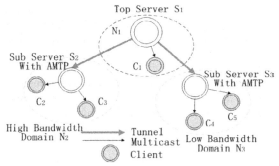

Fig. 7. TORM with Embedded AMTP Service

4.1   Measure of Quality

In the case of distance E-learning, we deal with compound multimedia documents, consisting of various media objects such as audio, video, electronic slides, etc. ATMP tries to maximize the quality of a user's perceptive experience with the limited network bandwidth available. We define CV(Content Value) to be the informational capacity of every media object. The Content Value could be determined by the four quantities listed below:

◆   TR(Transport Rate), bytes of a media object transported to the client per unit time.

◆   MTF(Media Type Factor), the measure of importance of various media objects.

◆   UPF(User Preference Factor), a weighted factor determined by user preferences.

◆   RCV(Relative Content Value), ratio of a transformed media object's CV over that of the original one. The original media object's RCV is 1, while the RCV for the transformed objects measures the degradation in quality resulting from the transformation.

Hence, the CV (Content Value) of a media object is:

$$CV = RCV * TR * MTF * UPF \tag{1}$$

And the Content Value of a compound document is:

$$CV_{whole} = \sum_i CV_i = \sum_i RCV_i * TR_i * MTF_i * UPF_i \tag{2}$$

where i enumerates all objects in the compound document.

After establishing the measure of quality, we argue that the question of adaptive transport for compound documents is by nature an optimization problem, with the CV_{whole} as the objective function, and various constraints which we are about to explore.

4.2   Constraints

➢   Temporal Constraint

The strict temporal constraint of real-time multimedia applications is the main factor to take into account. The overall principle here is that the transformation should in effect shorten the total delivery latency, i.e. the transformation overhead plus the delivery time of the transformed portion should be less than the delivery time of the original data. For a measure of the joint effects of size and operational complexity, the quantity CR (Comprehensive Rate) is introduced for each transformed media object, representing the actual rate of transmission. The following constraint needs to be satisfied for the summed CR of the compound document.

$$\sum_i CR_i \le B_{pc} \tag{3}$$

where B_{pc} is the total network bandwidth available between the proxy and the client.

➢   Terminal Capability

Terminal capability is determined by a host's hardware or software availability. Hardware factors comprise screen size, maximum color depth, storage capacity, CPU frequency, battery duration, sound card availability, etc. Software issues include the availability of media codecs, operating system load, and so on. Instead of adopting a quantified approach, we use a descriptive scheme based on rules.

➢   User Preference

The designers of Sameview have paid special attention to a user's personalized needs. In order to deliver customized data to individual users, we may resort to the technique of information filtering. The simplest approach is to have the users fill in a questionnaire, where they will be asked to subscribe interested categories of information. A better scheme is proposed by correlating the high-level semantics of data contents a user has accessed in history, so that an AI module will be able to draw inferences about the user's individual interests, and facilitate him accordingly in future learning experiences.

4.3   AMTP Algorithm

In order to cater to bandwidth requirements, terminal capabilities and user preferences, media data will undergo a series of transformations before they are transferred from an AMTP proxy to a client. Different types of operations include: media compression, format conversion, data filtering, etc. As a result, the Content Value of a media object, i.e. its perceived quality will be altered.

We generalize the optimization problem as follows:

$$\max \quad CV_{whole} = \sum_i RCV_i * TR_i * MTF_i * UPF_i \tag{4}$$

$$s.t. \quad \sum_i CR_i \le B_{pc}$$

Figure 8 demonstrates the interplay of the various quantities in the mathematical derivation. Whereas TR, MTF, UPF, and the terminal capability factor can be pre-determined, the RCV and CV for each media object will rely on the set of transformations chosen. The task, therefore, is to search the transformation space of the compound document, so that the resulting CV and RCV for each media object will maximize the objective function while satisfying the constraint inequality.

The inter-correlation between the media components within a compound document, however, results in a search space too large to be handled in finite time. As a tradeoff for feasibility, we propose a greedy algorithm which comes in two steps:

1. Regard RCV as a function of CR which we allot for each media object out of the limited bandwidth resource available, namely, B_{pc}. Assuming that the allotted CR for each media component can be fully utilized; we aim at maximizing the resulting CV* of the compound document.

2. Work out a transformation sequence for each individual media object, so that the allocated CR and terminal capability constraints are satisfied.

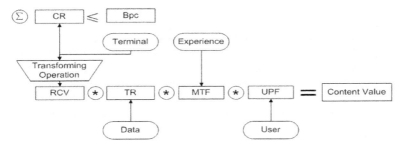

Fig. 8. How the various constraints affect the quality of the compound document

5   SameView

Based on TORM and AMTP, we have developed a desktop-based real-time interactive E-learning system named SameView. SameView embodies several distinct applications to enrich a user's learning experience in different aspects. A live audio and video feed will automatically switch between the teacher and a remote speaker. An enhanced whiteboard will allow participants to collaboratively view the courseware and make annotations. Moreover, all classroom activities can be recorded as a compound document for playback after class. With these facilities, a Sameview user will be privileged to enjoy everything an in-class participant experiences.

Figure 9 and Figure 10 are screen shots of SameView during a typical learning session. Figure 9 corresponds to the view on the speaker's side whereas Figure 10 is seen for a listener's part.

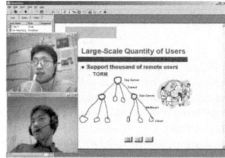

Fig. 9. SameView interface of the speaker   **Fig. 10.** SameView interface of the audience

The various functionalities of SameView will be detailed in the following sections.

5.1   Live Audio/Video

Live Audio/Video streaming enables the teacher and remote students to interact naturally as if in the same locality. With support from the AMTP presentation layer, the resolution and frame rate of the AV stream can be adjusted to ensure QoS on different network configurations.

Our present implementation of SameView allows only one AV stream at a time, i.e. only one speaker is brought to the focus of attention at any time with the AV stream. If several people attempt to speak at the same time, a coordination module will resolve the confliction according to a decided policy whose basic principles are listed as below:

- At the beginning of the session, only the teacher has the *token*, i.e. the right to speak;
- A remote participant wishing to speak can request token at any time during the class;
- The teacher may grant token to or take it back from one or more students at will; only token holding participants can acquire the *focus*, i.e. the AV channel;
- If no one is speaking, a token holding participant can snatch the focus by first starting to talk;
- Without the teacher's intervention, the person in focus will not release the AV channel until he closes his speech;
- When a speaker releases focus, it can be taken over by another talking participant if there is any;
- Again the teacher has the supreme power and can intervene at any time.

5.2   Synchronized Annotation and HTML Display

The whiteboard, which takes the place of the traditional blackboard, provides a digital space to accommodate the electronic handouts and the live annotations. Whereas the teacher can scribble freely on the board with a stylus as if working with a traditional blackboard-chalk combination, he can also benefit from its new digital features. The teacher and remote students can not only share a synchronized view of the board, but also work on it in collaboration. Electronic courseware can be exhibited, and various display properties such as font, color, object size, etc. can be altered at will. Remote students will need the teacher's permission before they could control the board.

There are two layers in the whiteboard, the HTML-extended layer, used for browsing HTML documents; and the event monitor layer, which deals with various on-board operations including annotation, illustration, and HTML browsing.

For the HTML-extended layer, the key design issue rests with the transport strategy of the HTML content, that is to say, how to exploit TORM to transmit the web documents. Here two strategies present themselves: we can either have each user obtain the web pages from the original web server; or have but one user who initiated the browse action communicate with the web server, and relay the web pages to all other SameView nodes. While the former scheme is not scalable as the number of users grows, SameView employs the latter scheme instead.

The event monitor layer, placed above the HTML-extended layer, provides two types of services including permission control and event capture. Only a token holding participant is allowed to operate the whiteboard. Operations from other participants are treated as illegal and discarded by the event monitor layer right away. Board operations caught by the event monitor layer will be dispatched to other nodes as event messages. Some fidelity-enhanced procedure can be realized so that the entire course of the operation can be reproduced vividly on a distinct host. For instance, when a teacher draws on the board with a stylus, remote students will actually witness the course of development with every stroke and curve. This offers a far richer user experience than, say, having the resulting pattern pop on to the screen in an abrupt fashion. It is in fact the notion of experience recurrence as opposed to object reappearance.

5.3   Live Record

Because a student may well want to review the lessons after class, it is a good idea to provide the users with a tool for recording the live classroom session. The recording is a natural process of courseware making. Generally any good courseware should involve an assortment of multimedia applications, so that a user will be fully stimulated in a learning experience. While it is a tricky and time-consuming business to produce good courseware with a general-purpose multimedia authoring tool, the recording feature of an RTIVC sets a new paradigm for courseware production.

The recorded archive can be viewed offline by an absent student to make up for the missed lecture. With the live record feature, an E-learning system not only abridges the spatial gap of traditional classroom education, but lifts the temporal limitation as well. Figure 11 is just a snapshot of SameView playing a recorded archive.

In designing the record tool, the key issue is how to organize and synchronize the numerous media objects into a compound document. SameView's live record feature captures a diversity of in-classroom activities, including streamed audio/video data and whiteboard operations. All recorded events will be time stamped in order to guarantee the playback synchronization. Whereas UWashington's virtual classroom restricts the recording facility to the server alone, SameView allows every participant to launch a customized recording session for his own convenience. The recorded compound document is structured as an XML file named ARS, which could be viewed using an embedded ARS player.

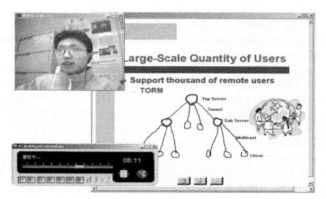

Fig. 11. Replaying a recorded classroom session

6   Tests

The testing of SameView has been performed on a systematic basis.

1) **Testing of TORM.** TORM was tested at first stage mainly by means of simulation. Using the Network Simulator--ns2 as a test-bed, we created various network topologies with different parameters regarding bandwidth, delay and loss rate. TORM was then examined in terms of its error recovery efficacy, scalability and robustness. Experimental results agreed well with TORM's initial design purposes, proving its feasibility as a transport layer infrastructure for large-scale multicast.

2) **Testing of AMTP.** AMTP was tested as a separate application before it was integrated into SameView. When a user requests a remote HTML page with several embedded media objects, a demo proxy will transform the media objects according to local bandwidth conditions, while ensuring the intactness of their high-level semantics.

3) **Testing of SameView.** After unit tests were performed on TORM and AMTP, SameView was tested under various network configurations as an integral application. The first set of tests was performed on the Tsinghua University campus network. When a teacher gave a lecture in the Smart Classroom[9], a group of remote students gathered in a computerized room, where a generic PC was used as a sub-server, and all remote students were connected to the sub-server as multicast clients. On a later occasion, we had a chance to test the software over the Internet. While the teacher

was still located on the university campus, the remote students availed themselves of the Internet either through ADSL or Broadband. All users were asked to give a subjective assessment of their experience with SameView, and general satisfaction was reported regarding the perceived quality of the audio, video and whiteboard presentation.

7   Conclusion and Future Work

In this paper, we presented an RTIVC system designed for large-scale deployment over the Internet. Our system was highlighted in the design of TORM, a transport layer multicast infrastructure, and AMTP, a presentation layer self-adaptive media transport policy. We presented our research in the field of human-computer interaction, by introducing SameView's multimodal user interface. With many enhanced pedagogical features, the system is well-designed for real-time interactive distance learning. Various tests have also confirmed the system's usability.

Our current and future work mainly involves two aspects:

1) **Self-organization of the TORM tree.** At present, the structure of a TORM tree has to be configured manually beforehand. It is expected that a self-organized TORM tree will soon be realized for minimized human intervention and a higher degree of error resilience.

2) **Semantics modeling.** We shall try to apply semantics modeling techniques so that a greater variety of semantics information will be extracted from the raw courseware and organized in a systematic way. The derived semantics model will then be exploited to better address a user's needs and preferences.

References

1. Real networks web site [Online]. Available: http://www.realnetworks.com
2. Microsoft's Windows Media web site [Online]. Available:
   http://www.microsoft.com/windows/ windowsmedia
3. Microsoft's NetMeeting web site [Online]. Available: http://www.microsoft.com/windows/ netmeeting
4. Stanford-online web site [Online]. Available: http://stanford-online.stanford.edu
5. Deshpande, S.G., Hwang, J.N.: A Real-Time Interactive Virtual Classroom Multimedia Distance Learning System. IEEE Transactions on Multimedia, Vol. 3, No. 4, December 2001.
6. Floyd S., Jacobson V., McCanne. S., et al: A Reliable Multicast Framework for Light-weight Sessions and Application Level Framing. In Proceedings of ACM SIGCOMM'95. Cambridge, MA US. 1995. 342–356.
7. Yang Y.D., Chen J.L., Zhang, H.J.: Adaptive Delivery of HTML Contents. Technique Report of Media Comupting Group, MSRCN, 2000.
8. Liao C.Y., Shi Y.C., Xu G.Y.: AMTM – An Adaptive Multimedia Transport Model. In proceeding of SPIE International Symposia on Voice, Video and Data Communication. Boston, Nov.
9. Shi Y.C., Xie W.K., Xu G.Y.: Smart Remote Classroom: Creating a Revolutionary Real-time Interactive Distance Learning System. In Proceedings of International Conference on Web-based Learning 2002, Springer LNCS 2436, p. 130.

Cultural Issues Relating to Teaching IT Professional Ethics Online: Lessons Learned

Elicia Lanham and Wanlei Zhou

School of Information Technology
Deakin University, Australia
lanham, wanlei@deakin.edu.au

Abstract. Over the last few years the number of fee paying international students attending Australian Universities has increased dramatically. However with the increasing number of international students enrolling in Tertiary education, awareness of their different learning styles has become apparent. Therefore the current way in which unit information is presented to students is no longer ideal and procedures are needed to be reviewed in order to keep up with the changing audience.

1 Introduction

In recent years there has been an increase in the use of the Internet as an educational platform in Tertiary education. The creation of online courses has meant that the student base for traditional courses has changed from local students to a combination of local and international students. This change in audience has meant that further investigation into students learning styles is needed to ensure that all students are able to complete the course successfully.

This paper will provide background information about online education, reporting on related research currently being conducted. Also presented are problems that existed for international and local students within this learning environment. The paper will conclude with lessons learned combined with guidelines to follow in order to lessen the severity of cultural differences between students.

1.1 Background

This paper provides an insight into the effects and issues involved in providing online courses to culturally diverse students. The Bachelor of Computing is a 3 year full-time degree offered at Deakin University. As part of the requirement to achieve the degree students are required to complete several core units each semester. One of the third year core units is Computers and Society and Professional Ethics, which is an on-campus, one semester unit.

W. Zhou et al. (Eds.): ICWL 2003, LNCS 2783, pp. 134–144, 2003.

The Deakin University 2002 Handbook [1] defines the goal of the Computers and Society and Professional Ethics unit as "… exploring the impact of Information Technology on society and investigating ethical and professional issues". At the completion of this unit, the students will have been exposed to the major ethical claims made against technology and will be able to assess and identify the issues involved. From this experience students will have developed their critical thinking, communication and research skills while considering these issues.

Deakin University is one of Australia's tertiary institutions that offer educational units via distance education. The Computers and Society and Professional Ethics unit (Computer Ethics) was part of the distance education program for the Bachelor of Computing offered by Deakin University since 1997. Generally at this time computing units offered via distance education in Deakin University, had paper-based study guides and readers, as well as web pages which contained up-to-date unit information and current announcements. The students also had access to their tutors via e-mail and telephone. However since 1997 we have had major technological advancement in the area of distance education. Therefore with the technology available today off-campus students are supported through web-based teaching technologies, such as: WebCT, FirstClass, Blackboard, etc. Student study guides are no longer provided in paper-based format, but instead have been converted into media documents. Another area that has improved since the introduction of web-based teaching technologies is communication. Through the use of the Internet, communication between off-campus students is easily achieved and therefore encouraged.

1.2   Unit Description

At the beginning of the semester, students were placed in groups to complete their tutorial requirements for the Computer Ethics unit. This format is much the same as that of students attending on-campus tutorial classes. The student groups are randomly generated, containing a mixture of both on and off-campus students. The student composition for this unit is quite mixed with a large number of International students participating in this unit. The percentage of International students enrolled in this unit on the Melbourne campus was approximately 50 percent of the total students. The majority of these international students were from Asia.

The Computer Ethics unit is a combination of two web-based platforms, WebCT and FirstClass. The inclusion of both applications caused initial confusion for students. Some students were unsure about what they had to do in each application, even though it had been explained that the WebCT site was their resource page, where they could access the information that they needed in regards to the unit; and the FirstClass platform was referred to as the discussion center, where students could interact with one another. The students were also required to use FirstClass to submit their assignments electronically. The complexity of having two online platforms running in parallel does not assist students with the cultural problems encountered when learning online, but rather adds to the confusion and uncertainty encountered.

The following communication tools were built into the FirstClass environment available for student communication:

- A message board for daily information updates posted by the instructors.
- Resource area, where students can post their responses and store completed work.
- Resume containing student information, which they enter themselves.
- Facility to conduct synchronous (real-time) communication.
- Social Club where students can discuss anything other than the unit.

Students received frequent e-mails from their instructors, providing them with updated class news, general class information and answers to common questions. This information was distributed via a global e-mail sent to all students enrolled in the unit. These bulletins were also posted in both WebCT and FirstClass; this ensured that all students were well informed about the unit.

With this unit there are no on-campus lectures or tutorials, the unit is run completely online for both the on and off-campus students. The on-campus students did not respond favorably at the commencement of the unit. In the University on-campus environment most units that students have completed during their degree have been instructor-centered, rather than the student-centered approach that online units require. Hence, participating students had to become accustomed to this new learning style and environment.

2 Related Work

Some researches have acknowledged that in traditional learning environments students from different cultures have different learning style. This paper hopes to identify whether these different learning styles still exist in online learning environments.

2.1 Cultural Issues

Several studies have indicated that different cultures have various levels of compatibility with different styles of learning. A number of researchers even claim that some cultures may embrace the online learning environment more easily than others.

The inclusion of multiple cultures in university courses means that a more flexible approach should be taken with the design of these courses to ensure that all students are able to reach the course goals [2]. This includes making use of various cultural ways of knowing, interacting, and teaching; and to promote the acceptance and equality of a variety of learning outcomes.

Nielsen (1996) [3] provides some guidelines for the interface design of internationally used environments. For example, ensuring that the interface does not contain icons that could be offensive to other cultures (e.g. a pointing finger); avoiding the use of visual puns to symbolize items on screen (e.g. using a coffee cup to indicate a cyber café where users can chat); desist from the use of metaphors (e.g. although they may be understood by local users, they might have a different meaning to international users); finally if content translation is planned, make sure that the content is translated in its entirety. By making use of these guidelines, we will be able to offer students an unbiased foundation. If students can understand the interface, then maybe they will be comfortable in the online environment.

2.2 Learning Styles

In online learning environments it becomes apparent that differences exist between cultures in the way they learn and their approach to learning. Conlan (1996) [4] identifies that the approach of many Asian students to learning is that of memorization and rote learning. This type of learning style is adopted in cases where students are presented with the learning content that they needed by their instructors/teachers and then they memorize (to reproduce) the required material. Whereas many Australian students, as well as others from similar Western backgrounds, have been encouraged to learn through the questioning of facts and understanding of concepts, rather than to reproduce the information. Due to this encouragement to understand concepts Australian students are more accepting of student-centered learning.

Munro-Smith (2002) [5] states that in a comparison of Singaporean and Australian students that students from Singapore prefer face-to-face interaction rather than the online interaction. Students in Singapore have been known to exchange their contributions in person and conducted editing around one computer. Australian students, on the other hand, prefer to conduct their communication through online channels only. In Singapore students prefer to print out the class material and use the material as instructions, whereas generally Australian students tend only to refer to online materials and then use their own ideas to apply that material to 'real' situations.

Cultural attitude towards knowledge acquisition will affect the way in which students are taught in society. According to Conlan (1996) [4], to "know" something for Asian students, often refers to being able to remember, repeat, reproduce, or recite the information in question. Whereas for Australian students, to "know" something is applied when the student has grasped the concept or is able to analyse the concepts fundamentals.

From these statements we can see that the reproduction and memorization of material is considered to be the correct way to learn in the Asian culture. Both papers [4] [5] agree that Asian cultures hold great respect for their teachers, therefore to ignore resources provided is seen as being disrespectful to teachers. Alternatively, in Australian culture to question the information and develop independent learning skills is deemed more important than the ability to reproduce information. We can see that from these two basic definitions that both cultures hold very different approaches and beliefs in learning styles. Therefore taking the one learning style fits all approach to e-learning does not seem appropriate.

Providing students with practical activities is an approach that could be used to increase student understating of the content. Hence, in the online environments students would be presented with the information content on screen, they would then have a set of activities or tasks, relating to the content, which they would be required to complete. This approach promotes the understanding and application of the facts, rather than the replication of them.

If we take another comparison of culture, this time between America and Finland, we can identify another set of attitudes towards learning. The paper written by LeBaron et. al. (2000) [6] identifies several cultural differences evident in the course run between these two countries. There was a distinctive difference between the participation between the Finnish and the Americans. It became quite obvious early in the course that the Americans were much more talkative than the Finnish. The students from Finland tended only to respond when they felt they had something worthwhile to say.

The students from America and Finland presented very different attitudes towards learning, this could stem from the fact that tuition for higher education in Finland is free and they are only assessed on a pass-fail basis. This is quite different from the pressure placed upon students in American institutions, to achieve high grades, and to pay for their education whilst studying. This difference in student pressures will be likely to have an impact on the outcome of their course.

In learning environments it is important not to make generalization in relation to student groups and cultural backgrounds as each student is individual and has different needs, this is even more important when we are dealing with online learning environments.

3 The Problem

The number of international students studying in Deakin University has been on the increase over recent years. Therefore the appearance of different student learning styles has become more obvious. It has been identified by some researchers that students from different cultures learn differently and have different approaches to learning. It has been recognised that the different learning styles become more apparent in the online learning environment. This difference is compounded through the Computer Ethics unit, ethics requires the application of morals and beliefs and as we know these factors differ considerably from culture to culture.

Teaching ethics online is an interesting topic, but when compounded with the globalisation and cultural diversity in the classrooms of today, the uniqueness of this topic increases. Ethics by itself is one of the more complex issues to teach, and teaching it to a multicultural group of students can produce some interesting results and responses. Gotterbarn (1991) [7] stated that psychologists have shown that the most effective method of teaching ethics is by discussing the issues with peers. Therefore providing an open environment where students can converse freely with one another provides the ideal platform to conduct this unit.

The combination of on-campus, off-campus and international students has provided a broad base for discussion in this unit. Students from each of these student groups will have different opinions, views and experiences to apply to the ethical situations given. However, within the student base each cultural group has its own specific set of values, ideas and beliefs that relate to their cultural needs. Children are raised up by their parents/guardians with a set of beliefs and ideas, from which they themselves have been raised. So when we put the subject of ethics, which relies on moral values, into an online environment, the results are interesting.

What is interesting about teaching ethics online is that we have access to different opinions, reasoning, and outcomes to the ones that we (ourselves) would produce. In terms of teaching ethics, sometimes it is hard to look beyond our own cultural beliefs to understand what other students are saying.

3.1 Cultural Differences

Due to the large number of international students enrolled in this unit, the response to tutorial tasks varied considerably, therefore enabling us to identify that the students were not all of the same cultural background. It was interesting to see that the opinions of students in relation to everyday situations varied in regards to their cultural beliefs, for example, one student posted a response regarding traffic lights. The student stated that they would not cross a red light (at a traffic intersection), not because of the road rules or the fact that they might have an accident but due to the fact that that if they did cross the red light then God would be displeased with them. This is not how most western cultures would view a red light, they would generally think about it in terms of obeying the road rules. These different perceptive on given situation are what make our cultures unique, we should use this information to broaden our own cultural awareness.

Towards the completion of the unit students were required to participate in a collaborative assignment online working in groups. The groups were arranged based on topics selected in the previous assignment, therefore the groups were a mixture of on-campus, international, and off-campus students. At the release of the groups on-campus students immediately approached tutors to ask if they could be put into groups with their friends to complete the major assessment. This normal request of students wishing to change groups was made interesting, due to the fact that nine times out of ten the 'friends' that they were asking to be placed with, were of the same cultural background as themselves. The students were trying to reorganize the groups so that they would be paired with other student who held similar values and ethical beliefs, therefore making the explanation of their ethical choices and positions easier.

For instance, during the semester students were required to read a passage of text about a situation, the students were then asked to make an ethical decision about what the outcome of the situation should be. Defining this outcome required students to make use of their beliefs, values, and what they have read; and apply them to the situation in order to derive at an ethical decision. It is in the justification and explanation of the student's answers that we can identify different cultural groups, due to their unique standpoints and opinions.

3.2 Students Online Difficulties

As this was purely an online unit both for the off-campus and on-campus students, there was to be no face-to-face contact. However it did not take long for on-campus students to visit their tutors. It was interesting to note that the ratio of international on-campus students to local on-campus students who sought out face-to-face help was approximately 8:1. This indicated that perhaps the international students were not as confident working in a student-centered environment than the local students. This is consistent with the information presented in papers [4] [5] [8] which identifies that Australian students were more accepting, comfortable, and confident working in the student-centered environment as opposed to Asian students who preferred the more traditional instructor-centered approach.

Another interesting fact in teaching this unit online is the need for constant validation that some students require about their work. This need is also evident in on-campus units but to a lesser extent, where students simply approach the instructor in class for help. In the online environment it became very obvious when one student is constantly sending messages asking if what they have done is correct. This reliance on instructor support and validation can also be linked to cultural issues. If we refer back to Asian culture, students follow the instructions their teachers provide them with very closely, therefore in an environment were the instructions require students to apply their own ideas this group of students may experience problems.

3.3 Ethics

Ethics is such a gray subject that it is often hard to determine the validity of a comment, judging which answer is "right" or "wrong" rarely applies. In ethics the correct answer comes down to the explanation and justification for the answer given. At the beginning of semester one student acknowledged this lack of right and wrong answers by saying, "In ethics if you argue your position well there are no wrong answers." This statement clearly identifies the view that in ethics, people have different positions and beliefs, therefore it is how you defend and provide support for your answers that counts.

Providing an explanation for their ethical decisions was an area where some students had trouble. Students knew immediately whether the problem presented to them posed an ethical issue or not, but they had trouble explaining the reason for their position. This could be due to their inability to express themselves using the language (English). Some students limited their responses in terms of word count due to their unfamiliarity with the language: for example, students only provided a few lines of thoughts in relation to complex topics without any explanation.

According to Coldwell (2000) [9] traditional computing units generally require students to use problem solving skills in a technological environment, calling on mathematical and programming skills as well as the ability to memorise content. However, the emphasis of the Computer Ethics unit differs considerably to other units previously completed by students in their Bachelor of Computing degree. In Computer Ethics the focus is on student collaboration and the sharing of ideas rather than the learning of technical skills. The technical–oriented students perceived the Computer Ethics unit as confusing, as they are not familiar with student-centered learning. In this unit however, students do not learn technical skills 'per sa' but rather are required to participate in discussion about issues relating to technical, social and professional situations, in a highly technical environment.

Another difference in running Computer Ethics online as opposed to other computing units is the emphasis on discussion. Traditionally the focus of programming units has been on the individual completion of work rather than on the combined input of students. However, Computer Ethics students are reliant on the members of their group to participate in the tutorial discussion in order for them to complete the unit successfully.

4 Lessons Learned

During the course of the unit it became apparent that certain areas of the online learning environment proved more troublesome than others to international students. These areas related not only to the content provided but also to the learning environment itself.

4.1 Creating a Suitable Social Environment

The idea behind this research is to provide all students with an environment that they can learn in. For instance, providing a single information session at the beginning of the semester for the International students will ensure that they hold the necessary information and skills required to navigate this web-based learning environment confidently.

Providing a social environment for the International students to discuss their problems and questions together could also be another means of improving their experience. This option is available in the FirstClass environment; however it is not fully utilized by the students. Often students will talk more freely about their problems to one another rather than with their instructor. This social environment could be used to discuss unit related problems or even general problems with settling into a new country.

It is important that when designing the unit we realize that the students who will be participating in the unit come from different backgrounds, therefore the environment can not be designed with one specific group of students in mind.

4.2 Cross-Cultural Design of Online Materials

When we combine international and local students in one learning environment, consideration is needed to ensure that all students are provided with a fair and unbiased learning environment. In paper [10], Collis and Remmers (1997) have defined two basic categories for educational web sites in relation to cross-cultural application:

- Category 1: Sites made for one context and its culture, but visited by those from other context and cultures.
- Category 2: Sites made specifically for cross-cultural participation.

They concluded that a majority of educational web sites today fit into the first category and that generally only those institutions specifically catering for cross-cultural education e.g. institutions that are fostering multinational educational partnerships, fit into the second category. However with the culturally diverse classes that we have in today's society we should be creating web sites using Category 2. The continued creation of Category 1 web sites demonstrates the lack of awareness to the increase of multicultural classes.

General items that should be taken into consideration when designing online materials, in order to reduce the effects on students from other cultures, include the following:

- Providing an environment free of colloquial language and cultural slang.
- Identifying items or language that may be offensive to other cultures.
- Identifying areas in which cultures learn differently, and make allowances for this in the learning outcomes.
- Providing an environment which ensures that all students are able to understand the material.

The above are just a sample of techniques that can be used to reduce the barriers between cultures in the classroom and in online environments. In the case of online learning environments providing links to general educational tools, such as, dictionaries, thesauruses, and spelling aids, as part of the unit resources will help to increase the understanding for all students, both international and local.

4.3 Combined Teaching Materials

The simple transfer of text-based information into online courses is not the answer; the materials need to be adapted to fit the online environment. It has been acknowledge that different cultures respond to the online environment with varying degrees of acceptance. Therefore we need to create a balance between the traditional methods of teaching and the new web-based learning technologies.

Students are confident in what they know, therefore, if we use the teaching methodology of the instructor-centered lectures combined with the teaching philosophy of on-campus tutorials, then we will have created a recognizable and familiar learning atmosphere online. By applying these methodologies and philosophies to the online environment we can use a combination of instructor-centered explanations with student-centered activities to strike a balance [4]. If we adopt this new philosophy into the online environment, we have a chance of improving student confidence in participating in web-based learning.

McLoughlin and Oliver (2000) [11] have assembled several design principles for use in culturally inclusive curriculum for online learners. These principles include, adopting a knowledge philosophy that is accepting of multiple perspectives; incorporating "real' learning activities that will build on existing knowledge, values, and skills; knowledge sharing to facilitate online learning communities; providing both internal and external support; encouraging students to be proactive in their learning; providing flexible learning goals to ensure that all students are able to achieve them.

Deakin University currently has in place several of these principals in online environments. The facilitation of online discussion (knowledge sharing) between students is encouraged and provided for in both WebCT and FirstClass. In these systems students are able to post messages to all students with the addition in FirstClass to specify group members or individual students. This interaction between students online can be used to improve the student's online skills, and participation in online discussion.

Support in any unit plays a vital role in student success; in the face-to-face (on-campus) environment support is a tangible thing, where students can approach the tutor/lecturer for help and guidance. In the online environment this support is less "real" and therefore is not utilized to its full potential. Therefore concrete support strategies need to be adopted in the online environment, whether it is peer-based or instructor-based support.

If the current approach is toward offering more units in the online environment then providing more opportunities for students to be proactive towards their education are needed. Making online studies part of the tertiary education experience from the beginning will improve students' skills and awareness of their learning environment. This initiation into the online environment could be limited to include simple online activities within units as a means of integrating student into online learning. Providing flexibility in the learning goals and being accepting of different student perspectives should also be integrated into online learning to ensure that all students receive the same opportunity to achieve these goals.

Taking the above principles into consideration when deciding what material to present in the online learning environment should help ease the difficulty in producing information that can be understood by all who read it. Obtaining all students understanding may seem unachievable, but by providing an unbiased base we have a good foundation from which to develop our online learning environment.

4.4 Future Work

The next stage in this research is to look generally at culturally diverse students participating in online studies and survey these students in order to formalise their opinions about problems encountered whilst learning using online environments. After the analysis of these results research will be carried out to produce a model aimed at accommodating student problems in using the online education environment.

5 Conclusion

At present there seems to be no major problems with putting courses online; however with the changing needs of society it is important that we no longer simply design our classes for local students. We must be aware of the diversity in classes and take into consideration the needs of all students. Designing and providing an environment that is understood by all students should be our highest priority. We have advanced enough to know that one type does not fit all and that adjustments are needed if we are to continue to promote global learning.

The dissolving of cultural boundaries in online learning will only occur if we first understand what those boundaries are. We have the technology to provide global education; the focus now must be placed upon ensuring that the educational content and resources we provide can be utilized by all students.

References

1. Deakin University, *Undergraduate Studies Handbook 2002*. 2001, Victoria, Australia: Deakin University.
2. Ngeow, K. and K.Y.S. Kong. *Designing Culturally Sensitive Learning Environments*. in *Winds of change in the sea of learning: charting the course of digital education*. 2002. Auckland, New Zealand: ASCILITE.
3. Nielsen, J., *International Web Usability*, in *The Alertbox: Current Issues in Web Usability*. 1996.
4. Conlan, F. *Can the different learning expectations of Australian and Asian students be reconciled in one teaching strategy?* in *Teaching and Learning Within and Across Disciplines, Proceedings of the 5th Annual Teaching and Learning Forum*. 1996. Murdoch University.
5. Munro-Smith, N. *A Tale of Two Cities: Computer Mediated Teaching & Learning in Melbourne and Singapore*. in *Winds of change in the sea of learning: charting the course of digital education*. 2002. Auckland, New Zealand: ASCILITE.
6. LeBaron, J., J. Pulkkinen, and P. Scollin. *Problems of Students Communication in a Cross-cultural, International Internet Course Setting*. in *Ed-Media 2000: World Conference on Educational Multimedia, Hypermedia & Telecommunications*. 2000. Montreal, Canada: Association for the Advancement of Computing in Education.
7. Gotterbarn, D., *A "capstone" course in computer ethics*. 1991, East Tennessee State University, Computer and Information Science Department: Johnson City, Tennessee.
8. Chin, K., Leng., V. Chang, and C. Bauer. *The use of Web-based learning in culturally diverse learning environments*. in *Proceedings of AusWeb2K, the Sixth Australian World Wide Web Conference*. 2000. Rihga Colonial Club Resort, Cairns.
9. Coldwell, J. *Is it possible to teach computer ethics via distance education*. in *ACM International Conference Proceeding Series: Selected papers from the second Australian Institute conference on Computer ethics*. 2000. Canberra, Australia: Australian Computer Society, Inc. Darlinghurst, Australia.
10. Collis, B. and E. Remmers, *The World Wide Web in education: Issues related to cross-cultural communication and interaction.*, in *Web-based instruction*, B.H. Khan, Editor. 1997, Educational Technology Publications: Englewood Cliffs, New Jersey. p. 85–92.
11. McLoughlin, C. and R. Oliver, *Designing learning environments for cultural inclusivity: A case study of the indigenous online learning at tertiary level*. Australian Journal of Educational Technology, 2000. **Vol. 16**(1): p. 58–72.

Perspectives on Creativity in Web Learning

Adriana Vivacqua[1], Francisco Mattos[1], Alberto Tornaghi[1], Jano M. de Souza[1,2], and Henrique Cukierman[1]

[1]COPPE/UFRJ – Computer Science Department, Graduate School of Engineering
{avivacqua, jano, hcukier}@cos.ufrj.br, franciscorpm@ig.com.br, tornaghi@uninet.com.br,
[2]Institute of Mathematics, Federal University of Rio de Janeiro
PO Box 68511, Zip Code 21941-972, Rio de Janeiro, RJ, Brazil

Abstract. Creativity is an important asset in today's fast changing environment. We believe it can and should be stimulated in educational environments, through the use of tools and careful design of activities and work groups. In this paper, we present and briefly discuss a checklist of eight activities to support creativity and should be applied when designing educational courses. We discuss the benefits of group work and present some educational perspectives to support it. We then relate creativity and collaborative learning and analyze a dynamic geometry system in relation to this checklist.

1 Introduction

The Internet has created a new reality for education, one where synchronous and asynchronous communication, long distance interaction and information exchange between students and teachers is relatively easy and accessible. The Internet brings to life the possibility of reaching greater numbers of people and providing high-level education at lower cost.

The rapid growth of the Internet and increase of competitiveness has also turned creativity into a major asset. Companies need to keep up with an ever-changing environment, in which changes come at great speed. To cope with these changes, they must be able to frequently redefine themselves in order to stay ahead in the market. For these reasons, creativity has become something companies look for in individuals. In this scenario, it is important that a student learn how to think and how to creatively solve problems, as opposed to simply learning conventional processes, from an early age. Collaborative, long-distance learning, coupled with creativity techniques might generate more creative individuals, better prepared to deal with today's challenges and to handle local problems in creative ways.

Ben Shneiderman [16] defines a creative cycle and a set of guidelines for the design of creativity support tools and interfaces. Some aspects are in close agreement with pedagogical theories. We explore how these could be applied to Web/Distance Learning settings and how these would work in collaborative learning situations. We analyze Tabulæ, a Dynamic Geometry teaching tool in relation to the guidelines.

In section 2, we introduce aspects of creativity and Shneiderman's guidelines. In section 3, we discuss educational approaches, followed by some previous work in

W. Zhou et al. (Eds.): ICWL 2003, LNCS 2783, pp. 145–156, 2003.

creativity and distance education. In section 5 we introduce Tabulæ and discuss how it may be used to promote creative learning and finish with a conclusion in section 6.

2   Aspects of Creativity

According to the dictionary, something is creative when it shows "imagination and originality as well as routine skill" (from the Oxford Paperback Dictionary, Oxford University Press, 1979). Among computer scientists, a commonplace definition seems to be that creativity is "something that deals with a process resulting in a novel and useful product" [3] or "the ability to produce new and original objects" [2]. Every definition emphasizes novelty, which implies the use of imagination.

An important aspect is that an act might be creative in a personal or societal level: if a student produces a bubble sort program without precious exposure to a bubble-sort algorithm, that is a personal creative work, even if not societal. This personal novelty (or discovery) is far more commonplace than societal novelty, which occurs when something never before experienced is produced [18]. We believe such personal creative acts can and should be stimulated in educational settings, in an effort to increase creative thought among students, in line with constructivist theories.

Many authors have tried to create models to map the creative process. It remains, however, an elusive topic. There are theories and studies on creative processes and factors leading to creative solutions to problems. Some models and computer systems have been proposed to assist in the performance of creative work and certain application areas have been identified. In the following subsection, we outline the creative cycle as proposed by Shneiderman [16].

2.1   The Creative Cycle

Csikszentmihalyi emphasizes the social aspect of creative work, describing an individual working within a domain, presenting work to the gatekeepers of that domain, who will judge whether it should be accepted to the domain as a creative contribution. He stresses the benefits of consultations with other domain experts and the necessity for dissemination within the field [5]. The existence of a social aspect of creativity has become widely agreed upon and Csikszentmihalyi's approach has been widely accepted, as scientists recognize their own research methods and the workings of their social research networks and domain areas. Inspired by Csikszentmihalyi's work, Ben Shneiderman defined a framework for generating excellence (GENEX), which describes four phases of creativity [16] and attempts to take into account the social aspects of the creative process. Note that creative work may require returning to earlier phases and much iteration.

The GENEX framework is founded on the beliefs that: (1) new knowledge is built on previous knowledge. This is in agreement with the basic premises of constructivism, that knowledge is constructed; (2) powerful tools can support creativity. This follows the lines of Piagetian thinking, whereby inquisitive interaction with the real world causes the development of intelligence; (3) refinement is a social process. According to Vygotsky, the interaction with peers causes the development of intelligence; and (4) creative work is not complete until it is disseminated.

The four GENEX phases are: (1) Collect – Learn from previous works stored in libraries, the Web and other resources. (2) Relate – Consult with peers and mentors at early, middle and late stages. (3) Create – Explore, compose and evaluate possible solutions. (4) Donate – Disseminate the results and contribute to libraries, the Web and other sources.

These are somewhat related to Nonaka's knowledge creation spiral, according to which there are two kinds of knowledge: explicit, which can be expressed in word and numbers and shared in the form of data, formulae, manuals and the like, and tacit, which is highly personal, hard to formalize and difficult to communicate: subjective insights, hunches, intuitions, etc. [10]. Knowledge creation is a spiraling process of interactions between explicit and tacit knowledge, which lead to the creation of new knowledge. This process is composed of four steps: (1) Socialization, which involves the sharing of tacit knowledge between individuals (relate); (2) Externalization, which requires the expression of tacit knowledge and its translation into explicit knowledge (donate); (3) Combination, which involves the conversion of explicit knowledge into more complex sets of explicit knowledge, also related to experimentation with problems and solutions (create) and (4) Internalization, which is the conversion of explicit knowledge into the organization's tacit knowledge (collect). In fact, knowledge management (KM) systems might provide useful insight into the construction of educational systems. KM frameworks have been proposed to integrate and share data and create collaborative work environments to increase user synergy and cooperation, such as SpeCS [13].

Analyzing some scenarios, Shneiderman identifies eight activities performed during the creative process, and suggests that an integrated creativity support tool should offer all of these. The activities and how they relate to the GENEX phases are shown in Figure 1. The relation shown is the primary one, but these activities could be performed at any of the phases.

Shneiderman's list follows, with a brief discussion of each of the activities.

- Searching and browsing digital libraries, the Web and other resources. Searching accelerates collection of information about previous work. Searches might also be performed to find peers or potential co-workers. A system should include tools for searching the web, dictionaries and other resources, including improved search tools for image, sound and video retrieval.
- Visualizing data and processes to understand and discover, invent or create relationships. Drawing mental or concept maps of current knowledge helps users organize their knowledge, see relationships and possibly spot missing items.
- Consulting with peers and mentors for intellectual and emotional support. An important part of collaborative work, peers can aid in problem solving and new idea generation (this is strongly related to concepts of peer learning introduced by Vygotsky, which will be explained in a later section). Consultation tools include email, chat and instant messenger applications.
- Thinking by free associations to make new combinations of ideas. Brainstorming or lateral thinking should be encouraged, in an environment where new ideas aren't immediately discarded.
- Exploring solutions: what-if tools and simulation models. Individuals should be able to conduct experiments and simulations about the implications of decisions and create several scenarios. Simulations open a person's mind to possibilities and

allow them to explore safely and to understand complex relationships. Simulations can be fun and popular, such as the computer game SimCity.

- Composing artifacts and performances step-by-step. The ability to easily build and change prototypes is very important. In this way, individuals can rapidly explore and refine their solutions to problems. Tools range from simple word processors to complex music composition tools.
- Reviewing and replaying session histories to support reflection. History keeping, or the capacity to record, review and save activities, is missing from many tools. The existence of a history feature allows users to return to previous steps, review a certain problem solving strategies, store frequent patterns and share them with peers and mentors.
- Disseminating results to gain recognition and add to the searchable resources. Once finished, work should be disseminated. One possibility is to send notifications to every person whose work influenced the project at hand or to others who referenced the same work. Dissemination tools include email, web pages, conferences, classes and publications.

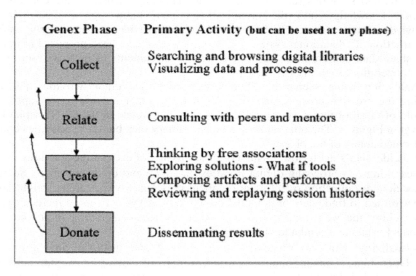

Fig. 1. GENEX phases and their primary relation to the activities

All of these steps can be performed by teams as well as by individuals working alone. When dealing with experts from different areas, one's ignorance in relation to another's domain of expertise can be used as a stimulus to creativity. This has been referred to as symmetry of ignorance. Bringing different points of view together and trying to create a shared understanding among all stakeholders can lead to new insights, ideas and artifacts [6]. This implies that work groups should be carefully chosen, so as to best leverage each person's strengths and weaknesses. This point is often overlooked, as most groups are formed at random or based on criteria such as friendship or personal relations, when different configurations might have generated better (and more creative) results. In these situations, it becomes necessary for individuals to instruct each other about their areas of expertise, externalizing their tacit knowledge. Externalization causes a person to move from vague mental conceptualizations of an idea to a more concrete representation of it, providing a means for others to interact with, react to, negotiate around and build upon it. It also provides an opportunity for the creation of a common language between parties.

3   Pedagogical and Educational Aspects

In this section we briefly outline three educational theories that are related to creative and cooperative learning systems. According to Freinet [Freinet, 75], cooperation is the driving force of educational processes. For him, cooperation and productive work are natural forms of interaction for students and therefore essential to any educational environment. Piaget [12], in his constructivist approach, states that a person builds his or her intelligence and knowledge as a result of the interactions with objects and the real world. When manipulating these objects and solving problems deriving from this interaction, a person develops his or her mental structures. Vygotsky [19] stresses the role of interaction between peers in the development of higher thought structures. He demonstrates that cooperation between individuals at different mental development stages not only facilitates, but also encourages intellectual growth. With these theories in mind, we see the potential for intellectual development that resides in the interaction between students mediated by their interaction with the computer (object).

Freinet suggests that the learning process should stem from necessary actions and through the production of objects that are useful to the apprentices. He emphasizes the value of an individual's production it's place in the greater scheme of things and that it can be modified and enhanced through their colleagues' interference [Freinet, 75]. One should note that his work presupposes collaboration not only between students but between teachers as well.

Piaget sustains that a person's intelligence is composed of structures that are developed by him or herself through the actions he or she operates on real-world objects. Development happens through a sequence of stages: sensorimotor; pre-operations; concrete-operations and formal operations. These are, in turn, divided into sub-stages. Evolution between stages happens through assimilation and accommodation in these structures and sub-structures. This evolution occurs because a person needs to structure and organize the information he or she receives from the environment. Intelligence is constructed as a structure necessary to support the knowledge produced by the subject in his or her interactions with objects and problems posed by the environment. These theories spawned constructivism. The name stems from the fact that knowledge is a mental construct, product of the interaction of a person with the environment [Piaget, 70]. This implies that educational institutions should offer students an environment that will lead them to work with real world objects, run experiments, interact with classmates, teachers and researchers and reach their own conclusions, registering and testing them with new experiments to verify their validity.

In Vygotsky's work, we find support for the establishment of groups and development of peer relationships. Vygotsky holds that there is a close relation between cooperation among peers and learning potential [Vygotsky, 89]. He defines "real development level" as the already established mental functions of an individual, stemming from the development stages already covered by the person. This is, therefore, the level of development verifiable through testing and direct problem solving, which the individual can handle by him or herself.

Vygotsky argues that, to understand what a person's real learning capacity is, the "zone of proximal development" must also be taken into account. He defines the "zone of proximal development" as the distance between the "real development level", usually determined through independent problem solving, and the "potential development level", usually determined through the solution of problems under the guidance of an instructor or in collaboration with more capable peers.

In the notion of "zone of proximal development", we find the importance of group study and the establishment of peer learning relationships. This "proximal development zone" is created when the individual interacts with others and observes how they handle and solve problems. Often these solutions are not reachable by the observer, but can be understood once they see peers or tutors reach them. Interaction with colleagues thus permits them to reach higher degrees of intellectual development.

More recently, proponents of Activity Centered Design build on Vygotsky's ideas and the concepts of distributed cognition and Activity Theory and view learning as a complex process in which an individual's cognition is defined by its relation to the material setting and the forms of social participation encouraged by these settings [8]. Thus, Activity Centered Design emphasizes the use of computer mediated environments to support and structure the interactions and interdependencies of an activity system, including interrelations between students, instructors, tasks they undertake and inscriptions they use. In Activity Centered Design, the focus is neither the teacher nor the student, but the design of activities that help learners develop the ability to carry out socially formulated, goal directed action through the use of mediating material and social structures.

4   Existing Systems

In this section we describe a few computer systems created to support creativity and web learning. Some online courses use email, online conferencing and web pages to enable group learning and activity development, in conjunction with face-to-face sessions. Communication and joint work over the Internet can be difficult for students and burdensome for teachers. These difficulties lead instructors to develop new strategies for group formation and ad-hoc problem solving when students have difficulties sharing knowledge or accessing each other's work. It has been argued that tools such as online discussion forums are powerful tools to aid in the development of critical thinking and decision-making abilities and that these forums are more inclusive than face-to-face ones, since they minimize the presence of more eloquent students and make participation more equalitarian [4].

Using a combination of traditional web technologies and tools, the CyberEd program, at the University of Massachusetts Dartmouth is an example of implementation and development of online education. Dartmouth offers university level courses on the Internet, and students enrolled in CyberEd courses receive college credits in chemistry, finance, history, commercial techniques and astronomy. Non-credit courses are also offered.

GRACILE (Grammar Collaborative Intelligent Environmet) is an example of an intelligent agent applied to Computer Supported Collaborative Learning [1]. An agent was developed to support the application of domain knowledge and effective collaboration between students. Agents mediate situations in which a student might learn from another while performing educational tasks. This usually means that the task requires the application of knowledge elements already internalized by other students that could also be internalized by him or her. These elements are usually relevant to the acquisition of more complex knowledge elements. GRACILE was designed for small (two to four students) heterogeneous groups.

Computer systems can facilitate creativity on at least two distinct levels: they can aid in knowledge gathering, sharing, integration and idea generation and they can enable the generation of creative artifacts in a particular domain by providing critical functionality in clear, direct and useful ways [9]. Most researchers recognize the importance of preexisting domain knowledge when solving a problem and the introduction of new, external knowledge when generating innovative solutions and many systems revolve around the management of existing knowledge and introduction of new knowledge in problem resolution. Creativity support systems range from kiosks at museums or exhibits to desktop design or composition systems.

Roast describes a system to support Active Reading, where the reader fills in blanks in the story [14]. Active Reading refers to how a reader's individual interpretation of a literary work influenced by its textual variants and how the reader may take the role of editor. Research is focused upon building tools to support creative understanding of a literary work and the articulation of that understanding in terms of alternative novel editions of the work being studied. In the system proposed, a literary piece is presented, with variant points inserted (displayed as question marks). The reader can "fill in the blanks" and then compare to other versions created to other users. Even though this system was created for literary researchers, to aid in the study of very old texts, which have been partially lost, it could certainly be used in an educational setting, with other kinds of texts and objectives (for instance, vocabulary practice and development).

Shibata and Hori [15] propose a personal creativity system, to support long-term idea-generation in daily life. Their system is essentially a knowledge management system, which allows a user to store and retrieve ideas when they are spontaneously generated. Their system consists of two subsystems: one for idea and problem management called IdeaManager and a personal information system called iBox, which stores notes, memos, papers, etc. When storing information on problems or ideas in IdeaManager, related information from iBox pops up on the user's screen, suggesting relations between the information. By showing related information, the authors hope to promote idea generation. This system has no formal educational pretensions. However, according to Freinet, work is a form of education. It could cretainly be used in group settings, to facilitate knowledge sharing between students, group problem solving and possibly help the generation of new ideas, following Vygotsky's approach.

5   Creativity and Web Learning

In this section we explore links between creativity and learning systems, and how these could be combined.

We believe that, in an educational setting, group activities should be designed in order to promote the eight activities as suggested by Shneiderman, and tools should be provided to support them. The eight activities, as explained earlier, are: search, visualize, consult, think, explore, compose, review, disseminate. If a particular educational software does not provide support for all activities, other supplementary tools may be used to fill in the needs. In addition, assignments should be planned to contemplate these activities. Furthermore, the instructor should carefully put together the student groups, in an attempt to enhance the quality of the work produced and provide externalization of ideas.

5.1   Case Study: Tabulæ

Tabulæ was developed to address the problem of teaching Euclidean Geometry using the Internet for synchronous and asynchronous communication [10]. Tabulæ is what is called "dynamic geometry" software, and it is built using client-server architecture. Dynamic geometry software is a system to aid in the study of plane geometry, which is based on the construction of geometric figures on a computer screen, as shown in Figure 2. Through a few icons it is possible to access commands that draw lines, circles, perpendiculars, parallels, reflections of figures, etc. It is also possible to move these constructs around using a mouse, without altering the predefined properties. Tabulæ permits the rapid creation of a virtual classroom, where each student receives, on his or her screen and in real time, the steps of the geometric construction the teacher is working on at the moment.

In Tabulæ, when objects are moved, geometric properties are observed. This is one of its greatest strengths: it allows a student to manipulate and experiment with abstract concepts, such as lines, points, angles, etc. as if they were concrete objects. It thus allows students to build constructs based on rules and properties they would otherwise not be able to manipulate, like medians and bisectors.

In traditional classroom settings, instructors construct their explanations on a blackboard, pointing out relevant issues as they appear. This process is static, that is, one cannot easily go back to a previous step or keep a history. Once they are erased, the constructs are gone. Tabulæ provides a blackboard for each student (on screen), on which the teacher can build each construct step by step, not necessarily following a predetermined guide. It allows the instructors to answer unexpected students' questions through exploration, composition and evaluation of possible solutions. It is desirable that students maintain control of their machines, so that they can experiment; propose variations to the solutions shown or disagree with a position, keeping an active and creative attitude. The students may save their constructs and those of the teacher and colleagues, in the same way they would copy the blackboard in a traditional class. Active participation allows each student to play the role of tutor (a temporary instructor) if the group feels the need for it.

These types of features allow students in different locales to create shared activities where each one is responsible for part of the process, creating animations to reflect this process that will later be discussed by the whole class. The whole group evaluates the process, which may lead to a new procedure that perfects the activity. Student participation is promoted by the teacher.

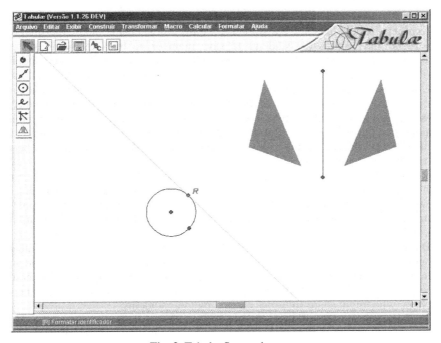

Fig. 2. Tabulæ Screenshot

These types of systems encourage students to participate in investigative activities and can be used so as to force externalization and the justification of results, which develops deductive reasoning. Tabulæ supports the eight creativity activities described earlier as follows:

Search: Tabulæ allows searching for constructs and properties others have created but doesn't directly support external searches. The instructor can propose activities that require some research, forcing the students to search the Internet or libraries for information. Educational activities should be designed in order to promote some external research.

Visualize: Tabulæ allows the students to visualize constructs and abstract properties in graphical form, and to perform operations on constructs that reflect on the graphics on their screen. In this way, a student might build new constructs and perceive relations between them.

Consult: Tabulæ permits sharing of one's screen with peers through the network. This enables the students to view each other's solutions and discuss them, to share problems or pieces of graphical objects. Better exchange tools are needed to enable further sharing and allow the students to reach their potential development level. Other media could be made available, such as video and audio and other communication methods, such as messaging.

Think: Tabulæ encourages creative thought by allowing free experimentation with constructs while class is going on and permitting the insertion of related external insights from other students or the instructor. It is a problem-solving environment. This could be enhanced with the introduction of related insights from the real world, such as the real-world application of the rules and properties being studied.

Explore: Tabulæ enables the student to apply rules, change and experiment with constructs, and permits the students to save them or go back to previous steps if necessary. In this fashion, a student may explore possibilities and create simulations without fear of making mistakes, and may save the best results for further exploration.

Compose: Tabulæ is a mathematical composition tool. It allows students to quickly build mathematical constructs based on geometric properties, formulae and rules, easily creating prototypes. They can create, experiment with and manipulate abstract constructs. These capabilities might be expanded to allow students to simulate real-world constructs using the mathematical ones, creating a link between the two knowledge areas.

Review: Tabulæ keeps the construction history and allows the creation of routines with animations that show the process of building mathematical constructs. This allows the students and teacher to review any given step and replay animations. This is an important feature, and could be enhanced through the use of annotations in the process.

Disseminate: Tabulæ supports sharing and externalization of constructs with peers through the tutor mechanism. In this fashion, a student takes the stand and shows what he or she has been working on, opening discussion on it. Dissemination could be wider. It should also occur between classes, different levels of students and between teachers, who might share solutions created by their students.

Regarding group formation, instructors need to know their students well to be able put together good working groups. When that is not the case, there might be a need for questionnaires or careful evaluation of a person's school history, hobbies, etc. Diversity should be sought after, in order to promote discussion and the introduction of external knowledge.

An experiment is currently being planned where a teacher will be at the Institute of Mathematics at the Federal University of Rio de Janeiro and the students will be at different schools of the public school network in Rio de Janeiro. In this experiment, the instructor will conduct a geometry class in which the main concepts will be formulated and discussed with the students. This may also be an opportunity to apply and verify the checklist in a real-world educational setting, proposing educational activities to fit the list.

6   Conclusion

We have presented some perspectives on creative work and explored how these might guide the design of activities in educational settings. We discussed a set of guidelines that we think should be followed when designing online courses. We believe that creativity should be stimulated from an early stage, in educational settings. As seen, there is a close relation between the phases in the creative cycle and the constructivist perspective of knowledge development, as well as a relation to Vygotsky's theories of peer development. We believe the activity checklist proposed by Shneiderman can and should be used to design educational activities. Through the exploration of these activities, we can propose computer-supported educational structures and activities focusing on experimentation and creative problem resolution and strongly based on constructivism and on collaborative learning. We believe these aspects haven't been fully explored yet.

We presented a computer system, Tabulæ, which allows teachers to quickly set up a virtual classroom, where each student views, on his or her own computer and in real time, the steps of the geometric construction the teacher is working on. During this process, students may modify the construct or add new elements and they may express opinions regarding the construction as well as questions and suggestions. Students may also send their work to colleagues and the instructor to share it and have it criticized. In analyzing Tabulæ, one can see that it has some creativity support features, but could be enhanced. One issue that comes to mind is the creation of construct libraries so students can archive and retrieve their and others' works. This would certainly increase the potential for exploration, as students would have the opportunity to explore and work on previous designs (including designs from previous classes) and build on top of them. Other improvements could be reached through the use of additional tools or creative design of activities. An interesting point to note is that Tabulæ has been proving very useful for teacher training. With the tools at their disposal, students are becoming more innovative and asking more questions. Teachers have had to become more flexible and learn to explain concepts in different ways, including sharing other students' works.

It should be noted that we're not looking to produce earth-shattering innovations in class. Rather, we aim for personal creativity, exploration and discovery. Stimulating creativity in educational settings, we hope to form more creative individuals, able to think in new ways and propose innovative solutions to problems. We believe the checklist will prove useful in designing educational systems that promote creativity.

References

1. Ayala, G. & Yano, Y.; Intelligent Agents to Support the Effective Collaboration in a CSCL Environment, Proceedings of the ED-TELECOM 96 World Conference on Educational Communications, June 1996, Boston, Mass.
2. Bonnardel, N.; Creativity in Design Activities: the Role of Analogies in a Constrained Cognitive Environment; Proceedings of Creativity & Cognition, 1999
3. Burleson, W. & Selker, T.; Creativity and Interface; Communications of the ACM, vol 45, n. 10; October 2002
4. Cahan, B; Adult Learning and the Internet: Themes and Things to Come, Adult Learning and the Internet: http://people.gactr.uga.edu/
5. Csikszentmihalyi, M.; Creativity: Flow and the Psychology of Discovery and Invention; Harper Collins Publishers, New York, 1996
6. Fischer, G.; Symmetry of Ignorance, Social Creativity, and Meta-Design; Proceedings of Creativity and Cognition, 1999
7. Freinet, C.; As técnicas Freinet da Escola Moderna, Editorial Estampa, Lisboa, Portugal, 1975
8. Gifford, B. & Enyedy, N., Activity Centered Design: Towards a Theoretical Framework for CSCL; Proceedings of the Third International Conference on Computer Support for Collaborative Learning, 1999]

9. Greene S.; Characteristics of Applications that Support Creativity; Communications of the ACM, vol 45, n. 10; October 2002
10. Guimarães, L.C.; Barbastefano, R. & Belfort, E.; Tabulæ and Mangaba: Dynamical Geometry with a Distance Twist. Annals of The 5th International Conference on Technology in Mathematics Teaching, Klagenfurt: ICTMT-5, 2001.
11. Nonaka, I. & Konno, N.; The concept of "Ba": Building a Foundation for Knowledge Creation, California Management Review, Vol 40, No 3, 1998
12. Piaget, J.; Genetic Epistemology, Columbia University Press, NY, 1970
13. Pinto, G. et. Al; Spatial Data Integration in a Collaborative Design Framework, Communications of the ACM, vol 46, no. 3, March 2003
14. Roast, C., Ritchie, I. & Thomas, S.; Re-Creating the Reader: Supporting Active Reading in Literary Research; Communications of the ACM, vol 45, n. 10; October 2002
15. Shibata, H. & Hori, K.; A System to Support Long-term Creative Thinking in Daily Life and its Evaluation; Proceedings of Creativity & Cognition, 2002
16. Shneiderman, B.; Creating Creativity: User Interfaces for Supporting Innovation; ACM Transactions on Computer-Human Interaction, vol 7 n.1, March 2000
17. Shneiderman, B.; Creativity Support Tools; Communications of the ACM, vol 45, n. 10; October 2002
18. Smith, D.K.; Paradice, D.B. & Smith S.M., Prepare your mind for Creativity; Communications of the ACM, vol 43, n. 7; July 2000
19. Vygotsky, L.S.; A Formação Social da Mente, Editora Martins Fontes, 3a Edição, São Paulo, 1989 (translated from "Mind in Society: The Development of Higher Order Psychological Processes")

Experience in Developing a General Education Website

Keith Chan

Department of Computer Science
City University of Hong Kong
cskeith@cityu.edu.hk

Abstract. This paper presents some experience in developing and evaluating a new Web Based Learning project which was launched to serve the wide public audience. Technological and pedagogical considerations were included in the design. The effectiveness can be improved by the use of pilot class study in the middle of the development stage. Results are found to be useful in fine tuning the final courseware product. Post-implementation evaluation is performed based largely on online user feedback, together with other observations derived from the server log records.

1 Introduction

Web based Learning has rapidly emerged as an important method for effective teaching-learning. WBL overcomes the limitations of time and space and enables rich information to be utilized as study materials through multimedia. This new media of learning also enables dynamic interactions.

Health organizations have taken part in creating web sites to educate the public for some years. Prior to year 2000, all sites came with largely text information plus still pictures, more or less like electronic versions of many printed pamphlets. They have yet to exploit the potential of multimedia and user interactivity. The rapid development of Web software tools provides various convenient ways to create lively multimedia Web courseware.

The Health Care and Promotion Fund in Hong Kong has funded several health education projects on Internet since 1997. Internet offers a rich, collaborative learning environment, available anytime and from anywhere. It is seen as offering a new cost-effective alternative to traditional health education channels. This new sex health education project is a co-operative venture between computer systems development and community health education personnel. It explores the many software techniques to incorporate various multimedia and user interactions into the web pages for more effective education. The Department of Computer Science of City University develops the web pages and provides computer technical support. Knowledge providers are recruited from the community. Editing advice on the course materials are actively sought from United Christian Nethersole Community Health Service as well as from the Department of Community and Family Medicine, Chinese

W. Zhou et al. (Eds.): ICWL 2003, LNCS 2783, pp. 157–167, 2003.

University of Hong Kong. Their expert assistance is essential to the success of this project.

This website covers a range of topics on sex related diseases plus some daily living like dating and friendship, surfing sex explicit webpages, etc. The main target audience is teenagers. This age group has been identified to be the most popular audience from previous health education webpage projects. Actually this age group presents the greatest challenge for the developers. If the WBL product works well with the teenagers, it will generally satisfy most of the other age groups as well. Therefore the design and evaluation of this project focus quite specifically on teenage school children. Measurements of the effectiveness are derived from user feedback as well as the server log records.

2 Design Considerations

One shortcoming of WBL is the lack of face-to-face communication between teachers and students. It will weaken the motivation of the students if the course materials on the Web are not designed accordingly. Providing constant motivation to students is a crucial factor to achieve success in Web based learning. [1]

Motivation is an essential factor to students' actual study process. Specifically, motivation is crucial because the course content is planned to change students' values and to modify their pattern of behaviour [2].

Constructivism is a very important theory in effective learning. It is generally considered in the design and planning. The basic principles include learner construction of meaning, social interaction to help students learn, and student problem solving in real world contexts [3, 4].

Needless to say, pedagogical perspective is also an essential design element for e-learning [5]. Dynamic multimedia is the modern tool which enables more user interactions. Web based learning enables rich information to be utilized as study materials through text, graphics, sound and animation. Therefore the potential of active learning is undoubtedly high.

This new site is targeted for the young Web audience in Hong Kong. In mid-1997, the estimated Web population in Hong Kong alone was about 500,000. The majority of frequent users were students and young professionals aged between mid-teens and mid-thirties. The population surpassed the one million mark quickly in year 2000 with a strong upsurge of young school children as a result of the government support on the use of computers in schools. In other words, the average age of the rapidly expanding cyber population becomes younger.

To arouse the interest of the massive young audience, we deploy some modern multimedia software tools to develop a number of dynamic interactive web pages including some interactive games. As edutainment tools, several games are designed to reinforce some of the main messages of individual topics. The use of technology is very appropriate because the cognitive learning approach can be promoted.

On planning the content, some guidelines need to be considered [6]. What are the audience's attitudes in learning this subject? What are the factors that can encourage or discourage their learning? From their perspectives, are the presentations effective to these unknown remote learners? What is the relationship between attitude, factors, and their perceived effectiveness?

One practical consideration is the wordiness of the content. Many young teenagers may not prefer to read long paragraphs of words on Internet. Therefore, most of the pages are reduced to easy to understand messages of less than a total of 100 words. Occasionally hyperlinks are provided for the audience to read other relevant websites available on the Web if they wish to find out more details.

The physical data transmission speed is another practical limitation. While audience are more and more able to enjoy the faster broadband service, there are still others who access through ordinary telephone lines. As the ordinary telephone line data speed capacity remains quite static, it usually takes about 10 seconds to download 100 Kbytes of data. However, the determination to accommodate the widest possible audience includes satisfying the many economic ISP account users. This adds extra challenge and constraint considerations to deal with multimedia web page development work.

Therefore in order to keep all the audience to stay in touch, we need to ensure the web site is download time friendly to the general audience. In other words, all the individual pages are restricted to less than the size of 100 Kbytes. Any page that exceeds this limit is modified before it can be put out for public viewing. Fortunately, there have been new breakthroughs in recent multimedia animation technologies which can substantially optimize the file sizes. Besides, despite the usual large audio file size, some simple audio effects are also introduced in several appropriate situations. Hopefully the lengthy downloading problem of using video files can be overcome soon.

3   Pilot Tests for Effective Courseware Deliverable

In general, the effectiveness of development projects is measured by evaluation after the webpage is implemented. Depending on the responses from the Web audience, sometimes the data can be so scattered that meaningful follow up assessment is not too possible. There are also many cases which the budget becomes too tight when implementation is complete.

Besides, the hit rates usually give quantitative measurement of the volume of visitors. Some sophisticated software may help to yield hints of some general trends of audience behaviours, but may not necessarily be related to effectiveness or other quality of the Web course content.

This project on sex health education is targeted specifically at the teenagers in Hong Kong. It explores the use of some pilot tests in the middle of the development stage. The feedback collected from these taste tests is used to assess the sensitivity of the intended future audience. The result from analyzing on their feedback may steer the direction of subsequent development to yield a more successful final courseware product.

In March 2002, when the draft copy of the first three topics were ready for viewing, they were migrated to a new account for pilot class test viewing. The pilot classes were arranged with two secondary schools. Each school arranged two classes of students at different levels for the pilot tests.

During the pre-test trial in the first school, certain character strings or substring combinations of file names were found to be on their filter lists. Fortunately the problem was not too complicated. Nevertheless, it took us a few hours to rearrange the necessary file name changes and then the website was ready for the first pilot class on the next day.

Both schools took a high initiation in running the pilot tests. The two different classes came from two different grades of each school. They were scheduled to take a sex education class session arranged in the computer laboratory classroom. Each student sat before a terminal to browse freely the three available topics. At the end of the computer lab session, the students were asked to fill in the questionnaire on paper.

Each class of about 40 students was then divided into several smaller groups for group interview and discussion. In the open forum discussion, many students were enthusiastic in giving opinions freely. Some students co-operated extremely well with their faithful written recording. But, some lower forms students were found to be somewhat less enthusiastic in discussion. There could either be an age factor or the topics might not stimulate as much of their interest.

The questionnaires and small group discussion were collected and analyzed. The feedback data were then studied, classified and prioritized by the development team for enhancements in subsequent months.

Both schools are co-educational schools. As the male female ratios were about the same, varying from 50/50 to 40/60, opinions were collected equally from teenagers of different ages and from both sexes in these pilot class samples.

Overall the students agreed that the presentation and/or media used in the Web courseware could raise their interest in studying this subject. As far as the mode of study, about half thought Internet was the best way and 85% believed Internet was a very good way to study sex education. As these students got used to normal class learning with a live teacher, the online interactive approach through Internet was rated as the best mode by just 20%, however 98% agreed it was a good approach.

The picture became cautious and deserved our attention when it came to another question. While 95% indicated they would recommend this website to their friends, only less than one third expressed they would definitely do it.

Nevertheless, different students might have different expectations. Some were looking for just knowledge information in some areas, while others wanted to know the correct way and attitude in the subject of sex matters. Interestingly some indicated their desire to know only things that were not mentioned in textbooks at schools.

Overall, the enthusiasm from the students exceeded our expectation. Feedback was being recorded for analysis purpose [7]. This interim pilot test study provided us face to face meaningful contact with the intended audience during the development phase. Such encounters with the young audience provide us greater audience's sensitivity which helps to fine tune our final courseware deliverables.

The pilot tests really serve the purpose to obtain useful feedback from the intended audience. As the usual post implementation questionnaire evaluation may take a long time to obtain the same amount of useful feedback, the earlier pilot test detection is definitely a very useful way to achieving quality and effective Web courseware for the Web audience.

We appreciate the enthusiastic participation from staff and students of the two pilot test schools. The school management's unhesitant strong support is very much the key to the success.

4 Post-implementation Evaluation

Evaluation is an immense challenge to any kind of research. In measuring effectiveness of Web based learning, evaluation goes beyond just "how much?", but rather to concern itself with the question of "what value?".

There are various channels of evaluation:

4.1 Web Server Log Records File

From this faithful diary of Website, the log records provide the most complete history of server file access traffic activities. Software programs can be written to interrogate the log records in order to produce various forms of statistical management reports. The record format is rather standard and simple. Each record comes only with the file name being downloaded, the time and the destinations. The names of the files used in the courseware can be structured in a way that all those belong to the same topic come under the same prefix name. In this case, we are able to determine how long a user surfs within the different topics.

The number of server log records for each day is really huge and amazing. Therefore, the hit rate alone for any website can be very impressive as Internet is open to everybody without restrictions. Understandably, there are always casual visitors who drop into the website for a rather short period. Unlike the visual advertisements, Web based learning courseware usually expects some attentive learning involvement from the audience in order to become any meaningful encounter. Judging from the timestamps difference when we send out our files of different pages, it is encouraging that a good proportion of serious visitors stay tuned with the site for a reasonable period which makes meaningful learning contact with these educational messages.

A good appreciation of the health and sex education messages usually takes certain minimum duration. From the log records information, we attempt to isolate the casual Web surfers from the more serious audience who spend sufficient time like a minimum of 60 seconds with at least one of the available topics.

One advantage of Internet is its global exposure. The destination addresses sometimes give us some good ideas of where the audience come from. Within the first month after it went public, some IP addresses from several overseas countries were recorded. The scope of influence is expected to grow gradually. Despite the language restriction, some individual users from various parts of the world also find this education web site useful to them.

4.2 Feedback File

The final product with five topics was released to the public in December 2002. A questionnaire page is added to collect feedback from individual users. It is designed for easy to use. Most questions are in multiple choice format which aims to minimize the typing for the users. Users are also encouraged to express their free personal opinions as well.

All replies via the online feedback page are saved electronically. Similar to our previous similar projects, only about one out of ten Web visitors took the efforts to go through the online feedback form. There were few visitors found in the first few days. But as soon as the link was published in Chinese Yahoo, high volume of visitors jumped in like floodgate being opened. The average of over one hundred non casual visitors each day is overwhelming.

For the first three months, the volume of feedback has been encouraging with 300 to 500 replies each month. As there is a consistent daily average of over ten feedback replies, the sample size from each month is useful for analysis.

Based on the sample, more than 70% of the respondents are aged between 10 and 19. The age distribution agrees reasonably well with the planned target audience. The introduction of several interactive course materials may contribute to the somewhat larger low teens audience. Another over 10% come from aged 20 to 24 which implies

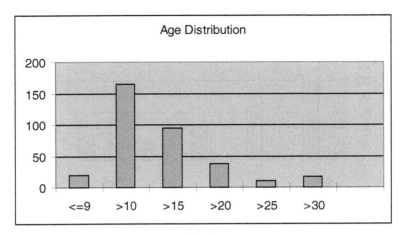

Fig. 1.

certain popularity in this age group also. As for the sex audience penetration, the male female ratio is 52:48 which indicates the website appeals quite equally to the Web audience from both sexes.

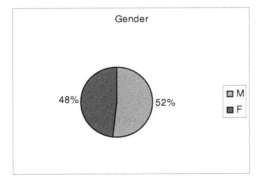

Fig. 2.

More than 50% of the respondents indicate their interests in viewing both the topics of Dating/ Friendship as well as Cyber Sex. From results of other previous projects, the first topic used to be the most popular topic for the young audience. Being the close second, the new topic on Cyber Sex is found to be very appealing to the modern young audience despite the title is not entirely pleasant to some female audience. On a closer examination of the audience by sex, 20% more female than male audience find the topic of dating interesting. But, on the other hand, 30% less female than male audience find the topic of cyber sex interesting. Nevertheless, both these topics have been the most visited topics by the young audience for the past three months.

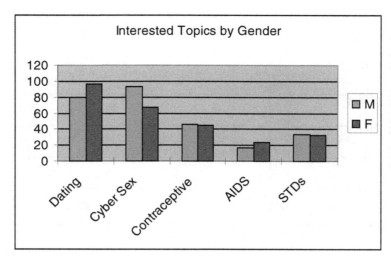

Fig. 3.

Besides dating and cyber sex, the topic on Contraceptive is visited by about 30% of the audience. The other two topics on diseases are relatively less popular. The young audience may not think these diseases are relevant to their daily lives or urgent to their friends and families. This is not too surprising as teenage school children may not be able to show much concern on diseases like AIDS or STD's. Anyway the topic on sexually transmitted diseases is well received by 20% of our audience and the one on AIDS is well received by 15%. Nevertheless, these health disease topics are rated useful or very useful by a decisive majority of their respective audience regardless of their popularity

As far as personal text comments, only several written comments are received each month. A few suggestions are saved for future considerations.

As the website is only listed in Chinese Yahoo. So at the beginning, the majority of our audience indicated their discovery of our website through Chinese Yahoo. However, some respondents began to quote other search engines after the first month. And others indicate their being referred by their own friends. These referrals are strong indication of some audience who have found the web courseware useful and worthy of recommendation.

4.3 Spontaneous Referrals

One popular way to promote a new website is to publicize actively through the media, including listing among a number of popular search engines. This undoubtedly can bring in good volumes of newcomers to the website for sometime.

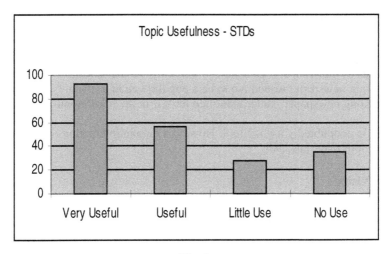

Fig. 4.

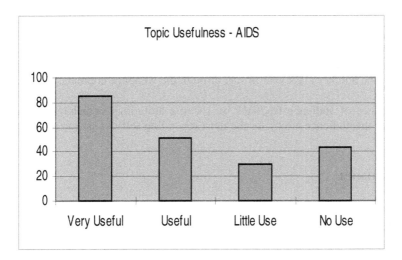

Fig. 5.

But for confirmation of the quality of courseware, it would have to take the active publicity from the audience rather than from the content providers. In the first three months, we recorded a good number of feedbacks from the audience indicating they were being referred to visit the new site by their own friends.

Starting from the second month, we recorded new indications that some were being referred to by their own parents, and some by their teachers. Since sex education is a rather sensitive issue among Chinese communities, the active referrals by concerned parents and teachers to their dear young partners are special breakthroughs from traditional culture. These referrals by mature audience are formidable signs of high acceptance of the courseware content and presentation on the Web.

Also in the second month, a few respondents indicated they were being referred to visit this site by newspapers. Despite the site aims at the teenagers in Hong Kong region, the first newspaper turned out to be a popular one in Taiwan. Nevertheless, the first Hong Kong newspaper reader identified herself in the third month.

E-Learning is undoubtedly a good tool. However, human interaction is still necessary in assessment of materials. [8]

4.4 Class Visits

Also in the third month, there were two instances where a teacher might make use of the availability and convenience to conduct a class visit to our website. In the first instance, there were half a dozen individual teenagers who sent their feedback to us within the same one hour period. A look up to the server log confirms all of them came from the same Internet service node. A conducted group visit to the Website is a clear recognition of the courseware being useful and effective.

Several days later, the online feedback file recorded an even larger group of teenagers within a 30 minutes period. All members of this larger group were confirmed to come from another Internet node address. Based on the server log file records, they were believed to be another class visit to surf through the webpage contents.

In the absence of audience feedback on specific attitudinal or behavioural changes, referrals by the audience are by far the most rewarding self-evaluation at this stage.

5 Conclusion

Using modern multimedia in delivering educational topics through Internet can be successful and persuasive than just texts and pictures. It will have a greater impact on the younger generations both locally and worldwide. The Internet can become the most influential technology in providing support to general education.

The effectiveness of Web based learning can be enhanced through listening to the intended audience. From this experience, the interim pilot class study can be instrumental to such success. The many referrals by the open audience as friends, concerned parents, and newspaper editors provide very positive assessments. The teachers who recommend the website to individual students or conduct group online visits are actually solid partners of Web based learning.

References

1. W. Jun, L. Gruenwald, J. Park, S. Hong "A Web based Motivation-Supporting Model for Effective Teaching-Learning" pp.44-55, Advances in Web Based Learning, 1st International Conference on Web based Learning, Hong Kong 2002
2. Jang, S "A study on Contents Development for Improving Learning Fulfillment", The Proceedings of KAIE, Vol 6, No.2, 2001 pp. 369–387
3. Abbey, B. "Instructional and Cognitive Impacts of Web-based Education", Idea Group Publishing, London 2000
4. Jonassen, D., Peck, K., and Wilson, B., "Learning with Technology: A Constructivist Perspective", Prentice Hall, Upper Saddle River, NJ, USA 1999
5. Ishaya T., Gussious S., Jenkins C.M. "Integrating Multimedia and Software Agents for Effective Web-based Learning" Web based Learning : Men & Machines 2002 pp. 80–92
6. Chan M. "The Effectiveness of Using Computer-Mediated Instruction in Distance Mathematics Education" Web based Learning : Men & Machines 2002 pp. 242–253
7. Chan K.   "Pilot Test for Effective Education Website" Proceedings of Hong Kong International Medical Informatics Conference, 2003
8. Mukherjee D. "Do Students actually Learn Online?" Proceedings of the Fourth IASTED International Conference on Computer and Advanced Technology in Education 2001, Banff, pp. 135–138
9. Chin F., Wong, C., Mak V. "Experience in Running a Flexible, Web-Based, and Self-Paced Course" Advances in Web based Learning, First ICWL 2002, Hong Kong, pp. 241–251

Interface Metaphors and Web-Based Learning

Sarah Guss

University of Melbourne and RMIT University, School of Business Information Technology,
239 Bourke Street, Melbourne, Victoria 3000, Australia
sarah.guss@rmit.edu.au

Abstract. In building an effective Web-based learning system, consideration must be given to not only the educational content and learning activities but also to the design of the human computer interface (HCI). When the interface is difficult to use it can interfere with learning. Whilst this is a critical aspect, the design of this element is often overlooked in the rush to get our materials on the web. The considered use of interface metaphors not only complements the overall HCI design process, but also allows the user to quickly move beyond the mechanics of the interface itself to the more important goal of learning the content. This paper provides examples of how interface metaphors have been used in software and discusses how we might leverage off their use in our future designs.

1 Introduction

In the rush to get on the web, Human Computer Interface guidelines and principles are largely being ignored [1, 2]. This results in the development of a web site that is difficult to use. The inherent problem is that a student, who spends time trying to understand the interface, wastes cognitive resources on navigation. This can interfere with learning the content [3]. Therefore it is critical that our learning web sites are designed with an interface that is easy to use.

The first fundamental design principle included in Apple Computer's *Human Interface Guidelines* is 'Use concrete metaphors and make them plain, so that users have a set of expectations to apply to computer environments' [4] (p3). Amongst Nielsen's [5] ten usability principles is the principle of 'speak the users' language' (p20). He suggests a way to achieve this is through the use of metaphors. Heckel [6] describes metaphors as leveraging off the users' knowledge. In one of her four high-level guiding principles for design of user interfaces, Preece [7] suggests the use of metaphors to 'maintain consistency and clarity' as they 'help to build and maintain a user's mental model of a system' (p488).

This paper discusses to what extent metaphors have been used in the interface, provides examples as illustrations and highlights aspects about metaphors that need to be considered in the design of web-based learning materials.

W. Zhou et al. (Eds.): ICWL 2003, LNCS 2783, pp. 168–179, 2003.
© Springer-Verlag Berlin Heidelberg 2003

2 Interface Metaphors

Metaphors are often used in speech to help illustrate or explain something that we cannot express literally. We also employ metaphors in teaching to help students understand new concepts. Intentionally or unintentionally, metaphors have also been used in software and now in pages on the Web. An example that immediately comes to mind is the use of the word web. The word helps describe the network of information that is available on the Internet. We take it for granted now, but when the concept was first introduced, it enhanced our understanding of the complex structure of the Internet. Other examples of familiar terms used for the Internet include information superhighway, bookmarks, virtual community, chat rooms etc.

Metaphors can be invoked through the use of a word or sentence and also through icons or graphics. Words such as file, folder, cut, copy and paste are words that have meaning in the real world. When these words are used in the digital world, their familiarity aids our use of the software. Icons representing these words invoke similar metaphors. It may be that individual icons such as the scissors ✂ for cutting, or a full screen graphic such as that shown below, invoke a metaphor. The graphic below, depicting a road with signs, is used as a site map. Colours can be used to further enhance connections between the old and the new, such as a yellow background used for an on-line yellow pages telephone directory [8]. Other colours such as red for stop (as in the case of the stop icon in Internet Explorer) and green for go can be used effectively. All these different elements can be employed in the interface to build a consistent overall look and feel for how to use the system.

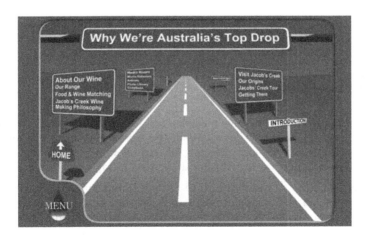

Fig. 1. Example from *http://www.jacobscreek.com.au/main.htm*

3 Metaphors Invoked through Terminology and Icons

Terms such as bookmark immediately present us with the idea that we can mark our current place so that we can return later. Browse or surf the web makes us think of skimming over the surface of the information (like browsing through the bookstore looking at book covers) in search of what we want. Electronic mail makes use of our familiarity with traditional mail by using icons and terminology based on this metaphor. In this software, an envelope is used to represent an email message 🖃 and an envelope with its flap up indicates the "letter" has been opened 🖂. The paperclip beside the letter 🖂📎 indicates that there is an attachment to the mail. The icons used for the mailbox 📭📬 are also recognisable. Without having to read any instructions, we immediately have an understanding of what is happening. Shopping web sites are another example in which we use a metaphor. We can "gather" things in our shopping cart/trolley 🛒 and view what it holds during our shopping "expedition".

People tend to think that metaphors are only invoked through pictures. Even though it is more likely that a metaphor will be visual in graphical user interfaces [9], metaphors will be invoked not only through the icons or graphics used in the interface but also through the terminology used. It may be the way the entire screen elements are constructed, and continued through with the use of the terminology that calls for the sense of familiarity. If the entire system is well designed beyond the initial screen, an overall understanding, or conceptual framework may also be formed. This provides us with an general "feel" for the way things work, enabling us to look beyond the one static screen and see the entire Web site or system in some kind of overall structure via an overarching metaphor.

4 Overarching Metaphors

The most well known overarching metaphor is that of the desktop. The desktop metaphor became more widely known when the Apple Macintosh was introduced. The metaphor invoked through the use of terminology surrounding an office environment was extended in the Macintosh desktop metaphor with the inclusion of icons to represent files 📄 and folders 📁. Apple Computer did this to provide an interface that enabled non-computer literate people, who were familiar with the way an office worked, to use the operating system with greater ease [4]. This wasn't the first interface metaphor employed. The first text editing software (precursor to word processors of today) employed the typewriting metaphor [10]. The spreadsheet programs of today were introduced using an accountant's ledger. The desktop metaphor has now become ubiquitous [11].

With each of these metaphors, desktop, typewriter and ledger, there was an underlying assumption that people worked in an office, or used a typewriter or had some accounting knowledge. However, if this is not the case, the user cannot rely on knowledge gained through experience and so the metaphor fails. If we are to build effective interfaces employing metaphors, we must make sure that the users can understand the metaphors we are implying in the interface. There is no point in using, for example, a desktop metaphor for children who have never experienced an office. A commonly used set of icons are those of a VCR but again if someone has never used anything resembling one, they will not understand how to use the buttons for play, rewind, fast forward etc. With the large number of international students who may be using our websites, even more careful thought needs to be given to choice of metaphors to ensure that the experiences we are drawing on are globally understood.

5 Examples of Interface Metaphors

Two examples of educational software that incorporate metaphors in the interface were created at the University of Wollongong. The first, *Investigating Lake Iluka*, uses a notebook metaphor. The notebook enables the student to keep notes about their investigations as well as to navigate by clicking on the "tabs" on the side of the notebook. Some of the other icons/metaphors included are the pencil for taking notes, the scissors for cutting (and pasting) and toolkits for selecting the necessary tools to take measurements.

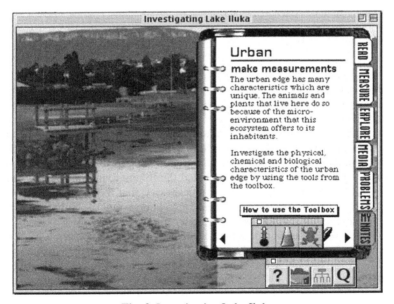

Fig. 2. Investigating Lake Iluka

The second example Exploring the Nardoo uses a Personal Digital Assistant (PDA) for navigation and taking notes. It also includes other metaphors such as a noticeboard holding the pictures of the regions to be explored, a filing cabinet containing tabbed folders that hold documents, a book with pictures that has chapters and a table of contents etc.

Fig. 3. Exploring the Nardoo

6   Case Study Evidence

Evidence was found by Smilowitz in 1996 [12], that the use of metaphors in interface design aided performance. Two experiments were conducted with subjects who were asked to find specific information on the Web but had never used a Web browser before. In the first experiment there were four different designs tested: two without metaphors used in the terminology (that is using terminology from the *Mosaic* software), one of which had icons, another with the library metaphor used in the terminology and then finally icons were added in to support this metaphor. To invoke the library metaphor, terms and icons reflected the things found in a library such as a reference section and bookmarks. The results showed that the use of icons seemed to have no additional value (with or without metaphors) but the subjects performed better with the metaphor invoked through the terminology.

The second experiment was designed to investigate which specific characteristics of the metaphor contributed to its success. In this experiment the conditions were the use of a library metaphor, a travel metaphor and a composite (combination of the travel and library) metaphor. The travel metaphor was invoked through the use of items such as travel log and shortcut. The results of this experiment showed that subjects performed best when using the library metaphor. The results from both experiments suggested that performance was aided by the use of a metaphor. The metaphor was invoked through the terminology used, rather than the icons and an integral metaphor was found to be better than a composite one [12].

7 Failure of the Interface Metaphor

Perhaps the travel metaphor used in Smilowitz's experiment may not have worked as well as that of the library because of the way it was implemented. That is the terminology used may have been inappropriate. For instance the word bookmark used in the library metaphor was replaced with the word shortcut in the travel metaphor and Reference Section was replaced with TourBook. These words do not seem to imply the same thing. In attempting to use the travel metaphor, the students may not have seen a relationship between the terms used and their task at hand. The problem may also have been that the travel metaphor was inappropriate altogether in this instance. (Although travelling does not seem inconsistent with what happens on the Internet.) Choosing an appropriate metaphor is not easy. The relationship between the metaphor used and the way the interface operates needs to be consistent or compatible [13].

The results of the experiments also led Smilowitz to conclude that an integral metaphor is preferable to a composite one. This is inconclusive, as the composite metaphor used may not have succeeded due to the fact that a library and travel seem to be totally unrelated. This situation of "mixed metaphors" might have created a sense of confusion – am I travelling across the web or am I searching a library? It would have been better to use a different combination with one used as the overriding or primary metaphor and a secondary one which could somehow be related to it.

A further example of poor implementation of an interface metaphor is that of the shopping trolley metaphor. To buy an item or put something in our shopping trolley you just click on the item or "buy" button. But if you want more than one of that particular item, you need to increase the number displayed next to the description of the item selected. The same problem occurs when you decide to take something "out" of the trolley, you need to set the number of items to zero [14]. A further example can be seen in the Macintosh desktop metaphor where the trash can is used to not only delete files but also to eject disks, which is confusing. For this reason Nelson argues against the use of metaphors [15]. He complains that once metaphors are used, every part of the interface must fit into the same metaphor. Cates [13] provides several successful examples where this is not the case. One example he gives is that of a book metaphor which includes a video control so that the user can listen to recorded sound. The other is of a map metaphor, which includes a magnifying glass to see an enlargement of the map.

Inconsistencies may also present problems but this is not always the case. The magnifying glass has been used successfully in a variety of software applications, but for different purposes. In *Microsoft Word* it is used on the print preview icon ⌕. In the *Microsoft Windows* operating system it is used on the ⌕ find file icon. What is important is the extent to which the metaphor helps the user know how the system will react in response to their actions [16].

An additional concern with respect to metaphors is the extent to which they are limiting, that is not showing the full scope of the software [5, 8, 17]. Nielsen provides the example of the wordprocessor, which uses the typewriter metaphor. The "search and replace" facility is available in a word processor, but not on a typewriter [5]. Another example of this is the clipboard used for cutting and pasting items. A physical clipboard allows us to attach a number of pieces of paper like the computer counterpart, but the computer clipboard also allows us to make multiple copies of a 'sheet of paper'. Rosenfeld also mentions the limitations from the opposite perspective [8]. For example, the physical library has a librarian to answer questions but (according to him) most digital libraries do not have this facility. Both limitations can be overcome by incorporating additional features in the design via complementary metaphors.

8 Choice of the Overarching Metaphor

The problem of trying to fit all the components of the interface to the one metaphor can be solved through the use of composite metaphors – that is, more than one metaphor. An underlying or primary metaphor provides the overall context, with auxiliary or secondary metaphors used to extend the concept [7, 10, 13]. The design of a composite metaphor is not easy. The greater the contrast between the underlying metaphor and the auxiliary metaphor, the greater the cognitive load it puts on the user to try to understand how the secondary metaphor fits in [13] . A composite metaphor was used in the development of software entitled *The Funeral of Edgar* [9]. The primary metaphor used was that of a funeral with secondary metaphors being eulogies and ghosts etc. The software was designed in this way in the hope that there would be better understanding of Edgar Allan Poe's poem *The Raven* through greater learner involvement with all aspects of the poem.

The design of this software went through a number of iterations [9]. The initial metaphor used was one of a bookshelf but there were activities (such as navigation) that did not fit into the bookshelf metaphor so the designers decided to use auxiliary metaphors. To do this without confounding the user, they felt they needed to choose a much better primary metaphor to contain the auxiliary or secondary metaphors. Since the main theme of the poem is death the next metaphor tried was that of a cemetery. Not satisfied that this metaphor allowed for sufficient engagement, they finally moved to a funeral metaphor. This resulted in the addition of a third dimension – time and provided a good overarching metaphor which could include many more secondary metaphors. In creating the funeral process, they felt that all the elements could be incorporated into the metaphor without causing confusion and allowing for more involvement and believability, expecting that this would be better for the students understanding [9]. The result of all of these iterations was the creation of a composite metaphor that included a primary metaphor with sufficient scope for allowing auxiliary metaphors that were complementary.

9 Metaphors and the Web

Siegel [18] calls metaphors used on the web 'vehicles of exploration' that 'guide a visitor and glue a site together' making it 'difficult to get lost' (p36). With Web based learning, the learner is presented with only one screen full of information at a time. This creates a need to remember the way all of these pieces of information fit together, thereby increasing the learner's cognitive load [19]. In order for the user to be able to navigate and learn from a system, it is necessary to provide a framework or structure so that the user can know what the boundaries and spatial distribution of things are [20]. The web-learner needs to be oriented – know where they are (and how they got there), where they have been and where to go next. Visual cues used on the web such as highlighted tabs, chapter headings or menu options help the learners orient themselves as far as where they are now, but it does not help answer the other questions. This is where a well-designed interface metaphor can be of great value. It can provide the subliminal support to the user, both for navigation and information structuring.

Quite a number of web sites use tabs. These seem to help the user's orientation by defining a structure; showing where the user is by having the selected tab highlighted; where they can go to by the other tabs being visible; and the full extent of the site (as long as there are no hidden levels). Blackboard and WebCT are two software packages which allow us to build on-line learning sites. Both of these use tabs in their interface. Another commonly used style with the same characteristics is shown in the web sites with menu bars on the sides of the page. (Sometimes these are better as they can show further levels by expansion of a menu item.)

Both of these metaphors, tabs and menu bars, seem to behave very much like a traditional book. They do not seem to represent the full power of what can be done over the Internet. Whether you are physically turning pages or electronically choosing to go to the next page by clicking on a tab or button, there is still the same level of interaction. They each have the same defined structure and each can be "put down" and another book or site can be "picked up" when you wish to move on.

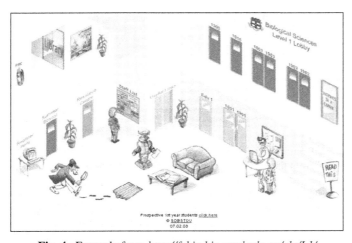

Fig. 4. Example from _http://fybio.bio.usyd.edu.au/vle/L1/_

Two examples that can be seen on the Web begin with a "front end" to the site. The Biology web site from the University of Sydney (see above) shows a "lobby" with different objects to click on to navigate to another level. For example, the lift labelled Useful Links takes the user to sites such as a Learning Centre and Student Services; the robot (Cyber-Tech) allows the user to ask questions; doors lead into "rooms" which provide access to study materials. Going to the Resource Centre opens up another similar room/screen but beyond that the site does not appear to carry the metaphor all the way through to other levels.

Another example (shown below) is that of the Business Computing 1 subject run at RMIT University. This begins with a reception area that has three modes of entry: on-line resources, administration and assessment.

Fig. 5. Example from *ISYS2056 Business Computing 1*

Fig. 6. Example from the second level of the *ISYS2056 Business Computing 1* resources.

At the next level for the on-line resources, the student can choose to take one of three pathways through the content. By choosing the calendar they navigate the weekly topics, choosing the book allows them to navigate by topic and choosing the factory allows them to move through by case study. The pathway they choose is represented at the underlying levels by a graphic watermark on each page. This gives some consistency through to the lower levels. However the designers are considering whether to further support the user's navigation by extending the metaphor through to the lower levels. The book metaphor could be extended by depicting a book with tabs (as in *Investigating Lake Iluka*) and using a table of contents. The calendar metaphor could be extended by allowing the user to choose a particular week by clicking on the appropriate date on the calendar and so on.

10   Learning Scaffolds to Support New Users

When using software or a web site for the first time, the student needs to be able to understand what needs to be done and to be able to predict how the software will behave in response to their actions, so that they can get on with gaining knowledge about the subject matter. Metaphors can help in this initial understanding of the system [10]. These support mechanisms or 'learning scaffolds' are necessary to begin with, but once they are no longer needed they should change and fade into the background [21] (p53).

The designers of *Investigating Lake Iluka* provided alternative means of navigation to that of the notebook metaphor. The user can also use the system through a "stack map", that is a hierarchical site map. Anecdotal evidence suggests that users, once familiar with the way the program works, move away from using the notebook metaphor and use the stack map as a quicker means of access. The more experienced user no longer needs the "scaffolds" and can use "short cuts" to move around the now familiar environment. Once the user has learnt the system the metaphor becomes less important and fades [7]. Many people who use the desktop metaphor today do not realize the significance of it and forget that it helped them understand what they were doing when they first were exposed to using an operating system.

Youth of today have no experience of a typewriter and therefore would not be able to draw on the typewriter metaphor in their initial use of a word processor. More than likely they would have had to learn how to use other things as well, such as the desktop or clipboard without understanding the intended metaphor behind them. Nevertheless, when something is unfamiliar, the user will try to make sense of it by relating to something they already know. In whichever way the user may have become familiar with the system in the first place, they then have a new metaphor that they can draw on in the future. Metaphors such as the desktop, shopping and VCR controls have become standards that we can leverage off in the future [2].

So it is in the initial stages that a metaphor can help or hinder the use of the software or web-based learning materials. If any icon or way the software operates is unfamiliar or different to what the students are used to, they will lose confidence and have difficulty working with it. This is where it is important not to "distract" our students from the learning through hard to use systems. This may happen because an icon invokes the wrong metaphor or the metaphor is unfamiliar. At a Teaching and Learning Forum, a speaker was showing a site, which included an icon representing a coffee mug. A number of audience members questioned its functionality. It was shown to only be there for "fun" and had no real purpose. It actually proved to be a distraction from the actual site. It illustrates the point that every element should be considered carefully as to how it fits into the users mental model of the system in order not to create confusion.

11   Conclusion

Regardless of individual preference and opinions, according to Marcus [22] *all* our communication involves the use of metaphors. As a consequence, he believes that interfaces will *always* include metaphors. Furthermore, whether an interface is intentionally designed to include metaphors or not, the user will most likely perceive metaphors in the interface [10]. Choosing the appropriate metaphor is not easy but if it is done with care, it can help the initial use of a system, whether web-based or not. Therefore, when designing our web-based learning materials, we need to consider carefully what metaphors we can leverage off to help the students' understanding of the system's interface. This will ensure that their cognitive resources are not wasted on learning how to use the system and instead be expended on the learning of the subject matter content.

So far there are no definitive guidelines for metaphor use in the interface. Extensive research needs to be conducted to investigate how metaphors can be used effectively in order to prepare such guidelines. Until then the following are reminders of what we should consider when using interface metaphors. Careful choice of metaphors should ensure that the metaphor helps, rather than hinders the student. Choosing the appropriate metaphor involves thought about the prior knowledge the students bring to the experience. We need to think about the students' education and cultural background as well as what other software or web sites they may have experienced. More than one metaphor can be used but there should be one overarching or primary metaphor with the secondary metaphor or metaphors used to extend it. The overarching metaphor should be broad enough to be all encompassing. The metaphor and the way each of its elements works should fit in with the user's prior experience. (Don't include "coffee cups" just because they look nice.) Consider the different ways metaphors can be invoked, not only through icons and graphics but also through the terminology used. The whole metaphor should be kept "in play" by "tying all the pieces together" through the consistent use of icons and terminology which support the chosen metaphor.

References

1. Anderson, R., Conversations with Clement Mok and Jakob Nielsen, and with Bill Buxton and Clifford Nass. interactions, 2000(january+february): p. 47–63.
2. Pearrow, M., Web Site Usability Handbook. 2000: Charles River Media.
3. Paolucci, R., The Effects of Cognitive Style and Knowledge Structure on Performance Using a Hypermedia Learning System. Journal of Educational Multimedia and Hypermedia, 1998. 7(2/3): p. 123–150.
4. Apple Computer Inc., Human Interface Guidelines: The Apple Desktop Interface. 1987: Addison-Wesley Publishing Company Inc.
5. Nielsen, J., Usability Engineering. 1993: Academic Press.
6. Heckel, P., The Elements of Friendly Software Design. 2 ed. 1991: Sybex.
7. Preece, J., et al., Human-Computer Interaction. 1994: Addison-Wesley.
8. Rosenfeld, L. and P. Morville, Information Architecture for the World Wide Web. Second ed. 2002: O'Reilly & Associates.
9. Bishop, M.J. and W.M. Cates, A Door is a Big Wooden Thing with a Knob: Getting a Handle on Metaphorical Interface Design., in Proceedings of Selected Research and Development Presentations at the 1996 National Convention of the Association for Educational Communications and Technology. 1996: Indianapolis. p. 80–88.
10. Carroll, J.M., R.L. Mack, and W.A. Kellogg, Interface Metaphors and User Interface Design, in Handbook of Human-Computer Interaction, M. Helander, Editor. 1988, Elsevier Science Publishing Company: North Holland. p. 67–85.

11. Myers, B.A., A Brief History of Human-Computer Interaction Technology. Interactions, 1998. **v**(2): p. 44–54.
12. Smilowitz, E.D., Do Metaphors Make Web Browsers Easier to Use?, www.baddesigns.com/mswebcnf.htm, 1996 (7 March 2001)
13. Cates, W.M., Designing Hypermedia is Hell: Metaphor's Role in Instructional Design, in Paper presented at the annual meeting of the Association for Educational Communications and Technology. 1994: Nashville, TN. p. 95–108.
14. Nielsen, J., Designing Web Usability. 2000: New Riders Publishing.
15. Nelson, T.H., The Right Way to Think About Software Design, in The Art of Human-Computer Interface Design, B. Laurel, Editor. 1990, Addison-Wesley. p. 235–243.
16. Blake, T., Adventures with Hybrid Systems: Integrating the Macintosh Interface with External Devices, in The Art of Human-Computer Interface Design, B. Laurel, Editor. 1990, Addison-Wesley. p. 289–297.
17. Cooper, A., About Face: The Essentials of User Interface Design. 1995, Foster City, CA: IDG Books Worldwide.
18. Siegel, D., Creating Killer Web Sites. 1996: Hayden Books.
19. Oren, T., Cognitive Load in Hypermedia: designing for the Exploratory Learner, in Learning with Interactive Multimedia, S. Ambron and K. Hooper, Editors. 1990, Microsoft Press: Washington. p. 125–136.
20. Semper, R., HyperCard and Education: Reflections on the HyperBoom, in Learning with Interactive Multimedia, S. Ambron and K. Hooper, Editors. 1990, Microsoft Press: Washington. p. 51–67.
21. Hsi, S. and E. Soloway, Learner-Centred Design: Specifically Addressing the Needs of Learners. SIGCHI Bulletin, 1998. **30**(4): p. 53–55.
22. Marcus, A., Metaphors and User Interfaces in the 21st Century. interactions, 2002. **IX.2**: p. 7–10.

Mapping Pedagogy to Technology – A Simple Model

Jo Coldwell

School of Information Technology,
Deakin University, Geelong, VIC, Australia 3217
jojo@deakin.edu.au

Abstract. As academics we are often encouraged to "go online" by our institution, by either moving or supplementing our teaching in an online environment. We have several options. We could simply attempt to replicate our face-to-face teaching, in effect changing nothing; we can enhance our face-to-face teaching with the available technology; or we can transform our face-to-face teaching by the available technology. The approach we choose will be determined by several factors, one of which will be our existing knowledge of the technological environment we are using. In this paper I propose a simple framework which provides novice eTeachers in particular with a simple mapping from classroom activity to technological functionality, reducing the need to have extensive technological literacy of the learning environment when designing online activities initially.

1 Introduction

In February this year, Deakin University launched Deakin Studies Online (DSO), its institution-wide learning management system (LMS) powered by WebCT Vista. Previously academics had a variety of applications available to them to support teaching and learning. These included TopClass, FirstClass, WebCT 3.6, custom-built systems and web pages, as well as email lists and bulletin boards.

Deakin University has been supporting distance education students in particular with online technologies since before the dawn of LMS's. The University has now prescribed that by 2004 all award courses will have a presence online consisting of at least "… unit information, a notice board, a resource repository and a means of communication between students and their lecturers." [4] Considerable time and money has been invested in the implementation of DSO, as well as providing appropriate initial training and ongoing professional development for all staff (both academic and administrative) who need access to the online environment.

Despite Deakin University's history with the use of online learning technologies, there is still a relatively large proportion of faculty who do not use online tools to support their teaching and, even worse, are not particularly computer literate. Reasons put forward for not using technologies range from discomfiture with the technology, a negative experience of previous attempts at going online, concerns regarding increased workloads, through to concerns regarding students' ability to access online materials.

W. Zhou et al. (Eds.): ICWL 2003, LNCS 2783, pp. 180–192, 2003.

Such staff will need to be coaxed into using the new online environment in a gentle and sympathetic way if the University's requirement for 100% basic presence online by 2004 is going to be met.

Moving any teaching activity into an online environment requires more than training in the online technology. The course designers may need to think outside the square of traditional pedagogies in order to add value to the students' learning experience. How far outside the square will depend very much on the confidence of the eTeacher as well as the eLearners. The imperative to go further online than the basic prescribed by the University will depend on many factors including the student cohort (such as distance education students), additional learning outcomes of the activity and so on.

In the following sections I elaborate on the approach I took when faced with the prospect of teaching online. I discuss briefly some pedagogies that lend themselves to online delivery. I develop the simple model by considering the basic components of eTeaching and online delivery and present a mapping of the components to the functionalities provided by most eLearning environments. I demonstrate the approach with reference to the eLearning environments that I am currently using to support my online teaching and indicate how the model has been used successfully to develop faculty's awareness of how LMS functionality can facilitate learning online.

2   Teaching Computer Ethics Online

The computer ethics unit (a core unit of study in the B. Computing degree) was designed for delivery to on-campus students in the traditional face-to-face manner. In 1997, I was given the task of converting the unit for off-campus delivery. The philosophy underlying the teaching in this unit is that students earning by doing and so discussions and collaborative work were emphasised. Initially I decided to concentrate on the group discussion aspect of the pedagogy. Having identified an appropriate tool (FirstClass conferencing software) to support the type of group discussions I wished students to undertake I had to convince the students to take part in them. Attendance at tutorials is compulsory for on-campus students and I naively thought that off-campus students could be coaxed into the online forum using a similar approach. Unfortunately, the off-campus students thought otherwise! This proved to be a tractable problem however, when I realized that carrots worked better than sticks and made tutorial participation an assessable component of the unit.

While running the unit for the first time I realized that the workload associated with running face-to-face as well as online tutorials could be minimized if one was eliminated. I could not remove the online tutorials unless I made major changes to the unit as approximately 50% of the students enrolled in the unit were off-campus. The alternative was to remove the face-to-face tutorials and move the on-campus students into the online forum. They too could benefit from the online experience. The following year I included these students in the online discussions as well. This proved to have some unexpected benefits. Many off campus students had never had the opportunity of studying in the same forum as on campus students and vice versa. Also, off campus students were more likely to be already working in the IT industry. Their input provided a very different perspective to the discussions than those held by groups of wholly on campus students. But again, a carrot had to be provided to overcome the wails of horror as on-campus students complained of being disadvantaged as their face-to-face contact with academics in the unit had been reduced. The carrot was the experience of communicating and collaborating in a formal manner in the online environment – a skill that could be added to their curriculum vitae.

More and more activities have been moved to the online learning environment to the point were this unit is fully online with no face-to-face contact. All learning activities are completed online, students working collaboratively in discussions, projects and other exercises in groups which cross temporal and geographic boundaries. Students undertake discussions, collaborative group work (including document preparation) and some assignment work in the online environment. They are encouraged to use online resources such as the library, reputable Internet sites and online study skills tutorials. Assignment submission, recording of marks and grades and return of markers comments are completed online. Communication with unit staff is online. Most communication and collaboration is undertaken in asynchronous mode to accommodate the various time zones that students live in. However, some tutor-student consultation occurs in synchronous chat rooms. The design of the unit online is described in detail in Coldwell [3].

The transformation process from a mix of face-to-face and online to totally online, has taken place over 4 years with further minor amendments happening with each offering of the unit since 2000. The process could have been considerably shortened if I had a better knowledge in the early design stages of what activities were possible to implement in an online environment. Unfortunately I discovered *how* to use the technology before knowing *what* was possible in the technology. Hence the trial and error nature of the transformation and the amount of time that it took to complete.

3 Some Pedagogical Theories and Models

Much has been written on pedagogies that support online teaching and learning. A variety of theories and models have been suggested and tested in the eLearning world and it is beneficial to look at some briefly before considering the generic components of eTeaching. The approach I have taken here is to select some key pedagogies that have influenced or been directly applicable to the online environment. The aim here is to highlight the key features of the pedagogies and models rather than investigating the educational philosophy underlying them. This will provide the basis of the eTeaching model introduced below. The material presented in this section is based on that presented in the Theory Into Practice (TIP) database [11].

3.1 Anchored Instruction

Anchored instruction is a paradigm originated by the Cognition & Technology Group at Vanderbilt (CTGV) and is attributed to John Bransford [1]. It is based on a general model of problem solving and has a strong emphasis on using technology to support learning. The main principles of the paradigm are that:

- learning and teaching activities are designed around a situation (the anchor) which may be a case-study or problem situation for example, and
- the student should be encouraged to explore the curriculum content in the context of the situation.

3.2 Conditions of Learning

Gagne [5] put forward the conditions of learning theory which proposes that there are different levels of learning each requiring different types of instruction. The major categories of learning are verbal information, intellectual skills, cognitive strategies, motor skills and attitudes. As detailed in Gagne, Briggs and Wager [6] the theory serves as a basis for designing instruction and, more importantly from the perspective of this paper, selecting appropriate media. The key principles of the theory are:

- different instruction is required for different learning outcomes,
- learning events impact on the learning in ways that constitute the conditions of learning,
- the type of learning outcome expected dictates the make up of instructional events,
- learning hierarchies define what intellectual skills are to be learned and how instruction is sequenced.

The theory emphasizes the enhancement of learner performance is achieved by ensuring learning activities are well defined. It is compatible with web-based courses.

3.3 Constructivist Model

Bruner's constructivist model [2] identifies learners as actively participating in the knowledge acquisition process by building on the framework of their current knowledge. It is diametrically opposed to the instructivist model which has traditionally been used in the classroom. The instructivist model is a static model of learning where the learning objects are designed and prescribed by the teacher, students assimilate facts and are assessed often by examination. This is the model which has traditionally been used to support distance education using paper-based materials.

Learning objects based on the constructivist model focus on problem-based activities and team-based learning for example, where students are encouraged to discover principles and actively participate in dialogue with the instructor. This theory is a general framework and is linked with many others such as Piaget's Genetic Epistemology and Vygotsky's Social Development theory. The key principles of the model are:

- instruction is related to the experiences and contexts that make the student willing and able to learn,
- instruction is structured so that it can be easily grasped by the student,
- instruction is designed to facilitate students extrapolating beyond the information provided.

3.4 Engagement Theory

Engagement theory has emerged as a result of Kearsley and Schneiderman's experiences of using online technologies to support their teaching, particularly for distance education and has been developed specifically with technology-based environments in mind. They suggest that the use of technology, while not essential for engagement to occur, facilitates the process that may be difficult otherwise. [12] Students participate in a meaningful way by interacting with others on realistic learning activities. The basic principles are that the learning activities:
- occur in collaborative teams
- are project-based, and
- have an authentic focus.

Kearsley and Schneiderman's [12] Engagement Theory is one often cited in support of online collaborative learning such as evidenced by Salmon's e-tivities [19].

3.5 Laurillard's Model of Instruction

Laurillard's model [13] is designed for technology-supported learning activities, but unlike Gagne's model, Laurillard's model emphasizes the collaboration and communication aspects of learning and is designed for use with interactive technologies. The model is actually a framework in which the importance of mediated and moderated communication between learners and teachers is emphasized. Delivery of information, or content, from teacher to student is secondary to the communication aspects. The framework defines the level at which teacher and learners are interacting as they move through a learning activity. It provides an insight into the type and depth of learning that will occur at each stage.

3.6 Situated Learning

Situated learning revolves around the notion that normally learning occurs as a function of an activity in some context and culture [14, 15]. A critical component of situated learning is social interaction. The main principles of this theory are that knowledge must be presented in a realistic setting, and that learning requires social interaction and collaboration.

Problem-based learning is a model based on situated learning and reflects how learning occurs in a real setting such as in the workplace. It was developed to support the training of medical students at McMaster University Medical School. Problem-based learning is the curriculum as well as the learning process. "The curriculum consists of carefully selected and designed problems that demand the learner acquisition of critical knowledge, problem solving proficiency, self-directed learning strategies and team participations skills. The process replicates the commonly used systemic approach to resolving problems or meeting challenges that are encountered in life and career." [16] The responsibility for learning lies with the student rather than the teacher which fits very well in a tertiary education environment. The problem is the core element of the problem-based learning process. It may be ill structured and have non-obvious solutions. The learning process demands that students acquire the knowledge needed to reformulate the problem into a tractable form. [7]

Situated learning is well suited to online learning environments, particularly when students need to seek knowledge, or content is delivered to them just-in-time.

4   Components of E-teaching

Whichever pedagogical model is chosen, or even combination of models, eventually the carefully designed learning objects have to be mapped to the virtual environment. The online activities are built using the functionality and tools provided by the learning environment (or developed as plug-ins or add-ons to the learning environment). But the range of tools available is limited. So how can the wealth of pedagogies suggested above be supported in a learning environment?

From the very brief exposition in the previous section, we can see that the basic components of eTeaching do not seem to differ much from one pedagogy or model to another. Each one has some element of content delivery, discussion and possibly collaboration. In an institution of higher education it would be safe to assume that there is also a high probability of an element of assessment. It is interesting to note that there is a strong emphasis on problem-solving, collaboration and realistic situations in the pedagogies, all of which can be facilitated in online environments.

Regardless of the pedagogy that is being used as the basis of learning activities, the basic components of any learning activity consists of one or more of:

- *Collaboration* including discussions, group work, as well as collaborative exercises requiring sharing of content and/or discussion
- *Communication* including one-to-one (student-to-staff), one-to-many (staff-to-students) and many-to-many (student-to-student) communications
- *Content delivery* such as study guides, lecture notes, study skills resources, readings etc.
- *Assessment* including assignments (individual or group), quizzes, tests, examinations, submissions and marking.

What distinguishes one pedagogy from another is the ability to build different relationships between the components and present them to the learner with a different focus or priority. For example, engagement theory is centred on the concept of discussions between students moderated by academic staff. Problem-based learning centres on a scenario which includes delivery of content, maybe released piecemeal, and possibly group discussions.

Taking a pragmatic approach there are two further components that are needed in order to be able to manage the classroom and students, regardless of whether this is in the context of real or virtual learning environments. These are:

- *Class management* including class allocations (real and virtual), record management, enrolments and so on.
- *Administration* such as rules for communication, access to personnel, unit assessment requirements, unit guides and so on.

Although not part of any pedagogy, without the management and administration components the teaching would be chaotic, particularly when talking in terms of hundreds of students participating in a virtual classroom! The ability to deliver unit guides and other administrative trivia is essential to students being able to complete their studies successfully Further, eTeachers need to be able to manage classes, campus dependencies in a multi-campus environment, class, tutorial and practical allocations, as well as record keeping including assignment results, class attendances and so on.

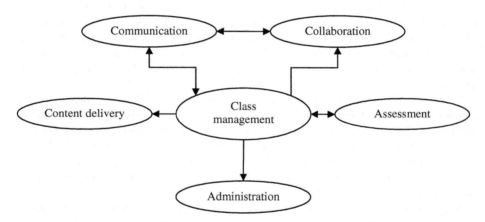

Fig. 1. A simple model of eTeaching

Figure 1 shows a simple model of eTeaching which incorporates each of the components described here. The model does not describe any particular pedagogy or model, but rather highlights the possible components of any learning activity. The linkages between components are a reflection of the major channels of potential information and communication flow between teacher and students, and between students, with the teacher being seen as the class manager (as well as teacher). This many not be strictly the case in all situations, but it suffices for the purposes of the model and following discussion.

The class management component is, in effect, where the eTeacher "resides" in the virtual environment. The arrows in the model represent the follow of information and/or communication from learner or teacher activity in one component to another. Flows can be from staff to student(s), between students, or from student to staff. The arrowheads in the model represent the direction of flow. For example, the eTeacher controls the delivery of content. Students access the content but, being a static resource, there are no communication flows back to class management. Similarly, the eTeacher sets up assessment, but in this case, once students have completed the set tasks, marks or grades are generated and are fed back (either automatically or manually) into the class record. Communication and collaboration are closely interlinked. Collaboration cannot exist without communication but the communication can occur without collaboration. The online tools used to facilitate collaboration are usually the same as those used to enable communication.

5   A Model of E-teaching

Joliffe, Ritter and Stevens [10] are quick to point out the shortcomings of a lot of Internet-based learning resources suggesting that:
   "… for the most part the Web is just a vast collection of semi-structured 'stuff' that has little to do with learning. When properly developed, however, Web pages do have the potential to be more than just information storage. When well designed and well structured [they] can guide learners through a variety of experiences including activities that present information, afford practice and provide feedback to inform them …" (p.19)
   In other words, the instructivist model still rules! Admittedly, they are referring to web pages, but nonetheless this is indicative of the norm. Deakin University has been quick to adopt new technologies to support distance education, but much of the web presence has been a means of delivering content to the students, without much regard to the pedagogical gains that could be achieved if more thought had been put into the design of the online presence. One notable exception is in the Faculty of Business and Law who took the opposite approach and concentrated on the communication possibilities of online learning systems rather than the more static approach. Their online pedagogy aligns well with Laurillard's model.
   Joliffe et al [10] also suggest that using the traditional pedagogical model approach to develop learning objects does not do justice to the potential of online technologies that support teaching and learning. Discussing the development of learning materials for a web-based environment, they suggest that more flexibility should be introduced into traditional models to "accommodate multiple goals and learning styles" (p.23) and provide a list of design considerations aimed at introducing added flexibility. They do caution however, that increasing the flexibility could result in increased costs and reduced learning outcomes. This suggests that moving towards a more constructivist model is beneficial to the learning outcomes for students if well managed.
   Herrington and Bunker [9] present a set of guidelines for online teaching developments that have been used at Edith Cowan University. The guidelines were developed in terms of three main areas: pedagogy, resources and delivery strategies. The pedagogy includes elements such as authentic tasks, opportunities for collaboration, learner-centred environments and so on. This still does not assist in the pragmatic translation of the elements to the tools and functions provided within the technology however.

When discussing a paradigm for creating a complete learning environment Harris [8] suggests that '... the content allows for the limitations of the [technology] while taking advantage of features inherent in the [technology]". (p. 140) But in order to take advantage of the features the designer needs to know what they are. But novice eTeachers often either do not know or do not appreciate the impact that any particular feature may have on, or contribute to, a learning activity. So let's consider what the common functions and tools (the features) are that exist in most learning environments. These include:

1. *(Content delivery)* a means of delivering content, either as web pages, pdf files or other standard format;
2. *(Content delivery)* some means of organizing content, such as a file system, or other systematic method such as icons on a web page linked to files;
3. *(Communication)* a means of allowing communication, synchronously via some form of online chat forum, and/or asynchronously via a bulletin board or discussion forum, or perhaps utilizing email or other messaging device;
4. *(Collaboration)* a means for students to work together, usually utilizing communication features and sharing of documents;
5. *(Assessment)* assessment tools such as self-assessment quizzes, tests and assignment submission tools;
6. *(Class management)* a class management tool which includes the ability to record grades and other characteristics of individual students;
7. selective release of learning objects depending on certain criteria being satisfied, such as date restrictions or student characteristics.

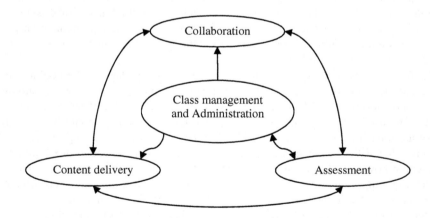

Fig. 2. Modified model of eTeaching

All of the components included in the simple model of eTeaching have a direct relationship with the functions provided in a learning environment except for administration. Administration however may involve communication, but is generally a matter of delivering administrative information to students, so can be seen as a non-discipline specific form of content delivery. Figure 2 demonstrates a simplification of the eTeaching model to reflect the overlap between communication and collaboration as well as that between administration and content delivery. The modified model can be used to more easily identify specific functionality to support specific pedagogies. For example, problem-based learning requires the controlled delivery of content as well as collaboration. Implementing an instructivist pedagogy online however requires the use of content delivery and assessment.

The one LMS tool that does not appear to be related to a specific component however is, in fact, the means of defining the relationships between students and learning objects, or between or within learning objects. All learning environments will support at least one pedagogical style. However, some form of selective release is essential if multiple pedagogies are to be implemented in the learning environment. Selective release is one of the keys to flexible online teaching. The other key is how learning objects can be organized within the technology. Some learning environments allow a single organizer tool for a particular component type. Others allow multiple types of organizer tools for particular component types. The most flexible allow multiple component types to be organized in multiple organizer tools. The more flexibility that is built into the presentation of learning objects in the technology, the more flexibility there will be for delivery using different pedagogies and models. However, the greater the flexibility of the technology the greater the confusion for novice users of the technology and the steeper the learning curve to become competent users of it.

We are now in a position to map elements of the model to the functions and tools provided by specific learning environments. For example, table 1 shows the mapping of the components of the eTeaching model to functions provided by WebCT Vista, the LMS that powers DSO. A similar table can be drawn up for any LMS. It does require knowledge of the LMS to compile, but can be used by teachers with little or no knowledge of the technology when designing their learning objects. The table provides support for a very basic presentation online and affords a starting point for novice eTeachers. Such information would most sensibly be supplement by exemplars that promote good online teaching practice for example to allow novices to envisage the required end result in the LMS.

The relationships between components, which define the pedagogy can be incorporated into the learning object by various means, some of which are mentioned here. The organization of the components in the environment, for example the order in which they appear on a web page, can foreshadow their relative importance. Organiser pages in WebCT allow the designer to build a hierarchy of elements, since organiser pages can be included in an organiser page. The way in which WebCT's learning modules present information in a sequence can be utilized to define the relationship between each element in the module. Selective release is used in WebCT to hide specific elements for example until certain criteria have been met such as a date or some characteristic of students such as a location or mark achieved in an assessment item.

Although I have described the technological mapping in terms of WebCT Vista, most LMS's provide equivalents to most of the functions and/or tools mentioned here.

Table 1. Mapping eTeaching activities to WebCT Vista.

Teaching component	WebCT Vista functions
Content delivery	Organiser pages, Learning modules
	Content pages
	URLs
	Media Library
Collaboration	Discussions
	Chat and Whiteboard
(communication)	(Mail)
	(Announcements)
Assessment	Assessment
	Assignments
Class management	Grade book
	Calendar
	Syllabus tool

6 Discussion

The model developed here will support the design of basic learning objects such as an online tutorial, an assessment task, a case study with supporting content, and so on. It provides a starting point for those with little or no technological background or online teaching experience to start designing their teaching programme online. Such developments may simply replicate some face-to-face activity but does afford sufficient information for the teaching to be supported by the technology.

Once teachers gain experience online and their confidence grows, they will start building more sophisticated activities than the model can support currently, using the more advanced tools provided in the learning environment, to enhance their teaching. No doubt many teachers will continue beyond the enhancement stage, using the technology to transform their teaching in innovative ways to support the varying needs of students studying in different modes and with different expectations.

Although the model has not yet been systematically evaluated, anecdotal evidence suggests that it has potential to achieve different goals. The model has been used in a seminar situation to provide academic staff in information technology related areas with an insight into a particular LMS quickly. It has been used, in a one-day workshop environment, to assist academic staff who have not used online tools previously, to consider ways in which the LMS could support their teaching. It has also been used, again in a seminar situation, to provide academic staff who do not have a strong IT background but have used a different online teaching environment previously, to translate their online skills to the new LMS environment.

7 Conclusions

There are many aspects of "going online" which have not been addressed here such as managing academic and student expectations, promoting good online practice, complying with copyright legislation and web accessibility guidelines, and so on. These are very important adjuncts to going online and must not be ignored if online teaching is going to be successful. Professional development activities would be expected to address these aspects, as well as basic training in the use of the online environment. But these are insufficient if the novice eTeacher cannot envisage the relationship between the components of teaching with which they are familiar and the functionality of the learning environment which may seem like a closed book to them.

I have presented here a model for eTeaching which facilitates access to the technology of online learning environments for novice eTeachers, providing the bridge between the pedagogy and the technology. It provides an opportunity for academics to get started in the online environment in a technologically non-challenging way.

References

1. Bransford, J.D. et al.: Anchored instruction: Why we need it and how technology can help. In D. Nix & R. Spiro (Eds.), *Cognition, education and multimedia*. Erlbaum Associates, Hillsdale, NJ (1990)
2. Bruner, J.: *The Process of Education*. Harvard University Press, Cambridge, MA (1960).
3. Coldwell, J.: It is possible to teach computer ethics via distance education! *Computer Ethics 2000*. Selected papers from the 2nd Australian Institute of Computer Ethics Conference (AICE2000). Canberra, November, (2000)
4. Deakin University: *Online Technologies in Courses and Units*. Internal policy document. (2002) Available: http://www.deakin.edu.au/dugs. Accessed 17th March, 2003.
5. Gagne, R.: *The Conditions of Learning* (4th ed.). Holt, Rinehart & Winston, New York (1985).
6. Gagne, R., Briggs, L. & Wager, W.: *Principles of Instructional Design* (4th Ed.). HBJ College Publishers, Fort Worth, TX (1992).
7. Gooding, K.: Problem Based Learning. Proceedings NET*Working 2001: from virtual to reality. Brisbane, Queensland, October 15-17, 2001. Available http://www.flexiblelearning.net.au/nw2001/. Accessed 15th March 2003.
8. Harris, D.: Creating a complete learning environment. In French, D., Hale, C., Johnson, C., Farr, G. (Eds.): *Internet based learning*. Stylus publishing (2000)
9. Herrington, A., Bunker, A.: Quality teaching online: putting pedagogy first. *Proceedings HERDSA 2002* Perth, July (2002)
10. Jolliffe, A., Ritter, J., Stevens, D.: *The Online Learning Handbook: developing and using web-based learning*. Kogan Page Ltd. (2001)
11. Kearsley, G. *Theory Into Practice (TIP) database*. Available http://tip.psychology.org/. Accessed 15th March, 2003
12. Kearsley, G., Schneiderman, B: Engagement Theory, *Educational Technology*, 38(3) 1998.
13. Laurillard, D.: *Rethinking university teaching: a framework for the effective use of educational technology*. Routledge: London (1993)

14. Lave, J.: *Cognition in Practice: Mind, mathematics, and culture in everyday life.* Cambridge University Press, Cambridge, UK (1988).
15. Lave, J., & Wenger, E.: *Situated Learning: Legitimate Peripheral Participation.* Cambridge University Press, Cambridge, UK (1990).
16. Maricopa Center for Learning and Instruction: *Problem-based learning.* Available http://www.mcli.dist.aricopa.edu/pbl/info.html. Accessed 15th March, 2003
17. Moss, J., Fearnley-Sander, M., Hiller, C.: Techno hero Fiasco. In Murphy, D., Walker, R., Webb, G. (eds.): *Online learning and teaching with technology: case studies, experience and practice.* Kogan Page (2001)
18. Salmon, G.: *E-moderating.* Kogan Page (2000)
19. Salmon, G.: *E-tivities: the key to active online learning.* Kogan Page (2002)

ATLAS: A Web-Based Software Architecture for Multimedia E-learning Environments in Virtual Communities

Marc Spaniol[1], Ralf Klamma[1], and Matthias Jarke[2]

[1] RWTH Aachen, Informatik V, Ahornstr. 55, D-52056 Aachen, Germany
{mspaniol|klamma}@cs.rwth-aachen.de
[2] Fraunhofer FIT, Schloss Birlinghoven, D-53754 Sankt Augustin, Germany
jarke@fit.fraunhofer.de

Abstract. Multi-perspective problem solutions, leading to an increasing complexity in creating authentic learning scenarios and collaborative learning strategies, have gained the focus of scientific research. In order to assist learners in virtual communities working with digital media artifacts we analyze the needs of communities in different scientific domains ranging from the humanities to engineering. We combine our results with a media theory developed in Germany's first interdisciplinary and collaborative research center on "Media and Cultural Communication". Based on the operational processes named transcription, localization, and addressing we introduce ATLAS, a web-based software architecture for multimedia e-learning environments in virtual communities. Further, we test metadata standards like MPEG-7 for digital media management in virtual communities. Exemplarily, we present the movie triage environment MECCA supporting an interdisciplinary community of scientists from the cinematic sciences, art history, and literature studies.

1 Introduction

For the past five years in our collaborative research center we have been studying the knowledge management strategies and learning processes in scientific communities in the humanities and engineering [KlJa99,BeKl01]. The center's scientific community covers all sorts of scientists, from cinematic scientists to philologists. Our research has led us to the assumption that learning and collaboration among learners in the humanities has a more discursive nature when compared to engineering. This process of knowledge creation by interpreting and discussing selected phenomena is leading to scientific progress, but is hard to formalize with conventional computer science methods. Two aspects being recognized among these communities are:

- The semantics of multimedia heavily depends on the discursive acts within the community of practice.
- Communities within the humanities use multimedia artifacts frequently.

W. Zhou et al. (Eds.): ICWL 2003, LNCS 2783, pp. 193–205, 2003.

This phenomena consequently lead to challenges for computer scientists in managing and presenting information in networked information systems. First, an evolving terminology is needed based on discursive processes and differences in the usage of terms in an area of specialization. We are seeking for opportunities in organizing terms of conversations within communities like ontologies, which have been specially designed to structure and organize discursive content. For computer science this results in a challenge of managing views allowing duplicate, redundant, or even contradicting descriptions to co-exist. The second aspect is the need for using multimedia artifacts for information presentation. Due to the ability of computer science to (re-) combine and organize digital media, we support scientists from the humanities with various fields of specialization.

Learning is a social system within the communities of practice [Weng98] that needs a tight interplay of communicative acts and the organization of knowledge. We have realized the need for computer supported communities in creating their evolving terminology of conversations in discursive processes. In a distributed setting this leads us to virtual communities and ontology management systems for virtual communities of learners. To satisfy communities' needs we have to find an opportunity in combing ontology management systems with multimedia artifacts as carriers of learning content. Consequently, virtual communities of learners need support in digital media processing that allow them to add multimedia with high-level semantics. In this paper we'd like to present and discuss different approaches for multimedia information processing in e-learning environments. The rest of the paper is organized as follows: In the next section we introduce the emerging theory of the community of practice we are cooperating with in our collaborative research center consisting of the concepts: transcription, localization, and (re-) addressing. Then we analyze current strategies on multimedia management in e-learning environments. Afterwards, we present the MECCA case study, a multimedia e-learning environment based on MPEG-7. The paper closes with a summary and an outlook on further research.

2   MM Management Strategies in E-learning Environments

The diversity of media allows learners to select information from various sources as well as to create content in heterogeneous formats. Especially, new media allows an even faster and more complex structuring (re-)configuration of information, making it more difficult for users to find the best fitting data set. When developing e-learning environments we are focusing on optimizing addressing of information in terms of content adaptability and functionality of the user interface. In contrast to approaches using low-level features by extracting semantic content as color, sound, or shape [Ciep01,SpFa02], humanist scientists communities need high-level semantic annotations to manage multimedia. There is also some research done on semantic indexing of multimedia [GrSr01], but it is missing features to manage divergent terminologies as it is needed for multimedia views. To overcome these challenges our colleagues from the humanities

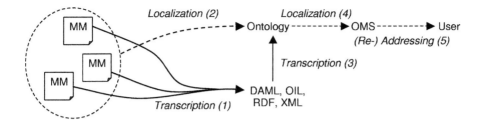

Fig. 1. Domain specific processing of MM files in ontology-based information systems

have developed the theory of transcription, localization, and (re-) addressing of multimedia. We are giving an overview on how these well-defined terms can be interpreted for the usage in computer science [Jark02]:

- Transcription is an operation to make media settings more readable [JaSt02].
- Localization is a transfer of global media into local practices [Fohr03].
- The term of (Re-) Addressing describes an operation that stabilizes and optimizes the accessibility of global communication.

Using these operational modes we will now analyze multimedia management strategies in e-learning environments. Basically, there are two strategies. Text and multimedia databases are approaches to handle data in a more or less unstructured manner in contrast to strict ontology management techniques.

2.1   Ontology-Based Information Systems

Ontology-based information systems have been developed to structure content and support information retrieval. They reach from simple catalogs to information system ontologies using full first order, higher order or modal logic [SmWe01]. Ontologies are based on modelling and abstraction of real world features [SSS*02]. The aim is to find a core ontology that can be modified to comply with specific settings [Guar98], which often results in a lack of flexibility since the structure of an ontology is too strict. For that reason, these systems are unpopular in some fields of applications, particularily where a somewhat individual classification of data is preferred. Experiences with other multimedia ontologies, like Dublin Core, lead to the insight that the effort of harmonizing relatively small ontologies often appears frightening and generates questions about scalability [DHLa03]. Surely, there is no alternative to merging of ontologies, which raises new scientific challenges. It requires considerable intellectual effort and is a learning process for individuals as well as their communities.

The problem is that an ontology has to fit into all user interpretations, which becomes obvious when an ontology creation is shared [DCGR98]. Hence, developing an ontology is usually guided by domain experts in an iterative, incremental and evaluative process. This is commonly done by an ontology engineer designing a common ontology by assessing users' and their community's needs. The

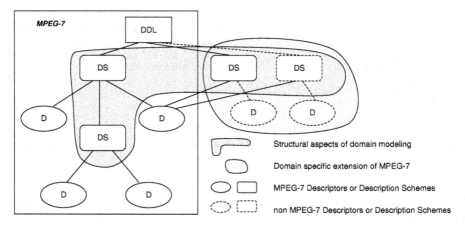

Fig. 2. Domain specific processing of multimedia information

understandability of the resulting ontology is questionable, since the used terminology is often (mis-) leading due to the user's field of specialty. Commonly, the lowest common denominator of terms has to be chosen. Overall, ontology-management systems mainly support the exchangeability of terminologies to find a common level of conversation, but lack an integration of multimedia content. For that reason, information-brokering systems have been built on top of them. They combine the advantages of strict ontologies and support multimedia retrieval. Still, the remaining problem is that information-brokering systems lack flexibility in a multi-user and distributed ontology creation process.

By means of figure 1, creation, organization, and presentation of e-learning content in an ideal ontology-based information system is being explained. *Transcription (1)* is used to make multimedia content better understandable for others. This can be done by annotating MM files and storing them e.g. in XML. The semantic enriched data are now ready for further processing. Now, a domain specific ontology is being used to structure the needed data. Therefore, an ontology engineer creates a *localized (2)* ontology assuming the needs of users in a specific domain. Semantic enrichment and categorization of MM files is performed in a second *transcription (3)* process, since the data has to be interpreted domain specific. All files are now *localized (4)* in an ontology management system (OMS) where they are stored for further processing. Depending on the user's interests - stored in an ontology related scheme - the MM files are presented to the user in a final *(re-) addressing (5)* process.

2.2   Ontology-Based Multimedia Management by MPEG-7

The MPEG-7 metadata standard [Mart02] is XML based and has been introduced by the moving pictures expert group (MPEG) [BYFe02]. MPEG-7 has

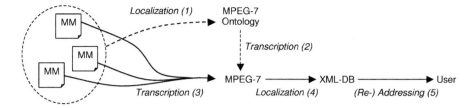

Fig. 3. Processing of MPEG-7 multimedia data by an underlying MPEG-7 ontology

been designed to describe multimedia content of different datatypes. Basic concepts of MPEG-7 are descriptors and description schemes (DS). Descriptors define syntax and semantics of each feature or metadata element, whereas the DS specifies the structure and semantics of the relationships between components. Additionally, the description definition language (DDL) allows the creation of MPEG-7 descriptors and DS. It provides a syntax to combine, express, extend and refine descriptors and DS [Hunt01].

MPEG-7 offers few means to manage content by strict formalizations just as ontologies do. Nevertheless, content management and personalization in an ontology-like structure can be managed by MPEG-7 (at least) twofold. The box on the left of figure 2 covers elements inherent in MPEG-7. They include the DDL, DS and descriptors, which can be freely rearranged. Pursueing a graph-based multimedia management strategy can be done fully compliant to the descriptors inherent in MPEG-7 ("MPEG-7 box" in fig. 2). Another possibility is to use structural aspects of the description schemes by interpreting the underlying tree-hierarchy and their nesting as a domain specific ontology. Usually, this requires the combination of newly defined DS and descriptors with those predefined by MPEG-7. Figure 2 indicates the latter approach as domain specific extensions outside the box capturing MPEG-7 inherent elements. Since these elements are also defined by the DDL and handled like those elements that are MPEG-7 inherent, validation and consistency checks can also be performed with those newly created components of a MPEG-7 schema. Since we are trying to achieve the best possible exchangeability of multimedia content we are developing MPEG-7 environments fully compatible to the basic set of MPEG-7 descriptors. This makes an exchange of content possible without further (mis-) interpretation of additional defined DS and descriptors.

Figure 3 clarifies the processing of multimedia content by an ontology stored as MPEG-7 graph. Based on a global view on multimedia (MM) files to be managed a *localized (1)* ontology is being developed. A core ontology is defined a-priori or by a collaborative ontology creation process [KSJa03] by interpreting (*transcribing (2)*) the MPEG-7 graph as an ontology. For a better understanding of the content MM files are *transcribed (3)* within the MPEG-7 descriptors. That allows us to combine the advantages of structural organization of content with unclassified metadata annotations. After that, the data is *localized (4)* in an

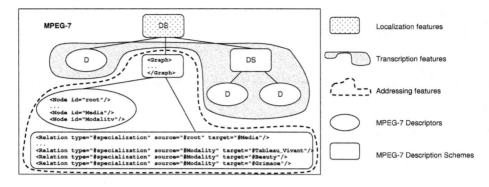

Fig. 4. MPEG-7 graph representation

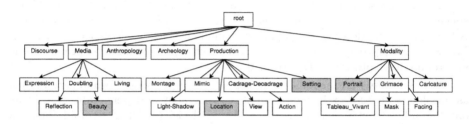

Fig. 5. Ontology stored in a MPEG-7 graph represented as a tree

XML database. From there it is accessible to all users in a final *(re-) addressing* *(5)* process using the classifications within the MPEG-7 graph as well as free text metadata annotations.

3   Building and Maintaining Ontology-Based Multimedia Management Systems

Adopting global media to a community's needs is the crucial aspect of localization, i.e. making media accessible and understandable for community members in their current practice. As we have discussed in the previous section, an ontology covering the terminology of the domain is needed to manage multimedia content in both cases. MPEG-7 is advantageous with respect to localization, transcription, and (re-) addressing, since it is capable of supporting all of it. At the top of figure 4 a DS responsible for localization in MPEG-7 ontologies enables us to integrate heterogeneous media. In general, we are able to integrate global media to local settings. What comes next are transcription features. They are used for adopting global media for a better understandability. Here, we are making use of standard MPEG-7 DS and descriptors that carry additional information in form of metadata in predefined tags. Finally, addressing in MPEG-7 is supported by

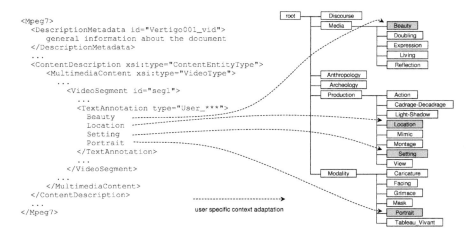

Fig. 6. Personalization and context adaptation in MPEG-7

an ontology being represented by the DS and descriptors in the lower section of figure 4. Exemplarily, we have filled in some nodes and relations, which are framed by the superordinate MPEG-7 graph description scheme.

The core of our MPEG-7 ontology multimedia management system is a MPEG-7 graph representation. In addition to media related metadata it consists of three components (cf. figure 4):

- The graph description scheme
- The descriptor(s) for node elements
- The relation description scheme

The graph description scheme contains all relevant information to define the structure and the elements of an MPEG-7 graph. It serves as an overall frame tagging all its sub elements. In general, nodes in MPEG-7 are optional. Any item referenced by a relation in a graph is automatically defined as a node (this is called an anonymous node). For the sake of clarity we have chosen the opportunity to define nodes directly. The descriptor for node elements defines the structure of the corresponding node elements. Each element is defined by its ID attribute. The relation description scheme can be used in two ways. One format is an external one that contains the relation apart from their related descriptions of the description scheme instances. The other format is an internal one that embeds the relation directly within the description of the source argument of the relation. In this case we have chosen the second opportunity. Figure 4 shows the application of the previously described technique with project specific annotations of the multimedia artifacts. Our internal relation description scheme specifies, within its relation elements, the type of the relation as well its source and its target attributes indicating the nodes joined by the relation.

The ontology represented as graph supports users navigating through digital media. In our case, we are using tree structures as s subset of a graph. Figure 5 shows a sample tree structure of an application ontology as a result of a discursive ontology creation process among cinematic scientists. The partially spanned tree of figure 5 indicates, by grey color, the corresponding categories of multimedia file. A related MPEG-7 document describing multimedia content (user has been made irrecognizable for the sake of privacy) is being shown in figure 6. All selected categories are represented in the body of the document. In order to support various communities, we are introducing an architecture supporting high-level semantic annotations of multimedia artifacts based on MPEG-7.

4   ATLAS: A Web-Based Community Software Architecture

ATLAS (Architecture for Transcription, Localization, and Transcription Engineering System) is a community management system handling multimedia artifacts in networked communities. The features of ATLAS are shown in figure 7. Based on our theory as a modification of Nonaka and Takeuchi [SKJa02], learning takes place when we successfully internalize the transcribed knowledge that has been created within our community. Creating new content for the community is done by writing reports, homework essays, etc. These multimedia artifacts are managed in a community repository together with community relevant information while all the metadata are stored in an MPEG-7 compliant XML repository. ATLAS components use both repositories. The measuring component is constantly assessing community needs by gathering and evaluating quantitative data. Searching, Browsing, and Personalization are components of the transcript engine, which allow a community to comment on existing media by using other digital media and thus addressing their own needs or stabilizing media addresses. This is done by metadata supported semantic zapping. Semantic zapping means metadata-mediated browsing, allowing easy access to semantic information by supporting retrieval of multimedia artifacts according to the learning task.

Strategies for efficient content management are crucial for e-learning environments since the amount of data can rapidly reach critical sizes. On the one hand there is the need of extensive and attractive multimedia presentations, but on the other hand network traffic should be reduced to speed up queries. Hence, we are applying a mix in storing the digital content on the client-side as well as on the server-side. On the client-side we keep the multimedia content, e.g. movies, on hard disk or on CD's that might cause disorders when accessed via the world wide web. On the server-side we have set up an Apache webserver situating an XML-database, which contains metadata on the digital content and associated collections compatible with MPEG-7. For that reason, we can easily transfer our content to and from other MPEG-7 based applications. User requests, e.g. by XQuery, result in an XML-file sent to the client. It contains the concerning metadata of the digital content to be presented in a Java-based MPEG-7 player. Since the implementation has been done in Java, ATLAS is platform independent

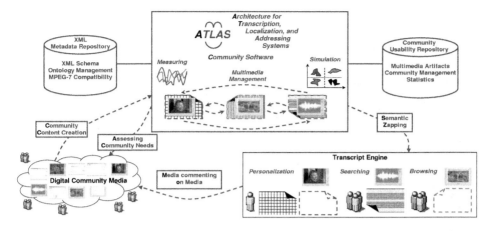

Fig. 7. ATLAS community software architecture

in general. The overall architecture is an extension of Grosky's metadata mediated browsing [GrSr01] and research on more detailed and performance oriented eventually layered digital media management architectures as in [BBH*02].

5   Experiences in Ontology-Based Multimedia Management

In our collaborative research center we are investigating the impact of digital media on learning processes in the cultural science communities. We are developing multimedia environments to make the learning process successful for both individuals and the community. Due to the interests of cinematic scientists in transcribing and commenting on multimedia artifacts, we are trying to combine those practices with methods of computer sciences as e.g. abstraction and categorization. Because of this, we have started a cooperation with cinematic scientists by jointly developing new information systems based on MPEG-7. This means that we have to reduce (or even close) the gap between unclassified semantic enrichment of multimedia and strict categorization of ontologies.

The MoviE Classification and Categorization Application (MECCA) is a high-level semantic annotation tool for multimedia artifacts. It serves as a multimedia environment for online video triages and collaborative ontology creation, which is a discursive and multistage process. The systems is based on MPEG-7 in order to enable scientists to develop concurrent classifications based on a distributed setting and to keep flexibility in multimedia content to be integrated. MECCA is being used in the cinematic sciences covering users having diverse educational backgrounds, like cinematic science, history of art, or graphical design. This community brings together users having various levels of profession such as full professors, research assistants, or students. Community members

Fig. 8. E-learning triage environment for cinematic science students (German version)

have different interests and point of views due to their educational background. In MECCA, users first take triages on the already existing multimedia content. In addition, users can add content compatible with MPEG-7. The next step is done by gradually annotating and classifying the data. Each users' classification scheme is kept in a separate MPEG-7 file. To retain the semantics of a multimedia file individual annotations and classifications are possible. This means that we allow redundant, overlapping, or even divergent views. These personal collections can be distributed and discussed among other community members. To detect differences between individually created ontologies and those of their community the system now checks the structures represented in the MPEG-7 graph representation based on tree-comparison algorithms. Concepts matching fully or partially can be detected as well as those showing divergence. In addition, MECCA allows users to reflect the decisions that have been made by back tracing as in [CTZa02].

MECCA is based on the constructivist learning environment "Berliner sehen" [Fend01]. Learners are stimulated to freely explore the content led by high-level semantics of the MPEG-7 content description and share their experiences in collections with others via the web. The front end of our video triage application (cf. figure 8) is an enhancement of its predecessor, the Virtual Entrepreneurship Lab (VEL) [KHJ*02]. Main improvements are an increased flexibility of the categorization panel and the integration of a search engine. The adaptive navigation toolbar allows displaying the underlying structure with respect to the cardinality of categories and components in the classification schema. To serve different classification systems further presentation styles from one-dimensional buttons to trees as well as combination of both can be selected. The search engine allows a comprehensive search on the users' collections or on the original content.

6 Discussion

We have received positive feedback from the scientists who used our e-learning environments because it allowed them to comment media on media. Based on that feedback, ATLAS has been designed to comply with this task. Due to discursive knowledge creation processes in communities of humanist scientists, there is an interest in exploring distributed classification processes. About one year ago, the MECCA project has been introduced to our colleagues from the humanities. Starting with meetings of 6-8 members, the community initially defined a classification scheme on a drawing table. Members liked to define a common vocabulary but some terms have been critically discussed since community members' disciplines cover a wide range. Hence, the overall community has rejected some terms since their interpretation might have been misleading to them. On the other hand, some special terms have been taken into the common classification scheme to allow specialists to classify the content in detail. These terms are not conflicting with the intuitive understanding of others, but due to their degree of specification into a subsection of the cinematic sciences, these patterns are rarely used. Hence, researchers are hoping that a computer-mediated system could detect those conflicts more accurately. Another aspect is that the hierarchy of professors, researchers, and students has been subliminal affecting the negotiation process. Hence, those members of the community being at the bottom of the hierarchy or belonging to a minority within the community are hoping that a computer-mediated classification process might give them a greater chance to push their interests.

Similar environments for communities in other areas of application - like plastics engineering - are currently being developed on the basis of ATLAS. All our environments allow the transcription of content in a guided but not prescripted way. By using ATLAS, a speedier software transfer in different areas of applications on the base of MPEG-7 has been made possible. The use of MPEG-7 has been crucial for the development of ATLAS. It allows users to express high-level multimedia semantics in a collaborative knowledge creation process. In addition, heterogeneous information can be contextualized since MPEG-7 gives us the opportunity to manage content of arbitrary digital media formats.

7 Conclusions and Outlook

We presented and discussed current approaches on digital media management. In our case studies we demonstrated that the use of MPEG-7, as a common ontology language both for the multimedia artifacts and the community vocabulary, allow a more authentic, transparent, and flexible knowledge creation process. We implemented a software architecture called ATLAS supporting application building by common services and unified repository handling. In making such environments compatible to the MPEG-7 standard, the maturity of digital media management increases. Yet, hosting virtual communities of learners is still in its infancy. For best exploitation of explicit multimedia semantics, we are currently researching on accessorily options that MPEG-7 offers.

Next steps include artifact transformation with parameterized XSLT (extensible stylesheet language transformation) scripts in our system. Another field of research is the implementation of an MPEG-7 hyperlink structure allowing to express and comment on relations of media files. Further research aims also at integrating streaming technologies into our learning environments. For that reason, we are currently investigating an integration of our Java applications in common browser technologies.

Acknowledgements. This work was supported by German National Science Foundation (DFG) within the collaborative research centers SFB/FK 427 "Media and cultural communication" and SFB 476 "IMPROVE". We'd like to thank our colleagues for the inspiring discussions.

References

[BBH*02] Berthold, H., Binkowski, F., Henrich, A., Hollfelder, S., Lindner, W., Marder, U., et al.: Architektur multimedialer Informationssysteme. *Informatik Forschung & Entwicklung 17(2)* (2002), pp. 77-89 (in German).

[BeKl01] Becks, A., Klamma, R.: Kooperative Dokumentanalyse in einem interdisziplinären Forschungskolleg. *Schnurr, H.-P., Staab, S., Studer, R., Stumme, G., Sure, Y. (eds.): Beiträge der Konferenz 'Professionelles Wissensmanagement – Erfahrungen und Visionen', Baden-Baden, 14.–16. March* (2001), pp. 289–307 (in German).

[BYFe02] van Beek, P., Yoon, K., Ferman, A. M.: User Interaction. *Manjunath, B. S., Salembier, P., Sikora, T. (eds.): Introduction to MPEG-7 – Multimedia Content Description Interface, John Wiley & Sons Ltd.* (2002), pp. 163–175.

[Ciep01] Ciewplinski, L.: MPEG-7 Color Descriptors and Their Applications. *Skarbek, W. (ed.): Computer Analysis of Images and Patterns, 9th International Conference, CAIP 2001 Warsaw, Poland, September 5-7* (2000), pp. 11–20.

[CTZa02] Chien, S.-Y., Tsotras, V., Zaniolo, C.: XML Document Versioning. *SIGMOD Record Vol. 30/3* (2001), pp. 46–53.

[DCGR98] Dieng, R., Corby, O., Giboin, A., Ribière, M.: Methods and Tools for Corporate Knowledge Management. *Proceedings of the 11th Banff Workshop on Knowledge Acquisition, Modelling and Management, KAW'98, Banff, Alberta, Canada* (1998).

[DHLa03] Doerr, M., Hunter, J., Lagoze, C.: Towards a Core Ontology for Information Integration. *Journal of Digital Information*, Volume 4, Issue 1, (2003).

[Fend01] Fendt, K.: Contextualizing content. In Knecht, M., v. Hammerstein, K. (eds.): Languages across the curriculum. *National East Asian Language Ctr., Columbus, Oh* (2001), pp. 201–223.

[Fohr03] Fohrmann, J.: Die Verfahren der Medien: Transkribieren – Adressieren – Lokalisieren. *In: Fohrmann, J., Schüttpelz, E. (eds.): Die Kommunikation der Medien, Tübingen, Niemeyer* (2003), (in German).

[GrSr01] Grosky, W.I., Sreenath, D.V.: Metadata Mediated Browsing and Retrieval in Semantically-Rich Cultural Image Collections. *Proceedings of the 2001 Tokyo Symposium for Digital Silk Roads, Tokyo, Japan, December 2001* (2001).

[Guar98] Guarino, N.: Formal Ontology and Information Systems. *Proceedings of FOIS'98, Trento, Italy, 6–8 June 1998* (1998), pp. 3–10.

[Hunt01] Jane Hunter: An Overview of the MPEG-7 Description Definition Language (DDL). *IEEE Transactions on Circuits and Systems for Video Technology, 11(6)* (2001), pp. 765–772.

[Jark02] Jarke, M.: Wissenskontexte. *Künstl. Intelligenz, Heft 1/02* (2002), pp. 12–18.

[JaSt02] Jäger, L., Stanitzek, G.: Transkribieren - Medien/Lektüre. *Wilhelm Fink Verlag, Munich* (2002), (in German).

[KHJ*02] Klamma, R., Hollender, E., Jarke, M., Moog, P., Wulf, V.: Vigils in a Wilderness of Knowledge: Metadata in Learning Environments. *Proc. of the IEEE Intl. Conf. on Adv. Learning Technologies, ICALT 2002, Kazan, Russia* (2002), pp. 519–524.

[KlJa99] Klamma, R., Jarke, M.: A Comparison of Engineering and Cultural Science projects. *ESCW-Workshop XMWS'99, Beyond Knowledge Management: Managing Expertise, Kopenhagen, Denmark* (1999).

[KSJa03] Klamma, R., Spaniol, M., Jarke, M.: Collaborative capturing and use of multimedia semantics in MPEG-7 based knowledge management systems. *Submitted to: IEEE Multimedia* (2003).

[Mart02] Martinez, J. M.: MPEG-7 Overview. *Intl. Organization for Standardization, http://mpeg.telecomitalialab.com/standards/mpeg-7/mpeg-7.htm*, (2002).

[SKJa02] Spaniol, M., Klamma, R., Jarke, M.: Semantic processing of multimedia data by MPEG-7 for capacious knowledge management. *Grosky, B. (ed.): Proc. of SOFSEM 2002 Workshop on Multimedia Semantics, Milovy, Czech Rep.* (2002), pp. 56–65.

[SmWe01] Smith, B., Welty, C.: Ontology: Towards a new synthesis. *Welty, C., Smith, B. (eds.): Formal Ontology in Information Systems, Ongunquit, Maine; ACM Press* (2001), pp. iii-x.

[SpFa02] Spevak, C., Favreau, E.: Soundspotter – A prototype for content-based audio retrieval. *Proc. of the 5th Intl. Conf. on Digital Audio Effects (DAFx-02), Hamburg, Germany* (2002).

[SSS*02] Schmitz, C., Staab, S., Studer, R., Stumme, G., Tane, J.: Accessing Distributed Learning Repositories through a Courseware Watchdog. *Proceedings of the E-Learn 2002 – World Conference on E-Learning in Corporate, Government, Healthcare & Higher Education* (2002).

[Weng98] Wenger, E.: Communities of Practice – learning, Meaning, and Identity. *Cambridge University Press, Cambridge, UK* (1998).

Streaming Audio and Video in Web-Based Learning: A Comparative Study of Three Systems

Nalin K. Sharda and Anil K. Hanumanula

School of Computer Science and Mathematics
Victoria University, PO Box 14428
Melbourne City MC, Victoria 8001, Australia
Nalin.Sharda@vu.edu.au

Abstract. We present three options for developing Web-based learning systems with audio and video. By including audio and video one can bring a web-based leaning system closer to a real-life classroom. However, it poses many challenges in courseware creation and delivery. The three options investigated for delivering audio and video are: RealSlideshow – a proprietary system by Real-Networks; SMIL – a language created by W3C; and HTML+TIME – a Microsoft solution. Web mounted tutorials – on the topic of Networked Multimedia – using these three approaches were developed and tested. While each solution has some advantages and disadvantages, the HTML+TIME system turned out to be most promising.

1 Introduction

Web-based learning is adding new modes of delivery to distance education. One of its most promising aspects is Education-on-Demand (EoD) [1], which refers to the ability of a remotely located student to participate in a course when and where suitable. The Web provides a universally accessible delivery mechanism for EoD. Nonetheless, the task of creating and delivering multimedia content poses many challenges.

Most distance education students feel a sense of disconnectedness when they have little or no face-to-face contact with their lecturers [2]. Video makes it possible to alleviate this problem to some extent. There are two options for video capture, storage and transmission, namely, analog video and digital video[1].

1.1 Analog Video

Analog video based systems have been used for many years in distance education. In such a system the lecture is delivered in a special hall equipped with video camera(s) operated by technician(s). Live video is transmitted to one or more remote sites. Stu-

---

[1] Henceforth video will refer to the combination of moving images and associated audio.

W. Zhou et al. (Eds.): ICWL 2003, LNCS 2783, pp. 206–217, 2003.

dents view the lecture synchronously. This mode of delivery relieves the students from the tyranny of distance but binds them to the specified lecture times. Of course, this analog video lecture can be saved on a videotape for later viewing. But the distribution of these video tapes adds another level of complexity to the logistics of running the distance education course.

1.2 Digital Video

Digital video provides all the possibilities that analog video does, plus some more features. The most important features of digital video include the ability to compress and transmit it over digital communications channels. For Web-based leaning systems it can be stored on servers with other lecture content. Inclusion of video poses many challenges in creating and disseminating this content. We explored the following three systems for combining digital audio and video with courseware, and tested their operation over the Web.

- RealSlideshow, by RealNetworks
- SMIL - Synchronized Multimedia Integration Language, by W3C
- HTML+TIME - Timed Interactive Multimedia Extensions, by Microsoft

In comparing these three systems we considered factors such as their ability to support multimedia content – especially video, ease of learning, ease of content creation, level of programming / scripting required, as well as initial and running cost.

1.3 Paper Outline

Section 2 covers the RealNetworks products for including streaming audio and video. Outline of SMIL (pronounced as smile) is given in section 3. Section 4 presents the HTML+TIME system. A comparison of these three systems is given in section 5, and section 6 gives the conclusions drawn from this project.

2 RealNetworks Products

RealNetworks have created a range of products for the delivery of multimedia content [3]. Their players are available gratis, but the software required for content creation are generally not. The cost depends upon the functionality of the individual product. The RealNetwork suite of products consists of a series of interlinked tool for creating media rich Web sites. The streaming media content created by RealNetworks' products is called RealMedia: RealText, RealAudio and RealVideo being its specific contents. Some of the main products used for creating RealMedia are described here, along with their pros and cons.

2.1 RealProducer

RealProducer converts audio and video into streaming media. It can also broadcast and stream live content. Content created with RealProducer can be published on the Web. RealMedia clips created by RealProducer are separately called RealAudio and Real-Video. RealProducer is a part of the RealNetworks RealSystem. RealProducer creates the clips, RealServer stores and transmits the clips, and RealPlayer displays the clips. An Internet server can be used to stream files by using the RealServer software. Real-Producer Basic is available free, but the advanced version called RealProducer Plus costs around US $ 150.

The process of creating a courseware with the RealProducer is one of the easiest of the three tools compared in this project. One of the main drawbacks of the RealNetwork products is their proprietary nature. This makes it difficult to get an 'inside' view of the products' operations and binds the user to the viewers provided by RealNetworks.

2.2 RealSystem Server

RealSystem Server is required for delivering RealMedia content over the Web. It can stream pre-recorded as well as live media. The content is delivered as streamed media. The client workstation receives the media in real-time, and does not have to wait for the entire clip to download before it begins playing. RealSystem Server Basic is free of cost and can serve 25 concurrent users. RealServer software includes the following components:

- Main software: Called rmserver.exe for Windows, and rmserver for UNIX.
- Plug-in files: Provide custom features created by third parties.
- Configuration file: A text file in XML format.
- License file(s) that control the features enabled on the RealServer.
- RealSystem Administrator: A Web-based console for customizing and monitoring RealServer.
- Tools: Such as the Java Monitor which allows monitoring how many clips are being served at a given time.

2.3 RealSlideshow

RealSlideshow creates presentations which the RealServer can send across the Internet [4]. RealSlideshow Basic version is free of cost. The RealPlayer is used to present these to the user. A presentation created with RealSlideshow can include images and audio that are mutually synchronised. A presentation created with RealSlideshow contains a collection of images as JPEG, GIF, PNG, or bitmap files. These images are combined with audio narration to create a streaming media presentation that is shown in a RealPlayer. With RealSlideshow text can be added to a presentation as captions that are read along with a slide. RealSystem uses the SMIL mark-up language to create the layout for the presentation. A screen image of the Networked Multimedia lecture created with RealSlideshow is shown in figure 1.

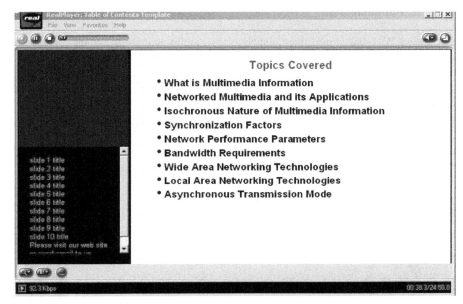

Fig. 1. A Screen shot of the Networked Multimedia Web-lecture created with RealSlideshow and presented with RealPlayer.

2.4 RealPresenter

RealPresenter software creates multimedia presentations from PowerPoint slides [5]. RealPresenter Basic is available gratis, but RealPresenter Plus costs around US $ 100. A presentation created with RealPresenter can include audio narration and video. The output can be played back with the RealPlayer software. RealPresenter converts PowerPoint slides to JPEG images. These images are displayed in the main region of the RealPlayer interface as the narration for that slide is played. A table of contents as the title of each slide is listed on the bottom left of the window. Clicking a slide title takes the user directly to that slide and accompanying audio voiceover. Since each slide is converted into a JPEG image, the dot points cannot be displayed one-by-one. Therefore it is not possible to synchronise the narration with the individual dot points.

3 SMIL – Synchronized Multimedia Integration Language

Synchronized Multimedia Integration Language (SMIL) is a text based markup language that can synchronizes and integrates multimedia content on the web [6]. SMIL was created by the World Wide Web Consortium (W3C), and is based on the Extensible Markup Language (XML).

3.1 SMIL Fundamentals

SMIL allows Web-based multimedia such as text, audio, animation, images, video and interactivity to work in unison. SMIL aims to produce cohesive multimedia presentations for the Web by combining the concepts developed with a number of other tools. For example, Macromedia Flash is a vector animation tool, that works fine with streaming audio but not with streaming video. RealNetworks RealMedia works well with streaming audio and video. SMIL combines the strengths of each one of these. Working with SMIL to develop Web-based multimedia is like building a mosaic, where the multimedia elements are the tiles and SMIL code the glue that holds them together. With SMIL, one can also create dynamic streaming presentations.

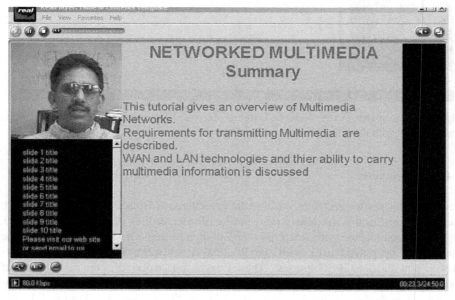

Fig. 2. A Screen shot of the Networked Multimedia Web-lecture created with SMIL and presented with RealPlayer.

Development of SMIL was led by the W3C, an independent international standards body that tries to create specifications beneficial to all parties involved. Unlike a proprietary technology owned by just one vendor, development of SMIL specification included many industry players as well as consumer interests. Nonetheless, SMIL has its limitations. A SMIL based presentation needs to use a player that can decode SMIL files. RealPlayer is one such widely used player. Oratrix's GRiNS Player is a full implementation of the SMIL 2.0 standard. Internet Explorer 5.5 supports a subset of SMIL 2.0.

3.2 Basic SMIL Syntax

SMIL code can be written with a simple text editor. A SMIL document controls where, how, and when multimedia clips are played. A few salient SMIL rules are:
- Every tag in a SMIL document must be closed.
- Tags without a corresponding end tag must be closed with a forward slash.
- Attribute values must be enclosed in double quotes.
- There should be no spaces around the equal sign for attribute values.
- SMIL documents are saved as .smi or. Smil files.
- No spaces are allowed in the file names; underscore can be employed.
- The use of HTML style comments is supported by SMIL.

A screen image of the Networked Multimedia tutorial created in SMIL is shown in figure 2. The player used for this is the RealPlayer.

4 HTML+TIME

HTML+TIME (Timed Interactive Multimedia Extensions) was first released in Microsoft Internet Explorer 5 [7]. Its aim is to add timing and media synchronization support to HTML code with the help of some XML-based elements and attributes. Images, video, and sounds can be added to an HTML page, and synchronised with HTML text over a specified time period. Therefore it can be used to create multimedia presentations with little or no scripting. As the author doesn't need to know scripting the focus is on creating the content instead of learning a programming language.

In HTML+TIME the author controls when and where multimedia objects appear on the screen. These objects can be text, still images, moving images, sound, and other HTML elements. One can specify an item to pop up on the page at a specific time, e.g. 11 seconds after the page loads, or to display at the same time as some other item, or at a time relative to the appearance of another item, or to appear and vanish in response to a user interaction, such as a button click. Play out duration, end time, or repeat count can also be specified.

4.1 HTML+TIME Attributes

An overview of the HTML+TIME system is provided here by exploring some of its salient features. It provides attributes to specify an element's timing behaviour. This section briefly introduces the **begin, dur, repeatCount, repeatDur**, and **end** attributes.

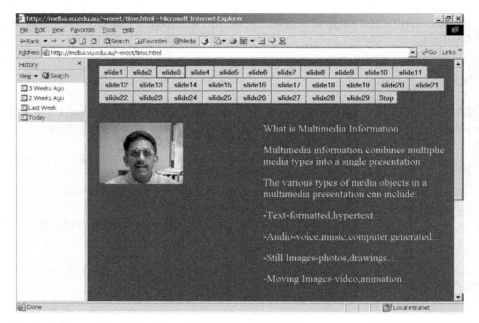

Fig. 3. A Screen shot of the Networked Multimedia Web-lecture created with HTML+TIME and presented with Internet Explorer.

The **begin** attribute specifies the time or times at which an element begins, relative to its parent's timeline. For example, **begin="4"** means that the element begins 4 seconds after its parent begins. Author can specify multiple begin times by separating them with semicolons. An element can also begin in response to an event like a button click or in relation to the beginning or end of another element. The special value **"indefinite"** means that the begin time is some time in the future and has not yet been resolved.

The **dur** attribute specifies the length of the simple duration, which is the basic duration of the presentation of the element. The **dur** attribute must be a single value greater than zero. The special value **"indefinite"** indicates that the duration should last forever. However, the duration can still be cut short by specifying an explicit end, using the **end** attribute or the end of the parent.

The **repeatCount** attribute specifies the number of times the element should repeat its simple duration. Fractional values such as 2.5 are allowed and indicate a partial repeat of the last iteration. The special value **"indefinite"** indicates that the repeat should last forever, subject to the duration of the parent.

The **repeatDur** attribute is similar to **repeatCount** but specifies the amount of time rather than the number of times to repeat the simple duration. For example, if **dur** specifies a simple duration of 5 and **repeatDur** is 12.5, then the simple duration will repeat two and a half times (12.5/5=2.5). The special value **"indefinite"** indicates that the repeat duration should last forever, subject to the duration of the parent.

The **end** attribute specifies the end of the active duration. As with begin, one can specify multiple end values separated by semicolons. The special value **"indefinite"** means that the end is sometime in the future and is yet to be resolved. An end time overrides the duration and can cut short or extend the duration.

In contrast to **dur**, which specifies duration relative to the element's begin time, end is an absolute time in relation to the element's parent's timeline. For example, if **begin="3"** and **dur="5"** and **end, repeatCount**, and **repeatDur** are not specified, then the element will end 5 seconds after it begins, which is 8 seconds on the parent's timeline. However, if **end="5"**, then the element will end at 5 seconds on the parent's timeline.

HTML+TIME provides a number of additional attributes that provide additional control over objects on the screen.

4.2 Development with HTML+TIME

A brief description of the development procedure is included here to provide a feel for the complexity of the development process with HTML+TIME. In this project a short interactive Web-based lecture was created on the topic of Networked Multimedia. It opens with a video in the left hand top corner synchronized with the text appearing on the right hand side. On the top three rows there are links which can be used by the user to interact with the presentation. This interactivity is enforced by the SMIL 2.0 **<excl>** element, which allows only one child element to be played at a time. If an element begins to play while another element is playing, the new element takes charge and the old element is paused or stopped. This makes creating interactivity much easier.

All HTML+TIME documents start with a template of basic markup. With the template in place next step is to prepare the structure of the presentation. Next one can bring in the video and text that make up the presentation. With text, video, sound in place next step is to establish the timing for the display of these elements. This done by specifying **begin, end,** and **dur** tags.

Once the structure is built and layout is created, it is time to add time containers such as **<par>, <seq>,** and **<excel>** elements. Through the use of the time containers and in particular <par> element, content are grouped to load and display as sets. This ensures that the media elements and text are grouped together logically and that the Internet Explorer will accept these transitions.

Once the presentation is structured and timed, layout for the video and text is created at desired locations on the Web page. The multimedia elements are positioned on the Web page using the style sheet. A backdrop is added for the presentation to be displayed against. A screen shot of the Networked Multimedia Lecture is shown in figure 3.

5   Comparative Study

This comparative study will consider capabilities of the three Web-based courseware development tools based on features that are most useful for distance education courses and students.

5.1   Resume Course Function

A course placeholder lets users save their place in an online course. The course placeholder allows the user to stop working on a course for a while, shut down the browser, and then at a later time resume the course where they had left off. When the user resumes the course, the course placeholder tool is used to take the user directly to the page of the course. This can be done by using HTML+TIME 2.0 but not by the other products.

5.2   Searching Within Course

Searching within a course allows users to find course material based on key words. Searching tools enable students to locate parts of the course materials on the basis of word matching. This can be done by using HTML+TIME 2.0, but involves some scripting.

5.3   Self-Progress Review

Student Progress Review tools enable students to plan for their workload and assignments typically through a course calendar. This may include the use of an online calendar. Student Progress Review tools enable the student to check marks on assignments and tests as well as their progress through the course material. In some tools there are additional provisions to support student workload planning as well by means of a calendar type of tool. This can be done by SMIL 2.0 and HTML+TIME 2.0 but not in the RealNetwork basic version.

5.4   Work Offline/Synchronize

The ability to work in a course environment offline is especially useful in situations where communication links are unreliable or expensive. This offline environment is essentially a local client application that embodies the important features of the online product without a constant connection to the Internet. This was not supported by the three Web-based lectures tested, as they required constant connection to the server.

5.5 Video Services

Video services enable real-time voice and video interaction as part of the course. These include tools for broadcasting video to those without a video input device. Some video services provide for two-way or multi-way video conferencing, which may be point-to-point connections or mediated through a central server. All three products support this. RealNetwork and SMIL 2.0 need a player to playback video. HTML+ TIME does not required any player, for the browser acts as the player, though Internet Explorer 5.5 or higher is required. Clarity of video in all cases is good. Synchronization of the video, audio and text elements was within acceptable limits. The ability to increase/decrease the screen size is available in RealPresenter and SMIL, but not in HTML+TIME.

5.6 Groupwork

Groupwork is the capacity to organize a class into groups and provide group work-space that enables the instructor to assign specific tasks or projects. Some systems also enable groups to have their own communications features like real-time chat and discussion forums. HTML+TIME 2.0 can do this by using some scripting.

5.7 Registration

Registration tools support the enrolment of students in an online course either by the instructor or through self-registration of the students themselves. The HTML+TIME 2.0 language can develop this feature by using some scripting.

5.8 Technical Specifications

All these three products requires same minimum configuration. But RealNetworks requires RealServer and SMIL requires some media server to stream the multimedia content over the web.

Ongoing costs are the main problem with the RealNetwork products because one must have a valid license. Start-up costs are the highest for RealNetwork products, but the basic versions are free. On the other hand, SMIL and HTML+TIME have none.

SMIL and HTML+TIME are Open Source, whereas RealNetworks products are not.

RealNetwork and SMIL work both with Internet Explore or Netscape. But HTML+TIME works with only Internet Explore and only with version 5.5 or above.

The vendors for RealNetwork products provide the technical support for their systems. For SMIL and HTML+TIME this is done by W3C and Microsoft respectively. RealServer provides a number of tools for the administrator to run the software. The ability to distinguish between syllables, points of emphasis, and discernable accentuations is called articulation. High ratings on articulation indicates that the listener can clearly identify a voice or sound and associate it with an individual or particular source. In RealNetworks and SMIL once the buffering is done, audio plays clearly. Even though in HTML+TIME there is no buffering, still the voice come out clearly.

Only in the case of RealNetwork products and SMIL there some delay because they are dependent on the player. Before playing streaming multimedia content the system takes some time to buffer the input stream.

The traditional telephone standard for perceptual lag is 150 milliseconds (ms). A break of less then 150 ms is beyond perceptual thresholds, and therefore represents acceptable lag. In the case of RealNetworks and SMIL there is a considerable amount of lag when we jump from one slide to another. In case of HTML+TIME this time lag is present only in case of a dial-up connection.

The ability of the software for scheduling communication events can be significantly degraded by an unreliable communications service. As RealNetworks products and SMIL depend on a server, at times they came to an halt requiring a reboot to play the media again. In the case of HTML+TIME this did not occur in any significant way.

6 Conclusions

We have presented a comparative study of three systems for including video in Web-based learning systems. RealNetworks products provide an easy to use proprietary solutions. SMIL is an international standard that depends upon third party players. HTML+TIME is Microsoft solution that requires only the Internet Explorer for presenting the Web-based lecture.

Some of the specific conclusions derived from this study are as follows:
- HTML+TIME is easily accessible over all types of connections because it depends only on the browser.
- Designing the interactivity in HTML+TIME is rather cumbersome because every interaction needs to be specified individually.
- Planning the layout is very easy and simple in RealNetworks products because it requires only dragging and dropping multimedia objects on the screen.
- Installation, authorization and registration are required in the case of RealNetworks products.
- Each of these can be started with low initial investment. There are no ongoing costs for HTML+TIME.
- SMIL and HTML+TIME took more time to create page layout design and content.
- RealNetworks products and SMIL load slowly as they depend on the player. HTML+TIME takes less time to load, since it depends only on the browser.
- The level of synchronization between audio, video and text is the best for HTML+TIME.

The current study focused on comparing properties of these three systems for content creation and delivery. While an overview of the comparison between their delivery characteristics was formulated, a detailed study on the Quality of Service obtained from these three solution will be conducted in the future.

References

[1] N. Sharda, *Multimedia Information Networking* (New Jersey: Prentice Hall, 1999).
[2] Anthony G. Picciano, *Beyond Student Perception: Issues of Interaction, Presence, and Performance in On-Line Course*, Journal of Asynchronous Learning Networks, July 2002.
[3] *Creation and Delivery Documentation*. RealNetworks, March 2003.
     http://service.real.com/help/library/index.html#credel
[4] Lynn Ward, *Creating Dynamic Online Lectures with RealPresenter*, Pointers and Clickers – ION's Technology Tip of the Month, May / June 2001.
     http://illinois.online.uillinois.edu/ionpointers/printerfriendly/ionpointers0501print.html
[5] *Introduction to RealPresenter*, RealNetworks Website. March 2003.
     http://service.real.com/help/library/guides/presenterg2/htmfiles/intro.htm
[6] Steve McCannell, *SMIL: Multimedia for the Masses*, Oct 2000.
     http://hotwired.lycos.com/webmonkey/00/41/index4a.html
[7] Patrick Schmitz (Microsoft), Jin Yu (Compaq/DEC), Peter Santangeli (Macromedia), *Timed Interactive Multimedia Extensions for HTML,(HTML+TIME) Extending SMIL into the Web Browser*. http://www.w3.org/TR/NOTE-HTMLplusTIME

Subdivision Feedback Based 3D Facial Modeling for E-learning

Yueting Zhuang, Congyong Su, Li Huang, and Fei Wu

College of Computer Science
Zhejiang University, Hangzhou, 310027, P. R. China
{yzhuang, su, lihuang, wufei}@cs.zju.edu.cn

Abstract. Online talking with facial animation is an alternative way of face-to-face communication for e-learning. In online talking faces field, facial modeling is very important. Available personalized 3D facial modeling systems cannot refine initial reconstructed 3D facial model automatically; therefore the output model is not very photorealistic. This paper proposes a subdivision feedback based personalized 3D facial modeling algorithm. After conventional facial modeling, in the feedback phase, quality of synthesized faces is estimated by facets' similarity metric between original face images and synthesized ones. Through subdividing the coarse facets locally and adaptively, we gain new personalized facial mesh. Using cylindrical projection and texture mapping in the forward phase once more, we obtain new facial model. Experimental results show that the model becomes more photorealistic after subdivision feedback.

1 Introduction

Web-based learning is different from traditional education. Face-to-face communication is carried out naturally among students and teachers in traditional education, but it is not commonly used in virtual education [1] and e-learning [2]. Students using a web-based learning system are likely to study alone and with relatively little classmate support [3]. Therefore, lacking of face-to-face interaction is a drawback of web-based learning.

Online talking with facial animation over the Internet is an alternative way of face-to-face communication. We propose a web-based face-to-face talking technique, and our aim is to build up a personalized face and speech communication system for e-learning. Firstly, an individualized 3D facial model should be constructed. Then a networked subsystem provides the networking support. Finally, a real-time speech subsystem performs the basic task of phoneme extraction from natural speech. In the receiver end, MPEG-4's FAP (Facial Animation Parameters) [4, 5] can be extracted from audio stream to drive the personalized 3D facial model with motion. Different people have different faces, so it's important to construct individualized facial model. In this paper, we mainly study how to create 3D facial model with a high degree of realism and personalization.

Available facial modeling methods can be categorized into two classes: (1) laser scanner based: Lee *et al.* [6] use laser scanner to directly reconstruct 3D facial model. It can generate fine grids. But the huge amount of 3D range data may bring a heavy

W. Zhou et al. (Eds.): ICWL 2003, LNCS 2783, pp. 218–229, 2003.

burden to the computation; (2) image-based: [7, 8, 9] use several face images and a sparse 3D facial model to build personalized shape model and facial texture. Through integrating shape with texture, it can obtain personalized 3D facial model. Their works are reviewed in the following paragraph.

Pighin *et al.* [7] create textured 3D facial models from photos of a human face. This algorithm must use several views of a human object to recover the camera poses and the facial geometry. Shan *et al.* [8] propose a coarse-to-fine deformable template strategy to localize some facial feature points in frontal view, but the synthesized face image is coarse in places. Tang and Huang [9] develop a template matching based algorithm to automatically extract facial features from the front and profile face images, but the mesh in his generic facial model is not dense enough to accurately represent the face shape.

In sum, most previous facial modeling algorithms lack a convenient mechanism to automatically improve the facial model based on input face images, i.e. input face images can't make corrections for output 3D model. Therefore 3D facial model's quality can't be guaranteed, for example, texture of face image is not continuous in color space, or generic facial model is too sparse to represent facial features in detail.

Based on the analysis above, we propose a new subdivision feedback based personalized 3D facial modeling algorithm, in which original input face images can be used to evaluate the 3D facial model reconstructed. Therefore we can make output model match input face images better, and then obtain more personalized and photorealistic result.

The rest of the paper is organized as follows. Section 1.1 gives the related work. In Section 2, we give an overview of our algorithm. Section 3 describes the forward phase of our algorithm. Section 4 presents the subdivision feedback based algorithm for generating 3D facial model. Experimental results are reported in Section 5, followed by conclusions and future work in Section 6.

1.1 Related Work

The current subdivision algorithms can be divided into global subdivision and local subdivision classes according to the subdivision area. They can also be divided into general subdivision and adaptive subdivision classes according to whether they are adaptive or not. A typical triangle facet based global subdivision algorithm is Loop's Loop [10] algorithm. Hoppe's view-dependent refinement [11] algorithm and Kobbelt's $\sqrt{3}$ subdivision [12] algorithm are two typical adaptive subdivision algorithms. Performing global subdivision requires complex data structures, because every vertex must know its neighbors and so does every triangle facet. Compared with global subdivision, local subdivision needs much less computations. To subdivide one facet, we only need to know this facet's vertex coordinate and normal. Vlachos *et al.* [13] propose a local subdivision algorithm, and present a formula when $lod = 3$ (level of detail). But this algorithm only performs same lod subdivision for every facet.

$lod = 3$ local subdivision algorithm subdivides one triangle facet into 9 small ones at a time. If we only subdivide a part of facets, it will be difficult to carry out subsequent crack filling. Therefore this paper improves local subdivision algorithm, and proposes $lod = 2$ local subdivision algorithm.

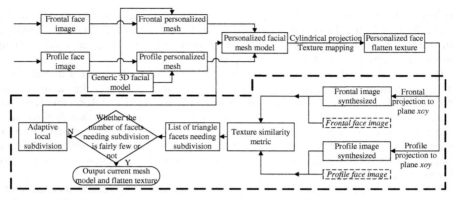

Fig. 1. Overview of 3D facial modeling based on subdivision feedback

2 Overview

As shown in Fig. 2, our algorithm has two main components:
(1) Forward phase:

Input two orthogonal face images, mark key feature points in images, then deform generic 3D face mesh model so as to match it with images' feature points using RBF-based interpolation function, thus generate initial personalized 3D facial mesh. Project 3D face mesh onto cylinder surface, and then use blending method to get personalized flatten texture from frontal and profile face images. Personalized 3D facial model is flattening texture combined with initial 3D mesh.

(2) Subdivision feedback phase (as shown in dotted box):

Project 3D model onto plane *xoy* to obtain synthesized frontal and profile face image. Calculate the corresponding triangle facet pairs' texture difference through comparing synthesized face images with input ones using histogram feature. Locally subdivide facets with large difference to get subdivided personalized 3D face mesh, then redo cylindrical projection and texture mapping so as to obtain flatten texture image in a new cycle. In the cycles of feedback procedure, the flatten texture becomes more and more smooth. After several times of feedback, the texture becomes smooth enough.

3 Forward Phase

We adopt revised Candide3 [14] model as the generic facial model. Candide3 model (see Fig. 2) can't cover profile face. In this paper, we change the position of feature points on the outer contour to make facial model cover profile. In addition, for the purpose of conciseness, our facial model (see Fig. 3) abandons redundant feature points that describe eyes, nose and mouth. From Fig. 3, it can be found that the revised facial model is able to represent main facial features.

Because Candide3 is compatible with MPEG-4, and our facial model is a revised version of it. Therefore our facial model makes the facial animation can be easily implemented by MPEG-4 FAPs (Facial Animation Parameters) and FDPs (Facial Definition Parameters) [4, 5].

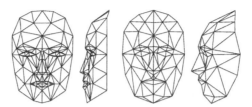

Fig. 2. Candide3 Model   **Fig. 3.** Our model

3.1   Deforming the Generic 3D Facial Model

The purpose of deforming the generic 3D facial model is to keep feature points consistent with input face images. Before deformation, we should mark the facial feature points by hand or some automatic ways. This paper chooses dot points in Fig. 4 as key feature points (points to be marked). The idea of deformation is enlightened by Pighin's discrete data interpolation algorithm [7].

Let p_k denote point marked, where $k = (1, \cdots, M)$. Let $p_i^{(0)}$ denote generic model's feature point, where $i = (1, \cdots, N)$. There is difference between coordinates of p_k and $p_i^{(0)}$. This paper denotes the displacement as $u_k \equiv p_k - p_i^{(0)}$, N as number of feature points, and M as number of points marked. In conditions that we know the displacement of points marked, we need to figure out other feature points' displacement by using an interpolation function. The interpolation function is defined as in formula (1), where $i = (1, \cdots, N)$ is feature point's sequence number, and $\phi(r)$ is radial basis function (RBF). This paper chooses $\phi(r) = e^{-\frac{r}{256}}$.

$$f(p) = \sum_{i=1}^{N} c_i \phi(\| p - p_i^{(0)} \|) \tag{1}$$

Let $u_k \equiv f(p_k)$, we get displacement of key feature points (points marked):

$$u_k = f(p_k) = \sum_{j=1}^{N} c_j \phi(\| p_k - p_j^{(0)} \|) \tag{2}$$

From formula (2), we obtain c_j, and substitute it into formula (1); therefore the displacements of other feature points are solved.

According to the above algorithm, the deformed mesh is attached to the orthogonal face images (see Fig. 4). We denote frontal and profile's image and mesh as (I_f, M_f) and (I_p, M_p) respectively.

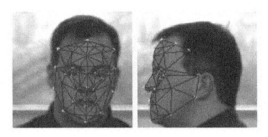

Fig. 4. Deformed mesh on the orthogonal face images

3.2 Personalized Facial Mesh Model Construction

This paper uses orthogonal face images to construct personalized 3D model. Let (X, Y, Z) denote the coordinate of feature point on 3D facial model. Let (x_f, y_f) and (z_p, y_p) denote the corresponding coordinates of the same feature point on frontal and profile face image. 3D coordinates are obtained from 2D coordinates using formula (3).

$$(X, Y, Z) = (x_f, (y_f + y_p)/2, z_p) \tag{3}$$

In this way, the personalized 3D facial mesh created is showed in Fig. 5.

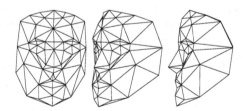

Fig. 5. Personalized 3D facial mesh

3.3 Cylindrical Projection

After we get the personalized 3D facial mesh, and before texture mapping, we need to do cylindrical projection for blending. On the assumption that most important facial features locate on cylindrical surface, we project facial mesh onto cylinder. Let

$p : (X_i, Y_i, Z_i)$ denote one feature point on 3D mesh. The cylinder's radius R can be obtained by formula (4).

$$R = \max(\max(X_i, \cdots, X_N) - \min(X_i, \cdots, X_N),$$
$$\max(Z_i, \cdots, Z_N) - \min(Z_i, \cdots, Z_N))/2 \qquad (4)$$

The cylindrical projection algorithm is as follows: (1) calculate frontal and profile image's dimensions; (2) calculate the smallest bounding rectangle of 3D mesh's projection onto xoz plane, then obtain R (see formula (4)); (3) transform coordinates of 3D model's feature point into polar coordinates, which cylinder's axis is polar origin, and R is polar distance. Then transform polar coordinates into cylindrical surface's Cartesian coordinates; (4) calculate every feature point's normal, then obtain angle θ of normal (see Fig. 6); (5) obtain smallest bounding box of projection texture from flatten cylindrical surface; (6) normalize coordinate $p^c : (x_i^c, y_i^c)$ of flatten cylindrical surface's feature point.

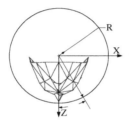

Fig. 6. Cylindrical projection

3.4 Texture Mapping

The procedure of texture mapping is as follows: (1) for each triangle facet T^c in cylindrical surface, let $p_1^c : (x_1, y_1), p_2^c : (x_2, y_2), p_3^c : (x_3, y_3)$ denote its three vertexes; (2) calculate bounding box $rect^c$ of T^c; (3) for each pixel $p^c : (x, y)$ in $rect^c$, obtain its barycentric coordinates $A : (\alpha, \beta, \gamma)$ of T^c (see formula (5)); (4) From A, obtain pixel coordinates $(x^f, y^f), (x^p, y^p)$ on frontal and profile image corresponding to p^c, each pixel value is pix^f, pix^p respectively; (5) blend pixels value of pix^f and pix^p, obtain flatten texture's pixel value $O_{i,j} = pix^f \cos^2 \theta + pix^p \sin^2 \theta$.

$$\begin{bmatrix} \alpha \\ \beta \\ \gamma \end{bmatrix} = \begin{bmatrix} x_1 & x_2 & x_3 \\ y_1 & y_2 & y_3 \\ 1 & 1 & 1 \end{bmatrix}^{-1} \begin{bmatrix} x \\ y \\ 1 \end{bmatrix} \qquad (5)$$

In formula (5), if $(\alpha, \beta, \gamma) \in [0,1]$, it means p^{ι} in T^{c}, vice versa. After texture mapping, we obtain flatten texture (see left image of Fig. 11.a). Integrating flatten texture with personalized 3D facial mesh (see Fig. 5), and displaying them through smooth shading, we gain personalized 3D facial model (see right images of Fig. 11.a).

4 Subdivision Feedback Phase

Because there is no comparison between original input image and output 3D facial model, the output personalized 3D facial model (see Fig. 11.a) is not very realistic. Facets lack of smoothness and facial texture is discontinuous in color space.

There are several reasons causing artifacts: (1) error exists in marking feature points by hand; (2) texture mapping is essentially the procedure of blending frontal and profile images. The blending procedure depends on normal of facet. Large difference may exist among the direction of neighbor facet's normal, which causes non-smoothness in neighbor facets.

For the sake of eliminating non-smoothness, the commonly used method is Laplacian smoothing [15]. But the results are not very ideal (see Fig. 11.b).

In this part, through measuring similarity between personalized 3D facial model's output texture and original image's texture, we find facets which have large color infidelity, and then subdivide them locally and adaptively. Using subdivision's inherent smoothing characteristic, we can obtain more photo-realistic texture (see Fig. 11.c).

4.1 Facet Similarity Metric

Some features can be used for image similarity metric. For example, color feature based color histograms, color correlation and color moments etc. In this paper, similarity metric is an independent module, which means various methods can be used when needed. For the sake of conciseness, we choose color histograms based similarity metric. Let nb denote bin number of color histogram. In Table 1's pseudo-code, we first calculate histogram of facet f_i of input image and f_i^s of image synthesized, and normalize each histogram. After that, we calculate Euclidean distance of the two normalized histogram and normalize the result (divided by $\sqrt{2}$).

The experimental analysis shows that we can choose $nb = 64$. If $S > 0.1$, we consider that the facet pair are very different, and append it to subdivision list Ls.

Table 1. Pseudo-code for facet similarity metric

$$h = hist(f_i, nb); norm(h);$$
$$h^s = hist(f_i^s, nb); norm(h^s);$$
$$S = EuclideanDist(h, h^s) / \sqrt{2};$$

4.2 Local Adaptive Subdivision with Feedback

This paper proposes a $lod = 2$ local subdivision algorithm that makes crack filling and long-thin triangle eliminating easily implemented. The algorithm is shown in Table 2.

Table 2. $lod = 2$ local subdivision algorithm

1. Select each edge's middle points of current triangle facet respectively. $M_{ij} = (V_i + V_j)/2$, M_{ij} denotes middle point, and V_i denotes facet's vertex.

2. Take M_{13} for example, project it onto the plane that is decided by vertex V_1 and its normal N_1, obtain projective point $P_{13}^1 = M_{13} - v_{13}N_1$, where $v_{13} = (M_{13} - V_1) \bullet N_1$; in the same way, obtain $P_{13}^2 = M_{13} - v_{31}N_3$, where $v_{31} = (M_{13} - V_3) \bullet N_3$.

3. Take P_{13}^1 and P_{13}^2's average as S_{13}, i.e. $S_{13} = (P_{13}^1 + P_{13}^2)/2$.

4. In the same way, obtain S_{23}, S_{12}.

The above algorithm can be implemented by formula (6). The effect of local subdivision is shown in Fig. 7.

$$w_{ij} = (V_j - V_i) \bullet N, \quad S_{ij} = \left(V_i + V_j - (w_{ij}N_i + w_{ji}N_j)/2\right)/2 \tag{6}$$

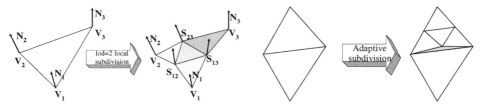

Fig. 7. $lod = 2$ local subdivision   **Fig. 8.** Adaptive subdivision creates crack

4.3 Crack Filling and Long-Thin Triangle Eliminating

If we only subdivide facets in list Ls (see Sect. 4.1), crack will appear inevitably (see Fig. 8). Junkins et al. [16] and Kobbelt [12] describe some crack filling algorithms, but problem still exists. They fail to consider eliminating long-thin triangles when doing crack filling. Chen and Medioni [17] explain that these degenerated long-thin triangles are undesirable since they do not represent local surface shape well and are often the cause of self-intersection on the mesh surface.

This paper proposes a crack filling and long-thin triangles eliminating algorithm solving this problem. See Table 3 for the procedure.

Table 3. Crack filling and long-thin triangle eliminating

1. Subdivide triangle facets in list *Ls* without considering crack generation.
2. After that, for three facets that are adjacent to a non-subdivided facet, there are three possible conditions: (1) only one neighbor facet is subdivided; (2) two neighbor facets are subdivided; (3) three neighbor facets are subdivided. See Fig. 9.a, 9.b, and 9.c. Note: we neglect the condition that none of the three neighbor facets are subdivided.
3. See Fig. 10 for effect after crack filling, There are no problems for Fig. 10.a and Fig. 10.c. But for Fig. 10.b, we must choose thick line l_t or dotted line l_d for connection.
4. Choose the shorter line between l_t and l_d to generate triangle. In this way, we can avoid long-thin triangle coming into being.

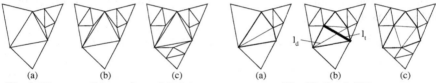

(a)	(b)	(c)	(a)	(b)	(c)

Fig. 9. Three conditions after subdivision   **Fig. 10.** Crack filling

The above algorithm is also suitable for facets on the border, in which crack can be filled according to Fig. 10.a and Fig. 10.b.

5 Experimental Results

Our experiments are conducted with a large number of images we captured with a Kodak digital camera and multi-view face images from Signal Analysis and Machine Perception Lab of Ohio University. We have implemented the prototype system of subdivision feedback based 3D facial modeling by using Visual C++ and Matlab. In the experiments, we compare the results of our algorithm (see Fig. 11.c) with those of Laplacian smoothing algorithm (see Fig. 11.b). The experimental results show that Laplacian smoothing can't eliminate facial texture's un-smoothness. Using our algorithm, the flatten texture becomes smoother. More results are illustrated with Fig. 12.

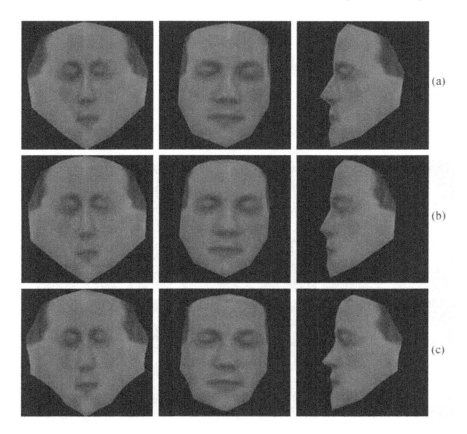

Fig. 11. (a) Result without subdivision feedback. From left to right: flatten texture, frontal face image synthesized, and profile one. (b) Result of Laplacian smoothing. (c) Subdivision feedback result.

6   Conclusions and Future Work

This paper proposes a new subdivision feedback based personalized 3D facial modeling algorithm. In this algorithm, we measure the texture similarity between original face images and those synthesized models, and then subdivide triangle facets that have significant difference. Our algorithm can make 3D facial model more photorealistic through overcoming traditional algorithm's open loop shortcomings.

The procedure of obtaining the 3D facial model is the first step of building the personalized facial communication system. Further research should be directed towards the other two steps: the networked subsystem and the real-time speech subsystem. The networked subsystem provides the communication layer so that speech and 3D facial model can be transmitted from one client to the other. The

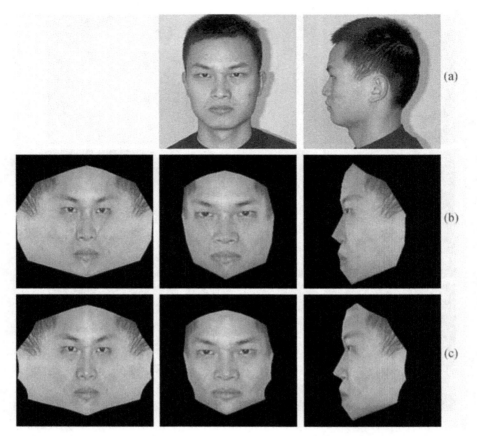

Fig. 12. (a) is the frontal and profile input. (b) is the result without subdivision feedback. From left to right: flatten texture, frontal face image synthesized, and profile one. (c) is the subdivision feedback result.

speech subsystem extracts the animation parameters, such as the lip movement and facial expression information from speech signal, and then applies them to a 3D facial model synchronized with the audio. The combination of above three steps provides a system to allow a real-time face-to-face communication with a high degree of realism and personalization over the Internet for e-learning.

Acknowledgements. We obtain some face images from Signal Analysis and Machine Perception Lab of Ohio University. We also wish to thank PhD. Zhongxiang Luo for helpful discussions.

The research described in this paper is supported by 973 Program (No. 2002CB312101), the National Natural Science Foundation of China (No. 60272031), Doctorate Research Foundation of the State Education Commission of China (No. 20010335049), and Natural Science Foundation of Zhejiang Province (ZD0212).

References

1. Chang, S.-K.: A Growing Book for Distance Learning. In: Proceedings of the First International Conference on Advances in Web-Based Learning (ICWL'02), LNCS 2436, Hong Kong, China (August, 2002) 3–18
2. Zhuang, Y., Liu, X.: Multimedia Knowledge Exploitation for E-Learning: Some Enabling Techniques. In: Proceedings of the First International Conference on Advances in Web-Based Learning (ICWL'02), LNCS 2436, Hong Kong, China (August, 2002) 411–422
3. Ou, K.-L., Chen, G.-D., Liu, C.-C., Liu, B.-J.: Instructional instruments for Web group learning systems : the grouping, intervention, and strategy. In: Proceedings of the Fifth annual SIGCSE/SIGCUE ITiCSE conference on Innovation and technology in computer science education, Helsinki, Finland (July, 2000) 69–72
4. ISO/IEC JTC 1/SC 29/WG11 N3055. Text for CD 14496-1 Systems MPEG-4 Manual. (1999)
5. ISO/IEC JTC 1/SC 29/WG11 N3056. Text for CD 14496-2 Systems MPEG-4 Manual. (1999)
6. Lee, Y., Terzopoulos, D., Waters, K.: Realistic Modeling for Facial Animation. In: Proceedings of SIGGRAPH'95, Los Angeles, California (September, 1995) 55–62
7. Pighin, F., Hecker, J., Lischinski, D., Szeliski, R., Salesin, D.: Synthesizing Realistic Facial Expressions from Photographs. In: Proceedings of SIGGRAPH'98, Orlando, Florida (July, 1998) 75–84
8. Shan, S., Gao, W., Yan, J., Zhang H., Chen, X.: Individual 3D Face Synthesis based on Orthogonal Photos and Speech-Driven Facial Animation. In: Proceedings of the 2000 IEEE International Conference on Image Processing (ICIP'2000), Vancouver, Canada (September, 2000) 238–241
9. Tang, L., Huang, T. S.: Automatic Construction of 3D Human Face Models Based on 2D Images. In: Proceedings of the 1996 IEEE International Conference on Image Processing (ICIP'96), Lausanne, Switzerland (August, 1996) 491–494
10. Loop, C.: Smooth Subdivision Surfaces Based on Triangles. Masters Thesis, Department of Mathematics, University of Utah (August, 1987)
11. Hoppe, H.: View-Dependent Refinement of Progressive Meshes. In: Proceedings of SIGGRAPH'97, Los Angels, California (August, 1997) 189–198
12. Kobbelt, L.: $\sqrt{3}$-Subdivision. In: Proceedings of SIGGRAPH'2000, New Orleans, Louisiana (July, 2000) 103–112
13. Vlachos, A., Perters, J., Boyd, C., Mitchell, J. L.: Curved PN Triangles. In: Proceedings of the 2001 Symposium on Interactive 3D Graphics, Research Triangle Park, North Carolina (March, 2001) 159–166
14. Ahlberg, J.: CANDIDE-3 -- An Updated Parameterized Face, Report No.LiTH-ISY-R-2326, Department of Electrical Engineering, Linköping University, Sweden (2001)
15. Lanman, D. R., Eng, B., Mayes, R.: Model-based Face Capture from Orthogonal Images. In: Proceedings of the First International Symposium on 3D Data Processing Visualization and Transmission (3DPVT'02), Padova, Italy (June, 2002)
16. Junkins, S., Hux, A.: Subdividing Reality: Employing Subdivision Surfaces for Real-Time Scalable 3D. In: Proceedings of Game Developers Conference 2000, San Jose, California (March, 2000)
17. Chen, Y., Medioni, G.: Surface Description of Complex Objects from Multiple Range Images. In: IEEE Computer Society Conference on Proceedings CVPR'94, Seattle, Washington (June, 1994) 153–158

3D Model and Motion Retrieval: The Extended Dimensions for Web-Based Learning

Yueting Zhuang, Yi Mao, Fei Wu, and Yunhe Pan

The Institute of Artificial Intelligence, Zhejiang University,
Hangzhou, 310027, P.R.China
yzhuang@cs.zju.edu.cn, {ymao,wufei}@zju.edu.cn,
panyh@sun.zju.edu.cn

Abstract. Traditionally, web-based learning techniques focus on the extensive use of multimedia data such as images, videos and audios. In this paper, we validate 3D model and motion retrieval as a part of e-learning architecture. New approaches, including a novel shape descriptor for arbitrary 3D polygon models, are proposed as initial solutions to these problems. Preliminary experiments demonstrate the promise of our methods, with potential applications in digital library, interactive learning, etc.

1 Introduction

As an alternative approach to the traditional classroom-based education, web-based learning offers incredible facilities to learners in that it is accessible to anybody, from anywhere, at anytime with self-paced instructions. This empowering methodology is changing the way that we are educated, that is, we are becoming life-long learners.

Web-based learning profits from a combination of learning portals, streaming audio/video, live web broadcast, interactive chats, desk-top video conference, digital libraries and search engines, etc. Of all these technologies, we are particularly interested in the teaching potential of multimedia data.

Mixing a multiplicity of media in the courses provides a powerful tool for developing a rich and comprehensive understanding of the knowledge presented. For example, when a biology teacher gives a class introducing horse's behavior, he might show an image to explain how the horse is like, play a clip of video to clarify the style it runs (remember how the film was born as a result of a debt), or listen to a sound clip of horse whinnying. Obviously, the effect of teaching this way would far exceed the practice using just plain text and oral explanation.

Pushed by the fast increase in the performance of affordable graphics hardware, 3D graphics has found its way into many mainstream applications. Due to the following reasons, we believe that 3D model databases will play a vital role in web-based learning. Firstly, the improved digital scanning techniques have made it possible to reliably and accurately digitize the external shape and surface characteristics of many physical objects. Secondly, 3D modeling tools, such as 3D Max and Maya, produce a large supply of publicly available 3D data sets. Thirdly, the World Wide Web has enabled fast and free access to distributed storage of 3D models. Lastly, but most importantly, the intrinsic interactive property of 3D models provides a natural way to

W. Zhou et al. (Eds.): ICWL 2003, LNCS 2783, pp. 230–240, 2003.

shift from a traditional instructor-centered learning platform to a learner-centered one, where it outperforms the other media types.

The Forbidden City Walkthrough [1] project has already demonstrated 3D models as a powerful web-based learning tool. Anyone who has never been to the Forbidden City only needs to have a networked PC to experience the magic of the ancient Chinese architecture. Compared with a documentary about the Forbidden City, 3D walkthrough provides more flexibility in that users can choose the palace to visit according to his or her own interest, without following the specific order posed by the filmmakers. Actually, it illustrates an example of active learning versus passive learning.

3D motion describes the movement of 3D objects. It can be regarded as an extension of 3D models along the time axis. The dynamic content of a 3D object as well as its appearance is captured in 3D motion, which further increases the power of 3D model as a means of web-based learning.

Among the wide variety of applications regarding 3D models and 3D motion, we are particularly interested in retrieving similar objects. It offers a special tool to augment digital library operations. Besides, it facilitates the making of educational films and provides easy data access for both medical training and designing issues. In a word, 3D model and motion retrieval constitute the extended dimensions for web-based learning.

The remainder of this paper is organized as follows. Section 2 summarizes the previous work related to 3D model and motion retrieval. An overview of the proposed approaches appears in Section 3. Finally, a brief summary and conclusion appears in section 4, followed by a discussion of topics for further study in Section 5.

2 Research Background

2.1 Shape-Based 3D Model Retrieval

The most straightforward way of 3D model retrieval is to analyze the shape similarity between different objects. The vast majority of previous work has focused on segmented objects in 2D images. Well-known descriptors include simple geometric attributes, digital moments, Fourier descriptor, elastic template matching, etc [2,3]. Direct extension of these descriptors to 3D space is not a trivial task since no explicit parameterization exists for arbitrary 3D surfaces.

Compared with 2D images, 3D models have no regular sampling of the corresponding object space. Therefore almost all the signal processing techniques that have been successfully applied to 2D images have no direct counterparts for 3D models. Besides, the increased dimensionality makes the issues of feature correspondence, optimal search, classifier construction and object recognition more complex. On the other hand, considerations of environmental setting, e.g. background, viewpoint, lighting, shadow, etc, can be readily released from 3D model related applications.

To sum up, there are a number of points worth elaborating when choosing the proper signature for description of 3D models. Firstly, it should reflect the intrinsic property of an object, namely, the shape content of the 3D model. Secondly, invariance properties such as similarity transformation invariance should be met.

Lastly, descriptors are supposed to be insensitive to degenerated models, robust against noise, and stable on tessellation.

Shapes have been compared for 3D objects on the basis of their statistical, topological or transformation properties. Here, we provide a state-of-the-art review of 3D shape descriptors.

Statistical shape descriptor is probably the most widely used technique. Examples include rotation invariant shape descriptor [4], shape histogram [5], digital moments [6], shape distribution [7], parameterized statistics [8], ray-based descriptor [9], and 3D shape spectrum descriptor [10]. They are usually easy-to-use and have little requirement of model regularity, but with limited discriminative power.

Topological matching is particularly useful when considering cognitive perception of a visual object. MRG [11] is constructed on the basis of geodesic distance and a coarse-to-fine comparison strategy establishes the correspondence between the parts of objects. Particularly, for objects of genus zero, local curvature distribution can be mapped onto the unit sphere using spherical resampling method [12]. However, such methods are time-consuming and not feasible to large database.

Transformation representation composes an important part of Digital Geometry Processing. Common tools include 3D Fourier Transform [13], Hough Transform [15], Spherical Harmonic Analysis [15], Wavelet Transform [16] etc. Normally, they cannot be directly applied to arbitrary surface models and the reconstruction to consistent or manifold surface has to be made with application-oriented concerns such as invariance properties, object representation and sampling issues.

Note that many approaches treat objects as a "point soup", where points are either sampled from surface or obtained by voxelization. Assuming unit mass per point, most previous work has merely explored the spatial location and relative position of these points.

2.2   3D Motion Retrieval

As far as we know, there has as yet been no systematic investigation of 3D motion retrieval. However, a number of studies exist on motion-based video retrieval which characterize video database using motion trajectory. They enlighten us on 3D motion retrieval since both areas use global motion information (either tracked over the duration of a video shot or obtained from motion capture data) as an indexing and search mechanism. Proposed trajectory modeling techniques include trajectory representation schemes (raw representation, curve representation, chain code representation and differential chain code representation)[17], spatial-temporal invariance [18] and wavelet-based sub-trajectory modeling [19].

Unfortunately, these motion representation methods are inadequate for description of complex 3D motions which work with motion captured data. This is because motion capture device is well beyond the expressive capability of conventional video camera. Specifically, objects can be no longer viewed as a whole and movements of different parts should be treated separately.

Among all the motion capture related areas, motion texture is the most similar to our work [20,21]. Intuitively, motion textures are those repetitive patterns in complex human motion. But they pay more attention to the feature of "liveness" and "personality" which tells the aspects of motion that are unique to a particular individual. That is, they are interested in subtleties in the same motion executed by different individuals where motion retrieval will simply mark as "similar".

To summarize, 3D model and motion retrieval are far under-explored in spite of their potential immense usage in web-based learning. In the latter section, we present our initial solution to these problems.

3 System Design and Implementation

In this section, we provide a detailed description of the methods we use to compute a measure of dissimilarities for 3D models and 3D motion.

3.1 3D Model Retrieval

We propose a novel shape descriptor, the "depth weighted normal map"(DWNM), for retrieving arbitrary 3D polygon models. The key idea is to incorporate normal, a natural representation for local curvatures, to give more cues about the shape content of 3D models. The shape signature is expressed as a statistical distribution of the surface normal weighted by their relative depth. The invariance properties of the descriptor are achieved by introducing uniform orthogonal sampling, per-object pose normalization and spherical harmonic analysis. Once we have computed the DWNM for two objects, the dissimilarity between them can be evaluated using any metric that measures distance between two distributions.

For each object, we put forward the following schemes for our approach:

1. **Per-object Pose Normalization.** We normalize the model into a canonical coordinate frame according to its first and second order moments, computed from the discrete approximation of the definition as [6] proposed. This procedure ensures that the principal axes of the models are aligned and the invariance property under Euclidean transformation is satisfied.

2. **Orthogonal Sampling of Normal Distribution** (Fig 1). We follow a spherical sampling technique for all the possible viewing directions and normal distribution. For convenience, we denote the viewing direction as $\omega_v = (\theta_v, \varphi_v)$ and the normal as $\omega_n = (\theta_n, \varphi_n)$. The function to evaluate normal distribution is defined as follows:

$$f(\omega_v; \omega_n) = \sum_i f_i(\omega_v; \omega_n), \quad i \in I \tag{1}$$

where I is the subscript set of the visible polygons P_i under viewing direction ω_v whose normal equals to ω_n.

We further define $f_i(\omega_v; \omega_n)$ as the depth-weighted area of the polygon P_i under orthogonal projection:

$$f_i(\omega_v; \omega_n) = \oint_{P_i} d_i(s) ds \tag{2}$$

where $d_i(s)$ is the depth of point s in P_i.

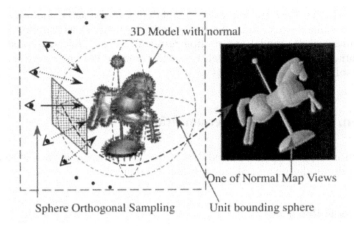

Fig. 1. Orthogonal sampling of the normal distribution.

3. **Spherical Harmonic Analysis along Viewing Direction.** To remove the dependence on the viewing direction, we compute the DWNM by further introducing spherical harmonic analysis:

$$h^f_{l,m,\omega_n} = \left\langle f(\omega_v, \omega_n), \ Y_{l,m}(\omega_v) \right\rangle \tag{3}$$

where $Y_{l,m}(\omega_v)$ are the spherical harmonic orthonormal basis functions with degree l and order m.

Our final representation of DWNM is the L_2 norm of the projection of h^f_{l,m,ω_n} onto the l-th rotation group acting on the space of spherical functions, and is formulated as:

$$DWNM(l, \omega_n) = \left\| \sum_{m=-l}^{l} h^f_{l,m,\omega_n} \right\| \tag{4}$$

This signature expresses the amplitude of l-th frequency component of a particular normal distribution from the initial function.

4. **Similarity Estimation.** The similarity is estimated by introducing χ_2 statistics for DWNMs of different models.

Using the spherical harmonic analysis, DWNM is not only reduced from 4D space to 3D space, but also achieves some useful properties. As is guaranteed by the preprocessing step, it is invariant with respect to translation, rotation and scaling. Since the amplitude of each spherical frequency component does not change when undergoing different viewing sampling sequence, we can confirm that it is independent of the viewing sampling mode. Furthermore, it is robust under tessellation, as we have taken into consideration the effect of surface area in weighting items.

We test our algorithm on 50 models collected from Internet. They are grouped into five classes, e.g. cars, fishes, flowers, lamps and toys, with ten models for each class. The experiments were run on a PC with P2 333MHz and 256MB memory. We have optimized experiment parameters and use a 256*256 rendering window and a sampling rate $N_v=8$ for viewing direction and $N_n=16$ for normal distribution. Here, we utilize OpenGL rendering functions to accelerate the computation of DWNM descriptor.

We compare the classification results in Table 1. Here, the FT (First Tier) column lists the percentage of top k-1 matches (excluding the query) from the query's class, where k is the size of the class. The ST (Second Tier) column lists the same type of result, but for top $2(k$-1$)$ matches. The NN (Nearest neighbor) column lists the percentage of test in which the top match was from the query's class. Overall, our system produces a top k-1 match for 76.8% of the models, a top $2k$-1 match for 93.3% of the models and a top match for 96% of the models.

Table 1. Classification result using DWNM and χ^2

Class	FT	ST	NN
Car	79.9%	96.7%	90%
Fish	98.9%	100%	100%
Flower	72.2%	97.8%	100%
Lamp	38.9%	72.2%	90%
Toy	94.4%	100%	100%

As we notice, the classification result for lamps is unsatisfying. Two reasons may account for it. First, the second-order moments used for rotational alignment scale quadratically with distance from the center of mass, thus small differences in mass distribution cause the principle axes to change significantly. As the descriptor is sensitive to local curvature, a small disturbance in dominant orientation, e.g. making the lamp chimney a bit flatter, will dramatically affect the content of the descriptor, and consequently the similarity estimation.

Our 3D model search engine allows a user to specify a query using an existing 3D model. For each query, it returns a set of candidates representing the first n best matching 3D models rendered with OpenGL. Compared with the thumbnail image approach to represent returned matched results, our system affords more interactivity at the expense of a quick load from disk storage. The user may click on any model to view its information of filename, vertex number, normal count, etc, and he may rotate the model around the origin or scale it to view details. Currently, our system doesn't support refinement of search by iterative queries of the database. Thus, we are motivated in building an interactive module to learn user preference in order to guide future similarity search.

3.2 3D Terrain: A Special Case

As a special case of 3D models, 3D terrain is useful for a number of applications such as navigation (Decide the route to fly from A to B in a simulated environment as the pilot training course requires), location (Where to build a base station and lay "Wired for Management"?) and teleoperation (viewing the environment while controlling the pace of remote machine operation).

What we are interested in is the Earth Data which models geography as a set of connective triangle meshes. Actually, it is a 2D plane with height value at every point of intersection of sampling grid parallel to geographical coordinates. Since Earth Data doesn't provide a closed form like 3D models and possibly can extend far out into distance, we have developed an algorithm to particularly deal with such problem.

Figure 2 demonstrates the details of our process [22]: (1) Simplification of the Earth Data using Quadtree based LOD (Level of Detail) algorithm. (2) For every triangle, compute a feature vector made up of the following components: the angle between the surface normal and z axis, volume of the tetrahedron formed by connecting each of the triangle's vertices with the origin and moments up to the third order. (3) Construct a strongly connected undirect graph with nodes representing feature vectors of every triangle and edges weighted by the Euclidean distance between feature vectors of the corresponding node pairs. (4) Cluster triangles using MST [23](Minimum Spanning Tree) algorithm and express each cluster by its centroid, thus dramatically reduce the dimensionality of signature. (5) Finally, index the Earth Data using SVM (Support Vector Machine) [24] so as to strike the right balance between the accuracy attained on the particular training set and the capacity of the machine.

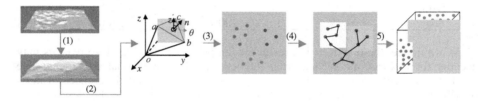

Fig. 2. Computing and indexing our shape descriptor for 3D terrain.

For this experiment, we investigate how well our system produces matches for the query entered. The subjects in this experiment are 60 examples of 3D terrain coming annotated as either "foothill" or "mountain". We design a "leave-ten-out" classification test which randomly chooses 25 examples from each class for training and averages classification results over all ten remaining models. The stopping criteria for the model simplification are the user specified triangle number. We learn from the experiment that 4000 is a suitable choice. The time complexity of the algorithm largely depends on the MST reduction procedure where optimization is required. We have compared MST with PCA (Principle Component Analysis) finding that MST outperforms PCA by 3 percent of precision (70% versus 66.7%) on average.

3.3 3D Motion Retrieval

To support searching for 3D motion, we first construct a hierarchical motion descriptor. The human body is modeled as a skeleton made up of 16 joints. We obtain the data from our motion capture system recording the motion trajectory of every articulation. To describe the mutual dependence of each joint, we use a convenient representation imposing a hierarchical relationship on these joints, where the position and orientation of each joint are specified relative to a "parent" joint. That is, a joint's configuration at any time can be described by a fixed translation and a rotation relative to the parent joint which is in turn defined in terms of its parent, all the way up to the root. Thus, our motion descriptor can be readily represented by a tree with 5 levels (Fig. 3). The root of the tree has full translational and rotational DOFs (degree of freedom) and describes global motion information. This kind of description is inherently compact, with constraints implicitly embedded. Besides, it provides a natural multi-resolution decomposition of movement which offers greater flexibility in building a tree-structured motion library.

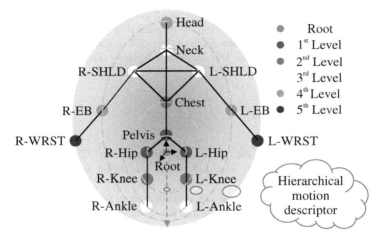

Fig. 3. Human Model and Top-down Hierarchical Motion Description. Note that the "parent" of a joint is the joint which is at a higher level and directly connected to with a bone (black line). The root is defined as the midpoint between L-Hip and R-Hip.

We hierarchically divide the motion library into subcategories using dynamic nearest neighbor cluster algorithm. The partition process will stop after six iterations. Each iteration utilizes the corresponding level of motion information. For example, the first iteration splits the library according to the data stored at the root node.

The main steps for computing clusters are as follows: (1) Adaptively extract key frames from a clip of motion data using unsupervised clustering. This procedure dramatically reduces the motion data to be compared and facilitates the following computation of dissimilarity measure. (2) Assign a similarity score to every pair of motions from current sub-library, using elastic matching between the series of extracted key frames. (3) Dynamically cluster the examples by performing the *single-linkage algorithm.*

Matches for the query are produced by a top-down hierarchical search strategy. At each level, K-Nearest-Neighbor algorithm is used to decide which class the query example belongs to in order to reduce the search space at lower levels. This procedure is repeated until the class is no longer separable. Then we perform elastic matching algorithm within this class and return the most similar results to users.

We test our key frame extraction algorithm on a motion clip with 195 frames of a human going over a small hurdle. The action is repeated four times. All clusters are decided before the 50th frame upon the finish of a complete cycle and no key frame is generated afterwards. For other tests, we have observed the similar results.

For this experiment, we use a test database with more than 450 motion clips. On average, for 75% recall value, our algorithm reports 85% precision value, which is a quite satisfying result.

4   Conclusions

In summary, this paper investigates issues in building a 3D model and motion retrieval system for web-based learning. The main contributions are: (1) a new shape descriptor based on statistical distribution of normal that is both discriminating and easy to compute. (2) new retrieval media including 3D terrain and motion, which are useful for applications such as pilot and cartoonist training but haven't been explored yet.

5   Future Work

This paper has just scratched the surface of research on 3D model and motion retrieval for web-based learning. The following are just a few of the topics that deserve further investigation:

1. **System integration:** currently, we are working on a system to support retrieval based on multiple 3D resources including 3D models, terrain and motion. This is particularly useful for students whose major is Computer Animation. We hope it would be easier to build an animation character and set movement to it using modeling tools incorporated with our system.
2. **Web oriented new query interfaces:** follow-up work should consider enabling browse and retrieval of 3D model and 3D motion through Internet by VRML plugged-in WWW-browser. Considerable amount of work has to be devoted to building a system with the full capability of model acquisition, shape analysis and similarity matching. Meanwhile, it is worthwhile to consider other methods for specifying 3D model and motion retrievals. For instance, the user may draw silhouette of an object and ask the system to retrieve similar models. And the spatial or spatio-temporal mode of an object's trajectory might be used to retrieve motions with the same moving style.
3. **New matching algorithms:** currently we are comparing whole objects, but it would be interesting to match partial objects as well. For example, upon submitting a head model, the system not only returns various head models including humans' and animals', but bodies containing heads as well.
4. **New applications:** it is necessary to investigate whether the proposed methods can be applied to other applications such as molecular biology, medicine and the related learning tasks.

We expect that in the near future analysis and retrieval of 3D models and motion will become ubiquitous and compose an important research area in web-based learning.

Acknowledgements. This work is supported by 973 Program (No. 2002CB312101), the National Natural Science Foundation of China (No. 60272031), Zhejiang Provincial Natural Science Foundation of China (ZD0212), Doctorate Research Foundation of the State Education Commission of China (No. 20010335049). We would like to thank Jun Xiao, Feng Liu for helpful discussion, 3D Café (http://www.3dcafe.com), Toucan Corporation (http://www.toucan.co.jp/), The 3D Studio(http://www.the3Dstudio.com) for providing free 3D resources, and Wei Chen for proof reading the paper.

References

1. http://www.intel.com/apac/gb/virtualcity/index.htm
2. A. Del Bimbo, *Visual Information Retrieval*, Morgan Kaufmann, San Francisco, USA, 1999.
3. M.S.Lew, *Principles of Visual Information Retrieval*, Springer, Germany, 2001.
4. M.T.Suzuki, T Kato, N.Otsu, "A similarity retrieval of 3D polygonal models using rotation invariant shape descriptors". *IEEE Int. Conf. On System, Man, and Cybernetics 2000*, Nashville, USA, pp. 2946–2952, 2000.
5. M.Ankerst et al, "3D shape histograms for similarity search and classification in spatial databases", *6th Intl.Symp. On Advances in Spatial Databases,* vol.1651, pp.207–228, 1999.
6. M. Elad et al, "Content based Retrieval of VRML Objects – An iterative and Interactive Approach", *The 6th Eurographics workshop in Multimedia*, Manchester, UK, Sept 2001.
7. R. Osada, T. Funkhouser, Chazelle, and D. Dobkin, "Shape Distributions", *ACM Transactions on Graphics*, Vol.21, No.4, pp.93–101, Oct 2002.
8. R. Ohbuchi, T. Otagiri, M. Ibato, and T. Takei, "Shape similarity search of three-dimensional models using parameterized statistics", *Proceedings of Pacific Graphics 2002*, pp. 265–274, 2002.
9. D.V.Vranic and D.Saupe, "3D Model Retrieval", *Proceedings of the Spring Conference on Computer Graphics and its Applications*, Budmerice, Slovakia, pp.89–93, May 2000.
10. T.Zaharia, F.Preteux, "3D Shape Spectrum descriptor", *Research report ISO/IEC JTC1/SC 29/WG11, MPEG 97 /M5242*, Melbourne, Australia, Oct 1999.
11. M. Hilaga, Y. Shinagawa, T. Kohmura, and T. L. Kunii, "Topology Matching for Fully Automatic Similarity Estimation of 3D Shapes", *Proceedings of ACM SIGGRAPH 2001,* pp. 203–212, USA, Aug 2001.
12. H.-Y.Shum, M.Hebert, and K.Ikeuchi. "On 3D Shape similarity", *Proceedings of CVPR*, pp. 526–531,1996.
13. D.V.Vranic and D.Saupe, "3D Shape Descriptor Based n 3D Fourier Transform", *Proceedings of the EURASIP Conference on Digital Signal Processing for Multimedia Communications and Services,* Budapest, Hungary, pp.271–274, Sept 2001.
14. T.Zaharia, F.Preteux, "Hough transform-based 3D mesh retrieval", *Proceedings of SPIE 4476 on Vision Geometry X,* San Diego, USA, pp. 175–185, Aug 2001.
15. T. Funkhouser et al, "A Search Engine for 3D Models", to appear in *ACM Transactions on Graphics*, Vol.22, No.4, Jan 2003.

16. E. Paquet and M. Rioux, "A Content-based Search Engine for VRML Databases", *Proceedings of Computer Vision and Pattern Recognition 1998*, S. Barbara, USA, pp.541–546. Jun 1998.
17. N. Dimitrova and F. Golshani, "Motion Recovery for Video Content Classification," *ACM Transactions on Information Systems*, Vol. 13, No. 4, pp. 408–439, October 1995.
18. S. Dagtas, W. Al-Khatib, A. Ghafoor and R. Kashyap, "Models for Motion-based Video indexing and Retrieval," *IEEE Transactions on Image Processing*, Vol. 9, No. 1, pp. 88–101, Jan. 2000.
19. W. Chen, S. F. Chang, "Motion Trajectory Matching of Video Objects," *Proc. of SPIE*, Vol. 3972, pp. 544–553, 2000.
20. Yan Li et al, "Motion texture: a two-level statistical model for character motion synthesis," *ACM Transactions on Graphics* Vol. 21, No. 3, pp.465–472, 2002.
21. Katherine Pullen, Christoph Bregler, "Motion capture assisted animation: texturing and synthesis," *ACM Transactions on Graphics* Vol. 21, No. 3, pp.501–508, 2002.
22. Yueting Zhuang, Xiang Liu, "Multimedia Knowledge Exploitation for E-learning: some Enabling Techniques", *The 1ˢᵗ International Conference on Web-based Learning (ICWL 2002)*, Hongkong, pp. 411–422, 2002.
23. http://www.cs.sunysb.edu/~algorith/lectures-good/node17.html
24. Burges C.J.C, " A Tutorial on Support Vector Machines for Pattern Recognition", Data Mining and Knowledge Discovery, 2(2), pp.121–167, 1998.

Design, Implementation, and Evaluation of a Digital Lectern System

Nikolai Joukov[1,3], Markus Fauster[2,3], and Tzi-cker Chiueh[1,3]

[1] Computer Science Department
State University of New York at Stony Brook
Stony Brook, NY 11794-4400 USA
{njoukov, chiueh}@cs.sunysb.edu
[2] Institute of Information Technology, University Klagenfurt
Universitatsstr. 65-67, 020 Klagenfurt, Austria
mfauster@edu.uni-klu.ac.at
[3] Rether Networks Inc.
99 Mark Tree rd. Suite 301, Centereach NY 11720 USA

Abstract. Deployment of asynchronous learning systems is still very limited and expensive due to the common use of digital video for recording and distribution of classroom lectures. Lectern II is a digital desk system that can transparently capture, through a touch-sensitive screen, all important lecture components during normal classroom lecturing activity without expensive video acquisition equipments. Lectures recorded through Lectern can be edited, automatically uploaded to a web server and viewed by students using a standard streaming media player. Since the average size of a one hour-long lecture is less than 10 MB, Lectern II lectures can be conveniently played even using a modest modem connection. Considering the total cost of a complete Lectern II system at less than $4,000, Lectern II represents the first Web-based course lecture recording system that has the potential to be widely used in the classrooms of universities and K-12 schools.

1 Introduction

For the last years, one can observe the emerging trend to choose the web as a medium for asynchronous learning systems [1]. Students can benefit a lot from the availability of means to review and repeat lecture material with the pace and at the time that is best suited for them. Therefore the effectiveness and convenience of classroom lectures can be dramatically increased [2]. Such systems typically use digital video as their main delivery medium, which delivers expressive, but also very expensive results. They are costly to produce, due to the dedicated hardware, software and personal necessary during recording and editing. The enormous size of the video streams recorded from lectures also creates problems for storage and especially delivery, because the high bandwidth requirements seriously restrict the accessibility of video-based material. In particular, they are out of reach to users that are connected to the Internet via ordinary modems. In fact, the bandwidth demands exceeding these typical

W. Zhou et al. (Eds.): ICWL 2003, LNCS 2783, pp. 241–252, 2003.
© Springer-Verlag Berlin Heidelberg 2003

for modems are common for all the current lecturing activity capturing systems (for example see [3]). Considering the problems outlined above, it is not surprising that deployment of such systems is very limited and that most lecture materials in the Internet are still only available as a series of lecture slides, therefore missing any additional information like speech or graphical annotations.

The Lectern project is dedicated to minimize the equipment and operational cost associated with course lecture recording and editing by refraining from the application of video capturing. According to the approach described in [4,5], Lectern uses the touch-sensitive screen technology to offer a "digital desk" to lecturer. This not only effectively captures voice, displayed slides and pen annotations, it has also shown to support the actual presentation process. The key advantage of the approach is that all significant components of a lecture, like sliding changes, speech and on-screen-remarks, can be captured effectively without the disadvantages of video recordings. The first generation of the Lectern system [4] still had a number of weaknesses. One problem was, that all slides had to be prepared as HTML files and that the system was designed around the assumption that would be rendered exactly the same on all possible operating systems and web browser settings. Aside from that, all system components were exclusively implemented for the Windows OS. And finally, the download of a custom player was required in order to play back the lectures. Keeping these drawbacks in mind, Lectern was completely redesigned while basically retaining its proven approach of capturing lectures: With Lectern II, whose architecture is described in [6], it is now possible to prepare slides using an arbitrary program running on the Windows platform, because a specially designed virtual printer is supplied to produce the internal slide sequence format. Once recorded, lectures can be edited and played back for review before they are finally converted into a Web ready format: All visual information is saved in a highly compressed rasterized form and audio is encoded using the MP3 format in order minimize space and bandwidth usage. All time dependent events (slide changes, on-screen remarks, mouse movements and voice) are coordinated using a combination of Synchronized Multimedia Integration Language [7] and the RealPix [8] format. In order to simplify upload, maintenance and online search of lectures, a set of optimized web server side tools is supplied. Recorded lectures can then be played back on most operating systems using freely available software and a modest modem connection simply by following a link to the lecture of interest.

The total cost of the hardware making up a Lectern II system is estimated to be less than $4,000, including a video projector, which is usually available in most of the lecturing environments. Since no expensive acquisition infrastructure is required and the production version of Lectern II consists of only two components, Lectern II is truly portable, and can be set up in almost every classroom in K-12 schools, colleges, or universities, and thus represents the first practical and economical asynchronous learning system for *everyday* use.

2   System Overview

2.1   Hardware Setup

Similar to the hardware set up described in [4] Lectern II consists of a high resolution touch-sensitive screen, a PC, a video projector, and a microphone (see Fig. 1a). However, a Tablet PC can substitute a touch-sensitive screen and a PC (see fig. 1b). Instructors carry out the entire lecturing activity using the touch sensitive screen, while its contents are mirrored on a big screen via the video projector. A digital pen is used to emphasize important points, draw illustrations and formulas, or simply attract students' attention to the location on the slide that is currently being discussed. Meanwhile, the voice is being recorded through a microphone. In the case when a Tablet PC is used the whole setup consists of only two pieces and thus can be conveniently carried by the instructor and easily shared among many classrooms.

 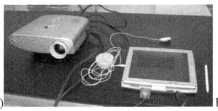

Fig. 1. Lectern II setup as seen by instructor. Setup consists of a touch-sensitive screen, digital pen, microphone, PC, and a video projector (a). A Tablet PC can substitute a touch-sensitive screen and a PC (b).

2.2   Slides Preparation

To simplify lecture preparation a special virtual printer driver was created. Thus, the lecture slides can be prepared in any program that can print on a printer on a windows platform. Once the slides are ready instructor can print them on the Lectern printer and the Lectern recording program is activated automatically. In fact, the Lectern printer is an EMF (Enhanced Metafile) [9] printer with a special print processor that extracts the slides from the spool in the vector EMF form. Subsequently, these slides can be rasterized and displayed on almost any system running Windows regarding of the screen resolution. An important additional benefit of this approach is that all the textual information in the slide can be extracted and made available for the context search by our own search engine and all web crawlers in general, making the slides content available for all of the popular search engines. The software drivers are designed for use with Windows NT, Windows XP and Windows 2000. Once generated, the prepared slide sequence can be repeatedly used.

2.3 Lectures Recording and Editing

One of the main goals of the project was to make the system easy to use while providing all the desirable functionality.

In general, the system operates in one of two modes: recording and editing a recorded lecture. In both cases the toolbar pops up on the side of the screen if a mouse or a pen is moved at the screen edge. Otherwise the toolbar is completely covered by the slide and will not obstruct slide's view.

In the recording mode the instructor can record/pause the lecturing process, choose a pen color, insert a new blank slide or create a copy of the current slide that is clean from pen remarks. As illustrated in Figure 2, a scrollable list of thumbnail slides' images is provided on the same toolbar to ease the slide navigation.

During the editing mode a prerecorded lecture can be played back and edited. The editing operations include cut to clipboard and paste from clipboard or another lecture. All the editing actions can be undone.

After the recording and editing is finished the lecture is saved in the vector format for subsequent editing operations and a set of files is generated and put on the Web through an automatic upload process.

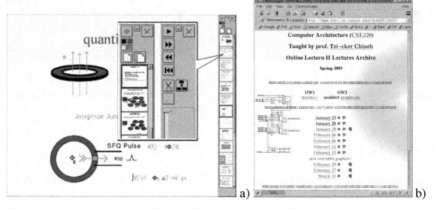

Fig. 2. a) The main screen of the Lectern II recorder/editor. The toolbar on the right pops up only if the mouse cursor or a pen is over the right edge of the screen. The inset shows the upper portion of the recording (on the left) and editing (on the right) mode toolbars. b) Links to the lectures are automatically updated with every new lecture upload.

2.4 Lectures Upload

After a lecture is recorded it can be uploaded to a web server automatically. There exist three ways to do so. Firstly, a lecture can be uploaded using a built in FTP client. Secondly, a standard HTTP file upload can be used. Thirdly, the output files can be uploaded using HTTP to a specially designed Lectern server. In the latter case a set of users has to be configured first. Each user's account is protected with a password against unintentional or intentional damage of recorded lectures. A user's index file is updated with every lecture upload while a template of the index file and lectures storage directory are associated with every user. The index file template is an arbitrary HTML file and thus it could be just a course web page as shown in fig. 2b.

2.5 Lectures Search

To easy the lectures navigation and enhance their accessibility a special search engine has been implemented. Thus, any student can find a desired lecture fragment using the keyword search. A preview of slides containing a specified keyword(s) is given together with the search results. To broaden the accessibility of the recorded lectures even more the contents of the slides are made accessible to the web crawlers and thus for all the popular search engines.

3   Streaming Playback

3.1 Lecture Representation

The Real Player [10] from the RealNetworks was chosen to be the recorded lectures player. The major reasons for this decision are that the player is free, available for all most popular operation systems, already installed by many users, and most importantly, provides support for the streaming playback of images. For this purpose the Real Player supports the RealPix (RP) file format [8]. Basically, this format allows specifying the screen location and time for a particular picture to be displayed. Pen remarks and erase regions are displayed over the background slide images at the times when they were put on the screen during the actual lecture.

Most importantly the RealPix format allows specifying the sizes for all the images to be played so that the Real Player itself can calculate the bandwidth utilization in advance and preload the data accordingly. This functionality can be further enhanced if a special streaming server [11] from the RealNetworks is used to send the data. The voice and the RealPix presentations are in turn synchronized by the means of Synchronized Multimedia Integration Language [7].

3.2 Lectures Statistics

Table 1 shown below contains information about the set of files generated from three lectures on "Wireless LAN-based Systems and Applications," which is an advanced course in the Computer Science Department of SUNY at Stony Brook and one lecture on undergraduate "Computer Architecture" taught in the same university. Note that the cursor was tracked only in the latter case.

Given statistics shows that the average bandwidth required is less than 18 Kbit, which is well below the speed of even a modest modem. The voice data accounts for more than 90% of the whole data volume. Therefore, all the images despite being saved in a rasterized form occupy less than 10% of the whole lecture. As soon as SMIL and RealPix files are loaded the Real Player can start the files download according to their position and size so as to make the bandwidth requirement as close to the average as possible. The typical startup latency is on the order of several seconds.

Table 1. Information about the set of files generated from three lectures on "Wireless LAN-based Systems and Applications," which is an advanced course in the Computer Science Department of SUNY at Stony Brook and one lecture on undergraduate "Computer Architecture" taught in the same university (rightmost column). Note that the cursor was tracked only in the latter case.

	Lec. 1	Lec. 2	Lec. 3	Lec. 4
Lecture duration (minutes)	77	99	118	72
Total files generated	539	429	1017	895
Total slides presented	44	51	17	6
Total size (KB)	9,930	13,172	14,902	9,173
MP3 file size (KB)	9,262	12,158	14,314	8,564
Total slide images size (KB)	512	880	178	40
RP plus SMIL file size (KB)	70	60	226	357

3.3 Synchronization Skew

In addition to the MCI voice time stretching problem described later, there is one more source of potential voice data lag behind the rest of the lecture data. It turned out that some existing MP3 players stretch the voice sampled at the rate proportional to 11.025 KHZ for about 7 seconds per 25 minutes. This problem was observed with Real Players for Linux and for Windows as well as with the Quick Time [12] player.

4   Recording/Editing System Implementation

All the Lectern recording/editing components were written with MS Visual C++ 6.0 using Windows32 API only. It is important to understand that many system design decisions are explained by the output format restrictions.

4.1   Slides and Remarks Handling

The internal slide representation is a list of GDI (Graphics Device Interface) calls in a form of Enhanced Metafile. The pen annotations or remarks are captured and stored differently depending on the platform used. The Tablet API [14] is used whenever it is available on the host system. By using Tablet API the pen drawings represent not only the lines drawn but even the pen pressure is captured. In case the Tablet API is not available the remarks are captured and stored as a set of points that are connected with lines when displayed on the screen. Every erase action made by instructor is sampled as a set of fixed size square regions that are required to be cleaned from all previous pen remarks. Thus, erase events are stored as a set of centers of the corresponding square regions. To play back an erase event a set of possibly overlapping square portions of the original slide is copied from the slide image stored in a memory buffer over the screen contents.

To create a Web-ready content all the screen images, remarks and erase regions are stored in a rasterized form. To minimize the size of the images, they are stored in an 8-bit indexed palette mode. The palette is constructed using a modified popularity algorithm [15]. Pen remarks are stored as transparent images of the corresponding pen-created line segments. The erase regions are stored as portions of the original slide image over which the pen eraser was applied. All the files are compressed and saved in Portable Network Graphics (PNG) [16] format using the libpng library. The playback time composition of the generated images is illustrated in figure 3.

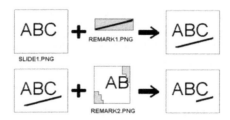

Fig. 3. Slides and pen remarks images composition. Top: a transparent remark image is put over a slide image. Bottom: putting a portion of the original slide over the previously composed image erases a part of the previously drawn remark. Erase region image is composed of several square fragments of the original slide. Grey color denotes transparency in this figure.

4.2 Voice Handling

Voice recording and playback is realized using the Windows Media Control Interface (MCI) [17]. All other voice related operations including cut and paste are done directly on the ADPCM voice data. The voice is sampled at 11,025 8-bit samples per second rate that is well above the human voice frequency range. Unfortunately, Windows MCI has a problem: recorded voice stream duration is longer than the voice recording time. The amount of MCI voice stretching depends on computer performance, but even on a 2.2 GHz PC with plenty of RAM there is a minute long lag of speech behind the presentation process at the end of a 2.5 hours long lecture. Recorded voice is resampled afterwards in order to solve the problem. Voice is compressed using Mpeg 2.5 Layer 3 format by the external Lame [18] program.

4.3 Cursor Tracking

As suggested by several instructors who used Lectern II system the mouse cursor is often used to emphasize certain slide locations while no drawings are made. Thus, it is essential to track and show the mouse cursor during the lecture playback. However, maintaining cursor image in the recorded lectures required removal of the cursor from its previous screen position as it moves. We had considered several alternatives to this problem. RealPix format does not provide support for outputting images by XORing two images. Representing the cursor as a transparent GIF movie that would erase itself after a timeout is not supported by Real Player either. Basically, the only way to erase a cursor using RealPix specification is to put an image over a cursor. However, we could not afford to create a separate image for every cursor movement, since this is a very frequent operation and the number of such images would be enormous. Fortunately, there is no problem to remove a cursor if it is not over a remark because the background image is already in the player memory anyway. Therefore, it costs just one short line of code to instruct the Real Player to show a portion of the slide over the rectangle containing a cursor. Therefore, we decide to "quantize" the cursor's position by moving the cursor position slightly, if necessary, so that it does not overlap with remarks and thus always have a cursor displayed over the pre-prepared slide image only. As a result of this optimization, the increase of the RealPix file due to the cursor tracking becomes very small. For example, for the lecture described in the last column of table 1 the total increase in the lecture size is less than 2%.

5   Backend Server Implementation

5.1   Lectures Upload and Maintenance

HTTP and FTP clients are built into the recording and editing subsystems of Lectern II. An instructor, is required to fill just a few entries and press one button for the whole upload process initiation. If the HTTP is chosen as the upload method the corresponding server is first probed for the presence of the Lectern II server software and only if it is not found a standard HTTP file upload method is tried. The Lectern II server upload part is implemented as a set of Perl [19] scripts. Therefore the server is platform and OS independent. The scripts are responsible for the communication with the Lectern II main program in the uploading process, placing the files in the appropriate directories and maintaining the search database and an HTML-based directory file that contains links to all uploaded lectures by the given Lectern II user. The directory file is created based on a template file that an individual user can customize, for example, it can be a course web page with automatically updated links to the recorded lectures with date and subject annotation.

5.2   Lectures Content Search Support

During the upload process an HTML file with all the textual information extracted from the slides is created and put on the server. This file is made accessible to the Web crawlers and thus for the majority of the Web search engines, including Google. The HTML file, in turn, has reference to the lecture that contains corresponding slides.

Because the indexing interval of the popular search engines is on the order of weeks there is a need to provide a separate search engine for users to search for the lectures immediately after the course lectures are recorded. We implement a special search engine to work with the Lectern II server. With this search engine, recorded Lectern lectures do not need to be made available on the global Internet. In addition, the output of the search engine contains previews of the slides that contain given keywords. Thus, end users can access a specific slide of Lectern lectures directly using the slide's keywords, without the need to visit an intermediate HTML page, as is the case if a general search engine is used. This search engine is implemented in Python language [20] and therefore is also platform and OS independent.

6 Evaluation

We have used the Lectern II system to record two courses in two consecutive semesters in the Computer Science Department of SUNY at Stony Brook. The first course, "Wireless LAN-based Systems and Applications" is an advanced course that was taught for 18 students in Fall 2002. The other course is a mainstream undergraduate "Computer Architecture" taught for 46 students in Spring 2003. The recorded lectures for the latter course are available at http://www.ecsl.cs.sunysb.edu/cse320/2003/ [21]. The third author of this paper is the instructor for both courses.

6.1 Evaluation by Instructors

The instructor of these two recorded courses feels that Lectern II introduces minimal intrusiveness in lecture delivery because of its excellent transparent recording capability, and that the learning effort required to familiarize with the system is relatively minor (10-30 minutes). An important advantage of Lectern II is that pre-prepared slides can be used as a background for drawing or writing. Notice that usually instructors are required to display slides on a screen while drawing the explanations on the blackboard separately. This arrangement is somewhat awkward because the light is usually dimmed in a room where projector is being used, and thus the blackboard usage is necessarily restricted. Another important feature of Lectern II is that it allows the instructor to sit in front of students during the lecture. This way both slides and students are visible to the instructor at the same time.

The fact that Lectern II allows an instructor to discuss a pre-prepared slide with the help of multiple remark slides is particularly useful because the instructor can leverage both statically prepared lecture slides and dynamically composed remark slides repeatedly in the course to cross-reference related concepts and examples. Also, the coloring and erasure capability of Lectern II also proves to be instrumental in making the lectures more effective. However, the instructor also thinks that Lectern II still has room for further improvement. The screen space available to the instructor is somewhat small, only 10 to 13 inches diagonally, which forces the instructor to adjust his "writing board space allocation algorithm" used in his previous teaching activities. In addition, writing/drawing on a touch-sensitive screen is still less effective than writing/drawing on a piece of paper or on the white/black board, despite the improvement in digital inking technology. However, after one to two lectures, the instructor is able to learn to adjust to this digital pen interface.

6.2   Usage Statistics Collection and Analysis

We use a specially designed system called Ktrack to monitor the usage statistics of the recorded lectures. Ktrack uses HTTP redirection mechanism to monitor access counts for any HTTP retrievable resources. The number of different students per day who used "Computer Architecture" lectures for the period from February 22nd to March 12th 2003 is shown in figure 4. This time interval is interesting because it contains three peaks of activity associated with a Midterm (Mar. 4th), a homework deadline that was postponed (Mar. 6th), and an actual homework deadline (Mar. 11th). There are 46 students in the class. From this figure we can conclude that students view Lectern lectures routinely on a daily basis. In addition, around 80% of the students reviewed the lectures as their final preparation step before the exam. Student's activity pattern during the midterm day is shown in figure 5.

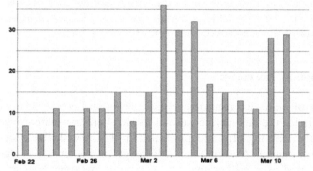

Fig. 4. Number of different students per day who viewed "Computer Architecture" course lectures during the period from February 22nd to March 12th 2003. Three peaks of activity are associated with: a Midterm (Mar. 4th), a homework deadline that was postponed (Mar. 6th), and an actual homework deadline (Mar. 11th). There are 46 students in the class.

Fig. 5. Number of different students who either downloaded lectures or viewed them online for the first time during the day as a function of the time of the day. The day shown is the midterm day (Mar. 4th). The fact that the midterm started at 5:30pm is well correlated with the figure.

6.3 Evaluation by Students

After the "Computer architecture" course was over we distributed a survey about Lectern II system among the students. We collected and analyzed 36 completed surveys. 34 out of 36 students strongly supported the Lectern system and recommended its use in other courses. Survey showed that majority of the students prefers to download the lectures for offline view. Table 2 shows the Lectern system usage statistics reported. Table 3 presents most popular reasons to view the recorded lectures.

Table 2. Distribution of students on the number of times they viewed recorded slides.

# of views	Never	Once or twice	<10 times	>10 times
% of students	8.3 %	13.9 %	30.6 %	47.2 %

Table 3. Most popular reasons to review recorded lectures.

Reason to view recorded lectures	# of students reported
Prepare for midterm	91.7%
Late for a lecture/missing a lecture	55.6%
Did not understand something during the lecture	50%
Work at homework	27.8%
Routinely review course material every week	19.4%

7 Conclusion

Lectern II is an easy to use and inexpensive course-lecture capturing system. The system not only allows regular lectures to be recorded transparently, but also enhances lecturing effectiveness in classrooms. Instructors can edit recorded lectures to add/delete materials and make them available over the Web without any additional human intervention. Lectern II includes an automatic backend to put recorded lectures on the Web, greatly simplifying such tasks as directory and keyword index preparation. The textual information from the slides is automatically extracted indexed, and made searchable through a special search engine tailored to Lectern II lectures. In addition, textual slides contents are accessible for standard search engines such as Google. Recorded material can be played back using a free streaming player via a modest modem link. Initial evaluation show that students and instructors found the system to be extremely useful and helpful. Students use the Lectern II system on a routine basis to review the course materials and/or catch up with missed classes.

There are several directions along which we plan to evolve the current Lectern II system. First, we will provide a richer set of presentation primitives to help instructors more effectively deliver their lectures. For example, Lectern II does not support PowerPoint-style animation, or display of relevant Web pages during course presentations. Second, we will deliver a more powerful backend facility that can automate the entire recorded lecture maintenance lifecycle, including storage, indexing, directory construction, archiving, usage tracking and management, and integration with other course management functions such as email communications, FAQ maintenance, announcements, homework distribution, and collection, etc.

References

1. Radford A.: The future of multimedia in education. First Monday, Vol. 2. 11 (1997)
2. Dutton J., Dutton M., and Perry J.: Do Online Students Perform as Well as Lecture Students? Journal of Engineering Education, Vol. 90. 1 (2001) 131–136
3. Comtasia Studio, http://www.techsmith.com/.
4. Chiueh T., Deng P.: Lectern: A Multimedia Course-Lecture Capturing and Playback System. proc. IEEE Multimedia, New York City, (2000)
5. Chiueh T., Wu W., Lam L.: Variorum: A Multimedia-Based Program Documentation System. proc. IEEE Multimedia, New York City, (2000) 155–158
6. Joukov N, Chiueh T.: Lectern II: A Multimedia Lecture Capturing and Editing System. to appear in IEEE Multimedia. Baltimore, (2003)
7. Synchronized Multimedia Integration Language, http://www.w3c.org/TR/smil20/
8. RealPix specification,
    http://service.real.com/help/library/guides/realpix/htmfiles/notice.htm
9. Enhanced Metafiles, Microsoft Windows SDK
10. Real One player, http://www.realone.com/
11. Helix Universal Server home page,
    http://www.realnetworks.com/products/server/index.html
12. Quick Time Player, http://www.apple.com/quicktime/
13. Windows Media Player, http://windowsmedia.com
14. Tablet PC API, Microsoft Windows SDK
15. Foley J. D., van Dam A., Feiner S. K., and Hughes J. F.: Computer Graphics: Principles and Practice. 2nd edition. Addison-Wesley, Reading, MA (1996).
16. Libpng library, http://www.libpng.org/
17. Media Control Interface, Microsoft Windows SDK
18. LAME project, http://lame.sourceforge.net/
19. Perl Language Website, www.perl.org
20. Python Language Website, www.python.org
21. Chiueh, T.: CSE320 Undergraduate Computer Architecture online lectures,
    http://www.ecsl.cs.sunysb.edu/cse320/2003/

User Learning Experience in Web-Based Systems:
A Case Study

Kamaljeet Sandhu[1] and Brian Corbitt[2]

[1]School of Information Technology
Deakin University, Geelong, Australia
ksan@deakin.edu.au
[2]School of Information Systems
Deakin University, Melbourne, Australia
bcorbitt@deakin.edu.au

Abstract. User learning experience may be considered as one of the prominent factors shaping the adoption of web-based systems. Web-based learners interfacing with large amount of information the rationale is to deduce the effect in the current web-based task environment. Understanding Web-based learner perception on the basis of the prior experience with information may provide insights into what constitutes in driving those perceptions and their effect in the current and future web-based learning process. The paper demonstrates theoretical context of user learning experience with information and proceeds in an attempt to distinguish factors in using web-based systems.

1 Introduction

User information experience in web-based systems learning is an important area that is gradually growing with introduction and adoption of web-based technology (i.e. WebCT, Firstclass, and Blackboard). The information available in web-based systems learning may be one of the determinants which direct the user in achieving the desired objectives that form the purpose of using the system. The user information requirements may be based from prior experience in similar or related traditional learning environment. Information search form the initial need in the activity to achieve the desired objectives, and hence the acquisition of information experience process. Information if not available to users in e-learning or traditional learning environments may direct the user in adopting the search process based on experience.

Web-based user services are generally perceived as being successful, but there has been little evaluation of how well the web meets its users' primary information requirements [1]. The freedom and flexibility offered by the Internet allow user's to connect to other websites of their interest and at the same time build upon their e-learning experience on the web. A number of researchers suggested that flow is a useful construct for describing interactions with websites [2][3][4][5]. Flow has been described as "the process of optimal experience" [2][6] achieved when sufficiently

W. Zhou et al. (Eds.): ICWL 2003, LNCS 2783, pp. 253–263, 2003.

motivated user perceives a balance between their skills and challenges of the interaction, together with focused attention [7]. The concept of flow is important because it has a clear set of antecedent conditions and consequences that have implications for web-based learning. User's information experience on a website, its impact, retention of that web-based learning experience can be related to the flow concept. For the flow state to be experienced the user must perceive skills and challenges to be in balance and above a critical threshold and the user must be paying attention. That is a user must be in state of learning. Hoffman and Novak [7] suggest that the consequences of flow in web-based environments relates to increased learning, increased exploratory and participatory behaviours, and more positive subjective experiences, that a critical objective of a commercial website is to facilitate the flow experience. Karahanna et al. [8] suggest that user's acquire personal experience and their own source of evaluative information in using the information system. Such an experience can have a strong affect on the user in remembering their learning experience on a particular website.

This study assumes that user's experience with information already exists in the traditional environment (i.e., offline). Understanding the traditional learning complexities of user experience with information and transforming it to the web-based environment is a challenge for both practitioners and researchers. The dimension and scale of such complexity in terms of technology and its alliance with information may provide an integration point where technology requirements may meet with the user's learning experience. Defining user learning experience with information is not an easy and straightforward process. Rather developing an approach to studying the learning experience process on the basis of web-based learning and user interaction is suggested. This paper specifically investigates issues related to user learning experiences in web-based learning adoption and the process involving continued use of web-based learning services. With technology constantly changing it will subsequently have an effect on the user's learning experience and perception.

User's engaged in web-based learning activities tend to focus on prior information experience and perception, especially from the offline environment. The effect of information on user experience in web-based learning on first time user's compared to the frequent user's will vary, a user with no experience can form high (or low) perception, especially via word of mouth communications. Such perceptions may behave differently from those developed via experience. Davidow and Uttal [9] suggest user's expectation is formed by many uncontrollable factors, from the experience of user's…to a user's psychological state. It is argued that a user web-based learning experience is formed and based on wider range of prior experiences that may be recalled or narrowed in a similar situation. The flow of information over the Internet is faster and communication between user's leads in enhanced learning. Understanding user's web-based learning experience and perception solely on the basis of online or offline experience would tend to limit the research dimension; rather a combination approach is adopted.

2 Methodology

The aim of the study is to investigate the adoption of web-based learning amongst users. This led to the development of converging lines of inquiry, a process of triangulation [10]. In the first instance discussions were held together with three senior staff members involved in implementing the web-based learning project. They included the executive director, IT Manager, and an outside Consultant. In the second round separate individual interviews are conducted with these participants. The third round of interviews was conducted with the admissions manager and separate individual interviews with two other staff members. Altogether six separate interviews with participants were held. Though the participant's gender is not a major factor for introspection, it coincided to balance, three males and three females. In the first round interviews the data collected were compared with the second round and third round interview data, for consistency, clarity and accuracy of the information. Interview data were also compared to test for the factors having effect on users with high and low performance in learning how to use the web-based system. This provided the advantage of not duplicating the data with just one set of evidence. The discussions and interviews were open-ended [10], the researcher in the beginning provided the topic, and the respondents are probed of their opinion about the events. The questions are directed towards user's learning experience with the web-based system. This led the users in reflecting their recent learning experiences with the system and demonstrating its effectiveness in the web-based task. It provides the opportunity of capturing rich information that is fresh and part of the user learning interface within the web-based system. It not only provides information about the user's learning experience, but also demonstrates the boundaries of the web-based learning system, in other words the scope of the system in providing enhanced learning is clearly reflected from the data the user's provided to what the system was capable of doing within the parameters. This approach took into consideration the users and the system context in understanding the web-based learning process. It provides important information from the user's perspective in the terms of the learning process available in the web-based system.

3 The Case Study

The case study examines the web-based framework of the University of Australia (UA)[1]. International students have the option to lodge an admission application through either of: web-based e-service on the Internet, phone, fax, or in person.

On receiving the application a decision is made by the staff on the admission status. Within this process the department is implementing an electronic delivery of its services on the website. Web-based e-service has been in use for the last two and half years. The complete process involves students making the application and the staff

---

[1] not the real name

processing applications on the website. The staff is currently using the web-based e-service and the paper-based system in conducting the tasks. Transition from paper-based to web-based e-service is believed by the department to be a significant step in the direction of moving the complete student admission process over the website and gradually removing the paper-based system. The users learning experience in adopting the web-based system is focus of attention in the study.

4   Evaluating User's Information Experience

The user perception of web electronic service is a burden and acted as a barrier to their work. The users learnt that it increased the workload, slowed the work process, and brought in complexity to the task. The department did not implement electronic services or introduce technology into jobs at the same time. The effect on user learning experience in using the e-service is not estimated when the system was being developed. Understanding the task sequence from start to finish, and integrating those functions into web-based learning process is missing. It lacks coherence. Individual users did not have consistent skills in learning how to use the system because of differing levels of expertise (i.e., user category). Specific expertise needed for conducting the task was lacking. Different task requires different skills when done on paper, doing it electronically requires different experience with information and knowing what was happening beyond the user's computer screen. In the paper-based system, it was known to the user how different process of a task and where information was stored and retained when needed, such as the filing, organizing, storing of documentation was systematically interconnected, in case of electronic service little was known by way what constituted as web-based e-service task process beyond the computer screen. Proper documentation providing information to the user's for referencing were either missing or unknown. The users didn't have learning experience in how to operate the system. One participant mentioned:

"User's had no confidence in the system and decision making." The users were asked to enter all information directly to the web. To expect a user to start using an electronic service without prior learning the user's experience is not perceive to be appropriate. Despite providing regular training the user resistance to use the electronic system increased. The following quote support this notion:

"There are quite a few fields where we can't use the web-based e-services." Martin, [11] suggest that user learning experience evolves, or ranges, from naïve (no system knowledge) through inexperienced to competent and finally to expert. On such basis user's can be divided into following categories: novice, intermediate, and experienced. It is important to remember that different categories of user's learning experience vary at different stages in performing the task. It is anticipated the user's are in a learning process and shift from one mode to another, with experience sliding up or down on the learning swing and the user experience varies, till they reach a point (see Figure 1, point A) where the learning experience flow is at the optimum level in doing the task.

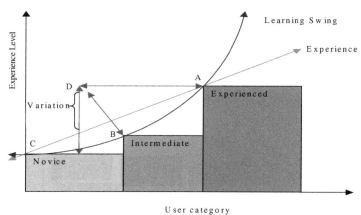

A- Optimum point; B- Improving point; C- Learning starting point;
D- Experience variation point

Fig.1. Learning-Experience Swing [12]

The assimilation and dissimulation of learning experience in conducting the web-based e-service task may provide the user an option in retaining that experience which can be remembered easily. A participant claimed:

"Need to rely on paper documents and another database to complete the task… have to use all…"

The information disclosed by the participant point to the fact that the web-based system was short from offering the user a learning process which if available would have gradually build on user's prior information experience, rather the user's were juggling with multiple sources to collect the information that was needed in completing the web-based task.

The experience attained in online or offline environment is likely to direct the user in retaining the most recent learning experience because this would be much easier to recall, provided that the information is relevant to the current context. Zemke and Connellan [13] posit that each learning experience, regardless of whether it's online or offline, sets the stage of expectations for future interactions. The user tends to focus on ease of use (more than the usefulness), familiarity, skills needed, website-to-website learning comparison, and on the task complexity. The task complexities can be defined in terms of navigation on the website, information search, transaction processing, and online support (i.e., help). A participant related this in terms of the web-based system as:

"System is not intelligent to check simple errors like spell checks, grammar checks…"

The statement referred to the user's learning expectation of the systems capabilities in terms of their prior experience. The user's had used this functionality in another system and expected to match with their prior information experience in the web-based system. The user's perceived experience about the current system being below its standard and not helpful in doing the task. It did not meet the user's information requirement for the task. Zemke and Connellan [13] developed a model (Customer Experience Grid, see Figure 2) to capture the sum total of a user learning experiences.

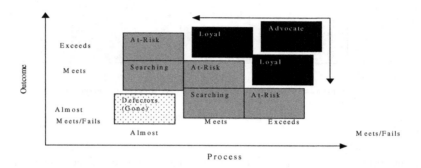

Fig. 2. User Experience Grid   (Adapted from [13])

The vertical axis of the user experience grid is the outcome the user receives, and offered on a website. On the horizontal axis the user's goes through the learning process to obtain the outcome, such as navigating the website, printing out information, looking for pricing, ordering a product etc. User compares similar outcomes on other website or in an offline environment in user transaction process. Zemke and Connellan [13] claim that the process – the way they are served – is what makes it into learning experience, positively or negatively for users. If the user's needs are not met on the process and outcome axes, they tend to go elsewhere, and hence called defectors. Similarly if the user's needs are met on one dimension and unmet on another, they are actively searching for an alternative on another website or in offline environment. This is supported in our study; the participants reported switching to the paper-based system, as the learning process and its outcome was easier to understand and follow. Zemke et al [13] suggest that to succeed on the website, it is important to consistently manage the total user learning experience (i.e. information experience) in the categories in upper three (black) boxes (see Figure 2). They claim to have successfully used the model at Dell Computers in understanding the total user's interaction. However, there is no quantitative data and analysis of the model that suggest how well the model works across web-based e-learning.

The user's interaction in computer mediated environment is an intense flow being a continuous variable ranging from none to intense [14][15][16]. The user's purpose of visit to the website may be perceived as more encouraging of exploratory behaviors than others [4]. If the website meets the primary information need of the user, it may positively affect the user in further progressing with the activity leading to a state of intense flow. It is likely that user's developing a high flow will visit those websites more regularly and for longer duration [17]. The state of intense learning flow was either missing or faced obstacles. The users weren't able to proceed with the task in the electronic environment. User may tend to reflect on the past experience for future interaction. A participant reflected this in a statement:

"The system is <u>not 100% ready</u>...""Adds on to the task...increases our task load."

It was believed that the users were loosing learning interest in the web-based system due to continuously being put down. To retain interest in a site, there should be enjoyment on the part of the user during the interaction of the site. A participant statement highlights this concern:

"If the system can be fixed it can be fixed, otherwise we will <u>continue using it as it is</u>."

It was known to the users that if the web-based system didn't work they could depend on an alternative system (i.e., paper-bases system) in doing the task. The shifting of learning experience between the paper-based and web-based emerged as a continuum on which the user viewed the web-based system effectiveness before proceeding with the task, which was based on an understanding from past experience. If the user felt the task could be (not only) performed and also completed they went ahead with the web-based system; otherwise they opted for the paper-based system. Any adverse feelings were filtered towards learning the web-based system at that time affecting the decision making to use the web-based system. Those claims were supported by participant statements:

"<u>Verifying information</u> on the Internet is not possible; we still have to check student's education credential in paper form"

"Site needs to <u>be improved with better features and functionality</u> that will make it <u>easier for us to use</u>."

In the flow state, the user's focus or attention is narrowed to a limited stimulus field, and irrelevant thoughts are filtered out. Csikszentmihaly [6] suggest that in a flow state the person becomes absorbed in the activity, while increasing his awareness of his own mental processes in the interaction with the web, the computer screen can serve as the limited stimulus field, focusing the individual's attention [5]. The user faced hurdles during the flow state affecting their learning in doing the task. A participant expressed this:
"Due to time out period that disconnect, the user has to reenter all the information once again...this <u>creates duplicity of information</u> for us...as the same user is reapplying again and it is hard to differentiate between the same application."

As users become more frequent users they place more reliance on learning from internal sources (memory) than external sources (advertisements, word of mouth, etc) [18] . Many researchers have noted the ways in which memory is biased [19]. Frequent events are easier to recall than infrequent ones [20]. Therefore remembering an event is biased by the availability of information within memory [18]. The mechanical process of conducting the task with the available tools on the website forms a basis of interactivity for the user and is similar to recalling frequent and infrequent events. Prior research suggests the application of tools to vary across different users from novice to advance [11].

The development of intelligent agents guiding the user in conducting the task from start to completion tends to improve the user learning interface and reduce uncertainty in learning and problematic experience. This has led to smart software taking over the task, reducing and limiting user's interactivity with the task, and completion of task within a few ticks and clicks of a mouse. The whole process tends to be reduced, removing the intricacies the user can encounter, and at the same time standardizing the users web-based learning across all domain and user developing a positive experience. The intelligent agent capability in storing and remembering user's transaction details, and displaying on revisits has also reduced the user's need to keep paper record of transaction, making it easier for the user in conducting the task with the availability of past, current and future information records available online. This has an effect on the user learning experience in using the traditional service where the information available is not swift and quick. A reliance on internal search means that the user's memory will have considerable influence on the formation of "learning expectancies" [19]. Hasher and Zacks [20] argue that the accuracy with which people encode information increases with the frequency of encoding. Although their research focuses on consumers' exposure to advertising, a parallel can be drawn with consumers' exposure to web-based e-learning. Similarly, Zeithaml et al. [21] in their study pointed to information gap on the basis of users learning experience with website that leads to providing incomplete or in accurate information to the users. It is anticipated that the application of intelligent agents in user interactivity will further enhance and integrate into the user learning experience with information, and become part of the user guidance in conducting web-based task. A participant directed the claim:

"If any information is missed, there is no way to check, there are no <u>compulsory fields </u>to inform of missing information."

Meuter et al. [22] report that 80% of the customer complaints are made in person to the company, either by phone or by visiting a service facility. This suggests that the when the user is effected with a problematic experience on websites, and to resolve the issue, the user adopts the traditional approach of face-to-face interaction, rather than online approach. The participant in the study evaluated the web-based task, and weighted its effectiveness by comparing it to the paper-based service.

"We can't offer admission letters to higher degree research students on the web-based system, as letter templates not there; we have to offer it on paper."

The degree of tolerance for web-based system may be intense due to the competitor's service being a click away [21]. The users are quick in changing over to paper-based service, which is believed competing with the web-based system. Thus user's tolerance level for web-based system, their immediate reactions to the service failure and their consecutive behavior, are interrelated and forms part of the user learning experience. A participant expressed:

"If the system can be fixed it can be fixed, otherwise we will <u>continue using as it is</u>."

When the web-based system fails it has fallen outside the user's zone of tolerance [23]. So far nothing is known about user's tolerance levels of web-based systems, or the user's propensity to complain about online service failures [24], and user's reaction to it. Zeithaml et al [21] claim that customers have no expectations, customers have been found to compare web-based service to competitor's services and to brick and mortar stores [22]; [25]. The degree of user's tolerance is not known. Another participant states;

"They are frightened for asking help if needed…rather they ask for help than provide wrong information."

It seemed there are considerable obstacles the user's developed in their learning experience to use web-based system.

5   Conclusions

In line with the preceding discussion it is suggested that web-based systems adoption takes into account the user learning experience that develops with user interaction with the system. Though prior studies even adopted the general technology user models like the TAM model [26][27][28], which is of significance, they do not take into account the user context issues on a commercial situation basis. To study web-based system from a user learning perspective centered context and combining it with adoption and acceptance models may enhance that understanding. To explore the context further, issues related to situation specific personalization of individual user learning needs in online and offline environment may be used to produce evaluation guidelines that would facilitate the adoption and continuation process.

Earlier studies investigated the adoption of web-based system in different contexts, but not provide insight into acceptance and continued use by users. Though a consumer may use a web-based system for the first time, its continued use relates to the success. The user's web-based learning experience may form an impression of the system in terms of how easy or how difficult it is to operate the system.

From the preceding discussion it has been clear that web-based system adoption is not a simple and straightforward process. Rapid development in technology delivery is gradually shaping the consumer learning in uptake and usage of this new innovation. The level of interaction from traditional services to web-based services and simultaneous use of both has laid a new set of implications for the universities, organizations, government, consumers, practitioners, and researchers. In understanding the new set of implications, initial research revealed that though uptake and use of this new innovation has been positive, its acceptance and continued use has been limited. The available research though identifies some main issues it lacks in understanding the impact of the critical success factors. Further research will attempt to explore a more structured understanding to web-based systems user learning within a referenced theoretical construct.

References

1. D'Ambra. J., and Rice, R.E. (2001). "Emerging factors in user evaluation of the world wide web." Information and Management 38: 373–84.
2. Csikszentmihalyi, M. and LeFevre, J. (1990). "Optimal experience in work and leisure" Journal of Personality and Social Psychology 56(5): 815–22.
3. Ghani, J., Supnick, R., and Rooney, P. (1991). "The experience of flow in computer-mediated and in face-to-face groups," Proceedings of the Twelfth International Conference on Information Systems, DeGross, J.I., Benbasat, I., DeSanctis, G., and Beath, C.M, Eds., New York, New York, December 16–18.
4. Trevino, L. K., and Webster, J. (1992). "Flow in computer-mediated communication: electronic mail and voice evaluation." Communication Research 19(2): 539–73.
5. Webster, J., Trevino, L.K., and Ryan, L. (1993). "The dimensionality and correlates of flow in human-computer interactions." Computer in Human Behavior 9: 411–26.
6. Csikszentmihalyi, M. (1975). "Beyond boredom and anxiety." Jossey-Bass, San Francisco.
7. Hoffman, D. L. and Novak, T, P (1996). "Marketing in Hypermedia Computer-Mediated Environments: Conceptual Foundations." Journal of Marketing Research. 60(7): 50–68.
8. Karahanna, E., Straub, D, W., and Chervany, N.L. (1999). "Information technology adoption across time: A cross sectional comparison of pre-adoption and post-adoption beliefs." MIS Quarterly 23(2): 183–213.
9. Davidow, W. H., and Uttal, B. (1989). "Service companies: focus or falter." Harvard Business Review (July/August): 17–34.
10. Yin, R.K. (1994). "Case Study Research: Design and Methods. Sage Publications, 2nd Edition.
11. Martin, M.P. (1991). "Analysis and design of business information systems." Macmillan Publishing Company, New York.
12. Sandhu, K., and Corbitt, B (2002). "Exploring an understanding of Electronic Service end-user adoption," The International Federation for Information Processing, WG8.6, Sydney.
13. Zemke, R., and Connellan, T. (2001). "E-Service: 24 ways to keep your customers when the competition is just a click away." American Management Association.

14. Day, H.I. (1981). "Play," in Advances in Intrinsic Motivation and Anesthetics, H.I.Day, Ed., New York: Plenum.
15. Berthon, P., and Davies, T. (1999). "Going with the flow: Websites and customer involvement", Internet Research: Electronic Networking Applications and Policy", 9(2): 109–116.
17. Berthon, P., Pitt, L., and Watson, R.T. (1996). "The World Wide Web as an advertising medium: toward an understanding of conversion efficiency", Journal of Advertising Research, 43–45.
18. Johnson, C. and Mathews, B.P. (1997). "The influence of experience on service expectations." International Journal of Service Industry Management 8(4): 290–305.
19. Foulkes, V.S. (1994). "How consumers predict service quality: what do they expect?" Rust, R.T., and Oliver, R.L, Service Quality, New Directions in Theory and Practice, Sage, Beverly Hills, CA.
20. Hasher, L., and Zacks, R.T. (1984). "Automatic processing of fundamental information: the case of frequency of occurrence", American Psychologist, 39, 1372–88.
21. Zeithaml, V.A., Parasuraman, A., and Malhotra, A. (2000). "A Conceptual framework for understanding e-Service Quality: Implications for future Research and managerial Practice." Marketing Science Institute, Working paper, Report no: 00–115.
22. Meuter, M. L., Ostrom, A.L, Roundtree, R.I., and Bitner, M.J. (2000). "Self-service technologies: Understanding customer satisfaction with technology-based service encounters." Journal of Marketing 64: 50–64.
23. Zeithaml, V. A., Berry, L., and Parasuraman, A. (1993). "The nature and determinants of customer expectations of service." Journal of the Academy of Marketing Science 21(1): 1–12.
24. Riel, A. C. R., Liljander, V., and Jurriens, P (2001). "Exploring consumer evaluations of e-services: a portal site." International Journal of Service Industry Management 12(4): 359–377.
25. Szymanski, D. M., and Hise, R.T. (2000). "E-satisfaction: an initial examination." Journal of Retailing 76(3): 309–22.
26. Davis, F. D. (1989). "Perceived usefulness, perceived ease of use, and user acceptance of information technology." MIS Quarterly 13(2): 319–40.
27. Davis, F. D., Bagozzi, R.P., and Warshaw, P.R. (1989). "User Acceptance of computer technology: A comparison of two theoretical models." Management Science 34(8): 982–1002.
28. Davis, F. D. (1993). "User Acceptance of information technology: systems characteristics, user perceptions and behavioral impacts." International Journal of Man-Machine Studies. 38(3): 475–87.

Use of Web-Based Live Demos in Computer Science Courses

Li Yang

Department of Computer Science, Western Michigan University
Kalamazoo, MI 49008, USA
li.yang@wmich.edu

Abstract. Web-based live demos were developed to remedy the lack of inter-action in most Web-based courseware. These demos were used as supplemental materials for students to reinforce what they have learned in class. Through the interaction with live demos, students are forced to think proactively and to use what they have learned in class to solve problems. Positive feedback from students indicates that Web-based interactive demos help students to understand key concepts and to improve their problem-solving skills.

1 Introduction

The World Wide Web and all of the technologies that are supported through its capabilities have made Web-based learning possible. Web-based teaching methods have been implemented in various disciplines with great success [5]. Web-based teaching tools are also used to enhance traditional face-to-face instructional techniques.

The use of Web-based techniques for teaching is attractive for several major reasons: First, distance education is much more effective with the use of the Web. Prior distance learning techniques relied on land-based mail systems to organize tests at distances. With Web technology, it is possible to update quickly Web-based materials and to use more effective Web-based testing methods. Another advantage of Web-based materials is that students throughout the semester can use the materials repeatedly as they review the course. Students can access these materials on their own time to fit their learning into their daily schedules. Finally, for the benefit of instructors, Web-based materials can be used repeatedly after their initial creation. The instructor for several section rotations can use the same Web-based materials if the materials do not need to be updated or only need to be updated incrementally with small advances.

Like most technological advances in education, Web-based learning tools have also negatives associated with them: From an instructor's point of view, Web-based educational materials take a long time to develop and implement. Very few instructors have the time and resources to create new materials. Furthermore, not all Faculty members are proficient at using computer software to generate robust educational materials. To avoid having to become capable users of the new computer technologies, many professors use off-the-shelf Web-authoring tools. An example is that almost every course now has an online syllabus, while very few have streaming video. Even if course materials are developed with more advanced features such as stream-

W. Zhou et al. (Eds.): ICWL 2003, LNCS 2783, pp. 264–270, 2003.

ing video, it is questionable how these simple repeats of classroom lecture are useful in students' learning. An example of this is the use of "talking head" boxes in Web pages where students can watch lecture materials. While it may be useful for students to review lecture materials in this manner, students are treated as passive learners and do not have any chance to interact with the instructor.

The quality of Web-based materials depends on the Web-based instructional authoring tools with which these materials are developed. In the current state-of-the-art, most Web-based course materials are written by off-the-shelf Web authoring tools for the purpose of easy presentation on the Web. There are currently three types of commonly used Web-based instructional tools – information posting, chat rooms, and streaming video. Information posting and chat rooms are most commonly used in Web-based instruction. Some of course materials are further furnished with video streams to allow students learn in a similar way as they learn in classroom. The advantage of using video stream is that the materials can be used many times without having to redo the preparation. In addition, students can review the lectures repeatedly which they cannot do in a traditional lecture. The major problems with streaming video involve time and the way that students use streaming video. Students that are able to view streaming video in real-time and that are able to ask questions to the instructor get all the benefits of being in a traditional classroom without having to physically be there. However, streaming video is often used by students who may not have access to real-time support of the instructor. The distance learners must often passively watch the streaming video without the interactive components of a traditional course. To address this issue, instructors have often offered online support for students using streaming video. Research has commented that it is very difficult to offer technical and informational support in such a teaching environment [9]. Without the interactive component, passively watching a streaming video is almost the same as using television in distance education. Students may feel that they are just watching another television program and give it the same amount of attention that television normally requires.

So far one can hardly claim that Web-based learning will replace the traditional classroom instruction. When the Web is used as a surrogate to replace face-to-face real-time interactions, as opposed to being used as a supplement to classroom teaching, the benefits of Web-based materials come at the cost of classroom instructional benefits. There just may not be a gain in learning over traditional methods. Some studies [1,4] have shown that students in a Web-based course performed worse than they performed in either a traditional lecture or using correspondence course materials. Other studies have shown the opposite, but they admit that students studied more when they were using the Web-based materials [8].

2 Developing Interactive Web-Based Demos

The above problems, unless being carefully addressed, could become serious burden of the deployment of Web-based instruction [7]. One common concern of these problems is how to efficiently develop quality Web-based course materials. Those online modules with chat rooms and streaming video simply deny the students' right of interaction with the courseware. They do not have the capability to excite students to learn interactively. In computer science, in particular, courses designed in this way do not encourage students to make intrinsic connections between theory, algorithms, programming, and applications. Each student is treated as a passive learner.

Acknowledging the above problems, we think that a key feature that is missing in most existing Web-based courseware is the introduction of interaction. Interaction needs to be introduced into the design of Web-based courseware. Web-based materials should invite students' interaction with the materials in a similar way as students' interaction with instructors in classroom. The full benefits of Web-based course materials seem to grow when students are able to take advantage of real-time interaction [6]. When theories are exemplified through interaction and visualization, interactive Web-based instruction methods will encourage students to become active learners, rather than treat all of them as passive learners. This will certainly promote and enhance students' understanding of contents.

This paper reports our work in introducing interaction into Web-based course materials and presents several demos we have developed. Rather than using the Web as a surrogate to replace traditional instruction, we use the developed interactive demos as supplements to classroom teaching. For on-campus students, the Web-based courseware will establish alternative sources of information and modes of learning in augment to classroom lecture. There are a few unique benefits of using the Web-based interactive materials as supplements to a traditional course: First, students can work at their paces. Second, they can have interactive materials that respond to student inputs, which is not possible in a printed book or in classroom. The interactivity are used to provide feedback to the students' input. Finally, there are other formats, for example, visualization and animation, for engaging students with Web-based materials that are not available in printed books.

Web-based demos were developed with a few objectives: First, the materials must be interactive so that students can receive feedback on their learning progress [3,7]. Second, the materials must be different from the lecture or the book [2]. If the materials are identical to information that students can get in other formats, students will only use one of the formats. Third, materials can also be used to instruct students that have different learning styles. In a lecture, we can only present materials in one format and one style, but Web-based materials can be varied among learning styles so that students can choose to use the ones that benefit them most.

From two years ago, students have consistently been encouraged to create Web-based interactive tutorials as course projects. This gives students interesting course projects which require creativity and imagination as well as knowledge and systematic thinking. To ensure the quality and consistency of results, the instructor gives the basic idea and the layout design. However, students are strongly encouraged to add additional features that they think useful to learning. The results are expected to be a set of demos with the underlying algorithms running live in backend and the results being presented to the user in real time through visualization and interaction. Students developed all Web-based demos presented in this paper. These developers commented that they benefited in many ways from working on projects as they created the Web-based demos. Some students also enjoyed developing the pedagogical approach to presenting their problem solution.

3   Examples of the Demos

A static format like this paper cannot demonstrate the interactive materials developed. We will show screen shots of several demos and describe the methodologies and features of these demos. These examples demonstrate huge demands of using visualization and interaction to develop live demos in higher education.

Fig. 1 shows screen shots of two example demos designed for a computer network course: (a) the CSMA/CD protocol used in the Ethernet, (b) link state routing by using Dijkstra's shortest path algorithm. Both are written by using Java applets. Each demo has clickable buttons and forms for the user to enter parameters. The demos show results with animation. These demos and explanations of course contents are organized according to the layers in the OSI network reference model. Fig. 2 shows the reference model where each layer is clickable to refer to further explanation of course contents and live demos. Fig. 2 also shows how a data packet at the application layer of the source is packaged by the underlying layers and how the data packet is delivered through bridges and routers to the application layer of the destination.

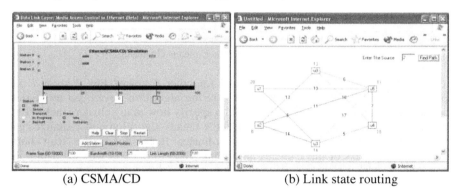

(a) CSMA/CD   (b) Link state routing

Fig. 1. Example demos to show principles in computer network.

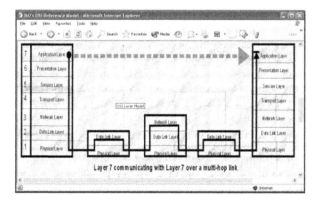

Fig. 2. The OSI reference model where each layer is clickable and links to detailed explanation and live demos.

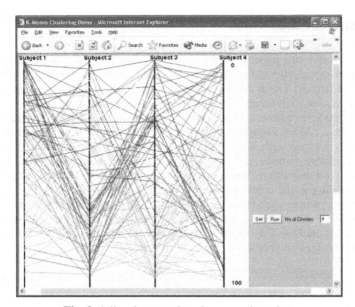

Fig. 3. A live demo to show k-means clustering.

Similar live demos have been developed for other coursers. Fig. 3 show a Java applet to demonstrate the k-means data clustering algorithm developed by students who took a data-mining course. Users need to specify how many clusters they wish to produce. The demo clusters data by using the k-means algorithm and visualizes each cluster with a different color in parallel coordinates. Each click of the 'Run' button will execute one pass of the k-means algorithm. Therefore, users will see data points change the clusters they belong. By running the demo, students will have a good idea on how the k-means algorithm works.

Computer graphics is another example course that can benefit from the supplementation of Web-based live demos. This is because of its demand for visualization and its challenge for 3D rendering. Traditional lecture-format learning in computer graphics falls short of conveying the 3D geometric principles that need to be mastered by students. When the author taught the model-view transformations, for example, he felt that the thumbs and fingers of both hands together are not enough to illustrate the model coordinate, the view coordinate, the relationships between these two, and the changes to be made to the corresponding matrix. In contrast, these concepts can easily be demonstrated by using Web-based demos.

Fig. 4 gives a screen snapshot of a live demo to show transformation, projection and lights in computer graphics. The demo was designed that it has three major windows: a 3D world-space view of geometric objects together with light and a camera describing what actually happens in the 3D real world, a 2D screen-space view which presents the finally rendered image and a command view which lists OpenGL functions. The 3D world scene is modeled and processed by the list of OpenGL functions to produce the finally rendered image. When a user moves an object or changes the values of the arguments of an OpenGL function, the changes will be reflected immediately in both the world-space view and the screen-space view.

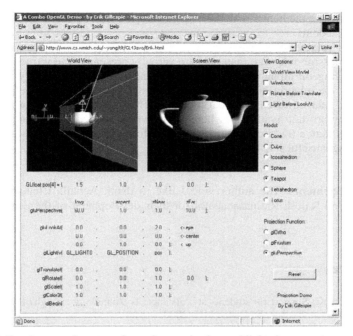

Fig. 4. A live demo to show transformation, projection and lights in computer graphics.

These demos were used as supplemental training materials for students to reinforce what they have learned in class. After class, students were asked to walk through these demos and to answer a list of questions. Some of these questions attempt to improve students' problem-solving skills by leading them through a series of small questions demonstrating how integrating individual small steps creates complex solutions. For example, using the demo presented in Fig. 4, students were asked how to put the camera at a specific location and how to create panning and zooming effects of the teapot by adjusting the parameters of the OpenGL functions. Through the interaction with these live demos, students are forced to think proactively and to use the concepts learned in class instead of just skipping ahead regardless of their comprehension.

4 Conclusion

Passive distance learning is one scenario where Web-based materials have been used successfully when face-to-face interactions are not possible. However, real-time interaction as students access the materials makes learning much more effective. When Web-based materials are used to supplement classroom lecture, they need to take advantage of the unique Web features that make them more useful instead of just replacing traditional learning methods. Interactivity is a way to make these supplemental Web-based materials useful. It provides an effective way to attract students' attention in their learning activities. We have developed a set of Web-based interactive demos as supplemental material. The development of these demos has given good projects to students.

Informal surveys of students have shown that most students are visual learners. However, classroom lecture materials are verbally presented and written on the board, heavily relying on alphanumeric representation. Visual students may have difficult time seeing the relationships between different ideas because all of the presented materials were relayed through verbal methods. The demos presented in this paper are visual. They are not available in books. The visual students may find these demos more useful than a traditional textbook. The informal feedback from students is positive as being a useful self-learning tool.

Acknowledgements. The author would like to thank Achalla Chandrasekhar, Erik Gillespie, and Rajesh Ratinasabapathi for their development of the demos presented in this paper.

References

1. Al-Ashkar, K.: Support for students at a distance: Is technology enough? Proceeding of the 2000 ASEE Conference. St. Louis, MO (2000)
2. Berge, Z. L.: Guiding principles in Web-based instructional design. Educational Media International, 35(2) (1998) 72–76
3. Bonk, C. J., Cummings J. A.: A dozen recommendations for placing the student at the centre of Web-based learning. Educational Media International, 35(2) (1998) 82–89
4. Collins, M.: Comparing Web, correspondence and lecture versions of a second-year non-major biology course. British Journal of Educational Technology, 31(1) (2000) 21–27
5. Khan, B. H. (ed.): Web-Based Instruction. Educational Technology Publications (1997)
6. Northrup, P.: A framework for designing interactivity into Web-based instruction. Educational Technology, (March-April 2001) 31–39
7. Pérez-Prado, A., Thirunarayanan, M.: A qualitative comparison of online and classroom-based sections of a course: exploring student perspectives. Educational Media International, 39(2) (2002) 195–202
8. Radhakrishnan, S., Bailey, J. E.: Web-based educational media: issues and empirical test of learning. WebNet'97, World Conference of the WWW, Internet and Intranet, (1997) 400–405
9. Simich-Dudgeon, C.: Developing a college Web-based course: lessons learned. Distance Education, 19(2) (1998) 337–357

Effective E-learning by Use of HCI and Web-Based Workflow Approach

Joseph Fong[1], Margaret Ng[1], Irene Kwan[2], and Macro Tam[1]

[1] Department of Computer Science, City University of Hong Kong, Hong Kong,
csjfong@cityu.edu.hk

[2] Department of Information System, Lingnan University of Hong Kong

Abstract. A web-based workflow system is proposed to help users study by e-learning anywhere and anytime. Basically, the Workflow based e-Learning System is a learning environment supported by workflow technology which provides a flexible learning solution. With the rapid development of Internet, distance-learning applications over Internet become more and more popular. The user interface of a system is often the yardstick by which the system is judged. An interface which is difficult to use will, at best, provide result with a high level of user errors. At worst, it will cause the software system to discard, irrespective of its functionality. If the information is presented in a confusing or misleading way, the user may misunderstand the meaning of an item of information. They may initiate a sequence of unexpected actions which even cause the system failure. In this respect, this paper focuses on the design principles and implementation of the Human-Computer Interface(HCI). We lay down the guideline for HCI design concept and principles, and evaluate the HCI design of a Workflow–based e-Learning application.

1 Introduction

This paper aims to apply the HCI design principles in the design and the implementation of workflow based e-learning system. We show the basic ideal of Workflow based e-Learning System and provide a practice experience to the designers and managers who face the challenges for building their own workflow based e-learning system. We then introduce the basic ideal and concept to designing, developing and deploying the new technology of e-Learning services. The deliverable includes a prototype Workflow-based e-Learning application system, its RDMBS database engine and database, and the workflow engine built on a Coldfusion web application server.

Conceptual models describe the important concepts in the problem domain from end user's perspective. On the system development point of view, it addresses all aspects of the system: data model, object design, business process, and rules. The following diagram describes the conceptual model of the Web-based workflow e-

W. Zhou et al. (Eds.): ICWL 2003, LNCS 2783, pp. 271–286, 2003.

Learning System. This is a top-down methodology. It begins by examining the higher-level structures in an e-Learning environment.

In general, the conceptual model of e-Learning system includes the following entities. The course (program, course, modules) , the person and queue (relation among the course) and assessment (the relation between course and person).

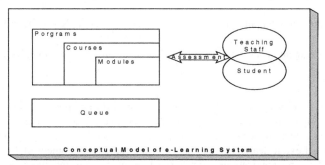

Fig. 1. Conceptual Model of e-Learning System

The e-Learning program, for example, a system administrator program on a popular database product may consist of 4 to 5 individual courses. It may be in a specified topic on database administrator or a common topic for database administrator or system developer. Before the student completes the program, the student must attend all components in design steps. It includes the introduction for database administrator, database management and the troubleshooting of problem. The Queue is the dependency or sequence of study. It records the prerequisite of a course, and ensures the student complete the program step-by-step. It informs the student the status of study. The difference between a Web-based workflow system and a linear system is the flexible sequence. In a linear system, the study flow is in a fixed order. In a Web-based workflow e-Learning System, it supports the concept of flexible learning pathways through subjects consisting of courses managed by a number of learning activities.

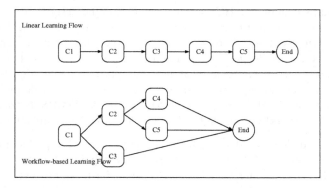

Fig. 2. Workflow approach on learning activities

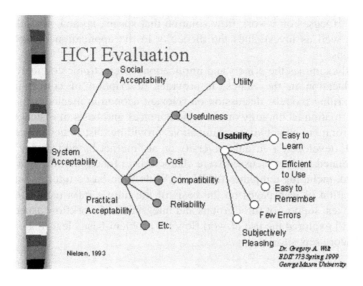

Fig. 3. HCI Evaluation criteria

2 Related Work

The workflow concept has evolved from the process in manufacturing and the office. Such processes have existed since industrialization and are products of a search for improvement in effectiveness and productivity. Previous research in workflow during the early 90s have been focused on Business Process Reengineering (BPR). These works mainly involved separate work activities into well-defined tasks, roles, rules and procedures which regulate most of the job tasks in manufacturing and office [1][2][3][4].

There has been a paradigm shift in workflow research from purely management oriented to information and technology oriented since the introduction of object-oriented concept, Internet and World Wide Web in the late 90s. Much research works in workflow design are increasingly popular in the arena of multi-media applications and system. For example: coupling object-oriented and workflow modeling in business and information process reengineering aim to integrate an OO method with a workflow analysis which take care of BPR and IPR [5]; making use of Artificial Intelligence influence on office automation to support design of a goal-based multi-agent workflow system for tasks coordination in organizational activities [6]. Until recently, more published research works are focused on the investigation and utilization of workflow design in networked web-based systems on various applications, including the application of workflow concepts and techniques in web-based learning. We have studied the following:

- [7] focuses on i-work flow solution that speeds up and streamline workflow as well as investigates the difficulty in the application of web-based solutions;
- [8] examines the effects and implications of electronic commerce on distance education in the States. It provides description of conventional distance learning models, discussion on relevant economic mechanism, impact of information technology on strategic alliances and basis of distance learning environment on network organizations providing distributed education.
- [9] developed a virtual university on an Internet-based learning environment. Related topics discussed were characteristic functionalities of a tutoring wizard, including templates for World Wide Web-based tutoring, automatic generation of web pages on the basis of the tutor's information filled in dialog boxes, support of tutor groups and integration of workflow aspects.
- [10] explored the use of workflow for problem-based learning on web hosting theory repositories.

On the development of web-based educational products, there are many research and commercial web-based educational products available in the computer industry. The most popular ones include Lotus LearningSpace, WebCT, BlackBoard, TopClass, etc.[11][12]. All apply the general HCI concept in their own design, and to increase the usability to gain competitive advantage. A competitive edge may be obtained if claim of reduced training cost and productivity gain are in terms of user friendliness.

As a result, there are several sociological factors to consider in software design. A task may have different behaviors to fit groups or individual users. Some aspects of this factor are related to privacy or value of information. For example, supervisors like to manage and control the information of their employees. Also lecturers can view and interact with their students' enrollment progress on our case study, the Workflow based e-Learning application.

The advent of the personal computer brought software products into use by the wider community, and the use of computers became an object of research by ergonomists, psychologists and others. The result was the emergence of the field of HCI which focuses on the users, and the usability of systems. A large proportion of HCI research has looked at commercial software packages such as word-processors [13] and the introduction of "user-friendly" operating systems[14]. In the age of Internet, HCI will affect the Web in the Web based application design.

Although there are a large number of software products in the Information Technology industry today, the number of software user interfaces with high usability is relative small. The most recent ACM Computing Curricula [15] recognizes HCI as a sub-area of Computing Science that requires core hours in every curriculum. This special issue is evident that the interest in HCI in academic circles continues to grow. Actually, most of the developer and researcher agree that good user interface design must take into account the needs, experience and capabilities of the system user. Potential users should be involved in the design process. Prototyping is essential for user interface development, and should be made available to users and the resulting feedback used to improve the user interface design.

Designer must take into account the physical and mental limitations of the humans who use the application. The most importance is the need to recognize the limitations of the operating platform. The web browser will affect the behavior of Internet application. At last, they avoid overloading the user with information.

Human capabilities are the basis for the design guideline discussed in the development of HCI topic. A longer list of user interface design guidelines is given by [16][17]. [18] also summarizes the guidelines into nine general principles and usability heuristics as evaluation of application usability.

HCI is strongly influenced by the fields of computer science, cognitive psychology and ergonomics (human factors). Its key concern is to understand and facilitate the creation of "user interfaces". This places the human and the machine on an equal footing as two interacting information processing systems where the output of one is the input of the other [19]. This cognitive science view of HCI has reached its limitation from the point of view of prominent HCI researchers such as [20]. It builds on and complements parts of two other academic disciplines:

➢   *Cognitive Psychology* – study the mental processes behind human behavior. That includes such things as perception, learning, accessing information, memory, and problem solving. Each of these mental processes is a factor in computer use.
➢   *Human Factors (or Ergonomics)* – study how the design of products affect people. It builds on cognitive psychology and complements this body of knowledge with ergonomics – the study of human capabilities and limitations vis-à-vis tool use..

3   Methodology for HCI and Web-Based E-learning Workflow System

The project objective is to study the HCI design principle and apply them in the design of workflow based e-learning system for an experiment.

Workflow Based-E-learning System

Workflow based e-Learning is a new IT solution for managing learning and teaching activities. It offers unique features allowing absolute flexibility of time management, material access and personal consultation during the study period for students and teaching personnel.

Workflow based e-Learning integrates individual components of study such as enrolment, learning and assessment into one fully system supported stream of activities called the integrated study process. In contrast to the traditional mode of teaching,

Workflow based e-Learning provides better access to and more effective interactions with teaching staff by providing system supported feedback sessions and personal guidance for students.

It offers a different learning approach than supported by other well-known online learning management systems. Rather than making all the course material and activities available to the student at the beginning of the course, Workflow based e-Learning coordinates their availability and completion by utilizing its embedded workflow functionality. It offers unique features to support individually tailored learning pathways and flexible study styles for students.

The environment provided by Workflow based e-Learning enables better interactions between students themselves as well as student and teaching staff necessary for effective active learning at the level of individual learning activity, course module, course or the whole degree. This feature prevents student isolation, often associated with on-line mode of study. Each course is associated with one or more workflow process templates that define the order of course activities. One of these process templates is assigned to each student when the student enrolls in the course.

We have found that there is a very logical mapping between e-learning application requirements and the workflow technology. Workflow technology offers many benefits that can potentially enhance e-Learning environment, such as[21]:

✓   By automating the learning process it can potentially improve student/teacher productivity.
✓   Provide continuous monitoring to all users.
✓   Support for individual planning of work schedule as well as the resource.
✓   Working at individual's own pace, users have options of choosing preferred working pathways.
✓   Management of information and knowledge sharing.
✓   Collaboration between users.

HCI Principles for Web-Based Workflow E-learning System

The following is a list of 10 basic principles that drive the design of our prototyping application. These "10 commandments" of human interface design are well known to most people who have ever read an interface design guide. However few are able to handle the entire job and various aspects of design through deployment[22]

● *Consistency*
A software application is expected to be consistent within itself and other software on the same platform in a few key areas. Consistency applies to the concepts, terminology, graphics and visual style and appearance of screens. Consistency also applies to interaction behaviors and use of user interface controls. Consistency is a major area of implicit and ambiguous expectations that is made explicit and measurable. This

allows users to learn something once, and then apply that knowledge again and again as they use the computer. In Web-based application software, we can keep the application visual consistent by applying the style sheet.

- *Aesthetic Integrity*

Aesthetic integrity means that information is well organized and consistent with principles of visual design. This means that things look good on the screen and the display technology is of high quality. Since people spend a lot of their time working while looking at the computer screen, design your products to be pleasant to look at on the screen for a long time. You may want to consider investing some of your resources in a graphic designer. The skills that a graphic designer can bring to your product design is well worth the expense.

Keep the graphics of the display simple. The number of elements and their behaviors should be limited to enhance the usability of the interface. Graphics--icons, windows, dialog boxes, and so on--are the basis of effective human-computer interaction and must be designed with that in mind. Don't clutter the screen with too many windows, overload the user with complex icons, or put dozens of buttons in dialog boxes.

Make sure to follow the graphic language of the interface and don't change the meaning of standard items. For example, if you sometimes use checkboxes for multiple choices and other times for exclusive choices, you dilute the meaning of the element.

Don't use arbitrary graphic images to represent concepts. When you add nonstandard symbols to menus, dialog boxes, or other elements, the meaning may be clear to you, but to other people the symbols may appear as something different and distracting. If you need symbols other than standard ones, use graphic images that convey meaning through representation, analogy, or metaphor.

- *Perceived Stability*

Computers often introduce a new level of complexity for people. If people are to cope with this complexity, they need some stable reference points. A good interface is designed to provide a computer environment that is understandable, familiar, and predictable.

To give users a visual sense of stability, the application uses a number of consistent graphics elements (frame, window border, and so on) to maintain the illusion of stability. Note that it is the *perception* of stability that you want to preserve, not stability in any strict physical sense.

To give users a conceptual sense of stability, the interface provides a clear, finite set of objects and a clear, finite set of actions to perform on those objects. Even when particular actions are unavailable, they are not eliminated from display but are merely dimmed.

- *See-and-Point, Not Remember-and-Type*

Computers are good at precisely remembering things like codes, commands names and lists of data. People are generally terrible at it. Instead of making users remember and type this sort of data, a HCI design application should always give them a list of valid possibilities and let them choose from it. Not only will the user's anxiety level drop, but also the developer is spared having to handle all the error conditions that arise when users guess wrong.

- *Direct Manipulation*

Good user interfaces allow their users to feel as if they are direct controlling the world inside the computer. Instead of abstracting out their work to a set of command words, they interact with them directly through the graphical interfaces.

Direct manipulation allows people to feel that they are directly controlling the objects represented by the computer. According to the principle of direct manipulation, an object on the screen remains visible while a user performs physical actions on the object. When the user performs operations on the object, the impact of those operations on the object is immediately visible. For example, a user can move a file by dragging an icon that represents it from one location to another or can position a cursor in a text field by directly clicking the location where the cursor should be placed.

- *Metaphors from the Real World*

The user interface model should be analogous to some real-world model which the user understands. The best-known metaphor is the desktop metaphor (Nutt and Ellis, 1980) where the user's screen represents a desktop. Similarly, a movie player application look likes a VCR. Other metaphors in common use include the various brushes and tools in paint programs, "inbox" for mail application, and even the all purpose trash can.

You can take advantage of people's knowledge of the world around them by using metaphors to convey concepts and features of your application. Use metaphors involving concrete, familiar ideas and make the metaphors plain, so that users have a set of expectations to apply to computer environments. For example, people often use file folders to store paper documents in their offices. Therefore, it makes sense for people store computer documents in computer-generated folders that look like file folders. People can organize their hard disks in a way that's analogous to the way they organize their file cabinets.

- *WYSIWYG (What You See Is What You Get)*

Don't hide features in your application by using abstract commands. People should be able to see what they need when they need it. For example, menus present lists of commands so that people can see their choices instead of having to remember and type command names.

People should be able to find all the available features in your application. If you find a need to initially "hide" features, do it in a way that gives people information about where they can find more choices. A stepped interface, by revealing relevant information to users in steps, shows the choice most users want most of the time while providing a way for the user to get more choices.

Make sure that there is no significant difference between what the user sees on the screen and what the user receives after printing. Let the user be in charge of both the content and the format (spatial layout as well as font choices) of the document. When the user makes changes to the document, quickly and directly display the results. The user shouldn't have to wait for a printout or make mental calculations of how the document shown on the screen will look when it appears on the printed page.

Unfortunately, on Web application development, it is not easy to achieve due to the underlying environment – Web Browser. An alternative solution on printing is to provide an "user friendly" print version of the information.

- *Feedback and Dialog*

Good programs never keep the user guessing, They react immediately when you perform an action, such as clicking a button. If something is going to take a long time, the computer keeps your informed about not only what it's doing, but how long it's expected to take. The users will greatly appreciate knowing how much longer a given operation will take before they can enjoy the fruits of their patience. As a general rule, most users like to have a message dialog box with a progress indicator displayed when operations are going to take longer than seven to ten seconds. This number is highly variable based on the type of user and overall characteristics of the application.

- *Forgiveness*

You can encourage people to explore your application by building in forgiveness. Forgiveness means that actions on the computer are generally reversible. People need to feel that they can try things without damaging the system; create safety nets for people so that they feel comfortable learning and using your product.

Warn people before they initiate a task that will cause irretrievable data loss. Alert boxes are good ways to warn users of this kind of situation. Note, however, that when options are presented clearly and feedback is appropriate and timely, learning how to use a program should be relatively error-free. This means that frequent alert boxes are good indications that something is wrong with the program design.

- *User Control*

Allow the user, not the computer, to initiate and control actions. People learn best when they're actively engaged. Too often, however, the computer acts and the user merely reacts within a limited set of options. In other instances, the computer "takes care" of the user, offering only those alternatives that are judged "good" for the user or that "protect" the user from having to make detailed decisions. This approach mistakenly puts the computer, not the user, in control.

The key is to create a balance between providing users with the capabilities they need to get their work done and prevent them from destroying data. For situations in which a user may destroy data accidentally, you can help the user by providing warnings, usually in the form of an alert box, to notify users of a potentially undesirable situation and still allow them to proceed, if they confirm that this is what they want. This approach "protects" users but allows them to remain in control.

4 Conclusion

In this paper, we have shown how a web-based workflow system can assist e-learning by providing more flexibility in scheduling study time and allocation of study modules at the student's leisure. The instructor can also tailor make appropriate coursework to the students depending on the student's learning capability. The workflow e-learning approach can provide a student centre learning environment for e-learning. We have described the development process of Workflow based e-learning (WFEL), and apply HCI Concept on the prototype development. To demonstrate the practice experience for the application development on Workflow based e-Learning solution, we outline the HCI principles and guidelines on software development, and the importance of the users involvement in software development cycle. A major objective is to guide a software developer who understands the basis of user interface development to design and implement better user interfaces more effectively. Designing a better user interface means achieving higher usability and user satisfaction on the software product.

Through the development of WFEL, we demonstrate the practical experience to developer on HCI software design. We describe the basic ideal of HCI principles, keep the thing real and important with user involvement.

The prototype of WFEL focuses on the student activities. The final product will place more effort on lecturer side. To enhance the interaction between the students and the lecturers, we provide tools to support individual learning tasks rather than the learning process. We also need to integrate technologies that support various aspects of the study process, for example, an interface to email system to alter the activities to the users.

In the future, the WFEL can be enhanced by adding a real world metaphor as the user interface model. The best-known metaphor is the desktop metaphor where the user's screen represents a desktop, for example, a bookshelf design on enrollment, or VCR like interface when playing the video material.

References

1. Georgakopoulos, D., Hornick, M. and Sheth, A., An overview of workflow management: from process modeling to workflow automation infrastructure, Distribution and Parallel Database. 3 119–153, 1995.
2. Agostini, A., DeMichelis, G., Grasso, M.and Patriarca, S., Reengineering a business process with an innovative workflow management system: a case-study, Journal of Collaborative Computing, 1(3) 163–190, 1994.
3. Mentzas,G.N, Coordination of joint tasks in organizational process, Journal of Information Technology.(8) pp139–150, 1993.
4. Dinkhoff, G., Gruhn, V., Sallmann, A. and Zielonka, M., Business Process Modelling in the Workflow Management Environment. In:P.Loulopoulos (ed) Business Modelling and Re-engineering. Proceedings of the 13th International Conference on the Entity-Relationship Approach, LNCS, Springer-Verlag, 881(Dec.), pp46–63, 1994.
5. Mentzas, G.N., Coupling OO and workflow modeling in Business and Information Process Reengineering", Information Knowledge Systems Management, 1999, Vol.1, Issue1, p. 63–85.
6. Mahling, Dirk E. and King, Ruth C., A Goal-Based Workflow Systems for Multiagent Task Coordination, Journal of Organizational Computing and Electronic Commerce, Vol.9, Issue1, pp. 57–83, 1999.
7. Howard, Courtney E., I-work, therefore I am, Electronic Publishing, Nov., 2002, Vol.26, issue 11, pp. 18–23, 2002
8. Lang, Karl R. and Zhao J. Leon, The Role of Electronic Commerce in the Transformation of Distance Education, Journal of Organizational Computing and Electronic Commerce, 2000, Vol.10, Issue 2, pp. 103–128
9. Mittrach, Silke and Schlageter, Gunter, A Tutoring Wizard Guilding Tutorial Work in the Virtual University, http://search.epnet.com/direct.asp?an=ED428701&db=eric&tg=AN, June, 1998.
10. Veen vander, Jan; van Riemsdijk, Maarten; Jones, Val and Collis, Betty, Theory Repositories, via the Web for Problem-Based Learning, Interactive Learning Environment, Dec.,2000, Vol.8, Issue 3, pp. 257–278.
11. Marshall University, Comparison of Online Course Delivery Software Products, Centre for Instructional Technology, http://www.marshall.edu/it/cit/webct/compare/comparison.html, 1999.
12. Jackson, B., Review of leading asynchronous, web based course delivery tools, http://www.outreach.utk.edu/weblearning/reviewasych.htm, 1999.
13. Card S, Moran T. and Newell, Erlbaum, The Psychology of Human-Computer Interaction, 1983.
14. Preece J, Human-Computer Interaction, Addison-Wesley. 1994.
15. ACM SIGCHI Curricula for Human-Computer Interaction, 2001
16. Shneiderman, Ben, Designing the user interface strategies for effective human-computer interaction, Addison-Wesley, 1992.
17. Maguire, M. C.: A review of human factors guidelines and techniques for the design of graphical human-computer interfaces. Comput. & Graphics, Vol. 9, No. 3, pp. 221–235, 1985.
18. Bickford, Peter, Interface Design – The Art of Developing Easy-to-use Software, AP Professiona, 1991.

19. Boulafia, A, Gould, E., Information Processing Vs Human Cognition: A Critical Review of Cognitive Approaches in IT and HCI, International Society for the Systems Sciences 39th Annual Meeting, Amsterdam, , pp. 293–304, 1995.
20. Norman D, Cognitive Artifacts in Designing Interaction: Psychology at the Human-Computer Interface, Cambridge, 17–38, 1991.
21. Lin, J., Ho, C., Sodiq, W. and Orlowska, M., "Using Workflow Technology to Manage Flexible e-Learning Services", Education Technology and Society 5(4), 2002.
22. Torres, R J, Practitoner's Handbook for User Interface Design & Development, Prentice Hall PTR, 2002

Appendix HCI Principles in WFEL

Fig. 4. *Consistency* : Applied frame across WFEL

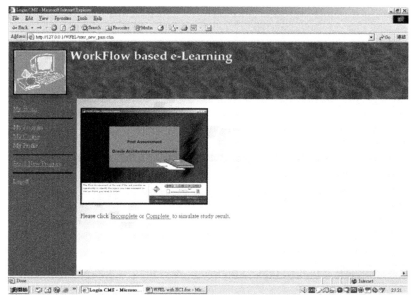

Fig. 5. *Aesthetic integrity:* Keep it simply for concentration

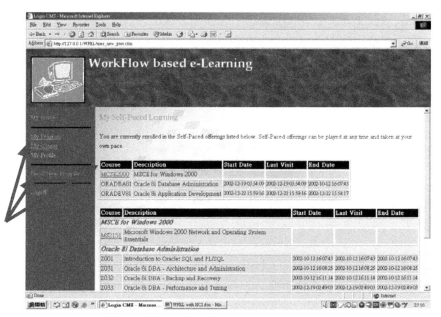

Fig. 6. Point-and-click, not remember-and-type

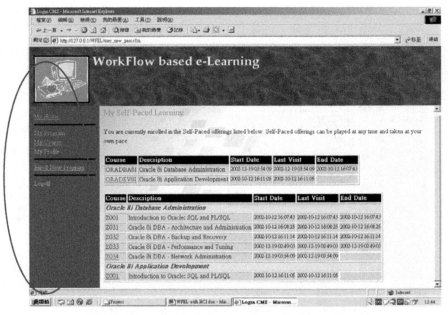

Fig. 7. *Direct manipulation:* Use Frame design on WFEL

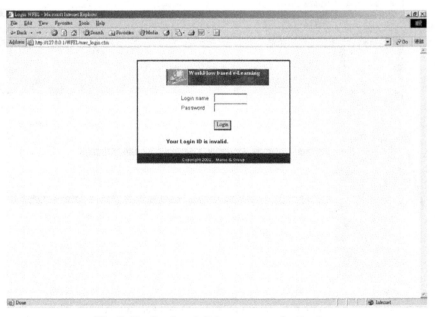

Fig. 8. *Feedback and dialog:* message feedback

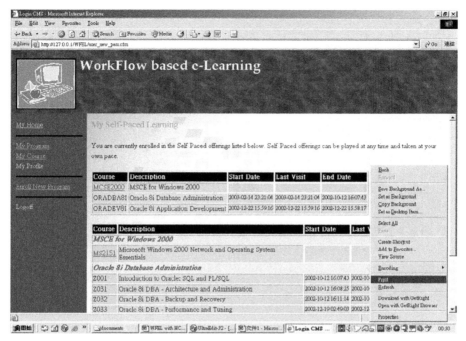

Fig. 9. *WYSIWYG*: Ensure the printing is as same as display

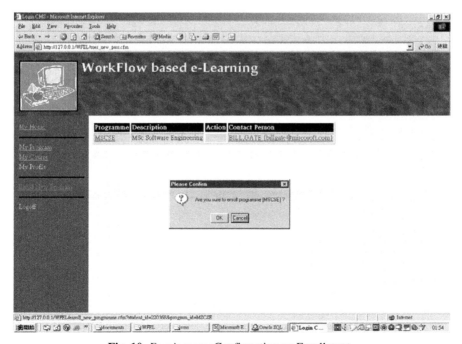

Fig. 10. *Forgiveness:* Confirmation on Enrollment

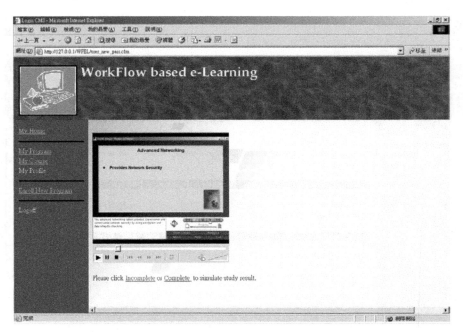

Fig. 11. *Metaphors:* Video metaphor screen in WFEL system

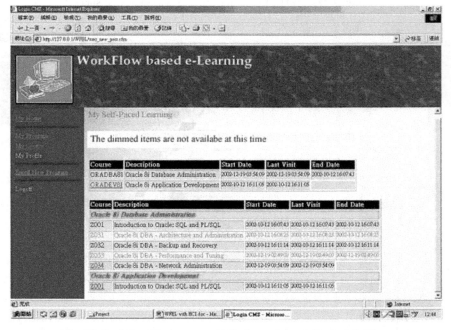

Fig. 12. *Stability:* Display unavailable items for stability in WFEL

Internet-Based Interactive Package for Diagnostic Assessment on Learning of Fluid Mechanics

Kwokwing Chau

Department of Civil and Structural Engineering, Hong Kong Polytechnic University,
Hunghom, Kowloon, Hong Kong
cekwchau@polyu.edu.hk

Abstract. Students in civil engineering and mechanical engineering fields may find the concepts of fluid mechanics abstract and have difficulty in grasping the real phenomena. Innovative learning methodologies are necessary to help arouse their interest. Yet, many web-based learning sites have common weaknesses including information being laid out basically in a textbook format and the lack of interaction. This paper delineates the development and implementation of a web-based interactive teaching package for diagnostic assessment on learning of fluid mechanics with an expert system approach, by employing the latest knowledge-based system technology and web production software. For each scenario of prompted answer from the learner, diagnostic assessment is performed by the system to determine the most probable shortfall or misconception of the specific learner on that particular topic. The package provides an opportunity of stimulating pedagogical environment to take care of engineering students in self-directed learning through interaction, application, and reflection.

1 Introduction

Fluid mechanics is a subject involving the fundamental principles of physical science and applied mathematics. By the nature of this subject, students in civil engineering and mechanical engineering fields may find the concepts abstract and have difficulty in fully grasping the real phenomena. Some innovative teaching and learning methodologies are necessary to help arouse their interest. This is in line with the prevalent goals of most universities for teaching and learning quality enhancement through the application of the latest technology.

As a result of advancements in the fields of computer and education technology, web-based learning (WBL) has been becoming a general trend in conventional higher educational settings [1-2]. The Internet has the potential for effecting fundamental changes in the design of pedagogical processes and the instructional system. The trend to couple the Internet in teaching and learning has been gaining momentum rapidly and learning availability over the Internet is increasingly expanding. An entire new industry of WBL has emerged to compete with these conventional instructional institutions [3-4]. In order to cope with this, most educational institutions at least attempt to conduct some forms of web-based instruction. It appears that new

W. Zhou et al. (Eds.): ICWL 2003, LNCS 2783, pp. 287–296, 2003.
© Springer-Verlag Berlin Heidelberg 2003

technology will build a new paradigm on education, with self-directed learning as a foundation strategy.

A retrospective review on the existing educational systems and the population of students under these systems demonstrates that quite a wide variety and deviation exist amongst different students. It seems to be a trend that the demand for higher education at different age groups, in particular adult age group, is escalating. It corresponds to the generally increasing expectation exerted by the society on better educational quality for the ultimate enhancement of productivity. Hence if the working adults desire to earn more money for improving their own living conditions, they have to upgrade themselves via various channels. Yet time constraints and places where they were residing usually impeded them [5]. Moreover, the traditional learning and training system is sometimes considered not effective enough since it offers little facility in tracking the progress of the student or keeping courseware up to date. It is suggested that simply to present materials to the students is not enough. It is extremely imperative to keep the records of the students to date and to monitor and record their progresses simultaneously. Monitoring should be undertaken on whether or not they have accessed the requisite information and whether or not they need to be chased at times [6]. Nowadays, novice technology has been invented, which is able to perform this student tracking activity in a convenient manner. WBL is rendering it possible for all the educators to deliver far more sophisticated and useful instructional programs.

Besides, recent advancements in artificial intelligence technology have rendered it possible for computer programs, by encoding knowledge and reasoning, to simulate human expertise in narrowly defined domains during the problem-solving process. A knowledge-based system (KBS), as a form of artificial intelligence technology, is capable to incorporate systematically the heuristic knowledge and expertise. By knowledge processing facilities, individual expert's knowledge could be stored under rule frame on a permanent basis so long as such rules are valid and update of such knowledge base whenever necessary is accomplishable over passage of time. The progress and development of KBS suggests that "machine expert" can play a vital role in decision making. It has been proven to be appropriate in furnishing solutions to domain problems that require considerable rules of thumb, judgment or expertise, in particular under the following types of classification, namely, education, diagnosis, interpretation, planning, and design. KBS has made widespread applications in a variety of domain problems and is proven to be capable of attaining a standard of performance comparable to that of a human expert [7-18]. Towards this direction, the present study indicates the necessity to go for extensive knowledge base on teaching and learning of fluid mechanics.

In this paper, the development and implementation of a prototype web-based interactive teaching package for diagnostic assessment on learning of fluid mechanics with a KBS approach, by employing the latest KBS technology and web production software, is delineated. Several up-to-date expert system shell and web production software including Visual Rule Studio, Dreamweaver, Java, JavaScript, Flash, PhotoShop and PhotoImpact, are employed. By using custom-built interactive graphical user interfaces, it is able to assist learners to acquire the much-needed knowledge in this domain area.

2   Web-Based Learning

In the present day, the society has entered into the information age, in which people strongly desire to obtain the information as soon as possible. The current technology is at such a stage that information released in the Internet is no longer restricted to text and graphics as usually presented in the traditional textbooks. The embedded material could be in a diversity of forms such as sound, animation, application, video, 3-D modeling or picture. An expanding multimedia communication system offers the advantage of furnishing diversified and enhanced delivery mechanisms of quality education. The student now has a potentially impressive myriad of study alternatives. This evolution into diverse learning opportunities has been prompted by the realization of a knowledge-based economy and associated technologies. The currently popular World Wide Web is characterized by the high speed in downloading, user-friendly graphic interface browsers and open standard, and portability between different operating systems and platforms.

It is generally acknowledged that effective instruction with technology must be driven by sound pedagogical principles, involve critical thinking, and provide a real community to students. Advocates of the use of new instructional technologies have asserted that these criteria can be, and have been, generally realized in an online environment. With the increasing quality and availability of technology, online learning has become rapid, effective, flexible, and convenient. In addition, technology has furnished the immediacy and range of interaction comparable with face-to-face learning. The proponent may confidently describe WBL as a viable alternative to conventional teaching at tertiary education sector. The flexibility and open infrastructure of Internet have been demonstrated to be able to act as a medium for developing learning application. For those individuals who would not have the chance or afford to further their education in a normal manner, WBL is able to furnish a cost-effective and flexible way and alternative opportunity of path to acquire lifelong education. It is apparent that the groups best served by WBL are individuals who have special demands, have family responsibilities, and work and reside in remote areas. WBL has a distant advantage that may render commute distance and time constraints of little or no consequence to students.

It should be aware that higher education is often shaped by debate among student, academics, politicians, and industrialists. In recent years, tight financial restrictions have forced educational institutions to become more efficient, demanding them to improve in areas including instructional quality, mode of study, access, and costs. Distance learning programs are evolving to satisfy, and to create new market demand. This expanded market renders it possible for educators to better serve working adults and those geographically and physically isolated from the campus. There exists strong demand for higher education to become more accessible, convenient, flexible, and effective for these individuals.

Besides, WBL furnishes the opportunity for interaction from the students, thus permitting them to acquire quality learning experiences to suit their specific demands or capabilities. WBL permits a student to enter and leave different course sections conveniently. They can freely and directly gain access to various parts of the course contents, and if they envisage any queries at any stage, they can point straight back into the relevant sections or into the references and back again. As such, it furnishes a dynamic and active learning environment and provides an opportunity of stimulating pedagogical environment to take care of engineering students in self-directed learning through interaction, application and reflection. Not only do they allow people work at their own pace from different locations and allow organizations to add their specific knowledge to tailor make the teaching materials, WBL has also been used in some organizations so as to raise the effectiveness of their education and training operations for the ultimate goal in enhancing the productivity.

3   Impact on Teaching and Learning

Concerns with the on-line program design are mostly pertinent to the relative novelty of the WBL environment. Queries have been put forward regarding the pedagogical quality that technology furnishes. Some educators may be concerned that WBL is neither personal nor interactive and is consequently less effective than face-to-face instruction. A serious criticism of WBL is that it fails to create an effective learning environment due often to poor design. The common weakness of many online learning sites is their misapprehension that information is equal to learning and material is laid out basically on the site in a regular textbook format. In such cases, learners are merely passively involved in electronic page turning when reading and sorting through material.

It should be emphasized that there exist different levels of WBL depending upon the degree of interaction offered. The lowest level of WBL includes a more objectivist philosophical orientation where instructional contexts are previously organized and simply displayed to the learner. The highest level of WBL comprises a more constructivist view where learners are encouraged to reorganize, manipulate and personally synthesize course materials. As such, the design of the learning experience under an active and dynamic environment is the cornerstone of quality WBL. The ideal WBL program would be user-friendly, interactive, satisfying, engaging, and responsive to learners' experiences. Besides, it would employ multimedia effectively, accommodate action, exploration, and reflection. The mere use of the World Wide Web does not automatically lead to efficacious quality instruction.

As a result of the necessity for active participation of learners in WBL, which is inconsistent with the more conventional passive learning role, it may require a shift in teaching paradigm. Instructors may need to adopt a more learner-centered approach to their teaching, with a role shift from authoritative teacher to facilitator. It is imperative to design WBL with learners in mind, with emphasis placed on collaboration and active learning. Under this constructivist approach, there is a shift away from didactic instruction towards discovery-based learning. A fuller set of contexts has to be available, which becomes part of the learning environment. They should cater for learners of wide-ranging perspectives and hence must be adaptable as the learner endeavors to create meaning from contexts. The opportunity for interaction results directly from the active role of the learner. Interactions are significant in that they render participation in the cycle of instruction, training, performance assessment, and improvement processes. They enable learners to tailor learning experiences to meet their specific capabilities or demands. Interactions allow clarification and the transfer of new ideas to existing conceptual frameworks. Moreover, they stimulate intrinsic motivation for learners by highlighting the significance of any novel information. In order to implement WBL efficaciously, new and responsive learning models, which would maximize technology for accomplishment of the teaching and learning transaction, are necessary to address the concerns of the learner and the challenges presented by the technology.

Technologies may furnish wealthy and flexible media for representing what students know and what they are learning. Yet they should function as intellectual tool kits that assist learners in establishing meaningful personal interpretations and representations of their environment. The objective thus becomes selecting the most effective tools to facilitate learning. In a technological society, academics should take a proactive role in the development and use of technology in the teaching process. New learning package should be developed by academics with technical support from computer programmers, which is founded on learner demands for quality content, delivery, and service that lead to desired learning outcomes.

4   Development Environment

It is not easy to compile an ideal web page if one is just using single web design software to create a web site. As such, in this case, several professional software programs, including Visual Rule Studio, Dreamweaver, Java, JavaScript, Flash, PhotoShop and PhotoImpact, are employed.

4.1   KBS Shell

In order to facilitate development of the knowledge base on fluid mechanics, KBS shell containing specific representation methods and inference mechanisms is employed. This system has been developed and implemented using a microcomputer-based KBS shell Visual Rule Studio [19], which is a hybrid application development tool under object-oriented programming design environment. This shell acts as an ActiveX Designer under the Microsoft Visual Basic 6.0 programming environment. Both production rules and procedural methods are employed to represent standard and heuristic knowledge on fluid mechanics. Rules are isolated as component objects, which are separated from both objects and application logic. As such, it produces objects that can interact with most modern development software. Rule development becomes a natural part of the component architecture development process. In addition, Visual Rule Studio is compatible with Active Server Pages and Microsoft Internet Information Server. In other words, the ruleset components can be deployed as part of a web server based application so that, with a web browser and Intranet or Internet access, it may virtually reach any users.

4.2   Web Production Tools

The main content, structure, frame, and most of the functions of the web pages are built by using the software Dreamweaver [20]. Some embedded programs, which are called applets, can be interactive taking user input, responding to it, and presenting ever-changing content. They are written in Java [21], which is a programming language that is well suited to designing software that works in conjunction with the

Internet. Besides, JavaScript [22] is employed to add some interactions to HyperText Markup Language (HTML), to allow for user interaction and feedback multimedia and animation, and to link HTML to other technologies such as Java and ActiveX. Flash [23] is used to produce the animation containing multiple scenes. It can create flash animations and interactive activities including vector graphics, interactive movies, buttons with actions, etc. It shows some interactive graphics, which make the web page more active and alive. PhotoShop [24], which is a pixel based image editing program, is employed to edit all the pictures and graphics in the web page of the package. PhotoImpact is used to perform some special effects in the pictures.

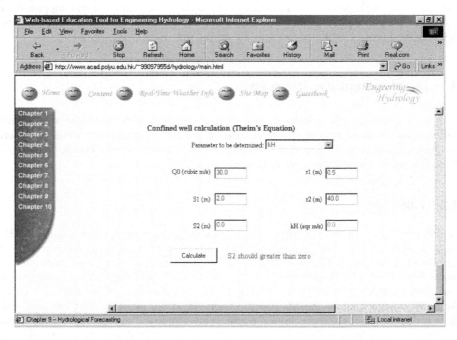

Fig. 1. Screen displaying the interactive "What-if" analysis on hydrology

5   Interactive Learning Package

In this study, a web-based interactive teaching package for diagnostic assessment on learning of fluid mechanics with an expert system approach is developed and implemented, by employing the latest KBS technology and web production software. In addition to the usual WBL techniques, including animation, friendly user interface, graphic presentation of teaching contexts, etc., the innovative idea in this project is the integration of KBS into the learning package so as to effect the desired interaction between the system and the learner.

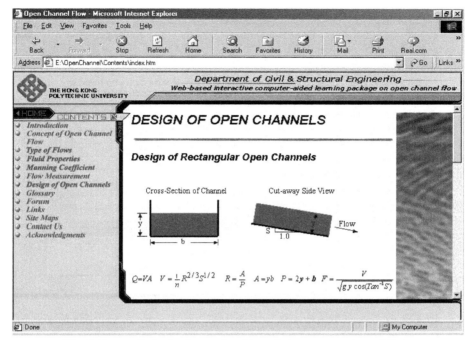

Fig. 2. Screen displaying instructional knowledge on open channel flow

The emphasis of the project is on the diagnostic assessment of learning performance and on the ensuing learning directive designed by the intelligent system, which depends on the response of the learner and the assessment outcome. Assessment exercises are carefully designed for each selected topic in fluid mechanics, covering all possible answers from the learner in mind. The covered topics include fluid at rest, types of flow, impact force, similitude, pipe flow, open channel flow, hydrology, hydrodynamics, coastal hydraulics, unsteady flow, and wind loading on structures, which are undertaken by different supervisors on the basis of their specialties. For each scenario of prompted answer from the learner, diagnostic assessment is performed by the system to determine the most probable shortfall or misconception of the specific learner on that particular topic. This heuristic knowledge can be represented by knowledge rules under the KBS approach.

So far the topics on hydrology, open channel flow, and fluid motion are included. Figure 1 shows the screen displaying the interactive "What-if" analysis on hydrology. Figure 2 shows the screen displaying instructional knowledge on open channel flow. Figure 3 shows the screen showing diagnostic assessment on the design of open channel. Figure 4 shows the screen displaying instructional knowledge on fluid motion. Upon the completion, the whole package will be tested rigorously through trial runs, evaluated and used by the engineering undergraduate students, who are the ultimate customers. Since it will be disseminated on the Internet, it may also be accessible by all engineering students in other local tertiary institutions, or even worldwide.

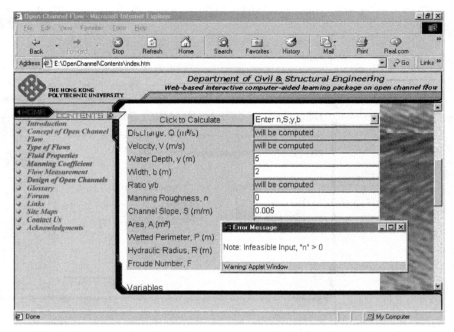

Fig. 3. Screen showing diagnostic assessment on the design of open channel

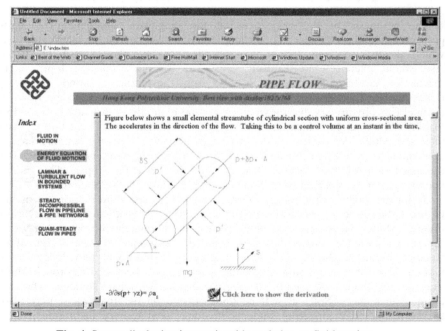

Fig. 4. Screen displaying instructional knowledge on fluid motion

6   Conclusions

This paper delineates the development and implementation of a prototype web-based interactive teaching package for diagnostic assessment on learning of fluid mechanics with an expert system approach, by employing the latest knowledge-based system technology and web production software. It is shown, from the preliminary results, that the application of the latest software, including Visual Rule Studio, Dreamweaver, Java, JavaScript, Flash, PhotoShop and PhotoImpact, are viable for this domain problem. It is demonstrated that various theories on hydrology, open channel flow, fluid motion, can be performed using this package through an active and dynamic learning environment. The flexibility and open infrastructure of Internet have been shown to be able to act as a media for developing learning application. The engineering students can gain deeper insight on this abstract subject through the interaction furnished in this package. It offers the possibility of providing a stimulating learning environment to engage learners in meaningful learning through reflection, application, and interaction.

References

1. Berge, Z.L.: Guiding Principles in Web-Based Instructional Design. Educational Media International **35(2)** (1998) 72–76
2. Wiens, G., Gunter, G.A.: Delivering Effective Instruction via the Web. Educational Media International **35(2)** (1998) 95–99
3. MacDonald, C.J., Stodel, E.J., Farres, L.G., Breithaupt, K., Gabriel, M.A.: The Demand-Driven Learning Model: A Framework for Web-Based Learning. The Internet and Higher Education **4** (2001) 9–30
4. Meyen, E.L., Tangen, P., Lian, C.H.T.: Developing Online Instruction: Partnership between Instructors and Technical Developers. Journal of Special Education Technology **14(1)** (1999) 18–31
5. Kearsley, G.: The World Wide Web: Global Access to Education. Educational Technology Review **5** (1996) 26–30
6. Maddux, C.D.: The World Wide Web: Some Simple Solutions to Common Design Problems. Educational Technology **38(5)** (1998) 24–28
7. Chau, K.W.: An Expert System for the Design of Gravity-type Vertical Seawalls. Engineering Applications of Artificial Intelligence **5(4)** (1992) 363–367
8. Chau, K.W., Albermani, F.: Expert System Application on Preliminary Design of Liquid Retaining Structures. Expert Systems with Applications **22(2)** (2002) 169–178
9. Chau, K.W., Albermani, F.: Knowledge-Based System on Optimum Design of Liquid Retaining Structures with Genetic Algorithms. Journal of Structural Engineering ASCE (in press)
10. Chau, K.W., Albermani, F.: A Coupled Knowledge-Based Expert System for Design of Liquid Retaining Structures. Automation in Construction (in press)
11. Chau, K.W., Anson, M.: A Knowledge-Based System for Construction Site Level Facilities Layout. Lecture Notes in Artificial Intelligence **2358** (2002) 393–402
12. Chau, K.W., Chen, W.: An Example of Expert System on Numerical Modelling System in Coastal Processes. Advances in Engineering Software **32(9)** (2001) 695–703
13. Chau, K.W., Cheng, C., Li, C.W.: Knowledge Management System on Flow and Water Quality Modeling. Expert Systems with Applications **22(4)** (2002) 321–330

14. Chau, K.W., Ng, V.: A Knowledge-Based Expert System for Design of Thrust Blocks for Water Pipelines in Hong Kong. Journal of Water Supply Research and Technology – Aqua **45(2)** (1996) 96–99
15. Chau, K.W., Yang, W.W.: Development of an Integrated Expert System for Fluvial Hydrodynamics. Advances in Engineering Software **17(3)** (1993) 165–172
16. Chau, K.W., Yang, W.W.: A Knowledge-Based Expert System for Unsteady Open Channel Flow. Engineering Applications of Artificial Intelligence **5(5)** (1992) 425–430
17. Chau, K.W., Yang, W.W.: Structuring and Evaluation of VP-Expert Based Knowledge Bases. Engineering Applications of Artificial Intelligence **7(4)** (1994) 447–454
18. Chau, K.W., Zhang, X.Z.: An Expert System for Flow Routing in a River Network. Advances in Engineering Software **22(3)** (1995) 139–146
19. Rule Machines Corporation: Developer's Guide for Visual Rule Studio. Rule Machines Corporation, Indialantic (1998)
20. Towers, J.T.: Dreamweaver 4 for Windows and Macintosh. Peachpit Press, Berkeley (2001)
21. Farrell, J., Gosselin, D.: Java Programming with Microsoft Visual J++ 6.0: Comprehensive. Course Technology, Cambridge (1999)
22. Barrett, D.J., Livingston, D., Brown, M.: Essential JavaScript for Web Professionals. Prentice Hall, Upper Saddle River (1999)
23. Kyle, L.: Essential Flash 5 for Web Professionals. Prentice Hall, Upper Saddle River (2001)
24. Margulis, D.: Professional PhotoShop 6: The Classic Guide to Colour Correction. John Wiley & Sons, New York (2001)

A Kind of Smart Space for Remote Real-Time Interactive Learning Based on Pervasive Computing Mode

Degan Zhang, Enyi Chen, Yuanchun Shi, and Guangyou Xu

Institute of Human Computer Interaction and Media Integration, Computer
Science Department, Tsinghua University, Beijing 100084, P.R.China
{gandegande,shiyc,xgy-dcs}@tsinghua.edu.cn

Abstract. As a kind of Smart Space, real-time interactive virtual classroom is
an important type of remote learning. However, available systems nowadays are
not adaptable large-scale user access and cannot accommodate heterogeneous
computing devices and different networks access either. Furthermore, these
systems are almost desktop-based. The Smart Classroom Project based on pervasive computing mode whose focus is on supporting software infra-structure,
context-aware computing, implicit human-computer interaction, interconnection
of computing device, etc. tackles the difficulties through these technologies: A
hybrid application-layer Multicast protocol, a dedicated software called
SameView, an augmented classroom called Smart Classroom, many kinds of
learning patterns' computing technology, interconnection learning via wireless
and wired communication protocol technology. So the teacher can instruct the
remote students just like face-to-face teaching in a conventional classroom. All
these developed technologies has been successfully integrated and demonstrated
in a prototype system. The efficiency of our researches has been tested by the
demo.

1 Introduction

The advances of personal computers and the Internet have laid the groundwork for the
revolution and the rapidly emerging era of intelligent, networked devices. This world
of connected devices offers new levels of customer service and computing capability.
Many new technologies introduce support for embedded mobile or fixed IP communications in the network, which will increase device-site capacity. Its embedded nature
also means that devices can be "always on the network", but only pay for services
when sending or receiving data. These changes are beginning to allow subscribers
access to the "invisible device applications". The migration paths from foolish-device
and smart-device to networking-device are clearly mapped out in many cases. However, as respective countries roll out their broadband networks and services, it will be
unlikely that the devices will offer the initial coverage that their existing smart-device
provide. Therefore, no matter what you do and no matter what you call it – pervasive
/ubiquitous computing, e-business, e-learning, or e-services, we are entering

W. Zhou et al. (Eds.): ICWL 2003, LNCS 2783, pp. 297–307, 2003.
© Springer-Verlag Berlin Heidelberg 2003

a new age of computing, namely, the era of pervasive computing era, which is studied only recently computing mode.

As we know, desktop and laptop have been the center of human-computer interaction since the late of last century. In this mode, people often feel that the cumbersome lifeless box is only approachable through complex jargon that has nothing to do with the tasks for which they actually use computers. Too much of their attention is distracted from the real job to the box. Deeper contemplation on valuable matured technologies tells us: the most profound technologies are those that disappear, which means they weave themselves into the fabric of everyday life until they are indistinguishable from it. We use them everyday, everywhere even without notice of them [Weiser 1991]. This inspiring view of prospect has been accepted and spread so fast and widely that in a short time of a few years, many ambitious projects have been proposed and carried on to welcome the advent of pervasive computing. There are a bunch of branch research fields under the banner of it, such as Mobile Computing, Wearable Computing, Nomadic Computing and also Intelligent Space, etc. The focus of this paper, Smart Classroom, belongs to the field of Intelligent Space.

It is obvious that the need for wider access to education, support for life long learning, and more part-time and remote real-time interactive learning (RRTIL). The Web/Internet provides relatively easy ways to publish hyper-linked multimedia content, and reach a wide audience. Yet, we find that most of the courseware are simply shifted from textbook to HTML files. Audience read from the book in the past and now read from the screen. However, in most cases the teacher's live instructing is very important for catching the attention and interest of the students. That's why Real-time Interactive Smart Space (RTISS), such as Virtual Classroom (VC), plays an important role of consequence in Distance Learning, where teachers and students located in different places take part in the class synchronously through certain multimedia communication system and can have real-time and media-rich interactions. However, to provide this type of Distance Learning in large scale still remains some barriers [Shi 2002]: It is not enough that adequate technologies to cope with large-scale access and adequate technologies to accommodate students with different network and device conditions in one session, such as wireless communication, mobile computing, nomadic computing, etc.

As a test bed and a prototype of pervasive computing mode, the Smart Space Project ["863" Plan of China] at our institute is a long-term project aiming at providing adequate technologies to overcome the above-mentioned difficulties in current practice of RRTIL and building an integrated system for the next generation real-time interactive distance learning in China. Currently we have made progresses in the following aspects: A software infrastructure based on pervasive computing mode, a dedicated software interface for RTISS called SameView and *a prototype system* have been developed.

The rest of the paper will be organized as following: First, discuss the focus problems of Pervasive Computing Mode. Then suggest the main scenario of smart space, later introduce a prototype system of our Smart Space Project – Smart Classroom. Finally give a conclusion.

2 The Focus of Pervasive Computing Mode

In researches of smart/intelligent space/environment, there are several relevant and challenging problems which is the focus problems of pervasive computing mode need to be solved, such as the Pervasive Computing software infrastructure, Context-aware Computing, Implicit Human-Computer Interaction, the inter-connection of computing devices on many different scales based on different layers' network protocol, the handling of various mobility problems caused by user's movement, application substrates, user interfaces issues etc. Although many projects have been conducted in the name of smart/intelligent space/environment, they have different emphases. Some focus on the integration of different sensing modalities, some aim at the adaptability of smart/intelligent space/environment to user's preference [Shi 2002], we developed special interest in exploring the impact of pervasive/ubiquitous computing to education. This leads to the prototype project of Smart Classroom.

2.1 The Supporting Software Infrastructure

In our point of view, there are several main different point of the supporting software infrastructure between the pervasive computing mode and traditional mode: It must manage the virtual space of computing network and physical space around the field at the same time. It must supply all kinds of functions and services, which are based on the space of daily life but not based on a special environment, the composing and structure of the software infrastructure are often changing. It must deal with the diversification of device, especially, including many mobile devices and wireless devices, that is to say, It must be adaptive to its object. It must be extendable, open and loose. etc.

As our opinion, the function and service of supporting software infrastructure should include as following:

(1) *Spontaneous discovery method of resource and services*. When a new device is brought into a space or new module us used in the old device, the infrastructure can know how to spontaneous discovery them and what is wanted to be interactive.

(2) *Adaptive interactive mechanism*. Because the resources of device are not same in a system, they may be embedded device, wearable computing device, basic components, etc. their computing capability, memory capability, interactive mode are too different. When the device is mobile or nomadic in the different environment, the interconnection problem is existed. the infrastructure can transform or translate the contents.

(3) *Coordination mechanism among modules*. As a distributed mode, the infrastructure can coordinate the relationship of association, communication, collaboration of modules, so Coordination mechanism among modules is more important to the whole function and services.

(4) *Toleration mechanism when the resource is not enough*. Because of the complexity, such as the scenario of movement in the different space between wireless communication device and fixed communication device, the scenario of spontaneous

cooperation among different modules, the error rate or loss rate is high, but the fault is temporary, the infrastructure can tolerate these cases and not stop, quit, or break down.

(5) *Privacy and security ensuring mechanism when spontaneous cooperation.* the infrastructure can not let the important information be modified, obtained by hostility, known by no authorization.

2.2 Context-Aware Computing

Although context information has been used in PC's computing mode, the content of it is fixed and set by manual and in pervasive computing, the content is changed with the task or event. Owing to the field/local of work environment, the complexity of its background is obvious, the dynamic change of context stands out. During the interaction, the importance of context is that : The same input, different context may be different annotation. The efficiency of interaction can be improved, so it distracts the user's attention within the less limit, which is the one of targets of pervasive computing. The physical interface under the pervasive computing mode is not private but shared by many users. In order to realize the individuation of interface and service, the context information is necessary.

The requirement to context-aware runs through each layer from lower hardware to upper application & interaction. As our opinion, the main technology of context-aware computing should include as following:

(1) *Obtaining of context information.* Context information is in different layer, both lower and upper, some can be obtained from the sensors directly, such as temperature, face character, some may be reasoned indirectly, such as normal state, abnormal state.

(2) *Modeling of context information.* In order to exchange the context information among different modules, system, environment, the model of context must be set up, including the expression method of context information, reasoning of uncertainty. The expression method must be common, which can permit the same context information be understood by different process module or agent. Owing to the noise and uncertainty of sensing data, the probability and statistic character of context information, the reasoning capability should be used frequently.

(3) *Management of context information.* How to query and store the context-aware information, how to schedule the context information, come a conclusion and supply the service actively, the management capability of computing platform is very important.

2.3 Implicit Human-Computer Interaction

Implicit human-computer interaction is distributed and attentive / proactive in fact. The former is that interactive interface of computing device is distributed in the 3D space, not in the front of a certain computer. The latter is that in this computing environment, the computer is not waiting for the controlling command passively, but supplying the individuation service passively in time according to what has been detected and recognized about the state of physical, emotion and cognition of the user and context-aware information. This is to say, the function and service of it should include as following:

(1) *Detection and recognition of user's physical state.* User's physical state includes user's biological character identification, position, gesture, vision angle, etc.

(2) *Detection and comprehension of events.* By the sensing data and context-aware information, the action of the user and the relative event are detected and recognized ,so the intention of the user is comprehended.

(3) *Detection and comprehension of user's emotion.* By the sensing data of audio, voice, etc, the emotion of the user is comprehended.

(4) *Fusion of multi-modal data.* Multiple sensors has been used, the sensing channel is multiple level, so the data is multi-modal, only by fusion, human-computer interaction may be done. This is the key technology.

(5) *Learning of user's action rule.* In order to supply individuation service, each user's custom and taste may be known by learning from the interactive data and recollection of user's calendar.

2.4 The Interconnection of Computing Device

The data exchange/switching is needed between different computing devices by different network, such as wireless infrastructure-based communication, multi-hop ad-hoc networks, dynamic topology without any infrastructure-based communication, Internet-based networks. Different computing devices are interconnected using IEEE 802.11x and Bluetooth technology, mobile devices may use GSM communication technology, also use GPRS, UMTS, DECT, etc. instead. Especially, although suitable routing protocols enable communication in multi-top ad-hoc networks, such as DSR, TORA, AODV, communication paths between sender and receiver can break when the network is topology is partitioned due to the movements of the nodes. Large-scale interactive applications have demanding requirements on underlying transport protocols for efficient dissemination of real-time multimedia data over heterogeneous networks [Kuo 1998]. Existing reliable multicast protocols failed to meet these requirements due to following reasons: (a) most protocols presume the existence of multicast fully-enabled network infrastructure, which is usually not the case for current Internet; (b) protocols that support multiple concurrent data sources only have limited scalability; (c) few of them have implemented end-to-end TCP-friendly congestion control policy.

Consider the following situation in a scenario which supports pervasive computing: In order to conserve energy, laptop A in the ad-hoc network initially communicates with laptop B using Bluetooth via the PDA. If B becomes unreachable, for example, when A moves out of the coverage of the Bluetooth network or when the PDA is switched off, communication is no longer possible. A's TCP connections will time out, even if B is still reachable using the IEEE 802.11x link. The reason is that a TCP connection is uniquely identified by a quadruple (IP address A, port A, IP address B, port B) and switching to another network interface results in a new source IP address related with this interface. However, it is also harmful to change the bindings of IP addressed to a networking device due to three reasons:

(1) *The mobile node becomes unreachable as the new address bound to the network interface might be topologically incorrect.*

(2) *The process of binding, unbinding, and the internal routing table is not very efficient.*

(3) *Caching of ARP information is not possible as the matching between IP address and MAC address changes after the modification.*

So a seamless and transparent switching mechanism between different networking interfaces is needed. Several service location protocols have been developed in the last few years. Among the most famous are Jini, UPnP, Bluetooth SDP, Salutation and SLP. Most service location protocols may be used in ad-hoc networks for pervasive computing mode. Some protocols, such as Jini, UPnP, even provide service access in addition to service discovery, in case of Jini even without the need of pre-configured drivers for a service. For ad-hoc network it is also important that a central service manager is not required because in a dynamic environment a centralized entity is always a single point of failure. So service location protocols that implement distributed service managers or enabling direct discovery of services at a particular device should be preferred in ad-hoc networks.

Seamless switching between different networks for different computing devices is a basic feature for improving the quality of a perceived service under the pervasive computing mode. However, the heterogeneity also implies that the services are also distributed over the accessible ad-hoc networks. Due to device mobility, the services need to be regularly discovered and their availability is not ensured as mobile devices can be frequently switched off and on by their users. For example, In the scenario described above, the laptop A has a connection to the Internet, using a gateway from ISP2.This gateway can be reached by means of IP routing via laptop B. If B is switched off A's connection to the internet terminates. In this case, the service location protocol running on A has to discover an alternative proxy providing Internet access service in the heterogeneous ad-hoc network. In this case a proxy form ISP will be used which can be reached via the other route. Afterwards, the network settings of a need to be reconfigured and the application must be restarted as the source address might have changed.

3   The Scenario of Smart Space on Pervasive Computing Mode

Fig. 1 depicts an example of the main scenario of Smart Space based on pervasive computing mode, such as Smart Remote Classroom, which is integrated into an overall scenario to enable a revolutionary real-time interactive distance learning practice. In this scenario, we have shown the communication mode by wireless network and INTERNET NETWORK. A reporter, such as teacher gives a report/class with natural ways in this Smart Space where could also exist local audiences/students, while the remote audiences/students connected by Internet access the report/class with SameView clients. The remote audiences/students can see the presented report/class materials, the annotations made during the report/lecture, the live audio/video in the

Smart Space and also can take the initiative to interact with the reporter/teacher, just like attending the space/classroom locally. Furthermore, the process of the report/lecture will be recorded as a multimedia courseware for playback after report/class. In addition, If several audiences/students have mobile computing devices, who can join in the report/class by wireless network, they may learn freely or discuss with other audiences/students or ask the reporter/teacher for questions, and so on.

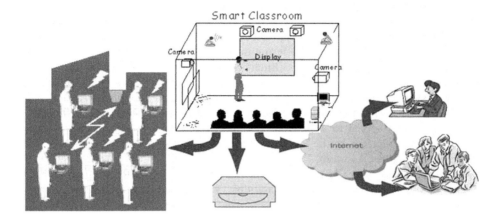

Fig. 1. The main scenario of Smart Space

In the smart environment of pervasive/ubiquitous computing, because of many interconnected computing devices and wide area network environment, collaborations of multi-user and multi-device can be the most important. And the support for collaboration is becoming a requisite of a smart space. The collaborative work support of a Smart Space can be categorized into two classes. One is the collaboration of multiple attendants within the Smart Space holding various computing devices, such as   pen-based devices, hand-held devices and wearable computer etc. The other is the collaboration of remote participants and local attendants. The demand for collaboration support is so obvious that many commonly observed tasks in a space, need the collaboration of multiple objects.

So the Smart Space is essentially a distributed parallel computing environment, in which many distributed software/hardware modules collaborate to accomplish specific jobs. Software infrastructure is the enabling technology to provide facilities for software components' collaboration. There are some candidate solutions to software infrastructure, such as Distributed Component-Oriented Model, like EJB, CORBA, DCOM, etc, and Multi-Agent Systems (MAS). In the context of Intelligent Environment, Multi-Agent System is more competent than Distributed Component-Oriented Model due to the following reasons: higher encapsulation level, faster evolution from design to implementation, easier development and debugging, and most importantly, more accordant to the need of dynamic reconfiguration and loose-coupling. The network of distributed software modules is conceptualized as a dynamic community of agents, where multiple agents, such as Facilitator agent, Facial-voice identification agent, motion-tracking agent, speech recognition agent, Virtual Mouse agent, etc. contribute services to the community.

4 A Prototype System of Our Smart Space Project

Smart Classroom, as a prototype system of our smart space project, is inspired by the research of pervasive computing mode. Smart Spaces are work environments with embedded computers, information appliances, and multi-modal sensors allowing people to perform tasks efficiently by offering unprecedented levels of access to information and assistance from computers [Smart Space]. Smart Classroom is just such a Smart Space deployed in a classroom [Xie 2001]. We augment an ordinary classroom with wall-sized displays, sensors, cameras and the associated computation and perception modules so as to allow the teacher in it access the SameView system transparently, rather than appeal to a desktop computer. By Smart Classroom, we actually extend the user interface of the SameView for teacher from a desktop computer into the 3-D space of the classroom.

The room setting is illustrated in reference [Xie 2001]. The teaching area of the classroom are augmented with two facilities: Mediaboard and Studentboard. Mediaboard is a physical embodiment of the shared mediaboard of the SameView software in the teacher's side, which is essentially a large touch-sensitive screen. Teachers can display prepared slides in this board and make or wipe scribbles on the slides with provided pens and erasers. Studentboard is a window to remote students, on which the image of remote students with presenter roles will be displayed and the video and audio of the remote student who has floor will be played here too. The student area of the classroom is just the same as any ordinary classroom, which can be occupied by local students. Around the classroom, there are near a half-dozen cameras, each with different usage. For example, some are used to recognize the action of the teacher and some are used to broadcast the live video of the classroom to the remote students. In addition, the teacher wears a wireless microphone to capture his speech. In Smart Classroom, the teacher no longer need to remain stationary in front of a desktop computer and to complete most of common tasks happened in a class, the teacher do not need to use keyboard and mouse. The natural teaching experience includes that Pen-based UI, Laser Pointer Tracking, Virtual Assistant, Biometric Character Based Login Process, Smart Cameraman and so on [Shi 2002].

4.1 The Software Infrastructure for Remote Real-Time Interactive Learning

The Smart Classrooms, just like many other similar smart space/Intelligent Environment setups, will assemble a good number of hardware and software modules such as projectors, cameras, sensors, face recognition module, speech recognition module and eye-gaze recognition module. It is unimaginable to install all these components in one computer due to the limited computation power and terrible maintenance requirements. Thus, a distributed computing structure is required to implement an Intelligent

Environment. We have currently completed a demo of the Smart Classroom (as Fig. 2). In order to an agent to communicate with each other, it should have a reference to the other peer. In order to make the system more loosely coupled and flexible, the reference binding should be created by some high-level mechanism. A usual implementation is binding by capability. That is to say, on startup, each agent should register its capabilities to some central registry, and when an agent needs some service, it could ask for it by describe the needed capabilities. However, the true challenge here is how to set up a framework for the description of the capabilities, which could enable a new agents to find out the exact semantic meaning of the capabilities advertised by other agents.

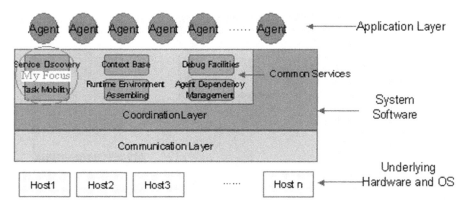

Fig. 2. A kind of software infrastructure for remote real-time interactive learning

The prototype/Demo system is composed of the following key components:

● *The multi-agent software platform.* We adopted a public available multi-agent system, OAA (Open Agent Architecture), as the software platform for the Smart Classroom. It was developed by SRI and has been used by many research groups. We fixed some errors of the implementation provided by SRI to make it more robust. All the software modules in the Smart Classroom are implemented as the agents in the OAA, and using the capability provided by it to communicate and cooperate with each other.

● *Multiple agents' realization.* The hand-tracking agent, which could track the 3D movement parameters of the teacher' hand using a skin color consistency based algorithm. It could also recognize some simple actions of the teacher's palm such as open, close and push. The same recognition engine had been successfully used in a project in Intel China Research Center (ICRC), which we have taken part in. The multi-modal unification agent, which is based on the work in the project of ICRC mentioned above, under a collaboration agreement. The approach is essentially based on the one used in Quickset as mentioned above. The speech recognition agent, which is developed with a simplified Chinese version of ViaVoice SDK from IBM. We carefully designed is developed with a simplified Chinese version of ViaVoice SDK from IBM. We carefully designed the interface to make any agents who need the SR capability could dynamically add or delete the recognizable phrases together with the associated action (an OAA resolve request indeed) when recognized. Thus the vocabulary in the SR agent is always kept to a minimum size according to the context of the time. It is very important to improve the recognition rate and accuracy. Some others have been finished except the service discovery agent and task mobility agent, which are ongoing research.etc.

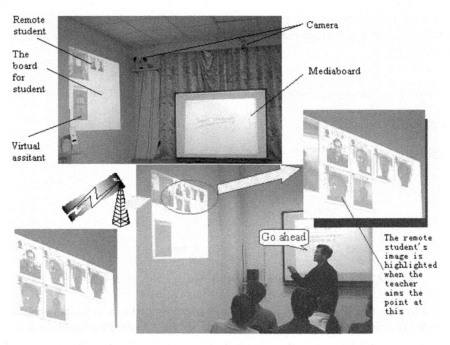

Fig. 3. A snapshot point of the SameView client

4.2 A Kind of Software for Remote Real-Time Interactive Learning: SameView

In order to support the remote real-time interactive learning, SameView is developed based on the proposed TORM and AMTM platform. Fig. 3 is a snapshot point of a SameView client. SameView provides a set of interaction channels for the teacher and local/remote students to efficiently achieve the goal of teach and learning [Smart Space]: shared Mediaboard which is a shared whiteboard capable of displaying multimedia contents, Live Audio/Video and Mutual Chat.

In the Smart Space, such as the Smart Classroom, real-time lecturing is a typical large-scale interactive application, where there may be hundreds or thousands remote students taking part in a virtual class. Reliable multicast is a useful network service but is also challenged research issue for the heterogeneity and the lack of full support of IP multicast in today's Internet infrastructure. Instead of following the traditional end-to-end model for reliable multicast, our research group developed a Totally Ordered

Reliable Multicast (TORM) protocol taking a hybrid approach that exploits both mobile/fixed IP Unicast and IP Multicast for data delivery. And during data forwarding, the Adaptive Multimedia Transport Model (AMTM) proposed is applied to dynamically trans-code the multimedia data for users with different devices and network capabilities.

5 Conclusions

Based on Pervasive Computing Mode, we have developed a set of key technologies for remote real-time interactive learning and make a new model of remote real-time interactive learning with following characteristics possible: (a) Able to accept large-scale user access the virtual classroom simultaneously with different network and device conditions. (b) The class can be recorded and turned into an ideal courseware for E-learning. (c) Support many kinds of learning patterns, such as mobile computing devices, wireless communication network environment. (c) Set up a channel of interconnection learning via uniformed communication protocol.

Of course, our project is not completed totally, such as service discovery, task mobility, so our work is continuously ongoing. Although we have made concrete achievements on each part of the project and the integrated system has been successfully demonstrated with controlled.

References

[Shi 2002] Yuanchun Shi, Weikai Xie, Guangyou Xu. Smart Remote Classroom: Creating a Revolutionary Real-time Interactive Distance Learning System. ICWL2002, Hongkong, Aug2002.
[Smart Space] http://www.media.cs.tsinghua.edu.cn/~pervasive.
[Weiser 1991]Weiser M. The computer for the twenty-first century. Scientific American, 1991, vol. 265, no. 3: 94–104.
[Kuo 1998] Kuo F, Effelsberg W, Garcia-Luna-Aceves J. Multimedia Communications: Protocols and Applica-tions. Prentice Hall PTR, 1998.
[Xie 2001] Weikai Xie, Yuanchun Shi and Guanyou Xu. Smart Classroom – an Intelligent Environment for Tele-education. In Proceedings of The Second Pacific-Rim Conference on Multimedia (PCM 2001),662–668, Beijing, China. Springer LNCS 2195.

Managing the Interactivity of Instructional Format and Cognitive Style Construct in Web-Mediated Learning Environments

Elspeth McKay

RMIT University, School of Business Information Technology
GPO Box 2476V, Melbourne, Victoria 3001, Australia
elspeth.mckay@rmit.edu.au

Abstract. The management of Web-mediated learning environments is complex. There are many ontological facets to account for in defining the interacting variables. Instructional designers need to be ready to correctly identify and unravel each variable [1]. A meta-knowledge processing model has been proposed to facilitate the courseware design process to enhance performance outcomes [2]. Research has already been carried out on each component, however very little is known about the interactivity of these components in a Web-mediated learning environment. While multi-sensory instruction is known to improve a student's capacity to learn effectively, the overarching role of knowledge-mediated human-computer interaction (HCI) has been poorly understood [3]. The purpose of this paper is to discuss this meta-knowledge processing model and its usefulness for Web-mediated learning platform design in general and in particular to identify the interactive effects of the cognitive style construct and instructional format on performance outcomes.

1 Introduction

The purpose of this paper is to promote the use of the meta-knowledge processing model (see Figure 3) to aid in the process of effective courseware design that initiate instructional outcomes that are predictable. The interactive effect of differences in cognitive style construct (*how we represent information during thinking and the mode of processing that information*) [4] and instructional format (*verbal(text)/image(pictures)*), have shown surprising results when applied to instructional materials that are solely paper based [5]. There is no research that can inform what happens with this interactive effect of individual differences in cognitive processing in a Web-mediated context. To compound the complexity of providing interactive courseware, there are additional challenges ahead for researchers to investigate how the effects of audio, colour and movement affect the learning performance outcomes. This paper provides a brief overview of the contextual issues involved in understanding the interactivity of Web-initiated instructional conditions and the cognitive style construct as a meta-knowledge acquisition process. This mechanism may explain how

W. Zhou et al. (Eds.): ICWL 2003, LNCS 2783, pp. 308–319, 2003.

individuals deal with the Web-mediated instructional format in terms of information processing, in the form of a speculated internal/external exchange process [6]. The discussion leads to a final conclusion, that reflects on how much work is ahead to uncover the best eLearning design and development specifications.

Web-mediated communications technologies seem to offer new instructional/learning opportunities. However, this view takes a pervasive approach to the individualised instructional requirements of diverse cohorts in Web-mediated learning programmes. Current thought on the multimedia technologies engaged in eLearning courseware development accentuates a presumed requirement for highly graphical (or visual) approaches to instructional formats. Unfortunately, providing textual displays will also encounter difficulties for the courseware designer. When the format involves screen-based textual displays, there are extra mitigating factors that involve an interaction between the learner managing the scrolling text and dealing with the comprehension of large amounts of information. While the so-called eLearning programmes may appear to enable a learner to proceed at their own pace [7], there is a common assumption made by instructional designers, that to facilitate eLearning, all learners are capable of assimilating the graphical material with their current experiential knowledge. There is little or no consideration for differences in cognitive styles!

Due to the far reaching effects of Web-mediated instructional systems (WMIS) in terms of development costs, let alone the HCI factors, there is often a need to accommodate co-existing instructional paradigms in any computerized learning/course authoring process. This inevitably requires a dynamic evaluation of task knowledge level requirements that responds appropriately to individual cognitive styles and the learner's knowledge acquisition requirements. Meta-knowledge acquisition strategies are thus essential to provide the mechanisms for the dynamic knowledge analysis necessary for knowledge-mediated instructional processes within Web-mediated learning environments. The complexity of the visual learning environment has been identified [8]. Prospects for an interactive customised learning shell, based on meta-knowledge have also been researched [2]. Unfortunately due to the abundance of technological choice, practitioners have been slow to implement educational research findings; however, progress can now be made in linking research outcomes to actual learning environments. The prospect of customised eLearning courseware, dynamically tailored to the requirements of individual students, has stimulated contemporary research into knowledge mediation. Consequently, the associated meta-knowledge acquisition strategies of learning contexts within Web-mediated instructional programmes can now be designed as synchronous and asynchronous learning frameworks.

Within the context of online asynchronous learning platforms, there is a noticeable shift from traditional teaching methods, which act as the sole content provider, towards a multiple mentor-guiding approach. This approach supports learners through the process of knowledge acquisition, but relies largely on the learners to direct the learning process themselves; reflecting a lack of understanding of the effect of computerized learning on the population at large. HCI is complicated, and Web-mediated courseware designers should ensure that careful attention is paid to sound and well-founded instructional design principles. In general terms, online courseware designers will need to be aware of the meta-knowledge acquisition process, relevant instructional strategies, and need to articulate the *conditions-of-the-learner*; specifically, drawing on comprehensive Web-based ontological models to direct the online learning experience that best achieves high quality instructional outcomes. It should be noted that understanding the *hierarchical structuring of knowledge* (ontological complexity) will be necessary to bring about the types of learning models that institutions and private consortia require [9].

This paper therefore presents a paradigmatic approach towards a knowledge-mediated learning environment. Aspects of instructional science, cognitive psychology and educational research are combined to articulate the ontological requirements of Web-mediated learning courseware. The discussion will firstly identify the cognitive style construct as an effective means to explain how human beings process information they receive. Next will be an outline of the research that has shown there are certain cognitive style dimensions that enable knowledge acquisition more readily than others. Then, an information processing framework is proposed to support the complexities of Web-mediated instructional environments. There is an explanation that spatial ability and notational transfer, involving the relationship of instructional format and the cognitive style construct may interact with particular tasks during the knowledge acquisition of abstract concepts. The WMISs' multimodal capacity is included to introduce the notion of cultural specificity as another important area for future research.

2   Cognitive Style Construct

The literature reveals research which distinguishes human ability to process information, as a combination of *mode of processing information*, and the *way people represent information during thinking* [10]. Moreover, there are two fundamental cognitive dimensions: Wholist-Analytic and Verbal-Imagery that affects performance in two ways. The first way, is in the way we perceive and interpret information we are given. While the second way is how we conceptualise related information already in our memory [11].

Cognitive style is understood to be an individual's preferred and habitual approach to organizing and representing information. Measurement of an individual's relative right/left hemisphere performance and their cognitive style dominance has been a target of researchers from several disciplines over the last decade. Different theorists make their own distinctions on an individual's cognitive differences [4]. The naming of their Wholist-Analytic (WA) continuum for example, maps to the cognitive categories used by other researchers. These well known terms are used frequently throughout the literature in a number of different research disciplines.

2.1 Wholistic/Analytic (Mode of Processing Information)

The Wholist-Analytic dimension defines that Wholist learners are able to perceive the whole concept, but may find difficulty in disembedding its separate facts [12]. Analytic learners analyse material into its parts but find difficulty in seeing the whole concept.

2.2 Verbal/Imagery (Mode of Representing Information while Thinking)

The Verbal-Imagery continuum measures whether an individual is inclined to represent information verbally, or in mental pictures, during thinking [13]. Verbalisers prefer and perform best on verbal tasks; while Imagers are superior on concrete, descriptive and imaginal ones [14]. When there is a mismatch between cognitive style and instructional material or mode of presentation, Riding argues that performance is deemed to be reduced. The suggestion is made here that as not everyone can see the same graphical detail presented in traditional materials, and therefore Web-mediated courseware design may also prove to be even more complicated. For instance, the well known graphical representation below that was first published in 1915 as a puzzle type picture to depict a multiple depiction of *a wife and a mother-in-law*. Without any prompting, some will see the profile of a young woman, while others will notice an old lady's face instead.

Fig. 1. Different Ways of Seeing [15, 16]

2.3 Complementary Style Dimensions

The full effects from the interaction of the cognitive style construct and instructional medium on learning in WMIS is unknown. There are few published studies which deal with the interactive effects of the cognitive style construct and multimedia delivery techniques, on performance outcomes [17]. However, courseware designers are well advised to examine the valuable contribution that has been made to enable comprehension of the differences in learning and behaviour as a complex human interaction [13]:1: *"The concept of style is an idea used frequently in everyday language. The concept has been used more technically in the psychological study of individual differences in learning and behaviour. In this respect it is used as a 'construct'. A construct is a psychological idea or notion...."*
According to Riding, the Wholist-Verbalisers are likely to utilize their dominant style for verbal representation of information, having the characteristic of both semantic coding and a degree of analytic facility as well as having an ability to internally proc-

ess what they see as imagery, which has both a pictorial quality and its associated wholeness. On the other hand, the Analytic-Verbalizer and Wholist-Imager combinations, are both less complementary, with the former having difficulty visualizing how facts and details fit into the bigger picture, and the latter unable to focus on detailed information [18]:210.

An investigation of the effects of instructional format (*textual metaphors* (T:1) or *graphical metaphors* (T:2)) on the performance of learning computer programming concepts (see Figure 2) has defied common assumptions about the effects of cognitive style and instructional outcome [5]. It shows that researchers should examine the interactive effects of the integrated cognitive style (ICS) construct sub-groupings (Wholist-Verbaliser, Analytic-Verbal, Wholist-Imager, Analytic-Imager) and instructional format on actual performance outcomes. Although the initial data analysis indicated that Wholists out-performed Analysts (dimension for mode of processing information), and Verbalisers out-performed Imagers (dimension of representation of information during thinking); closer examination of the full cognitive dimensions reveals that actually the Wholist-Verbalisers using the graphical treatment (T:2) were only 3rd in the performance level sub-grouping, with the Wholist-Imagers:T:2 and Analytic-Verbalisers:T2, being the top 2 sub-groups [5].

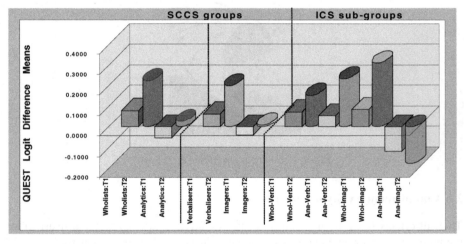

Fig. 2. Experimental Results

Conversely, given the relatively poor performance of the Analytic and Imager single category cognitive style (SCCS) groups (Wholist/Analytic, Verbaliser/Imager), it is not surprising that the Analytic-Imager ICS sub-groups performed badly. It is surprising that the results indicate that an Analytic-Imager would perform best with the textual treatment (T1). There are two interesting factors for the acquisition of programming concepts, which emerge from these findings. Firstly, is the suggestion, that in devising a prescriptive model for expressing concepts of computer programming in terms of content specific knowledge elements, there is a need to provide a notational representation of the instructional strategy with a mix of text and graphical metaphors. This instructional format will benefit most learners, including Verbalisers. Secondly, and the most striking, is that some learners (Analytic-Imagers) will perform better with a text-only instructional format.

3 Information Processing Framework for HCI

The means to provide Web-navigation exists, even at the most basic level, with well planned hyperlinks and floating menus. Yet novice-learners are often left to navigate Web-mediated courseware alone. Generic instructions will not provide sufficient information to reach a diverse mix of global learners in a WMIS. In a traditional learning setting there are three major components of a theory of instruction: methods, conditions, and outcomes [19]. Courseware designers need to be aware of these components to understand how best to articulate these components into a WMIS.

Methods are the different ways to achieve different learning outcomes under different conditions. For instance: methods can take the form of an instructional agent (maybe a teacher, or some other instructional medium), that directs its actions at a learner [20]. This context-mediated modeling tool could include an instructional conditions agent in an online context. *Conditions* are the factors that influence the effects of the instructional methods employed. Instructional conditions have a two-fold impact [19]. Firstly, courseware designers may be able to manipulate them as some conditions interact with the method of delivery to influence their relative effectiveness, such as instructional format. Secondly, there are instructional conditions that cannot be manipulated, and, therefore, are beyond the control of the designer, such as learner characteristics. This is the most complicated component in a WMIS. *Outcomes* are the various effects that provide a measure of value of alternative methods under different conditions, as they focus on instruction rather than on the learner [19]. Assessment practices in diverse cultures and learning domains will be studied using the model depicted in Figure 3. Note that the term conditions-of-the-learner [19] combines the interactive effects of the internal states of an individual and external events of the instructional delivery format on learning [2]; providing in eLearning environments the computer-mediated context. More work is needed to clarify how people respond the Web-based education.

The Meta-Knowledge Processing Model (Figure 3) articulates the complexity of the eLearning delivery environment [21]. The *Method of Delivery Transfer Agent* directs the *Instructional Conditions* according to the results of the *Learner Characteristics* (cognitive style) and *Event Conditions* (complexity of processing the learning material), and the *Measurable Instructional Outcomes*. Directions for choice of *Instructional Format* are given by the *Method of Delivery Transfer Agent* (or learner). Therefore it is useful to draw on this model as a courseware design tool to identify and thoroughly examine the characteristics of each component. For example, consider how the *method of delivery* (a palm pilot) would need to reflect the interactive effect of the expected learner profile *learner characteristics* (when the learners use English as a second language) and *instructional format* (the provision of sufficient conceptual translation opportunities to achieve the *measurable instructional outcomes*).

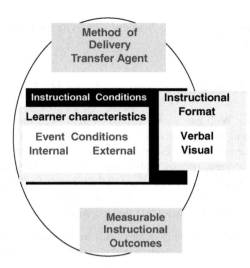

Fig. 3. Meta-Knowledge Processing Model

WMISs involve a complex pedagogical process that courseware designers struggle with. In the first instance, there should be an understanding of how the learners will deal with the instructional content. Next, is the recognition of the interactive effect of an individual's knowledge processing and the dimensions of their cognitive style construct. Finally, is the need for an awareness of how the dynamics of the Meta-Knowledge Processing Model will impact on the media engaged to bring about the instructional outcomes.

In most instructional programmes, it is not sufficient to say that one size fits all. The same can be said about the likely success of a WMIS. More work is needed by researchers to determine how dissimilar cognitive styles react, resulting in superior performance outcomes by learners with one cognitive style drawing on a particular condition of an eLearning instructional strategy, as opposed to another [21].

An explanation for how the Riding and Rayner [13] cognitive style construct interacts with a particular abstract or conceptual task that involves procedural programming knowledge may lie within the relationship of the instructional conditions' components as shown in Figure 3. It should be no surprise that individuals' performances vary on the strength of their cognitive style, and the task at hand. Because there is an interactive effect of graphical instructional metaphors on logical reasoning and spatial relations, a number of questions arise: can an explanation for this be found using between-item and within-item elaborations. Furthermore, can visual metaphors, used as internal/external exchange agents [6], have the same interactive effect (for some novice learners) in environments other than the computer programming domain? How will a WMIS impact on an individual's capacity to learn?

4   Spatial Ability and Notational Transfer

In the past, verbal (or analytic) ability was taken to be a measure of crystallised intelligence, or the ability to apply cognitive strategies to new problems and manage a large volume of information in working memory [22], while the non-verbal (or imagery) ability was expressed as fluid intelligence [23]. However, as electronic courseware lends itself to integrating verbal (textual) with non-verbal (graphical representations) and sound, instructional conditions that generate novel (or fluid) intellectual problems. Research into the effects of Web-based educational systems on knowledge acquisition must be carried out to provide instructional designers with prescriptive models that predict measurable instructional outcomes for a broader range of cognitive abilities. To this end an empirical experimental research methodology for cognitive performance measurement in a WMIS should be undertaken to facilitate the prediction of whether: the method of delivery affects highly-verbal/low-spatial learners, because they need a direct notational transfer agent [6]; or whether the instructional conditions disadvantage high-spatial/low-verbal learners, because they will be less able to pick out the unstated assumptions [6].

Picking out these important instructional variables for some types of instructional outcomes provides appropriate instructional environments for a broader range of novice-learners by means of an information-transfer-agent, thereby controlling the choice of instructional format and instructional event conditions. Isolating the key components of the instructional conditions provides the means to manipulate the method-of-delivery, which in turn may bring about a choice of information-transfer-agent (see Figure 4).

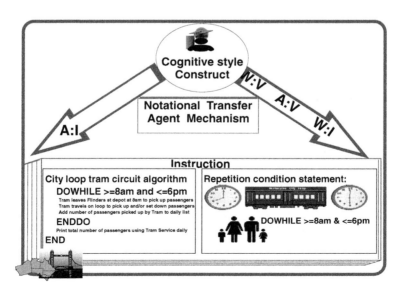

Fig. 4. Notational Transfer Agent

It is proposed that the external-representation of the instructional material may require a direct notational transfer of the symbol-system used for the instructional strategy (from the external representation of the instructional material to an internalised form in an individual's memory) [24]. For instance: the graphical details in a road map directly relate to the physical environment (in a 1:1 direct notation ratio, like the explicit representation of basic data-type rules in computer programming). Therefore, in a programming environment, another example would be that a real number must not contain a decimal point [6]. On the other hand, the embedded details in an abstract metaphor are said to require a non-notational transfer process. For instance, the programming loop shown as a graphical metaphor in Figure 4 requires a 2:1 transfer for the non-notational characteristics of the external representation to a single internal notational representation [6].

Taking this type of fine grained approach to locating the complexity of the ontological requirements will provide Web-designers with special insight. Courseware authoring that offers a WMIS without involving a customizable platform to individualize instructional strategies is much like implementing the closed systems of days gone by, and given the passing of time, this type of closed WMIS will inevitably fail [25].

5 WMIS and Cognitive Context

Multi-sensory instruction that involves choice of Web-mediated instructional media is emerging through the literature. Web technology has brought with it a resurgence of interest in knowledge acquisition through HCI. This important work began over four decades ago with the George Pask's famous conversation theory [26, 27]. Since then researchers have been wishing to develop learning systems that better resemble human beings. These attempts have been to have a computer mimic how humans think by establishing problem spaces, where there are a number of dimensions to deal with communication channels in a technical sense, while others characterise the complex nature of the system's cognitive ability [28]; [29]. While others concentrate on finding ways to develop interface technologies which posses multimodal capabilities to offer speech, and body language that includes: gestures, eye-gazing, lip motion and facial expressions [30].

Yet another Web-mediated instructional paradigm which is now popular are the instructional agent technologies. This research group is concentrating on bringing interactive interfaces which behave like human beings. However, in dealing with the technology aspects of HCI some of the importance of providing interactive learning systems which respond according to learner differences is lost. One such attempt to provide an intelligent tutoring tool which took a multi-sensory approach to the instructional strategies was a computer-based training (CBT) package called Cogniware launched in Taiwan (see Figure 5). Cogniware offers a range of instructional format (text, voice, and video) [31].

To exploit an individual's cognitive learning characteristics, Cogniware consists of a front end module that determines the learner's cognitive style, and offers a choice of instructional formats for the acquisition of programming concepts. Learners are encouraged to investigate the alternative instructional strategies. Cogniware is multisensory in the sense that the instructional strategies on offer provide the learning content in a range of alternative instructional modes. Figure 5 depicts a typical Cogniware interface with three instructional formats or separate viewing areas: graphical, textual, and voice. There are also cueing mechanisms for guided exploration, such as: directional icons, a learning module name tag, and an advance organizer screen.

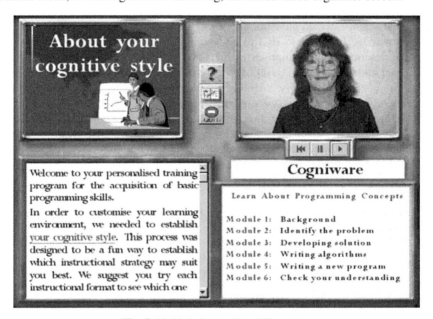

Fig. 5. Multiple Instructional Format

Research into the anthropocentric aspects of WMISs is scarce. However, it would appear there are many technological mechanisms to support the Web-mediated learning process per se; and certainly, the advent of the Web has far reaching effects for global connectivity.

6 Summary

This paper provided an overview of the contextual issues which surround the design of a WMIS. Management of the interactivity of the various aspects of multimedia and individual differences in a Web-mediated learning programme were explained. The meta-knowledge processing model was suggested to articulate the complex ontological requirements which involve aspects of instructional science, cognitive psychology and educational research. It has been suggested that rather than isolating the two dimensions of cognitive style (Verbal-Imagery (V:I), Wholist-Analytic (W:A)) to identify the representation of information during thinking (V:I), and the mode of processing information (W:A) as described by Riding and Cheema [4], courseware designers need to give consideration for the complete dimensions of the cognitive style construct that affect performance the most in respect to instructional media. Notational transfer, a phenomenon which occurs within a learner during a learning experience has been referred to in this paper as an internal/external exchange process [2]. More research should be done before we can be certain about the effectiveness of Web-mediated instructional systems, especially in multi-cultural settings.

It is expected that this research perspective generates considerable interest in the important relationships between cognitive psychology, educational research and instructional science, which have not previously been elaborated in a unifying context or meta-knowledge framework. HCI by its very nature brings together a number of professional practices. HCI comprises elements of computer science, cognitive psychology, social and organization psychology, ergonomics, human factors, artificial intelligence, linguistics, philosophy, sociology, anthropology, engineering and design [25]. Consequently there are many ways in which instructional designers will approach their work. However, it can only be through the synthesis of the shared knowledge gained from these different perspectives that true progress will be made towards efficient and effectively managed interactive online instructional environments.

References

[1]   Merrill, M.D. 1994. *Instructional Design Theory*, ed. D.G. Twitchell. New Jersey: Educational Technology Publications.

[2]   McKay, E. 2000. *Instructional strategies integrating the cognitive style construct: A meta-knowledge processing model (contextual components that facilitate spatial/logical task performance)*, in *PhD Thesis in Computer Science .& Information Systems*, Deakin University: Geelong, 3 Volumes.

[3]   Diana, E.M. and Webb, J.M. 1997. Using geographic maps in classrooms: The conjoint influence of individual differences and dual coding on learning facts. *Learning and Individual Differences*, **9**(3): 195–214.

[4]   Riding, R. and Cheema, I. 1991. Cognitive styles – an overview and integration. *Educational Psychology*, **11**(3&4): 193–215.

[5]   McKay, E. 2000. Measurement of cognitive performance in computer programming concept acquisition: Interactive effects of visual metaphors and the cognitive style construct. *Journal of Applied Measurement*, **1**(3): 257–286.

[6]   McKay, E. 2002. Cognitive skill acquisition through a meta-knowledge processing model. *Interactive Learning Environments*, **10**(3): 263–291

[7]   Schank, R.C. 2002. *Designing world-class e-learning: How IBM, GE, Harvard Business School, & Columbia University are succeeding at e-learning*. New York: McGraw-Hill.

[8]   McNamara, S.E. 1988. *Designing visual analysis training for the individual learner: An examination of individual learner differences and training content and procedures*, in *Faculty of Education*, Monash University: Australia.

[9]   McKay, E., Garner, B.J. and Okamoto, T. 2002. Understanding the ontological requirements for collaborative web-based experiential learning. in *International Conference on Computers in Education 2002*. Auckland, NZ: IEEE Computer Society. 356–357.

[10]   Riding, R.J. and Mathais, D. 1991. Cognitive styles and preferred learning mode, reading attainment and cognitive ability in 11-year-old children. *Educational Psychology*, **11**(3 & 4): 383–393.

[11] Riding, R. 1993. *A Trainer's Guide to Learning Design : Learning methods project report*, Assessment Research Unit, University of Birmingham: Birmingham.
[12] McKay, E. 1999. An investigation of text-based instructional materials enhanced with graphics. *Educational Psychology*, **19**(3): 323–335.
[13] Riding, R.J. and Rayner, S. 1998. *Cognitive Styles and Learning Strategies*. London: Fulton.
[14] Riding, R.J. and Caine, R. 1993. Cognitive style and GCSE performance in mathematics, english language and french. *Educational Psychology*, **13**(1): 59–67.
[15] Hill, W.E. 1915. My wife and my mother-in-law. *Puck*, Week ending Nov 6.
[16] Covey, R. 1989. *The Seven Habits of Highly Effective People*. NY: Simon & Schuster.
[17] Parkinson, A. and Redmond, J.A. 2002. Do cognitive styles affect learning performance in different computer media? in *7th Annual SIGCSE Conference on Innovation and Technology in Computer Science Education*. Aarhus, Denmark: ACM ISBN: 1-58113-499-1. 39–43.
[18] McKay, E. and Garner, B.J. 1999. The complexities of visual learning: Measuring cognitive skills performance. in *7th International Conference on Computers in Education: New human abilities for the networked society*. Japan: IOS Press. 208–215.
[19] Reigeluth, C.M., ed. 1983.*Instructional – Design Theories and Models: An overview of their current status*. 1st ed., ed. C.M. Reigeluth. Erlbaum: New Jersey.
[20] Landa, L.N. 1983. The algo-heuristic theory of instruction, in *Instructional-Design Theories and Models: An overview of their current status*, C.M. Reigeluth, Editor Erlbaum: New Jersey, 163–211.
[21] McKay, E. and Martin, B. 2002. The scope of e-learning: Expanded horizons for life-long learning. in *Conference Informing Science 2002 + IT Education*. Cork, Ireland: Mercer Press/Marino Books. 1017–1029.
[22] Hunt, E. 1997. The status of the concept of intelligence. *Japanese Psychological Research*, **39**(1 March): 1–11.
[23] Kline, P. 1991. *Intelligence: The psychometric view*. United Kingdom: Routledge.
[24] Goodman, N. 1968. *The Languages of Art: An approach to a theory of symbols*. New York: Bobbs-Merrill.
[25] Preece, J. 1994. *Human-Computer Interaction*. Harlow, England: Addison-Wesley.
[26] Pask, G. 1971. A cybernetic experimental method and its underlying philosophy. *International Journal Man-Machine Studies*, **3**: 279–337.
[27] Pask, G. 1984. Review of conversation theory and a protologic (or protolanguage), lp. *Educational Communications & Technology Journal*, **32**(1 Spring): 3–40.
[28] Coutaz, J. 1993. *The MSM Framework: A design space for multi-sensori-motor systems*, http://iihm.imag.fr/publs/1993/EWHCI93_MSM.ps.gz.
[29] Coutaz, J., Nigay, L. and Salber, D. 1994. *Taxonomic Issues for Multimodel and Multimedia Interactive Systems*,http://iihm.imag.fr/publs/1993/ERCIM93_Taxonomy.ps.gz.
[30] Waibel, A., Vo, M.-T., Duchnowski, P. and Manke, S. 1995. *Multimodal Interfaces*, http://tink.boltz.cs.cmu.edu/papers/multimodal/95.aij.ps.gz.
[31] McKay, E. 2000. Towards a meta-knowledge agent: Creating the context for thoughtful instructional systems. in *Paper presented at the 8th International Conference on Computers in Education/International Conference on Computer-Assisted Instruction (ICCE/ ICCAI 2000): New human abilities for the networked society*. Taipei: National Tsing Hua University, Taiwan. 200–204.

Intelligent Online Academic Management System

I. Ivanto, J. Wang, and F. Liu

Department of Computer Science & Computer Engineering
La Trobe University
Bundoora, Vic 3083, Australia
`liufei@cs.latrobe.edu.au`

Abstract. This paper introduces an intelligent web-based system which is an effective tool in the higher education sector for the purpose of students' academic advising and progress monitoring. It consists of functionality such as automated enrolment and enrolment variations, providing academic advices based on the student's personal profile and interests, creating study plan for the student according to his/her current stage, calculating credits and final signing off. The system contains a powerful inference engine which is based on PT-resolution (Resolution with Partial Intersection and Truncation) [9]. It periodically updates its database from the university's student administration system.

Keywords: PT-resolution, web-based, intelligent system

1 Introduction

In the higher education sector, a course coordinator's responsibility is mainly to help students in their subject selection during the enrolment and enrolment variation season, provide advices on course planing, and sign students' graduation forms. As the number of enrolments, especially the enrolments in Computer Science and Information Technology areas, has been dramatically increasing, this academic administration work becomes tedious, and sometimes, extremely time consuming.

The research presented in this paper attempts to utilise PT-resolution and web database technology to produce an intelligent online academic management system (IOAMS). Students and the course coordinator will be provided with an online system that acts similar to an intelligent organiser. The system will be responsible for searching and suggesting suitable subjects to the student; creating academic plan; collecting personal information from students, periodically downloading the students' academic records from the university's student administration system. In addition, through the system, students will be alerted about the compulsory subjects and the remaining credits points that are required to accomplish before the graduation. The system will also be used as an important communication tool between students and the coordinator. It provides email and messaging services (through the mobile phone network).

What made IOAMS outstanding from ordinary online systems is that it is intelligent and reliable. IOAMS has a powerful inference engine which is based on PT-

W. Zhou et al. (Eds.): ICWL 2003, LNCS 2783, pp. 320–326, 2003.
© Springer-Verlag Berlin Heidelberg 2003

resolution. The engine allows the system to conduct derivation to answer clients' queries. PT-resolution is a deduction strategy based on set theory. Unlike conventional deduction strategies [1, 4, 16] which are based on pattern matching and back-tracking, A PT-derivation calculates tuples to answer a query.

It has been proved that PT-resolution is sound [11] and complete [10] if the universe [7] of the problem is finite, therefore PT-resolution is the most suitable and reliable deduction strategy for IOAMS. It will not lead the derivation into an infinite recursion [9], and hence 'cut' [7] will not be used at any stage of the derivation.

2 PT-Resolution

This section presents the fundamental concepts and principles of PT-resolution. As previously indicated, IOAMS contains an inference engine which is the brain of the system. The inference engine is implemented based on PT-resolution. The fundamental principle of PT-resolution is to calculate the tuples which satisfy a predicate symbol to prove the goal [12, 13, 15].

In PT-resolution, the process of deriving tuples from equations [9] is defined as a PT-calculation (calculation with partial intersection and truncation). A PT-calculation is the fundamental unit of the PT-derivation. A PT-derivation is simply a sequence of PT-calculations finite or infinite.

PT-calculation is based on partial intersection and truncation which are set calculations [8]. It defines the P-domain for each predicate symbol, and converts the deduction to partial intersection and truncation. The following example illustrates this.

Example
Subject "Software Quality and Reliability" has a subject code *cse42SQR*, and it belongs to Software Engineering area, therefore
    inArea(cse42SQR, softwareEngineering)←
The P-domain *D[inArea]* (which is a set) contains all the tuples satisfying the predicate *inArea(X, Y)*. Consequently
    (cse42SQR, softwareEngineering) ∈ *D[inArea]*
cse42SQR has a pre-requisite which is "Fundamentals of Software Engineering" *cse21FSE*. So
    preRequisite(cse21FSE, cse42SQR)
and this can be translated as
    (cse21FSE, cse42SQR) ∈ *D[preRequisite]*

A subject can be recommended to a student if and only if the following conditions are satisfied
    (1) the subject is in the student's interested area; and
    (2) the student has the pre-requisite.

Hence

$$D[recommend(X)] \subseteq D[interestedIn(Y)] \cap \overline{D[inArea(X, Y)]} \cap$$

$$D[\overline{preRequisite(Z, X))}] \cap D[completed(Z)]$$

From the example, it is not difficult to see that pattern matching and back-tracking have been converted to partial intersection and truncation in the derivation, and hence the derivation is simply a sequence of set-calculations.

A PT-derivation is defined as follows.

Definition[9]
Let P be a logic program and

$$G : \leftarrow p_1(X_1^1,...,X_{k_1}^1) \wedge ... \wedge p_m(X_1^m,...,X_{k_m}^m)$$

be a goal of P. The PT-derivation on $P \cup \{G\}$ proceeds as follows.
Step 1. Mark all the equations as active.
Step 2. Iterate Steps 2 - 4 until at least one of the following termination conditions is satisfied.

Condition 1. The goal is proved.
Condition 2. No new tuple can be derived from the derivation.

If one of the conditions is satisfied, then go to Step 5.
Step 3. Apply the PT-calculation to the program.
Step 4. Mark all the saturated equations which have been selected in the previous calculation as inactive. Mark all new saturated P-domains and saturated equations which may arise.
Step 5. Prove the goal with the current P-domains. Any tuple which is in the P-domain, must satisfy the predicate symbol. Conversely, any tuple which is not in the P-domain, does not satisfy the predicate symbol.

3   System Design and Implementation

In this section, we will discuss the system requirements, overview structure, design, implementation and problem solving. We will emphases the inference engine which made the system intelligent.

3.1   Specification of System Requirement

System requirements are divided into two categories: functional and non-functional requirements.

Functional Requirements

The system is required to conduct
- User registration (registering staff and student users)
- Authorisation (allowing staff and student user login)

- Updating personal profile (allowing user to update their own personal details)
- Periodically updating the academic database through the university major administration system (periodically download academic records from the university databases)
- Error Handling (handling general errors, such as an error input, server breakdown, disconnection, etc.)
- Communication encryption and decryption

For student users, the system provides the following functionality
- Providing advices with subject selection (the advices are derived by the intelligent engine based on the current status of the student, available compulsory subjects and electives, and the student's profile and personal interests)
- Viewing subjects (offered subjects, exempted subjects and completed subjects)
- Viewing personal academic plan
- Updating personal details

For course coordinator, the system provides functionality such as
- Course management (updating details of the course structure)
- Subject management (updating details of a single subject)
- Credit point calculation (calculating a student's currently credit points)
- Completion checking (checking whether an individual student is eligible for graduation)
- Email and messaging services (sending email or mobile message to an individual student)

Non-functional Requirements

- Environmental requirement (IOAMS should be built efficient enough to handle queries with reasonable speed and accuracy under acceptable workload levels and normal server conditions)
- Maintenance requirement (IOAMS should also be built in such a way that system maintenance is easy and future enhancement is openly feasible)
- Platform requirement (IOAMS should be built as a platform independent application)

3.2 Design and Implementation

Based on the system requirement specification, the entire IOAMS is designed to have three tiers. The overall architecture is presented in the following figure.

There are two databases existing in the system – Personal Details Database and Academic Record Database. The Personal Details Database contains each student user's personal details such as student ID, family name, first name, home address,

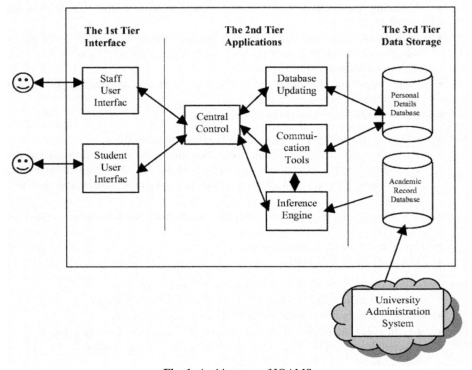

Fig. 1. Architecture of IOAMS

phone number, email address, course title, personal interested areas etc. Data stored in this database can be modified by the client – the individual student user. Academic Record Database contains each student user's academic record. This includes student ID, family name, first name, course code, enrolment data, exemptions, transcript, course plan etc. The student user has no writing access to the Academic Record Database. The database is updated directly from the university student administration system.

Staff User Interface and Student User Interface are the two user interfaces. Their functionality includes user registration, login and data input and output.

Central Control acts as the manager of the whole system. It takes client's request from the interface; invoke the corresponding sub-system to process the request; divert client's input data; and return the output data to the user interface. Another important functionality of the sub-system is to control the periodical academic database updating.

Communication Tools is mainly designed for staff users. It extracts the student's email address or mobile phone number from the personal details database when requested, and sends email to the student's account or short message to the student's mobile phone.

Updating database allows the client to modify his/her personal profile, and update the database accordingly.

Inference Engine is where logic derivations take place. As previously indicated, the inference engine is based on PT-resolution. PT-resolution is a deduction strategy based on set calculation rather than pattern matching and back-tracking. A PT-derivation is always finite if the universe of the problem is finite, therefore a PT-derivation in IOAMS is always finite.

4 Development Environment and Tools

Every effort has been made to make IOAMS platform independent. The system has been partially implemented by Ivanto [6] and has been utilised for experimental purposes.

Implementation was mostly done under Unix Solaris platform. The main database management system and the web server were also installed under the platform. However, Microsoft Windows NT 4.0, was also used to run required softwares for all of the design work. The final testing was completed under Unix Solaris platform where the server was generated.

PHP (version 4.2.0) [3, 22] is the implementation language. Libmcrypt (version 2.5.0) library [18, 20, 21] is used for the purpose of encryption and decryption. The system uses Apache (version 1.3.23) [17] as the web server and MySQL (version 3.23.49) [19] as the main database management system. In addition, Oracle 8.1.7 is also used to access the university student management database.

5 Conclusion

OIAMS is introduced in this paper. The system is designed and implemented to automate the tedious processes of enrolment and enrolment variations in the higher education sector and to act intelligently on study advising. The inference engine, which is the brain of the system, is based on PT-resolution. PR-resolution is a perfectly suitable resolution strategy for this particular system. As OIAMS has a finite universe, the derivation will always be finite, and consequently sound and complete.

The system, however, also has its limitations. It requires human involvement when conducting the student's initial enrolment, and so the initial enrolment is only partially automated. The system is implemented independently from the department academic management system, and consequently cannot share resources from the department system. Those are the areas we have been considering to address in further system development.

References

1. Apt K.R. and Doests K., *A New Definition of SLDNF-Resolution*, Journal of Logic Programming, Vol 18 1994, pp. 177–190.
2. Brewka G. and Eiter T., *Preferred Answer Sets for Extended Logic Programs*, Proceedings of Sixth International Conference on Principles of Knowledge Representation and Reasoning, 1998, pp. 86–97.
3. Castagnetto J., Rawat H., Schumann S., Scollo C. and Veliath D., "Professional PHP Dantsin E.et al., *Complexity and Expressive Power of Logic Programming*, ACM Computing Surveys, Vol 33, Num. 3, 2001, pp. 374–425.
4. Greiner R., *Efficient Reasoning*, ACM Computing Surveys, Vol. 33, Num. 2, 2001, pp. 1–30.
5. Hix D. and Hartson R., Developing User Interfaces: Ensuring Usability Through Product & Process, Wiley, 1993
6. Ivanto I., BappSci(IT) Academic Monitoring System, MSc minor project report, School of Computer Science & Information Technology, RMIT, 2002.
7. Lloyd J.W., *Foundations of Logic Programming*, Springer-Verlag, 1987.
8. Liu F. and Moore D.H., *Double Defined Logic Programming*, Proceedings of the Sixth Australian Joint Conference on Artificial Intelligence, 1993, pp. 27–32.
9. Liu F. and Moore D.H., *GOPT-Resolution and Its Applications*, Proceedings of the Eighth International Conference on Artificial Intelligence Applications, 1996, pp. 9–14.
10. Liu F., Moore D.H. and Wang J., *The Completeness of GOPT-Resolution*, Proceedings of the Second ECPD International Conference on Advanced Robotics, Intelligent Automation and Active Systems, 1996, pp. 92–98.
11. Liu F., Moore D.H. and Wang J., *The Soundness of GOPT-Resolution*, Proceedings of the International Conference on Genetic Algorithms, 1996, pp. 66–70.
12. Liu F. and Moore D.H., *Independence of Selecting Rule and Ordering Rule in PT-Resolution*, Proceedings of IEEE International Conference on Intelligent Processing Systems, November 1997, pp. 1082–1086.
13. Liu F. and Moore D.H., *An Implementation of Kripke-Kleene Semantics*, Journal of Information Sciences, Vol. 108, 1998, pp. 31–50.
14. Liu F., *Trigger Technique in GOPT-Resolution*, Proceedings of IASTED International Conference on Intelligent Systems and Control, 1999, pp. 9–14.
15. Liu F., PT(CP)-Resolution, Proceedings of IEEE International Conference on Fuzzy Logic, Vol. 2. 2001.
16. Pedreschi D., Ruggieri A. and Smaus J., *Classes of Terminating Logic Programs*, Journal of Theory and Practice of Logic Programming, Vol. 2, Part 3, 2002, pp. 369–418.
17. http://www.apache.org, "The Apache Software Foundation", 2002
18. http://www.zend.com/aboutphp.php, "Zend Technologies", 2002
19. http://www.mysql.com, "MySQL: The World's Most Popular Open Source Database", 2002
20. http://mcrypt.hellug.gr/#_libmcrypt, LibMcrypt: The Encryption Library Used by Mcrypt, 2002
21. http://www.php.net/manual/en/ref.mcrypt.php, Mcrypt Encryption Functions, 2002
22. http://www.phpbuilder.com, PHPBuilder.com - The Resource For PHP Developers, 2002

Collaborative Supervision of Machine Learning as a Tool for Web-Based Education: A Teaching and Learning Triangle

Steve Drew, Phil Sheridan, and Sven Venema

Griffith University, Queensland
{S.Drew, P.Sheridan, S.Venema}@griffith.edu.au

Abstract. Machine-learning applications often suffer bottlenecks due to inefficiency in the human-machine interface. A novel architecture design has been developed to allow expert supervisors to collaborate and cooperate in real-time to alleviate the effects of the bottleneck. Replacing supervisors with students, this architecture also allows for supervised training and collaborative learning of students as well as machine learners. Our attempts to provide Web-based courses to distance learners have highlighted the need for more effective use of the medium for education and appropriate tools to provide the necessary richness of experience. We present our design and an example application to demonstrate how we address some of the shortfalls present in Web-based, distance education.

Keywords: Web-based education, Distance education, Machine learning

1 Introduction

Griffith University runs a degree in Internet Computing where nearly all courses have a web presence of similar structure, helping students concentrate on "what to learn" rather than "how to learn". Addressing the need to adapt the Web-based degree program for effective distance learning highlighted the need for developing learning tools more suited to the medium. Key features are the provision of a high level of interaction, immediate communication and positive feedback to promote student motivation, interest and sense of achievement.

Web-based tools for self-paced learning often use the Web as a repository for information, or links to information, and as a means for organising course content, assessment items, feedback and results. Extra-tutorial communication amongst class members and tutors is often facilitated using applications such as Web forums, chat and email. In the class-based learning environment any shortfalls in the course materials or Web as a responsive teaching and learning tool are alleviated by face-to-face contact with the tutor and other students.

Every student has different needs based upon learning style and how effectively they make use of available communication channels. Multi-channel communication in the Web-enabled classroom might use a Web site to provide structure; web pages, spoken word and paper-based readings to provide content; supervised practical exer-

W. Zhou et al. (Eds.): ICWL 2003, LNCS 2783, pp. 327–338, 2003.

cises and hands-on tools with spoken explanations and one-on-one instruction to provide interaction. This classroom arrangement seems to provide for a wide range of students learning needs and tutors teaching styles.

Communication between the students and with the tutor is usually immediate and alleviates potential learning bottlenecks as they occur. Timely communication is the key for maintaining student interest, achievement and motivation to keep learning. Problems arise for many students when they are faced with distance education as many of the parallel communication channels available in a social setting are missing. Web-based course material is available online but immediacy and richness of communication and interaction can be lost. On the Web, as we know it today, elements such as body language, social dynamics and other group aspects of communication in classroom education are not easily provided.

Research into methods for collaborative supervision of machine learning has uncovered a system design that might effectively be used to enhance the distance learning experience. Fundamental to the design is the ability to share "awareness" of learning activities and to collaborate with tutors and other students through an interactive interface. The same collaboration interface and architecture that might connect machine-learning supervisors can be used to connect tutors to students for real-time learning supervision.

Inclusion of the machine learner into the educational architecture adds a novel and potentially revolutionary element to the instruction process. By incorporating a machine learner into the system, instruction can be given to students and machine at the same time. By completing online exercises students help the tutor to 'teach' the machine learner by supplying a rich source of learning examples. As the machine learner becomes more proficient it can take the place of the 'expert' tutor in some instances to provide feedback or validation of student learning outcomes.

To address an area of machine learning that suffers bottlenecks due to the slowness of the supervised training process, system architecture has been designed that distributes human effort. The same collaborative interface can also be applied to address some of the social shortfalls in web-based, distance education. A design and an example application for a web-based learning tool that provides a communication rich, real-time learning experience for selected class-based and distance education applications is presented. Issues relating to distance educational needs, machine/student learning architecture, communications infrastructure, machine learning as an education tool and future work in the area will be addressed.

2   Problems with Web-Based Education at a Distance

Appropriate design of the educational experience and the tools to be used is as important in the classroom as it is online or at a distance. In many cases lack of instructor access to resources, time or knowledge of educational design leads to poor learning experiences. Have you had one of those lectures? Susan Toohey [1] presents a simple model of the learning process (Figure 1) that can be used to assess the strengths and weaknesses of an education environment.

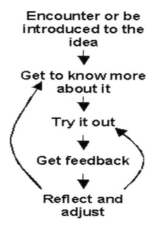

Fig. 1. A simple model of the learning process

Griffith University's development of an environment for flexible delivery of course material has addressed some of the lecture learning problems. Classes at Logan campus are limited to small groups (twenty-five to thirty-five) so that alternatives to bulk address are possible at any time and individual attention is possible. An entire campus has been designed around student centred learning and has been equipped so that communication is facilitated at many levels and through a range of channels.

To facilitate the initial encounter with new concepts, course material is available on the Internet and Intranet. All rooms are equipped with sophisticated audiovisual equipment so that material may be accessed for class sessions while with the tutor. Small groups allow effective polling of students to elicit experience and "knowledge" of the areas to be covered so that delivery may be tailored. From an early stage students are encouraged to collaborate and to use the Web as a research and communication tool to find out more about course related issues. Student-computer ratios are small and software is state-of-the-art so that putting Internet Computing into practice is eased. Small group teaching and accessibility of staff promotes feedback and guidance using face-to-face as well as asynchronous communications.

Problems still appear in this environment however, as many staff do not have sufficient knowledge of education principles to make use of different teaching modes. Taking staff from a traditional lecture-based campus and transplanting them into a new delivery environment without relevant educational instruction is a recipe for perpetuating the mini-lecture. Maintenance of Web-based course material can be extremely time consuming. Moore's law (computer processing power doubles every eighteen months) tends to work against educators in the IT area, as advances in hardware, software and application areas compound the course maintenance problem.

Our own experience has shown that as soon as a student chooses to enter distance education mode, access to the face-to-face (social) communication channels is effectively removed. The use of course material and delivery media that have not been adequately designed for the particular delivery mode compound teaching and learning problems. Interaction becomes mainly Web-based and assessment of the learning experience, using Toohey's model, needs to be adjusted. The modification of the learning process, below, occurs with much Web-based distance education. .

Introduction to course material is based upon Web and printed content as before, and relies mainly upon reading and diagrammatic comprehension for information transfer. Immediate interaction with classmates and the tutor for help and complementary or supporting information is not usually possible. Asynchronous communications like email, Web forums and chat might be used to some effect although the medium suffers the same limitations as before. In many cases the "getting to know more" phase is also limited to reading various text-based information sources without access to the immediacy of social learning elements.

Trying out new tools and putting new knowledge to the test without the aid of a tutor can be a lengthy process for students if instructions are insufficient, ambiguous or devoid of relevant examples. Feedback phase in practical situations is often limited to success or failure in getting technology to work. Lacking the immediacy of tutor or group feedback to consolidate process information and verify successes or failures can cause the learning process to become stilted. Without sufficient feedback and guidance, the reflection and adjustment stage can become an exercise in problem solving that is not aimed at the primary learning goal.

Hara and Kling [2] document a range of student's frustrations with Web-based distance education courses. Wegerif [3] noted that some students suffered problems with community belonging as the transition from "outsider" to "insider" is slowed by text-based social communication. Heath [4] noted student problems with:

  ▪ Maintenance of motivation and suitable pacing throughout course material
  ▪ Material was often presented of a type or in a manner that was unsuitable for the communication medium (page lengths longer than a screen, etc)
  ▪ Time for issue and response via email or forum is often too long and loses context and intention information in the process

There still exists some organisational resistance to change from the traditional lecture theatre and classroom delivery methods [5]. Reliance on research for promotion in most Australian universities certainly inhibits the general uptake of new teaching models and media for some staff. This leads to reluctance to learn what is needed to use the Web and related technologies effectively as a delivery medium rather than as just a new place to publish course notes. MacDonald [6] asks, "Is as good as face-to-face, as good as it gets?" and urges educators to design for and utilise the strengths of the new medium rather than focus on its weaknesses compared to classroom delivery.

Some features of successful instances of using the Web for education [7] include:

  ▪ Increased instructor satisfaction, encouraging further development of the educational experience
  ▪ Perception of social presence where there is a salience of personal interaction

- Learning communities where the environment enables group "paralanguage" activities through parallel communication channels and allows for directed interaction in real-time
- Incorporation of as many forms of participant interaction as possible to promote cognitive development and critical learning rather than "shallow" learning

In the following sections an innovative architecture design that addresses a number of the negative issues and attempts to promote the positive aspects is presented.

3   A Collaborative Learning Architecture

Imagine a radiography clinic where images are regularly processed and analysed by the radiologist. There are many possible sources and opportunities for mistakes in radiograph analysis and workload may be a contributing factor. In other situations a suitably experienced analyst may not always be locally available to process images when needed. Having access to an up-to-date expert system might streamline the professional's practice and even add the security of an immediate second opinion where needed.

Imagine a supervised machine learning system that might not only provide the analytical expertise of one specialist but a distributed community of specialists through the collaborative supervision of the learning process. Such a distributed system would be able to collate accurate training examples quickly to produce an expert system of unsurpassed ability. In the same way that experts might collaborate in real-time to produce training examples, student analysts might collaborate with experts to perfect their diagnostic skills.

Once developed, such a system as described above might be applied to distributed-supervision of machine learning in a number of areas where graphical information needs to be analysed quickly and accurately. Obvious areas include image analysis in astronomy, air-traffic control, industrial radiography, sonography, signal analysis as well as a range of other medical and industrial imaging applications.

In one application Akamai is taught to recognise breast tissue artefacts from mammogram pictures stored as graphics files. In a single supervisor system, the bottleneck in the machine-learning process is the collection of enough supervision input (learning examples) such that the machine has a high degree of accuracy (sensitivity and specificity) in its artefact recognition. It appears logical to explore the possibility of distributed and even real-time collaborative supervision of machine learning in order to improve the efficiency of this process.

Griffith University's Internet Computing Research Group headed by Professor ChengZheng Sun has had considerable success with development of collaborative editing tools as applied to text documents [8]. David Chen, from the same group has applied the same collaborative editing principles to editing of graphics images [9]. Initial exploration suggests that much of the theory and algorithmic process can effectively be adapted to the collaborative editing and processing of metadata structures related to graphics documents.

3.1 Collaborative Supervision and Machine Learning

Akamai is an artificial vision and machine learning system currently under development to help analyse images for visible features or artefacts. Machine learning is used to teach the system to link particular image artefacts to learning concepts. For example, a radiographic image might be analysed with the aid of a human expert supervisor in order to provide training examples to recognise certain image artefact types as "micro-calcifications" or other concept types.

Initial stages of machine learning require significant human input before the learning system gains enough "experience" and accuracy to move to an accelerated learning mode requiring less intensive supervision. Machine learning bottlenecks occur when significant numbers of training examples must be entered or learning outcomes verified by the human supervisor. Alleviation of the learning bottleneck requires a method for distributing the supervision tasks and parallelising the human effort in an efficient way.

A version of Akamai has been designed that allows human supervisors to communicate and collaborate in real time. In this model several images can be analysed concurrently to improve the rate of training example creation for a particular concept type. Collaborating supervisors may also apply their combined analytical effort to the analysis of a single image in order to improve training example accuracy and reduce error rate. This is an important feature as machine learning is limited by "noise" (inaccuracy) introduced by errors and inconsistencies in training examples.

Collaborative Akamai provides an environment where a group of human supervisors can be "aware" of each other's activities and analyses. Errors and inconsistencies are more likely to be detected and corrected in the group environment before a training example can be submitted to the machine learner. In early stages of machine learning, conflicting information detected by the machine learner needs to be referred to a supervisor for "conflict resolution". With distributed real-time supervision this might also be accomplished efficiently.

3.2 Collaborative Education and Machine Learning

Reviewing the elements of this system it becomes apparent that the same architecture used for distributed, collaborative supervision of machine learning could be effectively employed as an education medium for human learning. Changing perspective, a hierarchy of supervisors becomes a tutor and students; the interactive interface that allows mutual awareness of supervisors becomes a mechanism for student collaboration and student-tutor communication. Possibly the most novel adaptation is the role of the machine learner as an aid to education in distance as well as class-based learning.

A machine learner can be in different states dependent upon the amount of relevant training it has received. At one end of the scale, a machine learning system could take on the role of an expert system in a particular area. Its knowledge can be used to tutor students as well as select appropriate training examples to power-build student knowledge. Students' assessments of learning exercises can be compared to a library of historical analyses of the same case to build confidence and accuracy. With greater machine expertise comes the ability to provide immediate and specific feedback to maintain student motivation and guide the learning exercise.

As students reach expert status in their own right, and through interaction with an expert supervisor (instructor), their input will add to the learning examples thus increasing the potential of the machine learner itself. An "inexperienced" machine learner can be set up so that it monitors the learning process and educational history of a particular student. A student profile may be used to direct learning activities and to tailor the education process to suit the student's individual learning style.

Information can be accessible to experts and educators so that learning difficulties related to the technology or interface can be addressed and so that more specific learning problems can be targeted. On another level, the machine learns as the student learns so that learning examples can be created and shared. Combining the power of computer memory and calculation speed with student vision and intuitive approach to analyses creates a powerful learning environment. Add into the equation the ability to collaborate either asynchronously or in real-time with other students and the tutor and many of the social aspects of learning may be reemployed.

4 Collaborative Akamai – A Teaching and Learning Application

4.1 Operational Model for Collaborative Akamai

As a distributed machine-learning environment where individual supervisors are connected via the Internet, there are several possible modes of operation that the system might employ based upon different levels of:

- Awareness of other supervisors' operations
- Interaction amongst supervisors
- Collaboration between supervisors
- Need for conflict resolution
- Redundancy (repetition and validation) of analyses required
- Concurrency of operations and rule development
- Network service quality

Machine learning may be broken down into the collection of training examples, creation of an operational rule base, distribution of rules, and employing the newly created rules.

4.2   Learning Strategies in Collaborative Machine Learning

Consequences of uncertain lag time in Internet-based communications leads to the need to adopt a more responsive peer-to-peer model for collaborative image editing, conflict resolution and rule development. Sun and Chen [8, 9] both agree for collaborative editing of graphical images and text documents that a network of fully functional peers provides a more responsive system than relying upon individual servers to centrally complete key processing. With each peer fully capable of conducting graphical editing, learning data structure maintenance, conflict resolution, rule determination and related functionality; updates to information can be broadcast from one peer to each of the others as a minimal communication strategy.

What is presented here is a design overview for the operation of "Collaborative Akamai" in its various learning modes. Basic to the concept is the peer network with "key processors" that are responsible for the analysis, mark-up and intermediate data-structure information generated for a particular image at a particular time. In effect, learning mode should not impinge upon the collaborative effort and also should not add any degree of freedom that might affect the consistency of the mark-up information or the related data structure.

"Akamai" relies on human supervision to teach it how to "see" graphical artefacts in captured images and to relate them to particular learning concepts. An untrained system relies on the expert supervisor to navigate an image, aid the artificial vision sub-system in marking up artefacts that can be labelled to create training examples.

Akamai has three modes of operation, lazy, aggressive, and greedy. In the lazy mode, the supervisor drives the image analysis. In aggressive mode, Akamai navigates an image, creates an intermediate data structure, marks up the image, and attempts to distinguish between artefacts. In greedy mode Akamai attempts to recognise concepts and identify artefacts, and receives confirmation or correction from the supervisor as it goes.

Progression from lazy mode to aggressive mode represents moving of the learning process to a higher level. Each of the learning modes is more efficient than the one before as more of the previously validated machine learning and processing power can come into play to help complete the process.

In real-time, distributed mode with collaborative supervision of image analysis the machine learning process can be accelerated significantly over the single supervisor system. The question of how learning modes affect or are affected by collaborative supervision is addressed at this juncture to clarify the distributed system design process.

In "lazy" learning mode, human input and machine output can be distributed to all collaborators to create a training example based on collective human wisdom and experience. The fact that the machine is in "lazy" mode will be obvious to all through the shared graphical interface.

Similarly, in "aggressive" and "greedy" learning modes, the "key processor" is driving the vision or analysis process with the I/O apparent to all collaborating supervisors. Input required for correction and or confirmation can be input via the distributed interface as required and by mutual multi-supervisor consent.

No system is totally error-free as human error and inattention to detail will introduce "noise" into the system. Repeated, supervised validation will eventually reduce noise as errors are detected and corrected. A most important ability in each of the learning modes is the ability to "undo" any incorrect training example that is created and "undo" any effect that it may have by its addition to the rule-base. Any "doable" operation must have an inverse or be "undoable" which is a tenet to hold to for later development of this system.

For real-time analysis to be effective, there is benefit in having a reasonably strict process and procedure to guide the collaborative exercise. A set of mutual steps and objectives to guide all collaborators helps keep process efficiency high. Automating the guidance process to some extent is a point for future development. Images, served from a central repository are shared or divided and farmed to separate supervisors or supervisor groups.

With a highly interactive arrangement, much of the interpretation and analysis can be done collaboratively amongst the supervisors before committing a rule to the rule-base. There are two different social arrangements that might occur, one is where each of the supervisors is considered a peer with comparable knowledge to other supervisors. Decisions are made by consensus and consultation where there are distinct areas of expertise. This leads to the second arrangement where one supervisor is considered a leader and is considered to have superior knowledge or experience. In this arrangement non-trivial decisions are made by consultation and approval of the group leader. The second arrangement with a leader and subordinates is much like the teacher-student relationship or master-apprentice roles when dealing with practical work. For correctness the consultative communication must be open, candid and free.

4.3   Teaching Students Using Collaborative Akamai

By changing the social structure of the human collaborators from a peer network of experts to a supervised group of students the role of Akamai is effectively changed. An expert tutor can guide the learning experiences using the communication interface and by sharing awareness of his operation of the tools and image mark-up process with the student cohort. Encouraging students to collaborate in the exploration of the system can enrich experiential learning. Experiences of individual students are shared through the collaboration and communication interface for mutual benefit.

Experimentation with image analyses can be accomplished without having the supervisor online. By using the machine learning (expert) system in a greedy learning mode the student can view the analysis process needing only to add analysis information where required. By forcing an aggressive learning mode the student is required to verify and validate analyses made by the machine. Lazy learning mode allows the student to drive the analysis process for maximum interaction. Again, student collaboration can be used to effectively share the learning process. For future reference by students it is practical to store base images and related training example data structures in some repository at a central data server along with images.

Data structures, training examples and image mark-ups created during student learning need to be kept separate from the "expert" rule-base to eliminate "noise". Expert and student analyses can be compared for feedback and the expert system is used to demonstrate and critique the analysis process. Test images with known analysis outcomes can be analysed using student-created rule bases to test their completeness and accuracy. The collaboration interface is used to provide timely feedback to students from peers, the tutor and the machine itself.

Using Toohey's simple model of the learning process it is apparent that the student learning system addresses all of the stages with more even weighting. The instructor guides introduction to the study area in real-time and the first encounter with the system is hands-on. Getting to know more about the system and its processes is facilitated using the interactive interface to ask questions of the tutor and other collaborating students. Trying it out is a matter of following instructions and examples given in real-time and reacting to the relevant feedback offered by the system and collaborators. Reflection and adjustment is a quiet moment where the student's existing mental model of the system and experiential model merge to create a new mental model. From this point new exploration can proceed with greater effect.

Many of the frustrations expressed by distance education students are effectively eliminated using this learning tool, others still require careful design consideration. In particular, the technological issues must be overcome with careful user interface design; plentiful contextual help and well planned introductory sessions with the tutor. Mutual awareness provided through the interactive interface can provide timely tutorial assistance in the introductory sessions.

Using good user interface design principles [10, 11, 12] and concentrating on usability engineering [13, 14], issues such as missing or ambiguous instructions, poor navigation or insufficient state information can be rendered insignificant. Efficient data input and well-designed inter-peer communication strategies allow the new user to quickly gain proficiency. In this design, multiple communication channels are in use with graphical, textual and complementary information being blended throughout the learning session.

Using the interactive interface to share awareness of others activities allows all collaborators to contribute to the practical sessions. Interactions can range from student driven exploration to watch-and-copy; all of which may have tutorial guidance. In asynchronous communication mode, students are able to explore and experiment at their own pace to gain confidence and understanding of the system. Students are not limited to sole discovery in this mode as the machine learner [15, 16] can play a guiding or tutorial role to facilitate the student learning process.

An important implication of mutual awareness through the user interface is the ability for the tutor to provide timely feedback and gain accurate information on student progress. Tutor awareness of student progress allows for help, encouragement and allocation of specific learning tasks. In asynchronous mode, a suitably designed student modelling machine learner can also assess strengths and weaknesses to design a relevant learning strategy for the particular student.

5   Conclusions and Future Work

In this paper the concept of a collaboratively supervised machine learning system being used as a Web-based education mechanism for students is introduced. Student problems with current Web-based distance education systems have been highlighted and it is suggested as to how Collaborative Akamai addresses these problems.

References

[1]   Toohey, S., "Designing Courses for Higher Education", Society for Research into Higher Education, Open University Press, 1999.
[2]   Hara, N. & Kling, R., "Students' Frustrations With A Web-Based Distance Education Course", http://www.firstmonday.dk/issues/issue4_12/hara/index.html, 1999.
[3]   Wegerif, R., "The Social Dimension of Asynchronous Learning Networks", Journal of Asynchronous Learning Networks, Volume 2 Issue 1, 1998, http://www.aln.org/publications/jaln/v2n1/v2n1_wegerif.asp
[4]   Heath, E., "Two Cheers And A Pint Of Worry: An Online Course In Political and Social Philosophy", Journal of Asynchronous Learning Networks, Volume 2 Issue 1, 1998, http://www.aln.org/publications/jaln/v2n1/v2n1_heath.asp
[5]   Jaffee, D., "Institutionalized Resistance To Asynchronous Learning Networks", Journal of Asynchronous Learning Networks, Volume 2 Issue 2, 1998, http://www.aln.org/publications/jaln/v2n2/v2n2_jaffee.asp.
[6]   McDonald, J., "Is "As Good As Face To Face" As Good As It Gets?", Journal of Asynchronous Learning Networks, Volume 6 Issue 2, 2002, http://www.aln.org/publications/jaln/v6n2/v6n2_macdonald.asp
[7]   Richardson, J.C., "Examining Social Presence In Online Courses In Relation To Students' Perceived Learning And Satisfaction", Journal of Asynchronous Learning Networks, Volume 7 Issue 1, 2003, http://www.aln.org/publications/jaln/v7n1/v7n1_richardson.asp
[8]   Sun, C., "Undo as Concurrent Inverse in Group Editors", ACM Transactions on CHI, v9n4, Dec 2002, pp. 309–361
[9]   Sun, C., and Chen, D., "Consistency Maintenance in Real-Time Collaborative Graphics Editing Systems", ACM Transactions on CHI, v9n1, Mar 2002, pp. 1–41
[10] Alben, L. "Quality of Experience: Defining the Criteria for Effective Interaction Design." interactions, 3(3) May/June 1996.
[11] Dray, S., "The importance of designing usable systems", interactions, 2(1) January 1995, pp. 17–20
[12] Myers, B. A., "Challenges of HCI: Design and implementation", interactions, 1(1), January 1994, pp. 73–83.
[13] Neilsen, J., "Heuristic Evaluation", http://www.useit.com/papers/heuristic/
[14] Lee, S.H., "Usability Testing for Developing Effective Interactive Multimedia Software: Concepts, Dimensions, and Procedures", Educational Technology & Society 2(2) 1999. http://ifets.gmd.de/periodical/vol_2_99/sung_heum_lee.html
[15] Tsiriga, V. & Virvou, M., "Dynamically Initializing the Student Model in a Web-Based Language Tutor", (2002) http://citeseer.nj.nec.com/tsiriga02dynamically.html

[16] Tsiriga, V. & Virvou, M., "Initializing the Student Model using Stereotypes and Machine Learning", (2002) http://citeseer.nj.nec.com/tsiriga02initializing.html

[18] Garrison, D.R., "Computer conferencing: the post industrial age of distance education", Open Learning, 3–11, 1997.

[19] Gold, S., "A Constructivist Approach to Online Training for Online Teachers", Journal of Asynchronous Learning Networks, Volume 7 Issue 1, 2003, http://www.aln.org/publications/jaln/v5n1/v5n1_gold.asp

[20] Johnson, D. W., & Johnson, R. T., "Cooperation and the use of technology", In D. H. Jonassen (Ed.), Handbook of research for educational communications and technology (pp. 1017–1044). New York: Simon and Schuster Macmillan. (1996)

[21] Curtis, D.,D., & Lawson, M., J., "Exploring Collaborative Online Learning", Journal of Asynchronous Learning Networks, Volume 5 Issue 1, 2003, http://www.aln.org/publications/jaln/v5n1/v5n1_curtis.asp

[22] Dutton, J., Dutton, M., Perry, J., "How Do Online Students Differ From Lecture Students?", Journal of Asynchronous Learning Networks, Volume 6 Issue 1, 2003, http://www.aln.org/publications/jaln/v6n1/v6n1_dutton.asp

[23] Valenta, A., Therriault, D., Dieter, M., Mrtek, R., "Identifying Student Attitudes And Learning Styles In Distance Education", Journal of Asynchronous Learning Networks, Volume 5 Issue 2, 2003, http://www.aln.org/publications/jaln/v5n2/v5n2_valenta.asp

Mediator Based Open Multi-agent Architecture for Web Based Learning

Hongen Lu

School of Information Technology
Deakin University
221 Burwood Highway, Burwood
VIC 3125, AUSTRALIA
helu@deakin.edu.au

Abstract. Web based learning plays an important role in modern teaching environment. Many Web based tools are becoming available on this huge marketplace. Agent technology contributes substantially to this achievement. One of the fundamental problems facing both students and education services providers is how to locate and integrate these valuable services in such a dynamic environment. In this paper, I present a mediator based architecture to build open multi-agent applications for eLearning. An agent services description language is presented to enable services advertising and collaboration. The language exploits ontology of service domain, and provides the flexibility for developers to plug in any suitable constraint languages. Multiple matchmaking strategies based on agent service ontology are given to help agents finding appropriate service providers. The series of strategies consider various features of service providers, the nature of requirements, and more importantly the relationships among services.

1 Introduction

The World Wide Web has the largest collection of knowledge ever in man kind history. It is one of the most important resources in modern education. With the success of search engines, such as Google, and the vast acceptance of online learning systems, such as WebCT, students and teachers can search text and images efficiently. These tools are changing our learning process in schools and universities all over the world everyday. However, the Web has not reached its full potential. At its early stage, the Web is solely a huge collection of digital information. Nowadays, it is evolving into a huge growing marketplace for information providers and consumers. Agent technology makes a substantial contribution to this achievement.

However, how to find information providers and how to integrate information agents in such an open environment are new challenges. Information agents, such as Ahoy [6], ShopBot [3], and SportsFinder [5], are programs that assist people to find specific information from the Web. They are information service providers, which have the capabilities to find information for users, for example locating

W. Zhou et al. (Eds.): ICWL 2003, LNCS 2783, pp. 339–350, 2003.

a person's homepage, finding the cheapest available prices for music CDs, or finding sports results of a team or a player. For a novice user, a challenge is how to find these services; for an information agent, the challenges are how to locate the service providers, and how to communicate with them to solve its tasks cooperatively. This is one of the basic problems facing designers of open, multi-agent systems for the Internet is the connection problem — finding the other agents who might have the information or other capabilities that you need [2].

In [4], two basic approaches to this connection problem are distinguished: direct communication, in which agents handle their own coordination and assisted coordination, in which agents rely on special system programs to achieve coordination. However in the Web application domain, where new agents might come into existence or existing agents might disappear at any time, only the latter approach promises the adaptability required to cope with the dynamic changes in the environment.

2 Related Works

2.1 Ontology

Ontologies are content theories about objects, their properties, and relationships among them that are possible in a specific domain of knowledge [1]. In a given domain, its ontology clarifies the structure of knowledge in the domain. It forms the heart of any system of knowledge representation for that domain. Without an ontology, or the formal conceptualisations, there can not be any vocabulary for representing knowledge, let alone automatic knowledge reasoning and inference. An ontology gives the terms used in a certain domain, as well as their relationships. So that we can use these terms provided to assert specific propositions about a situation. For example, in computer science education domain, we can represent a fact about a specific unit: unit SCC303, Software Engineering, is a third year undergraduate unit, where SCC303 is an instance of the concept unit. Once we have the basis for representing propositions, we can also represent more advanced knowledge, such as hypothesise, believe, expect, ect. Thus, we can construct a domain ontology step by step to describe the world.

2.2 Web Service Description Languages

Web services are Web accessible programs and devices that not only provide information to a user, but to enable a user to effect change in the world. Web services are among the most important resources on the Web, and they are garnering a great deal of interest from industry. Many emerging standards are being developed for low-level descriptions of Web services.

- **WSDL.** Web Service Description Language provides a communication level description of the messages and protocols used by a Web service. WSDL is an XML format for describing network services as a set of endpoints operating on messages containing either document-oriented or procedure-oriented information. The operations and messages are described in abstract, and then bound to a concrete network protocol and message format to define an endpoint. Related concrete endpoints are combined into abstract endpoints (services). WSDL is extensible to allow description of endpoints and their messages regardless of what message formats or network protocols are used to communicate.

– **Semantic Web.** The huge collection of information on the Web is fare beyond a person's ability to search and index. So machine-understandable data is a high priority to automatic processing online information. Semantic web is a step to define and link data on the Web in a way that it can be used by machines not just for display purposes, but for automation, integration and reuse of data across various applications.

2.3   WebCT

WebCT is one of the leading on-line education tools. It provides teachers a powerful and convenient way to build up websites dedicated to publishing teaching materials for their subjects; meanwhile it is also a place for students to feedback their progress. No wonder WebCT is widely accepted in various levels of education institutes, especially for long distance learning. However, WebCT is a closed system. It can only let the teachers and students in the same university or in the same class to communicate each other. In this point of view, WebCT has not taken the full advantage of the World Wide Web, which now is a fast growing collection of services. WebCT is still based on the conventional client-server architecture. While the Web offers more flexible options, for example everyone on the Web could be an information provider and consumer at the same time. Peer to peer communication is becoming the mainstream of on-line publishing and marketing. I believe this is the future trend for on-line education, because in such architecture teachers and students can easily swap their roles and learn from each other. In addition, this architecture is open for everyone to join in.

3   Mediator Based Architecture

A mediator is a special kind of information agent acting as middle man to take as input, a request to find an agent that provides a service, and returns as output, a list of such agents and their cooperation relationships. A mediator also stores the services offered by different agents in the existing environment, and when a new agent is introduced into the environment it can register its capability to the mediator, using an agent service description language, if this agent wants its service to be used by others. Information agents also can unregister their services to the mediator when they want to quit the cooperation or exit. Also when an information agent receives a query or a subtask within a query that can not be solved by itself, it can request the mediator to find out other agents that have

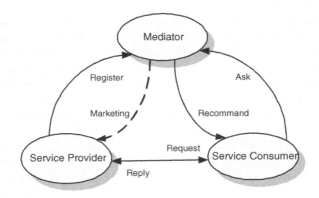

Fig. 1. Mediator Based Architecture

the capability or a set of agents who can work cooperatively to provide that service.

4   Agent Services Ontology

Since information agents are developed geographically dispersed over the Web, their capabilities are different from each other. SportsFinder [5] can find the sports results of golf, cycling, football and basketball etc. for users; while Ahoy [6] is good at locating people's homepages. In an application domain, such as Computer Science subjects, there exists a hierarchy relationship among these information agents. For example, information agent $\mathcal{A}$ can answer students' query about Software Engineering, while agent $\mathcal{B}$ is only capable of consulting on Risk Analysis, which is a part of the subject Software Engineering; in this case the service agent $\mathcal{B}$ can provide is a subset of agent $\mathcal{A}$, i.e. Service($\mathcal{B}$) $\subset$ Service($\mathcal{A}$).

To construct agent services ontology , it is necessary to identify their relations. Let S_i denotes the service of information agent $\mathcal{IA}_i$, and a service identifier to express in short what kind of service the agent can provide. For the above example, we have Service($\mathcal{B}$)={Software Engineering}, while Service($\mathcal{A}$)={Risk Analysis}.

- **Identical Service:** $S_1 = S_2$. This means the two services can provide the same function in spite of the fact that they may have different service names. As we know, information agents are being built over the Web using different programming languages and architecture. It is no surprised to have two agents running on different hosts that can offer the same service. Obviously, two identical services can substitute each other.
- **Subservice:** $S_1 \subset S$. This relationship characterises two services offered by agents, in which one service's function is only a part of another. For instance, an expert on C/C++ programming is good at tutoring lab project on Object

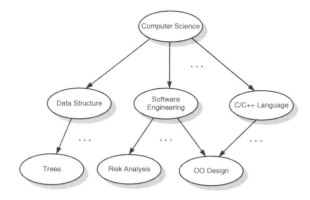

Fig. 2. Fragment of Computer Science Subjects Ontology

Oriented Design in Software Engineering unit; but he/she may not capable at formal methods in the same unit. In this point of view, the service offered by a tutor on C/C++, is only a part of a lecturer on the whole subject.

- **Substitute Service:** a service S_1 can be substituted by service S_2, $S_1 \leftrightarrow S_2$. From the above description, we know that identical service and subservice are two special cases of substitute service relationship. But the difference is that identical services can substitute each other, while the subservice can only be alternated by its "parent" service, not vice versa.

- **Partial Substitute Service:** $S_1 \cap S_2 \neq \phi$. This relationship describes two services that have some common subservices. In some circumstances, partial substitute services can be alternated with each other, such as where the service agent is offering, just by chance, the common subservice with its partial substitute service, that is, the agent is not offering its full service to others at the moment.

- **Reciprocal Service:** $\exists S = (S_1 \cup S_2)$ AND $(S_1 \cap S_2) = \phi$, then S_1 and S_2 are reciprocal with S. If two services are reciprocal, that means they have no subservices in common, but they can work together to offer a "bigger" service. From this definition we know that in case there is no current agent available to provide the "bigger" service, these two reciprocal services can cooperate as a single agent for this task. This gives us a message that by combining the current agents in a different manner, we can tailor the system to meet new requirements.

Agent service ontology gives a formal method to describe the relationships among agent services. An agent service ontology contains all the services of information agents as well as their relationships. Basically, a directed cyclic graph (DCG) is able to present the relations between agent services. The nodes in the graph present the services, and the edges are labeled with the service relationships. In Figure 2, a fragment of the ontology on computer science subjects is given, in sense of the content of the topic and their relationships.

```
<asdl> ::= ( service
                :service-id <name>
                :constraint-language <name>
                :input ( <param-spec>+ )
                :output ( <param-spec>+ )
                :input-constraints ( <constraint>+ )
                :output-constraints ( <constraint>+ )
                :io-constraints ( <constraint>+ )
                :service-ontology <name>
                |:<relation> <name>
                |:privacy <name>
                |:quality <name> )

<param-spec> ::= ( <name> <term> )
<relation>   ::= identical | subservice | substitute
                 | reciprocal | part-sub
<term>       ::= <constant> | <variable> |
                 ( <constant> <term>+ )
<constant>   ::= <name>
<variable>   ::= ?<name>
<name>       ::= <Identifier>

<constraint> ::= << expression in constraint-language >>
```

Fig. 3. Syntax for Agent Service Description Language in BNF

5 Ontology Based Agent Service Description

The proposed language in Figure 3 allows plugging in of an independent constraint language, that is the syntax of our ASDL is open at this point. This is described in the **constraint-language** field, which tells what language is used to present the constraints that should be hold on input, output and input-output. Also the **cap-id** field allows the specification of a name for this capability. The name for the capability is used to enable the middle agent to build a service ontology, and allows the **isa** field to naming a capability from which this capability will inherit the description. These two fields make it easier and simple to write a service description based on the already existed service ontologies, which is given as the value of **cap-ontology** field. The **privacy** and **quality** fields describe to what degree can other agents access this service and what the quality of this service is respectively. Depends on different domains, privacy and quality could be described in terms or functions.

6   Mediating Agent Services on the Web

Mediating is a process that utilise the knowledge on service domain to introduce service providers and consumers. Mediating is a high-level services matching and brokerage, in terms of level of knowledge applied, and directions of information flow. First of all, why do we need to mediate agent services on the Web? Let us look at the vast diversity of services that can be provided by agents all over the Web. Services are different in many aspects, I just name a few in the following:

- **Function.** It is obvious to note that different services have different functions. A sports agent has a totally different function to a shopping agent;
- **Constraints.** Even agents with the same function may impose different constraints on their input, output and input-output. For example, two lecturers both can be tutors on the subject, Data Structure and Algorithms, but one can only answer C questions, while the other is good at Java. Despite that they are able to consult on the same assignment question, but they require it in their capable language.
- **Quality and Privacy.** Quality and privacy are also varied from agent to agent, since they are run on different machines. Even when agents have the same function, due to the different implementations of the function, the qualities of their services may vary;
- **Names.** Agents may have different names despite the fact that they can provide the same service and have the same constraints and quality and privacy values.

The reasons that cause so many differences among agent services are mainly because of the open feature of the environment. Agents are developed over the Internet with heterogeneous architecture, and their functions vary from one to another. Due to diversity of agents, the requests of services are also various. In most cases, we can not expect that for a service request there is at least one agent to exactly provide that service, even through we suppose the service advertisement and request can fully express what the services are. In fact, a single agent can not have a global view of the whole system, it is not practical to do that, its request of service is also limited by the agent's "partial" knowledge of the environment.

7   Multiple Strategies for Services Matching

7.1   Type Matching

In the following definition, if type t_1 is a subtype of type t_2, it is denoted as $t_1 \preceq_{st} t_2$.

Definition 1. Type Match Let $\mathcal{C}$ be a service description in our ASDL containing: an input specification $I^{\mathcal{C}}$ containing the variables $v_1, \ldots, v_n$, and output specification $I^{\mathcal{O}}$. Let $\mathcal{T}$ be a service request in ASDL with input specification $I^{\mathcal{T}}$ containing variables $u_1, \ldots, u_m$, and output specification $O^{\mathcal{T}}$. $\mathcal{C}$ is type matched with $\mathcal{T}$, if

$$I^{\mathcal{T}} \preceq_{st} I^{\mathcal{C}} \text{ and } O^{\mathcal{C}} \preceq_{st} O^{\mathcal{T}}$$

where $I^T \preceq_{st} I^C$ means $\forall v_i \in I^C \exists u_j \in I^T$ that $u_j \preceq_{st} v_i$ and for $i \neq k$, $u_j \preceq_{st} v_i$, and $u_l \preceq_{st} v_k$, we have $j \neq l$.

This is the simplest strategy that only matches the types in the input and output fields of service advertisements against the correspondent field in requirements. It makes sure that a provider can take the inputs of requester, and its outputs are compatible with the requester's.

7.2   Constraint Matching

Definition 2. Constraint Match Let $\mathcal{C}$ be a capability description in ASDL with input constraints $C_I^{\mathcal{C}} = \{ C_{I_1}^{\mathcal{C}}, \ldots, C_{I_{k_C}}^{\mathcal{C}} \}$ and output constraints $C_O^{\mathcal{C}} = \{ C_{O_1}^{\mathcal{C}}, \ldots, C_{O_{l_C}}^{\mathcal{C}} \}$. Let $C_I^{\mathcal{T}} = \{ C_{I_1}^{\mathcal{T}}, \ldots, C_{I_{k_T}}^{\mathcal{T}} \}$ and $C_O^{\mathcal{T}} = \{ C_{O_1}^{\mathcal{T}}, \ldots, C_{O_{k_T}}^{\mathcal{T}} \}$ be the input and output constraints respectively of service $\mathcal{T}$. $\mathcal{T}$ is constraint matched with $\mathcal{C}$ if

$$C_I^{\mathcal{T}} \preceq_\theta C_I^{\mathcal{C}} \text{ and } C_O^{\mathcal{C}} \preceq_\theta C_O^{\mathcal{T}}$$

where $\preceq_\theta$ denotes the θ-subsumption relation between constraints. For $C_I^{\mathcal{T}} \preceq_\theta C_I^{\mathcal{C}}$ means $\forall C_{I_i}^{\mathcal{T}} \in C_I^{\mathcal{T}} \exists C_{I_j}^{\mathcal{C}} \in C_I^{\mathcal{C}}$ that $C_{I_i}^{\mathcal{T}} \preceq_\theta C_{I_j}^{\mathcal{C}}$ and for $i \neq k$, $C_{I_i}^{\mathcal{T}} \preceq_\theta C_{I_j}^{\mathcal{C}}$, and $C_{I_k}^{\mathcal{T}} \preceq_\theta C_{I_l}^{\mathcal{C}}$, we have $j \neq l$.

Since all the constraints are given in `constraint-language`, the details of θ-subsumption depends on the constraint-language. In first order predicate logic (FOPL), which is the constraint-language used in examples, constraints are a set of clauses. θ-subsumption in FOPL means there exists a substitution between two clauses.

7.3   Exact Matching

Exact match is most strict matching. It requires both the types and constraint fields are well matched. This strategy deals with the services that have the same functions but with different variable and type names. Considering the huge amount of Web-based applications which implemented over times and locations, there are many cases that developers may select different naming space.

7.4   Partial Matching

Definition 3. Partial Match Let $\mathcal{C}$ be a service description in our ASDL containing: an input specification $I^{\mathcal{C}}$ containing variables $V_{I_1}^{\mathcal{C}}, \ldots, V_{I_{n_C}}^{\mathcal{C}}$, and output specification $O^{\mathcal{C}}$ with variables $V_{O_1}^{\mathcal{C}}, \ldots, V_{O_{m_C}}^{\mathcal{C}}$, and $\mathcal{C}$'s input constraints $C_I^{\mathcal{C}} = \{ C_{I_1}^{\mathcal{C}}, \ldots, C_{I_{k_C}}^{\mathcal{C}} \}$ and output constraints $C_O^{\mathcal{C}} = \{ C_{O_1}^{\mathcal{C}}, \ldots, C_{O_{l_C}}^{\mathcal{C}} \}$. Let $\mathcal{T}$ be another agent service with the correspondent description parts as: input $I^{\mathcal{T}}$ containing variables $V_{I_1}^{\mathcal{T}}, \ldots, V_{I_{n_T}}^{\mathcal{C}}$, and output specification $O^{\mathcal{T}}$ with variables $V_{O_1}^{\mathcal{T}}, \ldots, V_{O_{m_T}}^{\mathcal{T}}$, and $\mathcal{T}$'s input constraints $C_I^{\mathcal{T}} = \{ C_{I_1}^{\mathcal{T}}, \ldots, C_{I_{k_T}}^{\mathcal{T}} \}$ and output constraints $C_O^{\mathcal{T}} = \{ C_{O_1}^{\mathcal{T}}, \ldots, C_{O_{l_T}}^{\mathcal{T}} \}$. We define $\mathcal{T}$ is partial matched with $\mathcal{C}$ if

$$\exists V^{\mathcal{T}}_{I_i} \in I^{\mathcal{T}}, \exists V^{\mathcal{C}}_{I_j} \in I^{\mathcal{C}} \text{ that } V^{\mathcal{T}}_{I_i} \preceq_{st} V^{\mathcal{C}}_{I_j}$$
$$\exists V^{\mathcal{C}}_{O_j} \in O^{\mathcal{C}}, \exists V^{\mathcal{T}}_{O_i} \in O^{\mathcal{T}} \text{ that } V^{\mathcal{C}}_{O_j} \preceq_{st} V^{\mathcal{T}}_{O_i}$$
$$\exists C^{\mathcal{T}}_{I_i} \in C^{\mathcal{T}}_I, \exists C^{\mathcal{C}}_{I_j} \in C^{\mathcal{C}}_I \text{ that } C^{\mathcal{T}}_{I_i} \preceq_\theta C^{\mathcal{C}}_{I_j}$$
$$\exists C^{\mathcal{C}}_{O_j} \in C^{\mathcal{C}}_O, \exists C^{\mathcal{T}}_{O_i} \in C^{\mathcal{T}}_O, \text{ that } C^{\mathcal{C}}_{O_j} \preceq_\theta C^{\mathcal{T}}_{O_i}$$

The above definition means for two capability descriptions, if some of their input, output variables have subtype relations, and there are constraint clauses in their input and output constraint specifications that are θ- subsumption, these two services are partial matched. Semantically, in some circumstances, i.e. the unmatched variables and constraints are irrelevant; the partial matched service is applicable.

7.5   Privacy Matching

Due to a service provider agent's privacy restriction, the matching result actually is sent to the service provider instead to the service requester. In other words, the provider agent wants to control the communication with consumers, it does not want to expose itself before knowing who are requesting its service. For instance, when recruiting for qualified software developers, some companies may not like their names known by their competitors, so they ask the agencies (middle agents) to keep their privacy. After the agency provides them with the resumes of potential experienced programmers, they can decide whom they would like to interview. Compared with other "conventional" matching strategies, privacy matching actually matches a service advertisement against service requests each time, while all the other strategies are vice versa; the information flow is different; the result of matching is transferred in a different direction. From the mediator's perspective, privacy matching is a service for capability providers. It supplies service request information to providers to help them marketing their services.

7.6   Cooperative Matching

Matching is a process based on a cooperative partnership between information providers and consumers. In cooperative matching process, the mediator first tries to find out from the current available information agents who have the capability that the query agent (information consumer) is asking for. In case no available agent can fulfill the queried service singly, the mediator will infer the relationships among available services, according to the domain ontology, to find a set of available information agents that can cooperate in some way to provide the requested service. This strategy requires an arbitrary amount of deduction and knowledge to match any given service and request. It exploits service ontology, knowledge on the application domain, to discover the hidden relationships among currently available services. It returns the agents contact information and their relationships.

8 TutorFinder: An Open Online Learning Tool

One great advantage of Web based learning is its openness. Everyone on the Internet can participate the learning and education process at any time they like. Traditional computer aided instruction (CAI) systems based on client-server architecture can not cope with this requirement. In order to take the full advantages offered by the Web, a new trend of online learning is open systems architecture, which introduces middleware to solve the connection problem.

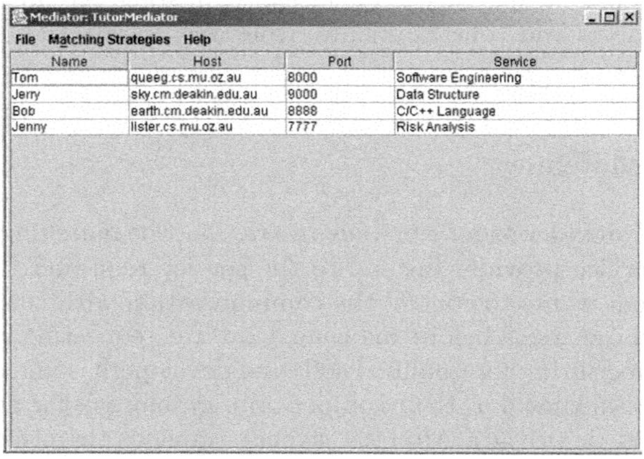
Mediator: TutorMediator
File Matching Strategies Help
Name Host Port Service
Tom queeg.cs.mu.oz.au 8000 Software Engineering
Jerry sky.cm.deakin.edu.au 9000 Data Structure
Bob earth.cm.deakin.edu.au 8888 C/C++ Language
Jenny lister.cs.mu.oz.au 7777 Risk Analysis

Fig. 4. Tutor Mediator

Based on the above mediator architecture and strategies, TutorFinder, an online tool for students and lecturers to locate suitable tutors, is presented in this section. TutorFinder is a mediator based open system. Any new available agent, who is able to offer services related to a specific eLearning subject, can register or advertise its ability to the TutorMediator, shown in Figure 4, who acts a middle man to mediate services requests and advertisements. This paradigm is open to any educators who wish to make their tools public over the Internet; in addition it is also open to any learners who are seeking some kind of helps. Service requests and advertisements are written in the proposed agent services description language, which can be easily plugged into any agent communication language. TutorMediator applies the multiple matching strategies to find out a or a team of service providers to inform to a consumer. The matching process can be reversed as a marketing campaign, in case the service provider would like to remain unknown until it knows who are seeking its services, and then the provider will target its marketing to the potential consumers. This procedure is depicted in Figure 1 as the dash line labeled with "Marketing".

8.1   Services Description and Matching in TutorFinder

The presented agent services description language based on ontology provides a meaningful tool for service providers to express their capabilities. This is critical in a Web based learning environment, considering the open nature of eLearning. Using this language, online learning service providers can prescribe what kind of services they can offer to the community. For example, a Web service dedicated to answer students' queries on subject SCC303 Software Engineering can register its service to the above TutorMediator in the following format:

```
( service
    :service-id SCC303Tutor
    :constraint-language fopl
    :input ( (SCC303Question ?question) )
    :output ( (Answer ?answer) )
    :input-constraints (
        (elt ?question Question)
        (SubjectIn ?question SoftwareEngineering) )
    :io-constraints (
        (Correct ?question ?answer) )
    :service-ontology ComputerScience )
```

In this description, we know that the service SCC303Tutor takes questions in subject SCC303, Software Engineering, as input, and gives the correspondent answers. It requires an input to be a valid question defined in Computer Science Subjects ontology, and the question should be in the topics of Software Engineering; on these conditions, SCC303Tutor is able to give a correct answer. Please note that the constraints in this example are written in First Order Predicate Logic (FOPL), which is specified in constraint-language field. Actually, developers can choose any formal languages independent from ASDL to write constraints, and simply specify it in this field.

The ontology of Computer Science subjects is not only exploited in service advertising, in which it defines all the terms and their relationships used in the description, but also in service matching. Here I present a scenario in Figure 4.

In this scenario, there are four information agents available, and they can provide tutoring services on subjects of Software Engineering, Data Structure, C/C++ Language, and Risk Analysis to students. These four agents can be located at different universities and institutes. When a student or an agent requests services on Computer Science, TutorMediator can recommend a provider, or a list of service providers working as a team in case that the requested service can not be accomplished by any single agents. Considering a student who is doing a programming project on Object Oriented Design and Analysis, at the current situation, there is no single agents has the capability on OO Design and Analysis programming; but this requested service can be achieved by two agents Tom and Bob, who have the expertise on Software Engineering and C/C++ Language respectively, working cooperatively as a team. So by exploiting service ontology and cooperative matching strategy, TutorMediator can reply the student's query with Tom and Bob's contact information, as well as their relationship in forming the team. Without ontology and various matching strategies, this can not be achieved. Powered with knowledge on the domain and a series of matching strategies, TutorMediator in our architecture is not a conventional middle agent, but an intelligent mediator who can reason and refer service providers' relationships, and guide them into cooperation.

9   Conclusion

The proposed agent service description language gives a flexible method for developers to plug in a suitable independent constraint language; it is more expressive for service quality and the privacy of service providers. The mediator, TutorMediator, in the presented open multi-agent architecture serves as middle agent that not only solves the connection problem, but also infers the cooperation relationships among information agents, this will direct service providers to forge a cooperation to answer a user's query. In such a way, tutoring agents can improve their capabilities, and online learning system becomes open and more scalable. This architecture with the service description language and matching strategies provides a solution to build open online learning system step by step. It also enables developers to integrate new tutoring services with legacy eLearning systems, since the architecture and language are open. This is critical for the success of online education, because both the educator and learner can take the full advantage of the World Wide Web, which gives people the freedom to pursue education from anywhere at anytime.

References

1. B. Chandrasekaran, John R. Josephson, and V. Richard Benjamins. What are ontologies, and why do we need them? *IEEE Intelligent Systems*, 14(1):20–26, January/February 1999.
2. Keith Decker, Katia Sycara, and Mike Williamson. Matchmaking and brokering. In *Proceedings of the Second International Conference on Multi-Agent Systems (ICMAS-96)*, December 1996.
3. Robert B. Doorenbos, Oren Etzioni, and Daniel S. Weld. A scalable comparison-shopping agent for the World Wide Web. In *Proceedings of the First International Conference on Autonomous Agents*, 1997.
4. Michael R. Genesereth and Steven P. Ketchpel. Software agents. *Communications of the ACM*, 37(7):48–53, July 1994.
5. Hongen Lu, Leon Sterling, and Alex Wyatt. Knowledge discovery in SportsFinder: An agent to extract sports results from the Web. In *Methodologies for Knowledge Discovery and Data Mining, Third Pacific-Asia Conference (PAKDD-99) Proceedings*, pages 469–473. Springer, 1999.
6. Jonathan Shakes, Marc Langheinrich, and Oren Etzioni. Dynamic reference sifting: A case study in the homepage domain. In *Proceedings of the Sixth International World Wide Web Conference*, pages 189–200, 1997.

Intelligent Characters of Web-Based Learning Platform*

Zhan Xu[1], Qinglin Zhang[1], Ailisha Li[1], and Weiyuan Wang[2]

[1] School of Psychology,
Southwest China Normal University,
400715 Chongqing, P R C
{xuzhan, zhangql, pno1}@swnu.edu.cn
[2] Opentec Ltd Limited, Australia
weiyuanw@opentec.com.au

Abstract. An important issue of web-based learning is to realize self-adaptation in individual learning with respect to individual characteristics of learners. In this paper we present a web-based learning platform based on the learning theories of educational psychology. The platform and courseware are developed and experimented in the high schools and the result shows that the system demonstrated certain characters of intelligence in web-based learning, being able to judge like an expert teacher in instruction process. The platform is capable of not only providing individual learning but also enhancing students' motivation, interest, autonomy and meta-cognitive ability.

1 Introduction

Web-based learning is being developed rapidly in recently years. It is getting more and more popular because Internet gives us the best hope for the less expensive, more accessible, higher quality education [1] (Jones, 1999). This form of instruction can meet the needs of many for whom conventional education is inappropriate or unavailable [2] (John Stephenson, 2001).

To take the advantages of web to instruct involves not only the web technology but also more importantly the further development of the principles of pedagogy and psychology during the course of web-based learning. In fact, the tendency for new technologies to be seen as heralding a revolution in educational methods and then consistently failing to make an impact has been noted [3] (Mayes, 1995). We believe that new technologies alone, however effective in other fields, don't inevitably cause fundamental changes in education. New theories of pedagogy and psychology are necessary to effectively deploying the new technologies in education to achieve the best results.

Generally speaking, web-based learning has two main forms. First is collaborative learning. That is, the students construct their own knowledge systems by the way of solving problems in collaborating with others. The second one is individual learning. The students acquire the knowledge by themselves. Most of web-based teaching sites

---

* The work has been sponsored by the Ministry of Education, P R C (project DBB010510).

W. Zhou et al. (Eds.): ICWL 2003, LNCS 2783, pp. 351–359, 2003.

provide both forms of learning. While there are many researchers focusing on how to realize the communications between students and teachers and the communications among students through solving problems by collaboration [4] (Jonassen and Land, 2000), this paper discusses the self-adaptation in individual learning.

2   Individual Web-Based Learning and Psychological Theories

Individual learning stems from the behaviorism. In order to overcome the disadvantages of learning in the traditional class, Skinner proposed a method of programmed learning [5] (Skinner, 1954). The main steps of programmed learning include selecting goal, fixing the pace, timely feedbacks and controlling by machine [6] (Xiaozhen Zhang, 2000). Programmed learning is effective in teaching because it costs less time and learners enjoin it [7] (Hanna, 1971). After so many years programmed learning has not been abandoned yet and it is also being adopted in some web-based learning. In programmed learning, the information is presented in the form of small nodes followed by some reinforcements. The learner must master the former content before they learn the next content. The communication can be enhanced through tests. If the learner fails the test, he/she has to go back to the former knowledge node and go it over again. Many web-based learning sites were built on the principle of programmed learning. Some researches indicate that programmed learning takes less time than traditional learning and is welcomed by the students. Such a learning theory falls into the behaviorism category, and may best suit teaching of the basic knowledge and skills (Abbey, 2003) [8].

Following behaviorism is cognitive psychology that regards the learning as the interaction result of stimulus and inner cognitive process. It proposes that the structure of knowledge should be directly presented during the learning process. For instance, a research on concept formation shows that it is an interactive process [9] (Bruner, Goodnow & Austin, 1956). Knowledge may not be useful until learners master it. In order for the learner to grasp it, knowledge need be presented as knowledge notes one by one. Thus, the research outcomes of cognitive schema, web structure of cognition, the concept formation, motivation theories and meaningful learning all may find their uses in web-based learning.

Constructivism regards learning as the initiative process to form the knowledge and understand the new by empirical structure. Individuals use the assimilation and confirmation to adjust their knowledge structure [10] (Piaget, 1954). Structural psychologist thinks the knowledge is acquired by the interaction between individual and environment, not by teaching. The spiral development of cognition is followed the way of meaningful structure. The theory insists of learning by tasks, meaningful learning by discussing the problems, designing realistic problem condition, letting the students experience the challenge similar to the real world and learn the knowledge [11] (Kekang He, 1997). The structural psychology didn't discuss the individual problems, but focuses on the self-control during the learning process. The main functions of teachers are guiding and consulting. Web-based learning most are student-centered. Web-based learning from constructivism is suitable for higher learning. It demands that learners are more responsibilities for their own learning [12] (Perkins, 1991). Structural learning theory becomes the important one to web-based learning. Now, the design and creation of curriculum and web-based learning are mainly based on this theory. The model of individual web-based learning can be improved with the development of the theory.

3   Intelligent Characters of Yuanlin Web-Based Learning Platform

Some researchers believe there are not many differences between web-based learning and traditional learning. Web-based learning is simply an extension and further development of traditional learning. It should be viewed as a tool or a kind of support to traditional learning. The researchers who hold such a view, however, ignore the inevitable conflict between the "in the same pace" of the tradition learning and individual differences. Web-based learning can better solve the individual problems than traditional learning. Teachers should aim at the students' difference in terms of knowledge background, learning goal, learning ability and so on. Furthermore, non-cognitive factors such as the learner's motivation, interest, emotion, autonomy and so on should not be ignored. As a result, teachers should set different goals, contents, paces, ways of testing and measures of remedy. At the same time, they should consider how to prompt the learner's learning by kinds of valid means. All of these parameters should be variable and adjustable. In this way, the students will find their own comfortable ways to learn.

Yuanlin Web-based Learning Platform (abbr. as YWLP) is designed on the basis of psychology theories. It not only has the collaboration learning function but also can realize the individual learning by aiming at the different characters of learners. It is capable to judge like expert teachers and gives advices. Learners may either accept the advices or refuse them and take their own pace. The process of such individual learning is presented and analyzed as follows.

3.1   Goal Selection and Learning Mode

When individual learners contact the web-based learning at the first time, they will have different knowledge backgrounds, learning abilities, motives and goals. To teach students in accordance of their own aptitude should aim at the different characters of the learners. If learners choose the goals suit for themselves, they will know the goals. They will have high level of motivations, work efficiently, and take the challenges. Consequently, it will bring out the feelings of success, efficiency and inner interests.

YWLP allows the course designer to set different goals according to different educational levels. The levels will be lined up by the content difficulty. Learners should firstly select their learning goals (see Fig. 1.). Learners who choose different goals will meet the different knowledge nodes, requirements and tests. For example, learners A and B choose the goal 1 (the learning goal of novice) and goal 2 (the learning goal of expert, more difficult than goal 1) separately. The contents what they will learn are different. Learner A will not have to learn some contents what learner B has to learn.

YWLP supplies two different learning modes for the learners. One is to choose from the catalog of the contents that are not completed grasped. This is suitable for the learners who have better background knowledge and meta-cognitive abilities. The other is to learn the content systemically. The web-based learning platform will present instructions and tests systemically according to the respective contents and sequence set in advance. It also supplies feedback and make intelligent judgment automatically according to the students' responses. This mode is suitable for most circumstances, especially for learning new contents.

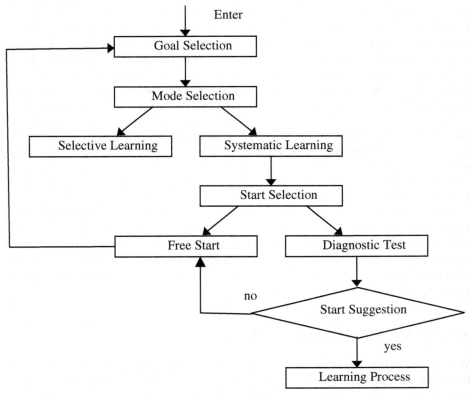

Fig. 1. Goal selection and start selection model

3.2 Intelligent Judgment to Individual Learning Start

The first problem solved by YWLP is to determine the starting-point from which the learner begins his/her studies after the learning objective is chosen. The system will decide the learner's starting-point by conducting automatic diagnosing tests. The system automatically compiles a series of diagnosing tests. At the end of tests, the system will make judgment of the learner's starting-point.

With these diagnosing tests, the system may know the learner's current status, that is to say, what the learner has mastered and what problems the learner has. For an instance, a learner is going to study high school physics course. The system may diagnose how well the learner masters the knowledge of physics at the junior middle school level and how much the learner knows the knowledge of high school physics. Learners will receive various feedback data after they have the diagnostic test. It just reflects that individuals' current status is different from each other. YWLP web-based instruction system will automatically provide advice according to the results of diagnosing tests. Learners will start learning once they accept the advice. Certainly learners may refuse the advice of the system and decide their own starting-points.

3.3   Intelligent Judgment to Individual Learning Process

The instruction procedure of YWLP course is made up of the instruction of a series of knowledge nodes. Specifically, there are exercises, instruction, games, simulation, problem solving and so on. A learner will study the lecture, which includes files, pictures, audio files, video files and flash, and have the respective test in order to master each knowledge node.

Experts' support, colleagues' feedback and related data are available for the learner during the course of learning. This is similar to the general web-based instruction systems. The critical difference, however, is the way of evaluation and the remedies after the evaluation.

YWLP may propose different requirements, including understanding, memorizing, using, applying skillfully, and applying synthetically or creatively, with regard to different features of knowledge nodes. Therefore various requirements are put in the lecture and the test of knowledge nodes. In our opinion, for a given knowledge unit, the learner may not memorize it even if he/she understands it; he/she may not use it even if he/she memorizes it; he/she may not apply skillfully even if he/she can use it; he/she may not apply synthetically even if he/she can apply it skillfully. Or the learner cannot synthesize thinking strategies. Different knowledge nodes have different requirement. It is necessary to evaluate the learning at different levels.

YWLP provides two different types of tests, test I and test II, in order to guarantee that the most basic and general knowledge nodes can be mastered and applied skillfully. Test I requires the learner to master the knowledge nodes while Test II requires the learner to master the knowledge nodes skillfully. The learner's speed of response is recorded during the test. For those who do not meet the requirement, the system will automatically provide relevant exercises until they are able to meet the requirement.

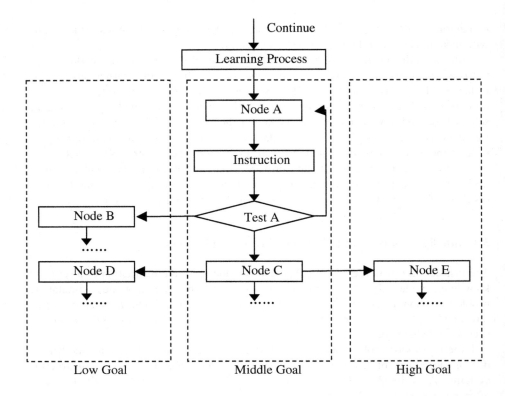

Fig. 2. Individual learning process model

YWLP provides timely feedback when a learner fails the test of some knowledge unit. YWLP may also make intelligent judgment and find out what difficulties the learner has and what can be done to overcome them. Fig. 2 shows, for an instance, that the learner fails test A. The learner may re-learn Node A. It is, however, possible that Node A is not the reason for the failure. The real cause to the failure is that the precedent Node B or D is not mastered well enough. The system will automatically advise the learner to review Node B and Node D. the learner is free to decide whether accepts the advice or not.

The judging capability of computer is derived from the design of web-based courses. Designers, normally experienced teachers, are required to construct relationship of all knowledge nodes, that is, cognitive network of knowledge nodes. In Fig. 3, for example, there is some intrinsic relation among the knowledge nodes. Node B and D are the predecessor of Node A. In other word, Node B and D are more basic that Node A in term of construction. Node E is the consequence of Noda A and C. Such a node network is similar to human cognition network and proved by some researches. Stimulating recall of prior learning can be as simple as reminding learners of what was studied the day before, or last week, in class. This is often observed in the quick review with which many teachers start their daily courses. In some instances, however, simple reminders are not enough. It then becomes necessary to reinforce the prerequisite knowledge or skills by some practice activity [13] (Gagne and Driscoll, 1988). An example can be seen in the following protocol, taken from Driscoll and Dick's observations of a grade-8 science teacher about halfway through an instructional unit on light and lenses [14] (Driscoll and Dick, 1991).

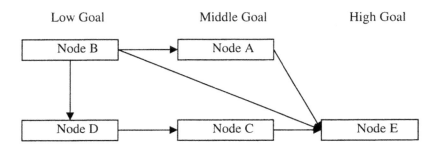

Fig. 3. Part of knowledge node network

The evaluation subsystem of YWLP pays much attention to the quantitative evaluation during the learning process. The evaluation is dynamical and quantitative throughout the course of learning. There are two index of quantitative process evaluation. One is the score of learning progress, which means the quantity of knowledge nodes mastered by the learner. Another is the score of learning quality, which means how good the learner masters the knowledge nodes. The hypothesis is that learning quality of some knowledge unit can be judged if the learner successfully passes the test of the respective knowledge unit. That is, the learner may score full if he/she passes the test at the first time. The learner may score half if he/she passes the test at the second time. The learner may score quarter if he/she passes the test at the third time. The learner scores zero if he/she fails at the fourth time. It can be expected that two learners might be scored 600 of learning progress, but their scores of learning quality are different. Learners may know one's scores of learning progress and quality as the scores approach full. Learners may compare one's scores with others, too. This kind of evaluation method will help to motivate and maintain learning motivations, and timely evaluate the gap between the current status and objective status.

Besides, learners' objective is changeable. Learners may change his/her objective. YWLP can dynamically advise learners to adjust the objective if the score of learning quality of some learning stage does not meet the requirement of certain instructional objective. For an instance, there are three objectives, primary, middle and senior-set, in some web-based course. A learner chooses the middle objective at the beginning. If his/her score of learning quality is beyond the standard after a period of learning, the system will automatically advise the learner to "adjust your objective to a senior one". If his/her score of learning quality is below the standard, the system will automatically advise the learner to "adjust your objective to a primary one". Certainly it is learner who decides whether or not to accept the system's advice. Learning contents and tests will be adjusted respectively with regard to the changes of learning objectives. As a result, YWLP is capable to make judgment as an expert teacher does.

4 Conclusions

It can be seen that YWLP is capable to make intelligent judgments during the course of individual learning. Learning process may be dynamically adjusted with regard to individual differences of every learner.

Comparing with the other web-based teaching platforms, YWLP can provide not only general functions shared by other platforms, including cooperative learning, support online, courseware administration and so on and so forth, but also the function of intelligent support for individual learning.

YWLP has been used in teaching practices. We developed network courseware of math, physics and chemistry in high schools in the Western China. It proves that YWLP can offset the shortcomings of instructions in the traditional classroom. The mean scores of the different classes in the pre-test and post-test are seen in Table 1. After statistic analysis, there were not significant difference in the pre-test between the experimental class and the contrastive class in the three subjects. When we finished the experiment throughout one term, something interesting happened. The mean scores in other two subjects increased but were not significant on statistics. However, significant difference in the post-test was found in chemistry. The mean score (74.3) of the experimental class is significantly higher than it (67.5) of the contrastive class (significance < 0.05).

Table 1. Comparison of mean score of the different classes

	Class	Pre-test	Post-test
Math	Experimental	86.3	111.7
	Contrastive	88.6	112.4
Physics	Experimental	56.9	76.0
	Contrastive	56.8	72.1
Chemistry	Experimental	70.6	74.3
	Contrastive	66.7	67.5

Additionally, after the experiment we made an investigation into the effects of YWLP on non-cognitive factors. The statistic data showed that the students' motivation, interest, autonomy and meta-cognitive ability have been enhanced significantly. Most of the learners reported that because they were promoted to master knowledge and skills they can control their learning. Although there are still more problems to solve in YWLP, it is clear that the intelligent character of TWLP in individual instruction is helpful for learners to make best progress and develop their potential as much as possible.

"…the best teaching occurs when educators make choices about learning environments, learning tools, and learning experiences based on strategies drawn from a board knowledge base" [15] (Norton & Wiberg, 1998). YWLP provides students a good chance to choose how to learn individually with their own comfortable style.

References

1. Jones, G. R.: Free Market Fusion. Cyber Publishing Group, Incorporated (1999)
2. John, S.: Teaching and learning online. Kogan Page: London (2001)
3. Mayes, J. T.: Learning technologies and groundhog day, in Hypermedia at work: Practice and theory in higher education, eds Strang, W., Simpson, V. B. and Slater, D. Canterbury: University of Kent Press (1995)
4. Jonassen, D. H. and Land, S. M. (eds).: Theoretical foundation of learning environments. Lawrence Erlbaum, Mahwah NJ (2000)
5. Skinner, B. F.: The science of learning and the art of teaching. Harvard Educational Review, 24(2) (1954) 86–97
6. Xiaozhen Zhang: Multimedia and network courseware. Southwest China Normal University Press (2000)
7. Hanna, M. S.: A Comparative investigation of three models of instruction in organization if ideas. Unpublished doctoral dissertation. University of Missouri, Columbia (1971)
8. Abbey, B. (Ed.): Instructional and Cognitive Impacts of Web-Based Education. Hershey, Idea Group Publishing, PA(2000)
9. Bruner, J. S., Goodnow, J. J., & Austin, G. A.: A study of thinking. (3rd ed.). John Wiley & Sons, New York (1956)
10. Piaget, J.: The construction of reality in the child. Basic Books, New York (1954)
11. Kekang He: Computer assisted education. China Higher Education Press (1997)
12. Perkins, D. N.: What constructivism demands of learner. Educational Technology 31(9) (1991) 19–21
13. Gagne, R.M., & Driscoll, M.P.: Essentials of learning for instruction (2nd ed.). Englewood Cliffs, Prentice-Hall, NJ (1988)
14. Driscoll, M. P., & Dick, W.: What do textbooks contribute to learning? Unpublished raw data (1991)
15. Norton, P. & Wiberg, K. M.: Teaching with technology. Harcourt Brace & Company (1998)

Knowledge Refinement Tools to Support Inductive Learning by Inquiry Examples

Feng-Hsu Wang

Department of Computer and Communication Engineering
Ming-Chuan University, Taiwan
fhwang@mcu.edu.tw

Abstract. This paper presents a machine learning approach to develop computer-assisted learning supports for inductive learning tasks. Several machine-learning techniques are developed to evaluate student's learning results, promote learning and achieve better results by giving better hints during the learning process. The learning supports can be exploited to provide individualized guidance in the context of learning classification knowledge by inquiry examples. Integrated with the learning supports, a knowledge refinement process is proposed, and a web-based system, named ALBIX (Active Learning By Inquiry Examples), was implemented so that students can actively construct, verify and refine their classification knowledge in an interactive manner. The knowledge refinement process is supported by four machine-learning modules, which are knowledge retraction module, knowledge evaluation module, knowledge diagnosis and knowledge remediation module, respectively. Finally, the learning supports presented in this paper are shown to be effective to their design purposes through a set of simulation tests. A small-scaled prototype testing also showed that teachers and students might be interested in such a kind of learning strategy.

1 Motivation and Research Purpose

One of the creative capabilities of scientists is the ability to turn data (observations) into knowledge, that is, the capability for knowledge discovery. Students can experience the knowledge discovery process by engaging themselves in scientific activities such as data collection, observation and analysis of real world data from different perspectives, to derive and test their own knowledge. In such an individualized and constructive learning scenario, we need a proper tutoring system [1] equipped with appropriate tutoring and diagnosis tools to support such kind of creative learning.

This research is aimed to develop computer-assisted learning supports that could be exploited to provide individualized guidance in learning classification knowledge. Classification knowledge is composed of features and pattern description rules. Educational domains such as medical clinics, global climate patterns, and taxonomy are typical domains that require students to study samples so that they can learn the classification knowledge. In this paper, a knowledge refinement process is proposed, and a

W. Zhou et al. (Eds.): ICWL 2003, LNCS 2783, pp. 360–371, 2003.

web-based system, named ALBIX (Active Learning By Inquiry Examples), was implemented so that students can actively construct, verify and refine their classification knowledge in an interactive manner. The knowledge refinement process is supported by four machine-learning modules, which are knowledge retraction module, knowledge evaluation module, knowledge diagnosis and knowledge remediation module, respectively.

The knowledge extraction module automatically builds an initial knowledge model from learning results of students. The knowledge model comprises a categorical feature space and pattern classification rules. The knowledge extraction module performs two tasks related to machine learning techniques. First, the feature reconstruction problem refers to reconstructing categorical feature concepts from student's feedbacks to numerical features. A feature reconstruction method based on alpha-cuts of fuzzy sets is developed for numerical features. The second is the rule extraction problem. A rule extraction method based on rough set theory [2][4] was proposed for deriving pattern classification rules [8] with the reconstructed categorical feature spaces. One advantage of rough set theory is that it is useful for data sets of both large and small sizes. This is especially important in the context of this research because the data sets for analyzing are collected from students' testing results, which might not contain a large number of data items.

The knowledge evaluation module verifies the knowledge model by applying the knowledge to classify the examples in the database. Diagnosis of student's knowledge (classification rules and conceptual features) is based on the evaluation of how well the knowledge applies to the samples in the database. Appropriate samples that are useful in leading effective modification of the knowledge can hence be decided and selected. A diagnosis and remedial instruction strategy based on the maximum-utility policy is proposed to decide the most effective knowledge modifiers and accordingly the most appropriate inquiry examples according to the evaluation results of the knowledge model. The remedial module can also generate proper suggestions and hints to guide the student through the knowledge refinement process.

In the following, we focus on the design of the learning tools and demonstrate how machine learning techniques can be applied to support active learning by inducing inquiry examples We have implemented a prototype tutoring system for the domain of global climate classification by integrating all the tools we had built. The learning supports presented in this paper are shown to be technically effective through a set of simulation tests. A small-scaled prototype testing also showed that teachers and students might be interested in such a kind of learning strategy. However, more complete experiments need to be conducted to investigate the pedagogical effects of this system on student's learning outcomes.

2   A Web-Based Environment for Learning by Inquiry Examples

We had designed and implemented a web-based collaborative learning environment named CILSE-GCE [7] for global climate pattern exploration. The task domain there is inherently a scientific classification problem. Students are expected to induce climate classification rules by collecting and observing climatic features of city samples of the world. A visualized data investigation subsystem based on GIS (Geographic Information System) technique is developed to help students to make observations, data collections and feature comparisons between city samples of the globe. Through the GIS environment students could observe real world data in different perspectives and induce their own classification rules. Figure 1 shows a screenshot of the GIS visual environment, where the climate information could be displayed with different colors in different feature layers covering the globe. Specific information of city samples is accessed through the hot links associated with the corresponding city points in the screen. In summary, the learning system was designed with the intention not only to teach students the target knowledge, but also the scientific ways of exploration.

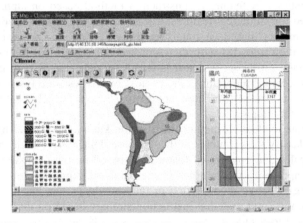

Fig. 1. A screenshot of the Visualized Climatic Data Viewer

To evaluate the learning results of students, they have to go through a series of tests, putting down their answers about what climatic patterns they think are important for predicting the climatic patterns, the feature spaces and the reason why. For example, Table 1 shows a student's answering sheet in which a student decided to adopt four condition features to predict the climate pattern. The information hidden the answer sheets is valuable in evaluation of the knowledge states of students. For example, what is the student's concept of "moderate" Year_AT (average year temperature), and what is the student's rule for predicting the "rainforest" pattern.

Table 1. An example of a student answer sheet. Table entries containing * indicate don't-care attributes from the student's viewpoint.

Answer #	Year AT	Year TD	Precipitation	Latitude	Pattern
Item-1	*	small	abundant	low	rainforest
Item-2	*	small	abundant	low	rainforest
Item-3	moderate	moderate	*	middle	temperate wet
Item-4	*	small	scarce	high	rainforest

3   The Knowledge Refinement Process and System Architecture

Figure 2 shows the knowledge refinement process. The student starts the knowledge refinement process by entering into the knowledge exhibition phase. In the knowledge exhibition phase, the knowledge model is exposed in explicit forms so that the student and the system can have a common foundation for interaction. In this research textual rule format is adopted to represent the pattern classification rules, while a simple trapezoid fuzzy set is used to display a numerical feature concept. In the knowledge evaluation phase, the system evaluates and verifies the explicit knowledge model against the sample database. The knowledge evaluation module performs diagnosis of student's knowledge entities (pattern classification rules and conceptual features) based on the evaluation of how well they apply to the samples in the database. Appropriate samples that are potential in leading students to effective modification of their knowledge are decided and selected. This involves consideration of numerous possible alternatives of knowledge modifiers to improve the prediction accuracy of the classification rules, and then chooses among them the most effective one that would results in the greatest improvement.

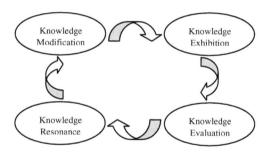

Fig. 2. The knowledge refinement process

In the knowledge resonance phase, students have to refine the current knowledge model by investigating and studying the suggested inquiry samples to explore possible refinements of the knowledge model. After making a decision on how to refine the knowledge model, students could exploit a knowledge editor provided by our system to modify the knowledge model. This process is repeated until an approved evaluation condition is met or it is found by the evaluation module that no further improvements can be done on the knowledge model. In the latter case, an evaluation summary report will be generated, indicating the model's effectiveness in terms of prediction accuracy and number of rules used. After that, the next learning target for the student can be prescribed, and a new knowledge refinement process can then be started again.

Figure 3 shows the system architecture that supports the aforementioned knowledge refinement process. Given the current learning target, the Knowledge Testing Module selects appropriate test items from the sample base based on specific testing policies. The Knowledge Extraction Module uses machine-learning methods to re-construct the student's knowledge model by extracting the feature concepts and pattern classification rules from the student's answer sheet. The Knowledge Evaluation Module then evaluates and verifies the knowledge entries, and makes a decision on selecting which remedial samples and suggestions for student guidance. The Knowledge Editing Module is a knowledge editor that helps students to refine their knowledge content. All the modules are integrated via the Interactive Tutoring Module that interacts with the student.

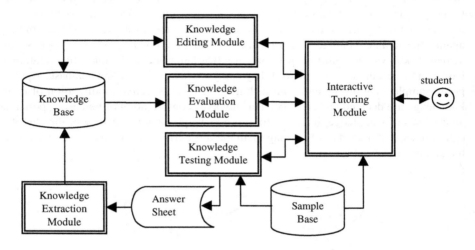

Fig. 3. Architecture of the ALBIX tutoring system

4   Machine Learning Methods for Knowledge Model Construction

4.1   Extraction of Classification Rules from Answer Sheets

A knowledge extraction method for pattern classification rules based on rough set theory [2][4] has been proposed and applied in this system [8]. Two knowledge extraction methods were designed based on lower approximation set and upper approximation set of the rough set theory [2], respectively. A set of simulation experiments is conducted to evaluate the capability of the knowledge extraction modules. The simulation results show that it is hard to extract "just-the-same" rules using current knowledge extraction methods. Nevertheless, The rough set based methods, especially the upper-set algorithm, perform significantly well to extract "almost-the-same" rules. Besides, when inconsistency exists in the student rules, the upper algorithm can deal with the inconsistency problem very well. Finally, to improve the rule extraction effectiveness, the rule extraction algorithms should use only those features that students had really adopted in the testing records. This will contribute much especially to the extraction of inconsistent student rules. For more details, the readers may refer to [8].

4.2 Reconstruction of Categorical Feature Concepts

Consider the numerical attribute "Latitude" in the answer sheet shown in Table 1. Assume four data points can be collected from the table entries, i.e., (5° N, low), (3° N, low), (35° N, middle), and (67° N, high). The problem of feature concept extraction is to construct a fuzzy set for each linguistic term used by the student in the answer sheet. For example, the constructed fuzzy sets for the "Latitude" feature might look like those shown in Figure 4.

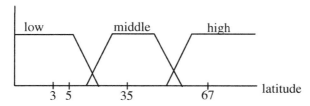

Fig. 4. An example of fuzzy feature concept derived from student answer sheet

In the sequel, we outline the feature extraction algorithm that is based on computing the alpha-cuts of each fuzzy feature using the entropy function as a criterion for partitioning the numerical attribute domains [3][6].

Phase 1. Generation of Data Intervals for a Given Numerical Feature F

(1) Sort the n data points in an ascend manner according to the numerical feature value. Store the sorted data in the array $P[1...n]$, and let $P(0)=\text{Min}(F)$, $P(n+1)=\text{Max}(F)$ be the minimal and maximal values of the feature domain, respectively.

(2) For each linguistic term A of F, collect data points with term A from P and put them in the array $A_X[1...m]$, and let $A_X(0)=\text{Min}(F)$, $A_X(m+1)=\text{Max}(F)$ be the minimal and maximal values of the feature's domain, respectively.

(3) Compute the midpoint of each consecutive two data points in A_X, and store the results in A_M. Specifically,

$$A_M(i) = [A_X(i-1) + A_X(i)] / 2, \quad i = 1 .. m+1,$$

and let $A_M(0)= A_X(0)$, $A_M(m+1)= A_X(m+1)$. Note there are totally $m+1$ midpoints, which are $A_M(1), A_M(2), ..., A_M(m+1)$, respectively.

(4) Form $m+1$ intervals from the $m+1$ midpoints in A_M. Specifically, let interval $I_k:(A_M(k-1), A_M(k))$, $k=1, ..., m+1$. Let I_A be the set of these intervals.

(5) Delete those intervals containing no data points, and have it merged with neighboring intervals.

Phase 2. Compute the Membership Function of Each Interval I for the Feature Concept A.

(1) Compute the entropy (denoted by n_A') of each interval I:

$$n_A' = -k \log k , \tag{1}$$

where k is the proportion of data points with linguistic term A in the interval I.

(2) As a result, the membership degree of the interval I with respect to A (denoted by E_A^I) is computed as

$$E_A^I = \frac{\left(\dfrac{1}{n_A^I}\right)}{\sum\limits_{A' \in F}\left(\dfrac{1}{n_{A'}^I}\right)}, \qquad (2)$$

where A is the target feature concept and A' is the other feature concept (linguistic term) of feature F. Store the computed membership interval degrees in A_p array.

Phase 3. Construct and Smooth the Fuzzy Set A.
(1) Let $\Phi=\{\alpha\colon \alpha \in A_p\}$ be the set of membership degrees appear in A_p. Then the α-cut of fuzzy set A (denoted by A^α) is defined as

$$A^\alpha=\{I | E_A^I \ge \alpha, I \in I_A \}. \qquad (3)$$

(2) Define the fuzzy set A as

$$A(x) = E_A^I,$$

where $I \in A_p$ and I is the interval that contains x and has the maximal membership degree among those intervals containing x.
(3) Apply the linear regression technique to further smooth the membership function.

An Example
Consider the example for "Latitude" feature as shown in figure 5. Take the feature concept of X as that target feature concept. From those midpoints ($\diamond$s) we have formed "five" intervals. Note that since I_1 contains no data points, it will be merged with the neighboring interval I_2.

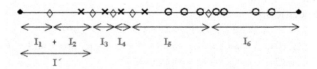

Fig. 5. The formation of data intervals for data points collected from student's answer sheet.

Next compute the membership degree of each interval for the target feature concept X. By (1), we have

$$n_x^{15} = (-1/4) * \log (1/4) = 0.1505 \,，\, 1/ n_x^{15} = 6.6445,$$
$$n_o^{15} = (-3/4) * \log (3/4) = 0.0937 \,，\, 1/ n_o^{15} = 10.6724.$$

Therefore by (2) we have

$$E_x^{15}=6.6445/(6.6445+10.6724)=0.3837.$$

At last, as I_6 contains no X data points, we have $E_x^{16}=0$.
Finally Let $\Phi=\{0, 0.3837, 1\}$ be the result set of all membership degrees computed for the intervals of the target feature concept X. Then by (3) we have

$$X^1 = \dot{I} \cup I_3 \cup I_4 \,,$$
$$X^{0.3837} = \dot{I} \cup I_3 \cup I_4 \cup I_5 \,,$$
$$X^0 = \dot{I} \cup I_3 \cup I_4 \cup I_5 \cup I_6 \,.$$

As a result, the constructed fuzzy set for the target feature concept X is shown in figure 6(a), which are composed of discrete rectangle areas. In this research we apply the linear regression technique to further smooth the membership function, which have a more general data description capability than the discrete one has. The resulting membership function will be a trapezoid-shaped fuzzy set, as the one shown in figure 6(b).

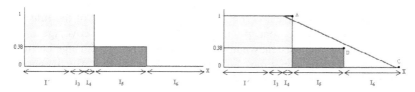

Fig. 6. (a) The discrete fuzzy set for X constructed based on the α-cuts of the data intervals. (b) The smoothed membership function by applying linear regression.

Simulated Performance Results

To evaluate the effectiveness of the feature concept reconstruction algorithm, simulation tests are performed using the following similarity measurement proposed in the literature [5][9].

$$S_{w1}(A,B) = \frac{\int\limits_{x \in S(A) \cup S(B)} (1 - |A(x) - B(x)|)\,dx}{|S(A) \cup S(B)|}, \tag{4}$$

One thousand fuzzy sets of three target feature concepts, low, moderate and high, are generated randomly. Each fuzzy set is viewed as a student's feature concept. Besides, we generate numerical test items with sizes of 25, 30, 35, …, 100, respectively. These test sets with different sizes were used to investigate the number of test items on the accuracy of the feature reconstruction algorithm. Given a fuzzy set and a test item, the decision of the suitable categorical value adopted to encode the numerical item is determined by the fuzzy set with the highest membership degree with respect to that numerical item. The results show that the average similarity Sw_1 of the reconstructed feature concepts for "low" and "high" are both above 0.88, and they are almost independent of the item sizes between 25 and 100. The average similarity Sw_1 of the "moderate" feature concept is 0.76, which increases slightly as the number of test items increases. In summary, the simulation results showed that the feature reconstruction method is effective with a reasonable amount of test items.

5   Knowledge Diagnosis and Remediation Module

5.1   Common Deficiency Types of Classification Knowledge

Two sources of knowledge deficiency are identified in this research. The first comes from erroneous structure of pattern classification rules and the other comes from the deficient feature concepts. Both of the deficient knowledge sources will together hinder the effectiveness of the knowledge model, which is often measured by the *false positive* and *false negative* error rates. Erroneous rule structures include *too general or too specific* rule conditions. Some modifications on the rule conditions are often required to increase the effectiveness (i.e., accurate prediction rate) of the rule. On the other hand, deficient feature concepts may be due to improper coverage of feature domains or due to the inconsistency among the feature concepts. Change on fuzzy sets of feature concepts may sometimes be needed to increase the effectiveness of the knowledge model.

5.2   Evaluation of Knowledge Model

Given a classification rule in the knowledge model, we propose a utility measurement to assess the effectiveness of a rule in predicting the target patterns. Let $P(r)$ and $N(r)$ be the set of positive samples and negative samples, respectively, with respect to a given rule r. Then the utility of the rule is defined as

$$utility\ (r) = \frac{\displaystyle\sum_{s_i \in P(r)} d(s_i, r)}{|T|} + \frac{N(r) - \displaystyle\sum_{s_i \in N(r)} d(s_i, r)}{|T|}\ , \tag{5}$$

where $T = P(\mathrm{r}) \cup N(\mathrm{r})$ is the set of all samples, and $d(s_i, r)$ is the degree to which the sample s_i matches the fuzzy conditions of the rule r. Specifically, let $\wedge_j F_j = v_j$ be the left-hand side (fuzzy conditions) of a rule r, where F_j be the fuzzy feature and v_j is a linguistic value of feature F_j. Hence, $d(s_i, r) = \min_j \mu_{(F_j = v_j)}(F_j(s_i))$, where $F_j(s_i)$ is the numerical value of sample s_i in feature F_j. The utility measurement in (5) shows that a positive sample will generate a positive effect of increasing the rule utility, and a negative sample will generate a negative effect of decreasing the rule's utility. A rule matching no negative samples will have a utility increased by $N(r)/T$, which justifies the rule's capability of ruling out negative samples.

5.3   Strategy for Generating Inquiry Samples

Peter Goodyear [1] pointed out the importance of inquiry samples in helping students focus on critical aspects of the knowledge model. In particular, by controlling one factor at a time, several samples can be presented to reveal the effects of that factor on the prediction outcome. Therefore, the system adopts the one-time-one-variable policy to evaluate the utilities of classification rules and determine the most effective modifier on the rule to achieve maximal utility increment. The rule with the largest utility that is still "incomplete" is first selected as the target rule for refinement. A rule is incomplete if there exists a rule modifier that can increase its utility. Once the proper knowledge modifier is decided, the corresponding samples that reflect the effects of the modifier will be presented to the student in order to guide his/her refinement process. Figure 8 shows the process of automated generation of inquiry samples.

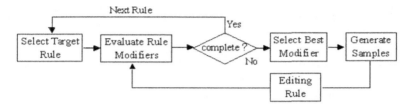

Fig. 7. Process of automated generation of inquiry samples.

We adopt the following knowledge modifiers in handling the two sources of classification errors.

(1) Some positive samples may be excluded by a rule (false negative errors) due to over-specific rule conditions and/or feature concepts. For this situation, we consider the *Condition Deletion* modifier and the *Feature Intensify* modifier. The Condition Deletion modifier tries to cover those positive samples by removing a condition of the rule, while the Feature Intensify modifier does this by increasing the matching degrees of those positive samples against a condition $F_j=v$ via intensifying the membership function of $\mu_{F_{j}=v}$. The method to intensify a feature concept is described later.

(2) Some negative samples are included by a rule (false positive errors,) due to over-general rule conditions and/or feature concepts. For this situation, we consider the *Condition Addition* modifier and the *Feature Lessen* modifier. The Condition Addition tries to rule out those negative samples by adding a new condition into the rule, while the Feature Lessen modifier does this by decreasing the matching degrees of those negative samples against a condition $F_j=v$ via lessening the membership function $\mu_{F_{j}=v}$. The method to lessen a feature concept is described later.

(3) The last rule modifier is the *Condition Change* modifier, which may change a rule condition of the form $F_j=v_1$ into $F_j=v_2$, $v_1 \neq v_2$. In some situations, the rule utility may be increased via the Condition Change modifier because some positive samples are covered and some negative samples are excluded.

For a given rule, the above five modifiers are evaluated respectively, and the modifier resulting in the maximal utility increment will be selected. Inquiry samples that best reflect the selected modifier will be generated and presented to the student. Due to the limitation of the paper size, we discuss only the feature intension and feature loosening modifiers below. To intensify a feature concept $F=v$ of a rule predicting pattern p, positive samples that are outside of the maximal potential range of the feature concept are first collected. The smallest numerical range that covers those positive samples in the feature F shapes a new range for the feature concept $F=v$. The new membership function of $F=v$ is formulated by scaling horizontally the original one along the new range. The concept of scaling membership function is depicted in figure 9. First, cut points with membership degree of 0.5 are first computed from the original membership function, which are point a and b, as shown in figure 9. Three uncovered positive samples are collected and the smallest range to cover them is [a', b']. By scaling the old membership function horizontally along its both sides such that the point a reaches point a', and point b reaches point b', we obtain a new membership function that is more strengthened and higher utilized than the old one.

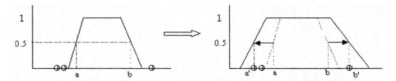

Fig. 8. An example of feature intensification by expanding the membership function.

To lessen a feature concept $F=v$ of a rule predicting pattern p, negative samples that are inside of the maximal positive range of the feature concept are first collected. The largest numerical range that covers only positive samples and none of the negative samples in the feature F forms a new range for the feature concept $F=v$. The new membership function of $F=v$ is formulated by shrinking horizontally along both sides of the original one to the new range. Figure 10 shows the basic idea of lessening membership function. First, maximal positive range of the feature concept are computed, which are point a and b, as shown in figure 10. Two covered negative samples are collected and the largest range to uncover them is [a', b']. By shrinking the old membership function horizontally along its both sides such that the point a reaches point a', and point b reaches point b', we obtain a new membership function that is more lessened and higher utilized than the old one.

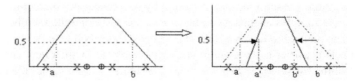

Fig. 9. An example of feature lessening by shrinking the membership function.

6 Conclusive Remarks

The knowledge refinement methods and supports developed in this research are shown to be effective in a set of simulation experiments [8]. Four teachers and four high school students were invited to test the system. Some empirical testing results show that teachers and students are highly interested in such a kind of tutoring system.

However, some students also express the frustration confronted in various high level learning activities such as making decision on selecting and defining relevant feature concepts. Response time is another issue that the users concern about. Since about 1700 samples are collected in the database, too much time was spent in evaluating the effectiveness of the knowledge modifiers, which would make the interaction responses too slow. Hence we are working on improving the knowledge evaluation process by designing faster matching algorithms, and by reducing the sample size with a reasonable amount of typical samples. In summary, the preliminary results showed that it is worthy to conduct more complete experiments to investigate the effects of the system on student's learning performance.

References

1. Goodyear, P. Teaching Knowledge and Intelligent Tutoring. ABLEX Publishing Corporation (1991) 203–229
2. Lingras, P. J., Yao, Y. Y.: Data Mining Using Extensions of the Rough Set Model. Journal of the American Society for Information Science 49(5) (1998) 415–422
3. Liu, X.: Entropy, Distance Measure and Similarity Measure of Fuzzy Sets and Their Relations. Fuzzy Sets and Systems 52 (1992) 305–318
4. Pawlak, Z.: Rough Sets. Intern. J. of Computer and Information Sciences, 11(5) (1982) 341–356
5. Pappis, C. P., Karacapilidis, N. I.: A comparative assessment of measures of similarity of fuzzy values. Fuzzy Sets and Systems 56 (1993) 171–174.
6. Wu, T.-P., Chen, S.-M.: A New Method for Constructing Membership Functions and Fuzzy Rules From Training Examples. IEEE Transactions on Systems, Man, and Cybernetics-part B 29(1) (1999) 25–40
7. Wang, F.H.: On the Design of an Intelligent Exploratory Environment for Geographic Climates on WWW. Computer Networks and ISDN Systems, 30 (1998) 699–700
8. Wang, F.-H., Hung, S.-W.: (2001). On Application of Rough Data Mining to Automatic Construction of Student Models. In: Cheung, D., Williams, G. J., Li, Q. (eds.): Advances in Knowledge Discovery and Data Mining. Lecture Notes in Artificial Intelligence, Vol. 2035. Springer-Verlag, Berlin Heidelberg New York (2001) 161–166
9. Wang., W.-J.: New Similarity Measures on Fuzzy Sets and on Elements. Fuzzy Sets and Systems 85 (1997) 305–309
10. Zadeh, L. A.: Fuzzy Sets. Information and Control 8(3) (1965) 338–353

Toward Supporting E-learning and Providing E-teaching Services for E-world

Andrzej M. Goscinski and Jackie J. Silcock

School of Information Technology
Deakin University
Geelong, Victoria, Australia

Abstract. We are entering the e-World. One special part of it is an e-University that supports e-Learning and provides e-Teaching services. Graduates must be well prepared for working in, with and through the e-World. e-Learning and e-Teaching services are necessary to support modern students learning and help academics to provide excellent teaching. This document reports on the School of Information Technology' initiatives, projects, courses and systems that lead toward e-Learning and e-Teaching in preparation of graduates for the e-World. The major lesson of our work toward supporting e-Learning and providing e-Teaching services is that the School's (the authors believe higher education) greatest asset is intellectual capital (human capital), not intellectual property.

1 Introduction

The influence of Information Technology on business, industry and the whole society is growing. Traditional ways of doing business, carrying out production processes are being changed as the result of introducing both computers and computer networks; and information technology based methodologies, techniques and procedures. A computer has become an integral part of work environments. Companies do business via the Internet. Many businesses employ people and allow them to work at homes that have a connection to the Internet. General public has started doing banking, shopping and communicating with institutions and their friends via the Internet. The world has been made smaller – the world is becoming the e-World.

Many universities in their wisdom are preparing students for the e-World; they are choosing to support students who cannot come to their campuses because of work, distance or family requirements; their decision to be competitive or being forced by financial factors have intensified their effort to support student learning processes and provide teaching services using resources, tools and methods of information technology. These universities have embarked on the development path of e-Learning and e-Teaching – the use of Internet technologies in learning and teaching. This path is complex as there is a need to not only provide basic lecture materials on the Web but also to develop new methodologies and teaching methods, which have a computer and a network in their core. Furthermore, there is a need to create a study environment for students who wish to acquire knowledge and skills far away from university campuses, when studying at home or work environment, as well as to provide support for those students who wish to come to campuses – full and flexible delivery of

W. Zhou et al. (Eds.): ICWL 2003, LNCS 2783, pp. 372–382, 2003.

courses should be provided to both groups of students. One of the problems that e-Learning and e-Teaching should solve in pursuing flexible offering of course, where there is no border between on- and off-campus study, is to create an environment of sharing a spirit of a university and being within, and working in groups, which on-campus student either appreciate or take for granted. This could only be achieved if multimedia services via broadband networks are commonly used.

University students must be well prepared and constantly enriched to take advantage of e-Teaching and participate in e-Learning and graduates must be made ready for working in, with and through the e-World.

The School of Information Technology has been one of the major creators and builders of systems leading toward e-Learning and e-Teaching, and offering through them services to prepare graduates for the e-World. This paper reports on the School's initiatives, projects, courses and systems in this area. In this document some references are made to the Deakin University wide projects leading toward some information technology infrastructure and services, as they form a basic for the School's work.

This document addresses the following issues. Firstly, it shows a relationship between e-Learning and e-Teaching; and modes of study from the School's point of view. Secondly, it presents opportunities to learn to use computing technologies that allow Deakin students to take advantage of e-Teaching and participate in e-Learning; on-campus access to hardware and software, and access to email and the Internet. Thirdly, it briefly characterizes basic tools (systems) that support students in their learning activities and teaching services of the School of Information Technology. Fourthly, it demonstrates how information and communications technologies are used in core educational processes in the School of Information Technology in support for students from disciplines other than information technology. Fifthly, it reports on opportunities for students to learn about information and communications technologies in the School's computing areas of specialization. Finally, it stresses the costs of the development and offering of e-Teaching, participating in e-Learning services and preparing Information Technology students for the e-World.

2 E-learning and E-teaching vs. Study Mode

There are two very important questions to be asked: Is it necessary to distinguish between off-campus (distant) students and on-campus (traditional) students? Which group of students is e-Learning and e-Teaching for?

Some economy and education rationalists argue that it is possible to save a lot of money having all students who study in off-campus mode, who are supported by ordinary tutors and use some study materials (learningware) developed in house (by a small group of academics, who never see students even to test their study materials) or bought somewhere. There is no need for lecture theaters, seminar rooms, laboratories and offices.

The pure off-campus model
- may be well suited to some entry level training whereas learning and hands-on laboratories still best work in a classroom setting;
- requires self discipline by the learner as a computer (PC) provides many distractions (e.g., games);

- is educationally unsound as academics who developed study materials could not test their educational features; and
- is not welcome by many students as they continue to need and want support from an academic.

Some traditionalists argue that real learning takes place in a classroom environment in the presence of and with support provided by academics. Although the pure on-campus mode may support student learning very well,
- learning is completely replaced by teaching – i.e., the student is an empty vessel waiting to be filled;
- it is expensive; and
- it does not suit all students, as some cannot come to a campus because of work or family commitments.
  Our study and experience have led us to the following conclusion:
- both modes of study can exist if Internet support is offered and academics provide efficient support;
- both modes should be mixed to save resources and to suit all groups of students, and offer flexibility throughout life-long learning of students.
  Thus, e-Learning and e-Teaching should be a natural approach to support both on-campus and off-campus students to order to offer courses in a flexible manner.

3 Opportunities for Students to Access Information and Communications Technologies

All Deakin students have the opportunity to acquire Information Technology knowledge and skills at two different levels. Basic introductory level training is provided to all students during the Orientation week. Some students may still not have been exposed to Information Technology at all previously. This training is defined by Information Technology Division and addresses use of the Deakin computer network and basic productivity skills such as using email and accessing the Internet. The training is provided by the best second and third year Computing students. In providing this training, the second and third students are given the opportunity to acquire some basic teaching skills, improve their communication skills, which are of prime importance to provide good professional services.

The second level, also offered to all Deakin students, is based on the study materials developed and tested by staff of the School of Information Technology. Through first year teaching programs students have an opportunity to gain essential information technology knowledge and computer literacy skills including use of email, accessing and using online services, word-processing, using and building spreadsheets, using and developing database management systems as well as preparing effective presentations using PowerPoint software. These computer literacy skills are becoming as necessary as reading, writing and arithmetic!

All Deakin students, in particular, off-campus students, receive a CD that contains basic software that allows them to learn about the University, IT services and access IT services provided by Deakin. Further, all Deakin students (both on- and off-campus) have 24-hour access to Deakin IT servers and laboratories. All computing laboratories comprise the latest models of PC that run Windows 98, Windows NT, Windows 2000 and Windows XP. The Deakin computers are connected by local and metropolitan networks and are also connected to the Internet.

The laboratories are located in two main types of areas: general access areas on all Deakin campuses and within the Schools of Deakin. The latter are designed to meet specialized needs and comprise specialized hardware and software. Laboratories within the School of Information Technology, which support teaching in Computer Networks, Operating Systems, Distributed Systems and Communication Security, can be disconnected from the University network to avoid any disruptions should any error occur during laboratory classes and to ensure security of the network is maintained.

Computers linked by a network are also provided in student dormitories. Students are able to use any computer in laboratories, dormitories and at home, and all these are provided with e-mail and Internet services.

4   Tools for Administrative Dealings with Students

Information Technology has become a core-enabling tool of the School of Information Technology enriching all aspects of the teaching and learning process. Students can access study guides, lecture notes, class information, assessment methods and results. Assignment tasks are available electronically; assignment solutions are submitted via networks from laboratory or home computers. Assignments are marked and returned electronically. Students communicate among themselves and with lecturers and tutors using on- and off- line computer supported communication facilities such as WebCT, FirstClass, and e-mail systems.   Unit evaluations are carried out at the end of each semester via a Web tool developed within the School. The data is processed automatically within the tool and the outcomes can be accessed, using passwords, by students, lecturers and tutors. Communication with on/off campus students is facilitated through email and other specialized teaching and learning tools such as WebCT. Students are not limited by physical locality.

5   Using Information and Communications Technologies in Support of IT Students

This includes access to learning resources by electronic means, and using electronic instructional and assessment media. Note, that providing distance education will not be regarded as an advantage per se. Evaluation of distance education will be as for any other kind of educational work: to what extent are information and communications technologies appropriately provided and used?

Some of the off campus study materials are accessible electronically by both on and off campus students, as are lecture, tutorial and other learning resources (although via restricted sites to protect intellectual property and copyright).

Computing units are delivered electronically. Students in Johannesburg, Broome, Hong Kong, Darwin, and London use the same materials as on-campus students in

Geelong or Melbourne. With two decades experience delivering units electronically, the School of Information Technology provides the same complex advanced information technology laboratory exercises to remote students on their home or work computers as on-campus students experience in laboratory sessions. Electronic meeting places allow off-campus students to mingle with each other and with on-campus students, providing depth to the educational experience that cannot be provided by student-teacher interaction alone. Students obtain rapid feedback from tutors and lecturers via email and electronic newsgroups. Electronic delivery also enhances on-campus students' education, providing twenty-four hour a day access to course materials, rapid remote access to academic staff and access and interaction with a highly diverse student population including practicing professionals from around the world. Automated computer managed learning systems provide instant feedback whenever and wherever students wish to access it.

The School's units in information technology are informed by both research and industry practice. The University has recognized the international standing of the School's research by forming a priority area of research on information technology for the information economy. The School's staff actively advises some of the nation's leading companies on the use of information technology in the e-World.

6   Opportunities for Students to Learn about IT&T

This topic includes the use of information and communications technologies as professional tools, but perhaps more importantly it focuses on learning about implications for professional practice. For example, what opportunities do business students have to learn about the 'e-commerce revolution'? Do teacher education students consider how technologies might change the delivery and character of education?

Deakin students are provided with many opportunities to learn about Information and Communications Technologies and their implications in the students' area(s) of specialization. These opportunities include:

- IT&T (computer and network) literacy, which is created in the form of single subjects (units);
- Major study in Computing/e-Systems/Multimedia Technologies;
- Bachelor courses such as the Bachelor of Computing, offered by the School of Information Technology;
- Coursework based postgraduate courses in IT&T, for instance, Graduate Diploma of Computing, Master of Information Technology; offered by the School of Information Technology;
- Research based postgraduate courses in IT&T leading to PhD and DTech (Doctor of Technology) degrees (also offered by the School of Information Technology).

In order to promote the Internet, its role and importance for education, business and industry, the School of Information Technology, as early as 1995, organized a set of workshops that comprised a 40 minute lecture and 1.5 hours laboratory (hands-on-exercises). 200 high school principles and teachers and 40 business and industry specialists attended these workshops. Such workshops are still being organized for elderly citizens, Internet groups, parents and teachers. As a follow-up, some high schools received Internet access through Deakin University. Academics and postgraduate students assisted schools and businesses to develop their home pages.

Although IT&T literacy units are geared towards teaching elementary IT skills and provide foundational IT knowledge, students from diverse disciplines are provided the opportunity of investigating the role and impact of IT in their own disciplines. This is achieved in two ways. First, by dividing a subject (unit) into two parts, IT&T oriented offerings by the School of Information Technology usually span 9 weeks and the applications and impact of IT&T on a given discipline is offered concurrently by academics from these disciplines. Secondly, it is achieved through open-ended assignments. Students nominate the topic or area they wish to investigate. While they have to meet core competency requirements of the specific unit, the contents of their final submission should reflect their home discipline interests.

Some disciplines require more than just basic knowledge and skills as provided by IT&T introductory units. For instance, health students in the Faculty of Health need knowledge and skills related to databases, engineering students in the Faculty of Science and Technology need programming knowledge and skills as well as an understanding of computer architecture and operating systems. These units are available to them through the School of Information Technology.

Students of other disciplines are encouraged to take a major study in IT&T, which comprises eight (8) units. Students of Engineering, Accounting, Commerce and Education use this approach in particular to enrich their study and be better prepared for the e-world.

Students who are interested in IT&T careers are offered the following courses:

The Bachelor of Computing, with streams in Applied Computing, Computer Science and Software Development, Information Systems and Multimedia Technology, has been re-accredited by the University and the Australian Computer Society (ACS). It satisfies the requirements for professional membership at the highest level. This course is designed to enable students to work in a professional capacity in the computing industry and any area where IT&T is used. It provides a sound foundation and up to date knowledge of computing technology, prepares students for a professional life and, at the same time, fosters continuous learning and development to efficiently address, influence and propose technology changes. The course also aims to help students develop essential workplace skills. These include problem solving skills, management of human resources and physical assets, working in groups and skills enabling students to communicate effectively with clients.

The Bachelor of Computing curriculum has been developed to innovatively and effectively embrace students' existing mastery of the e-World. The School's Introduction to Software Development unit is a typical example of this approach. The current generation of students comes to tertiary study with extensive knowledge and experience of information technology. These students have grown up in the information age. In contrast, much Information Technology education is grounded in traditions developed when computing was a novelty and most students had little knowledge of the technology. Instead of ignoring it, the School's first computer programming unit Information to Software Development leverages student's extensive knowledge of using computers. Instead of starting with the low level details of programming and programming languages, this unit starts with the familiar Windows user interface and works back from that well understood starting point to the principles, techniques and skills that underlie the development of the software. Students learn the same material as covered by traditional first programming units, but do so in a manner that integrates it into the electronic world that they know. Our experience has demonstrated that this enables students to more readily understand and master the very complex and abstract subject matter.

The curriculum for a new degree, the Bachelor of Information Technology, is currently being accredited. This new degree will have four streams: Computer Science and Software Development, e-Systems, Multimedia and Information Modeling. It is characterized by set of twelve (12) common core units, eight (8) stream core units and four (4) elective units. This course will prepare graduates for the e-World even better.

Another innovative program has also been introduced, the Bachelor of Information Technology (BIT) leading to Honours, which is designed to create elite graduates in the field of IT&T and is a joint venture between the Schools of Information Technology and Information Systems. It is expected that many of the graduates from this program will become the future IT&T leaders in Australia. As an integral component of the course, students will work with two industry sponsors during their second year, so gaining essential workplace skills that will ultimately make them very employable within an industry that has a serious skills shortage.

The Master of Information Technology (MIT) is designed to enable students to continue working in a professional capacity in business, industry and government bodies using leading edge computing technology. To this end the course, through specialized streams aims to provide up to date knowledge of recent developments in computing and network technology and at the same time foster continuous learning and development in order to efficiently address, influence and propose technology changes. Graduates will be able to perform their existing roles more effectively in business, industry, government bodies and other organizations, in order to provide better services, achieve better performance and lower costs. Through a range of teaching and learning strategies the course covers technical and theoretical foundations of topics and gives students the opportunity of applying this knowledge in practice. Students are offered a choice of units, allowing them to tailor their studies to their individual interests and needs while still meeting the academic requirements of the course.

People who wish to change their career path and professionals who have significant relevant work experience have access to the Graduate Certificate of Computing or the Graduate Diploma of Computing within the MIT course. The Graduate Diploma/Graduate Certificate of Computing enables graduates to take up IT&T related jobs in business, industry, government bodies and the education sector.

Some students, mainly those who have achieved excellent results during Honours study, enroll in research based PhD and Master Courses. Research topics of PhD and Master students reflect the "hottest" topics and research specialization of staff of the School of Information Technology, such as cluster and grid computing, data mining, parallel processing on computer clusters, e-business systems, communication risks and technologies and information technology for the information economy.

Experienced professionals from industry and businesses who satisfy the entry requirements can enroll in DTech courses. These students carry out innovative research that addresses industry and business needs generated by IT&T technologies. Students are supervised by specialists of the School of Information Technology and relevant industry or business.

The 'e-commerce revolution' is addressed within Deakin at two major levels: the technological level addressed by the School of Information Technology, and management and sociological level addressed by the School of Information Systems.

The School of Information Technology introduces the issues and solutions even in an introductory unit that is offered to all Deakin students. Students of the Bachelor of Computing program can study the e-business issues by taking units such as Information Systems in Organizations, Electronic, Business Systems, Data Mining, Distributed Systems, and Computer Security. Students of the Master of Information Technology course can specialize in e- business by taking one of the course streams that comprises four advanced units.

Not only do education students learn about the impact of IT&T on the delivery and character of education, but also all Computing students in the School of Information Technology experience the issues associated with the changing image of education and learning by enrolling in units, which are offered via the Internet. Their experience helps to shape the delivery and character of e-education by providing constructive comments and suggestions while learning in the environment. In particular, they experience that FirstClass and other communication technologies are used as learning tools to facilitate transmission of knowledge. Not only do students have to learn to navigate the tool itself initially, they also have to accommodate the limitations as well as utilizing the advantages of electronic communication. These skills are highly transportable to any computer supported collaborative work environment that is increasingly being used within large, distributed organizations. By exposing students to a range of tools, such as email, WebCT, FirstClass etc. we increase their competency with them and facilitate their acceptance and use of new tools.

7 Specializations in Aspects of the E-world

The 1996 edition of the Good Universities Guide listed just three specializations (with a total of three courses) in the broad area of e-commerce, the Internet, and multimedia. The current edition lists 14 specializations ranging from desktop publishing and electronic commerce to interactive multimedia and network publishing, with dozens of courses. How is the University positioning itself in relation to this kind of curriculum innovation?

Computing courses offered by the School of Information Technology directly cover the areas of e-commerce, Internet, and multimedia.

- e-commerce issues are dealt with at the technological and risk areas in units of the Bachelor of Computing. In particular, the current Information Systems stream comprises Information Systems in Organizations, Electronic Business Systems, Data Mining, Distributed Systems; and Computer Security. Advanced units that cover the above subjects are offered in the Graduate Diploma of Computing course. One area of specialization of the Master of Information Technology is devoted to e-commerce;

- The Internet is covered in an introductory unit offered by the School of Information Technology. Students who enroll in this unit acquire knowledge of communication via the Internet, its basic services such as WWW, email, file transfer and have the opportunity of hands on experience with these tools. The Internet is addressed at the advanced level in the computer network unit.

Furthermore, students learn how to program internet-based, distributed applications using the Java programming language. The issues of the Internet are also addressed in the Distributed Systems unit. The impact of this network and its technologies on business, industry and society are addressed in these and other units, in particular, when e-commerce topics are dealt with. One stream of the Master of Information Technology stream is devoted toward network computing, where the Internet is a major area of interest from the point of view, of both technology and its impact on business, industry and society.

- Multimedia Technology is one of the four streams of the Bachelor of Computing course. Students are offered the opportunity to acquire knowledge and skills that allow them to design and develop multimedia applications, use networks to support such applications and understand the impact of this technology on business and industry activities.

8   Challenges of E-learning and E-teaching

Some believe that a university can became a university of the 21st century, and eventually an e-University, if there is a uniform infrastructure based on basic PC- and 100Mbps network infrastructure, some services for administrative dealings with students, some good editorial services, and Web based materials for individual course units. Some academics believe that the changes underway within universities and higher education are strictly about putting content on-line. They also fear that they will not be needed anymore. That would be a fast and very inexpensive solution.

However, the achievement of e-Learning and e-Teaching and the preparation of students for the e-World are much more complicated and expensive. This is because there is a need for the following three elements:

- a very high quality computer and network infrastructure to be provided by telecommunication companies;
- appropriate prioritization and investment strategy of a university, which are needed to synthesize new learning and teaching methodology, develop and/or purchase software and equipment, employ new academic and support staff who are able to build necessary systems and offer services to students; and
- high quality academics and support staff.
  Here we only address the last two elements.
  Students (off- campus as well as on-campus) these days expect much more than on-line access to unit materials and communication with their lecturers via e-mail. Furthermore, it is possible for students to use "learningware" for self study, however, the majority of them, even as our experience shows, will continue to need and want support from academics. There is a need to provide interactive web sites that could enhance students' learning. Also, "anyplace-anytime" technologies are needed to provide flexibility and support to life long learning of students.

Dealing with students and their learning problems on-line requires excellent knowledge of a study material and learning techniques as well as web site support tools. Students wish to participate in meetings and this opportunity must be created. This requires both excellent on-line conference environment and skills, which must be exploited by academics to support different kinds of meetings (e.g., tutorial-type, brainstorming, problem solving).

We have academics, offices, laboratories – we will continue to have them even when the changes underway would reach the state of e-Learning and e-Teaching. In particular, we will need excellent academics that would be able to find ways and implement them for themselves and their professional colleagues to make instruction more about learning and less about teaching.

This leads to another issue, which is how to "keep on board" academics that have initiated and continue to make possible the changes leading toward e-Learning and e-Teaching. They are able to identify the productivity of instruction from the point of view what is learned, how long it takes to learn and at what cost. They are our greatest assets.

We have achieved a lot in carrying out projects leading toward e-Learning and e-Teaching. However, we know little about how students learn when they use and are supported by these new technologies. Furthermore, while we have embraced these new technologies there has been no time to develop a culture for the e-World.

9 Conclusion

Whether we like it or not we will become a part of the e-World, in particular by becoming an e-University. Our contribution to building it is through the provision of an environment that offers e-Learning opportunities to students and provides e-Teaching services.

The School has learned that the development of an e-Learning and e-Teaching environment is expensive and cannot be seen as something that could be supported by basic infrastructure and putting unit content on-line. It requires vision, good planning, leadership, some enthusiasts of e-Learning and e-Teaching, support of academics, technical and administrative staff, and a lot of work

The School of Information Technology is on an excellent path, based on well-defined plans that leads toward e-Learning and e-Teaching. Our experience shows that e-Learning and e-Teaching is for students who study in both modes of study, on-campus and off-campus. The School has acquired, developed and efficiently used tools (systems) that support students in their e-Learning activities and academics in providing e-Teaching services. Academics of the School use information and communications technologies in core educational processes in support for students from disciplines other than information technology. Despite the fact that Computing is a laboratory discipline academics and technicians of the School have developed information and communications systems that create excellent opportunities for students to e-learn about information and communications technologies in computing areas of specialization. As the outcome of these initiatives and work, students that take our courses and units are well prepared to work in the e-World.

It is important for all academics who wish to embark on projects involving e-Teaching and e-Learning to distinguish between the electronic delivery of a large number of documents to students and teaching of students. The delivery of documents ignores the large role played by the sharing of inferred knowledge that occurs in face-to-face lectures, tutorials and discussions between academics and students [1]. We need to examine ways to capture and replicate this type of teaching and learning in an e-Environment. We would all do well to consult educationalists on this.

Academics need to evaluate these teaching methods and compare the success of these students and their reaction to this environment with the face-to-face environment in order to improve the student's learning experience and outcomes. In particular, we need to examine the learning outcomes for cohorts of students from different backgrounds and age ranges in order to identify different requirements of different students. In the School of Information Technology we have long accepted only student who are older than twenty one years old for off-campus units. Anecdotal evidence suggests that these more mature students are more successful when studying in an independent and electronic environment.

What we have re-learned now, when carrying our work toward e-Learning and e-Teaching, is that the School's (the authors believe higher education) greatest asset is intellectual capital (human capital), not intellectual property. Education cannot exist without human communication and resource sharing – the Internet provides excellent leverage for both of them. The School has embarked on the e-Learning and e-Teaching path and demonstrated that student learning and our teaching have been greatly improved due to the computer and Internet based services. However, the School cannot be asked to spend more time and go for the next step toward e-Learning and e-Teaching unless there is a real support to do this. This is not one group of academics and support staff individual game – it is an institutional game. Furthermore, the benefits of e-Teaching and e-Learning should be looked at very critically. This issue has also been addressed by other researchers e.g., [2].

References

[1]   Veljko M. Milutinovic, Nikola Skundric, Will Distance Learning Create a Global University? IEEE Computer 36(3): 98–100 (2003).
[2]   Charles A. Shoniregun, Sarah-Jane Gray, Is E-learning Really the Future or a Risk? Ubiquity (10) (April 29 – May 5, 2003).

A Framework for Evaluation of Learning Effectiveness in Online Courses

Alan Y.K. Chan, K.O. Chow, and Weijia Jia

Department of Computer Science,
City University of Hong Kong, Hong Kong
{csachan, cspchow, itjia}@cityu.edu.hk

Abstract. One of the hottest research topics today in higher education is E-Learning. Different issues and challenges such as pedagogical, technological, social, cultural, ethical and economical have been addressed in this context by many researchers. While online courses have always been a common approach to E-Learning, it is essential to develop some measurements in the form of quality assurance systems in order to reflect their learning effectiveness and improve the quality of teaching and learning. Therefore, a framework for evaluation of learning effectiveness in online courses is proposed in this article. A case study is presented to illustrate the use of the framework in a study programme. Finally, possible improvements and future directions of the framework are discussed in the conclusion.

1 Introduction

This article is about the evaluation of learning effectiveness in online courses. Section 2 describes the framework for evaluation of learning effectiveness in online courses, highlighting the implementation of online courses, the factors in learning effectiveness, the approach to evaluation methods and the implications of evaluation results. Section 3 is a case study that illustrates the use of the framework in a study programme. Section 4 concludes the article with a summary and a discussion about possible improvements and future research directions.

1.1 E-learning Trends

The rapid growth of the Internet and other emerging technologies has brought a new era of E-Learning in higher education. There are an increasing number of these technologies used to enrich the learning experience in higher education. Online courses have always been a common approach to E-Learning. Online courses provide an active learning environment and this shift in learning process can transform pedagogy with the use of online technologies. Many higher education institutions have been delivering online courses in conjunction with traditional classroom in their efforts to

W. Zhou et al. (Eds.): ICWL 2003, LNCS 2783, pp. 383–395, 2003.

improve learning effectiveness. However, online courses should not be viewed as another means of accessing the same materials and methods used to present in a traditional classroom [1]. It requires a different array of preparation, infrastructure, technical support, technology expertise, and course methodology [2]. Careful considerations of the use of supporting technologies in online courses would encourage learning and improve students' performance. In order to demonstrate the learning effectiveness in online courses, it is essential to develop some measurements in the form of quality assurance systems. Course evaluation is one of the essential educational delivery components to improve the quality of teaching and learning [3]. It can be used to evaluate the effectiveness in teaching and learning. Examples of course evaluation include questionnaires, databases and log files which are often used to capture data from users about their perceptions and learning activities within the online courses. Analysis of these evaluation results would help instructors to refine their teaching strategies and methods, thus enhance the quality of teaching and learning.

1.2   Framework Outline

The outline of the framework for evaluation of learning effectiveness in online courses is shown in figure 1 below. The framework consists of four major components, namely online courses, learning effectiveness, evaluation methods and evaluation results, which are described in detail in section 2. The processes between each component within the framework include implementation, feedback, analysis and implications, which are illustrated in the case study in section 3.

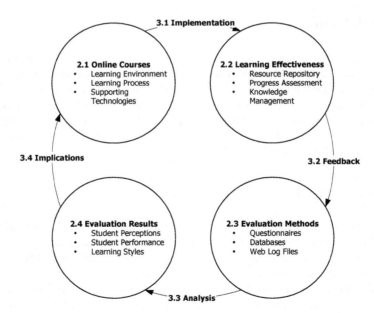

Fig. 1. Framework for evaluation of learning effectiveness in online courses

2 Online Course Evaluation Framework

This section describes the four underlying components of the online course evaluation framework, namely online courses, learning effectiveness, evaluation methods and evaluation results.

2.1 Online Courses

Online courses differ from traditional classroom in many aspects. Their differences in terms of learning environment and learning process are discussed. With the emerging Internet technologies in recent years, a growing number of e-learning software systems are being developed and used in higher education. Supporting technologies in online courses such as learning management system, synchronous/asynchronous communication, content management and student portfolios are also described in this sub-section.

Learning Environment. Online courses support high quality learning by offering different kinds of environments such as synchronous or asynchronous or both. Some environments and approaches facilitates student learning while others impede it [4]. For example, computer-mediated communication such as threaded discussion cannot effectively substitute for certain specific properties of voice communication, especially the intimacy and the spontaneity of response [5]. A traditional classroom only provides a face-to-face learning environment where instructors can direct and take active immediate role in class at a fixed time and place. In online courses, both instructors and students can teach and learn regardless of time and location. Online courses provide alternative opportunities for current on-campus students to take classes that they could not take otherwise due to time conflicts with other courses or work [5].

Learning Process. Learning process can be self-paced, independent, collaborative and continuous in online courses. In traditional classroom, it is often instructional where the instructors transfer the knowledge directly to the students. It does not reflect the students' understanding of the knowledge effectively. However, the dynamic nature in the online courses supports better communication such as self-reflections and peer-to-peer reviews. This change in communication transforms the learning process where knowledge is constructed actively by cognition [6].

Supporting Technologies. Learning management system (LMS) is one of the most mentioned E-Learning technologies. LMS is defined as a distinct, pedagogically meaningful and comprehensive system by which learners and faculty can participate in the learning and instructional process at anytime and any place [7]. For example, WebCT, one of the well-known LMS developed by the Department of Computer Science at the University of British Columbia, is a web-based application to create an online learning environment. WebCT is a powerful tool designed to create a versatile

OLE and has become rich in both features and usage [8]. It can be used to create an entire online course or to publish materials that supplement courses that use an online component [9].

Synchronous and Asynchronous communications are important features in LMS. Synchronous communication can be achieved with the use of Chat room and White-board where instructors and students interact with each other at real time. Asynchronous communication is supported with the use of threaded discussion and internal mail. These tools can promote text-based communication. The opportunity for reflective interaction can be encouraged and supported, which is a feature not often demanded in traditional classroom settings where discussion is often spontaneous and lacks the reflection that is a characteristic of asynchronous online interactions [1]. Collaboration and discussion are advantageous in LMS because they make students more central to the learning process [10]. Active interaction and participation are essential for both instructors and students to enhance their learning experiences, which cannot be achieved in a traditional classroom.

Content management capability of the LMS must be able to organize different kinds of content materials of the online course such as teaching and learning instructions, lesson objectives, multimedia video and audio clips, hyperlink and book references and glossaries, etc. The development of these web-based materials should be of high quality in order to encourage students to learn online. Support staff for content development may be required because instructors may not have the expertise and skills to create these content materials. A team approach is recommended for the creation of web-based materials [11] where instructor is the designer and support staff is the developer of the content materials.

Access logs and databases of the LMS provide a powerful tool in capturing the students' activities and their learning process in the online courses. These data can be analyzed and presented in the student portfolios, which are the development of learning resources such as questions, writing notes, homework, self-reflection and diary [12]. Student Portfolios allow instructors to better understand the progress of the students, thus improve instructions and guide their learning.

2.2 Learning Effectiveness

Online courses offer a new opportunity to deliver education with an aim to improve quality of teaching and learning. Online courses provide a different kind of learning environment for instructors and students. They can be accessed regardless of time and location. They also provide new learning tools that cannot be found in a traditional classroom. However, it is not to say that online courses can replace the traditional classroom. The hybrid approach may be used to enhance the learning experience when proper teaching and learning strategies are applied. This sub-section describes the learning effectiveness in online courses, particularly resource repository, progress assessment and knowledge management.

Resource Repository. There are many different kinds of learning resources on the Internet such as reference links, online glossary and dictionary. These resources can be high-quality, multimedia, web-based materials consisting of video clip and Flash animation. They can surely encourage students to learn other than reading text from lecture notes and books. The use of hyperlinks and search engines can effectively organize these resources in online courses. Instructors and students can access in a timely manner and evaluate the usefulness of these different learning resources.

Progress Assessment. Student portfolios can be used to track the students' progress in online courses, evaluate their performance and promote learning outcomes [12]. Student portfolios consist of activities such as interaction in chat room, participation in discussion forum, reading in online materials, reflection to learning resources, etc. They provide a collection of the students' work assembled over a period of time. They encourage the critical thinking and decision making of the students and provide an effective communication channel and media for them to interact with others.

Knowledge Management. Discussions and ideas are not recorded in a traditional classroom. This type of implicit knowledge is important in learning. The communication tools such as threaded forum and chat room in online courses provide a convenient method to capture this knowledge. Instructors can moderate the discussion with immediate and consistent feedback. This will encourage the students to participate actively and improve the quality of learning.

2.3 Evaluation Methods

Evaluation of learning effectiveness in online courses can help instructors to refine their teaching strategies, thus enhance the quality of learning. It is necessary to develop some measurements in the form of quality assurance systems in order to demonstrate the learning effectiveness in online courses. In this sub-section, several evaluation methods such as questionnaires, databases and web log files are discussed.

Questionnaires. Questionnaires are widely adopted in course evaluation to capture information about learning experience from students. For example, they are used to evaluate the usefulness of learning resources [13], the effect of asynchronous discussion forum [14] and the adaptation of learning tools in LMS [15]. The design of the questionnaires to evaluate the learning effectiveness in online courses should focus on three aspects, namely the impacts on teaching and learning (Process), the involvement of instructors and students (People) and the capabilities of online tools in LMS (Technology).

Databases. Databases are primarily used in online courses to store data and information such as learning resources, discussion topics and their relationships to the students. The presentation of data extracted from the databases can be organized into the format of student portfolios to allow instructors to keep track of the students' learning progress. For example, student portfolios are developed using frames (functions) such as reports, notes, questions, homework, self-reflections, agendas, plans and journals, which are stored in databases [12]. Thus, the records and their relationships in the databases can be built into student portfolios for evaluating the learning effectiveness in online courses.

Web Log Files. One of the criteria of learning effectiveness in online courses is the availability of the LMS platform. Most LMS platforms are running in a web server such as Apache and IIS. In order to effectively manage a web server, it is necessary to obtain feedback about the activity and performance of the web server as well as any problems that may be occurring. Most of the web servers provide very comprehensive and flexible logging capabilities such as access log. The logging mechanism is quite complicated and will not be discussed in this article. The server access log records all requests processed by the server, including information such as the IP address of the clients, the date and time of the requests, the location and the referrer of the resources.

2.4 Evaluation Results

The analysis results from the evaluation methods can reflect the learning effectiveness in online courses. These results have implications for the overall effective design of learning strategies, policies and online tools. Implications of student perceptions, student performance and learning styles are discussed in this sub-section.

Student Perceptions. The feedback of the students from the questionnaires can provide an in-depth understanding of their perceptions of learning effectiveness in online courses such as the ease of use and accessibility of the LMS, the organization of course content, the usefulness of online tools and other comments about the impacts on their learning. These perceptions can be used to refine the teaching and learning strategies and to enhance the functionalities of online tools, thus improving the quality of learning.

Student Performance. The development of student portfolios to track their learning progress allows instructors to monitor their performance and ability in critical thinking and decision making. The assessment of the student progress allows instructors to refine their short-term learning goals and re-align student learning in the right direction.

Learning Styles. The access frequency and sequence from the analysis of web log files provide a good indication of how students adapt the learning style in online courses. For example, the access sequence of online tools may indicate their importance to learning effectiveness. Understanding the students' learning styles can not only provide an individualized instruction satisfying their diverse needs, but also carry a more equitable evaluation in online courses [16].

3   Case Study: Online Courses in a Study Programme

This section presents a case study to illustrate the use of the proposed framework. The case study describes the processes of evaluation in a study programme where online courses have been implemented as a supporting component in conjunction with tradition classrooms in their efforts to improve learning effectiveness.

3.1   Implementation

A course template was developed and organized into eight functions, namely Information, Schedule, Download, Content, Reference Link, Glossary & Online Dictionary, Discussion and Assessment. The course template was used in each of the online courses. This would save time and effort for setting up the course structure and allow consistency in user interface of each course. The content materials were prepared in advance before it became available to students. The update of content materials was an ongoing and continuous process in order to reflect any changes in the online courses. Table 1 describes the details of each function. Figure 2 below illustrates the design of the course template.

3.2   Feedback

The target group of users for the online courses was the year-one and year-two students from a part-time study programme. A questionnaire to evaluate the effectiveness of the online courses was conducted. The response rate in both classes was around 67% (see Table 2). The purpose of the questionnaire was to evaluate the usage frequency, the LMS, the organization and the functional effectiveness of the online courses.

3.3   Analysis

The student usage of the online courses is summarized in Table 3. At least 90% of the students have accessed the online courses with average login over 100. The technical support for students using online courses was minimal as they are good in computer literacy. The participation in the discussion forum was not active. The results show that the average number of articles posted and read were insignificant when compared to the class size. The forums were not moderated and the instructors were passive and did not provide timely response. Thus, collaboration and interaction among students were not encouraged. It is essential that the instructors take the initiative and keep the discussion flow going in the asynchronous environment.

Table 1. Description of functions in online courses

Function Name	Description
Information	Displays the details of the course such as syllabus, outline, contacts of lecturer and tutor, textbooks and reference books.
Schedule	Consists of a timetable and a calendar. The timetable outlines the details of the lectures and tutorials. The calendar was a tool from the LMS showing all the announcements such as public holidays and academic events.
Content	Provides web-based multimedia course materials. Students could browse the online notes using a tree-like table of content. Learning tools such as forum, glossary and links can be attached to each chapter of the online notes.
Download	Allows instructor to disseminate their lecture slides, tutorial handouts and recommended articles.
Reference Link	Serves as a bookmark for the course. Lecturer-reviewed websites are listed here to allow students to access course-related information.
Glossary & Online Dictionary	Serves as a reference material for students to look up technical terms.
Discussion	Consists of threaded forum, chat room and whiteboard. It allows the instructors and the students to interact and communicate asynchronously and synchronously.
Assessment	Consists of Assignment, Quiz and Self Test. Students can submit their homework online. Instructors can conduct survey and short quiz to evaluate the student performance.

Fig. 2. Design of the course template

Table 2. Response rate of the questionnaire

	# Students	# Response	% Response
Year I	66	44	67%
Year II	47	32	68%
Total	113	76	67%

Table 3. Student usage in online courses

	Course				
	A	B	C	D	E
Number of Students	68	68	67	46	113
Students accessed	68	66	61	46	113
Access ratio	100%	97%	91%	100%	100%
Total login	12119	9753	8950	6386	3377
Average login	178	148	147	139	30
Total articles posted	0	0	7	12	0
Average articles posted	0	0	0.1	0.3	0
Total articles read	0	53	365	416	0
Average articles read	0	0.8	6	9	0

Usage Frequency. The result shows that students frequently access the online courses while they are attending lectures and tutorials in classroom. Table 4 summaries the usage of the online courses. Over 60% of the students spent more than one hour per week. Over 50% of the students accessed the online courses at least five times per week.

Table 4. Usage frequency

Hours spent per week		Number of accesses per week	
Hours	Percentage	Frequency	Percentage
0 – 1	34.2%	0 – 2	19.7%
1 – 2	42.1%	3 – 4	22.4%
2 – 3	9.2%	5 – 6	17.1%
3 – 4	5.3%	7 – 8	14.5%
> 4	9.2%	> 8	26.4%

Learning Management System. A LMS is used to support the delivery of the online courses. Over 80% of the students felt that the LMS is user friendly and easily accessible on the Internet. It is important that the LMS provides a functional and stable environment to encourage students' participation. Table 5 summaries the evaluation of the LMS in the online courses.

Table 5. Learning management system (LMS)

	Very Easy	Easy	Fairly Difficult	Difficult	Very Difficult
Ease of Use	21.1%	61.8%	14.5%	2.6%	0.0%
Accessibility	19.7%	61.8%	6.6%	7.9%	3.9%

Course Effectiveness and Organization. More than 80% of the students found the effectiveness and the organization of the online courses were better than average. Table 6 summaries the evaluation of the effectiveness and organization of the online courses. Online courses allow students an alternative mean to access information about the course when students cannot attend lectures and tutorials due to time conflicts. They also provide extra learning tools that cannot be achieved in classroom. Good organization is needed in order to be more effective in online courses.

Table 6. Course effectiveness and organization

	Very Good	Good	Average	Bad	Very Bad
Course Effectiveness	3.9%	38.2%	46.1%	10.5%	1.3%
Course Organization	3.9%	19.7%	64.5%	9.2%	2.6%

Functional Effectiveness. The functions in the online courses can be divided into three categories, namely Content, Communication and Assessment. The result shows that Content functions are more effective than Communication functions, which in term are more effective than Assessment functions. Table 7 summaries the evaluation of the effectiveness of the functions in the online courses.

Table 7. Functional effectiveness

	Strongly Agree	Agree	Disagree	Strongly Disagree	N/A
Content	3.9%	71.1%	15.8%	2.6%	6.6%
Communication	2.6%	50.0%	28.9%	13.2%	5.3%
Assessment	0.0%	44.7%	36.8%	13.2%	5.3%

Comments. The positive comment about the online courses is that they allow self-paced studying, provide centralized learning resources and can be accessed at anytime and any place. However, a lack of high quality web-based content materials and inadequate response from instructors discourage students using online courses. Moreover, the students found the study load had not been decreased with the use of online courses.

3.4 Implications

The evaluation results show that there is a high access ratio of students and the online courses are effective and well organized. The LMS platform is user-friendly and easily accessible. The content tools are used more often than the communication and the assessment tools. There is a lack of high quality web-based content and inadequate responses from instructor. The workload has not been decreased with the use of online courses. The implications of these results are discussed below.

Enhance the Value of Learning Resources. Students frequently access the learning resources such as lecture notes in online courses. However, these resources from traditional classroom should be viewed as reference materials. It is essential to develop high-quality, interactive, multimedia, web-based learning content to encourage students' learning. Instructor's recommended learning resources such as articles, journals, papers and reference links can be useful readings for students. A mechanism to review these resources by students can also increase their values and students' participation.

Utilize Other Online Tools. Instructors mainly use the online courses to distribute their teaching materials. That is why the content tools are accessed more often than the communication and the assessment tools. They can use the assessment tools to allow students doing assignments online. This will reduce their workload from marking the assignments.

Develop a Knowledge Forum. Inadequate responses from instructors result in low participation from students in the discussion forum. Instructors can take an initiative role and define learning topics for students to post their comments and opinions. This will encourage students to express their thoughts and create a knowledge base about the topics. When students cannot attend classes, they can access the forums and keep up-to-date with others.

4 Conclusion

This article describes a framework for evaluation of learning effectiveness in online courses and illustrates the use of the framework with a case study. It also highlights the implementation of online courses, the issues in learning effectiveness, the approach to evaluation methods and the implications of evaluation results. From the case study, a lack of online tools for developing student portfolios restricts the assessment of student progress and performance. Students' learning styles are also not reflected due to insufficient information from the web log files.

Based on the current framework, possible improvements may include the development of standard templates for evaluation questionnaire and the use of Web Mining techniques on web log file to explore new knowledge about learning effectiveness in online courses. The framework may also be adopted for the evaluation of teaching effectiveness in online courses for further research directions.

References

1. Rovai, P., Online and traditional assessments: what is the difference?, The Internet and Higher Education, 3(3), 2000, 141–151.
2. Monolescu, D., Schifter, C., Online Focus Group: A Tool to Evaluate Online Students' Course Experience, The Internet and Higher Education, 2(2-3), 2000, 171–176.
3. Reid, C., Reflections on using the Internet for the evaluation of course delivery, The Internet and Higher Education, 4(1), 2001, 61–75.
4. Lieblein, E., Critical factors for successful delivery of online programs, The Internet and Higher Education, 3(3), 2000, 161–174.
5. Schifter, C., Teaching in the 21st Century, The Internet and Higher Education, 1(4), 1999, 281–290.
6. Cheng, C.C., Construction and Evaluation of a Web-Based Learning Portfolio System: An Electronic Assessment Tool, Innovations in Education and Teaching International, 38(2), 2001, 144–155.
7. Dringus, L., & Terell, S., The framework for directed online learning environments, The Internet and Higher Education, 2(1), 1999, 55–67.
8. Clark, J., A product review of WebCT, The Internet and Higher Education, 5(1), 2002, 79–82.
9. Kaiden, R., A review of WebCT, The Internet and Higher Education, 5(4), 2002, 399-404.
10. Clark, J., Stimulating collaboration and discussion in online learning environments, The Internet and Higher Education, 4(2), 2001, 119–124.
11. Savenye, C., Olina, Z., Niemczyk, M., So you are going to be an online writing instructor: Issues in designing, developing, and delivering an online course, Computers and Composition, 18(4), 2001, 371–385.

12. Chen, G.D., Liu, C.C., Ou, K.L., Lin, M.S., Web Learning Portfolios: A Tool For Supporting Performance Awareness, Innovations in Education and Teaching International, 38(1), 2000, 19–30.
13. Brown, M., Doughty, G., Draper, S., Henderson, F., McAteer, E., Measuring Learning Resource Use, Computers and Education, 27(2), 1996, 103–113.
14. Vonderwell, S., An examination of asynchronous communication experiences and perspectives of students in an online course: a case study, The Internet and Higher Education, 6(1), 2003, 77–90.
15. Grabe, M., Sigler, E., Studying online: evaluation of an online study environment, Computers and Education, 38(4), 2002, 375–383.
16. Lee, M.G., Profiling students' adaptation styles in Web-based learning, Computers and Education, 36(2), 2001, 121–132.

Incorporating Motivational Elements in a Web-Based Learning Environment for Distance Students: A Malaysian Experience

Zoraini Wati Abas

International Medical University, Sesama Centre, Plaza Komanwel, Bukit Jalil,
57000 Kuala Lumpur, Malaysia
zwabas@imu.edu.my, zwabas@pc.jaring.my

Abstract. The Internet has prompted educational institutions world wide to deliver their distance learning programmes via the Web. Malaysian institutions are following suit. However, the success of Web-based distance learning programmes is largely dependent on how well we keep the students sufficiently interested, energized and enthusiastic to complete the degree requirements. There are techniques that designers and instructors can use to make the virtual learning environment attractive and meaningful. As such, the virtual learning team at the International Medical University developed a motivation model based on Horton's recommendations for a motivating environment to help sustain the students' interest. VENuS (Virtual Education for Nursing Sciences) was developed not only using the systematic model of instructional design but had also applied the motivation model. The paper describes the application of the model and highlights the feedback received on the prototype.

1 Introduction

There are tens of thousands of distance learning courses offered by educational institutions around the world. It appears to be the trend. Many institutions are using the Internet to reach out to their students. The technologies most often incorporated include the World Wide Web and communication tools such as threaded discussions, chat rooms, electronic blackboards and electronic mail (e-mail). In short, online distance learning, has gone virtual to reach out to wider groups of audiences in far away places. And, distance learning is popular among working adults because it provides them the flexibility in obtaining a degree or to upgrade their paper qualifications.

However, in spite of the promises and potential benefits offered by the Internet, not all virtual learning environments have included some of the essential pedagogical elements necessary to help keep the student numbers in. As Sir John Daniel, the Vice Chancellor of The Open University once stated, "Much of the commercial hype and hope about distance learning is based on a very unidirectional conception of instruction, where teaching is merely presentation, and learning is merely absorption. The Open University's experience with two million students over 25 years suggests that

W. Zhou et al. (Eds.): ICWL 2003, LNCS 2783, pp. 396–410, 2003.

such an impoverished notion of distance education will fail – or at least have massive drop-out problems." [1]. And, as Jackson and Anagnostopoulou found in their review of current research, online approaches should not dictate pedagogical changes [2]. The pedagogy employed in virtual learning environments appears to be the principal variable affecting the nature and quality of teaching. Hence, in the effort to design and develop a virtual learning environment for the International Medical University (IMU), past efforts and experiences were reviewed so as not to repeat mistakes. Instead, an effort was made to look for the best of recommendations.

1.1   Distance Learning in Malaysia

The most widely known distance-learning programme in Malaysia is that offered by the University Science of Malaysia (USM) for more than the past twenty years. It is today, still, largely tradition-based using print and a small portion of ICT or the Internet. However, the newer Malaysian universities such as Unitar (Universiti Tun Abdul Razak) established about six years ago and the Open University of Malaysia (OUM), established about two years ago, have incorporated the Internet in a significant way to deliver their distance learning programmes.

Other universities (a total of 16 public and 21 private universities) are quickly following suit to meet an increasing demand for distance learning among Malaysian adults as they seek to gain additional qualification while working or while waiting for the country's economic situation to improve. This growing demand has led to a marked increase in the number of distance programmes offered by both the public and private colleges in Malaysia. It is to be noted that locally, the popularity of Internet has grown exponentially in the last decade. The number of Malaysian Internet users has risen from a few hundred to over four million out of a population of 24.79 million people.

1.2   Distance Learning for Malaysian Nurses

Recently, the Malaysian government announced that at least ten percent of the 32,000 non-graduate nurses [3] in the country needs to be upgraded and has urged the nurses to obtain a Bachelor's degree in nursing while working. This has prompted the International Medical University (IMU) to help meet the ministry's needs by offering the programme via distance. Distance learning is believed to be most appropriate because in-service nurses are generally unable to secure study leave or to obtain a leave of absence from work due to the severe shortage of nurses in Malaysia. The health ministry is thus expectant that the solution is in the form of distance learning programme. The upgrading of the nursing profession will provide better quality nurses and will help meet the more sophisticated demands from the public for better quality healthcare and also to support a thriving healthcare industry.

In view of the advantages offered by the Internet, a web-based learning environment was designed for the nursing programme at the IMU. This mode of learning is also expected to contribute to the Malaysian government's National Information Technology Agenda (NITA) to help spur the development of the K-based economy. It is thus also perceived that the nursing profession will benefit more from their exposure to an online learning environment. All the new hospitals that have been recently built or being built will be equipped with the latest in technology and will be paperless. Hence, it is even more imperative to develop a group of nurses who will champion the use of ICT as well as establish an ICT using culture where they work [4].

2 Design of the Virtual Learning Environment

Designing an effective virtual learning environment for any form of learning is both an art and a science. It requires the understanding of sound learning principles and the selection of only the appropriate technologies. According to Alexander and Boud, for example, much of the potential of online learning is being lost because too much of the pedagogy of online learning has been transferred unreflectively from didactic traditional teaching where the computer substitutes for the teacher and textbook as conveyors of information [5].

It is important to ask, "How can instructors exploit technology to promote improved learning?" Another important question is "What is it that we want to do and how will technology support it?" It should not be a situation where looking at the capabilities of the technology, we determine how the learning process should be fitted in. An example is where class notes or a videotaped lecture is transferred to the Internet. What is more important is the strength of teacher-student and student-student interactions, how students are engaged in the learning process, particularly in collaborative learning [6]. The latter is where communication tools such as threaded discussions can be effectively used.

To a certain extent, the wide availability of Learning Management Systems (LMS) such as Blackboard, Top Class, Lotus Learning Space and WebCT has made the task of designing virtual learning environments somewhat easier. Creators are prompted to include certain sections in the virtual learning environment that would support the pedagogical needs of distance students. This includes features or sections such as course content, e-discussions, chat, e-mail, whiteboard, self-assessments, grading information and calendar. However, these are mere tools. They will only be effective if the designer and instructor can employ the tools to support good pedagogical principles and to provide the motivation distance students require.

For a virtual learning environment to succeed in meeting the needs of distance learning, it must be attractive, motivating and meaningful. How the designer and instructor incorporate teaching, learning tasks, activities, content, information or communicate any other curricular related matters to the student will make a huge difference. The significance of creating an environment that attracts, motivates and provides for meaningful learning is especially important to keep attrition rates low. As Horton suggests, it is important that instructional designers, web developers and instructors use techniques to keep students interested, energized and enthusiastic [7]. It is not about using the best or the latest technology. It is about choosing the most appropriate technology that will support the various pedagogical requirements so that we can incorporate, within it, features to achieve effective learning using motivational techniques recommended by Horton. In short, a motivating environment is particularly important in the case of distance students to help keep attrition rates low.

2.1 Design Guidelines

Virtual learning environments should have high standards of quality but it must also be easily accessible, motivating and provide interactivity for students [8]. The need to achieve the balance between these elements is clear but not so easy to achieve. While most technology platforms are able to support the most sophisticated elements such as video clips, animation, sound effects, music, voiceovers, photographs and drawings, they may not necessarily be the key elements required to succeed. What is the use of having multimedia files if students have slow access to the Internet and find the time taken to download and finally view these files take too long and hence frustrating? Similarly, what is the use of providing collaborative learning opportunities when students and instructors are unaware of the value, unsure of the process and benefits?

For web-based courses, elements that must be accounted for in the overall design are in the following six areas: administrivia (e.g. syllabi, schedules, contact information, course objectives and expectations), course content (e.g. textbooks, readings, lectures, video/audio tapes, graphics and images), interaction (between student and instructor and among students), additional learning resources, monitoring of the learning process and final assessment of attainment of course learning objectives [9].

Horton states that for students to succeed in distance learning, self-discipline and motivation plays a key role. He found that dropout rates are as high as 85%. It implies that we cannot assume that all students will come properly motivated or continue to be motivated as they move from one course to another or from one semester to another. In fact Horton observes that web-based learning demands high levels of motivation and this means a virtual learning environment must motivate students. The instructional design team must consciously plan to include high levels of motivation as they develop the web-based learning system. Horton believes that motivation is a key element that will contribute to a student's success in the distance-learning environment. In the review of the literature, many others in the field echo this [10]. Hence, the focus of this paper is on providing the motivational aspects in the virtual learning environment.

Preparation of the learning environment and materials for distance learning is usually the task of an instructional development team comprising at the very minimum; an instructional designer, a web developer, graphic/multimedia artist and subject-matter expert. The instructional designer applies the universal ADDIE (Analyze, Design, Develop, Implement, Evaluate) instructional design model. While the ADDIE model is a widely adopted universal model for the development of learning materials, sound pedagogy need to be employed during the process of developing a virtual learning environment such as VENuS at the IMU. This is where Horton had the most impact on the author who is the instructional designer, during the process of designing VENuS. It is without a doubt that good instructional design of web-based education significantly improves what instructors deliver to students and enhances learning objectives. While different learning objectives require different learning strategies, courses need to be structured and organized to involve students in the learning process in the most effective way. It was found that Horton's recommendations on how to create a motivating environment for students were the most apt and practical. Hence, the recommendations became the basis for developing some of the detailed features of VENuS, the virtual learning environment for the IMU's distance learning programme for nursing.

2.2 Design and Development of VENuS at the IMU

VENuS (see Fig. 1) is the learning platform for the IMU's distance learning programme for nursing. It is designed by a team comprising full-time subject-matter experts, an instructional designer and a Webmaster. For graphics related work, the team taps the artistic talents from the IMU's Chief Knowledge Officer's Office. Two members of the VENuS team had prior experience designing OLIS (Online Learning Interactive System) for the medical students of the IMU. The instructional designer and Webmaster have graduate degrees in Instructional Technology and have had vast experience in the field, teaching as well as developing technology-based learning materials.

Fig. 1. The entrance page to VENuS where students and instructors log in to access the contents of the nursing programme

The learning management system used to develop VENuS is WebCT. When designing VENuS, much consideration was given to the preparation of a student-friendly and motivating environment. The motivation model based on most of Horton's recommendations was applied. These are described in the next section.

Students can access VENuS via the Internet from wherever they are. An initial survey with the first cohort group of the IMU's nursing students indicate that everyone had a computer at home although not all were experienced in using the Internet. This also means that not everyone had an e-mail address. However, based on the survey conducted during their pre-course orientation, everyone was prepared to upgrade their home computer and subscribe to an Internet Service Provider.

2.3   Motivational Elements in a Virtual Learning Environment

In the attempt to understand Horton's concerns and recommendations relating to the factors of motivation for an effective learning environment, the author created a visual model in the form of a wheel (see Fig. 2). Most of Horton's recommendations were considered, particularly those that were applicable for the nursing programme. The author organized Horton's recommendations into four main areas: Communication, Content and Activities, Community and Reinforcement. Each area comprises Horton's recommendations that, when implemented, is believed to provide a student-friendly environment that will provide an incentive to the students, encourage, as well as discipline them.   Each area is discussed below.

Communication. Communication is one of the keys to successful learning. Creating a warm and welcoming atmosphere is an underlying principle to creating a learner-friendly environment and is a key factor in distance learning (see Fig. 3). There are four other areas of concern: setting clear expectations, requiring commitment from the student, intervening when the student is not on track and encouraging students to seek help. In setting clear expectations, the student needs to be told what is expected of them and they also should be encouraged to convey what they expect from the course. Items that need to be communicated are how the course will be organized, what are the learning outcomes, what and how many learning activities will there be, what are the assignments, how and when will the student be assessed, what is the passing mark, and what will happen if students do not meet the minimum requirements (see Fig. 4). Additional questions are what and where are the resources and who can they ask if they need clarification.   This is no different from the way courses should be conducted full-time on campus.

It is expected that a distance student will be distracted at work and at home compared to a full-time student on campus. It is believed that asking the students to be committed to the goals of the course when they register and to declare that they will complete the course requirements will help them stay more focused. Identifying unmotivated students early and re-motivating them as soon as the problem is recognized is another recommendation by Horton. Some of the signs of unmotivated students include being late with assignments, not answering messages, giving negative comments about the course, instructor, or other students, not submitting optional assignments and suddenly performing poorly in tests.

Students need to be encouragement to seek help.   Providing them an avenue to discuss their problems without being embarrassed or intimidated will help them to be open with their problems and to be responsive to suggestions on how to find solutions. This can be via e-mail communication with their instructor or mentor, a phone call or meeting in person with someone they can trust and seek understanding from.   Dealing with such students will require the instructor's understanding, proper advice and counseling as well as follow-ups.

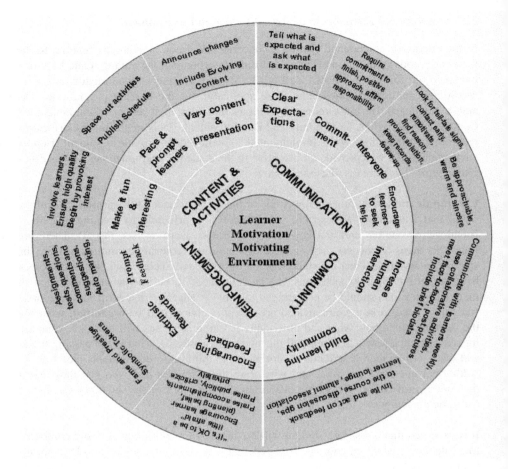

Fig. 2. A model developed to ensure student motivation or the design of a motivating environment for web-based learning. It includes recommendations by Horton. There are four areas of focus: Communication; Content and Activities; Community; and Reinforcement

Content and Activities. Horton suggests that the online learning environment should be fun and interesting for students. Learning should be a pleasure and the process enjoyed by students. Designers should ensure that students are started off in the right way. In VENuS, this was accomplished by provoking interest in the subject, for example, by setting a scenario, telling a story, asking a question, showing a picture that creates curiosity, or by stating a meaningful problem that the material will solve.

Students who feel involved in the learning process will be motivated and benefit from the learning process. Interactivity should be part of the design where students do more and read less. Giving more examples or familiar case studies and scenarios that the students can relate to would be effective. And, Horton cautioned designers

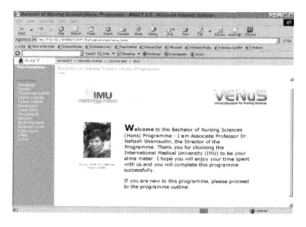

Fig. 3. The Welcome Page that greets students after logging into VENuS. The welcome message from the head of the nursing programme has been edited to reflect a warm and a student-friendly environment.

to consider the incorporation of multimedia materials only if appropriate and practical. It should justify the download time.

Undoubtedly, the contents and resources provided should be of high quality. The content should be accurate, credible, organized and clear. There should be no misspellings, grammatical errors or lapses of logic. A more effective presentation of the contents and materials presented at the Web site can be achieved by having a consistent and attractive layout utilizing an appropriate visual design scheme (see Fig. 5).

The content and presentation should be varied, for example by adding new content. If that happens, an announcement at the course home page or in a discussion thread should be made. Content should also be evolving. Horton suggests the use of discussion groups, FAQs and tips, news, and lists of useful Web sites or resources. All these are expected to motivate students to visit the Web site frequently.

It is also important for students to be able to space out their learning activities such as readings and assignments. This is particularly helpful to distance students who have a full-time job and a family to manage as well. A course schedule (see Fig. 6) can be provided to help students organize themselves in line with time management principles. Instructors should ensure the practicality of the various learning activities.

Community. Perhaps the most important need for distance students who will feel lonely and isolated from their instructors and peers is the need to feel belonged to a learning community. This could be in the form of online student lounges (see Fig. 7) such as chat rooms or threaded discussions where they are able to keep in touch with their peers and instructors. It could be a place that invites students to give feedback to the course or to discuss general learning issues. Nevertheless, online learning needs to be supplemented with face-to-face meetings such as tutorials and this where the six regional centres identified by the IMU in various parts of the country come in. Online,

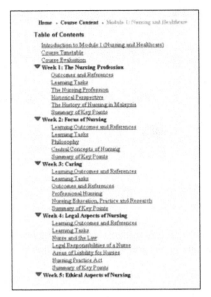

Fig. 4. Part of the Table of Contents for a course delivered through VENuS. The topics or sections for each week are broken down into Learning Outcomes and References, Learning Tasks, List of Sub-topics and Summary of Key Points. The weekly content is more organized, systematic and clear to the student. Note that a general introduction to Module 1 of the course, the course timetable and the course evaluation are also provided.

the learning atmosphere should be kept as humanistic as possible. Students should be invited to introduce themselves and to have their personal homepage published t the Web site. Another useful feature of virtual learning environments is the use of threaded discussions for collaborative learning to bring out issues and problems where students discuss with each other. The role of the instructors is to facilitate or moderate the discussions to help students keep on track and to finally weave in the topics discussed to provide more meaningful learning.

To promote collaborative learning whereby students are engaged in the online discussions with their tutor and fellow students, marks should be given and made part of the formative course assessment. The nursing curriculum committee had decided that the marks given would be based on the quality of postings rather than on the frequency or length of postings. An evaluation matrix is being developed for this. Collaborative discussions will comprise at least 10 percent of the total course marks.

Reinforcement. This is another important principle of learning. Students need to be informed that they are on the right track, doing the right things and performing within expectations. Instructors could encourage students by confirming that the student's fear and anxiety about their course and performance are to be expected. What is more important is that they take steps to remove their fear or anxiety and become a member

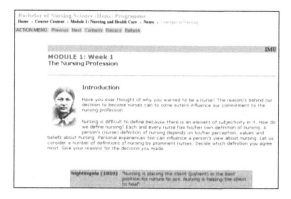

Fig. 5. Part of the content page. The layout and colour scheme are applied consistently throughout the content pages

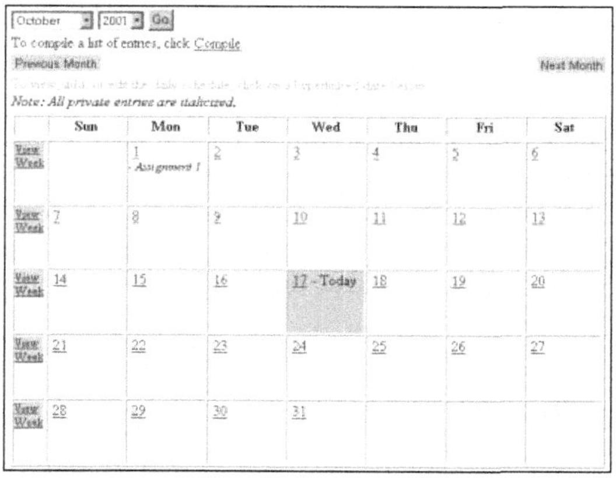

Fig 6. A monthly calendar provided in the VENuS learning environment to help students manage their time and to focus on their learning requirements. A weekly calendar is also available online

of the online learning community, contributing to each other's learning process. Students should be praised publicly to encourage others but criticized privately to prevent unnecessary embarrassment. Public praises can be achieved in the discussion groups and criticisms can be given to the student via one on one communication such as e-mail or discussed in person.

Students should receive prompt feedback on their learning tasks or activities such as assignments, tests and projects. Self-tests could be provided at the Web site to enable students to gauge their own learning. This also includes responding to students within an acceptable period of two or three working days to personal e-mail communication from students or postings to the discussion groups. Another reinforcement technique to motivate students recommended by Horton is the use of extrinsic rewards such as

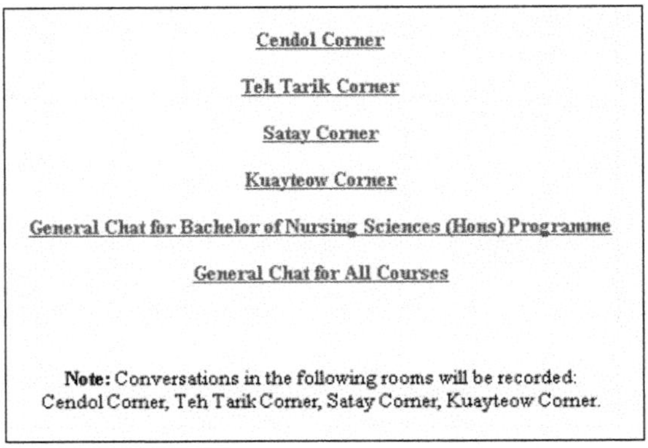

```
Cendol Corner

Teh Tarik Corner

Satay Corner

Kuayteow Corner

General Chat for Bachelor of Nursing Sciences (Hons) Programme

General Chat for All Courses


Note: Conversations in the following rooms will be recorded:
Cendol Corner, Teh Tarik Corner, Satay Corner, Kuayteow Corner.
```

Fig. 7. Student lounges for informal communication among students to provide a sense of community. Each corner will have a graphical icon in the final version of VENuS. Formal threaded discussions on learning issues are provided in another section

fame and prestige or symbolic tokens. Examples are Student of the Month awards in which the student's photo, profile and accomplishments are displayed in one section of the Web site or certificates or recognition awarded for various accomplishments such as the Best Online Discussant. The next section highlights the feedback received from the students to VENuS during one of the VENuS evaluation sessions. The feedback will reveal some of the motivational elements that have been incorporated based on the model presented in Fig. 2.

2.4 Feedback from Students

The IMU is awaiting approval from the National Accreditation Board nursing before it can begin its nursing degree programme . VENuS was developed ahead of time to demonstrate to members of the evaluation panel from the board how the virtual learning environment will provide the content and learning activities. VENuS was first introduced to potential students during a two-week pre-course orientation programme of the first cohort group of nursing students who will be sponsored by the Ministry of Health. They were provided with hands-on activities, particularly on how to access and use VENuS, how to e-mail messages and attachments, post their messages to the discussion group and how to benefit from the links to the Internet. They were also taught how to create a personal homepage comprising a one-page biodata for inclusion at the Web site. Following their initial feedback, the VENuS User Guide for students was further improved and another guide on "How to Succeed as an Online Student" was written to deal with motivation issues. These would be distributed to the students upon registration as well as made available online in VENuS.

Following the pre-course orientation, more contents were added to VENuS. Next, a group of eight potential students were invited to spend half a day at the IMU to use VENuS and to provide their feedback to the use and features of VENuS. A one-page questionnaire containing four open-ended questions were administered. These were filled and returned as soon as they have completed their assessment of VENuS. Their use of VENuS was also observed to determine other difficulties so that steps can be taken to overcome them. They were invited to give feedback to four questions:

- "What do you like most about VENuS? Think in terms of features, content, navigation, overall environment, etc."
- "What do you find most difficult to do/manage in VENuS?"
- "What do you think are some of the challenges that students will face when using VENuS?"
- "If there are two things that we should improve in VENuS, what would they be?"

When asked what they liked most about VENuS, their comments include:
- well-designed
- very good
- provides social interaction
- opportunity to create home page
- instructions are concise , clear and easy to follow
- content easy to read
- discussions will develop critical students
- participation in discussions will allow students to evaluate own strengths and weaknesses
- simple yet captures attention
- communication with course mates and lecturers
- interesting features suitable for nurses and paramedics
- direct communication with facilitator
- allows faster feedback

Responses to the second question were much fewer. Respondents who were probably new to computers and the Internet commented having difficulty getting into the e-discussions, e-mail and e-chat facilities. In contrast, one person commented that there was really nothing difficult because time and repeated usage will solve the problem of using the interactive features of VENuS.

Some of the challenges given were interesting. One was worried about the amount of time she would need to spend on VENuS considering that she had a job and a family to look after. Another concern was on how frequent students would need to participate in the collaborative discussions. One respondent felt it was a challenge for students to understand the topic well enough before going into the discussions. They need to be able to think critically. Another was concerned about accessibility from the home, particularly in connecting to the Internet via telephone lines, as lines are busy at times. Another concern was of not being sure how to submit assignments and how to get feedback from the lecturers.

When asked for suggestions to improve VENuS, the few comments were to ensure that the pre-course orientation be continued to provide hands-on experience to familiarize the students with the virtual learning environment. One person suggested that the language in the content pages be simpler for them to understand. Another suggested that assessments should be based on knowledge development, critical thinking

and research-based assignments. This issue needs to be researched further as a significant portion of the course marks will be given to examinations.

Based on an earlier survey to determine their level of computer and Internet knowledge and skill, it was found that 5.8 percent of the 89 respondents have never used a
computer before the pre-course orientation programme. A majority, that is, 68.2 percent of the respondents have never used e-mail, and 52.3 percent have never used the
Internet prior to the orientation programme. The students were mostly in the early to
late 40s. The pre-course orientation programme had included training in the basic use
of MS Word and MS PowerPoint as well as the Internet in general and VENuS in
particular. The survey also aimed to determine their PC ownership and access to the
Internet. Most, that is, 89.9 percent of the 89 respondents have a PC at home. About
38 percent had access to the Internet from home and a majority of the cohort group of
students ,that is, 77.7 percent of them needed technical assistance when using the
computer at home.

3   Summary and Conclusion

Distance learning offerings are on the rise to meet the increasing demands of the matured and working adults who appreciate the flexibility in getting a degree. Many
institutions are offering their programmes through a Web-based learning environment
that incorporates the use of various communication tools such as e-mail and threaded
discussions. However, it has been found that drop out rates among distance learning
students are high leading to the recommendations by educators to include motivational
elements. It is believed that motivated students will stay in the programme until they
graduate. Hence, instructional designers and instructors need to incorporate motivational elements into the design of virtual learning environments.

The paper reported the IMU's experience in developing VENuS, a virtual learning
environment designed to deliver the university's distance-learning program for nursing. The VENuS development team considered most of the motivational elements
recommended by Horton. These are represented in the form of a diagram (see Fig. 2).
The motivational elements fall into four main areas: communication; content and
activities; reinforcement and feedback. Horton's recommendations in each of these
areas have been highlighted. How they have been incorporated into VENuS has been
shown in several screen captures (see Fig. 1, Figs. 3 to 7).

The first cohort group of nursing students attended a pre-course orientation programme for two weeks, during which they were given the opportunity to use VENuS.
The team also observed their behavior to detect any difficulty, technical or otherwise,
in using VENuS. This led to the improvement of the VENuS User Manual and the
writing of a guide on "How to Succeed in Distance Learning." A second round of the
evaluation of VENuS by students were conducted four months later. Students' gave
very favourable feedback with regard to the learning environment and the contents of
VENuS. Some concerns were related to technology, that is, whether they would be
able to connect to the Internet from home due to their newness to the Internet or busy
telephone lines. Another concern was whether they would manage, as part-time stu-

dents, to spend time online and to actively participate in the collaborative discussions. However, based on the feedback received, it was realized that these discussions were considered appropriate and students indicated that they look forward to being part of the discussions. They were also concerned with how they would be assessed. They suggested more emphasis on the evaluation of higher levels of cognitive knowledge or critical thinking, for example, to be evaluated for assignments based on readings and research rather than on examinations.

As the team consulted additional reports of other distance learning practitioners and implementers, it was realized that the use of technology has to be carefully planned in. It is not be used to hype up the value of distance learning. In short, use high tech but ensure a high touch environment. It appears that instructors need to re-orientate their instructional styles so as to be able to leverage on innovative technology but at the same time, ensure that students are completely comfortable in a high-tech learning environment. It is necessary, for example, to provide new online instructors the experience of being in a collaborative online learning environment. The role of the instructor in discussion forums is crucial to the success of online collaborative learning. It is thus suggested that instructors enroll in one of the many online discussion groups on the Web to familiarize and appreciate the process of engaging students in web-based collaborative learning.

The most important element in the distance-learning environment is the student, who, isolated and at a distance from their instructors and course mates, need much more support from the institution than regular on-campus students. This can be achieved by providing a motivating environment that will provide them the incentive, encouragement and help them develop the perseverance to succeed. While VENuS was designed to incorporate motivational elements, further research needs to be carried out to determine how these elements have helped students feel encouraged to stay focused and to gain confidence in what would have been a lonely path to obtaining further education.

References

1. Martin, P.W.: LII Backgrounder on Distance Learning. Retrieved March 12, 2003 from the World Wide Web http://www.law.cornell.edu/background/distance/background 99.htm
2. Jackson, B., Anagnostopoulou, K.: Making the Right Connections: Improving Quality in Online Learning. In Stephenson, J. (ed.): Teaching and Learning Online: Pedagogies for New Technologies. Kogan Page London (2001)
3. Chua, J.M.: Speech delivered at the opening ceremony of the International Nursing Conference: Advances in Nursing Practice, 4 October, 2002, The Legend Hotel, Kuala Lumpur (unpublished)
4. Abas, Z.W., Shamsuddin, N., Phua, K.L.: How Prepared are Malaysian Nurses for Online Distance Learning? Informing Science Proceedings. Retrieved May 25, 2003 from the WorldWideWeb
   http://ecommerce.lebow.drexel.edu/eli/2003Proceedings/docs/082Abas.pdf (June, 2003)

5. Alexander, S., Boud, D.: Students Still Learn from Experience when Online. In: Stephenson, J. (ed.): Teaching and Learning Online: Pedagogies for New Technologies. Kogan Page London (2001)
6. Teaching at an Internet Distance: The Pedagogy of Online Teaching and Learning. The Report of a 1998-1999 University of Illinois Faculty Seminar (December 7, 1999). Retrieved March 12, 2003 from the World Wide Web
    http://www.vpaa.uillinois.edu/reports_retreats/tid_download.asp
7. Horton, W.: Designing Web-Based Training. John Wiley New York (2000)
8. Berge, Z.L., Collins, M., Dougherty, K. Design Guidelines for Web-Based Courses. In Abbey, B. (ed.): Instructional and Cognitive Impacts of Web-Based Education. Idea Group Publishing London (2000)
9. Fisher, M.M. Implementation Considerations for Instructional Design of Web-Based Learning Environments. In Abbey, B. (ed.): Instructional and Cognitive Impacts of Web-Based Education. Idea Group Publishing London (2000)
10. Powers, S. M. Guan, S. Examining the Range of Student Needs in the Design and Development of a Web-Based Course. In Abbey, B. (ed.): Instructional and Cognitive Impacts of Web-Based Education. Idea Group Publishing London (2000)

Assessment Management Using Software

Jason Wells

School of Information Technology Deakin University, Victoria, Australia
wells@deakin.edu.au

Abstract. Web based learning is providing new and innovative environments to facilitate the delivery of course material to increasing numbers students, but most of the effort is centered around the presentation of the learning material and creating environments where student interact with this material and each other. Despite the changes the web based learning environments have delivered, little attention has been given to improving the management and process of assessment. This paper introduces a new software application designed to take advantage of the web based environments and addresses the management overheads associated with assessment whilst improving the feedback to students. Initial investigations indicate significant benefits can be achieved by using software to manage the assessment process. A detailed description of the software is provided and two case studies presented that highlight the software's application and confirmed benefits when used to conduct and manage assessments.

1 Introduction

With the introduction of web based learning environments and the increasing use of computers in the learning process opportunities exist to improve the management and methods of assessment. Much of the effort and focus of application development in the educational field seems to focus on developing tools to present, deliver and communicate educational content to the students. Greater numbers of students can be accessed and incorporated into the learning environments increasing the workload associated with assessment but little effort has been applied to providing the tools required by the learning staff to manage and assess the students.

The web based learning environment provides a number of opportunities to utilise and take advantage of the structure and culture it provides. Web based learning requires students to have a computer and an Internet connection. They are required to read their email and gather material from the learning environment. They are generating electronic documents and submitting them electronically via systems provided or custom solutions. They are becoming used to completing their studies online and in electronic form. Assessment on the other hand is not keeping pace and is not considered a major priority. A recent Computer Assisted Assessment (CAA) Centre survey found that the majority of staff were using CAA for formative and diagnostic assessment, not summative assessment, thereby not reducing their marking burden at all [8]. Despite some successes, such as that reported by the University of Luton [1], the vast majority of marking is still a manual process.

W. Zhou et al. (Eds.): ICWL 2003, LNCS 2783, pp. 411–422, 2003.

2 Assessment

Assessment of students is a major task undertaken by all teachers, lecturers and trainers at all education levels. Assessment generally involves making judgements about students work based on a set of instructions relating to a particular subject. It can be defined as the process of obtaining information that is used to make educational decisions about students, to give feedback to the student about his or her progress, strengths, and weaknesses, to judge instructional effectiveness and curricular adequacy; and to inform policy. [10]

The assessment process may consist of a number of tasks. These include:
- Creating assessment material, test, exams, assignments etc
- Conducting the assessment
- Collection and storage of the submissions
- Marking of the submissions
- Recording marks and grades
- Delivery of feedback and results to the students

The type of assessment, the number of students, the bias, experience and attitude of the assessor, the turn around time, expectation of the student are just some of the factors that may determine the quality and effectiveness of the assessment.

The submissions produced by the students can take many forms. They may be essays, short answer questions, diagrams, drawings, programs, databases, spreadsheets and so on. They may be submitted in electronic form as one or more files or as hard copy documents.

The methods used to assess the student's work are as equally diverse and generally left to the assessor to determine the assessment criteria. Marks are allocated and recorded for each student. Submissions and feedback containing some sort of grading and associated comments are then returned to the students. Students then review their results and if they feel they have been unfairly treated can request a remark and marks adjusted accordingly.

This whole process is very important both for the educational process and the students. It is time consuming and potentially fraught with dangers. Every assessor develops their own customised methods to complete the assessment process and record, manage and deliver student results. [3]

For the assessment to meet both the student and assessors needs a number of factors must be considered.

- The criteria for marking must meet the objectives of the course
- The marking must provide a measure of the learning
- The marking should provide effective feedback to the student

There is the pressure on assessors to provide accurate and meaningful evaluation procedures for student work against a background of increasing staff: student ratios, External Subject Review requirements and Teaching Quality Assessments. [12] There is the requirement to ensure that marking and feedback are always consistent and there is an increasingly short amount of time for external examiners to view. Individual lecturers are trying to deal with ever increasing amounts of assessment within a time bottleneck, which is a consequence of this individual approach to marking (Lecturer-to-student approach). [3]

Regardless of the type of assessment, the nature and number of students, there exists an opportunity to provide tools and methods that improve the management of the assessment process while also improving the feedback to the students.

3   Current Technology

Currently there is little in the way of software that attempts to meet the demands of the assessment process. Two applications exist that attempt to fill the software void in this area.

Markin32 is a Windows program which can import a student's text for marking by pasting from the clipboard, or directly from an RTF or text file. Once the text has been imported, Markin32 provides all the tools a teacher needs to mark and annotate the text. When marking is complete, the teacher can export the marked text as an RTF file for loading into a word-processor, or as a web page so that students can view the marked text in a web browser. Marked work can even be emailed directly back to the student, all from within the Markin32 program. [2] This application is designed to mark and annotate text submission such as an essay, short answer questions etc.

Mindtrail is a Windows program that allows the marker to construct a detailed marking proforma or "knowledge tree," complete with marking scales, check boxes and comment fields. Individual assignments are evaluated via the marking guide, producing a mark of that assignment and an individual marking report. Mindtrail improves the quality of both the marking process and the feedback given to students, but according to Stevens and Jamieson a major difficulty is encountered when constructing the knowledge tree. "This proved to be a laborious task, taking over four hours to prepare for each of the two major assignments."

They also found that "explicit construction of the marking guide assisted in focusing on the important issues of the assignment and hence provided for a more 'objective' marking process" and "It forced the marker to focus on the point at hand, thus reducing the influence of other items outside that point, such poor grammar and spelling or 'flashy' presentation". [6]

4   The Application

As a consequence of having to deal with the demands of managing and assessing ever increasing student numbers, an application titled 'Markers Assistant' was developed in an attempt to fill the software void that exists in this area.

Markers Assistant is a Windows based application developed to provide a more efficient and flexible method of managing, assessing and delivering results to small to large numbers of students. It was designed to automate as many components of the assessment process as possible, whilst maintaining and improving the feedback to the students within a reasonable timeframe.

The goals of the software were as follows:
- provide automation that retrieves student submissions and presents them via a pre-determined application;
- provide a flexible marking guide GUI that only requires the identification of the criteria and or and assessment of an items value;
- automate the collation of results within the application;
- provide facilities to deliver student results via email;
- provide facilities to collate final marks summaries;
- enable all data collected to be saved and retrieved via a project file.

Generally assessment is created and marked based on a set of criteria. This criteria identifies areas within the submission that are considered important and generally have a mark associated to reflect the level of importance. Markers Assistant displays a marking criteria or marking guide in the form of checkboxes organised in a hierarchical configuration. The marking guide also provides the basis for feedback to the students regarding their submission.

A marking guide loaded into the software provides the assessor with a series of checkboxes and associated descriptions (Fig. 1). Generally the marking guide criteria are organised in hierarchical groups where the high level criteria must be met before other items within that criteria are considered. Grouping allows marking guides to be set up that orders information into related topics, making it easier to interpret, speeding up the marking process. Markers identify the higher-level criteria and work down through the criteria as required. If the high level criteria are not met then the remaining items in the group are not considered and marks deducted accordingly. The first level represents a major concept or criteria that must be met in order for subsequent lower levels to be included.

Individual students are identified by information supplied via a student list consisting of a unique identifier, such as student number or id and an associated email address if results are to be delivered via email. Students can be found either by identifying them in a drop down menu or by searching all or part of their ID or email address.

The student identifier is used through out the process to identify a particular student and also can be used to organise and retrieve student submission automatically if the student submissions are stored electronically in student directories identified by the student identifier.

The application searches for a directory in a given base location and if a match is found, opens the directory and returns the file specified or the closest match. For example you may setup the environment to find the first occurrence of a '*.doc' file in a student directory and present the file to the assessor using Microsoft Word.

Marking consists of checking the marking guide items where the student has met the criteria, adjusting the allocated mark to a one that represents the assessor's judgment of the criteria and adding any comments and adjustments to the submission. Each time a checkbox is switched the marks are adjusted accordingly. Comments can

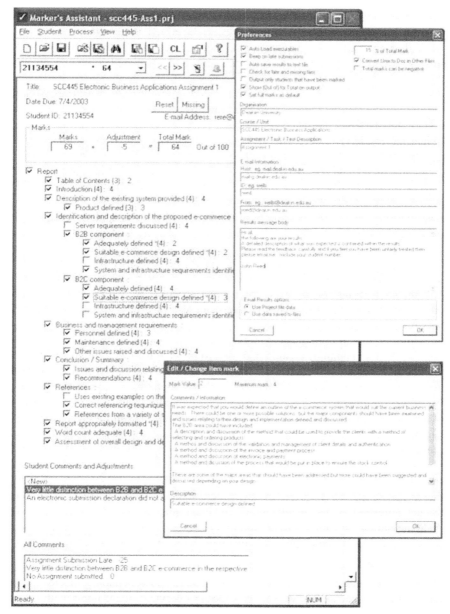

Fig. 1. Example marking guide, Preference and Edit item dialog.

be added against an individual item in the marking guide or as a general comment that relates to the submission as a whole. These comments may also have an adjustment value associates with them that will either increase or decrease the overall mark for a student. All comments entered are stored in a general repository and can be applied to a different student if required. All comments can be edited or deleted.

A marker navigates from student to student via next and back buttons or via the drop down menu or search facility. Student results and associated comments are stored within a project file and can be retrieved at any stage.

At any time the assessor may save the marking completed to a project file that saves all the information generated so far. The project file can be reloaded at any time to restore the marking completed.

When the marking is complete all results can be emailed to the students or files generated and printed. Results are collated in the form of a text file containing the assessment criteria and the associated mark the student received for each item in the criteria. Any comments relating to the assessment were also included. A log file is kept for each email that is sent to students.

The marking guide provides the basis for the feedback the students receive. Each item in the marking guide is tagged to indicate whether the student met or lost marks for the criteria. If comments relating to the criteria exist, the item is tagged with a comment number the student can reference for further explanations on why they lost marks. All comments relating to particular items are stored and presented to the student if the student did not meet the criteria or lost marks for the criteria. The student identifies the comments that relates to them and also has the benefit of seeing where other students had problems.

In addition to item comments, general comments that relate to the overall assessment of each student can be created and used to provide feedback to the student. Each comment added is stored against the particular student and is also placed in a store where it can be reused if it is relevant to another student during the marking process. A list of all comment made for all students is available for analysis.

A major advantage of storing assessment results and data in an electronic form is the ability to provide a variety of analysis. A basic requirement of the assessment process is to provide results summaries of all assessment performed. Traditional methods of assessment do not allow the analysis of comments and marks associated with individual criteria within the assessment. The software enables statistics to be gathered and output on a variety of assessment items. These include a criteria mark, comment adjustments and a total mark for each student. Statistics for all students include the number students marked, number of zero and full marks, the average mark and the min and max mark. Item statistics indicate which item was attempted and the average mark for each.

This type of analysis can be used to gain a better understanding of any teaching strengths and weaknesses as well as provide an overview of all items within an assessment for all students.

Results can be collated into a summary for each student in the form of comma-separated file suitable for most spreadsheet and database formats. The summary provides a mark breakdown and a final mark for each student and if you provide a % value for the submission as a preference, the application will also calculate and output the % mark for each student. If more than one assessment is used to formulate the final mark or grade the application can produce a summary of all individual assessment and produce a summary and final mark calculation for each student. Each project file is identified for each assessment and processed by the application. It is again valuable to provide the % mark each assessment represents as this will result in a final grading calculation.

A number of features added reduce the chance of losing data. Backup projects are automatically created in the background, as each student is marked and backup projects created when the application is closed. The project file is saved as text and can be interpreted outside of the Markers Assistant environment.

5   Case Studies

Markers Assistant has been developed over a four year period and has been used within a variety of subjects within the School of Information Technology at Deakin University. The following case studies outline two types of assessment tasks managed using the application. They highlight the various issues encountered and the solutions that were developed to meet the needs of the assessment tasks.

5.1   Introduction to Software Development SCC104

This unit was based around the assessment of students' ability to apply programming concepts using the Visual Basic programming language. As part of the course the students were required to submit eight programming assignments in a 13-week period. Around 430 students were enrolled in the course over four campuses. Processing and marking the 430 * 8 assignments required a solution that automated as many components of the marking process as possible, whilst maintaining and improving the assessment feedback to the students.

Each submission consisted of a Visual Basic (.vbp) project file and one or more source files depending on the requirements of the assignment. Assignments were submitted electronically via a custom submission system developed at Deakin University. Assignments were grouped in directories identified by:

Assignment Number->Student Number->[assignment files]

The software is designed to accept a series of parameters that identified the location of the files, an application that would be run to view the files (in this case VB.exe) and any command line arguments the application may require.

Student assignments were automatically retrieved and presented based on the current student being marked. In the Visual Basic example, the student's project file was used to compile, run and present their assignment to the assessor.

Facilities were provided to view the contents of the each file in the student's submission directory in text form. This enabled the assessor to inspect the code in all files quickly and simply, further speeding up the marking process (Fig. 2.).

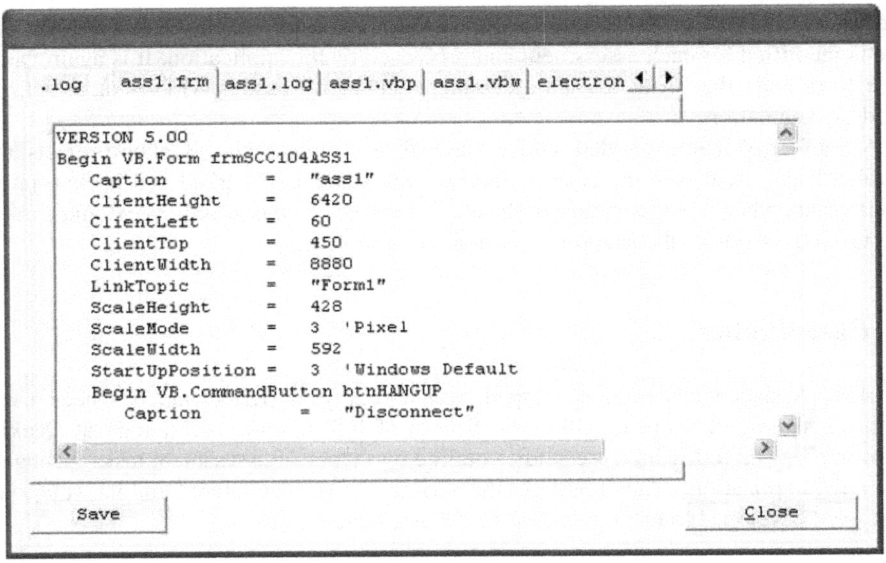

Fig. 2. Other Files Dialog

The application proved very valuable during the unit as it provided a superior method of managing the student results as opposed to traditional means considering the number of students and assessment tasks required. The student assignments stored electronically and ordered in a structured way combined with the ability of the software to automate the assessment process enabled over 3,440 individual assessments to be viewed, processed and results delivered within the specified turn around time of one week for each of the eight assessment tasks.

Marking was distributed to the 10 markers in the form of a project files created by the software. Equal numbers of students were allocated and stored in project files and distributed to the markers. Each marker completed their assessment then saved and returned the project file to the principle assessor for compilation and analysis. The ability to create, distribute then compile project files returned from markers enabled the primary assessor to examine and adjust the assessments as a group providing a greater level of consistency and accountability.

Frequent requests were made by students to review their submissions after they received their results. The application was easily able to retrieve and present the requested submission and associated marks and comments by reloading the respective project file. If adjustments to the assessment were required, these were made directly and the results saved back to the project file and results emailed to the student.

Summary results were not generated until the end of the semester, when all assessment was complete. All eight project files were loaded and summary of all assessable items for each student produced for finalisation.

5.2 Computers and Society and Professional Ethics SCC306

This unit consisted of 336 student based over four campuses. Students were required to submit three written assignments in essay and short answer formats, submitted via electronic means as Microsoft Word formatted documents or in some cases printed documents.

The assessment of essays and short answer questions requires the assessor to make judgments regarding the student's submission against criteria that is not easily definable. This posed some problems for the software as the checkbox type arrangement only enabled either a right or wrong type of assessment and not judgment based assessment where marks can be adjusted to represent a grading for each item within the criteria. Adjustments were made to the software to allow the associated mark for each item in the marking criteria to be adjusted. The assessor selects the item and a dialog is presented enabling them to adjust the mark associated with the item to between 0 and the maximum value assigned in the marking criteria.

In addition facilities were added to enter a comment associated with the item that could be used to identify reasons why marks were deducted or suggest the right answer or outline the general approach expected. This enabled the assessor to build a collection of reasons why marks were lost or more valuable, a collection of information that explained and quantified the information that would have been considered desirable to answer the particular item (Fig 1).

It was felt, that while using the software, the assessor tended to focus on the elements of the assessment that were incorrect or lacking. This tended to build a list of negative statements and did not really provide adequate feedback to the student. Research has found that feedback centered on the correction of errors does not support learning. Therefore, it was considered more important to provide examples of good work or highlight information that was important, required or desired in order to gain the marks for the item. [5] This tended to educate the students rather than the traditional method, which merely explains where and why they lost marks. [13] This also compensated for the inability of the software to annotate and make comments with the submission text. Further enhancement to the software will enable the marker to annotate and save the submission and then later automatically attach the annotated submission to the student's results so they can open their assignment and read any comments made within the document in addition to the marking criteria and associated marks and comments.

6 Results

Research indicates that feedback or knowledge of results has been shown to have a positive effect on performance [4][7], but with larger class-sizes and increasing workloads, the time staff can devote to giving students detailed feedback on their work has been substantially eroded. [9] Special attention was devoted to ensuring the software design centered around providing meaningful feedback to the students and not just on the process of assessing the submissions.

Anecdotal evidence suggest that a well written marking guide and informative comments that focus on educating and not criticising the students work does provide meaningful feedback based on research and feedback received from the students. The marking guide identified the expectations of the assessment and the associated marks provide a measure of the student's effort in meeting the expectations. In addition to the marking guide, each item could be tagged with a comment to provide information that explains or quantifies the expectation for that particular item.

It was found that these comments are best focused on the information that was required by the assessment criteria rather than a criticism of the student work or reason why they lost marks. It was felt that the student given a correct answer would not only identity where they went wrong for themselves but also discover what was required or was a correct answer. This method proved to be a more efficient method of providing feedback, as the comments did not result in a catalogue of criticism but simple a solution that applied to all students.

As part of the SCC306 unit evaluation performed at the end of semester 2, 2002, students were asked to evaluate and comment on the feedback they received for their assignments. Of the 336 students, 137 students responded. All responses to the survey were anonymous.

Question: How do you rate the assignment marking feedback you received?
- 5.8%   very poor
- 6.6%   poor
- 34.3%   average
- 38.0%   good
- 15.3%   very good

Students were invited to make comments regarding the marking feedback. It was not compulsory to make a comment.

Question: Please add comments or suggestions you have regarding the assignment marking feedback?
Responses:
- "The assignment feedback was excellent. From the feedback, I was able to see where I went wrong and how I could have fixed the problem. Excellent part of the unit"
- "This unit had more that I have seen in the last five."
- "The best I have had in my three years at Deakin."
- "I did not understand all the explanations, but then I realised that I had not fully understood the task. I thought I had, but the assignment feedback made me aware that I was wrong in assuming that I had a perfectly grasp of what was expected."
- "Details of why marks were lost were vague and offered no insight into how the assignment could be improved to right the same faults that may occur in future assignments"
- "It was pretty good and all the briefings were given where we went wrong."
- "There was substantial feedback, but it was very general."

Further investigation via unit evaluations will be performed to identify specific information to evaluate the feedback students receive as a result of using the application.

A major problem of manual assessment exists where assessment is distributed to more than one assessor. The potential for inconsistency exists and generally it is very difficult to review the assessment environment for each student after they have been assessed. A major benefit of the software is the ability to divide the assessment environment into individual projects containing a unique list of students that are distributed to each assessor. The assessors complete the marking and return the saved project file. The software collates each individual project into one complete project. A review of the entire assessment can be completed where each submission and associated marking and comments are retrieved and can quickly be compared with other students to ensure consistency and potential plagiarism cases identified and investigated. This also provides a level of accountability to both the assessor and student as the marking for all students can be retrieved and viewed against the all other students in a standard environment.

The use of this type of application has an enormous capacity to speed up and improve the management and assessment of student submissions. If you consider the assessment process is not just the marking of submission but a management issue with many associated tasks, the software proved very valuable in all components of the assessment process, especially when the class size is large. In all cases where the software was used it was felt that the turn around time from submission to delivery of the results was shorter than using traditional means. Assessment review requests were dealt with more efficiently and overall the management of the results was not a task in addition to the marking process but a consequence of using the software.

An important characteristic of good assessment information is its consistency, or reliability. [10] The structured process provided by using software in assessment improves the consistency of the assessment as each assessor views a structured, well-defined, consistent marking guide. More accuracy should be expected from the assessors as consistency within the marking guide and process was enforced within the environment. Comparison between submissions was quickly and easily available enabling any perceived or suspected inaccuracies to be checked and adjusted.

A major problem for all institutions managing students on a variety of locations is the delivery of results. Traditionally results have to be created and saved as individual files and either emailed or printed and mailed to the students. This is a time consuming task that is subject to human error. The application managers both these tasks automatically. This facility proved extremely valuable, reducing the workload and associated stress generally experienced with teaching and assessment.

The application removes much of the complication from assessment by automating many of the tedious tasks of assessment. This allows the assessor to focus on the assessment not the process. A variety of options allow the assessment task to be tailored to meet the assessment demands. Student submissions stored in electronic form can be retrieved and presented using a predefined application. Marking guides are reused for all students. Results are automatically stored for retrieval in a variety of formats. Comments applied to student during the marking process are stored and can be reused for all students.

To provide a greater understanding of the effectiveness of the application, further research is being conducted that will examine anecdotal evidence collected so far.

Additional features are under development that will further improve the environment and functionality of the application. These include:

- Extend system to allow annotated attachments to the results
- Extend to output HTML formatted documents that provides more interactive feedback
- Provide remote server access and database connectivity
- Provide facilities to create and edit a marking guide within the application
- Extend the statistics output
- Provide plagiarism detection facilities

References

1. Bull, J and Stephens, D.: The use of Question Mark software for formative and summative assessment in two universities. Innovations in Education and Training International 36 (2) (1999) 128–136.
2. Creative Technology. (2002) http://www.cict.co.uk/software/markin/index.htm.
3. Stephens, D., Sargent, G., Brew, I.: Comparison of Assessed Work Marking Software: Implications for the Ideal Integrated Marking Tool (IMT). (1999)
4. Erez, M.: Feedback: A necessary condition for the goal setting-performance relationship. Journal of Applied Psychology 62. (1977) 624–627.
5. Gibbs, G., Simpson, C.: Retention Interim Report. (2002)
6. Stevens, K., Jamieson, R.: The Introduction and Assessment of Three Teaching Tools (WebCT, Mindtrail, EVE) into a Post Graduate Course, Journal of Information Technology Education, Vol 1. No. 4. (2002)
7. Locke, A., Latham, P.: A theory of goal setting & task performance. Englewood Cliffs, NJ: Prentice Hall. (1990)
8. Martin, N.: Web-based assessment. Testing Times. 1 (4) April 2001. (2001) 1-7
9. Race, P.: The Art of Assessment. New Academic, SEDA publication, Vol.5. Issue 3. (1995)
10. Dietel, R., Herman, J., Knuth, R.: What Does Research Say About Assessment. (1991)
11. Stiggins, R.: Student-Centred Classroom Assessment. New York, Merrill. (1994)
12. Thomson, A.: Growth is blamed for fall in standards. Times Higher Educational Supplement No.1486 (2001) 8
13. Bruner, J. Beyond the information given. London: George Allen & Unwin Ltd. (1974)

Using the Web as a Source of Graded Reading Material for Language Acquisition

Alexandra L. Uitdenbogerd

School of Computer Science and Information Technology, RMIT University
GPO Box 2476V, Melbourne 3001, Australia
alu@cs.rmit.edu.au

Abstract. Reading has been shown to be an important component of foreign language acquisition. However, to efficiently use reading for this purpose requires an extensive collection of graded reading material. I propose using the Web as a supplementary reading source. In this paper, I describe potential applications that present reading material to learners, and I pose research questions that will lead to an effective application. Important issues include the measurement of readability of text in order to match text difficulty to the level of the learner, profiling the learner, and whether there is suitable reading material for learners on the web. I summarise related prior work in computer-assisted language learning (CALL) and foreign language reading skill acquisition, and report on some preliminary results on readability measurement. In particular, for foreign language reading, sentence length is well-correlated with readability, but vocabulary has a more complex relationship.

1   Introduction

Reading is an important means of increasing foreign language skill and has been shown to increase vocabulary [13]. A frequently used resource for language learning is the graded reader, that is, a text in the target language that has been especially written for language students of a particular standard. One common type of reader is the reduced vocabulary reader, and is available for many languages. Typically, there is an assumed basic vocabulary of a defined number of common words. Most of the text will be written using this basic vocabulary, and any extra words used in the text will be defined on the page in which they occur, or in a vocabulary list at the back of the book. These readers allow a student to read fluently in the target language, and thereby increase their comprehension and enjoyment.

While there are several publishers that publish readers, generally the quantity of reduced vocabulary reading material is limited, particularly for languages other than French, German, English, Italian, Spanish and Russian (published by Easy Readers, Teen Readers, Hachette, Oxford University Press and others). I propose to develop a means of automatically providing reading material based on a user's current skill-level, where the source of the reading material is the vast quantity of text available on the Internet. This application could be used to

W. Zhou et al. (Eds.): ICWL 2003, LNCS 2783, pp. 423–432, 2003.

provide further supplementary reading of current material in the user's target language. In this paper I discuss past work in applied linguistics and computer-assisted language learning (CALL), and propose a system for presenting graded reading material from the web. I describe research questions related to the implementation of the application, and present the results of an experiment on readability of text in French as a foreign language.

2   Language Learning and Readability

Theories about language learning have gone through several changes in the last century. Each of these changes has led to dramatically different approaches to the teaching of languages. In this section I first discuss practices in language teaching related to reading. I then examine the measurement of readability of text and reading skill level.

2.1   Language Learning and Reading

Traditional teaching focused on grammatical rules, drills, and analysis of texts. However, even in 1909 some teachers and authors believed that students should have available to them texts of a suitable difficulty to be read for enjoyment (for example MacMillan and Co published a series of French readers, consisting of authentic texts adapted for foreign language learners [7]). Once Michael West published the results of his experiences teaching English in India in 1926 by using English word frequencies, further experiments were carried out in teaching French. Gurney and Scott ran an experiment over two years in an English secondary school, using texts adapted on the basis of word-frequencies. These were shown to be very useful in improving reading skills of students [5]. The stories that they provided in the "Oxford rapid reading French texts" series, were based on French stories written for native readers. These were reduced in vocabulary using the lists published by Vander Beke [3].

For many years it was believed that students should first learn purely by listening and speaking, with reading and writing taught a considerable while later [11]. This theory was influenced by discoveries that children tend to learn language structures in a specific order. Initially they pick up certain words, then later they start to reason about language, leading to certain mistakes, such as "I goed", then further rules are learnt. Interestingly, the order in which language is learnt has more in common with the order that other children learn language than it ressembles the language to which they are exposed. Further, foreign language speakers follow a similar pattern of acquisition.

Since that time it was discovered — or perhaps rediscovered — that students can pick up reading in a foreign language much sooner than taught according to the methods of the time [11], and that extensive reading improves vocabulary and comprehension much more effectively than intensive reading of texts [4]. Problems with reading in a foreign language have been analysed from various perspectives, leading to the adaptation of textbooks to make them easier for foreign language learners to read [2], and novel techniques for introducing foreign language reading, such as intermingling the native and target language [17]. More recently, the use of computers for text presentation has been shown to provide several advantages (discussed next section).

A common strategy for making reading materials suitable for foreign and second language readers is to adapt existing texts that are in the target language. The techniques that are typically used include: choosing a base vocabulary, mostly based on word frequency, substituting words in the text with those that are within the base vocabulary, providing a gloss for essential words that cannot be substituted, removing idiom, minimising homonyms, and simplifying tense and grammatical structures [2,8].

To provide suitable reading material at any stage of learning, the readability of a text needs to be determined, that is, how difficult the text is to read for the learner. Teachers select texts for students by estimating their difficulty. While many teachers may assess texts in an informal manner, others make use of a formula.

The applied linguistics field has provided a variety of metrics that attempt to calculate readability. The metrics are usually based on word and sentence length. Some metrics also make use of word frequency, counts of grammatical constructs and other measures.

One popular technique amongst users is the Fry readability graph (discussed by Klare [12]). Users calculate the number of syllables and the number of words in a piece of text and then determine the reading level by looking up the figures in a graph.

The Flesch formula for reading ease (RE) as described by Davies, is given as:

$$RE = 206.835 - (0.846 \times NSYLL) - (1.015 \times W/S) \ , \tag{1}$$

where NSYLL is the average number of syllables per 100 words and W/S is the average number of words per sentence [6].

Another popular formula, developed by Dale and Chall in 1948, makes use of a vocabulary list in addition to sentence length:

$$S = 0.1579p + 0.0496s + 3.6365 \ , \tag{2}$$

where p is the percentage of words on the Dale list of 3,000, and s is the average number of words per sentence. The resulting score represents a reading grade. It was shown to be more consistent than the Flesch score in experiments. Klare provides us with a comprehensive survey of readability formulae, including those discussed here [12].

An alternative approach used by applied linguists is to assess the ability of people who read the text to answer comprehension questions based on the material. This test, plus the cloze test, in which the learner needs to fill in missing words in a piece of text, are used to assess the learner's reading skill level. These same methods are also the most common ways of validating readability formulae.

3   Computer-Assisted Language Learning

Early computer-assisted language learning (CALL) programs did little more than provide drill practice, or use "programmed learning" techniques for language learning. Unfortunately, these techniques appeared at a time when the language teaching paradigm had shifted more to a communication-based paradigm as opposed to a grammatical approach [16].

Since then, computers have been used for a variety of activities that encourage language use, such as: a kind of hangman game, where the user guesses words in a sentence instead of letters in a word [16]; adventure-style games, where the user enters short sentences to solve a mystery or accumulate points.

A more recent trend is the use of corpuses, that is, collections of text, for language learning. Students use software to produce concordances for a word that they are interested in. All occurrences of the word in a corpus are presented, giving the students many examples of how the word is used [10].

The Textladder project allows the educator to provide a collection of texts to the software, which then determines the order that the texts should be presented to users for reading based on vocabulary [9]. However, this ordering of text is unlikely to correspond to the order of reading difficulty. The experiments discussed in this paper show that other factors such as sentence length may have a much greater influence than vocabulary, except in special circumstances. My vision of a web-based reader application is closely related in concept to Textladder except that the source of the text is the Internet's vast collection of text.

In other research into online reading, it has been found that full glossing aids in both comprehension and vocabulary acquisition of learners [14]. Further, presenting the same material on-line was more beneficial than printed materials [1]. The use of more than one method of representing the meaning, such as images, audio and video, also enhances vocabulary acquisition [1].

4   Application Requirements

The cited research tends to support the benefits of an application that provides graded reading material from the web. For best effect, it should provide access to glossaries to any words that the user wishes to check.

I expect the web application to track a user's vocabulary in the languages that they are studying. Each time the user logs onto the website, they should be able to do any of the following things:

- Define their vocabulary knowledge in some way.
- Check definitions of words occurring in a piece of text.
- Select reading material from a ranked list of web pages, and read it.
- Choose a specific kind of vocabulary that they would like to improve through reading, for example, spoken, business, or academic vocabulary. These all have slightly different typical word frequencies.

- Provide a list of words that they would like to learn through reading at their level, for example, technical words from a subject area that the user is studying, or required vocabulary from a language course.

The application should track which pages have been read, along with their last modification date, so that identical pages will not be presented to the user unless specifically requested.

Methods that could be used to determine the user's level of reading skill include:

- Check a list of words in the target language, and mark them as known or unknown. This method can be used to either determine the exact list of words known by the user, or to estimate words known based on the frequency of words from a sample list that are known.
- Read sample text and indicate whether they want text that is easier or harder. This technique can be combined with a measure of general readability. The user's preferred level of readability can be used to select texts.
- Complete cloze tests on text, that is, fill in the blanks in a text. This technique has long been used to determine a person's level of comprehension [15].

A further enhancement of the application could be the use of relevance-feedback to fine-tune the assessment of readability. Similarly, the use of collaborative filtering techniques could allow users to benefit from other users' experience of the available texts.

5   Implementation Issues

In order to provide such an application, an index of web content must be maintained, in addition to user data stored in a traditional database. Web crawlers would be required to collect web pages for insertion into the index. Words would need to be extracted and stored into the index. Most of these aspects are not new in terms of the technology required. Depending on the criteria used for selecting text, the types of queries to the term index may differ somewhat from those of other search engine applications. For example, if the user's vocabulary is taken into consideration, the number of query terms is likely to be large (and increasing over time).

Many search engines apply stopping to their indexes, that is, they don't index common words. For this application, if user vocabulary is used as a measure, it will be important to index these common words. Similarly, stemming, that is, the removal of suffixes, is likely to be inappropriate. On the other hand, very rare terms would be less useful for indexing. The main issue with regard to this application is the nature of the query compared to a typical query presented to a search engine. At this stage it is unclear whether user-specific vocabulary will help in finding suitable documents. If it does, then indexes on vocabulary could be useful. Otherwise, an index on general readability may be sufficient.

If an approximate vocabulary is determined through some means, such as presenting words of different word frequencies to the user and estimating known vocabulary, then a different kind of measure is used. The vocabulary is no longer specific, so it is possible to use a general ranking based on word content. This essentially sorts documents into vocabulary complexity order.

However, if word frequency is the basis of the ranking, and readability is largely based on the percentage of words that are known, then it is not entirely clear that a single-valued ranking will represent the document readability for the user adequately. For example, suppose a user knows the 1000 most frequent words in the target language. In one document 95% of the words may occur in the set of 1000 most frequent words, and the remaining words may be quite infrequent. In another document, 95% of the words may come from the set of 1100 most frequent words, but the rest of the words may be more frequent than those in the first document. What has been established through language learning research is that a person needs to know about 95% of the words in a text to be able to read it with sufficient understanding to guess the words that are unknown (discussed by Ghadirian [9]). What we don't yet know is whether vocabulary is more or less important than other measures of readability, and whether this would differ greatly amongst users in ways other than general skill-level. The experiments discussed in the next section begin to shed light on these issues.

6   Experiments

There are several questions I wish to answer. First, are the measures of readability developed several decades ago the best ones to use for online text? These were mainly developed for assessing printed material and many were simplified for easy manual use. Second, do the same measures apply to different languages? Some studies do exist on specific languages [12]. Third, more specifically, do different measures apply if the learner is reading in a foreign language rather than their own? Most previous studies used children of different ages reading in their native language when developing readability formulae. In general word frequency and word length are inversely related, and longer sentences are more complex than shorter ones, but some established measures use the number of syllables per word, which may differ markedly for different languages or definitions of syllable. Fourth, is there sufficient reading material of a wide range of readability on the web? In this section I report on experiments that explore readability measures for readers of French as a foreign language.

The aim with this experiment was to determine which were the most important factors for readability for readers of French as a foreign language. In an initial exploratory study, I experimented with a small collection of French texts. A set of 10 books for which the number of known words out of the first 100 words was approximately 98 was used as a data set. A word was classed as "known" if I believed I could translate it.

Before analysing the text further, I ranked the readers in terms of perceived difficulty. There seemed to be three obvious levels of difficulty amongst the readers, with the majority (six) falling in the middle group. However, I gave each reader a unique ranking. I then determined the number of words per sentence for approximately the first 100 words of the text. Where there were less than six sentences in this amount of text I continued until the length of six sentences was determined.

Despite each of the texts having the same percentage of known words, there was a large range in perceived readability, from easy to very difficult. When comparing the words per sentence ranking with that of perceived readability, there seemed to be a fairly close correspondence. There was not quite such a correspondence between readability and word length, however.

I investigated this further with three human subjects ranking nine texts each. These texts were randomly selected from a collection consisting of graded readers, classic French literature, books written for French children, and for French adults, however, the majority (21 out of the 27 ranked texts) were written or adapted for students of French. The subjects had each studied French for several years at either secondary or tertiary level and had not actively maintained their knowledge. Two defined themselves as novices and the third as intermediate.

Once each human subject ranked their nine texts in order of readability I compared the ranking with several measures. These are described below.

Words per Sentence. The number of sentences in the first 100 words was counted. The number of words that made the final sentence complete was added to the 100 words, then this total was divided by the number of sentences.

Vocabulary Knowledge. At this stage this is based on the number of words that I couldn't define out of the first 100 words in each text. In future experiments the human subjects will judge this as well as readability. However, this measure came up with interesting results despite the author bias.

Word Complexity. The number of words within the first 100 of the text with more than two syllables. Determining this is problematic, especially for French. In this instance I decided to not include the usually silent final vowel as a separate syllable, despite this being sounded in some regional accents and in singing in French. This measure is also used in the SMOG formula.

Visual Factors. As the visual appearance of the texts was not held constant in this experiment, additional factors observed are the relative font size, amount of text per page, level of illustration, and type of vocabulary support.

Results. In Table 1 we can see the Spearman ranking correlation coefficients for the human subject's rankings of texts versus various measures. Each subject's ranking correlates to a statistically significant extent with that produced by the words per sentence measure. Vocabulary rating, however, was only significantly correlated with human ranking for those subjects (2 and 3) that rated themselves as novices.

Table 1. The result of comparing each human subject's ranking of 9 texts with several measures of the text. Figures represent the Spearman ranking correlation coefficient. For 9 items, values over 0.6 are considered to be related with a confidence factor of 95%. In addition, the correlation between the different measures on each set of text is shown. For interest, the author's ratings of a fourth set of texts is included.

Measure	1	2	3	Author
Words per sentence (w)	0.73	0.68	0.72	0.85
Vocab Rating (r)	0.13	0.87	0.80	0.59
w versus r	0.25	0.67	0.73	0.5
Person 2 judging person 1's texts				
Words per sentence (w)	0.93			
Vocab Rating (r)	0.01			

Discussion. The experiment revealed an interesting result, that vocabulary is less important than words per sentence in determining the difficulty of French texts for (English-speaking) learners of French. More specifically, it appears to be consistently important, whereas vocabulary is only important in some special cases.

The experiment leads to two possible hypotheses. The first is that the skill-level of the learner may be a factor in determining the most important variables for readability. It may be that the majority of texts were incomprehensible to the novice learners, so that their judgements were more likely to be based on their ability to recognise words instead of their ability to understand the sentences. To test this a further experiment was performed in which person 2, whose ranking correlated most highly with vocabulary, was given person 1's set of texts, which don't have a high correlation between vocabulary rating and words per sentence. To test the consistency of person 2's ranking assessment, he was then asked to rank the set of books he originally ranked (several weeks earlier).

The result of this further experiment is also shown in Table 1. Person 2's ranking of the second set of books correlated very highly with sentence length and not at all with vocabulary. Further, when reassessing his first set of texts he was highly consistent (correlation coefficient 0.96). Therefore we can conclude that the assessor's skill level is not likely to be the reason for the difference in correlations, and that human rankings are repeatable.

The second hypothesis is that vocabulary has a more complex relationship with words per sentence in assessing readability. The correlation between words per sentence and vocabulary rating in the three sets of texts varies from 0.25 to 0.73. Coincidentally the lowest correlations correspond to the lowest correlations of vocabulary with human ranking. It may be that vocabulary is only a good indicator when it correlates with sentence length.

The results also lead to questions regarding the nature of the ideal graded reader. Currently the main types are those based on vocabulary size, and those that use a general level classification such as intermediate and advanced. It may be that the vocabulary size is less important than the sentence simplification once students achieve a certain level, and that a stated readability level that describes this would give students a better guide than the stated vocabulary size.

As far as the web-based reader application is concerned, it may be that all that is required is a readability measure for each document, and a corresponding assessment of the learner requesting the reading material. However, vocabulary-based selection of texts can be driven by the user's desire to learn specific word lists, and thus still be a useful element of a reader application.

7   Summary and Conclusions

In this paper I described a novel application that provides reading material of a suitable level of difficulty from the vast collection on the internet. I believe that this application is feasible, at least to a practical level. Some aspects of the application would make use of existing search engine technology, however, the uses of the text are different and may lead to different indexing and searching techniques being required for efficient operation.

In order for this application to be effective, suitable readability measures are needed. I tested various measures against judgements by non-native readers of French text. It is very clear that a simple measure based on words per sentence is sufficient to consistently obtain a correlation of over 0.68 with human rankings of the texts. Other factors are less clear-cut and I conclude that the internal consistency of vocabulary and sentence length within the text may cause significant variation in readability results. I hope to examine this issue further in the near future. I raised many research questions and issues regarding this application, only some of which have been addressed. In future work I hope to further define a readability metric for foreign language readers and discover the best techniques for implementing the web reader application.

Acknowledgements. I thank James Thom and Justin Zobel for providing useful feedback. I also thank George Mitri, Theresa Wallner and John Harnett for their assistance with experiments.

References

1. K. Al-Seghayer. The effect of multimedia annotation modes on l2 vocabulary acquisition: a comparative study. *Language Learning and Technology*, 5(1):202–232, January 2001.
2. J. C. Alderson and A. H. Urquhart, editors. *Reading in a foreign language.* Applied linguistics and language study. Longman, 1984.
3. G. E. Vander Beke. *French Word Book,* volume 15 of *Publications of the American and Canadian Committees on Modern Languages.* Macmillan, 1929.
4. T. Bell. Extensive reading: speed and comprehension. *The Reading Matrix,* 1(1), April 2001.

5. L. Boutinon. *La mission de Slim Kerrigan.* Oxford rapid-reading French texts based on word-frequency. Oxford University Press, London, 1931. D. Gurney and G. C. Scott, editors.

6. A. Davies. Simple, simplified and simplification: what is authentic? In Alderson and Urquhart [2], chapter 9, pages 181–198.

7. F. R. de Chateaubriand. *Les aventures du dernier abencerage.* Siepmann's French Series for Rapid Reading. MacMillan and Co, London, 1909.

8. H. E. Ford and R. K. Hicks. *A new French reader.* J. M. Dent and sons Ltd, London, 1931.

9. S. Ghadirian. Providing controlled exposure to target vocabulary through the screening and arranging of texts. *Language Learning and Technology,* 6(1):147–164, January 2002.

10. S. Hunston. *Corpora in applied linguistics.* The Cambridge Applied Linguistics Series. Cambridge University Press, Cambridge, 2002.

11. M. Kellerman. *The forgotten third skill.* Pergamon Press, Oxford, 1981.

12. G. R. Klare. Assessing readability. *Reading Research Quarterly,* X:62–102, 1974.

13. G. Krantz. *Learning vocabulary in a foreign language: a study of reading strategies.* PhD thesis, University of Göteborg, Sweden, 1991.

14. L. L. Lomicka. "to gloss or not to gloss": an investigation of reading comprehension online. *Language Learning and Technology,* 1(2):41–50, January 1998.

15. W. L. Taylor. Cloze procedure: a new tool for measuring readability. *Journalism Quarterly,* pages 415–433, 1953.

16. J. H. Underwood. *Linguistics, computers, and the language teacher.* Newbury House Publishers, Inc, Massachusetts, 1981. Revision of thesis (doctoral) – University of California, Los Angeles.

17. D. M. Weible. Teaching reading skills through linguistic redundancy. *Foreign Language Annals,* 6:487–493, 1980.

Modelling the Adoption of Web-Based Mobile Learning – An Innovation Translation Approach

Arthur Tatnall[1] and Bill Davey[2]

[1]Victoria Graduate School of Business, Victoria University, Melbourne, Australia
[2]School of Information Technology, RMIT University, Melbourne, Australia

Abstract. The potential of mobile computing applications in learning is clear, but to have any of this potential realised is problematic. Before a new educational technology can be used it must be adopted. Conventional approaches to innovation suggest that adoption decisions are related mostly to the characteristics of the technology, but we think the process is much more complex than this and find these approaches too simplistic. In this paper we apply the principles of innovation translation theory to the process of adoption of mobile computing in web-based education.

1 Introduction

Web based mobile computing is penetrating a wide variety of fields [1–3]. Writers are now starting to examine the possibilities for educational delivery and management [4, 5]. But there is a problem. Even if its developer can show through a wealth of well researched evidence that this innovation will greatly improve the learning process, there is still no guarantee that it will be used, as many curriculum designers and educational technologists have discovered, to their cost.

Innovation diffusion theory [6] suggests that the acceptance of a new product or process is mostly due to the characteristics of this product or process. Experience tells us that many technologies have had more imagined uses in education than are ever realised. In this paper we will show that the application of innovation translation theory can be useful in investigating the introduction of new electronic technologies in education and learning.

2 E-learning as an Innovation

Innovation involves getting new ideas accepted and new technologies adopted and used. The introduction of new methods of e-learning into an organisation should thus be considered as an innovation. The first step to investigating this process is to examine and identify the factors inside and outside the organisation that support, and those that stand in the way of the adoption of these new methods. Our research has shown [7-9] that acceptance of an innovation is affected more by the complexity of the interactions between the *people* within the organisation than any supposedly

W. Zhou et al. (Eds.): ICWL 2003, LNCS 2783, pp. 433–441, 2003.

objective characteristics of the innovation itself. We will argue that to accommodate these complexities and to provide a useful socio-technical perspective, an innovation translation model [10] dealing with the interactions of human and non-human actors within the organisation provides an effective approach.

The more commonly known theory of innovation diffusion [6] suggests that there are four main elements to adoption: characteristic of the innovation itself, the nature of the communication channels, the passage of time, and the social system through which the innovation diffuses [8]. Rogers argues that the attributes and characteristics of the innovation itself are particularly important in determining the manner of its diffusion and the rate of its adoption, and outlines five characteristics of an innovation that affect its diffusion: relative advantage, compatibility, complexity, trialability and observability. We have argued [7], however, that this approach to innovation is rather too simplistic and that a better model would put more emphasis on the people involved.

Borrowing ideas from innovation translation in actor-network theory [10–13] we will argue that, rather than just the technology, *people* are very important, as they may either accept an innovation in its present form, modify it to a form where it becomes acceptable, or reject it completely. "If we know one thing about innovation and reform, it is that it cannot be done successfully *to* others." [14] An innovation translation approach has been shown to be useful in considering ICT (information and communications technology) innovation in small business [7] and in education [15–18].

Recent research has illustrated some of the complex processes people go through in deciding whether or not to adopt an educational technology [19], and we have argued that these can, in some ways, be related to an ecology [9, 20]. In this paper, however, we will incorporate some of the concepts of innovation translation into discussing the adoption and use of e-learning in organisations. Using a socio-technical approach such as this enables identification of factors that do not emerge from traditional approaches to innovation theory.

3   Innovation Translation and Actor-Network Theory

The innovation translation approach to innovation originates in actor-network theory (ANT) and draws on its sociology of translations. In ANT, translation [21] can be defined as: "... the means by which one entity gives a role to others." [22: 229]. Using an innovation translation approach to consider how the adoption of web-based mobile learning occurs, it is necessary to examine the interactions of all the actors involved. First, however, this requires identification of these actors. It is also important not to ignore the influence of the many non-human actors including computers, modems, Web browsers, Internet service providers, e-mail documents and Web pages. In trying to understand this adoption it is useful to see these interactions in terms of negotiations, not just between humans but also involving non-humans.

Actor-network theory [10, 21, 23] attempts impartiality between all actors, whether human or non-human, and makes no distinction in approach between the social, the natural and the technological. Using an actor-network approach all the factors (both human and non-human) influencing adoption of web-based mobile learning are seen as actors, and the combination of all of these in terms of networks. It is a feature of actor-network theory that the extent of a network is determined by actors that are able to make their presence *individually felt* [24] by other actors.

Research in technological innovation is often approached by focusing on the technical aspects of an innovation and treating 'the social' as the context in which its adoption takes place: assuming that outcomes of technological change can be attributed to the 'technological' rather than the 'social' [25]. On the other hand some would argue for social determinism which holds that social categories can be used to explain change. This concentrates on investigation of social interactions, relegating the technology to context. Bromley [26] argues that as long as 'technology' is seen as a distinct type of entity which is separate from 'society' the question will always need to be asked 'does technology affect society or not?' One answer to this question is that it does, but this leads us to the technological determinist position of viewing technology as autonomous and as having some essential attributes [27] that act externally to society. The other answer: that it does not, means that technology must be neutral and that individual humans must assign it their own values and decide on their own account how to use it. This view is close to a social determinist position. Bromley maintains that neither answer provides a useful interpretation of how technological innovation operates, and argues against an either/or stance like this. He argues that we should abandon the idea that technology is *separate* from society.

Rather than recognising in advance the essences of humans and of social organisations and distinguishing their actions from the inanimate behaviour of technological and natural objects, ANT adopts an anti-essentialist position in which it rejects there being some difference in essence between humans and non-humans [11]. To address the need to treat both human and non-human actors fairly and in the same way, ANT is based upon three principles: agnosticism, generalised symmetry and free association [23]. The first of these, agnosticism, means that analytical impartiality is demanded towards all the actors involved in the project under consideration, whether they be human or non-human. Generalised symmetry offers to explain the conflicting viewpoints of different actors in the same terms by use of an abstract and neutral vocabulary that works the same way for human and non-human actors. Neither the social nor the technical elements in these 'heterogeneous networks' [24] should then be given any special explanatory status. Finally, the principle of free association requires the elimination and abandonment of all a priori distinctions between the technological or natural, and the social [22, 23]. As Callon [23: 200] puts it: "The rule which we must respect is not to change registers when we move from the technical to the social aspects of the problem studied."

Actor-network theory has been used to investigate the success of a number of technological innovations and, in particular, to describe a number of heroic failures, several of which are listed below. Grint and Woolgar [25] have used ANT to explain the Luddite movement in England last century. McMaster et al. [28] have applied it to the adoption of a particular approach to systems analysis by a local council in the UK, and Vidgen and McMaster [29] to car parking systems. Latour has used innovation translation to describe the life and death of the revolutionary Parisian public transportation system known as Aramis [10]. An innovation translation model has also been used in several studies of curriculum innovation including those of Nespor [30], Gilding [31], Bigum [17, 32], Busch [18] and Tatnall [15].

Grint and Woolgar [25] note that an actor-network is configured by the enrolment of both human and non-human allies, and that this is done by means of a series of negotiations in a process of re-definition [23] where one set of actors seeks to impose definitions and roles on others. In an innovation translation model the movement of an innovation is in the hands of people [10] whom may react to it in different ways. Instead of a process of transmission we have a process of continuous transformation [10] where getting an innovation accepted calls for strategies aimed at the enrolment of others.

4   Improving the Chances of Adoption

The proponents of actor-network theory make no claim that ANT can be used to predict the outcome of adoption decisions by using innovation translation techniques. In fact, they would claim that the very complexity of the interactions makes it extremely unlikely that successful prediction is possible. We believe, however, that while not attempting prediction, it is possible to enhance the likelihood of successful adoption by paying attention to the lessions suggested by ANT.

The process of ANT analysis results in identification of a number of human and non-human actors and their networks of interactions with other actors. The interactions of some of these actors will soon be, on the whole, seen as working to enhance the adoption, while some others will be seen as acting to oppose it. We are not, of course, suggesting any simple relationship here where all actions of a given actor always enhance or always oppose. We are not even suggesting that every actor can easily be placed into one or other of these categories. What we are suggesting is that it is likely that there will be some overall trend that can be identified.

Suppose that, as one of the actors, a manager wants to facilitate the adoption of a specific new technology. We would then argue that he should begin by identifying these classes of actor (- those generally opposing adoption and those generally enhancing it). If he works to assist those that generally enhance the chances of adoption, and works against those who would generally oppose it [33], then the overall changes of adoption will be enhanced.

We are, of course, not speaking here of predicted certainties, just actions that may improve the likelihood of adoption. Use of this technique then gives a very practical relevance to the use of a translation approach to consideration of the adoption of technological innovations.

5   Two Situations Involving Mobile E-learning

To facilitate discussion within this short paper we will introduce two concrete examples of innovation and, by applying innovation translation theory, attempt to show the advantages of our suggested approach.

Consider first an example of mobile e-learning in a factory situation. A factory equips each employee with a Tablet PC fitted with wireless networking (- probably IEEE 802.11b or something similar). This contains delivery software and a profiling program for the particular employee. As an employee moves through the factory they will use different machines. For each machine the operating procedures and safety considerations are built into the machine and are made available through wireless networking. Software on the machine recognises the Tablet PC of a new operator and automatically downloads content to the Tablet. The employee then has delivered the learning package resident in the machine they are closest to. The Tablet PC configures this to what it has determined to be the learning style of the employee. Is adoption of this innovation likely and if so, how might we best implement the system?

Secondly we will consider another example of a mobile e-learning and information provision, this time related to educational management. Each teacher spends some time in curriculum development but much of their time in classrooms delivering classes. Each teacher is equipped with a Pocket PC (- something like a Compaq iPAQ or a Palm Pilot) and a mobile phone, each equipped with Bluetooth technology. The mobile phone also has a WAP (Wireless Application Protocol) interface using GPRS (General Packet Radio Service) technology. When the teacher is in the classroom she is able to use the mobile phone to contact the office intranet and to download relevant information about the job, the curriculum, and the students. In particular she is also able to download e-learning materials relating to the particular class, topic or student. Will she make use of the learning materials if they are delivered in this way, or will she wait till she gets back to the office to look at the printed manuals?

6   Applying Innovation Translation to Mobile E-learning

6.1   Mobile E-learning in a Factory

The first step in an actor-network analysis is to identify as many as possible of the (human and non-human) actors. In this case some are obvious: factory employees, management, factory machines, learning packages, Tablet PC, wireless networking, delivery software, profiling program. But there may well also be other actors. The way we then proceed is to interview the human actors and to investigate the non-human actors. We 'interview' the non-humans by looking at instruction manuals, speaking to various humans about them, investigating how, and why, they were built and any other techniques that simulate an interview situation. One of the things that will arise in these 'interviews' is the existence of other actors we did not identify earlier. We then proceed to 'follow the actors' [10] in determining what is important and what is not.

Discovering networks of associations and interactions comes next. In this case we might begin with the interactions between management and workers. If the employer-employee relationship in this company is such that the workers are suspicious of any initiative coming from management then this is likely to be significant. At this stage we attempt not to judge the likely consequences to potential adoption, just to note this interaction. Most of the other interactions are between the factory workers and various non-human actors. We would investigate how they use the machines; is this simple and straightforward, or is it difficult and clumsy? What about the interactions with each of the computer-based technologies? How does the employee interact with the learning package? Does the employee find this interaction stimulating, frustrating, difficult, irrelevant, or what? Do they like using the Tablet PC? Do they find carrying it around a nuisance? Does it sometimes get lost? How does management view these technologies? Do they have any interactions with them? Why did they purchase a particular brand of Tablet PC? Was it the best, or just the cheapest? How did they decide on the learning package? Why did they decide to use mobile technologies rather than a training room? There are many questions that need to be asked, and from the answers a general picture will be built up of the relationship between the employees, the management and the various technologies.

The researcher using actor-network theory would investigate all of these interactions and look at how successful they were. They would look for potential problems, like the management imposing new situations on workers who were not happy to respond. Potential problems also exist with the various technologies. For instance there may be an unacceptable level of radio frequency interference inside the factory of a type that makes using wireless technologies an unreliable activity.

After the analysis is complete, can management make use of the results to enhance the chances of adoption? We would argue that by addressing issues of concern in the interactions between the various actors that they can, and should, do so. Perhaps they need to address a radio-frequency interference problem. Perhaps they need to ensure that the learning materials are more intuitive and easy to use. Perhaps they need to ensure that there are convenient places for factory workers to leave their Tablet PCs when they are not in use. If there is a problem between management and workers then they should certainly address it, but one could question whether this would happen now if it had not happened before anyway.

6.2 Mobile E-learning and Educational Management

The potential actors that can be quickly identified in this second example are students, school teachers, school principals, classrooms, mobile phones, Pocket PCs, Bluetooth technology, WAP, GPRS, e-learning materials, student information and curriculum information. But are all these potential actors able to make 'their presence individually felt' [24] by other actors? It may be that students, although very important in the overall school situation, are not relevant to this one. If they are not able to have any influence on the use of this new system, and are not directly affected by it then they should not be considered as actors.

Like the previous example, the associations and interactions between the principal and the teachers are of interest, and will be relevant in this analysis. Again, like the previous example, most of the other networks of interactions are between human and non-human actors. Do the teachers find the technology easy to use? Do they find that it interrupts their work? Is the student information material provided of use to these teachers in the classroom, or would they get as much value from it back in the staffroom? Similarly with the curriculum materials; are these needed 'on the move' or would they be more use when the teacher is preparing work in their office or back at home?

Interactions between sets of non-human actors are also significant. Does GPRS work properly with WAP, and do both work seamlessly on the mobile phones provided? Can the curriculum materials be usefully delivered on the small screen of a Pocket PC? Are the Pocket PCs reliable? Does the carrier chosen for the mobile phones provide uninterrupted service in this area all of the time?

To improve the likelihood of adoption a school principal could usefully consider these interactions, identifying those likely to cause problems. Perhaps the use of the available curriculum materials should be de-emphasised if this is not found to be of use when the teacher is in action in the classroom. Perhaps instead, the provision of student information should be made the main use of the system.

What we are arguing here is that with a good grasp of what the interactions and associations actually are, we are in a much better position to facilitate adoption of a new technology. There is, of course, still no guarantee that this adoption will successful, but we suggest that the chances of success can be thus enhanced.

7 Conclusion

The main advantages of using an innovation translation model to consider whether or not a new e-learning approach is likely to succeed in an organisation relate to a presumption of complexity and interaction. What we are suggesting is that concepts of complexity and interaction in this field can be usefully applied to a consideration of an e-learning implementation. We also argue that use of such a model offers an opportunity to improve the chances of successfully innovation through the ways that the new e-learning method is implemented.

In any field it is necessary to use language in framing research questions and in offering explanations. The innovation translation approach goes a long way towards accommodating complexity and the use of this approach can provide good insights into whether or not a mobile e-learning innovation is likely to be adopted. Furthermore it can be used to facilitate this adoption.

References

1. Porn, L.M. and Patrick, K., *Mobile computing acceptance grows as applications evolve.* Journal of Database Management, 2001. **12**(2): p. 36.
2. Stevenson, S., *Mobile computing places data in the palm of the hand: Devices deliver real-time access to information.* Ophthalmology Times, 2001. **26**(4): p. 15.
3. Rodger, J.A., Pendharkar, P.C., and Khosrow-Pour, M., *Mobile Computing at the Department of Defense.* 2002, Hershey, PA: Idea Group Publishing.
4. Tolson, S.D., *Wireless Laptops and Local Area Networks.* Technological Horizons in Education, 2001. **28**(11): p. 62.
5. Tolson, S.D., *Simple Internet Access and Management.* Technological Horizons in Education, 2001. **28**(6): p. 28.
6. Rogers, E.M., *Diffusion of Innovations.* 4th edition. 1995, New York: The Free Press.

7. Tatnall, A. and Davey, B., *Understanding the Process of Information Systems and ICT Curriculum Development: Three Models*, in *Human Choice and Computers: Issues of Choice and Quality of Life in the Information Society*, K. Brunnstein and Berleur, J., Editors. 2002, Kluwer Academic Publishers / IFIP: Assinippi Park, Ma. p. 275–282.
8. Tatnall, A., *Modelling Technological Change in Small Business: Two Approaches to Theorising Innovation*, in *Managing Information Technology in Small Business: Challenges and Solutions*, S. Burgess, Editor. 2002, Idea Group Publishing: Hershey, PA. p. 83–97.
9. Tatnall, A. and Davey, B., *Information Systems Curriculum Development as an Ecological Process*, in *IT Education: Challenges for the 21st Century*, E. Cohen, Editor. 2002, Idea Group Publishing: Hershey, PA. p. 206–221.
10. Latour, B., *Aramis or the Love of Technology*. 1996, Cambridge, Ma: Harvard University Press.
11. Latour, B., *The Powers of Association*, in *Power, Action and Belief. A new sociology of knowledge? Sociological Review monograph 32*, J. Law, Editor. 1986, Routledge & Kegan Paul: London. p. 264–280.
12. Latour, B., *On Recalling ANT*, in *Actor Network Theory and After*, J. Law and Hassard, J., Editors. 1999, Blackwell Publishers: Oxford. p. 15–25.
13. Law, J., ed. *A Sociology of Monsters. Essays on power, technology and domination.* 1991, Routledge: London.
14. Fullan, M.G. and Stiegelbauer, S., *The New Meaning of Educational Change.* 2nd edition ed. 1991, New York: Teachers College Press.
15. Tatnall, A., *Innovation and Change in the Information Systems Curriculum of an Australian University: a Socio-Technical Perspective*, in *PhD thesis*, Education, Editor. 2000, Central Queensland University: Rockhampton.
16. Tatnall, A. and Davey, B. *How Visual Basic Entered the Curriculum at an Australian University: An Account Informed by Innovation Translation.* in *Challenges to Informing Clients: A Transdisciplinary Approach (Informing Science 2001).* 2001. Krakow, Poland.
17. Bigum, C., *Solutions in Search of Educational Problems: Speaking for Computers in Schools.* Educational Policy, 1998. **12**(5): p. 586–596.
18. Busch, K.V. *Applying Actor Network Theory to Curricula Change in Medical Schools: Policy Strategies for Initiating and Sustaining Change.* in *Midwest Research-to-Practice Conference in Adult, Continuing and Community Education Conference.* 1997. Michigan State University.
19. Naidu, S., Cunnington, D., and Jasen, C., *The Experience of Practitioners with Technology Enhanced Teaching and Learning.* Educational Technology & Society, 2002. **5**(1): p. 23–34.
20. Tatnall, A. and Davey, B., *ICT and Training: A Proposal for an Ecological Model of Innovation.* Educational Technology & Society, 2003. **6**(1): p. 14–17.
21. Law, J., *Notes on the Theory of the Actor-Network: Ordering, Strategy and Heterogeneity.* Systems Practice, 1992. **5**(4): p. 379–393.
22. Singleton, V. and Michael, M., *Actor-Networks and Ambivalence: General Practitioners in the UK Cervical Screening Programme.* Social Studies of Science, 1993. **23**: p. 227–264.
23. Callon, M., *Some Elements of a Sociology of Translation: Domestication of the Scallops and the Fishermen of St Brieuc Bay*, in *Power, Action & Belief. A New Sociology of Knowledge?*, J. Law, Editor. 1986, Routledge & Kegan Paul: London. p. 196–229.
24. Law, J., *Technology and Heterogeneous Engineering: The Case of Portuguese Expansion*, in *The Social Construction of Technological Systems: New Directions in the Sociology and History of Technology*, W.E. Bijker, Hughes, T.P., and Pinch, T.J., Editors. 1987, MIT Press: Cambridge, Ma. p. 111–134.

25. Grint, K. and Woolgar, S., *The Machine at Work - Technology, Work and Organisation.* 1997, Cambridge: Polity Press. 199.
26. Bromley, H., *The Social Chicken and the Technological Egg: Educational Computing and the Technology/Society Divide.* Educational Theory, 1997. **47**(1): p. 51-63.
27. Tatnall, A. and Gilding, A. *Actor-Network Theory and Information Systems Research. 10th Australasian Conference on Information Systems (ACIS).* 1999. Wellington: Victoria University of Wellington.
28. McMaster, T., Vidgen, R.T., and Wastell, D.G. *Towards an Understanding of Technology in Transition. Two Conflicting Theories. Information Systems Research in Scandinavia, IRIS20 Conference.* 1997. Hanko, Norway: University of Oslo.
29. Vidgen, R., T. and McMaster, T., *Black Boxes, Non-Human Stakeholders, and the Translation of IT through Mediation,* in *Information Technology and Changes in Organizational Work,* W.J. Orlikowski, Editor. 1996, Chapman & Hall: London. p. 250-271.
30. Nespor, J., *Knowledge in Motion: Space, Time and Curriculum in Undergraduate Physics and Management.* 1994, London: Falmer Press.
31. Gilding, T., *Student Construction of a Knowledge-based System as an Actor Network,* in *School of Education.* 1997, Deakin University: Geelong. p.198.
32. Bigum, C., *Boundaries, Barriers and Borders: Teaching Science in a Wired World.* Australian Science Teachers Journal, 1998. **44**(1): p. 13-24.
33. Lewin, K., *Frontiers in group dynamics.* Human Relations, 1947(1): p. 5-41.

Adaptive Educational Hypermedia Based on Multiple Student Characteristics

Herman D. Surjono* and John R. Maltby

School of Multimedia & Information Technology, Southern Cross University
PO Box 157, Military Road, Lismore NSW 2480 Australia
{hsurjo10, jmaltby}@scu.edu.au

Abstract. The learning process in Adaptive Educational Hypermedia (AEH) environments is complex and may be influenced by aspects of the student, including prior knowledge, learning styles, experience and preferences. Current AEH environments, however, are limited to processing only a small number of student characteristics. This paper discusses the development of an AEH system which includes a student model that can simultaneously take into account multiple student characteristics. The student model will be developed to use stereotypes, overlays and perturbation techniques.

Keywords: Adaptive educational hypermedia, multiple characteristics, student model.

1 Introduction

The World Wide Web (WWW) has become a powerful environment for distributing information and many educational providers are using it to deliver knowledge to an increasingly wide and diverse audience. One of the initial approaches to delivering instruction via the Internet was to use web-based instruction (WBI). WBI is a hypermedia-based instructional program that utilizes the attributes and resources of the WWW to create a meaningful learning environment [1]. However, many WBIs are still oriented toward classroom style student groups that are expected to be homogeneous in terms of knowledge, motivation, learning styles, etc. Internet sites that use simple WBI tend to convey the same hypertext pages to every student, irrespective of the student's ability and background knowledge. This inflexibility provides many students with a less than optimum learning curve.

Students who study a course on the Internet tend to be more heterogeneously distributed than those found in a traditional classroom situation. Where this is the case, learning material should, if possible, be presented in a more personalised way. This problem is being addressed by the development of *Adaptive Educational Hypermedia* (AEH) systems. These systems combine ideas from hypermedia and intelligent tutoring systems to produce applications that adapt to meet individual educational needs. An AEH system dynamically collects and processes data about student goals, preferences and knowledge to adapt the material being delivered to the educational needs of the student [2]. Currently, however, most systems are capable of processing only a small number of student characteristics [3]. Since the learning process is influenced

---

* On study leave from the Dept. of Electronic Engineering, Yogyakarta State Univ., Indonesia

W. Zhou et al. (Eds.): ICWL 2003, LNCS 2783, pp. 442–449, 2003.

by many factors, including prior knowledge, experience, learning styles and preferences, it is important that the student model of an AEH system accommodates such factors in order to adapt accurately to student needs. This paper proposes the design of an AEH system with a student model that will simultaneously take into account multiple student characteristics.

2 Adaptive Educational Hypermedia

Adaptive hypermedia technology is actually a combination of two distinctive technologies, those of hypermedia and adaptive systems. According to Brusilovsky [2], adaptive hypermedia systems (AHS) can be defined as all hypertext and hypermedia systems that accommodate some user characteristics into the user model and apply this model to adapt various visible aspects of the system to the user. Three key components of the system are hypertext/hypermedia, the user model and the ability to adapt the hypermedia using the user model. According to De Bra [4], an AHS builds a user model by observing the user's browsing behaviour or by testing to determine what the user's background, experience, knowledge and interests are. These user characteristics are then used by the system to individualize the knowledge presentation. The presentation is adapted to the user model, and the user model is constantly updated as the user reads and interacts with the presentation.

Adaptive educational hypermedia (AEH) is one of the earliest applications of AHS and currently the most popular application in the field of adaptive systems. The advances of Internet technologies and the acceptance of distance learning have pushed many researchers and educators to develop educational hypermedia systems. Some interesting AEH that use the Web as a development platform include ELM-ART, InterBook, and 2L670. One of the most well-known general-purpose adaptive hypermedia systems is called AHA and it has been used to develop several educational adaptive hypermedia applications [5].

Two of the main advantages of Web-based instruction are classroom and platform independence: AEH extends these advantages by offering learners personalised instruction in a distance learning setting. Being adaptive is important when students have different needs, preferences, abilities, interests, behaviour, knowledge, etc. In addition, student knowledge and experience evolve over time in a student-dependent manner: students who have similar needs at the start of a course may follow very different paths and learning curves.

The basic components of existing AEH systems are the *domain model*, the user or *student model* and the *adaptation model*. The domain model is the subject area for which the adaptive hypermedia is intended as a resource, the student model is a collection of student characteristics and the adaptation model describes the parts of the hypermedia system that can be adapted and the circumstances under which this adaptation is to occur [6].

The main component of the AEH system is a student model that stores and processes relevant student characteristics. The student model maintains up-to-date information about each student's goals, background knowledge, etc. The system gathers information by asking the student to fill out questionnaires or achievement tests and by observing the browsing behavior of the student. The more precise and correct the student model, the more advanced the types of adaptation that can be supported.

In terms of method and technique for providing adaptation, Brusilovsky [7] identified two major areas: *adaptive presentation* (content adaptation) and *adaptive navigation support* (link adaptation). *Adaptive presentation* is the general term for techniques used to adapt the content of a web page based on the user model. These techniques include adaptive text presentation and adaptive multimedia presentation. *Adaptive navigation support* is the term for techniques used to modify the links accessible to the user at a particular time. These techniques include: direct guidance, adaptive link sorting, adaptive link hiding, adaptive link removal, adaptive link disabling, adaptive link annotation and map adaptation [2].

Most current systems are capable of considering only a small number of student characteristics for the adaptation [3]. According to Carver et al. [8] current student models normally limit characteristics to a single dimension. AES-CS [9] is an adaptive educational system that includes accommodations for cognitive styles in order to improve student interactions and learning outcomes. INSPIRE [10] is an adaptive system that monitors learner's activity and dynamically adapts the generated lessons to accommodate diversity in learner's knowledge state and learning style. NetCoach, an authoring system which supports the development of adaptive hypermedia, uses relations between visited pages and learner responses to test items [11]. AHA uses the fact that each student visits a specific page to update an estimate of his/her knowledge [12]. Whilst this is a practical approach, it has a major disadvantage: clearly, it is difficult to measure a student's knowledge simply by monitoring pages visited as it is not sure whether or not the student has really read and understood the information on each page.

3 Student Model Based on Multiple Student Characteristics

The student model for the proposed AHS will be developed using techniques of stereotyping, overlays and perturbation. Stereotyping, where students are assigned to a specific group or stereotype, is one of the simplest of student modelling techniques. There are two types of stereotyping: *fixed* and *default*. In *fixed stereotyping* students are cast according to their performance into a predefined stereotype that is determined by academic level. Default stereotyping is a much more flexible approach: at the beginning of a session the students are stereotyped to default values, but as the learning process progresses and student performance data is obtained, the settings of the initial stereotype are gradually replaced by more individualized settings [13].

The overlay is a classic student modelling technique. An overlay model is a student modelling technique in which student performance is considered to be a subset of expert knowledge in the subject domain [14]. In order to use the overlay model, the domain knowledge must be able to be broken down into generic items such as rules, concepts, facts, etc. Basically, the model estimates the level of mastery of each item in the domain that is considered to be fully mastered by an expert. The perturbation model is an extension of the overlay model that represents the student's knowledge as including possible misconceptions as well as a subset of the expert's knowledge [15]. This extension allows for better remediation of student mistakes, since the fact that a student believes something that is incorrect is pedagogically significant.

In the construction of the student model, many different aspects can be taken into account, such as the existing student knowledge of the application domain, the cognitive and learning styles of the student, and the student goals, preferences and background. The student model will build a student profile that stores information for each student. Profile updating (in the case of overlay models), or an assignment of a student's characteristics to a profile (in the case of stereotype models), requires access to the information that the student gives to the system [16]. This information can be collected by querying the student or by observing his/her actions.

The learning process in an actual AEH environment is complex and influenced by many characteristics of the student. It is therefore important to consider accommodating as many of these characteristics as possible into the student model in order to generate an accurate adaptation. However, many student characteristics have been identified in the literature; it is therefore important to select for use in the student model only those characteristics that directly influence student achievement in the learning process, otherwise the design of the student model will become unnecessarily complex. The student characteristics to be considered in the proposed system are knowledge, learning styles, experience, background and preference. Other characteristics such as age, sex/gender, race/ethnicity, demographic data, interests, etc are not taken into account as they are considered significantly less influential to student achievement.

Information about student characteristics is generally initialised either with default values or by querying the student. Thereafter, it is maintained by the system and students may be able to review or edit their own profiles. Student actions and events at various conceptual levels, such as mouse clicks, task completion and requests for help, are reported by the application to the student profile as well. An analysis engine combines the student profile with other models of the system to derive new student information. The analysis engine can update the student profile with the derived information or initiate an action in the application. Constructing the student model, analysing a student profile and deriving new information can be done by using, amongst others, Bayesian techniques, logic-based techniques, machine learning techniques, stereotype-based techniques and inference rules [17].

Most of the existing AEH systems consider only student knowledge as a means for providing adaptivity. Student knowledge is a variable with a different time-dependent value for each student. Thus adaptive systems must evaluate student knowledge at appropriate stages throughout the learning process, recognise the changes in knowledge status and then update the student model accordingly. Assessment tests that are part of the educational material can include special questions to assess the learner's level of performance.

Typically, a student's learning style is initialised through the submission of a questionnaire the first time the student logs onto the system. This allows the learning style to be automatically determined and stored in an individual student model. Alternatively, the learning style can be directly initialised or updated by the student, who is offered the option to select his/her dominant learning style based on information provided by the system about the general characteristics of the different learning style categories.

Finally, information stored in the student model is a valuable resource which enables a tutor to monitor progress and study student attitude; in addition, a quantitative evaluation of learners' preferences, in terms of the time spent, performance, help request frequency, etc., can provide useful information about the quality of the material used.

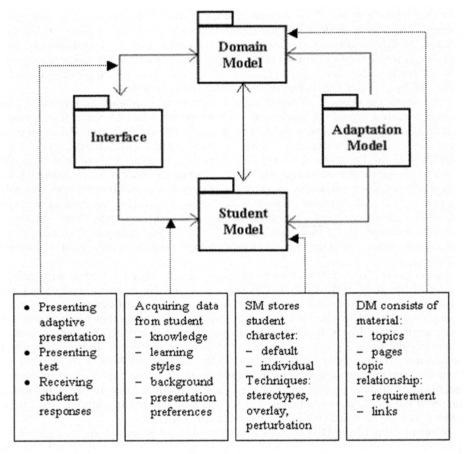

Fig. 1. The system architecture

4 System Architecture

The proposed system architecture is documented at high-level in Figures 1 and 2 using the UML notation. It consists of four major components: the interface, the student model (SM), the domain model (DM) and the adaptation model (AM). Students will interact with the system through the interface in the form of a web browser such as Microsoft Internet Explorer. The other modules of SM, DM, and AM will reside in a web server that supports a Java environment. The system architecture depicted in Figure 1 is composed from all components that are represented as packages, the standard UML grouping mechanism.

Stereotyping is initially used to store information whilst the system waits to gather something better; then the overlay method is employed. The conceptual model of the SM is shown in Figure 2.

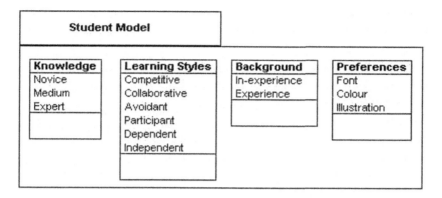

Fig. 2. The conceptual model of the student model

The initial knowledge level of each student will be obtained from tests that are presented at the beginning of the first session. From the student responses collected by the system, the SM will assign a particular value to the student regarding his/her knowledge level. Students may choose not to do the initial test and in this case the SM will assign a default value to the student knowledge. Whilst the learning session is progressing the system will present an achievement test every time a student has completed a particular topic. The test score will update the student knowledge level in the SM. This knowledge level will then be used by the adaptation model for controlling the presentation of learning materials.

In order to learn optimally, especially in a distance learning environment, students must be aware of their own learning style. However, sometimes it is difficult for students to determine what their learning style is. The system will gather information about each student's style by presenting a questionnaire at the beginning of the learning session. There are many different categorizations of learning style inventories available in the literature. The Grasha-Riechmann Student Learning Styles Scale (GRSLSS) is ideal for assessing student learning styles in a college-level distance education setting [18]. The GRSLSS identifies six dimensions of learning styles as follows: *competitive* (compete with other students), *collaborative* (believe they can learn by sharing ideas), *avoidant* (uninterested by what happens in class), *participant* (eager to take part in class activities), *dependent* (need structure and support) and *independent* (like to work alone). Student scores for each of these dimensions will be stored in the SM so that they can influence the way the material is to be presented to the student.

The SM will also take into account the existing computing experience of the student. The system will offer selected questions to obtain an estimate of this experience. Students with little or no computing experience will receive special treatment until such time as their skill improves. The treatment will consist of presenting basic guidance on how to proceed, answer questions and do certain learning tasks; it will be employed only until a student has improved his/her skill to the necessary level. The final characteristics to be taken into account will be presentation preferences such as font, colour, illustration, etc.

The domain model (DM) contains a collection of learning materials. A course module implemented in the system can be divided into a number of topics with a particular value for each according to the level of difficulty. Each topic consists of several pages depending upon its complexity. The relationship between one topic and another can be expressed in terms of requirements such as pre-requisites, depending upon the nature of the topic. Students working on a particular topic can undertake tests at any time to evaluate their achievement for that topic. In order to advance to another topic which is at a higher academic level, students must pass a threshold score that is determined in the relationship rules.

The proposed AEH will be developed in the domain of electronics theory (a subject familiar to one of the authors) and targeted at university level students who are learning principles of electronics. Reasons why electronics is appropriate for use in web-based learning environments include the desirability of allowing students to practice and apply principal theories interactively and to provide immediate time-saving feedback to prevent students learning incorrect concepts. The uniqueness of this system compared to existing web-based learning systems for electronics theory is the capability to adapt the presentation to individual student needs. More specifically this system will take into account multiple student characteristics as a basis for providing the adaptation, so that the system will perform adaptation to students' needs more individually and accurately. This benefit is hoped to be the main contribution to the field of web-based learning systems.

The adaptation model (AM) contains adaptation and relationship rules. The adaptation rules describe how a page is presented to the student according to his/her own SM. Each time the student is assigned a score for a test, the SM will update his/her level of knowledge. In the proposed system, the level of knowledge will not be updated if the student is just accessing pages without undergoing a test; it is necessary to make sure that a student has understood a pre-requisite topic before advancing to a further topic. The relationship rules describe how any page or topic is related to other pages or topics in the DM.

The implementation of the AHS will use the following technologies. The student model and domain model will be implemented using XML/XSL files and a MySQL database. XML (Extensible Markup Language) and XSL (Extensible Stylesheet Language) technologies allow content to be separated from the presentation. XML is used to store the content and XSL is used to present pages with different layouts. The PHP scripting language will be used to present a dynamic content within a static document and is also appropriate for reading information from web forms and maintaining sessions between web pages. These sessions have to be maintained in order to store and update student names, browsing behaviour, student history and other student specific information in the student model. The adaptation model and interface will be implemented in a Java environment and enhanced by JavaScript and other graphical based software.

5   Conclusion and Future Work

Most existing AEH systems utilize student models that take account of only a small number of student characteristics. We contend that such models can provide only limited adaptability for the host application and, as such, do not optimize student learning for individual students. Since the learning process in an actual environment is complex and influenced by many aspects, it is important to consider these aspects in the design of an adaptive web-based learning system. Accordingly, research has commenced into prototyping an AEH system that incorporates a multi-dimensional student model to accommodate multiple student characteristics such as knowledge, learning styles, backgrounds and preferences.

References

1. Kahn, B.H., *Web-Based Instruction (WBI): What is it and why is it?*, In *Web-Based instruction*, B.H. Kahn, Editor. 1997, Educational Technology Publications: Englewood Cliffs, NJ. p. 5–18.
2. Brusilovsky, P., *Methods and techniques of adaptive hypermedia.* User Modeling and User Adapted Interaction, 1996. **6**(2-3): p. 87–129.
3. Carro, M.R. *Adaptive Hypermedia in Education: New Considerations and Trends.* In *the 6th World Multiconference on Systemics, Cybernetics and Informatics.* 2002. Orlando, Florida.
4. De Bra, P., *Adaptive Educational Hypermedia on the Web.* Communication of the ACM, 2002. **45**(5): p. 60–61.
5. Calvi, L. and A. Cristea, *Towards Generic Adaptive Systems: Analysis of a Case Study.* Adaptive Hypermedia & Adaptive Web-Based Systems, 2002. **LNCS 2347**: p. 79–89.
6. Pascoe, R. and A. Sallis. *A Pedagogical Basis for Adaptive WWW Textbooks.* In *North American Web Developers Conference.* 1998.
7. Brusilovsky, P., *Adaptive Hypermedia.* User Modeling and User Adapted Interaction, 2001. **11**: p. 87–110.
8. Carver, C.A.J., J.M.D. Hill, and U.W. Pooch. *Third Generation Adaptive Hypermedia Systems.* In *World Conference on the WWW and Internet (WebNet 99).* 1999. Honolulu, Hawaii.
9. Triantafillou, E., A. Pomportsis, and E. Georgiadou. *AES-CS: Adaptive Educational System based on Cognitive Styles.* In *the Workshop on Adaptive System for Web-based Education, held in conjunction with AH'2002.* 2002. Malaga, Spain.
10. Papanikolaou, K., A., et al. *INSPIRE: An INtelligent System for Personalized Instruction in a Remote Environment.* In *Third Workshop on Adaptive Hypertext and Hypermedia.* 2001. Berlin: Springer-Verlag.
11. Lippitsch, S., S. Weibelzahl, and G. Weber, *Adaptive Learning Courses in Pedagogical Psychology The PSI Project and the authoring system NetCoach.* Künstliche Intelligenz, 2002. **3**(02).
12. De Bra, P. and L. Calvi. *AHA: a Generic Adaptive Hypermedia System.* In *the 2nd Workshop on Adaptive Hypertext and Hypermedia HYPERTEXT'98.* 1998. Pittsburgh, USA.
13. Kay, J., *Stereotypes, Student Models and Scrutability*, In *Proceedings of Fifth International Conference on Intelligent Tutoring Systems*, G. Gauthier, C. Frasson, and K. VanLehn, Editors. 2000, Springer-Verlag: Montreal. p. 19–30.
14. Beck, J., M. Stern, and E. Haugsjaa, *Applications of AI in Education*, In *ACM Crossroads Student Magazine.* 1996.
15. Mayo, M.J., *Bayesian Student Modelling and Decision-Theoretic Selection of Tutorial Actions in Intelligent Tutoring Systems*, In *Computer Science.* 2001, University of Canterbury.
16. Cannataro, M., A. Cuzzocrea, and A. Pugliese. *A Probabilistic Approach to Model Adaptive Hypermedia Systems.* In *1st International Workshop on Web Dynamics (in Conjunction with the 8th International Conference on Database Theory).* 2001. London, UK.
17. Kules, B., *User Modeling for Adaptive and Adaptable Software Systems.* 2000. [Available On-line] http://www.otal.umd.edu/UUGuide/wmk/, Accessed 17 December 2002.
18. Grasha, A.F., *Teaching with styles: A practical guide to enhancing learning by understanding teaching and learning styles.* 2002, Pittsburgh, PA: Alliance Publishers.

Distributed Web-Based Critiquing of Electronically Submitted Assessment

Penny Baillie-de Byl

Department of Mathematics and Computing
University of Southern Queensland
Toowoomba, Queensland, 4350, Australia
penny.baillie@usq.edu.au

Abstract. The increased use of Internet technologies in education has in the past, been primarily focused on the student's needs. Very little research and development has looked at the course management and administrative needs of the teacher. It is usually the case that when learning management systems (LMS) are introduced into a course, the teacher's work load is increased. The assessment critiquing tool (Classmate) discussed in this paper has been developed with the teacher in mind. The tool manages the distribution, critiquing, mark recording, feedback generation and final grading of electronically submitted assignments through an online environment designed to marry with existing LMS technology. This paper will investigate the architecture of Classmate, illustrate its use and discuss the advantages of the systems use.

Keywords. Online assignment submission management, Authoring tools, Electronic submission, Distance learning, Large-scale class management

Glossary. As it is common for different Universities to refer to the same entities using differing terminology, for clarity we will precede the content of this paper with the language used herein. A single class in which a student is enrolled will be referred to as a *course*, the manager of this course will be called an *examiner* and a *marker* is a person that evaluates a student's work. The term *marking* is defined as a process undertaken by a marker in which a student's work is critiqued for the purpose of determining a grade.

1 Introduction

The escalation of the Internet has caused dramatic growth in the number of online applications and development tools for educators [1]. Developers such as WebCT (http://www.webct.com) and Blackboard (http://www.blackboard.com) provide suites of software that assist teachers in developing online course content by suppling turn-key applications that offer content presentation, interactive learning environments and student activity tracking. The focus of online education has changed from the simple reproduction of teaching materials on webpages to the goal of motivating students to become interactive learners [2]. However in the rush to enhance ways of delivering

W. Zhou et al. (Eds.): ICWL 2003, LNCS 2783, pp. 450–461, 2003.

pedagogical materials electronically, the administrative role of the examiner has all but been forgotten.

One fundamental administrative role performed by an examiner is that of managing student assignments. This task includes assignment collection, critiquing, providing feedback to the student and recording the grades as well as (in large-scale classes) managing a team of marker's (performing the same critiquing procedures) while having to ensure the feedback to students is timely, useful, justified and consistent among a team of markers. Popular learning management systems such as WebCT and Blackboard provide very little automated assistance in performing this task.

Enter the computer science department examiners.

For a time extending back to before the popular use of the Internet, in a time of emails and file transferring (FTP) in the late 1980s, small groups of examiners at various international educational institutions, working independently, saw the potential of this new global network working in conjunction with their own computer programs to assist them in their administrative tasks. This saw email and FTP being used to transfer electronic versions of student work[1] between markers and the storage of student results in simple distributed database/text files. These systems have experienced a natural evolution as use of the World Wide Web has increased.

One such development was automated marking systems designed to reduce the examiner's workload whilst still assessing students' knowledge. Contemporary online teaching environments provide a plethora of these types of assessment tools. However, while methods such as multiple choice, matching, fill-in-the-blank and formulaic questions lend themselves to online education and automated marking [3], the primary disadvantage of these assessment methods is their poor ability to accurately reflect student learning [4].

Although it is possible to integrate a more accurate means of testing a student's knowledge and understanding (for example, essays and projects [4]) into an online teaching environment [5], the advantages of using contemporary online education environments ends after the electronic submission. The expert judgment of the respective examiner is essential in marking and critiquing work [6]. Many online educators shy away from electronic submission of essays and projects because of the level of technical expertise required to disseminate, open, critique and administer them [4].

While the motivation in using technology in teaching has been to enhance the student's learning experience, the premise for automated or semi-automated assessment systems has been an attempt at significantly reducing the workloads of examiners with relation to repetitive and trivial assessment related tasks. Allowing electronic submission of assignments may reduce the time it takes for assignments to arrive at the examiner's doorstep, however it does not reduce other assignment management and critiquing tasks inherent of marking any essay or project (on paper or in electronic form). Many commercially available learning management systems (LMS) such as WebCT, Blackboard, Top Class and CourseInfo and institutionally develop systems

---

[1] At this time the majority of student work presented in electronic format was that of computer science students who had access to the technology and from the nature of their studies worked with computer files.

such as Submit [7], NetFace [8] and AMS [9] provide methods for submitting assignments utilising the Internet, however, the assistance they provide to the examiner after submission is limited.

This lack of foresight may help fuel the fire for researcher's such as Noble who has claimed that virtual universities are doomed to fail due to their shoddy attempts at automation by administrators [10]. If manual systems are to be replaced with online systems, the applications need to mirror current practice, reduce workload and integrate with other administrative systems. Beyond the process of assignment submission, acceptance of assignments in electronic format by examiners will rely on a system that addresses the shortcomings in the assignment critiquing and management process [11]. These include 1) inconsistent feedback given among markers; 2) administering the return of feedback to students; 3) the double handling of student results from personal spreadsheets into university databases; 4) the tracking of marking progress without elaborate administration and continued communication with the markers in large-scale classes; and, 5) sometimes lengthy turn-around time of assignments from submission to feedback.

Preston and Shackelford [12] suggest the ideal online marking system would 1) place emphasis on the students submitted work, 2) allow a holistic view of the submitted work, 3) provide quick and easy navigation between sections of the work, 4) highlight syntax to improve readability, 5) provide markers with a logical and consistent means of critiquing, 6) allow for student by student or problem by problem marking, 7) separate the interface of the system from the implementation, and 8) automate grade submission and file downloading and uploading.

This paper outlines the *Classmate* system which addresses these issues. Classmate allows a team of markers to assess students' work in an organised, virtual marking and critiquing environment providing timely, valuable and consistent feedback to the students. The system consists of a collection of agents that semi-automate the marking of assignments. The paper begins with an overview of the current literature in online assessment practices. This is followed by a discussion on the Classmate architecture and its use. The paper concludes with a look at future developments for the system.

2   Related Work

Developing automated assessment systems is not new in computing disciplines. Examiners who work within the computing domain have the necessary skills to design and write programs for their own use. It would be uncommon to find a computing department at a university that did not have its own course specific student batch processing systems whether they are for automated marking or final grade calculations. These types of narrow-focused systems, while perfect for the course for which they were designed, are difficult to modify for broad usage in other disciplines and courses. In addition, as Internet companies have seen the value in developing sets of generic teaching tools as learning management systems (LMS), much of the work developed within the computing departments has been overlooked but not superseded.

In 1995, Dawson-Howe [7] described a command-line system called *submit*. This system prompted computing students to run compilation examples and sample runs (testing) of their programs in the Unix environment. As the programs were tested and compiled a script of the session was recorded. When completed, the script and the files would be submitted into a central repository for collection by the examiner. This program became a standard on most version of Unix and implemented in many computing departments world-wide. The electronic submission component of the *submit* program has been outdated by the web-based graphical user interfaces of LMS's such as the *dropbox* provided by Blackboard. However, the prompting for testing and compilation has not.

There are now a plethora of other applications that provide students with the means of transmitting an electronic file to their course examiner [13]. Blaine and Petre [14] describe an electronic marking system that accepts electronically submitted assignments and forwards copies of the assignments to a marker. The marker uses Microsoft Word to critique the work with a specially formatted template that presents inserted and deleted parts of the original file in a different font. The marker returns the files to the marking system which returns the feedback to the student, enters the student's grade into the university student database and sends the marker a receipt.

A more structured approach to marking is given in [15] where the Grading Environment (GE) system is described. This system has been designed to improve the reliability and consistency of student performance evaluations among a group of markers by guiding them through the marking process. The system takes the traditional pen and paper based approach to marking and places it on the screen. Each marker is asked a series of evaluation questions about the students' work. Through point and click interaction the system evaluates the students' work and calculates a grade for the student. The system also uses the marker's responses to set remedial work for each student based on the errors in their assignments. The system was designed for marking computing students' programs although it can be adapted for other courses. Other systems such the one described by Mason & Woit [16] allow annotations to be entered into the assignment files via a structured webpage. The webpage allows the marker to enter a comment into a textfield and this comment is further programmatically inserted into the student's submission. This allows single lines of text to be added in the student's file. However, the marker cannot correct or modify existing lines.

Classmate builds on the ideas developed in the before mentioned systems, marrying electronic submission and a grading environment with file management, course team management and automated student feedback in an online environment. It provides both a free format method of critiquing students' work along with a structured grading template [17]. The architecture of this system will now be discussed.

3   Overview of Classmate

A conceptualisation of the Classmate system is given in Fig. 1.

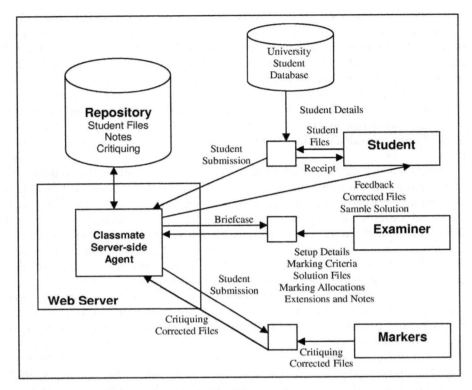

Fig. 1. The Classmate System

Classmate currently resides on the web server in the Department of Mathematics and Computing at USQ. The system was written using a mixture of C/C++, Perl and Java to give it the greatest flexibility. The system consists of 4 main agent entities. The main server-side agent works to manage student submissions, administer student receipts, distribute submission to markers and collate marker critiques. The smaller agents are distributed as necessary and act as clients on the user's machines. The agents are independent of any database system and currently reside over a file/directory structure. This makes the system modular (other system parts can be added) and platform independent.

The use of Classmate begins with Agent A being used by the examiner to setup the course details. This agent asks the examiner a number of pertinent questions, such as the number of assignments, the assignment due dates and the names and ids of the markers. The examiner must also provide the agent with a file containing a list of the students enrolled in the course and their contact details (including an email address). For each assignment the examiner can give Agent A a list of the marking criteria for an assignment along with the associated sub-marks for each. The examiner can also provide a solution file with answers to the assignment. The view presented to the examiner by Agent A is called the *Briefcase* (shown in Fig. 2).

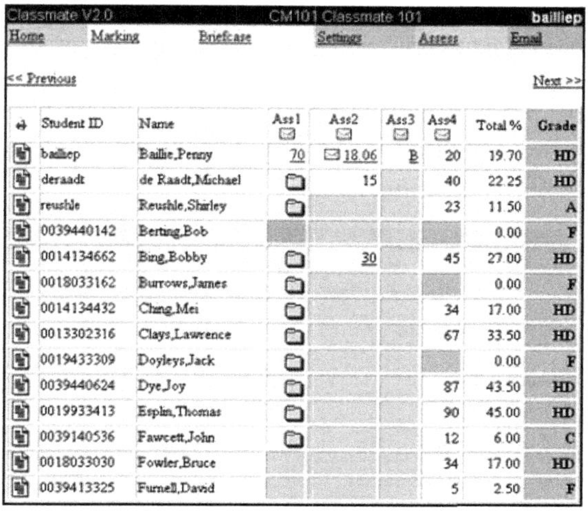

Classmate V2.0		CM101 Classmate 101					bailliep
Home	Marking	Briefcase	Settings	Assess	Email		

<< Previous   Next >>

	Student ID	Name	Ass1 ✉	Ass2 ✉	Ass3 ✉	Ass4 ✉	Total %	Grade
	badhep	Baillie,Penny	70	✉18.06	B	20	19.70	HD
	deraadt	de Raadt,Michael	📁	15		40	22.25	HD
	reushle	Reushle,Shirley	📁			23	11.50	A
	0039440142	Berting,Bob					0.00	F
	0014134662	Bing,Bobby	📁	30		45	27.00	HD
	0018033162	Burrows,James	📁				0.00	F
	0014134432	Ching,Mei	📁			34	17.00	HD
	0013302316	Clays,Lawrence	📁			67	33.50	HD
	0019433309	Doyleys,Jack	📁				0.00	F
	0039440624	Dye,Joy	📁			87	43.50	HD
	0019933413	Esplin,Thomas	📁			90	45.00	HD
	0039140536	Fawcett,John	📁			12	6.00	C
	0018033030	Fowler,Bruce				34	17.00	HD
	0039413325	Furnell,David				5	2.50	F

Fig. 2. Briefcase View of Classmate

In the Briefcase view, the examiner can see a list of their students and the status of each assignment. If an assignment is waiting to be marked, it is displayed as a folder icon. If the assignment has been marked, a result will appear in the appropriate column. The Classmate system also allows the examiner to set cutoffs for grading and these are calculated automatically and displayed.

When a student wishes to submit an assignment, they download Agent B. This agent uses their student login id to access the universities central student database using LDAP. The agent displays these details to the student and provides them with a list of assignments and due dates from which to choose and submit their work. The student's details and submitted files are streamed to the Classmate server-side client for storing in a repository located, for security reasons, outside the realm of the web server. Before a marker can access the students' submissions and commence marking, the examiner must interface with Agent A in order to allocate students to specific markers. Until this is done, Agent C will report to the marker that they have no assignments to mark. Agent A will allow the examiner to manually assign students to markers, however for very large classes where this is impractical, the examiner can simple tell the agent what the maximum allocation (in numbers) for each marker is and the agent will randomly assign students to markers. Having done this, the agent reports back to the examiner the actual number of students that was allocated to each marker. At this time the examiner has the opportunity to make manual adjustments to the allocations as they see fit.

4   Classmate's Distributed Critiquing Process

Once students have been allocated to a marker, the marker can obtain a view of their student list from Agent C. The view, called the Marker's Briefcase, is similar to the examiner's Briefcase of Figure 2 but with restricted administration functionality. The marker can use the mouse to select a student's work to mark (by clicking on the folder icon). On selection, Agent C presents the marker with a list of submitted files (shown in Fig. 3). If the submitted file is a zip file, the marker can ask the agent to unzip the contents of the file. When this request occurs, Agent C contacts the server-side agent who performs this task and provides Agent C with an updated list of the unzipped files to present to the marker.

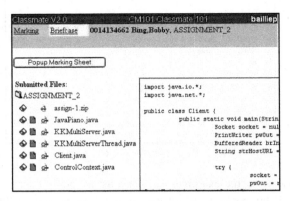

Fig. 3. The marker's view of submitted files.

The marker can view the contents of the file, through Agent C, by clicking on the filename. Agent C then requests the contents of the file from the server-side agent. The server-side agent accesses the file from the repository and streams it to Agent C for display. The file is displayed to the marker in an authoring textbox (shown on the right in Fig. 3 and enlarged in Fig. 4). For security reasons, the marker cannot modify the originally submitted file and therefore can ask Agent C to request a copy of the file for editing. Agent C relays this request to the server-side agent. The server-side agent creates a copy of the original file and transforms the file into Rich Text Format (RTF). The RTF file is sent back to the marker via Agent C. The RTF file was chosen as it allows different coloured text to be entered.

As the marker critiques the student's file with comments and corrections, any text entered by the marker appear in red (comments are displayed in Fig. 4 beginning with "//->" for the readers benefit). Currently Agent C is capable of presenting plain text, HTML and RTF in its authoring textbox. For other submitted files, the marker has the option of downloading them to their own computer and opening them with the appropriate software (e.g. Word or Excel Documents). If the marker makes corrections to these downloaded files on their own computer, they can upload them via Agent C back into the repository.

The authoring tool also has a facility to record frequently made comments (FMC). This saves the marker time when multiply students need to be given the same comments about parts of their work. It also allows the marker to be consistent in their remarks across all students. The FMC box at the bottom of the authoring tool records the FMC at the request of the marker. As Classmate is a distributed critiquing system, these FMC are made available to all markers. Selected FMC are simply dragged from the FMC box into the authoring window and can be inserted at any location within the text.

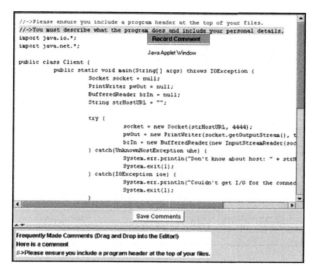

Fig. 4. Classmate's Online Critiquing Authoring Tool

The major difference between Classmate and other *dropbox* type electronic submission systems is that the submitted work stays in the repository during the marking process. This means that the marker knows where the file is at all times (not in a sub directory on their own computer or on a floppy disk in their office). Unlike in a paper based system if the marker goes missing [19] the assignments do not go with them. Feedback and error corrections are entered directly into a copy of the submission. This copy also resides in the repository. The result of managing the marking of student submissions in this manner means that the marker's comments and notes are recorded with the submission and associated grade. This differs from traditional marking methods where annotations written on paper that describe and justify a student's grade for an assignment are usually lost [15].

In addition to critiquing the files in the authoring textbox, the marker also completes a marking criteria sheet (shown in Fig. 5). This sheet is generated by Agent C from the criteria entered in by the examiner. The marker fills out the sheet by clicking on tick boxes and entering numeric values. Once completed, Agent C calculates a total number of marks for the student and sends the details to the server-side client for storage. The marker or examiner can revisit the marking of an assignment at anytime and make adjustments as necessary. The total calculation also takes into consideration any extensions given by the examiner. Agent C obtains extension information and the time stamp of the student files, compares them and calculates a deduction if applicable.

When the marker is satisfied with the assignment mark, they can inform Agent C to complete the electronic assessment cycle by sending the assignment feedback to the student. This process begins when the marker clicks on an *envelope* icon displayed

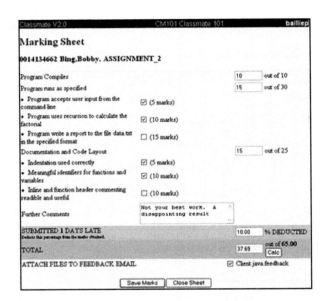

Fig. 5. Classmate's Marking Sheet

next to the students work (see Fig. 2) in the Marker's Briefcase. Agent C sends this request to the server-side agent. The server-side agent accesses the student's files and critiquing, generates a feedback letter and emails this letter along with any marker corrected files and the sample solution to the student.

5 Discussion

The Classmate system has been in use since 1994 in differing formats. The latest evolution (as discussed in this paper) is being implemented for the first time in semester 1 of 2003. To date, the Classmate system has been used by ten markers. Of these, five were surveyed. From the results of a survey conducted to get feedback on the Classmate system from the markers, the system has proved useful in:

- reducing repetitive and trivial assessment related tasks (such as computer code compilation);
- providing markers with the flexibility to mark assignments anywhere, anytime without having to have all the submitted files on their own computer;
- managing the administration of electronic submission among a group of markers;
- providing an interface that allows markers to mark an assignment via a coherent interface (no matter what the file format) in a traditional manner (red pen on paper) and keeping within the examiners guidelines;
- presenting real time information on the progress of assignment marking and the status of student submissions to the examiner via the web interface; and

- reduces erroneous student grade data through the agents' management of results collection, the emailing of feedback to students and the uploading of result data directly into appropriate university administration systems

Although markers were asked their opinion of the Classmate system with respect to other electronic systems, only 1 of the 5 markers surveyed had had experience with other systems. The markers reported a reduction in assignment turnaround time from 3 weeks for a paper based system to 4 days using Classmate. This is not unusual in other electronic submission management systems [18] and it could be fanciful to think that a further reduction in this timeframe is possible. In our own investigations with the Classmate markers, some reported that they did not start marking the assignment as soon as it arrived. This meant that the turnaround time was increased simply because the submitted file sat idle on the server for a couple of days (or even weeks in some cases). One keen marker had a turnaround time of 1 day. This was made evident in a class after the submission due date when a couple of students commented with surprise that they already had their assignment marks back. All markers found that the Classmate system reduced some of the repetitive and trivial tasks associated with marking. 50% of the markers commented that the annotation system allowed them to cut and paste frequently used annotations, thus reducing marking time. They performed this task using a opened text editor and cut and paste comments from the editor into the submission. In the new version of Classmate, the Agent C keeps track of the marker's annotations and provides the marker with a drag and drop list with the authoring textbox shown in Figure 3. 40% of the markers noted that marking assignments was a repetitive task and that no system could eliminate this, however the automation of grade recording and the emailing of student feedback greatly reduced these tasks.

Several markers agreed that the amount of feedback given on paper was usually superior to electronic forms of marking, however they made a note that the Classmate system did allow them to put as much feedback with the assignment as they would on paper. 80% of the markers believed the consistency and quality of feedback was better than paper-based submissions. Finally, all markers agreed that Classmate reduced the amount of erroneous student data as results are recorded within the system at marking time and uploaded to the university systems. The current version of Classmate uploads data into the universities Peoplesoft database where as examiners using the WebCT platform still need to manually transfer their marks out of WebCT and into Peoplesoft.

The success with acceptance of Classmate among markers can be attributed to the interface design being modelled on the paper based system. Classmate attempts to add value to the electronic submission management and marking process with semi-automated processes while allowing markers to interact with the students' work in a traditional manner.

6   Conclusions and Future Work

Classmate has proven affective in providing examiners and markers with a semi-automated electronic submission management system. Classmate endeavours to streamline the process of marking electronically submitted assignments while not placing restrictions on the content of these assignments. To date, Classmate has been used primarily for the marking of programming code as it was developed in the environment of a computer science department. The latest version of Classmate is now being trialed by a surveying examiner for the management of Excel spreadsheet assignments. Classmate's independence from a database and platform makes it ideal for integration with WebCT and Blackboard like systems. For example, the student list displayed in the briefcase could be easily populated with an API call to Blackboard. The assignment files could as easily be streamed by the server-side agent to Agent C simply by informing the server-side agent of the file structure of the WebCT dropbox.

The focus for future developments of Classmate will be to upgrade the agents. It is planned to implement a learning mechanism in the marking Agent C. Over time, the agent will learn to identify repetitive mistakes in assignments and be able to add commentary feedback to assignment files before the marker attends to them. For example, a common mistake in CSC1401, Programming in C, is the improper use of recursive programming. The agent, with assistance from the marker, will learn how to identify recursion and subsequently semi-automate the marking of a group of assignments by pre-assessing and adding appropriate feedback. After an agent learns a critiquing procedure from one marker, it will communicate this with other marker's agents via a central knowledge base, thus distributing the knowledge of one marker among the marking team. The distribution of expert knowledge within the agents and the storage of this knowledge would then be available for use in marking future assessment tasks and new offerings of a course.

In addition, the agents will be configured to take advantage of new mobile computing technologies (for example, webslate technology [20]) giving markers a greater range of freedom when interacting with Classmate. The traditional 'pen and paper' approach to marking submissions could be replaced with a webslate and stylus.

Although Classmate and systems like it have been in use for the past ten years, not a lot of progress has been made in moving the domain of online assessment management systems forward. It seems that duplicate and hybrid systems evolve from time to time, but without any real progress. The future task of researchers in this domain should be to examine the scope of use for such systems beyond the confines of computer science departments and first year programming subjects and to scrutinise the requirements of examiners from other subject areas on their current processes and needs. Only then will such systems and methodologies find their way into commercially available learning management systems.

References

1. Lever-Duffy, J., McDonald, J. & Mizell, A., 21st The Century Classroom: Teaching and Learning with Technology, Allyn and Bacon, Boston. (2003)
2. Trotter, A., From Science and the Workplace Come New Tools of the Trade, Technology Counts '99, http://www.edweek.org/ sreports/tc99/articles/tools.htm. (1999)
3. Goldberg, M., Online T(esting): Some Observations, http://www.webct.com/OTL/ ViewContent?contentID=2339239. (2000)

4. White, J., Online testing: The Dog Sat on My Keyboard, Proceedings of the 13th Annual ICTCM, Atlanta, 2000, Addison-Wesley, London. (2000)

5. Ritchie, D., Hoffman, D., Incorporating Instructional Design Principles with the World Wide Web, Web-based Instruction, Badrul Khan (editor), Educational Technology Publications, Englewood Cliffs, New Jersey, (1997) 135–138.

6. Korb, K., Kopp, C., & Allison, L., A Statement on Higher Education Policy in Australia, Technical Report CS97-318, http://www.csse.monash.edu.au/ publications/1997/tr-cs97-318/policy.html. (1997)

7. Dawson-Howe, K., Automatic submission and administration of programming assignments. ACM SIGCSE Bulletin, (1995) 27(4), 51–53.

8. Thompson, D., WebFace Overview and History.
    http://mugca.cc.monash.edu.au/ ~webface/history.html. Monash University. (1998)

9. Byrnes, R., & Lo, B., A Computer-Aided Assignment Management System: Improving the Teaching-Learning Feedback Cycle, http://www.opennet.net.au/cmluga/byrnesw2.htm. Southern Cross University. (1996)

10. Messing, J., Can Academics Afford To Use E-Mail?, e-JIST, 6(1),
    http://www.usq.edu.au/electpub/e-jist. (2003)

11. Baillie-de Byl, P., An Online Assistant for Remote, Distributed Critiquing of Electronically Submitted Assessment, Tech-Report SC-MC-0304, Department of Mathematics and Computing, U.S.Q. (2003)

12. Preston, J. & Shackelford, R., A System for Improving Distance and Large-Scale Classes, in ACM SIGCSE Bulletin Inroads, Ireland, (1998) 30(4), 193–198.

13. Darbyshire, P., Distributed Web-Based Assignment Management, in Web-Based Learning and Teaching Technologies: Opportunities and Challenges, Idea Group Publishing, Hershey, (2002) 198–215.

14. Blaine Price, Marian Petre, (1997), Teaching Programming through Paperless Assignments: an empirical evaluation of instructor feedback, Proceedings of Integrating Technology into Computer Science Education, SIGCSE Bulletin, 29(3), Gordon Davies (editor), September 1997, pp 94–99

15. Preston, J., Evaulation software: improving consistency and reliability of performance rating. Proceedings of ITiCSE '97,Uppsala, Sweden, ACM, New York. (1997)

16. Mason, D & Woit D., Providing Mark-up and Feedback to Students with Online Marking, ACM SIGCSE Bulletin, (1999) 31(1), 3–6.

17. Joy, M & Luck, M., Effective Electronic Marking for On-line Assessment, Proceedings of ITCSE98, Dublin, ACM Press, New York, (1998) 134–138.

18. Jones, D. & Behrens, S., Online Assignment Management: An Evolutionary Tale, Proceedings of HICSS03, Hawaii. http://cq-pan.cqu.edu.au/david-jones/Publications /Papers_ and_Books/OLA_Evolutionary/. (2003)

19. Price, B. & Petre, M., Teaching Programming through Paperless Assignments: an empirical evaluation of instructor feedback. ACM SIGCSE Bulletin, (1997) 29(3), 94–99.

20. McDonell, J., webPads, a presentation at QUESTnet 2001, Gold Coast,
    http:// http://www.usq.edu.au/its/webslate/. (2001)

In-Process Quantitative Evaluation for Network-Based Learning

Qinglin Zhang[1], Ailisha Li[1], Jiayi Hu[2], and Weiyuan Wang[3]

[1] Department of Psychology, Southwest China Normal University,
400715 Chongqing, PRC
{zhangql, pno1}@swnu.edu.cn
[2] Department of Psychology, Southwest China Normal University,
400715 Chongqing, PRC
hujianyi996@hotmail.com
[3] Opentec Ltd Limited, 6 Lyon Park Road,
North Ryde, NSW 2113, Australia
weiyuanw@opentec.com.au

Abstract. This paper analyses the features of quantitative evaluation in network-based teaching, introduces an in-process quantitative evaluation model[1] for intelligent network-based teaching, and discuss its implementation and performance in the Yuanlin intelligent network-based teaching system.

1 Introduction

Network-based education is developing surprisingly as information technology advances rapidly. Increasingly, we are facing the use of the Internet as an aid to learning (Oliver & Omari, 1999) [1]. It has become a challenge to traditional school education (Stephenson, 2001) [2]. Network technology will be an important tool for educational reform and development worldwide. As is mentioned in *Outline of Curricula Reform of Elementary Education* promulgated by the Chinese Education Ministry, we must promote the popularity of information technology in teaching practice and realize the integration of information technology into curricula; we must change teachers' pedagogic methods and the way of presenting teaching contents, the way of learners' studying, and the way of interacting between learners and teachers, and provide learners with various education circumstances and helpful learning tools.

Network-based education systems need be intelligent in order to meet the above requirements. Current network-based education systems worldwide, however, are far from being intelligent. They cannot meet learners' requirements of efficient and independent learning online (Chao, 2002) [3]. Online evaluation and assessment should be part of the learning-teaching process, embedded in student activities and in the inter-

---

[1] The work has been sponsored by the Ministry of Education, P R C (project DBB010510).

W. Zhou et al. (Eds.): ICWL 2003, LNCS 2783, pp. 462–472, 2003.
© Springer-Verlag Berlin Heidelberg 2003

actions between learners and teachers (Harasim et al, 1996) [4]. Evaluation involves judging the effectiveness and worth of programs and products (Reeves, 2002) [5]. In fact, vendors, designers and instructors appear to struggle with conceiving of evaluation as anything more than a multiple-choice test (Angelo & Cross, 1993) [6]. With regard to measurement, evaluation and feedback of learning online, almost all existing systems adopt some sort of terminative evaluation. They often include a database with considerable contents for test and items may be chosen from the database according to certain principles to compile test papers and implement grading or scoring methods. Terminative evaluation cannot provide with timely feedback. Specifically, they can neither provide with quantitative feedback betimes on the gap between a learner's goal and the progress and quality of his/her present learning, nor point out what causes difficulties to the learner and how to overcome them. Besides, there is a common problem in existing network-based teaching systems: they are unable to provide learners at different learning levels with different teaching methods and advices, unable to efficiently help learners who have different learning goals, abilities and starting-points. According to Bloom's view (Bloom, 1973) [7], The main reason why many learners do not achieve excellent academic performance is not because of their lack of intelligence, but the absence of appropriate teaching circumstance and reasonable helps. If we provide with good learning environment, most learners will become quite similar on learning abilities, progress and motives for further study. Here learning environment includes individual instructions.

The network-based teaching systems should focus on providing learners at different learning level with this kind of learning environment as much as possible. The precondition of achieving this objective is to develop an effective quantitative evaluation model for network-based teaching that not only provide exams at end of learning, but also evaluates learners' performance during the process of learning.

When designing intelligent network-based courses, the designers should keep in mind such matters as below. The first is how to provide learners with timely and quantitative feedback about the gap between a learner's goal and current learning. The second is how to automatically analyze and detect learners' difficulties of learning, as an excellent teacher provides students with individual instructions. Network-based courses should be able to inform learners of why they cannot master the knowledge in the course. For an instance, the reason is whether a learner does not know related knowledge, or the learner does not understand new knowledge; whether a learner can understand new knowledge but unable to remember them, or the learner can understand and remember new knowledge but cannot use them skillfully; whether a learner can understand and skillfully use new knowledge but the knowledge has not been instantiated nor generalized by the learner, or the learner can meet all the above requirements but lack strategies to apply the knowledge flexibly. The third is that network-based teaching system should be able to choose pertinent pedagogy methods automatically, to provide learners with advices and feedback on learners' goals. For a student whose goal is to go to top-ranking universities, the system can judge the appropriateness of the learner's goal and give some suggestion. For example, the suggestion may be that your present goal is too higher and you may suffer excessive difficulties, frustration, worries and disappointments if you do not change your goal to go to general universities.

When the learner accepts the suggestion, the system will provide respective learning contents at the level for entering general universities. When the learner makes great progress at the new level, the system will automatically advise him/her to adjust the goal back to going to top-ranking universities again. The system will also help the learner in mastering knowledge and skills necessary to pass the examination.

With the above consideration, it is necessary to develop an in-process quantitative evaluation for intelligent network-based teaching systems.

In-process Quantitative Evaluation Model or IQEM for network-based teaching can meet the above need. The functions of this model include: being able to guide and enlighten learners to choose appropriate learning goal, procedure and process, being able to provide learners with timely supervision, feedback, and record learners' progress at the goal level. Learners can monitor, adjust and control his/her own learning on the basis of the information provided by the system. In this way learners are helped to choose the most appropriate learning contents and procedure and make best progresses. As a result, each individual's potential will be best deployed and learning quality will be improved.

The rest of this paper introduces IQEM model and its implementation in Yuanlin intelligent network-based teaching system.

2   In-Process Quantitative Evaluation Model for Network-Based Learning

The earliest quantitative evaluation was implemented by teaching machine. Teaching machines propose that content is arranged in small steps, which progress from simple to complex. It requires a response from the learner in order for teaching machine to carry on teaching. Teaching machine suffers from one serious flaw: it is boring (Driscoll, 2000)[8]. Besides, teaching machines cannot automatically and quantitatively evaluate the progress in learning process. Therefore this issue has been remaining as a hot topic.

Current online learning systems fall into four paradigms according to the variations in the locus of control and task specification (Stephenson, 2001)[2]: (a) teacher-controlled, specified learning activities (Dee-Lucas, 1999)[9]; (b) teacher-controlled, open-ended or strategic learning (Mason, 1998)[10]; (c) learner-managed specified learning activities (Paolucci & Jones, 1998)[11]; (d) learner-managed, open-ended or strategic learning (Bonk, Angeli &Hara, 1998)[12].

Generally, web-based learning models can be classified as behavioral or cognitive (Jonassen, 1993)[13]. The effectiveness of the Internet in learning will be a function of web-model alignment and the appropriateness of the model to a particular learning situation (Lin & Hsieh, 2001)[14]. Current systems emphasize the influence of control focus and content specification on learning activities, but fail to answer the question how to improve learning efficiency. Comparing with general systems, the

IQEM model (to be defined below) is capable of enhancing learners' learning efficiency. Firstly, general systems fail to distinguish learners with different learning capabilities and different knowledge structure. As a result, when learning is designed with the same requirements and at the same pace for every learner, some learners have difficulties in learning independently and making progress, meanwhile other learners may not find challenges in learning. They are restrained in developing their potentials. By contraries, IQEM is capable of distinguishing various types of learners, structuring contents on the basis of the differences, and providing relative tests as well. Thus, IQEM system is effectively promoting learners in the optimal way. Secondly, in general systems, tests are always made at the end of one section or even one chapter. It becomes hard to find out learners' difficulties until the end of one section or even one chapter. Consequently, it takes a great amount of time to remedy. Oppositely, IQEM is capable of doing diagnostics and tests. The errors made by learners can by detected and fixed timely. Learning efficiency can be greatly improved by providing learners with pertinent and timely feedback. Thirdly, general systems provide learner with tests and marks at the end of one section or even one chapter while IQEM progressively accumulate scores. By the way of accumulative scoring, IQEM contributes to timely reinforcement, and consequently continuous drive for learning. Learners' curiosity can be elevated so that learning efficiency will be enhanced. Fourthly, general systems pay much attention to lecturing knowledge itself, but ignore the instruction of thinking methods and learning strategies. IQEM embodies thoroughly the emphasis on the instruction of thinking methods and learning strategies.

Below we present IQEM, an In-process Quantitative Evaluation Model for network-based teaching. In general, IQEM can be defined as a framework or system that can automatically and immediately provide learners with quantitative feedback on the gap between learners' goals and their current learning status including location, progress and quality, automatically detect and analyze learners' difficulties as excellent teachers do in the individual instructions, timely inform learners why they cannot understand the knowledge, and automatically choose pertinent pedagogy strategies and provide learners with positive advices.

The model is explained in more details below.

2.1 Addressing Processing

It is during the process of self-adjustment instead of evaluation at the end of long learning periods or terms that quantitative evaluation can help to detect learners' shortcomings. The IQEM model can automatically provide learners with assessments, feedbacks and constructive suggestions betimes. Consequently, learners will continuously adjust their behaviors or goals according to the assessments, feedbacks and constructive suggestion from the system, and approach their goals step by step.

2.2 Setting Goal

The IQEM model allows designers to set goals at different levels.

Tolman believes that behavior is guided by purpose (Tolman, 1948) [15]. The effectiveness of instructional goals for enhancing academic performance has been debated since the 1960s. Gagne (1985) [16] argued that informing learners of goals would help them to be ready for learning. Besides, goals can also provide a framework of contents for learning that will eventually be tested. Obviously, explicit and accurate goals in network-based learning are necessary.

The IQEM model starts with setting appropriate goals. The model allows designers to set goals at different levels so as to suit different groups of learners. For example, there could be three goals for senior high school students to choose. The low-level goal is to graduate from school. The goal of secondary level is to pass the entrance examination for general universities. The goal at the third level is to pass the entrance examination for top-ranking universities.

Once a student selects his goal, the learning contents and requirements should be in accordance with the selected level. As a result, the learning contents and requirements for those students who select the goal of secondary level will be different from that of students who select the goal of low-level. The designers of network-based courses should design different contents and requirements for different levels of goals. For example, the requirements for the goal of lower level are to know, understand and remember some knowledge, while the requirements for higher level of goal are to comprehend the knowledge and skillfully, creatively apply them, instead of just understand and remember the knowledge. Setting different levels of goals is the precondition to evaluate learning quantitatively and accurately. With such goals it becomes possible to efficiently guide learning process and to help learners to approach their goals. These goals will stimulate learners' internal drives to learn, which results in effective learning and good performance.

2.3 Giving Feedback Timely

The IQEM model is capable to present feedbacks at any time during the process of learning.

As learners monitor their progress toward their goals, they make evaluation or judgments about their performance, about their self-efficacy for reaching the goal, and about their personal goals in light of their current achievements (Bandura, 1997)[17] (Zimmerman & Schunk, 1989)[18]. Timely feedback becomes critical when learners are monitoring their progress. The IQEM Model is capable to present feedbacks at any time during the process of learning. In this way, learners can self-evaluate the gap between their performance and their learning goals, and adjust their own learning strategies, procedures or goals in time.

2.4 Giving Feedback Accurately

The IQEM model gives feedback accurately. The knowledge of results provides feedback on the quality of particular performance, and the knowledge of progress provides feedback on the performance over time (Driscoll, 2000) [8]. The In-process Quantitative Evaluation Model is able to accurately inform learners of the gap between learners' goals and their current progresses. In the model, knowledge node means the least knowledge unit that can be learned independently. Teaching contents of one lecture might be made up of many knowledge nodes. With regard to the learning of specific knowledge nodes, the system is able to inform learners how well the knowledge nodes have been commanded by them. If learners have not mastered the nodes well enough, the system is able to precisely suggest what their problems are, and why they failed to know, understand, remember, use skillfully, or apply the knowledge creatively and comprehensively. The system can also suggest what remedies may be taken. For an instance, it could be o review knowledge nodes that have been learned before but not been remembered by them.

As mentioned above, knowledge nodes in the IQEM model refer to the small knowledge chunk in web-based learning. They are different from traditional knowledge points in that the knowledge nodes are more detailed and well structured.

2.5 Motivating Students' Behaviors

The IQEM model provides the information of the gap between learners' goals and their progress, which can motivate learners more effectively. Specifically, the functions of in-process quantitative evaluation model include timely finding out the progress of a learner, providing learners with encouraging feedback and suggestions, effectively maintaining learners' self-efficacy, developing learners' self-confidence, motivating learners to achieve, and fully developing learners' potential. As Bandura proposed, self-efficacy is a belief system that is causally related to behavior and outcomes. That is, people make judgments about their abilities to perform certain actions to achieve a desirable outcome (Bandura, 1977,1982) [19] [20].

3   Yuanlin Intelligent Network-Based Teaching System

The Yuanlin Intelligent Network-based Teaching System or YINT is developed based on the In-process Qualitative Evaluation Model presented in the previous section. The system can offset the deficiencies of the most existing web-based teaching systems by providing in-process quantitative evaluation. The system can also help learners to fully develop their potentials.

3.1 Introduction to YINT System

The YINT system includes two subsystems: IDesigner and OnlineTeacher. IDesigner is designed and built for the authors or designers of network-based courses. IDesigner allows the authors to integrate different network-based course components into complete courses. With the IDesigner tools, authors or designers can create various courses efficiently and creatively by the way of designing the course framework (for example, setting different learning goals, contents and detailed requirements of these goals), specifying knowledge nodes, constructing a network of the knowledge nodes, integrating multi-media contents and so on.

One of the key factors for the YINT's success is the in-process quantitative evaluation model built into the system. The system allows one to set different levels of learning goals, construct the dependency network of knowledge nodes based on the levels of goals, specifies knowledge nodes, and proposes grading regulations as well. It is easy for users to realize the mechanism of dynamically quantitative evaluation. Therefore, it is helpful to establish a system of self-determination learning.

Most current use of network-based teaching transfers traditional lecture-based methods to the online environment (Bourne et al, 1997) [21]. In the virtual learning settings, learners are as much responsible for the quality and amount of leaning as the instructor. YINT provides an online teacher that embodies the knowledge and experience of traditional instructor (McQuillan, 1994) [22]. The Online Teacher is to provide services to learners. Online Teacher is capable to record, measure, analyze and judge learners' progress. It can also automatically suggest the most appropriate learning goals and starting-point in the network of knowledge nodes. When learners start the procedure controlled by the system, the system can automatically present necessary knowledge nodes with regard to learners' goals, record learners' progress, provide evaluation scores, and measure the gap between learners' goals and their current status and progress. It can also present feedback on learners' performance during the process of learning. The system is helpful to implement individual learning. It guarantees that every leaner can learn the most opportune knowledge at the most suitable pace, so as to fully develop learners' potentials.

3.2   In-Process Quantitative Evaluation of YINT

The in-process quantitative evaluation of YINT allows one to design the contents and goals (requirements) in accordance with different levels of goals.

Bloom (1956) [23] suggested that the cognitive goals of the learning of knowledge could be graded as six levels of knowledge, comprehension, application, analysis, synthesis and evaluation. The YINT system modifies Bloom's taxonomy and sets up a new system of cognitive goals based on research of modern cognitive psychology. This new system of goals includes different levels of goals as knowing, understanding, memorizing, using skillfully, as well as applying comprehensively.

According to this new system of cognitive goals, designers of network courses should firstly specify how many necessary knowledge nodes should be mastered and assessed based on levels of learning goals, contents of textbooks and standard of network-based courses.

Secondly, designers should determine different requirements of different knowledge nodes in term of the features of knowledge nodes and the relationship between knowledge nodes and learning goals, and standard of network courses Designers may, then, develop multi-media contents, compile test papers, and provide with feedback.

3.3 Implementation of the IQEM Model in the YINT System

The subsystem of YINT system, Online Teacher, provides two learning modes: self-determination learning and systematical learning. Self-determination learning is also viewed as self-management leaning. It refers to a process that learners themselves detect and determine knowledge nodes to learn, choose appropriate learning process and strategies, as well as manage their own behaviors in the light of learning goals determined by them. Online Teacher allows learners to determine what to learn in the index of knowledge nodes. Learners may choose knowledge nodes at any point (for example, of one chapter or of one section), and choose any specific knowledge nodes.

This approach is helpful to enhance learners' consciousness of the relationship between their goals and the rest of knowledge nodes to be required to master. Learners will be better aware of that how much knowledge nodes has been mastered. Learners' abilities of reflection and self-control will be improved, too. This approach is crucial to develop learners' ability of meta-cognition which is crucial for learners' academic achievement.

On the other hand, the limitation of this approach is that it depends on learners' positive attitude and outstanding ability of meta-cognition. Therefore, the most appropriate learning strategy for learners with poor academic performance previously should be systematic learning.

The evaluation method of systematic learning in Online Teacher is based on the in-process quantitative evaluation model presented previously. The system can detect how much knowledge nodes the learner has mastered. The system can, then, give suggestion on learning goals and starting-point of learning. Besides, the system can present necessary knowledge node one by one as the learner intends (the learner, at the beginning, maybe reject the suggestion). The learner is asked to pass the tests of knowledge nodes one by one. But is not necessary for the learner to study all the multi-media contents of every knowledge node. The system is able to grade dynamically in term of the result of the test. The learner will receive feedback. If the learner passes the test, the system will provide encouragement to him/her. If the learner fails the test, the system can provide with feedback and remedy. This way of evaluation can help learners who have met difficulties in learning to offset their shortcomings.

On the basis of the new system of goals, the YINT system is designed to be able to evaluate the learner's performance in the test of every knowledge node and give two kinds of scores: the score of learner's progress and the score of learning quality. When the learner finishes a test, the system can make grading on the learner's progress and learning quality in the light of the evaluation index.

As for score of learner's progress, the learner will score four if he/she passes the test of a knowledge node at the first time, score two if he/she pass the test of a knowledge node at the second time, score one if he/she pass the test of a knowledge node at the third time, score zero if he/she fails the test of a knowledge node at the third time. This way of scoring helps to prevent learners from guessing randomly the answers because their scores will be quite low if they guess randomly. It also helps to develop learners' positive learning attitude.

If the preceding scores are too low to be capable of encouraging subsequent learning, the system will score by the way of dynamic adjustment. This refers to adjusting the preceding score according to the learner's performance in learning of the latest two chapters. In this way, the score of the quality of learning will fluctuate as the quality of learning varies. Scores will better motivate learners to study. If they achieve better performance, their internal motive and self-efficacy will be improved. Internal motives to any thing are learned. Internal motives will not occur until people succeed in doing something and believe one's ability on these aspects.

Table 1. Comparison

Items	General network-based teaching systems	YINT system
Learning goals	To provide same learning goals, contents, paces, ways of evaluation and remedies to learners of different academic performance. It cannot be adjusted dynamically.	To provide different learning goals, contents, paces, ways of evaluation and remedies to learners of different academic performance. It can be adjusted dynamically.
Scoring standard	To adopt terminative evaluation, providing only one way of scoring. This way of scoring cannot provide timely feedback. Learners might have misgiving because of preceding academic performance. It cannot motivate learners. Dynamic adjustment is hardly realized.	In-process quantitative evaluation is adopted, including scores of progress and quality. Score of quality can be adjusted dynamically. Scoring is timely, accurate, detailed. Scores can better motivate learners.
Learning requirements	Same requirements for all students.	Different requirements in accordance with different levels of learning goals.
Teaching styles	Individual learning is not actually realized. Learners' experiences are same.	In view of individual difference among learners, the system simulates individual tutoring. Self-determination learning is possible.
Features on the aspect of intelligence	Interaction between learners and system is primary	On the basis of interaction between learners and the system, the system can record learners' progress, fully make use of data. The system possesses knowledge, experience and ability of judgment similar to expert teachers. It can analyze, evaluate and diagnose learners' difficulties.

Another function of the YINT system is to evaluate the appropriation of learners' goals in the light of their scores of progress and quality. At some stage of learning process, the system can automatically calculate the learner's score of learning quality. If the system believes the learner's current goal is inappropriate, it will suggest the learner to set a higher or lower level goal. The learner is allowed to reject the advice with a view to developing the learner's belief of self-determination. If the learner sets a higher level of goal, the system will help him/her to learn all preceding knowledge nodes, which have not been presented on the lower level of goal, but necessary for this new goal. The learner may, then, learn the subsequent knowledge nodes. If the learner sets a lower level of goal or rejects the advice of a higher goal, the system will present the related knowledge nodes on the basis of the goal selected by the learner.

4 Comparison YINT System and General Systems

The advantages of YINT system over general network-based teaching systems include quantitative design of learning process, timely feedback, accurate goals, as well as individual teaching. The system successfully implements in-process quantitative evaluation and dynamic analysis in network-based learning.

Table 1 presents the difference between YINT system and general network teaching systems.

The in-process quantitative evaluation built in the YINT system is still at its trial stage. Further research and practice of this model are required in order for it to be used widely in intelligent network-based teaching systems.

References

1. Oliver, R., Omari, A.: Using Online Technologies to Support Problem Based Learning: Learners' Responses, Australian Journal of Educational Technology, 15(1), (1996) 58–79
2. Stephenson, J.: Teaching & Learning Online: Pedagogies for New Technology, Kogan Page Limited, London (2001)
3. Chao, M.: The Monitoring of Network-based Learning. In: China Distance Education. 7 (2002) 35–38
4. Harasim, L., Hiltz, S. R., Teles, L., Turoff, M.: Learning Networks: A Field Guide to Teaching and Learning Online. MIT Press, Cambridge MA (1996)
5. Angelo, T. A., Cross, P. K.: Classroom Assessment Techniques (2nd Ed.), Jossey-Bass, San Francisco (1993)
6. Reeves, T. C.: Keys to Successful E-learning: Outcomes, Assessment and Evaluation. Educational Technology. 42(6) (2002) 23–29
7. Bloom, B. S.: Recent Developments in Mastery Learning, In: Educational Psychologist. 10 (1973) 53–57
8. Driscoll, M.P.: Psychology of Learning for Instruction (2nd ed.), Allyn & Bacon A Pearson Education Company, Massachusetts (2000)
9. Dee-Lucas, D.: Hypertext Segmentation and Goal Compatibility: Effects on Study Strategies and Learning. International Journal of Educational Telecommunications, 5(4) (1999) 225
10. Mason, R.: Models of Online Courses, ALN Magazine, 2(2) (1998)
11. Paolucci,R., Jones, T. H.: A Research Framework for Investigating the Effectiveness of Technology on Educational Outcomes, www.sapioinstutite.org (1998)

12. Bonk, C.J., Angeli, C., Hara, N.: Content Analysis of Online Discussion in an Applied Educational Psychology Course. Unpublished Manuscript, Center for Research on Learning and Technology report, Indiana University at Bloomington (1998)
13. Jonassen, D. H.: Thinking Technology: Context Is Everything. Educational Technology. 31(6) (1993) 35–37
14. Lin, Binshan, Hsieh, Chang-tseh (2001) Web-based Teaching and Learner Control: A Research Review. Computers & Education. 37 (2001) 377–386
15. Tolman, E.C.: Cognitive Maps in Rats and Men. In: Psychological Review. 55 (1948)189–208
16. Gagne, R.M.: The Conditions of Learning (4th ed.), Holt, Rinehart & Winston, New York. (1985)
17. Bandura, A.: Self-Efficacy: The Exercise of Control. W.H. Freeman. New York. (1997)
18. Zimmerman, B., Schunk, D.: Self-Regulated Learning and Academic Achievement: Theory, Research, and Practice. Springer-Verlag. New York. (1989)
19. Bandura, A.: Self-Efficacy: Toward a Unifying Theory of Behavioral Change. In: Psychological Review. 84 (1977) 195–215.
20. Bandura, A.: Self-Efficacy Mechanism in Human Agency. In: American Psychologist. 37 (1982) 122–147
21. Bourne, J. R., McMaster, E., Rieger, J., Campbell, J. O.: Paradigms for Online Larning: A Case Study in the Design and Implementation of an Asynchronous Learning Networks Course. Journal of Asynchronous Learning Networks. 1(2) (1997) 1–9
22. McQuillian, P.: Computers and Pedagogy: the Invisible Presence. Journal of Curriculum Studies. 26(6) (1994) 631–653
23. Bloom, B. S., Engelhart, M.D., Furst, E.J., Hill, W.H., Krathwohl, D.R.: Taxonomy of Educational Goalives, Handbook I: Cognitive Domain. McKay, New York (1956)

A Web-Based System to Teach Computer Operating System Theories and Usage to Elementary School Students

Sujin O[1], Woochun Jun[2], Le Gruenwald[3], and Sukki Hong[4]

[1] Seoul Kyungdong Elementary School, Seoul, Korea
osjin@orgio.net
[2] Dept. of Computer Education
Seoul National University of Education, Seoul, Korea
wocjun@ns.snue.ac.kr
[3] School of Computer Science
University of Oklahoma, Norman, OK, USA
ggruenwal@ou.edu
[4] Division of Business & Economics
Dankook University, Seoul, Korea
skhong017@dankook.ac.kr

Abstract. Recently ICT (Information Communication Technology) education has been adopted for elementary school students in Korea. ICT education is classified into two categories: literacy education and application education. However, only application education is emphasized in the current ICT education curricula. The computer operating system is a core topic in ICT literacy education, and thus it is necessary to teach the right concepts and basic knowledge of computer operating system from early childhood. In this paper, a Web-based computer operating system teaching-learning system for elementary school students is designed and implemented. The system has the following characteristics: first, the basic contents on operating systems necessary for elementary school students to understand are organized and classified into various stages and areas depending on students' prior knowledge and study plan, second, user-friendly interfaces are designed and implemented to facilitate students' learning, third, the system can help teachers keep track of students' progress and easily guide students.

Keywords: Internet, operating systems, Information Communication Technology

1 Introduction

Recently ICT has been adopted in many educational areas. ICT education is education based on computers and communication tools for collecting abundant information and for supporting individuals' study depending on their progress anytime anywhere. The purpose of ICT education is to provide a means to gather and analyze information necessary to each person, and let everyone use this capability to enjoy active and creative life [2]. ICT education is classified into two categories: literacy education and

W. Zhou et al. (Eds.): ICWL 2003, LNCS 2783, pp. 473–484, 2003.
© Springer-Verlag Berlin Heidelberg 2003

application education. Literacy education is education about computers and information communications, while ICT application education is education about applying ICT to various courses, such as science and languages [6].

Due to the current ICT curricula that are more concerned with ICT application education, literacy education has not been emphasized. The lack of literacy education enables students to have superficial and unessential knowledge on computers [9]. Operating systems is one of the main elements in ICT literacy education. However, education on operating systems has been ignored in the current ICT curricula. The existing teaching-learning methods for operating systems encourage students to learn the basic concepts by heart and are not systematic in contents' structures.

In this paper, we present a Web-based operating system teaching-learning system for elementary school students. The system has the following characteristics. First, the basic concepts of operating systems necessary for elementary school students are organized into various areas and stages depending on students' prior knowledge and study plan. Second, user-friendly interfaces are designed and implemented to facilitate students' learning. Third, the system can help teachers keep track of students' progress and guide students at ease.

This paper is organized as follows. In Section 2, we discuss the basic concepts and related theories on operating systems as well as introduce and analyze the current ICT curricula. In Section 3, we present the design of our operating system teaching-learning model for elementary school students. We also describe the implementation of our model in Section 4. Finally, we give conclusions and further research issues in Section 5.

2   Theoretical Backgrounds

In this section, we present the basic concepts and functions of operating systems, organize the topics related operating systems in the current ICT curricula of elementary schools, and discuss the existing works.

2.1   Operating Systems

An operating system is a set of programs that lies between application software and hardware. It is the fundamental software that controls access to all other hardware and software [1,5]. The term *system software* is sometimes used interchangeably with operating system. However, system software means all programs related to the coordination of computer operations. That is, system software includes the operating system but also includes programming language translators and other utility programs [1].

The operating system performs a variety of technical operations as follows [1].
-   Communicating with peripherals
    The operating system always includes routines that take care of the details of communications with peripherals transparently.
-   Coordinating concurrent processing of jobs

In multi-user environments, there are several jobs running concurrently. When a computer has only one processor, the computer takes advantage of idle time of one job by working on another job. The operating system must take care of various situations for the concurrent processing.

- Memory management

When several jobs are running concurrently, the operating system needs to keep track of memory usage and makes sure that no jobs invade other's area.

- Resource monitoring, accounting, and security

The operating system keeps track of each user's time, pages printed for accounting purposes. It also should monitor resources for ensuring privacy and security.

- Program and data management

The operating system should locate and access files requested by users and other programs.

- Coordinating network communications

Many modern operating systems are designed to handle various network communication tasks.

Table 1. The purposes of ICT education [6,7]

Categories	ICT education purposes
Understanding knowledge-based society	- Understanding the concept of information - Understanding characteristics of knowledge-based society - Cultivating information communication ethics
Understanding computers	- Understanding the organization and principles of computer operations - Understanding various kinds of software for operating computers - Understanding and utilizing operating system
Understanding and using information processing	- Understanding and utilizing information processing - Understanding and utilizing word processors - Understanding and utilizing spreadsheet software - Understanding and utilizing presentation software - Understanding and utilizing authoring tools for multimedia information
Understanding and using information communication	- Understanding information communication - Understanding and utilizing the Internet - Searching, analyzing and processing information - Evaluating information searched

2.2. The Current ICT curricula in Elementary Schools

The purpose of ICT education is to provide students with information processing and problem-solving capabilities so that they can improve their life in the current knowledge-based society. This purpose can be classified into four categories as shown in Table 1.

In addition to the purposes of ICT education in [6,7], Table 2 shows the purposes of ICT education for elementary school students.

Table 2. The purposes of ICT education for elementary school students [6]

Areas	ICT education purposes
Understanding knowledge-based society	- Understanding the concept of information - Understanding the importance of information in knowledge-based society - Understanding the basic information communication ethics
Understanding computers	- Understanding hardware components in computers - Understanding how to turn on/off computers - Understanding various kinds of software - Understanding the basic concepts and usage of operating system - Understanding how to take care of floppy diskettes
Understanding and using information processing	- Understanding the basic concepts of information processing - Being familiar with keyboards - Being familiar with the basic operations in word processors - Being familiar with the basic operations such as addition, subtraction, multiplication and division in spreadsheet software - Being familiar with the basic functions of presentation software - Drawing a simple picture using graphic editors - Removing virus using vaccine programs
Understanding and using of information communication	- Understanding the basic concepts of information communication - Understanding how to search information using search engines - Understanding how to send/receive e-mail

As we discussed above, computer literacy education should be included in an ICT curriculum. However, in elementary schools, computer literacy education including operating systems has not been emphasized. Students usually use application software without understanding the basic principles of operating systems.

2.3 Analysis of Some Representative ICT Curricula

In this section, we present some representative curricula.

1) TEKS-Texas Essential Knowledge and Skill for Technology Application [10]

TEKS recommends computer science contents for elementary, middle and high school students. In TEKS, computer education is classified into four categories: basic operations, information acquisition, problem solving, and communication. Based on TEKS, contents dealing with operating systems are extracted as shown in Table 3.

2) NETS – National Educational Technology Standards [8]

NETS has recommended various technology standards for students and teachers since 1993. The contents can be classified into six categories: ① basic operation and concepts, ② social, ethical and human issues, ③ technology productivity tools, ④ technology communications tools, ⑤ technology research tools and ⑥ technology problem-solving and decision-making tools. The contents related to operating systems are shown in Table 4.

3) Computer Science Final Report [11]

'Computer Curricula 2001 Computer Science Final Report" [11] published in 2001 has suggested 13 core areas in computer science curricula. Basically it aims at high school students. Based on the recommendations, the study contents related to operating systems are command language and its use, files and disk management and, networks.

Table 3. Contents related to operating systems in TEKS

Steps	Contents
K – Grade 2	- Understand the basic terminologies of computers - Understand how to create and store a file - Understand how to use input devices
Grade 3 –5	- Understand how to use some options dealing with files - Understand the basic commands - Understand how to use application software for problem-solving
Grade 6-8	- Understand the basic concepts of operating systems - Understand the principles of the basic functions of computers

Table 4. Contents related to operating systems in NETS

Grade	Contents
K- grade 2	- Understand the basic terminologies of computers - Understand how to use input devices, output devices, and monitors
Grade 3-5	- Use input devices such as keyboards effectively

2.4 Related Works

Some works have been presented in the literature [3,4,12]. In [4], a Web-based information literacy cultivation system was developed and applied for elementary school students. The work is basically concerned with information search and related activities. The system in [12] provides multimedia-based lectures aiming at adults, which may not be good for elementary school students since various types of interaction have not been provided sufficiently.

The system in [3] provides some contents related to operating systems for elementary school students. The system presents how to use Windows 98. However, the system does not deal with the basic concepts of operating systems.

3   Design of the Proposed Teaching-Learning System

3.1   The Design Principles

The principles of our system design are as follows.

First, we organize and classify the contents that are suitable for elementary school students.

Second, a student-centered user interface is designed. Since the user interface is very important in message delivery, we consider various student's needs and characteristics. For this purpose, we adopt multimedia such as dynamic images.

Third, the system is designed to support student's self-directed study. Students can check their progress and select areas and stages of their choice, and examine their study results. Therefore, students can decide their progress for themselves.

Finally, for teachers, this system is designed to check students' progress and results quickly. It is also designed to help teachers manage study contents, evaluation results and BBS (Bulletin Board System) easily.

3.2   The Study Contents of Operating Systems

Based on the contents from TEKS [10], Computer Science Final Report [11], and NETS [8], we organize the contents for elementary school students as in Table 5.

Table 5. Contents related to operating systems

	Theory	Understanding operating systems	Concepts of operating systems
Operating Systems	Practice	Managing files and disks	The basic operations of operating systems
			Managing files (including creation, copy and deletion, etc)
			Managing folders (including creation, copy and deletion, etc)
			Managing disks (including formatting and copying, etc.)
		Setting	Using control panel
		Removing virus	Understanding computer virus
			Prevention and remedy program

In addition to Table 5, we refine the contents as follows. Based on some representative curricula in Section 2.3, we divide the contents into three stages depending on student's grade and the advancement of student knowledge. The first and second stage is for grades 1–4 and grades 5–6, respectively. The contents of the third stage include advanced concepts and practice for any grade. The contents of each stage are connected smoothly. We also classify the contents into three areas: understanding operating systems, functions of operating systems, and virus. Table 6 shows the refined contents.

3.3   The Structure of the Proposed Teaching-Learning System

The proposed Web-based system is designed to support student's self-directed study and has the following characteristics.

First, the system provides study progress charts for each student so that students can check their own progress.

Second, the system supports teachers to check students' progress by various tests.

Third, the system supports various communication tools, such as chat and BBS, so that students can communicate with other students or their teacher anytime.

Fourth, the system records students' study history, such as the number of connections per week, average connection time, so that the teacher can keep track of the study process of each student.

The proposed system has basically two modules: student module and teacher module. Also, our database has three major contents: student information, study contents information, and study results of each student. Fig. 1 shows the overall menu structure of our system.

1)   Student module

Students are required to login the system first before using the system. Students can check their own progress and choose study areas and stages. Then, students can study each unit. During their study, student can use BBS or chat for further discussion or questions. After the unit study, students can evaluate their study results. Fig. 2 shows the menu structure for students.

Table 6. The refined study contents for operating systems

Stages & areas	Elements	Contents of stage 1	Contents of stage 2	Contents of stage 3
Understanding operating systems	Concepts of operating systems	-Understanding the basic terminologies. -Understanding the basic concepts and roles of operating systems	- Being aware of the importance of operating systems in computers	- Understanding the development history of operating systems
	Kinds and roles of operating systems			
Function of operating system	Managing files and folders	- Understanding what an operating system can do	-Managing files -Managing disks Understanding principles of CPU operations -Managing Peripherals Concepts of processing	-Understanding main memory management -Understanding concepts of virtual storage -Understanding the concepts of paging and segmentation -Understanding the concepts of file systems
	Managing disks			
	Managing input/output devices			
Virus	Understanding of computer virus	- Understanding the concept of computer virus	- Understanding how to prevent computer virus -Using remedy programs for virus removal	
	Prevention and usage of remedy programs			

2)   Teacher module

The teacher is supposed to manage the overall information about students, such as personal history and study grade. Our system is designed to help teachers manage the study contents, evaluation results and BBS easily. In our system, like students, a teacher should login first. After login, the teacher can check students' progress in his/her class and provide advice to students depending on the contents the students finished studying or the evaluation results. The teacher can check student's progress by identifying test scores for each area and stage, discussions on email and BBS, etc. Also, the teacher can answer students' questions via BBS or chat. Fig. 3 shows the menu structure for teachers.

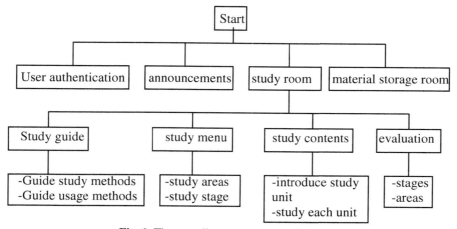

Fig. 1. The overall menu structure of our system

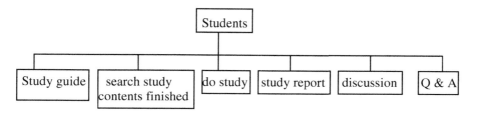

Fig. 2. Menu structure for students

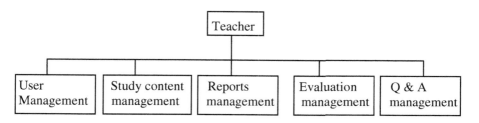

Fig. 3. Menu structure for teachers

4   Implementation of the Proposed Teaching-Learning System

4.1 System Development Environment

The proposed system is implemented as follows. We adopt the script languages PHP 4.0 and JavaScript for our implementation. Flash MX is the authoring tool we used to provide dynamic images. Apache is used for Web server. The Website address of our system is http://comedu.snue.ac.kr/~nadajin.

4.2 Major Screens

1) Initial screen

Fig. 4 shows the initial screen of our system. Each user is required to login first. After login, diverse menus are displayed depending on users. In case of a teacher, in addition to the basic menu, the menus for membership management, study contents management, report management, and Q & A management are shown.

2) Study guide screen

In this screen, the main menus for study contents of operating systems are presented. Based on these menus, students can search study contents they have finished. Students also can choose the next study contents including areas and steps in each area. After their study, students are guided to submit their study results on BBS. Fig. 5 shows the study guide screen in our system.

3) Study area selection screen

After user authentication, students are faced with menus for selecting four areas on operating system study. These four areas include the concept area, functions of operating systems, practice of usage, and virus area. If a student chooses one area, the student is required to select one of the three stages depending on their progress. Fig. 6 shows the study area selection screen.

4) Study stage selection screen

In this screen, students can choose one of the three stages, stage 1, stage 2 and stage 3, depending on their grade and progress. After the selection, a menu for unit study is displayed. Fig. 7 shows the study stage selection screen.

5) Unit study screen

After choosing the study areas and stages, students can select a study unit of operating system contents. Fig. 8 and 9 show the screens of the basic concepts and functions of operating systems, respectively.

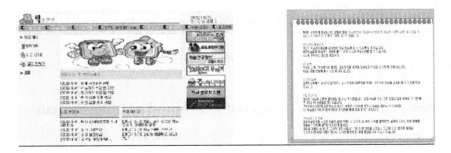

Fig. 4. The initial screen   **Fig. 5.** Study guide screen

Fig. 6. Study area selection screen   **Fig. 7.** Study stage selection screen

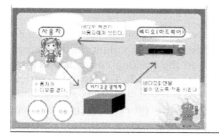
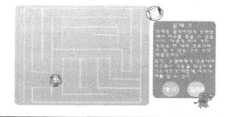

Fig. 8. Screen of the basic concepts   **Fig. 9.** Screen of functions of operating systems

4.3   Guide for Practical Use of the Proposed System

In this section, we present some guidelines for both students and teachers to follow so that they can use our system effectively.

1)   Guideline for Teachers

In schools, it is difficult for teachers to teach operating systems due to lack of knowledge and adequate materials for elementary school students. In order to teach the operating system contents successfully, it is very important to select adequate contents for students and apply teaching methods. This is due to the fact that operating systems is a difficult and broad subject.

In this system, the study contents are organized according to the advancement of student knowledge. Also, in our system, teachers can store and retrieve students' test scores and other results. Based on these results, teachers are supposed to give advice to each student. Also, teachers are required to check students' progress regularly and give quick responses to students.

2)   Guideline for Students

The proposed system provides various theories and practices of operating systems for different levels of students on the Web. In this system, students can check the study contents they have finished and select the next areas. After each unit, students can check their progress for themselves. If they fail to achieve their study goals, they can repeat the same contents as often as they wish.

This system provides various types of interactions (student-to-students, student-to-teacher, and student-to-experts) in order to achieve the study goals. Thus, students are supposed to use various communication tools such as e-mail, chat and BBS, whenever they need some assistance. Also, students are required to check their progress through formative tests.

5 Conclusions and Further Work

Although operating systems is an important area in ICT literacy education, it has been ignored in schools due to lack of teachers' knowledge and adequate contents. In this paper, we designed and implemented a Web-based operating system teaching—learning system for elementary school students.

In order to teach operating systems effectively for elementary school students, organizing study contents and teaching methods is very important. In this sense, we organized and classified study contents based on the existing curricula, such as the Computer Science Final Report [11], TEKS [10] and the ICT education curriculum [6]. We designed this system to support students' self-directed study so that students can learn the theories and practices depending on their progress. In order to support self-directed study, we provided various types of interactions and diverse examples for students. We also designed a multimedia-based user interface for ease of use. For teachers, this system was designed to check students' progress and results quickly. In addition, this system was designed to help teachers manage study contents, evaluation results, and BBS easily.

The proposed system will be extended as follows. First, we will choose and refine the terminologies for elementary school students. Second, we will continue to refine the user interface according to the advancement of student knowledge. Finally, we have a plan to develop various evaluation strategies and methods.

References

1. Beekman, G.: Computer Confluence, 3rd edition (1999)
2. Eduict: http://www.eduict.net (2001)
3. Edupia: http://www.edupia.com (2002)
4. Kang, I.: The Development and Application of Computer Education Curriculum for Information Literacy Cultivation for Elementary School Students, Master thesis, Korea National University of Education (2001)
5. Koo, Y.: Operating System, Ihan Press (2000)
6. Korea Ministry of Education: Guideline for Practical Use of ICT for Elementary and Middle School (2000)
7. Korea Ministry of Education: 1998 ICT in Education (1998)
8. National Educational Technology Standards: http://cnets.iste.org (2002)
9. Shin, E.: Research on Computer Science Curriculum for High School Students, Master thesis, Korea University (2002)
10. Texas Essential Knowledge and Skill for Technology Application: http://www.tea.state.tx.us/teks/ (1997)
11. The Joint Task Force on Computing Curricula IEEE Computer Society Association for Computing Machinery: http://computer.org/ education/ cc2001/ final/ cc2001.pdf (2001)
12. The Korea Educational Broadcasting System: http://www.ebs.co.kr (2002)

Developing Learning Objects through Concepts and Contexts

Sean W.M. Siqueira[1], Mª Helena L.B. Braz[2], and Rubens N. Melo[1]

[1] Catholic University of Rio de Janeiro, Computer Science Department,
Rua Marquês de São Vicente, 225, Gávea,
22453-900, Rio de Janeiro, Brazil
{sean, rubens}@inf.puc-rio.br
[2] Technical University of Lisbon, DECivil,
Av. Rovisco Pais, Lisbon, Portugal,
mhb@civil.ist.utl.pt

Abstract. The Internet has promoted several changes in the world, including on education. People have been more interested in learning, which makes developing higher quality content material even more important. In addition, people want to satisfy their learning needs according to their personal characteristics such as knowledge background and learning style. Therefore, nowadays there is a great interest on reusable learning content material and adaptive systems. Learning metadata standards contribute to achieve such reusability through the idea of learning objects. However, there is no guidance on how to develop learning objects, but only on how to describe them. The work presented in this paper proposes a model for structuring knowledge (concepts, demonstrations and interactions) in learning objects according to their context, representation and composition. This approach enables increased reusability and adaptability while providing better structured content material.

1 Introduction

We are living on what has been called the Information Age. There is an overload of information that is getting more difficult to filter, manage and assimilate. As a consequence of this high amount of information readily available and easily accessible we want to be able to use it in an efficient and effective manner to pursue our goals.

The development of the Internet has accelerated this process. Not only, the Internet has become a great resource of information but also the access to this resource is easy and affordable. This is the main reason why the Internet has caused many changes on several business areas.

In parallel to all this revolution, Education has also been re-discussed. New theories and paradigms have been developed and new methodologies have been tested. The Information Age and its environment of rapid changes have increased the importance of life long education and the Internet has provided mechanisms for advancing tech-

W. Zhou et al. (Eds.): ICWL 2003, LNCS 2783, pp. 485–496, 2003.

niques and methodologies. In addition, changes like personalization of services and content that the Internet has endorsed in the business area are also being propagated to education.

In order to provide education, it is necessary to develop learning content material. However, developing high quality material is expensive and time consuming. It has led to a demand for reusability in order to enable reduction of costs and time for material development.

The use of well-structured descriptions of the content material (metadata) has contributed to a better search of the desired material, thus facilitating content reuse. However, as these descriptions are not unique it is necessary to provide ways to enable interoperability among metadata structures. This is particularly important when considering that there is a movement towards globalization where organizations need (or want) to cooperate to each other,

To enable interoperability of learning content, organizations such as IEEE, IMS Global Learning Consortium and ADL have worked to develop technical standards, recommended practices and guides for learning technology. In general, their main focus is on describing learning content (e.g., [1], [2] and [3]).

Although these valuable efforts are being used worldwide and have proved their efficiency and efficacy, there are still some problems on how to structure learning objects. The general approach consists on having already developed several learning objects (i.e., learning content materials) and to define their metadata in order to allow their reuse on different educational and training programs.

The work described in this paper presents a conceptual framework that considers facts to be learned according to theory and practice, i.e. concepts, stories (knowledge experiences) and phenomena. In addition, a more critical view is also expressed through interactions. However, in order to use these concepts, phenomena and interactions in a learning activity it is necessary to place them into a context. Finally, an application enables representing such knowledge and it is possible to sequence/animate it. Therefore, besides improving content reusability and adaptability, our approach also provides guidance in the development of learning objects and activities.

This paper is organized as follows: Section 2 describes our proposed architecture of schemas for Learning Objects. Then, in section 3 we present the concept of Knowledge Manifold, which is reorganized and restructured to be used in our conceptual framework. In this section we also present the fact schema. Section 4 describes the context schema, which represents the environment in which learning occurs. Then, Section 5 presents other schemas and their integration to the overall architecture. Section 6 presents the relationships of the schemas, showing therefore how they are associated. Finally, Section 7 presents some final remarks.

2   The Proposed Architecture of Schemas

In order to improve reusability it is desirable to have high granularity in learning objects. However, breaking up content usually leads to losses in meaning. Considering these aspects, it was decided to adopt an architecture of schemas (or conceptual frameworks) in order to be able to define semantically richer learning objects although with high granularity. It was also seen as an important aspect to be able to apply underlying concepts of learning into the development of learning objects.

In our architecture of schemas (Figure 1) we consider as a "fact" everything that is to be learned, i.e., concepts, experiences and experiments. However, a fact is related to a context that represents the environment in which the fact occurs. Therefore, the interpretation of a fact is dependent on its context.

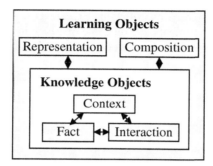

Fig. 1. Architecture of Schemas for Learning Objects

Facts and context are subject to interactions, i.e. in order to enable better understanding of facts according to their context it may be necessary to discuss over the facts and their environment. These discussions are represented through interactions that also allow the evolution of facts and contexts. Notice that this component is more important when a critical thinking approach of learning is considered. Thus it is not an essential component, but it has increased on significance over the years as education shift from teacher-oriented to student-oriented.

Learning occurs through the representation of facts, their context and respective interactions. Representation provides media representation so that it is possible to learn facts and interactions through an application. It is also an important aspect because it enables adaptability according to learners' styles and abilities. The representation component is the most affected by technology since it is the representation of application mechanisms that are used to present information (facts and interactions).

Finally it is possible to compose facts, interactions and contexts (knowledge objects). It allows a more sophisticated knowledge representation because we organize information into more complex units that will originate learning objects, i.e., the physical learning objects (content material files) and respective metadata.

We consider the fact and the context schemas the most important because they are responsible for describing concepts and experiments as well as the environment on which learning is going to happen. Therefore, they are going to be detailed separately in sections 3 and 4 respectively.

3   Concept of Knowledge Manifold and the Fact Conceptual Framework

For the fact schema, in our work we have adopted the concept of Knowledge Manifold. According to Ambjörn Naeve [4], an idea (concept) is a representation of a subjective experience. Knowledge Manifold (Figure 2) is the collection of such ideas within each individual that are constantly calibrated with their surroundings in a multitude of different ways. It is based on the fact that the mind works part deductively, by theorizing – part inductively, by collecting experiences. A theory creates expectations that often lead to experiments, the outcome of which in turn can verify or contradict the corresponding theoretical predictions, thereby influencing the conceptual evolution of the theory itself.

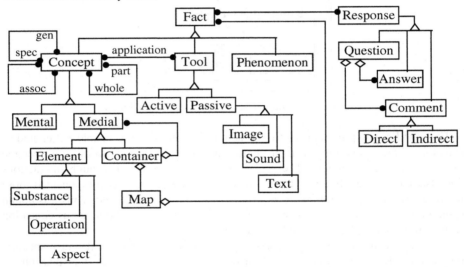

Fig. 2. Conceptual classification of a Knowledge Manifold

Facts can be theoretical or practical, hence involving concepts and/or can express experiences. Tools can present a concept.

Concepts can be inward ideas (mentally expressed) or outward ideas (medially expressed). There are different kinds of relationships among concepts: generalization/specialization, part/whole and associations.

A concept can be an element or a container (i.e., a set of medial concepts). An element concept can be a substance (i.e., describes something that remains unchanged during the transformational changes – just like a noun), an operation (i.e., describes a process of change/transformation – just like a verb) or an aspect (i.e., describes some type of invariant property of a substance – just like an adjective). A container concept has associated maps that are related to facts.

A tool is an application that presents facts. It can be passive in such a way that is expresses the idea through an image, a sound or a text; or active presenting a simulation or experience.

Facts are associated to responses that can be of type question, answer or comment, and a comment can be direct, i.e. expressed in multimedial form, or indirect, i.e. expressed in the form of a link (address).

Since we see the educational process as an application of the Knowledge Manifold, we use the structuring of facts to represent knowledge to be learned. We adapted the conceptual classification of a Knowledge Manifold in order to define the fact conceptual framework (Figure 3), i.e. the fact schema of the Figure 1. The extensions are represented through gray boxes and dashed lines.

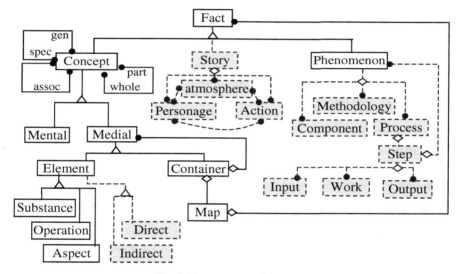

Fig. 3. Fact conceptual framework

We represent facts to be learned according to three different approaches: theory, story and practice, i.e., concepts, knowledge experience and experiments.

Story represents stories or cases. A story is composed of personages, descriptions of the environment (atmosphere) and actions. The personages execute actions that occur in a specific atmosphere.

Notice that interaction and representation aspects such as response and tool that are depicted in the conceptual classification of a knowledge manifold (see figure 2) are not represented in the fact conceptual framework (figure 3). They will be represented in other appropriated conceptual frameworks (interaction and representation conceptual frameworks). Therefore, this is the reason for response, questions, answers and comments or tool, active, passive, image, sound and text are not included here.

We extended the element concept in order to allow its representation directly or in the form of a link (address), i.e., indirectly. In addition, as presenting an experiment involves components that are processed according to a specific methodology, these are the extensions for phenomenon that we have defined in the fact conceptual framework (figure 3). A phenomenon is composed of component, methodology and process. A process is composed of steps that have input, processing/work and output. A step can be more complex, involving other phenomena.

In order to enable better understanding we present an example *in italics. We could represent the fact that a dog barks loud to a mailman in a house. The concept could be medially represented through a container of a dog (element substance), bark to (element operation), loud (element aspect volume), mailman (element substance), in a house (element aspect place). In this case we would have the (definitions of the) concepts dog, to bark to, loud, mailman, and in a house. However, it could also be presented through a story, with personages (dog and mailman), atmosphere (in a house) and an action (to bark). Finally, we could represent it as a phenomenon with methodology (observation of a mailman delivering mails in a house), components (dog and mailman) and a process (s1: the mailman is arriving and we look for the dog; s2: the mailman arrives and the dog starts barking; s3: the mailman deliveries the mail and the dog keeps barking; s4: the dog keeps barking and we measure the volume of the barking; s5: the mailman leaves and the dog stops barking).Other representations could also be possible, such as having the same story plus the concept mailman. It only depends on what it is going to be taught.*

4   Placing Learning Concepts and Experiments into a Context

After defining the fact conceptual framework, representing concepts, stories and experiments, it is necessary to define a conceptual framework for context.

Hawryszkiewycz [5] says that learning objects take a new meaning in their context and can better add to knowledge if they are placed in a context. Naeve [4] emphasizes this importance when he says that separating between knowledge-components and learning-strategies is complicated by the fact that any given answer implies a pre-judgement of the context within which the question was formulated. This creates a 'strong dependency' between what is being presented and under what kind of circumstances it is being presented, which represents a hardwired relationship between knowledge-content and learning-strategy.

According to the Webster's Dictionary, context is the environment in which an event occurs. Therefore, the learning context is the environment in which the facts to be learned occur.

We represent a learning context (Figure 4) through the knowledge area, learning goals, learning level, requirements / prerequisites, moments, places and experiences that are related to the fact.

A context can be simple or complex. In the latter case it represents a composition of contexts.

Area represents the knowledge area. Goal represents the learning goal. Level represents the learning level. Requirement represents the learning requirements or prerequisites. Moment and Place represent respectively temporal and spatial aspects related to the fact.

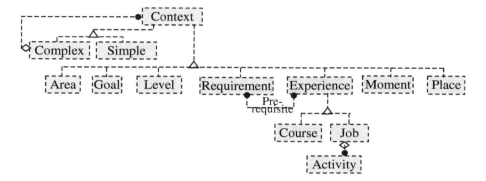

Fig. 4. Learning context conceptual framework

Experience presents academic and work experiences related to the fact. An experience in which the fact is inserted can represent a course and/or a job. A job involves activities, some of which can contextualize the fact. The requirement for learning a fact can be a specific experience.

In order to enable better understanding we present an example *in italics. We could represent several different contexts. A simple context would be representing only one aspect such as level (novice, intermediate, advanced) or area (veterinary). A complex context could have an area (veterinary), a goal (to understand dogs reactions under mailman presence), a level (advanced), and requirement (to know concepts such as dog, mailman, barking, house, and that normally a dog barks; and previous experience on animals psychology). The learning will provide experience on working with mailmen to avoid bad reactions on dogs. The place is in a house while the moment is when the mailman is near the house. Notice that several variations of this context are possible.*

5   The Other Conceptual Frameworks

In this section we present the remaining three conceptual frameworks/schemas (interaction, representation and composition) of the proposed 5-schema architecture that was described in section 2.

Interactions allow a better understanding of the concepts, knowledge experiences (stories) and experiments as they enable a critical discussion over the facts. Since facts are inserted into a context, these interactions must also consider the context. Figure 5 represents the interaction schema. Notice that it is part of the conceptual classification of a knowledge manifold. However, it was extended in order to express more semantic related to the messages.

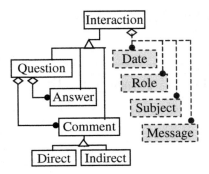

Fig. 5. Interaction conceptual framework

In order to enable better understanding we present an example *in italics. Questions over the example experiment in the second context (the complex one), could be: date = march 13ʰ, 2003; role from = professor John; role to = all students; subject = specific case?; message = Is it a characteristic of a specific kind of dog?. Then student Mark could answer in the same day to the professor that he has made experiments with three races of dogs and they all behaved the same way, barking loud; while student Mathew could comment in the next day to all students that he believes that trained dogs do not have the same behavior.*

As described in section 3, the concepts, stories and experiments are expressed in the fact schema and are related to the environment in which learning occurs (expressed in the context schema – see section 4). The interactions allow the discussion over such facts, thus improving learning. However, it is necessary to represent all these components (facts, context and interactions) through a media. Figure 6 shows the representation conceptual framework.

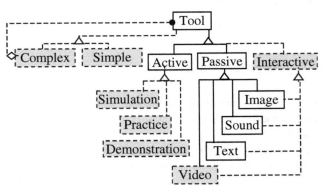

Fig. 6. Representation conceptual framework

A tool can be simple or complex. In the later case, it is composed of other tools. A passive tool conveys information through different types of sensing media, most often visual images, sound, text or video. However, through an active tool it is possible to perform experiments of different kinds, for instance simulations, demonstrations or practices. Finally, the representation conceptual framework also includes interactive tools that can be available in text (e.g., email, newsgroup, discussion forums and textual chats), sound (e.g., voice over IP and phone calls) and video (e.g., videoconference).

In order to enable better understanding we present an example *in italics. A simple tool could represent the concepts of the first example in the beginner level context through a video. The second context could have a complex tool to through practice enable the student learning the experiment and through a text interactive tool enable discussions.*

Finally, we need to enable compositions of the represented facts, interactions and their context. Figure 7 presents the composition conceptual framework. Composition is achieved through animation or sequencing of knowledge objects and corresponds to an ordered aggregate of facts, interactions and contexts.

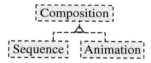

Fig. 7. Animation/Sequencing conceptual framework

In order to enable better understanding we present an example *in italics. Considering the second example of context, we could have the representation of the story through a video, which would give the motivation to the experiment. Then the sequence would be the experiment though practice followed by discussions. The next step could be defining the reasons for this behavior of dogs.*

6   Integrating the Conceptual Frameworks

Since we have defined the schemas (or conceptual frameworks), it is necessary to determine their relations.

A knowledge area (represented in the context schema) is defined through a concept defined as a fact or it can be defined through a direct description. It is related to fact and response, since they refer to a knowledge area. This area can slightly adapt a generic concept, so it is important in the definition of the context.

The learning goal can be expressed through fact-objectives, i.e., facts can describe other facts' goals, or through a direct description. By well-established and disseminated learning goals related to a specific fact or participating of a specific interaction the learner can feel more motivated. In addition, knowing the learning goal and objectives enables a better organization of learning as a whole.

It is possible to express requirements/prerequisites through facts or experiences, i.e., relations between fact and requirement define a fact that is prerequisite of other specified fact. Similarly, relations between requirement and experience define an experience that is prerequisite of a specified fact. In addition, the prerequisite facts and experiences allow better and easier understanding of what is to be learned.

The relation between fact and experience expresses how learning the fact can contribute to the learners' experience. Analogously, the relation between interaction and experience expresses how participating of the interaction can contribute to the learners' experience.

The relations between moment and place with fact and interaction represent temporal and spatial aspects of learning.

Facts and interactions are represented through the use of tools. Concepts and stories are passive tools while phenomena are active tools and interactions are interactive tools. The context can help in the choice of the best representation tool, for example the concept to bark can be represented by a image in conjunction with a sound for a little child while it is enough a text for a teenager (context level).

The learned sequence of knowledge objects (facts and interactions) defines what has recently been learned and what is to be learned, so that it makes learning the fact simpler and motivates the learner. The relation between animation and context as well as the relation between animation and representation allows better sequencing and animation through the same or complementary contexts or representations. Notice that animations generally occur when simpler concepts are considered (e.g., animation of pictures composing a story).

7   Conclusion

In this paper we presented a novel approach for developing learning objects based on an architecture where semantic aspects are emphasized. This architecture is centered on the idea of knowledge objects (concepts, stories and phenomena, plus interactions embedded in a context). These knowledge objects are represented and possibly composed in order to originate learning objects. The resulting learning objects allows better structuring of what is to be learned as well as better definition of related learning activities. Therefore, besides improving content reusability and adaptability, our approach also provides guidance in the development of learning objects and activities.

We started studying learning objects and their application in learning environments. Then we have seen that the development of learning objects could be better structured thus allowing more reusability and adaptability. Therefore, we initiate the process of defining the underlying concepts (hence defining the schemas).

The definition of the schemas was not only based on the concepts about knowledge manifold but also received an important input from the generalization of a previously proposed metamodel that was defined in the context of marketing activities [6] [7]. The generalization of the concepts for a generic environment allowed a deeper discussion on the schemas for developing learning objects.

In addition, a previous proposal of an architecture of schemas for learning objects based on the conceptual architecture of data warehouse systems [8] enabled the perception about the need for more structured learning objects than the considered in the available standards proposals.

In [9] we proposed a configurable environment for e-learning systems that we are going to instantiate. The work described in this paper is part of the database schema definition for this e-learning environment, in which we try to apply a better knowledge-structured approach.

During the development of our proposal we have found some interesting works. Song [10] presents a metadata model for learning objects. Although it is related to the description of learning objects instead of knowledge that is embedded in learning objets, it considers some similar concepts, such as the need for structuring content, carrier (representation), neighbor (context and composition) and intensity (context).

Rodriguez, Chen, Shi and Shang [11] present the idea of open learning objects (OLO), in which is considered an interface to export the results of learning objects-to-learner interaction and for learning object adaptation. It considers InnerMetadata that is the collection of layered metadata mechanisms that are used to describe the OLOs, their adaptive features, and the learning interaction tracing. It presents five layers for OLOs that look somewhat similar to our proposed architecture of schemas for learning objects. However, they do not consider learning context and their work is on describing learning objects to enable better learner interaction and learning object adaptation, while our work is based on the knowledge representation of what is to be learned so that better learning objects can be developed.

Hawryszkiewycz [12] presents how to integrate learning objects into learning contexts. This is a complementary work to our proposal, since besides considering the context of facts and interactions, it will be also necessary to consider the context of learning objects.

Finally, Elisabeth H. Wiig and Karl M. Wiig [13] describes the importance of conceptual learning, in which is emphasized the use of conceptual maps. We consider this is an important work that is related to the definition of facts and their sequencing in our proposal. Therefore, we consider it as a complementary work to our proposal and further study will be necessary.

We are just at the beginning of what we expect to be an important contribution for e-learning but a lot of work is still to be done. Some of the future works involve the detailing of the other database semantic components such as learner and course conceptual frameworks; the use of ontologies for improving the usability, efficiency and efficacy of the proposed schemas; the development of automatic behavior and intelligent guidance throughout the development of learning objects in order allow an easier and faster structuring; and more detailed tests of the proposed schemas.

Acknowledgements. The authors would like to thank the database technology group from PUC-Rio (TecBD) and the e-learning technology research group from ICIST/DECivil who actively participated on modeling discussions and the definition of the conceptual frameworks. This paper was partially supported by CNPq Brazil – Brazilian National Research Council, through a PhD bursary, and FCT Portugal – Foundation for Science and Technology, through the Multi-annual and Programmatic funds of ICIST.

References

1. IMS Global Learning Consortium, Inc.: IMS Learning Resource Meta-Data Information Model – Version 1.2.1 Final Specification. (28 September 2001)
2. Advanced Distributed Learning Initiative: Sharable Content Object Reference Model (SCORM^{tm}) – Version 1.2 – The SCORM Overview. (1 October, 2001)
3. Learning Technology Standards Committee of the IEEE: Draft Standard for Learning Object Metadata. Institute of Electrical and Electronics Engineers, Inc. (15 July 2002)
4. Naeve, A.: The Garden of Knowledge as a Knowledge Manifold – A Conceptual Framework for Computer Supported Subjective Education. CID – Centre for User Oriented IT Design, Nada Dept. Computing Science, KTH - Royal Institute of Technology, Stockhom, Sweden (1997)
5. Hawryszkiewycz, I.T.: Integrating Learning Objects into Learning Contexts. Proceedings of the International Conference on Dublin Core and Metadata for e-Communities, Florence, Italy (2002) 217–223.
6. Siqueira, S.W.M., Silva, D.S., Uchôa, E.M.A., Braz, M.H.B., Melo, R.N.: An Architecture for Database Marketing Systems. Proc. 12th Database and Expert Systems Applications, Munich. Lecture Notes in Computer Science. Berlin Heidelberg: Springer-Verlag (2001) v. 2113, p. 131–144.
7. Siqueira, S.W.M., Silva, D.S., Braz, M.H.B., Melo, R.N.: A Metamodel for Integrating Data to Database Marketing Systems. Proc. 3rd International Conference on Information Integration and Web-based Application & Services, Linz. (2001)
8. Siqueira, S.W.M., Braz, M.H.L.B., Melo, R.N.: E-Learning Content Warehouse Architecture. Proc. IADIS International WWW/Internet 2002 Conference, Lisboa (2002) 739–742
9. Siqueira, S.W.M., Braz, M.H.L.B., Melo, R.N.: E-Learning Environment Based on Framework Composition. Poster presented at the 3rd IEEE International Conference on Advanced Learning Technologies (2003).
10. Song, W.W.: A Metadata Framework for Description of Learning Objects. ICWL 2002, LNCS 2436 (2002) 31–43.
11. Rodriguez, O., Chen, S., Shi, H., Shang, Y.: Open Learning Objects: the case for inner metadata. Proc. WWW2002 Education Track, Hawaii, USA (2002), Available at: http://www2002.org/CDROM/alternate/693/
12. Hawryszkiewycz, I.T.: Integrating Learning Objects into Learning Contexts. Proc. International Conference on Dublin Core and Metadata for e-Communities, Firenze (2002) 217–223.
13. Wiig, E.H., Wiig, K.M.: On Conceptual Learning. Knowledge Research Institute, Inc. Working Paper (1999).

Building Reusable and Interactive E-learning Content Using Web[1]

C. Bouras, M. Nani, and T. Tsiatsos

Computer Engineering and Informatics Dept., Univ. of Patras, Greece
Research Academic Computer Technology Institute, Greece, 61 Riga Feraiou Str. GR 26221
Patras GREECE, TEL: +30 261 0 960 375, FAX +30 261 0 996 314
{bouras, nanim, tsiatsos}@cti.gr

Abstract. This paper presents the design of a web-based learning content authoring tool as well as the way learners can access courseware material, within the scope of a personalized, yet social, learning environment for vocational training. The authoring tool is intended to be part of the instructional component of the VirRAD European project, where the learning process is inspired by the principles of the Mindful Learning theory and supported by an intelligent learner modelling system. It will enable the creation of Radiopharmacy-related learning content that can be easily accessed and reused. In addition, it will facilitate the monitorship of the users' learning activities.

1 Introduction

Nowadays that the use of Internet has been expanded widely and the time and place limitations are considered as an obstacle to the traditional classroom-based training, technology-based learning, otherwise e-learning, gain continuously the interest of scientific community, organizations and governments. In the recent past, a great number of e-learning platforms has been introduced into the market [1], showing different characteristics and services, according to the pedagogical approach they follow for serving their end-users needs as well as the technological solutions they adopt to support the learning process. The swift growth of technology that is observed the last decade facilitates the incorporation of new services and functionalities in such platforms that could not be even conceived few years ago. As a consequence, e-learning environments are now able to efficiently manage just-in-time learning content [2] as well as pedagogical aspects related to the training process [1].

E-learning environments are expected now, more than ever, to deploy and manage learning content that can be easily searched and retrieved during an auto-learning phase as well as to be reused for different educational purposes. Content's reusability is considered as a crucial factor for the effectiveness of an e-learning system as not only reduces the efforts that have to be paid for the redesign of the learning content but also contributes to the avoidance of content duplication [1]. Moreover, the wide variety of learning resources may disorientate learners from choosing content that best meets their needs, according to the previously gained knowledge. To overcome this

---

[1] This work was supported by VirRAD/IST-2001-32291

W. Zhou et al. (Eds.): ICWL 2003, LNCS 2783, pp. 497–508, 2003.

learning obstacle, it is essential to allow the learners to easily locate and access the content of their preference.

Another important functionality that up to date e-learning environments are expected to expose, is the monitorship of the users' interactions with the content [1]. This enables the system to gather information about the learning resources' usage as well as to track and report on learners' progress and performance. Students are then able to consult, at any time, the results they have reached and, consequently, to monitor their preparation level. This information can, also, be exploited by the system in an attempt to diagnose the learners' needs [2] and advice them on the most suitable learning content [1].

A first step towards content's accessibility is the description of the learning resources in a consistent way using metadata. Metadata, or "data-about-data", are defined as the attributes required to fully and adequately describe a learning resource regardless of a specific learning context or a specific educational purpose. Furthermore, as mentioned in [2], the reusability of the learning resources presupposes the presence of an advanced knowledge management system able to categorize, enrich and integrate learning resources. It is, therefore, fundamental for the application of web-based learning to attach metadata to the learning resources. Hopefully, the last years, a lot of effort has been put on the development of learning technology specifications towards this need. Organizations, such as IEEE Learning Technology Standards Committee (LTSC) [3], IMS Global Learning Consortium (IMS) [4] and Advanced Distributed Learning (ADL) initiative [5], have presented remarkable outcomes regarding the development of standard metadata rules able to point out the real semantic content of the learning resources.

A web-based courseware authoring tool, as part of an integrated e-learning environment, able to develop accessible and reusable learning resources, is considered not only valuable for serving effectively the learner's needs but also for facilitating the whole learning process by allowing the monitorship of the learner's interactions with the content. It is one of the technological means that the environment should exploit in order to serve the pedagogical approach it adopts and manage just-in-time learning content.

This paper is dedicated to the design of such a tool, within the scope of a virtual learning environment for vocational training on the radio-pharmacy field. The section 2 of the paper presents briefly the VirRAD European project, in terms of the objectives and expected outcomes, whereas section 3 focuses on the instructional component of the system. Section 4 is dedicated to the design of the authoring tool, as it is envisioned to function, as well as the way in which learners can access the learning material. The fifth section is engaged with implementation considerations. Finally, some conclusion remarks together with the envisioned next steps are presented.

2   The VirRAD Project

VirRAD (Virtual Radio-pharmacy) [6] is envisioned to be a virtual learning environment for the vocational training of individuals on the radio-pharmacy field. The learning process will be inspired and conducted under the theories and principles of the Mindful Learning theory as well as other contemporary learning or instructional design theories. Mindful learning theory questions seven myths of the traditional learning and supports experiential learning, enhances learning process through creative distraction and presents an alternative view point, encouraging more flexible learning [7]. Within VirRAD, a multi-layer, meta-cognitive learner modelling system will support the learning process by encouraging individuals to communicate and collaborate with each other, facilitating the learning content access according to each learner's needs, and offering pedagogical advice on the learning material usage. The environment, where the learning process will be realized, will be a virtual space enabling the communication and collaboration among the individuals both in a synchronous and an asynchronous manner.

To meet the aforementioned objectives, VirRAD system has been divided into four main areas, namely Public Website, Community, Instructional Component and Project Internal Site [8].

- The Public Website constitutes the VirRAD's introductory component aiming to invite potential users to the system. It will provide general information on Radio-pharmacy as well as the means for the users to contact the VirRAD team.
- The Community site provides a series of tools for the communication, collaboration and information exchange among the radio-pharmacist's community members. These tools offer functionality such as personal card, library, text chat, virtual conference, forum, news, links, events, adverse reactions reporting system and glossary of terms.
- The Instructional Component of the VirRAD system aims to support and facilitate the access to the learning material through an intelligent learner modelling system, as well as to encourage and facilitate interactions among learners, authors and mentors. The Instructional component will be further discussed in subsequent sections.
- The Project Internal Site provides functionality similar to the Community's but it applies, mainly, to the project members.

3   Instructional Component of the VirRAD System

The Instructional component of the VirRAD system concerns learner-learner, learner-mentor, and learner-system interactions as well as the access and the creation of the VirRAD courseware. Within this area, the users of the system can undertake three types of roles: learner, mentor or author.

Each learner has his/her own personal learning profile (e.g. determined through introductory assessments or further registration). S/He can access the available e-learning material, make use of the VR Laboratory (that is subsequently described) and be supported by mentors and the learner modelling system.

Mentors derive from the real radio-pharmacists' community and have as main task to support the learners into the instructional component. This is realized in two main modes: asynchronously, via e-mail, or synchronously in the 3D Virtual Teaching Laboratory (this is also described in the next paragraphs).

Authors are members of the VirRAD community that have as main task to provide Instructional material to the learners in the instructional component. They can submit and modify instructional material as well as to attach and edit metadata to the learning resources.

The main functionalities the instructional component provides, are:

- *The VR laboratory:* It is a 3D simulation of a radio-pharmacy laboratory, where learners, represented by 3D avatars, can experiment on radio-pharmacy equipment by carrying out specific learning scenarios. The VR Laboratory can be accessed either in a stand-alone or in a multi-user way (VR Teaching Laboratory). In the first case, a learner can interact with the radio-pharmacy equipment and get pedagogical advice by the system or send an e-mail to a mentor requesting further explanations. In the second case, learners can meet, communicate and collaborate with each other and with mentors, as well as get support by mentors on the usage of the 3D simulated radio-pharmacy equipment.

- *The learning management element:* It provides tools for the creation and integration of learning objects and courses into the VirRAD courseware. This element facilitates the access to the courseware and monitors the learners' interactions with the instructional material, while offering them pedagogic advice by means of the intelligent learner modelling system. Learners are able to conduct self-assessments as well as to create, access and edit their own personal academic records, which exchange data with the learner modelling system. The last is divided into two main parts: an active and a static one. The active part is mainly responsible for monitoring and analyzing the learner's interactions with the learning material, while the static one (database) stores information and statistics about the learning activities experienced by a learner. This information is used by the system with the intention to offer pedagogic advice to the learner's best advantage. Furthermore, mentors can support learners by monitoring their personal academic records, answering to their questions via e-mail, suggesting informative learning resources or inviting them in the VR teaching laboratory for further discussion.

- *The courseware:* It comprises the learning content of the VirRAD system. The topics of the content are mainly targeted on the radio-pharmacists' community and therefore they focus on the preparation, manipulation and quality control of potentially hazardous radioactive material. VirRAD system will support a wide variety of content types, such as exercises, slides and 3D simulations (e.g. elution of a generator and contamination monitoring). The courses will be composed of learning objects, which will be accessible and reusable and they could be linked to more than one course.

This paper is dedicated to the design and development of the third functionality. Therefore, the structure of the e-learning content as well as the tools for creating and accessing courses are described in detail, in the following sections.

4   VirRAD's Courseware

The courseware within VirRAD is intended to serve the need of the radio-pharmacy community members for just-in-time learning content related to radio-pharmacy. The courseware elements, also called content model components, should be easily merged and aggregated to produce a modular repository of training material, whereas they need to be attached with descriptive information for facilitating their easy access and reuse. Furthermore, according to the Mindful Learning theory, the learners' interactions with the learning material should be tracked by the VirRAD's learning management element. These interactions include the time a learner spends on a learning resource, other similar learning resources the learner selects to view, the content type (e.g. vide or text) delivered to the learner as well as answers to assessment questions. The following subsections present the VirRAD supported content model components and their metadata elements, the way these components can be aggregated to form larger units of instruction as well as the means that enable their access and monitorship in terms of learners' interactions.

4.1 Content Model Components

The VirRAD system distinguishes three types of learning content model components, which are involved in the courseware development process. These concern "Assets", "Learning Objects" (including assessments) and "Courses" and they are defined as follows:

- *Assets:* Assets comprise the basic constitutive element of the courseware. They refer to raw media files that can be viewed by a web browser, such as slides, flash objects, exercises and 3D simulations.
- *Learning Objects/Assessments:* A learning object refers to the learning content launched by the learning management element and delivered to the end-user during a courseware learning experience. It can be either a collection of one or more assets or an assessment object. Assessments may contain a question of at least four types, namely multiple-choice (true-false and multiple answer are also included), matching, fill-in-the-blank and open short answer questions (including short paragraph questions).
- *Courses:* One or more learning objects or even courses can be aggregated together to form a cohesive unit of instruction, i.e. a course, dedicated to radio-pharmacists' needs. Within a course, the learning objects and courses will be listed sequentially in an author-defined order. Using a course as part of another course, authors can develop courses nested in any depth and, thus, apply learning taxonomy hierarchy.

4.2 Metadata Elements

In order to allow the application of web-based learning and fulfill the requirements for accessible and reusable learning content within VirRAD, there is the need to attach metadata elements to the three previously described content model components. As already mentioned, the scientific community and industry engaged in e-learning technology area has presented a variety of specifications regarding learning resources metadata. The most significant of them are the IEEE 1484.12.1 Learning Object Metadata (LOM), approved on June 2002 as an IEEE-SA standard, the IMS Learning Resource Metadata Specification and the SCORM Specification.

As described in [3], LOM defines the attributes required so as to fully and adequately describe a learning resource. The IMS Global Learning Consortium based on LOM and slightly modifying it, has developed the IMS Learning Resource

Metadata Specification. Finally, the SCORM Specification references the IMS Metadata specifications and applies its definitions to the SCORM' s three content model components. This mapping provides "the "missing link between general specifications and specific content models" [5].

From the above it is clear that the SCORM specification has precedence over the other aforementioned specifications, as it refers to them while making one step further. This is, actually, the main reason why more and more learning technology products tend to be compliant with it [9].

SCORM specification maps the metadata elements to its three content model components, "Assets", "SCOs" and "Content Aggregations", by defining which elements are mandatory, optional or reserved by the system. Assets, SCOs and Content Aggregations are defined as follows [9]:

- *Assets:* They concern learning content in the most basic form that can be delivered in a Web client. Web pages, images and text are few examples of assets.
- *SCOs:* A Sharable Content Object (SCO) is a collection of one or more assets that can be launched by a Learning Management System (LMS). However, as opposite to an Asset, a SCO can communicate with the LMS thus allowing the LMS to track down the learner's interactions with the content.
- *Content Aggregations:* It concerns a content structure that can be used in order to aggregate Web-based learning resources into cohesive instructional units (e.g chapters and courses), define the structure of this unit and associate learning taxonomies. The content structure defines the sequence according to which the learning content will be presented to the user.

As mentioned above, a SCORM-conformant LMS can track the learner's interactions with the content by exchanging information with SCOs. These interactions include the majority but not all the interactions that need to be tracked down according to the Mindful Learning theory. In particular, open short answer questions are not defined in the SCORM specification, whereas information about the alternatives content types (e.g. video or text) the learner selects to view is limited to audio and text preferences only. SCORM supports many more interactions, which, however, are considered out of the VirRAD scope. Using the SCORM Run-Time Environment [5] for exchanging all the necessary information between the delivered learning content and the VirRAD's learning management element, presupposes the extension of the data model proposed by ADL initiative, the implementation of the appropriate (scripting) functions that need to be incorporated into the content, as well as the extension of the ADL's Application Programming Interface (API) to implement the new functionality. Instead, and in attempt to create an auspicious but still simple web-based authoring tool, we appose our solution to simplify the whole process.

In order to apply SCORM conformant metadata to the VirRAD's content model components, we assume the following interrelations:

Table 1. Interrelations between VirRAD and SCORM content components

VirRAD content component	SCORM content component
Asset	Asset
Learning Object (including assessments)	SCO
Course	Content Aggregation

VirRAD system will support all the mandatory elements for each of the aforementioned content model components so as to assure full compliance with the SCORM Metadata specification. Furthermore, the learning resources will be provided with some optional SCORM metadata elements, which are considered necessary within the scope of VirRAD, as well as with an additional one, called "storyboard". This has been introduced for VirRAD's purposes with the intention to describe what happens in a learning resource. Metadata elements are grouped into nine categories, namely General, Lifecycle, Meta-metadata, Technical, Educational, Rights, Relationships, Classification and VirRAD specific.

4.3 Creating Courseware

The courseware material within VirRAD concerns Assets, Learning Objects and Courses targeted to the learning needs of the radio-pharmacist's community members. This subsection presents the way these components are brought to light, during the authoring process.

As already mentioned, assets constitute the basic element of the courseware and they can be of various types. Authors will have the responsibility to upload them into the system (in particular to the Web Server) and enrich them with at least all the mandatory metadata elements, as they have been defined by ADL initiative. Thereafter, authors can assemble one or more assets so as to create Learning Objects (LOs).

In the case where the LO is intended to be an assessment, authors can select one of at least four question types to insert into the assessment. The available question types are envisioned, but not restricted, to be multiple-choice (this also includes true-false and multiple answers questions), matching in two columns, fill-in-the-blank and open short answer questions (this also includes short paragraph questions). Authors need, also, to define the correct answer to the question (or keywords that the answer should include) and, conditionally, the maximum time a student is allowed to view the assessment object until s/he supplies an answer. This information can be used by the system in an attempt to monitor and report on learners' progress and performance. Moreover, assessments may be enhanced with an asset, located in the Web Server, for illustrative purposes (e.g. a graphic).

In the case where the LO is intended to be a collection of one or more assets, the author is provided with a title list of all the assets available in the system's Web server. S/He can, then, select the asset(s) s/he intends to incorporate into the LO and define the way this object will look. This process is facilitated by an ease-to-use graphical user interface, which aims at alleviating the authoring process by minimizing the author's programming efforts.

In both cases, the whole process terminates with the metadata provision. Thereafter, the system incorporates some scripting functions into the content with the intention to supply the learner modelling system with the appropriate information that it needs to be aware of according to the Mindful Learning theory.

Creating a course within VirRAD involves the aggregation of one, or more, Learning Objects (or even courses) together and the attachment of, at least, all the mandatory metadata elements required to fully and adequately describe this content component. These metadata elements aim to describe the course in a particular context, related to Radio-pharmacy. The way in which authors can aggregate learning resources to develop a course within VirRAD has been inspired but is not identical to that described by IMS Content Packaging and SCORM specifications, due to simplicity reasons. Though, authors can still apply learning taxonomy hierarchy.

In particular, when an author selects to create a course for VirRAD's purposes, s/he will be provided with a list of all the available LOs and courses. S/He can then select the learning resources that the course will consist of, as well as the sequence in which they should be presented to the learners (see Fig. 1). As they are allowed to encapsulate courses in another course, authors are able not only to apply learning taxonomy hierarchy but also to consecutively create larger and larger units of instruction.

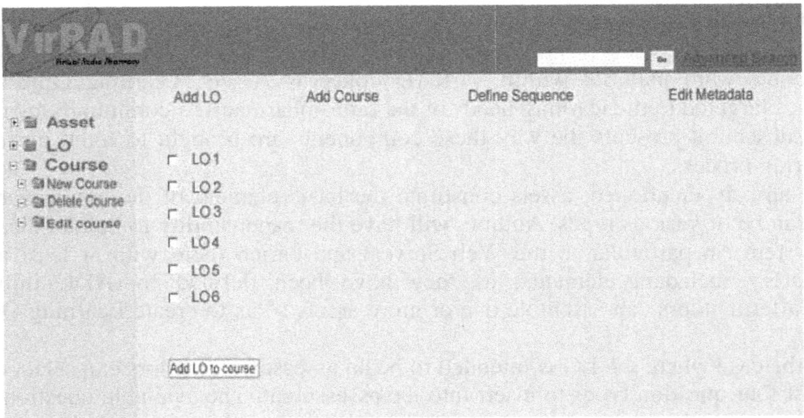

Fig. 1. Adding LOs to a new course

Besides uploading assets into the system and gradually creating learning objects and courses, authors have also the ability to modify the attached metadata elements, as well as the various learning objects and courses. However, any changes to the learning material are not readily available during content authoring or access, unless approved by the Editorial Board (members of the real radio-pharmacists' community that are involved in the VirRAD project as partners).

4.4 Access to Courseware

Any community's member registered as a learner can access the VirRAD's courseware from the Public Web Site. The general access page for all the courseware provides the means for the learners to choose a mode of learning, links to all the available courses approved by the Editorial Board, as well as searching facilities.

Learners can select between two modes of learning while experiencing a course. These concern the "browse mode", where learners are able to jump from topic to topic as they wish, and the "study mode", where learners are motivated to follow the pedagogical advice, provided by the learner modelling system. If the learner accepts the pedagogical advice, s/he can be transferred to another element of the course or part of the community area. In study mode, the learner modelling system will monitor the learners' activities such as what course material they access, for how long as well as their response to assessment questions. This is expected to be the usual mode of using the learning material.

Learners can view the contents of a course by clicking on its title within the general access page. They are, then, redirected to a new web page, which contains the course's table of contents in one frame (in the from of a hyperlink tree) and the real learning content in another frame. The table of content is built dynamically according to the course's structure as it has been defined by authors and stored in the courseware database. Moreover, when a user clicks on the course's title or a topic within the course, a list of links to learning resources that the clicked resource relates to appears in another frame of the browser window (see Fig. 2). The list of related resources is built based on the resource's metadata elements (in particular the elements contained into the Relationships category).

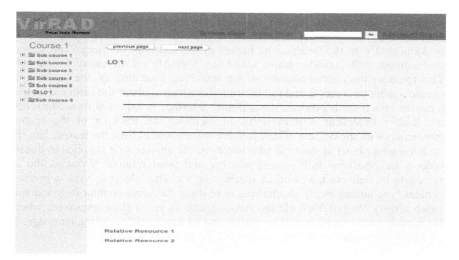

Fig. 2. Accessing courseware within VirRAD using browse mode

Users can navigate through the learning objects contained in a course or encapsulated courses, by (a) selecting a topic from the table of contents, (b) using the "Next page", "Previous page" navigation buttons, (c) following the pedagogical advice or d) following a link form the list of the related resources. The last two ways may guide the learner to another course. The title (hyperlink) of an already visited learning object is highlighted so as to keep the learners informed of all the learning objects they have been delivered. While experiencing a course, learners can change the mode of learning (browse or study) or search for a learning resource.

Learners can search and retrieve assets, learning objects and courses by supplying indicative keywords. As the three content model components within VirRAD are described using metadata, the keywords are searched within these metadata elements. Learners have also the ability to define advanced search criteria such as the title, the type or the author of a learning resource.

5 Implementation Issues

The VirRAD system will be based on a client-server architecture. The picture bellow (Fig. 3) presents the part of the system's architecture that is engaged to the courseware element. There the following three components can be distinguished:

- *Web client:* Learners will be able to access the learning content as well as other VirRAD's services through a browser window. Authors can upload assets and create or modify learning objects and courses through a browser window too. The VirRAD system will come with a variety of user interfaces in order to manage the various functions.

- *Web Server:* The Web Server is used, among others, for storing the content of the courseware as well as for storing and executing the scripts of the scripting environment. The Web Server interacts with the browser window using the HTTP protocol and with the database by means of the scripting interface. The scripting environment will provide almost all of the VirRAD's courseware functionality. This includes the implementation of the searching functionality, the building of a course's table of contents and the information retrieval about the resources a LO or a course relates to. Moreover, the scripting interface is expected to send events to the learner modelling system so as to facilitate the tracking of the learner's interaction with the content. These involve the amount of time the learner has spent on a learning object at the time s/he leaves it, the answer s/he supplies to question objects and the time this occurs, whether and what relative resources the user selects to be delivered, as well as whether or not s/he selects to view a particular content type among many alternatives describing the same content (e.g. video and video script). Within VirRAD the Apache web server will be exploited, whereas the scripting environment will be mainly drawn upon PHP scripting language. The events to the learner modelling system will be sent through XML.

- *Courseware Database:* The database management system constitutes the core of the whole system where the majority of the information available is stored and organized. Information related to the courseware element will be stored in the "Courseware Database". This includes information about the available learning resources and their relationships, the metadata elements and data about learner's activities needed by the learner modelling system. VirRAD will exploit the MySQL database server.

- *Learner Modelling System:* The learner modelling system facilitates the access to the learning material, encourages the communication, collaboration and information exchange among learners while offering them pedagogical advice. It exchanges information with the learners' personal academic records and the database and accepts XML events sent through the scripting interface.

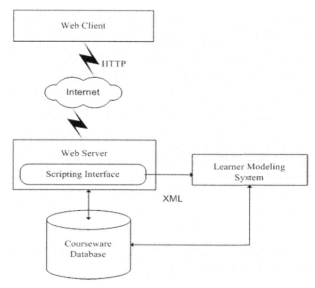

Fig. 3. System Architecture concerning the courseware functionality

6   Conclusions and Future Work

The swift growth of technology allows up-to-date e-learning environments to incorporate a wide variety of services and functionalities, which enable them to effectively manage just-in-time learning content as well as pedagogical aspects related to the training process. Learning content's accessibility and reusability are considered essential to the success of such an environment as they obviate the danger of the content's duplication, while smoothes the progress of the access to the learning material. E-learning environments are, also, expected, more than ever, to monitor the learners' interactions with the content so as to track and report on their progress and performance in addition to advice learners to their best advantage.

Metadata constitutes an important attempt towards learning content's accessibility and reusability. In particular, SCORM specification regarding metadata references the most significant learning technology specification towards this need, while making one step further by linking the metadata elements to particular content model components. The learning content within VirRAD involves three model components (Assets, Learning Objects and Courses), which will be attached with SCORM conformant metadata as well as with an optional, VirRAD specific, metadata element.

The web-based authoring tool we have presented is designed to assemble learning resources in a highly modular way and attach them with the appropriate metadata elements. Moreover, this tool allows the creation of assessment questions that facilitate the monitorship of the learners' interaction to the content. The learner modelling system will exploit this information in an attempt to offer pedagogical advice to the learners, to encourage them to communicate and collaborate with each other as well as to facilitate the access to the learning material. Besides the authoring tool, special attention is paid to the learning content access. Learners will be provided with all the means that will help them navigate through a courseware element or access content according to their previously gained knowledge.

The proposed web-based authoring tool as well as the way the learning material will be accessed, constitute an attempt towards e-learning environments' requirements to deploy and manage accessible, reusable and traceable learning content. Our next steps involve the implementation of this tool and functionality within the scope of VirRAD. During this phase, special attention will be paid on the minimization of the programming efforts required by the VirRAD' authors. For the implementation the Apache Web Server, a MySQL database server and the PHP scripting language will be exploited. Furthermore, client-side JavaScript and Cascading Style Sheets could also be used to provide a more flexible, user-friendly and intuitive graphical user interface.

Acknowledgements. We would like to thank all the VirRAD partners for their collaboration and contribution to our work.

References

1. Francesco Colace, Models for E-Learning environment evaluation: a proposal, SSGRR 2002, L' Aquila, July 29–August 4 (2002)
2. Lytras, M. D. and A. Pouloudi. E-learning: Just a Waste of Time. In Strong, D., Straub, D. & DeGross, J.I. (Eds) Proceedings of the Seventh Americas Conference on Information Systems (AMCIS), Boston, Massachusetts, pp. 216-222 (2001a)
3. IEEE Learning Technology Standards Committee (LTSC), http://ltsc.ieee.org
4. IMS Global Learning Consortium, Inc, http://www.imsproject.org
5. Advanced Distributed Learning (ADL) Initiative, http://www.adlnet.org
6. Virtual Radiopharmacy – VirRAD (IST-2001-32291), http://www.virrad.eu.org/
7. E. J. Langer, The Power of Mindful Learning, Perseus Books (1997)
8. Ch. Bouras, El. Giannaka, V. Kapoulas, M. Nani, Th. Tsiatsos, "Building e-learning communities: The case of VirRAD", ICALT 2003, July 9-11, 2003, Athens, Greece (2003) (to appear)
9. Ch. Bouras, M. Nani, Th. Tsiatsos, "A SCORM-conformant LMS", ED–MEDIA 2003, Honolulu, Hawaii, USA, June 23–28 (2003) (to appear)

Design and Implementation of VPL: A Virtual Programming Laboratory for Online Distance Learning

Alvin T.S. Chan[1*], Jiannong Cao[1], Chi-Kin Liu[1], and Weidong Cao[2]

[1]Internet and E-Commerce Laboratory,
Department of Computing
The Hong Kong Polytechnic University
Hung Hom, Kowloon, SAR of Hong Kong
[2]Department of Mathematics,
Jiangsu Institute of Education
Nanjing, Jiangsu, China
[*]Contact Author: cstschan@comp.polyu.edu.hk

Abstract. The virtual programming lab (VPL) project described in this paper offers is designed to facilitate Internet access to application software. It emulates a real computing laboratory environment that promotes group learning and project management. The laboratory resources are situated at the university and are centrally controlled. Users of the virtual programming laboratory include students, tutors and administrators of the system. Users can be located at different geographical locations and remotely access applications through the Internet. The virtual programming lab design is based on a distance education concept. This paper focuses on the design and development of the runtime modules within the VPL framework. These runtime modules provide underlying services that drive the launching of applications, file management and communications services. In addition, this paper presents an evaluation of the performance of the system.

1   Introduction

The growth of the Internet over the last few years has promoted many areas of web development including education. E-learning has become one of the fastest moving trends and is expected to play an ever more important role in the provision of distant education.

Web education makes distance learning effective and flexible. Students can learn according to their own schedules and, if necessary, follow a non-linear approach to acquiring knowledge based on their own capabilities. Students can access course materials anywhere at anytime. They can download lecture notes, communicate with the instructor via email, and sit examinations on the web. Already, there are popular e-learning software packages that support online lecturing and tutoring and considerable effort has been put into providing web-based learning and teaching.

All of this notwithstanding, it is not a simple matter to find reports that address the important issue of providing students with convenient online access to programming

W. Zhou et al. (Eds.): ICWL 2003, LNCS 2783, pp. 509–519, 2003.
© Springer-Verlag Berlin Heidelberg 2003

facilities. Indeed, students who currently wish to access a particular item of software are invariably required to physically go to the computing lab to do it, and up until now, solutions to this problem have either been   ad hoc or have required special-purpose web programming facilities [1][3].

The virtual programming laboratory system (VPL) enables users to launch programs at remote servers located in the laboratory and provides ease and better use of laboratory software resources. By providing wide area access through web infrastructure, VPL allows more students to remotely use the software located within the laboratory. An additional benefit of VPL is that it allows students to share resources and remote files with others. By providing a channel for users to communicate with their peers, VPL promotes collaborative learning.

2   Challenges in Laboratory-Oriented Learning

Advances in Internet technologies have led to new types of teaching and learning projects. Mostly, these projects have been limited to the dissemination of teaching materials, but   some projects have tried to provide more attractive and Internet-informed features that support interactive, customized, and collaborative teaching and learning. Such Internet-informed projects have included providing a laboratory-learning environment on the web. This is an important step, as practical work plays a central role in learning science subjects. The aims of laboratory work are often synonymous with the aims of science courses [1] and aided learning. A laboratory with software access promotes learning because it allows students to apply concepts in practice. Yet the use of software in physical laboratory settings presents a number of challenges in terms of efficient and effective teaching.

Currently, little work is found on either ad hoc or special purpose web programming facilities that support virtual programming environment [2]. When students need to use lab-based software or have a discussion with project members, they are required to be physical present in a computer lab, causing students to waste time traveling and arranging meetings.

In short, laboratory resources are not leveraged effectively and uniformly. One reason for this is that software and application usage in laboratories often depends on course assignment workloads and project deadlines, so laboratories (and consequently software) have a very uneven usage pattern over a term. Similarly, usage tends to be very high during "normal" lab hours, while resources are under-utilized during off-peak hours, especially weekends. A further reason for ineffective and uneven leveraging of laboratory resources is geographical, in that the license usages are always distributed unevenly.

Instructor/tutor led laboratory sessions usually have an excess of materials to present. This may lead to students needing extended lab hours to complete their assignments. In these circumstances, instructors/tutors too, may face difficulty to managing their workloads, and find themselves unable to simultaneously run their courses and appropriately respond to students. Obviously, this can damage both teaching and learning and teacher and student morale.

A final problem is that software installation and configuration also consumes large amounts of time in the physical laboratory that could otherwise be spent on more productive learning activities.

The aim of the Virtual Programming Lab (VPL) [4] project is to solve each of these problems by enabling any student with access to a computer with a web browser and a connection to the Internet to gain access to laboratory resources, wherever, whenever. There are three desirable characteristics of the virtual learning environment [5] that are applicable to this project:

1. Supported and customized individual lab environment

2. Real-time and non-real time group usage of the virtual lab environment

3. Collaboration and learning between lab users

The VPL project supports these three characteristics. Users are assigned accounts to store their individual environment information. System support is provided for users and administrator to customize and manage their virtual lab environment. Within the virtual environment, users can interact with each other via built-in collaborative tools to promote interactive learning.

The VPL system also provides a statistical log of software usage patterns. An integrated mechanism to monitor the software usage patterns and user behavior are provided. The former is important for planning of resources, while the latter may be used as a basis to monitor students learning experience and behavior.

File management is also addressed in this project. The files in the VPL system can be stored in the local or remote machines. A simple job such as "opening a folder" involves many processes such as distinguishing the location of the file, connecting to the remote site, mapping to the remote user account and getting the file information. The file management function handles these complex tasks for the user. The user does not need to know the file location before copying the file. If a remote file is copied to local folder or vice versa, the file transfer between local and remote is necessary and should be performed transparently.

3   VPL Design

The purpose of the VPL system is to create a seamless laboratory environment that supports online distant learning. Because of the lack of laboratory simulation projects that allow remote program launching, the VPL system is designed to provide such functionality and a standard platform for user interaction.

Fig 1 shows the network infrastructure between clients and lab machines. The VPL system allows users to access the lab machine software through a thin client no matter what type of hardware, be a pc, laptop or PDA.

The overall system architecture adopts the typical 3-tier approach where the graphical user interface is located at the client tier, the virtual lab runtime API at the middle tier, and the database at the 3rd tier. The client side includes some components that provide access to the virtual lab runtime. The middle tier manages the virtual programming lab and provides APIs to access the database and the lab machine. The third tier stores information and resources in the system (see Fig 2).

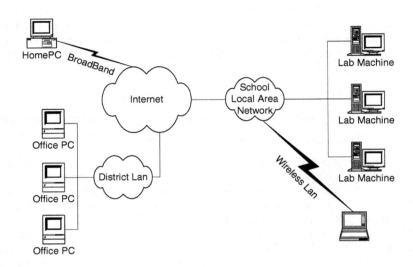

Fig. 1. System context of VPL

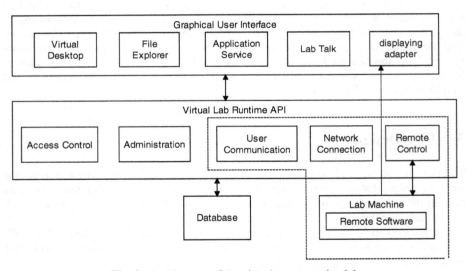

Fig. 2. Architecture of the virtual programming lab

This paper focuses on the virtual lab runtime part which is highlighted in dotted lines as shown in Fig 2. The runtime will appear as a set of software packages that bundled together to provide Java API access to service provided by the VPL system.

3.1   Design of VPL Runtime System

The design of the VPL runtime system can be broken down into five parts:

- File management subsystem—provides remote file management function for applications. The purpose of the subsystem is to enable the seamless transfer of files between local and remote systems operating in a graphical user interface. The component is designed to be modular so as to support open programming interfaces, where future applications can be built easily based on the API provided by this system.

- Communication subsystem—provides the communication function between users of the VPL system. In particular, it supports important functions to enable users to interact and collaborate with one another using tools such as messaging, chat and file attachments.

- Remote application launching—provides a remote software application launching function. This component forms an important part of the VPL system. It provides remote launching of software that is installed in the laboratory and to make it available to users accessing it via de facto standard web browsers. It is made up of a client applet and a corresponding terminal server which implement X protocol for remote terminal control.

- Usage monitor—designed for backend support and acting as a repository for real time usage monitoring. The component provides logging of activities that are performed by end users in terms of the pattern of software usage. This information is important to provide support for collaborative learning, where the usage monitor can inform end users who are concurrently using the same software. In such cases, users can choose to interact with one another. Knowledge of the usage patterns of users would also be useful in planning future software purchases and deployments.

- Administration subsystem—provides administrative functions that are similar to a real-life laboratory, providing facilities for users to be added or deleted, and application access rights to be granted.

The above sub-systems work in tandem to provide the collective functionality of the VPL runtime system.

4   Implementation and Performance Evaluation

A prototype of the VPL system is being implemented on a web platform hosted by the J2EE web application server. The implementation part follows the design as described in section 3. In this section, we discuss issues and techniques of implementing the VPL runtime system, including the file management sub-system, the communication sub-system, the usage monitor and the remote application launcher.

This project is implemented mainly in a Microsoft window and Linux environment. Java™ language is the main programming language used. The software platforms used include the Oracle 8.1.7 relational database server, Oracle9i application server (J2EE compliance) and SonicMQ messaging server.

Also discussed are the collaboration with a backend database and case study on how to make use of the VPL runtime system.

4.1   Deployment and System Architecture

The system architecture of the VPL system includes a client pc connecting through the Internet to one web server and an application server.

The Client PC
The client pc contains two applets that are downloaded from the web server. Both of the applets are digitally signed.

The VPL applet contains necessary classes for running the virtual desktop graphical user interfaces and classes for connecting to backend services. It directly connects to the lab machine remote file system. In the deployment diagram, a remote file object is shown on the client PC. Physically, the remote file resides in the lab machine. The VPL applet is responsible for getting data from the database by connecting to the web/application server.

The displaying adapter applet is used to draw remote application graphical user interfaces on the client side. Shown in Fig 3 is a screen shot of the virtual desktop and the execution of a remote application GIMP.

The Web/Application Server
The web/application server is Oracle9i application server. It contains a web server to store web pages for the VPL system and an application server that is capable for running Java Servlet and Java Server Page (JSP). Java Servlet and Java Server Page are server side programming based on the Java standard enabling dynamic website building and connection to backend enterprise services. The message queue server is SonicMQ, it is used to provide message-based communication between client and server applications.

The Database Server
The database is based on the Oracle8i server. It is located within the school campus Intranet. In this way, both the web/application server and the lab machines will have direct access to the database by use the Java JDBC connection to the server.

The Lab Machines
Lab machines are computers providing remote software applications to remote users. They are located within the school campus Intranet. There are two system servers running in each of the lab machines: 1) a remote file server, a file server which provides remote file management functionality and 2) a usage monitor, which is a server program that keeps track of which program is being used and by which user. The usage status is updated to the database server.

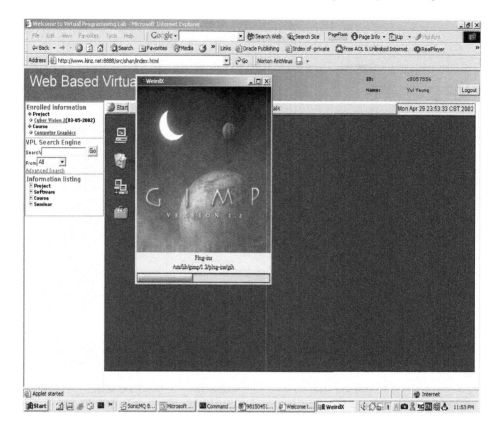

Fig. 3. Screen shot of VPL

The deployment diagram for the VPL system is shown in Fig 4. When the applet is started on the client side, it connects to the database though the web server and registers itself to the message queue server. There may be a number of lab machines working together to provide software usage monitoring. The usage monitor at the lab machine periodically connects to the database server to update the software usage status.

4.2   Experiments

To verify and evaluate the VPL system, we have set up an experimental test bed to measure the performance in terms of the delay in launching remote applications. The experiment focuses on the lab machine connection speed as shown in Fig 5.
The following software is used to measure the network performance on the client side and to measure the system resources usage on a Linux lab machine.

1.   Network Smart Lite 1.0 (Build 385) is used to measure throughput, latency and, data sent and received. This application can be used on the connection with a LAN card.

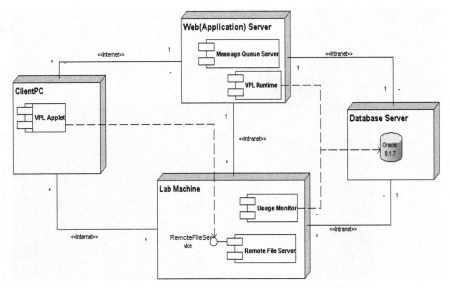

Fig. 4. Deployment diagram for the VPL system.

	Lab machine	**Computer at school network**	**Computer outside school network.**
Processors	Pentium III 500 MHz	Pentium III 500 MHz	Pentium III 600 MHz
Memory	256 MB PC-100	256 MB PC-100	512 MB PC-100
Network connection speed to Lab machine	Not Applicable	100 Mb/s LAN	1.5 Mb/s broadband or 56 kb/s dialup connection
OS	Mandrake Linux 8.0	Window 2000 professional edition	Window 2000 professional edition
Screen Resolution	Not Applicable	1024 * 768	1024 * 768
Color depth	16k bit color	16k bit color	16k bit color

Fig. 5. Confguration of experiment machine.

2. Qcheck version 2.1 is used to measure latency when using a dialup connection.
3. Xosview is used to monitor the system resource usage in a Linux system such as CPU time, physical memory usage and swap memory usage.

The experiment was conducted at three different connection speeds. The throughput and response time were measured using Qcheck version 2.1. The results are summarized below.

	Measure by Network Smart Lite and Qcheck	
	Throughput	**Latency**
School LAN	More than 10 Mbit/s	Less than 10 ms
Broadband LAN	Around 350 Kbit/s	Around 20 ms
Dialup connection	Around 30 Kbit/s	Around 150 ms

Fig. 6. Lab. machine throughput and latency

This experiment tests the launching times of three different types of software applications operating at different connection speeds. The purpose is to demonstrate the performance of the remote application as it launches in different network environments. The launching time is defined as that period between the moment of double clicking on an application icon and the moment when the application is ready to accept input. The launching time of each application, was measured five times. The average launching times is displayed in the table below.

Launching time	**JDeveloper 9i**	**Gedit**	**Xterm**
Local	24 sec	1 sec	0.7 sec
School LAN	28 sec	3 sec	2.5 sec
Broadband	54 sec	35 sec	33 sec
Dialup	> 5 minutes	75 sec	52 sec

Fig. 7. Program launching times s in different environments

Three applications were launched, Jdeveloper 9i, Gedit and Xterm. Of the three, Jdeveloper 9i is the most graphic- intensive application, followed by Gedit, then Xterm. This explains the exceptionally long delay in launching the Jdeveloper program as compared with others when operating over a dialup network (see Fig 13). The launching time difference decreases, however, as the connection speed increases and the bottleneck due to bandwidth availability becomes less of an issue.

5   Conclusion

This paper focuses on the development of runtime modules for VPL. With a well-defined interface established between the subsystems, the runtime modules have been developed to provide core mechanisms for driving the operations of the VPL system. We have successfully developed core modules that support remote application launching through the use of an X-protocol. To bind the remote application to a web terminal, a telnet mechanism was developed and implemented to transparently and remotely launch Unix-based applications over the web. To support seamless access of the files repository on both local and remote machines, a file management module was developed to allow the intuitive and efficient transfer of files between the

Program launching times delays: various software

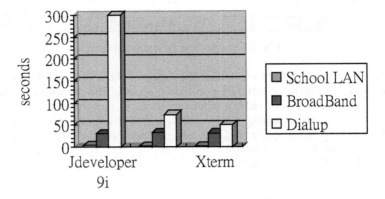

Fig. 8. Program launching time delays: various software

directories. The need to provide project-based messaging to allow student collaboration resulted in the development of the communication module. Based on the Java Messaging System, it allows a seamless exchange of messages between students and is configurable according to on topic/ project group.

While the core modules have been successfully developed, we believe there are several enhancements that can be incorporated to increase the robustness and usability of VPL. These include:

- **Firewall compatibility:** The VPL system should support users behind a firewall. This can be accomplished using the HTTP tunneling technique.
- **Intelligent load balancing:** The system implemented in this project involves only one lab machine. In order to support a larger number of users, a load balancing scheme based on lab machine CPU/RAM consumption levels and network utilization levels should be applied to the VPL system.
- **Automatic server discovery and monitoring:** the system involves several servers and is inherently complicated. Therefore, an automatic server monitoring and discovery platform is needed. A technique such as heartbeat listening could be applied to this system.
- **Peer to Peer computing:** The existing VPL system supports only message transfer between users. More intuitive communication channels such as web conferencing and white boards should be developed. More work should also be done to facilitate project collaboration such as screen and file sharing.

Acknowledgement. This project is supported by the HK Polytechnic University Teaching and Learning Grant LTG00-01\DLTC\COMP05.

References

1. Hboffstein A., Lunetta V., "The role of the laboratory in science teaching: neglected aspects of research.", Review of education research, 52, p.201–218.
2. Glenn W. Rowe, Peter Gregor, "A computer based learning system for teaching computing: implementation and evaluation", Computers & Education 33 (1999) p. 65–76, Pergamon
3. A. Di Stefano, F. Fazzino, L. Lo Bello, O. Mirabella, "Virtual lab: A Java Application for distance learning", 0-7803-4192-9/97/$10.00 © 1997 IEEE
4. Jiannong Cao, Alvin T.S. Chan, Weidong Cao, Cassidy Yeung, "Virtual Programming Lab for On-line Distance Learning", Proc. 1st International Conference on Web-based Learning (ICWL'02), Aug. 2002. Hong Kong. Lecture Notes in Computer Science (Springer-Verlag).
5. Sam K.P. Ma, Michael Rung-Tsong Lyu, "A web-based customized virtual learning environment" APWEB'99 http://www.cse.cuhk.edu.hk/~lyu/student/

A Framework to Support Schema Matching in E-learning

Marvin B.L. Tan[1,2], Angela E.S. Goh[1], and Robert K.L. Gay[2]

[1] Centre of Advanced Information Systems, School of Computer Engineering,
Nanyang Technological University, Singapore 639798,
[2] ASP Centre, NTU Innovation Centre, Singapore 637722
{ps7726426d,asesgoh}@ntu.edu.sg, eklgay@aspcentre.org

Abstract. Interoperability between eLearning systems can be achieved through adoption of standards. However, the differences in the data models provided by eLearning systems and learning standards mean that mediation is required to achieve interoperability. With the pervasiveness of relational databases and XML in eLearning systems, we propose a mediation framework that maps between the relational database schemas in eLearning systems and eLearning standards defined in XML Schema. This framework consists of a Schema Matcher Module, a Translation Module and a Mapper Tool. All three modules integrate to provide mapping of schemas and translation of data between the two sources for eLearning systems.

1 Introduction

The Internet has revolutionized eLearning by enabling the mass distribution of learning resources and capabilities throughout organizations. Today, all you need is an Internet connection to access widely available learning resources and commercial learning systems. At the same time, the emergence of learning standards has an indisputable impact on the evolution of eLearning systems.

Learning standards took off with the emergence of XML [1] and numerous learning standards consortia [2]. Today, there are standards that influence various aspects of eLearning ranging from sequencing to learners' profile tracking. XML, a W3C Internet standard, has established itself as arguably the most popular data interchange format. Its self-describing nature and the widespread availability of related tools have encouraged its use in the integration of legacy and enterprise systems as well as interoperation between heterogeneous information systems. As such, the use of XML to encode learning standards helps to ensure that these standards can be accessed and adopted easily. So why do we need learning standards?

Standards are necessary to ensure that information is kept in a format that is understood by various communities. Today, consumers expect interoperability in the form of standards-compliance to be present in the eLearning systems they adopt. As the development of courseware is extremely time-consuming, users therefore want assurances that such courseware is "exportable" to other

W. Zhou et al. (Eds.): ICWL 2003, LNCS 2783, pp. 520–531, 2003.

platforms, especially when they change or upgrade their learning systems in the future. The adoption of learning standards has become an essential step in the eLearning business.

Currently, many learning systems use their own proprietary data models which are different from that of learning standards. It is necessary to reconcile these models. Hence, we propose a mediation framework which assists in transforming an existing data model to one that conforms to learning standards.

This paper is organized as follows. In Section 2, the paper will briefly describe the current eLearning trends and various global efforts in the establishment of learning specifications. Following that, Section 3 will examine some related work. Section 4 will describe our proposed framework, which derives design-time mappings between the schema of an existing relational database(from a eLearning system) and an XML Schema[3] (for a learning metadata standard). At the same time, there are additional functions that aid in the integration of eLearning specifications into existing systems. The framework will focus on semantic interoperability and the use of metadata vocabularies to bridge different data sources effectively. Section 5 describes the implementation of the framework and some preliminary evaluations. Last but not least, Section 6 discusses some issues encountered and presents our conclusions.

Our framework focuses on metadata since this is required by query processing facilities to identify and retrieve learning content. We select relational databases (RDBMSes) as the main data store over Native XML databases (NXDs) as most learning systems still employ the former over NXDs.

2   Current Trends on Global Learning Standards Establishment

Over the past few years, numerous organizations have been working on various aspects of eLearning standards, ranging from metadata to accessibility. While some of them are working towards international approval with the help of groups such as ISO and IEEE, most of them already have draft releases of specifications adopted by a number of LMSes. Table 1 (taken from [2]) shows the areas of learning standards that some of these organizations are involved in.

The IMS(Instruction Management System) Metadata Specification[4] is one of the first metadata specification drafted specifically for eLearning. It is being adapted and extended by various organizations such as CanCore (http://www.cancore.org) to reflect their localized needs. Other organizations, such as ADL (Advanced Distributed Learning Initiative - http://www.adlnet.org/) and AICC (Aviation Industry CBT (Computer-Based Training) Committee - http://aicc.org), recommend the coupling of IMS's metadata specification with their own content packaging or interfacing specifications. The establishment of standards is only the first step to interoperability. The next step is to implement and enforce such standards.

Table 1. Areas of involvement of various organizations in eLearning standards/specifications establishment

	IMS	ADL/ SCORM	Dublin Core	Prometeus	IEEE	BSI/ISO	ARIADNE	AICC
Metadata	Yes	-	Yes	-	Yes	Yes	Yes	-
Content	Yes	Yes	-	-	Yes	-	-	Yes
Enterprise	Yes	-	-	-	Yes	-	-	-
Learner Information	Yes	-	-	-	Yes	Yes	-	-
Question & Test	Yes	-	-	-	-	Yes	-	-
Accessibility	Yes	-	-	-	-	-	-	-
Learning Design	Yes	-	-	Yes	-	-	-	-
Collaboration	-	-	-	-	-	Yes	-	-
User requirements	Yes	-	-	Yes	-	-	-	-

3   Related Work

Our work spans a few areas of research, namely – XML Data Integration, Interoperability via standards and eLearning but it focuses mainly on Schema Matching. Currently, we have yet to see a similar framework within the eLearning domain.

While it is not easy to translate from the XML data model to the relational model, it is undeniably more difficult to perform matching between the two models since the former can be performed in the absence of full semantics. Mapping approaches are usually structural as compared to matching. Even in "semantic" mapping efforts such as [5] and [6], the "semantics" cited are primitive "semantic constraints" such as structural relationships and concepts found in "graphs", "trees" or other structural models. In our research, while we refer constantly to research efforts on mapping of data sources, the approaches are somewhat different. The main focus of our project is in "Schema Matching".

3.1   Generic Schema Matching

Excellent surveys of generic schema matching applications can be found in [7] and [8]. In particular, three related projects are of interest as they examine diverse approaches of schema matching. The first, [9], presents a RDF-based architecture for semantic integration of heterogeneous information sources. As part of the Hera project [10] targeting at multimedia information sources, this framework is similar to our schema matcher, in that it provides an additional abstraction layer using RDF between the wrappers and the actual schema matching engine. However, users must provide the mapping rules manually, using a language known as LMX [11].

The second [12] is a system that employs and extends current machine-learning techniques to "discover semantic mappings" between multiple data sources semi-automatically. The wide range of machine learning techniques and statistical methods employed makes this system an extensive matcher. However, the main drawback is the need for training (as with most machine learning based approaches such as the one in [13]) and this means that an initial corpus of "unbiased data" is required from different data sources. Such training data is difficult to come by in the "real world".

The last project, Cupid [7], can be described as a generic schema matcher adopting a wide range of schema matching techniques. It is distinguished from the rest by its use of various techniques in a hybrid matching approach. However, in the paper, there was no evaluation of any kind. There were only some "real world" examples, taken from standard sources such as XML purchase orders from www.BizTalk.org . Although these are useful examples to evaluate and demonstrate the features of such frameworks, they do not provide a clear picture of how imperfect actual "real world" examples would be.

4   A Mediation Framework for Relational Database Schemas-XML Schemas Mapping

Our framework consists of three main components, namely: the **Schema Matcher Module, Mapper Tool Module** and the **Translation Module**. The Schema Matcher Module allows users to perform semi-automatic matching between an XML Schema and a relational database schema. The Mapper Tool Module enables the refinement of mappings suggested by the Schema Matcher and the Translation Module allows the import and export of learning objects to/from database records based on the mapping definitions. The entire framework may operate with any LMS, which employs a relational database as its main data store. However, the operations of the framework will be kept independent of the LMS's internal functionalities. An overview of the mediation framework is shown in Fig. 1.

To demonstrate the practicality of our framework, we present a scenario outlining the use of the framework:

"An eLearning system could be present either as an in-house system for users within the company or it could be a product deployed in the intranet or internet for hundreds of clients. The system was developed before the current eLearning standards took shape."

Proposed Solution: A team of developers will integrate the existing system with the framework to provide interoperability with other eLearning systems by supporting standards. The only point of integration between the framework and the existing eLearning system is the relational database through a standard database interface. A possible sequence of operations (with the corresponding data flow indicated in Fig. 1) is as follows:

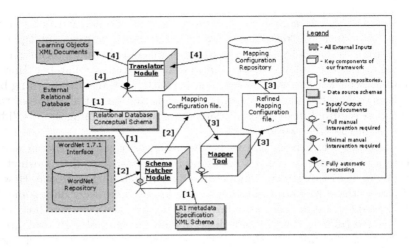

Fig. 1. Conceptual Framework for the Mapping of Learning Standards Metadata Specifications to/from Relational Databases

1. Initially, the developers adopt a particular learning metadata standard (e.g. IMS) and provide the path of the relational database and the IMS Metadata XML Schema to the Schema Matcher Module.
2. With the help of WordNet 1.7.1 [14], the Schema Matcher Module will match the XML Schema with the relational database. At the end of the matching process, a mapping configuration file is produced.
3. Using the Mapper Tool, the developers may then refine the mapping between the two data sources and the 'final' mapping configuration file is stored in a mapping configuration repository.
4. At a later date, a batch of IMS-compliant learning objects becomes available. The Translation Module retrieves the previously-prepared mapping configuration and translates the metadata of the learning objects into database records.
5. The content from the learning objects may now be used as part of the eLearning system.

This is an example of a typical application of our proposed framework. The next few sections will describe the main components of our framework in detail.

4.1 Schema Matcher Module

Given the path of 2 schemas, the module produces two corresponding abstract tree structures and performs lexical, structural and datatype matching with the help of a lexical repository, WordNet [15]. This matcher module will then provide the full list of suggested mappings to allow users to further refine them.

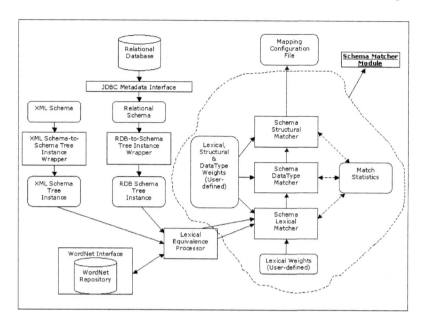

Fig. 2. Overview of Schema Matching Process

Details of the schema matching process are provided in Fig. 2. The overall functionality of this module is summarized as follows. This component comprises of several reusable components to prepare the original schema for matching at a later stage. The first stage involves a pair of wrappers which retrieve the schemas from the data sources in their native forms and repackage them into a common format (Schema Tree Instances). In this case, the XML Schema document is read by the XML Schema wrapper and transformed into a Schema Tree instance. For the relational database, a JDBC interface is required by the relational schema wrapper to retrieve the relational schema for transformation to a Schema Tree instance.

The Schema Tree Instances are abstract tree structures used to model schemas from both relational databases and XML Schemas. The use of a common structure and its extension to different data sources reinforce reusability. In the next stage, the Schema Tree instances are passed to a lexical equivalence processor. This processor produces a list of lexically-equivalent words for each leaf node of the abstract tree structures. The list is generated with the aid of the WordNet [15] repository. Currently, our implementation only produces the lexical list for one tree (XML Schema tree) and not the other. This is because preliminary tests have shown that the inclusion of the lists for both structures has not improved the accuracy of the matcher significantly. Instead, it has introduced two more iterations of matching to be performed. Hence, a single list for the XML Schema elements is a more efficient approach.

The final tree structures are then passed to the combinatorial matcher. There are 3 matchers - lexical, structural and data type. The lexical matcher confers scores to various kinds of lexical matches between the names of the leaf nodes of both structures. The structural matcher looks out for similarity between the tree-paths as well as sibling and ancestry information between leaf nodes. The data type matcher checks for equivalence between the data types and simple constraints of the leaf nodes. Different weightages will be assigned to the matchers and the scores will ultimately be tallied and the best matches suggested. Developers may then review the matches as well as the intermediate results along with other possible matches. At the end of the process, the relevant matches are confirmed and a mapping configuration XML document, containing a list of "XML element-to-relational database field" mapping pairs, is generated.

4.2   Mapper Tool Module

Since automatic mapping strategies are impossible until a general consensus is reached on the understanding of the semantics for concepts and terms, manual tools are extremely important in the integration and interoperation of information sources. The Mapper Tool provides an intuitive graphical interface which allows developers or domain experts to refine existing mappings and amend the incorrect ones.

By reading both schemas using the respective schema wrappers described in Section 4.1, this tool provides 2 trees for the developer to select correspondences manually between leaf nodes of the trees. This tool may also read in an existing mapping configuration XML document for the editing of existing mappings.

4.3   Translation Module

The Translation Module (TM) is the only module which processes data instead of schemas. It provides a physical bridge between the relational data source and the XML data source. The translation procedure is as follows:

1. The incoming XML learning object is validated against its underlying schema and is parsed into a DOM tree.
2. The Mapping Configuration XML document (MCXD) is read, retrieving the list of mapped data source pairs.
3. While iterating through each mapped-pair within the MCXD, each XML element is extracted, with its literal values retrieved. At the same time, the relational field portion of the mapped-pair for each mapping is broken down into a "database name, table name, field name" format.
4. The literal values (from the XML elements) are categorized according to the name of the relational tables they are to be inserted into.
5. For each table, identifiers are generated for the primary keys that were not matched in the mappings.
6. The generated identifiers are propagated to every foreign key related to the primary keys.

7. For each table, an "INSERT" statement is created, combining all the fields mapped along with their literal values.
8. System executes the entire list of "INSERT" statements via a JDBC interface. (This step must be performed in a sequence so that insertions into relations with foreign keys are preceded by insertions into relations with corresponding primary keys.)

5   Implementation and Evaluation

5.1   Implementation

A prototype of our framework has been developed in Java. The relational data source used is a MySQL database. Fig. 3 shows a screenshot displaying the results and statistics of the Schema Matching process. These statistics include the scores for the individual matching components as well as the matched terms from the lexical matcher. Fig. 4 shows a screenshot of the Mapper Tool in use.

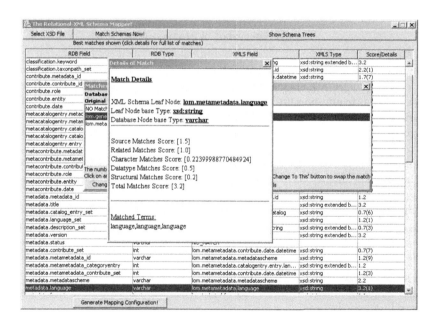

Fig. 3. Screenshot of the Results from the Schema Matcher Module

5.2   Evaluation

During our evaluation of the Schema Matcher Module, there were three main groups of test cases (relational database schemas). The first group consists of

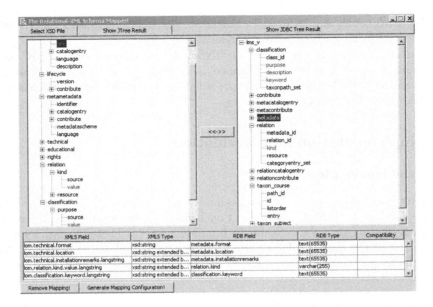

Fig. 4. Screenshot of Mapper Tool

"artificially-generated" relational databases, derived by manually mapping existing learning metadata specifications. The second group comprises of database schemas taken from existing LMSes. These LMSes range from commercial enterprise-level systems to readily available evaluation off-the-shelf LMSes. The last group are metadata repositories (such as the UNCW Digital Library – http://aa.uncwil.edu/dl) on the Internet that are IMS specifications-compliant and serve as a form of an online LMS. The XML schemas were either from the IMS specifications or other variants such as the LRI (Learning Resource Identification) specifications[16].

Evaluation is only performed on the Schema Matcher Module while only testing is performed on the other two modules as they are supporting tools for the framework. The following metrics were used to evaluate the Schema Matcher Module.

1. Percentage of correct best matches
2. Percentage of incorrect best matches, with the correct best matches suggested as possible matches
3. Percentage of incorrect best matches, with the correct best matches NOT suggested as possible matches

Preliminary evaluation was performed on about 6 pairs of schemas and the average percentage of correct best matches was 67%, while the other two metrics shown above posted averages of 28% and 5% respectively. That meant that an average of 95% of matches was returned as possible best matches. The mapper tool was then used to map the remaining unmatched fields. The maximum deviation from the mean results in all three metrics did not exceed more than 5%.

This showed consistent performance across schemas from different sources. The results could be explained by the lack of "true semantic support" and that will be discussed in the next section. More details on the evaluation can be found in [17].

6   Issues Encountered and Conclusions

6.1   Issues Encountered

The major issues encountered, which reduced the accuracy of the "semi-automatic schema matching", were the lack of semantic support and common standards in the definition of schemas. Currently, there are only machine-readable semantics for a small range of concepts. While it is true that the terms taken from WordNet to support the matching process are semantically-related, the actual matching performed is more lexical than semantic. The matcher actually matches the fields using various forms of lexical similarity rather than using the actual meaning of names. Ontologies may be used to represent the semantics of concepts but there is a lack of agreement regarding the semantics within the same domain as well as across different domains. Large scale standardization projects are currently trying to bring these semantics into general consensus and it will be some time before semantics and concepts may be freely "accessible" for semantically-enabled applications.

In addition, the lack of standardization in the definition of schemas is also a major problem. While lexical ontologies similar to WordNet may be used to define the semantics of concepts, the definition is often confined to "single words". Often, many field or element names of schemas are created from different root terms, e.g. "cost_price" or "ShippingAddress". Sometimes, the new word formed takes on semantics from both root terms but at times, it is possible to end up with a word that has an entirely new meaning. More advanced NLP (Natural Language Processing) techniques will be required to distinguish word boundaries and separate multiple root terms. The massive number of possibilities and combinations of such cases makes it difficult for common concepts and terminologies to be defined. In addition, non-standard abbreviations are often used to define field names. For example, "shipping address" may be defined as "ShipAddr", "Ship_Addrs" or "ShpAddress". Other examples include cases where unique record identifiers are given names like "pk" or "rid".

The lack of proper semantic support and standardized naming conventions for schemas often undermine the accuracy of lexically-based schema matching drastically and it is left to the other techniques such as "structural matching" to identify the possible matches. As such, generic automatic schema matching is extremely difficult to perform. We expect accurate results to only come from schema matching within specific domains as domain-based information may be used to improve performance. Hence, at present, the availability of effective manual mapping tools is extremely important for the success of data interoperation and integration applications.

6.2   Conclusions

The field of eLearning requires a great deal of interoperation in order for knowledge and instructions to be disseminated more efficiently. With the help of standards and frameworks such as the one proposed, interoperability will be facilitated more effectively. This in turn will reduce the number of learning management systems becoming legacies. The preliminary results reveal that there is a lack of proper semantic support and standardized schema definition conventions. However, the presence of manual tools and other useful functions will still help to improve interoperability between different learning systems through the use of standards. To improve the accuracy of the automatic mediation process, our future work involves the incorporation of domain-specific thesauri, abbreviation libraries and other useful aids. In addition, we will also be investigating how ontologies may be incorporated to improve interoperability between eLearning systems.

References

[1] Bray, T., Paoli, J., Sperberg-McQueen, C., Maler, E.: Extensible Markup Language (XML) 1.0. The World Wide Web Journal **2** (1997) 29–66
[2] CETIS: Who's doing what? Technical report, CETIS (Centre for Education Technology Interoperability Standards),
    http://www.cetis.ac.uk/static/who-does-what.html (2002)
[3] World Wide Web Consortium (W3C) http://www.w3.org/TR/xmlschema-0/:
    XML Schema part 0: Primer. (2000)
[4] IMS Global http://www.imsglobal.org/metadata/index.html: IMS Learning Resource Meta-data Specification Version 1.2. (2001)
[5] McBrien, P., Poulovassilis, A.: A semantic approach to integrating XML and structured data sources. In: Conference on Advanced Information Systems Engineering. (2001) 330–345
[6] Lee, D., Mani, M., Chiu, F., Chu, W.W.: Net and cot: Translating relational schemas to xml schemas using semantic constraints. In: 2002 ACM CIKM International Conference on Information and Knowledge Management. (2002) 282–291
[7] Madhavan, J., Bernstein, P.A., Rahm, E.: Generic schema matching with cupid. In: 27th International Conference on Very Large Data Bases, VLDB. (2001) 49–58
[8] Rahm, E., Bernstein, P.A.: A survey of approaches to automatic schema matching. The VLDB Journal: Very Large Data Bases **10** (2001) 334–350
[9] Vdovjak, R., Houben, G.J.: RDF-based architecture for semantic integration of heterogeneous information sources. In: Workshop on Information Integration on the Web. (2001) 51–57
[10] Houben, G.J.: HERA: Automatically generating hypermedia front-ends. In: Third International Workshop on Engineering Federated Information Systems EFIS. (2000) 81–88
[11] Maruyama, H., Tamuran, K., Uramoto, N., Tamura, K., eds.: Chapter LMX: Sample Nontrivial Application. In: XML and Java. Addison-Wesley (1999) 97–142
[12] Doan, A., Domingos, P., Halevy, A.Y.: Reconciling schemas of disparate data sources: A machine-learning approach. In: ACM SIGMOD Conference. (2001) 509–520

[13] Berlin, J., Motro, A.: Database schema matching using machine learning with feature selection. In: Fourteenth International Conference on Advanced Information Systems Engineering. (2002) 452–466

[14] Beckwith, R., Fellbaum, C., Gross, D., Millers, G.A.: WordNet: A Lexical Database Organised on Psycholinguistic Principles. In U. Zernik (Ed.) Using On-line Resources to Build a Lexicon. Hillsdale, NJ: Lawrence Erlbaum Associates (1992)

[15] Miller, G.: Wordnet: An on-line lexical database. International Journal of Lexicography (special issue), Computational Linguistics, 18(1) **3** (1990) 235–312

[16] LTSC, ed.: Specification For eLearning Framework Part 2: Learning Resource Identification. Singapore Productivity and Standards Board (2001)

[17] Tan, M.B.L.: A mediation framework to support schema matching in elearning. Technical report, CAIS, NTU Singapore (2003)

Exploring the Foundations of Practicing Online Collaboration

Ruth S. Raitman, Wanlei Zhou, and Paul Nicholson

School of Information Technology
Deakin University
221 Burwood Highway
Burwood VIC 3125
Australia
ruth@deakin.edu.au

Abstract. In collaborative learning, instruction is learner-centered rather than teacher-centered and knowledge is viewed as a social construct, facilitated by peer interaction, evaluation and mutual support [1]. Such computer supported collaborative learning (CSCL) enables and encourages learners to confer, reflect and help to develop meaningful learning in an environment where significant learning can be achieved through interactions supported by electronic communication and discourse [2]. This paper proposes a theory that supports educational collaboration in a *peer-to-peer* computing environment, thus blending the two disciplines.

1 Introduction

For the purpose of further detailed investigation and continued research in the area of collaboration, it is imperative to clearly define all relevant keywords.

For example, the terms collaboration and cooperation both represent different aspects of interactive learning, yet are often loosely referenced within the one context. Collaboration is a philosophy of interaction and personal lifestyle whereas cooperation is a structure of interaction designed to facilitate the accomplishment of an end product or goal [3].

Collaborative learning is student centered and focuses on the process of students working together and sharing the authority to empower themselves with the responsibility of building on their foundational knowledge [4]. An exact answer is not required and the final results cannot necessarily be predicted.

In contrast, when learning cooperatively, the authority remains with the instructor, who retains ownership of the task [5]. Students are employed to produce a designated solution based on the instructor's requirements.

W. Zhou et al. (Eds.): ICWL 2003, LNCS 2783, pp. 532–541, 2003.

1.1 Computer Supported Collaborative Learning

Crook [6] suggests that there are 4 ways in which the computer technology plays a part in the interaction; interaction at the computer, interaction around the computer, interacts related to computer applications and the interaction through computers. This last means of interaction lends itself to further investigation about collaboration, which is mainly based on the written language.

Thus, Computer Supported Collaborative Learning (CSCL), first noted in the early 1990's, is the development of collaboration by means of technology to augment education and further research. It focuses on how collaborative learning supported by technology can enhance peer interaction and work in groups, and how collaboration and technology facilitate sharing and distributing of knowledge and expertise among community members [7].

1.1.1 Conceptual Framework

Suggesting a constructivist framework, Puntambekar [8] believes that learning is constructing knowledge from one's experiences, as opposed to receiving information directly from the outside sources. He proposes the following four principles as the basis of constructivism:

1. Learners construct their own understanding
2. New learning depends on current understanding
3. Learning is facilitated by social interactions
4. Meaningful learning occurs within authentic learning tasks

This framework allows students to reflect on their ideas and solutions, which will aptly relate to their explanations and justifications. Collaboration with other students will provoke further activity, make the learning more realistic and stimulate motivation [9]. Consequently, the students will augment their own understanding of the domain knowledge.

The constructivist approach to CSCL focuses on the individual in the context of social interaction. The socio-cultural approach focuses on the relationship between the individuals, and the shared cognition approach to CSCL focalizes the environment, which includes a physical context as well as a social one [10].

1.1.2 Challenges of CSCL

There are however, challenges involved with research into CSCL. Firstly, the *effects of* technology refer to what one has learned and can then convey it further using a computer. Yet, the *effects with* technology refer to what one could achieve in synergy with a computer, clearly producing a greater effect, which would otherwise not be possible [11]. These parameters need to be clearly defined on the outset.

Secondly, there are variations within the research procedures. This includes the length of the study, the number of students participating in the research, the student's ages, and the size of the experimental groups [7]. In the past, researches have addressed issues, such as learning tasks, sociocognitive effects of CSCL, complex reasoning and levels of argumentation. They have considered inquiry processes, collaborative knowledge building, motivational aspects in CSCL and the effects of stress, which can effect participation.

And thirdly, collaborative research remains complex due to all the different technologies used. Whether it be varied applications, simulation programs or networked learning environments [12], research into this field remains quite involved, with the need to establish concise boundaries.

1.1.3 Collaborative Knowledge Building

Stahl [13] suggests that in fact, 'knowledge building' would provide collaboration with a more accurate understanding, as opposed to 'learning'. Learning, never seen, but existing everywhere, can be in the form of a conscious activity, or a non-conscious activity. However, realistically, the outcomes of the learning experience can be statistically insignificant, with no directly developed consequences apparent [14]. Yet, collaborative knowledge building refers to particular occurrences that are clearly identifiable, as a result of groups constructing new knowledge.

1.2 Peer-to-Peer (P2P) Computing

Traditionally, networks consist of a common computer, known as the server, and many clients all on their own individual PCs, receiving information and accessing shared resources. However, since the PC has an increased processing power, it has gained the strength to act as a server or a client, thus facilitating peer-to-peer computing [15].

A comprehensive P2P software package, such as Groove, allow clients to effectively use tools which include text chat, audio chat, a discussion board, files, a notepad, a shared Web browser, online file storage, a group calendar, photo storage, a contact list, instant announcements and messaging among selected or all participants, and even an audit trail [16].

Additionally, P2P boasts an architecture that supports the building of self appointed teams, thus allowing members to participate in forums, and perhaps cross academic or corporate boundaries. A hierarchical or departmental structure need not apply in this environment where officially, no boundaries apply. Clearly, all peers are limitless in what they can achieve. They are able to suitably collaborate with one another in this environment, thus providing a basis for CSCL.

2 Synchronous vs. Asynchronous Communications

The P2P platform can add functionality to working with documents and to communicating, in both synchronous and asynchronous instances. It provides decentralized data storage and can be useful when working offline, thus synchronizing all work later in a central server. Alternatively, it can allow students to share a space online and conduct learning sessions together.

Communicating in real time creates a synchronous environment, where the following tools support interaction: voice and video conferencing, shared whiteboards and live presentation tools, application sharing, live assessment testing and voting, audience control, chat and perhaps breakout rooms for smaller groups [17]. They are ideal for activities such as brainstorming, group decision-making, and remedial coaching, since these activities need rapid interaction and feedback, and tend to be of a lower quality if spread over a longer period of time. This synchronous environment also supports the theory that the role of eye contact in video-mediated communication is important to augment and facilitate joint problem solving, and it assists in achieving improved results [18].

There are however, some disadvantages to synchronous learning. All participants, who may be globally dispersed, must be available at the same time, which could consist of incorporating many different time zones – perhaps a scheduling nightmare. And for all that administrative organization, a productive session may only last for one hour, aspiring to keep the learning value at a peak. Also, when contributing in a chosen language, participants who are not proficient in speaking or typing in that specific language may be reluctant to partake in the session due to a feeling of ill confidence or dominance by other language proficient participants.

An asynchronous learning environment (ALN) allows participants to learn at the pace and the times best suited to their individual needs [1]. Working in an elapsed time as opposed to real time, students are given the opportunity to carefully reflect on relevant issues, construct and format their contribution with no immediate pressure to perform, and allow students to research the material at their own speed [17].

Both synchronous and asynchronous sessions should be implemented in online learning environments. The asynchronous activities would allow the student to work through the material, with time to reflect and do individual research. Yet the synchronous session would be most advantageous if held at time intervals, to encourage peer-to-peer and peer-to-tutor communication, supporting a rapid response and a period of quick coaching.

3 Facilitation

Although student feedback can be in the form questions, suggestions or requests for clarification, it appears to be as essential as the learning itself in a collaborative environment [19]. The main function of the tutor / facilitator is to

- Keep the group on task
- Focus and deepen the inquiry
- Guide the synthesis of information toward decision making and problem solving
- Resolve disputes among participants
- Critique work

The facilitator has the ability to offer expertise in the relevant field, friendship in the learning environment when students can benefit from the socially humane input, authority, and the command to reward or punish the progress with grading, recommendations, grants etc. [20].

There are other real issues that the facilitator must devote attention to: forming the groups of appropriate size and assessing the levels of intelligence, dealing with members who are not contributing, unmotivated, bossy, resistant, abusive, and instilling in the members a sense of responsibility, which will ultimately rely on them being accountable for all their actions and input [21].

When considering the efficient use of computer technology in terms of maximizing its collaborative potential, it is worthwhile reflecting on an experiment, which was performed in Michigan. A 'room', the Capture Lab, was designed and built to provide a computer supported collaborative environment for 151 participants [22]. The purpose of this research, which consisted of two tasks, was to analyse the sequences of interaction over time (task related), and examine other non-task related dimensions, such as the participants' optimism, negativity, dominance, submissiveness and emotional expressiveness.

Upon completion of the case study, there were 3 significant observations that were evident:
1. If the technology is used without group process feedback, then there is a substantial reduction in socio-emotional interactive sequences
2. If the technology is used with group process feedback, then there is a significant increase in socio-emotional interactive sequences
3. If the group process feedback is given without technology, then there is a significant reduction in socio-emotional interactive sequences

4   Current Research

At present a case study is being conducted to research the fundamentals of online collaboration in a newly implemented P2P educational environment. This also includes the platform objectives, the case study members, and the assessment of the P2P collaborative e-learning environment.

4.1   Research Case Study

Computing Project is a unit offered by Deakin University, and its main goal is to allow groups of students to demonstrate the synthesis of the knowledge, methodologies and other skills acquired during their studies, through means of collaboration.

This unit has been chosen as the basis of the study, with the emphasis on the project structure. In fact, the content remains irrelevant. However, the unit requires a project to be completed for assessment in an online environment, utilizing a collaborative methodology to develop information resources. In groups of ten, students will have to utilize communication skills, teamwork skills, analysis and design skills, implementation techniques, system testing and quality control, writing skills and project management skills.

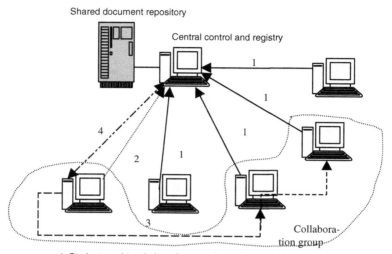

1. Students register their preferences for on-line projects
2. Project leader seeks members with certain criteria
3. An on-line project group is set up and collaboration starts
4. Periodically reporting and controlling.

Fig. 1. P2P collaboration in the controlled facilitation model

Figure 1 and 2 illustrate how students will be communicating with each other using two different models: Controlled (with a centralized control and registry) or monitored (with a registry only) facilitations. They will have the opportunity to utilize the P2P Collaboration Platform (installed in every computer participating in the collaboration) in order to arrange and identify with their groups (see Section 4.3). Meanwhile, they will be able to communicate directly with each other, consult the Internet and its facilities, and thus accomplish their goals. The P2P platform will then gather all shared documents and save them in the repository.

In the controlled facilitation model, students first register to the central control about their preferences for projects. The project leaders then solicit from the registry the students who are willing to do a certain project and with some required skills and criteria. The group will be formed with the help from the central control. Once a group is formed, it will carry out the collaborations itself, with a periodically reporting process to the central control and a periodically controlling process from the central control to the group.

In the monitored facilitation model, the project leader calls for participation of an on-line project among all students. Students then respond to the call if they wish to be enlisted. The leader then selects the members and notifies these selected members to start a collaboration. The leader also periodically reports the progress of the project to the Registry.

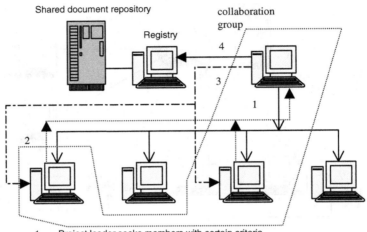

1. Project leader seeks members with certain criteria
2. Students reply to the request from the leader
3. An on-line project group is set up and collaboration starts
4. The leader reports to the Registry periodically.

Fig. 2. P2P collaboration in the monitored facilitation model

A student evaluation and satisfaction survey will be conducted at the end of the semester unit. Conclusions will be made, relating to usability, usefulness, accomplished research, and the collaborative environment. Were there any apparent communication patterns that evolved from the case study? Were the students put into appropriate groups that enabled them to collaborate to their full potential? Full face to face interviews are conducted followed by detailed questionnaires, which cover issues related to anxiety, motivation, tension, satisfaction, the sense of responsibility, the development of skills, file and data access and their overall feeling of completion and success.

4.2   The Agents

In order to facilitate online collaboration in a P2P learning environment, the following 5 agents will exist:

- Interface agent – to act as a go between the students, the university and the other agents
- Analytic agent – to facilitate the learning process

- Communal agent – organize the groups taking personal goals and preferences into consideration
- Pedagogical Content agent – to provide the Analytic agent with further educational activities when required
- Collaborative agent – support and maintain the group work

Communicating via the *Interface Agent*, the *Communal Agent* is embedded in the P2P infrastructure and will group the students according to suitability, taking the following preferences into consideration:

- The selection of people joining the group
- The choice of assignment topic and theme
- The grouping of different required skills within the group
- Time zone compatibility for synchronous sessions

Monitoring the student behaviour and keeping track of all relevant details achieve this. The agent is then able to recognize all recurring actions, and offer the student a setting that is manageable and conducive to their learning practices.

4.3   The P2P Collaboration Platform

This platform enables the students to retrieve files from another student who most recently viewed the content. In fact, the request was made to the server, but to minimize packet transfer, the platform identified that Student E can transfer the file most efficiently. This P2P application gains value by peers sharing and receiving their vast resources as a key element. In fact, the aim is to essentially *hide* the central server / platform from the students, and let them interact dynamically with each other.

Additionally, there are other factors that have been considered. This platform will support the ongoing challenge of file sharing among the collaborating participants, and distribute the data comfortably. And what about enforcing rules of social responsibility? Well, these protocols are clearly defined in the onset of the unit sessions, and can be monitored by the existing facilitator. For the purpose of the unit, the collaborating groups contain no more than 10 members, so protocols can be suitably monitored.

Congestion management has been implemented, and it carries the support of Deakin ITS, should the need arise. All firewall and router arrangements are concealed so the students are oblivious to all the technical issues, and can concentrate on their academic goals. This also ensures that non-members are excluded from the group, and unnecessary or inappropriate content is not accepted, thus ensuring a scalable and secure system.

Furthermore, this P2P structure enables data caching to deal with the load sharing issues and to support the bulk data transmission.

5 Conclusion

Although much research has been done in collaboration and P2P computing separately, there remains a gap in the merging of these two fields of study. This paper proposed a powerful new environment whereby students can discover, create, query and share their knowledge and resources. With a combination of synchronous and asynchronous sessions as selected by the members, they have been offered a platform to further their research, as well as utilize their facilitator in the most effective and valuable way. Comprehensive guided member reflections will tribute the effectiveness of this new P2P collaborative platform in the field of education.

References

1. Keynes, M., *Supporting Collaborative Learning in Asynchronous Learning Networks.* 1997, UNESCO: England.
2. Oliver, R., A. Omari, and J. Herrington. *Developing Converged Learning Environments for On and Off-Campus Students Using the WWW.* in *ASCILITE.* 1998.
3. Panitz, T., *A Definition of Collaborative vs Cooperative Learning.* 1996, London Guildhall University.
4. Myers, J., Cooperative Learning, 1991. **11**(4).
5. Bruffee, K., *Collaborative Learning: Higher education, interdependence, and the authority of knowledge.* 1993, John Hopkins University Press.
6. Crook, C., *Computers and the collaborative experience of learning.* 1994, Routledge: London.
7. Lipponen, L., *Exploring foundations for computer-supported collaborative learning.* 2002, University of Helsinki: Finland.
8. Puntambekar, S. *An integrated approach to individual and collaborative learning in a web-based learning environment.* in *Computer Support for Collaborative Learning 1999.* 1999. NJ: Lawrence Erlbaum Associates.
9. Veerman, A. and E. Veldhuis-Diermanse. *Collaborative learning through computer-mediated communication in academic education.* in *Euro CSCL 2001.* 2001.
10. Jaques, P., et al., *Using Pedagogical Agents to Support Collaborative Distance Learning.* 2002, Federal University of Rio Grande do Sul.
11. Salomon, G., D. Perkins, and T. Globerson, *Partners in cognition: Extending human intelligence with intelligent technologies.* Educational Researcher, 1991. **43**: p. 22–25.
12. Hall, R., N. Miyake, and N. Enyedy. *Proceeding of CSCl '97.* in *The Second International Conference on Computer Support for Collaborative Learning.* 1997: Lawrence Erlbaum Associates.
13. Stahl, G., *Contributions to a Theoretical Framework for CSCL.* 2002: Germany.
14. Russell, T., *The No Significant Difference Phenomenon.* 1999, Mindspring Press.
15. Cross, J., *eLearning Forum Update: Peer-to-Peer,* in *Learning Circuits.* 2001.
16. Rossi, L.C.D., *Online Collaboration and Exchange.* 2002, Robin Good.
17. *Delivering Learning Online - A Course for Facilitators.* 2002, Australian Flexible Learning Framework for the National Vocational Education and Training System 2000–2004.
18. Joiner, R., et al., *Evidence from a series of experiments on video-mediated Collaboration: Does eye contact matter?*

19. Cockrell, K.S., J.A.H. Caplow, and J.F. Donaldson, *A Context for Learning: Collaborative Groups in the Problem-Based Learning Environment.* The Review of Higher Education, 2000. **23**(3): p. 347–363.
20. *Online Facilitation.* 2002, elearnspace.
21. *Instructional Development Experiences, Applications and Solutions for Cooperative and Collaborative Learning.* 2003, Hong Kong University.
22. Losada, M., P. Sanchez, and E.E. Noble. *Collaborative Technology and Group Process Feedback: Their Impact on Interactive Sequences in Meetings.* in *Computer Supported Cooperative Work.* 1990.
23. Coldwell, J. and J. Wells. *Students perspective of online learning.* in *Quality Education @ a Distance.* 2003. Geelong.

Synchronous Graphic-Interaction in CSCL

Xinyu Zhang, NianLong Luo, and Dongxing Jiang

Computer and Information Management Center, Tsinghua Univ., Beijing, 100084
zxy@cic.tsinghua.edu.cn

Abstract. During the development of CSCL, a high demand on Synchronous Graphic-Interaction was promoted. The traditional interactive means such as BBS, chatting room and electronic whiteboard can hardly meet this demand completely. This paper proposed and implemented an experiment system supported by Synchronous Graphic-Interaction with which the interactive graphic/character information used in CSCL can be safely exchanged, processed, displayed for the long-distant teachers/students.

1 Introduction

CSCL (Computer Supported Co-Learning) is a very important aspect of the modern Long-Distance Teaching [1]. In CSCL, the synchronous communication only by character is far from to meet the demands of CSCL because a lot of issues are closely related to the graphics. For one group researching on flow chart of control program or a mechanic design, it is difficult to communicate the members' ideas without the Real-Time communication based on the graphics since they may live or work in different locations.

CSCW (Computer Supported Co-Working) systems established between different departments or R&D centers of the super international companies, has already enhanced their working efficiency and competency of their products. But the similar system is still far from the realization in the CSCL system in universities because of the considerable expense.

The main interactive means in CSCL for the either the full time students or part-time students in universities includes BBS which is mainly based on Telnet Protocol, chatting room which is mainly based on Web, and the electronic whiteboard which is mainly based on Java.

- **BBS Based on the Telnet Technology**

BBS is an important on-line Real-Time means of interaction. Users attending the discussion need to log in a distant server by Telnet protocol, and then entered the BBS system. As a new fashion, BBS system provided people with user management, article passing/reading, Real-Time discussion, emails and message board. However, since the Telnet is only a protocol used in logging in distant UNIX sever, the BBS system

W. Zhou et al. (Eds.): ICWL 2003, LNCS 2783, pp. 542–549, 2003.

seems just a character terminal without any multimedia ways. As a result, it's hardly to communicate with necessary pictures.

- **The Chatting Room Based on WEB**

Chatting room is a popular means of communicating; users got the information and knowledge that they wanted by browsing all kinds of web pages. Although it provide some simple face symbols that are defined by the system and can't be changed by user, the amount of the information that chatting room can deliver is still limited.

- **Electronic Whiteboard Based on the Java**

Electronic Whiteboard is a WWW multi-user discussion system based on Client/Server mode, which means that an applet application program written in Java is embedded in the Web pages, and the serving programs run in the server at the same time. Since electronic whiteboard is limited by the Java functions, and could only transfer some simple geometry figures such as dot, line, rectangle, circle, it can hardly deal with some complex figure such as mechanic picture used for CAD or circuit diagram used for Protel.

After systematic exploration in CSCL, we designed and implemented a system that worked effectively in a serial of experiments.

2 System Architecture Overview

As a system based on TCP/IP Protocol and Client/Server model, the system architecture is presented in the Fig. 1.

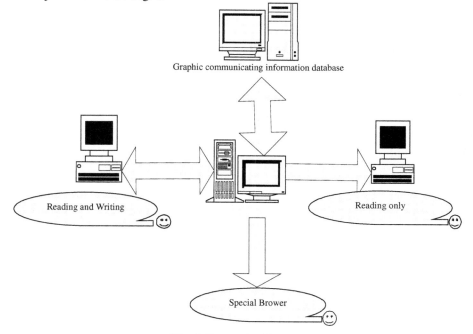

Graphic communicating information database

Reading and Writing

Reading only

Special Brower

Fig. 1. System Architecture

Graphic/character communicating information database: System selected Oracle database as the Figure communicating information database whose main functions are:

- Storing all the related information, including users' name, password, rights for accessing and so on;
- Acting as the center memory, saving the graphic and character information of the Real-Time discussion into the specific character string sequence that can be downloaded when necessary.

On Server: After logging in the server, users can make use of software to communicate with each other, such as AutoCAD, Pro/E, which are provided by server. In the process of discussion, server provided the background service by transferring discussion information from a client to another. According some rules specified, it transformed the Real-Time graphic and character information to the specific character string sequences that were sent to "Graphic communicating information database" and were stored there then.

On Clients: Clients provided the interfaces for logging, inputting, displaying the graphic/character information without saving them.

Specific browser: Only the legal users who have already logged in could use the specific browser. Since the clients didn't save any Real-Time information, all the discussion information is saved in the graphic/character interactive information database with the specified format of character string sequence. The only way for users to backup their discussion information is by using this specific browser to download them from graphic/character interactive database and translate them to create their own "notebook".

3   The Implement of the System

Server monitored the application from Client, and established the Socket connection between server and clients. Once upon the connection is established, the communication and discussion began.

3.1   The Implement of Server

Creating a TCP/IP server by adding a Tserversocket component to the Form or Data Module. When Server listened the application from Clients, request for connecting from clients was accepted by the server, and then this Tserversocket can control the dialogue between the Socket in Server and the Socket in Client.

3.2   The Implement of Client

The application program could become a TCP/IP client by adding a TclientSocket Component to the Form or Data Model. When a connecting request promoted by a Socket of client was listened by the server, the connection would be automatically established to begin the dialogue between server and clients.

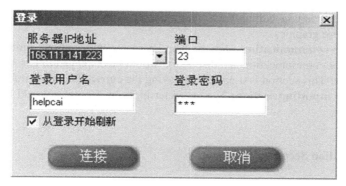

Fig. 2. Users Logging Interface

3.3   Users Logging on Interface

In this interface, Users can input the user name, password, the IP address and the corresponding Port address of server, and then get the response from server after clicking the "connect" button.

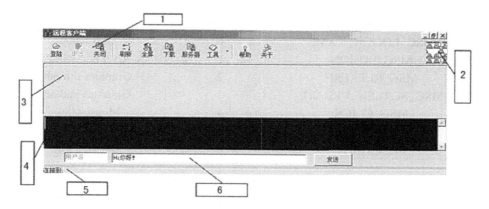

Fig. 3. Users communicating interface

3.4   Users Communicating Interface

1. Toolbar: There are a few buttons respectively used for downloading files, setting clients interface, Refreshing and so on。
2. Dynamic displaying mark: This mark is used for displaying whether this client is requesting a connection to server.
3. Figure communicating section: The graphics used for communicating or discussion would be displayed in this section. Users who had the right for reading/writing

with the corresponding editing tools that were also displayed in this section could modify all these graphics.

4. Character communicating section: The character information coming from the server used for communication and discussion would be displayed in this section.

5. Status Bar: This section is used for displaying the current condition information.

6. Character inputting section: The character input by the users would be displayed in this section.

3.5 Information Security

The information security is always important for some research group who need to keep their discussion/research content secret. Our system implemented this security with a serial of specific measurements.

Defining the types of information: The information transferred between the server and clients was divided into several kinds that were respectively given one special identifier to represent this kind of information [2]. There are totally more than six identifiers that are presented as following.

Table 1. Defining the types of information

Information Type	Identifiers	Notation
MSG_LOGON_NAME	0	User name
MSG_LOGON	1	User password
MSG_REFRESH	2	Graphics refresh
MSG_SCREEN_UPDATE	3	Graphics update
MSG_CLICK	4	Mouse click
MSG_FILE	5	File download
MSG_CHAT	6	Chatting log

Information Conformity: According specified regulations, the information transferred between Server and Clients as well as the representing codes were translated into special character string sequence that would be sent a bit later [3]. For instance, before sending graphic information from a server to a client, a function SendMsg () must be defined first:

```
Procedure TServerForm.SendMsg(MsgNum: integer; const
MsgData: string; Socket: TCustomWinSocket);

  var

    s : string;

  Begin
```

```
    s := IntToByteStr(MsgNum) + IntTo-
ByteStr(Length(MsgData)) + MsgData;

Socket.SendText(s);

End;


SendMsg(MSG_REFRESH, tmp, Socket)。
```

The information preprocess (In client): The information transferred from Server to Client is a serial of special character string sequence that must be preprocessed to recognize. The function ProcessMessage()used to preprocess the character string sequence is defined as following:

```
Procedure TServerForm.ProcessMessage(const Msg: string;
Socket: TCustomWinSocket);

    var

        MsgNum, x, aa, I, rc: integer;

        bmp        : TBitmap;

        tmp,usertype, Data      : string;

    begin

    CurSocket := Socket;

    Move(Msg[1], MsgNum, sizeof(integer));

    Data := Copy(Msg, 9, Length(Msg));

    if MsgNum = MSG_REFRESH then begin

    ...............

    End;

    End;
```

4   Experiences and Results

Our system has been successfully run in the LAN. The experiment environment is presented in Fig. 4.

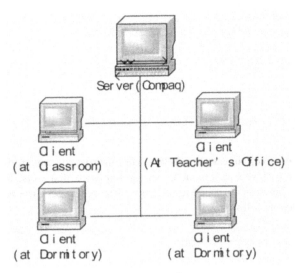

Fig. 4. Experiment environment

- One Compaq server with AutoCAD2000 installed in was located in the CAI Center Lab. in campus.
- Four Pentium III computers acting as the clients were respectively located in student dormitory, classroom, and administration office. All these clients were installed graphic communicating clients software but without any AutoCAD2000 software installed in them.

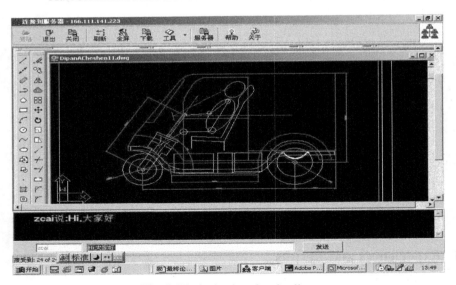

Fig. 5. Displaying interface in client

In this experiment, one teacher and four students need to discuss an Auto design drawing. Teacher and student promoted their own ideas or suggestions, which were presented both in characters and in graphics, to improve the Auto drawing. All the information was displayed in the teacher's and the students' screens synchronously. The operating/displaying interface is presented in Fig. 5.

5 Conclusions and Further Development

As mentioned above, our system is a real time communicating system by which information of both graphics and character could be exchanged based on TCP/IP Protocol. With our system, the CSCL could be applied in much more areas, and become more powerful. The features of our system are:
- Compatible with the Windows OP and necessary application software;
- Real-Time exchanging the complex graphics, can meet the demands of technology design to some extent;
- Real-Time saving the interacting and discussion data that can be browsed as references in the future;
- Setting user rights so as to help the user management.

Our system is just at the beginning; the future further work is presented as following:
- Real time discussion/communication by voice;
- Simultaneous discussion/communication of different topics by different groups.

References

1. Shen Ruimin, Chen Wei: DISCUSSION – a Discussion System of Distant Education Based on WWW, Calculator education application and educational reform., 1997
2. Liu Feilong: Use Java to establish electronic whiteboard based on Internet, Computer world, 1998
3. Shi Wei: Windows Sockets Rules and Applications-Windows Networking Program Interface, Shanghai Transportation University Publishing Company, 1996

Author Index

Lecture Notes in Computer Science

For information about Vols. 1–2688
please contact your bookseller or Springer-Verlag

Vol. 2689: K.D. Ashley, D.G. Bridge (Eds.), Case-Based Reasoning Research and Development. Proceedings, 2003. XV, 734 pages. 2003. (Subseries LNAI).

Vol. 2690: J. Liu, Y. Cheung, H. Yin (Eds.), Intelligent Data Engineering and Automated Learning. Proceedings, 2003. XXI, 1141 pages. 2003.

Vol. 2691: V. Mařík, J. Müller, M. Pěchouček (Eds.), Multi-Agent Systems and Applications III. Proceedings, 2003. XIV, 660 pages. 2003. (Subseries LNAI).

Vol. 2692: P. Nixon, S. Terzis (Eds.), Trust Management. Proceedings, 2003. X, 349 pages. 2003.

Vol. 2693: A. Cechich, M. Piattini, A. Vallecillo (Eds.), Component-Based Software Quality. X, 403 pages. 2003.

Vol. 2694: R. Cousot (Ed.), Static Analysis. Proceedings, 2003. XIV, 505 pages. 2003.

Vol. 2695: L.D. Griffin, M. Lillholm (Eds.), Scale Space Methods in Computer Vision. Proceedings, 2003. XII, 816 pages. 2003.

Vol. 2696: J. Feigenbaum (Ed.), Digital Rights Management. Proceedings, 2002. X, 221 pages. 2003.

Vol. 2697: T. Warnow, B. Zhu (Eds.), Computing and Combinatorics. Proceedings, 2003. XIII, 560 pages. 2003.

Vol. 2698: W. Burakowski, B. Koch, A. Bęben (Eds.), Architectures for Quality of Service in the Internet. Proceedings, 2003. XI, 305 pages. 2003.

Vol. 2699: M.G. Hinchey, J.L. Rash, W.F. Truszkowski, C. Rouff, D. Gordon-Spears (Eds.), Formal Approaches to Agent-Based Systems. Proceedings, 2002. IX, 297 pages. 2003. (Subseries LNAI).

Vol. 2700: M.T. Pazienza (Ed.), Information Extraction in the Web Era. XIII, 163 pages. 2003. (Subseries LNAI).

Vol. 2701: M. Hofmann (Ed.), Typed Lambda Calculi and Applications. Proceedings, 2003. VIII, 317 pages. 2003.

Vol. 2702: P. Brusilovsky, A. Corbett, F. de Rosis (Eds.), User Modeling 2003. Proceedings, 2003. XIV, 436 pages. 2003. (Subseries LNAI).

Vol. 2704: S.-T. Huang, T. Herman (Eds.), Self-Stabilizing Systems. Proceedings, 2003. X, 215 pages. 2003.

Vol. 2705: S. Renals, G. Grefenstette (Eds.), Text- and Speech-Triggered Information Access. Proceedings, 2000. VII, 197 pages. 2003. (Subseries LNAI).

Vol. 2706: R. Nieuwenhuis (Ed.), Rewriting Techniques and Applications. Proceedings, 2003. XI, 515 pages. 2003.

Vol. 2707: K. Jeffay, I. Stoica, K. Wehrle (Eds.), Quality of Service – IWQoS 2003. Proceedings, 2003. XI, 517 pages. 2003.

Vol. 2708: R. Reed, J. Reed (Eds.), SDL 2003: System Design. Proceedings, 2003. XI, 405 pages. 2003.

Vol. 2709: T. Windeatt, F. Roli (Eds.), Multiple Classifier Systems. Proceedings, 2003. X, 406 pages. 2003.

Vol. 2710: Z. Ésik, Z, Fülöp (Eds.), Developments in Language Theory. Proceedings, 2003. XI, 437 pages. 2003.

Vol. 2711: T.D. Nielsen, N.L. Zhang (Eds.), Symbolic and Quantitative Approaches to Reasoning with Uncertainty. Proceedings, 2003. XII, 608 pages. 2003. (Subseries LNAI).

Vol. 2712: A. James, B. Lings, M. Younas (Eds.), New Horizons in Information Management. Proceedings, 2003. XII, 281 pages. 2003.

Vol. 2713: C.-W. Chung, C.-K. Kim, W. Kim, T.-W. Ling, K.-H. Song (Eds.), Web and Communication Technologies and Internet-Related Social Issues – HSI 2003. Proceedings, 2003. XXII, 773 pages. 2003.

Vol. 2714: O. Kaynak, E. Alpaydin, E. Oja, L. Xu (Eds.), Artificial Neural Networks and Neural Information Processing – ICANN/ICONIP 2003. Proceedings, 2003. XXII, 1188 pages. 2003.

Vol. 2715: T. Bilgiç, B. De Baets, O. Kaynak (Eds.), Fuzzy Sets and Systems – IFSA 2003. Proceedings, 2003. XV, 735 pages. 2003. (Subseries LNAI).

Vol. 2716: M.J. Voss (Ed.), OpenMP Shared Memory Parallel Programming. Proceedings, 2003. VIII, 271 pages. 2003.

Vol. 2718: P. W. H. Chung, C. Hinde, M. Ali (Eds.), Developments in Applied Artificial Intelligence. Proceedings, 2003. XIV, 817 pages. 2003. (Subseries LNAI).

Vol. 2719: J.C.M. Baeten, J.K. Lenstra, J. Parrow, G.J. Woeginger (Eds.), Automata, Languages and Programming. Proceedings, 2003. XVIII, 1199 pages. 2003.

Vol. 2720: M. Marques Freire, P. Lorenz, M.M.-O. Lee (Eds.), High-Speed Networks and Multimedia Communications. Proceedings, 2003. XIII, 582 pages. 2003.

Vol. 2721: N.J. Mamede, J. Baptista, I. Trancoso, M. das Graças Volpe Nunes (Eds.), Computational Processing of the Portuguese Language. Proceedings, 2003. XIV, 268 pages. 2003. (Subseries LNAI).

Vol. 2722: J.M. Cueva Lovelle, B.M. González Rodríguez, L. Joyanes Aguilar, J.E. Labra Gayo, M. del Puerto Paule Ruiz (Eds.), Web Engineering. Proceedings, 2003. XIX, 554 pages. 2003.

Vol. 2723: E. Cantú-Paz, J.A. Foster, K. Deb, L.D. Davis, R. Roy, U.-M. O'Reilly, H.-G. Beyer, R. Standish, G. Kendall, S. Wilson, M. Harman, J. Wegener, D. Dasgupta, M.A. Potter, A.C. Schultz, K.A. Dowsland, N. Jonoska, J. Miller (Eds.), Genetic and Evolutionary Computation – GECCO 2003. Proceedings, Part I. 2003. XLVII, 1252 pages. 2003.

Vol. 2724: E. Cantú-Paz, J.A. Foster, K. Deb, L.D. Davis, R. Roy, U.-M. O'Reilly, H.-G. Beyer, R. Standish, G. Kendall, S. Wilson, M. Harman, J. Wegener, D. Dasgupta, M.A. Potter, A.C. Schultz, K.A. Dowsland, N. Jonoska, J. Miller (Eds.), Genetic and Evolutionary Computation – GECCO 2003. Proceedings, Part II. 2003. XLVII, 1274 pages. 2003.

Vol. 2725: W.A. Hunt, Jr., F. Somenzi (Eds.), Computer Aided Verification. Proceedings, 2003. XII, 462 pages. 2003.